Social Work Practice with Older Adults

Social Work Practice with Older Adults

An Evidence-Based Approach

Dawn Joosten-Hagye

University of Southern California

 cognella® | ACADEMIC PUBLISHING

Bassim Hamadeh, CEO and Publisher
Amy Smith, Project Editor
Abbey Hastings, Associate Production Editor
Emely Villavicencio, Senior Graphic Designer
Sara Schennum, Licensing Associate
Natalie Piccotti, Senior Marketing Manager
Kassie Graves, Vice President of Editorial
Jamie Giganti, Director of Academic Publishing

Cover images: copyright © 2018 iStockphoto LP/Rawpixel.
copyright © 2013 iStockphoto LP/Aldomurillo.
copyright © 2017 iStockphoto LP/FatCamera.
copyright © 2017 iStockphoto LP/PeopleImages.
copyright © 2017 iStockphoto LP/FatCamera.
copyright © 2018 iStockphoto LP/FG Trade.

California Social Work Education Center, "Competencies Selections," *CalSWEC Curriculum Competencies*, pp. 1-6, 9, 12-15. Copyright © 2017 by CalSWEC. Reprinted with permission.

Council on Social Work Education, "Assess Individuals, Families, Groups, Organizations, and Communities," *Specialized Practice Curricular Guide for Gero Social Work Practice*, pp. 89-90. Copyright © 2015 by Council on Social Work Education. Reprinted with permission.

Printed in the United States of America.

ISBN: 978-1-5165-2801-1 (pbk) / 978-1-5165-2802-8 (br)

BRIEF CONTENTS

Detailed Contents

Chapter 4
Aging in Place   75

Chapter 8
Chronic Illness and Disability 197

Chapter 11
Loss, Grief, and Bereavement 279

Chapter 12
Caregiving 309

Chapter 13
Mezzo Practice   335

Chapter 14
Macro Practice   361

PREFACE

The Goal

The purpose of this textbook is to prepare social workers and other related professionals at undergraduate and graduate levels for effective clinical practice with older adults and families in micro-, mezzo-, and macro-level practice settings. This textbook was written to serve as a foundation for social work students and related professions to draw from in considering the application of best practices from start to finish with older adult clients in micro, mezzo, and macro contexts. It is intended to be used by instructors as a teaching guide for training students in social work and related professions to work effectively with older adults. This textbook fills an important gap among existing textbooks on older adults by addressing the key domains of social work practice in each chapter. A unique feature of this textbook is the emphasis on evidence-based practice. Students learn how to identify appropriate evidence-based and best practice treatment options for older adults and how the process of shared decision making empowers older adults to select culturally preferred and meaningful treatments. Case studies are presented in each chapter as tools for instructors to engage students in both the discussion and application of the key domains of social work practice required to work effectively with older adults in different contexts and settings. Informed by intersectionality theory, in each chapter, students learn how to first consider the context and intersecting diversity factors of the older adult client, which will be used along with a biopsychosocial/spiritual assessment to inform treatment planning. This context not only provides instructors with an opportunity to lead students in discussions about context and intersectionality of an older adult client, but it also serves as an opportunity for instructors to build on and reinforce students' engagement and assessment skills by further training them in advanced skills of synthesizing contextual, intersectional, and biopsychosocial/spiritual assessments when formulating a treatment plan and how to identify appropriate evidence-based interventions and best practices for treatment that establish a goodness of fit for the client.

Another feature of this textbook that benefits both students and instructors is the emphasis on interdisciplinary collaboration and interagency coordination of services when intervening with older adults. In each chapter, students are provided with suggestions for presenting their assessment of an older adult during interdisciplinary team planning meetings. Instructors can further guide students to consider the role of the social worker as an interdisciplinary team member in different practice settings with older adults similar to or different from the case study presented in the chapter. Similarly, each chapter presents a guide for framing community resource and interagency coordination of services for older adults. Another added benefit in this textbook, often missing in others, is the addition of potential legal and ethical issues that may present in practice, as well as transference and countertransference, and strategies for addressing and managing them, respectively. This feature presents students with an opportunity to consider their role as advocate when legal and ethical issues present in different contexts and settings. It is also intended as a reminder of the importance of self-care and managing countertransference to prevent compassion fatigue and, equally important, to prevent it from impacting the older adult client negatively. Instructors can guide students in further discussion of how to address legal and ethical issues in their state or county or within a certain practice setting/context with older adults.

Another aspect of this textbook that makes it different from others about social work practice with older adults is the emphasis on both issues and opportunities typically encountered when working with older adults and their families that are often not found in one textbook. For example, homelessness and sexual health (Chapter 3); wellness, prevention, and health promotion (Chapter 4); aging in prison settings (Chapter 5); long-term care planning (Chapter 9); advance care planning and end-of-life issues (Chapter 10); mezzo practice advocacy skills (Chapter 13); and macro practice advocacy skills (Chapter 14). It also includes technological resources that students can access to learn more about the key topics highlighted and share them with older adults and their families. Each chapter includes discussion questions that instructors can use to engage students in class discussion and exercises to further apply the content from the chapter to practice with older adults. Students are provided with self-reflection questions as well to increase their insight into their own perceptions and understanding of the topics presented in the chapter.

The book begins with a description of evidence-based practice. Chapter 1 sets the context for evidence-based practice and introduces the domains of clinical practice followed in Chapters 3 through 12. Chapter 2 highlights key theories for aging populations and assessment approaches. Key domains for effective practice outlined in Chapters 3 through 12 include assessing context, biopsychosocial/spiritual assessment, diversity—cultural competence/spirituality/LGBT/sexuality, interdisciplinary team roles and planning, evidence-based interventions, assessing/monitoring evidence-based treatment outcomes, community resources/interagency coordination, transference and countertransference, technological resources, and legal/ethical considerations. Each chapter highlights the Council on Social Work Education (CSWE) Gero Competencies and skills students need to successfully engage, assess, intervene, evaluate, and provide advocacy at the micro, mezzo, and macro levels with older adults and their families. The textbook includes a template for social work geriatric assessment and case studies to illustrate its use in different contexts of clinical practice. Screening tools and approaches are also presented in select chapters. The textbook highlights key theories that inform assessment and interventions with older adults and provides suggestions on how to apply each theory to an older adult client. Chapters 13 and 14 present the context for mezzo and macro level practice as well as key strategies and skills social workers for mezzo and macro level practice and advocacy. Supplemental tools for instructors include PowerPoint presentations, quizzes, and a sample syllabus. Tools for students include flash cards, key words, learning objectives, critical thinking activity/discussion questions, and self-reflection exercises.

Introduction to Evidence-based Practice

Evidence-based practice involves the expertise of a social work clinician to engage, assess, treat, and evaluate desirable outcomes for a client and family system. It involves all phases of social work practice: engagement, assessment, intervention, treatment planning, treatment, and termination. Specifically, evidence-based practice with older adults is informed by clinical expertise to navigate the context of the client's presenting problem, the best research evidence for the intervention that establishes a goodness-of-fit to address a client's presenting problem, relevant human behavior theory to understand developmental needs and theory related to evidence-based interventions, the client's preferences for treatment and engagement in shared decision making for a desirable treatment and outcome, and continual monitoring of the effects of the intervention on the desired outcome. In social work, evidence-based practices are defined as "interventions for which scientific evidence consistently shows that they improve client outcomes" that reflects both best research evidence and clinical expertise as well as the preferences and values of patients/families (NASW, 2017, p. 1). The profession of social work is mandated to stay up to date with best practices, research evidence, knowledge in the field, and evaluation of practice by the National Association of Social Workers (NASW) Code of Ethics (1999). Evidence-based practice promotes the philosophy of lifelong learning and requires critical thinking, expertise, and leadership on the part of the clinician to seek best practices that can be brought into different clinical settings to provide the best fit for the client.

The roots of evidence-based practice stem from medicine. It originated in the 19th century in Europe and is best defined in medicine as "the conscientious, explicit, and judicious use of current best evidence in making decisions about the care of individual patients" (Sackett, 1996, p. 71). According to Gibbs and Gambrill, evidence-based practice includes the following steps: (1) "an individual assessment and a well formulated question," (2) "a technically efficient electronic search for external research findings related to practice questions," (3) "deciding if the evidence applies to the client," (4) "considering this evidence together with the values and expectations of clients," and (5) evaluating the outcome of the applied intervention in a single-subject case study design (2002, pp. 453–454). Ideally, a standardized assessment is used to measure the desirable outcome at multiple times before and during the treatment delivery. A baseline measurement of the desirable outcome should occur prior to the implementation of the evidence-based intervention and at multiple times throughout treatment to monitor the efficacy of the intervention and determine whether the desirable outcome has been met, the treatment is not working (i.e., outcome is getting worse), or the client should be prepared for termination (i.e., the desirable outcome has been met).

To guide clinicians in evidence-based practice, Haynes, Devereaux, and Guyatt (2002) developed an updated conceptual model to inform decision making that includes: the clinical state and circumstances of the client/family, research evidence, the patient's preferences and actions, and the clinical expertise of the clinician (Figure 0.1). The clinical state and circumstances include a "patient's clinical state, the clinical setting, and the clinical circumstances they find themselves in when they seek medical attention" (Haynes, Devereaux, & Guyatt, 2002, p. 37), which can include a variety of physical, psychological/mental, social, environmental, contextual, and financial factors in the field of social work.

FIGURE 0.1. An Updated Model for Evidence-Based Decisions

The patient preferences and actions include the following considerations: views on options for treatment available to them, personal values and beliefs about treatment and the need for treatment, the extent to which a client may be willing to or resistant to avoid risk factors, medication adherence, insurance and other health/behavioral health-related resources, health care insurance, and family support (Haynes, Devereaux, & Guyatt, 2002). In addition, social workers assess a patient's preference for treatment, whether individual or group; the setting they prefer—inpatient or outpatient; community-, faith-, or diversity-based—and prior attempts to address the presenting problem, outcomes, and satisfaction with previous interventions.

Research evidence for social work practice includes randomized clinical trials with the intervention with a target population similar to that of our client. One challenge is that many evidence-based interventions may not have been tested with our target client population—the role of social workers in making cultural modifications and testing evidence-based interventions is key for building the knowledge base of the profession. A risk that comes with modification involves fidelity of the treatment intervention. Such modifications should, therefore, be carefully considered against best evidence and research on attempts to date.

Clinical expertise refers to the skills and expertise of the clinician and "must encompass and balance the patient's clinical state and circumstances, relevant research evidence, and the patient's preferences and actions if successful and satisfying result is to occur" (Haynes, Devereaux, & Guyatt, 2002, p. 37). For social work, skills include training in generalist and specialized practice, trainings and certifications in evidence-based practices, licensure, and experience in working with a population as well as the conditions/issues a population commonly seeks treatment for. In social work practice, two key areas are brought into the context of evidence-based practice, as noted by Gilgun (2005): the person of the practitioner and clinical wisdom. The four cornerstones of evidence-based social work practice identified by Gilgun include: (1) "research and theory," (2) "practice wisdom, or what we and other professionals have learned from our clients, which also includes professional values," (3) "the person of the practitioner, or our personal assumptions, values, biases and world views," and (4) "what clients bring to practice situations" (2005, p. 52). The model complements the former evidence-based models as the NASW Code of Ethics in social work requires both the integration of research and theory with practice. It further incorporates the professional values and clinical wisdom and insight into clinical expertise. Like former models, it recognizes the clinical state, circumstances, and action of the client, or what the client brings into the therapeutic relationship. Lastly, it considers the biases, world views, and assumptions the social worker brings into the therapeutic relationship, a key requisite for identifying and managing countertransference as it presents in the therapeutic relationship.

Acknowledgments

I am appreciative and grateful for the support and assistance I received from Cognella Publishing, my colleagues, and my family. I benefited from the invaluable support and feedback from both Kassie Graves, editor, and Amy Smith, project editor, as well as the team at Cognella Publishing. I am thankful for the encouragement and support of my colleagues from the University of Southern California, Suzanne Dworak-Peck School of Social Work who continue to inspire me: Bruce Jansson, Iris Chi, Julie Cederbaum, Erik Schott, Kristen Zaleski, Eugenia Weiss, Kim Goodman, and Suzanne Wenzel. I am thankful for the ongoing support from my husband, Steve; daughter, Crystal; and son, Adam. And lastly, I am thankful for the more than 9,000 older adults and their families who welcomed me into their homes, hospital and skilled nursing home rooms over the past 19 years, as well as the interdisciplinary team members I worked with. Learning from older adults and members of the interdisciplinary team has been a true honor and highlight of my clinical social work practice. This book is dedicated to the older adults with whom I have worked with and those in the future with whom I will work to improve their well-being and quality of life.

References

Gibbs, L., & Gambrill, E. (2002). Evidence-based practice: Counterarguments to objections. *Research on Social Work Practice, 12*(3), 452–476.

Gilgun, J. F. (2005). The four cornerstones of evidence-based practice in social work. *Research on Social Work Practice, 15*(1), 52–61.

Haynes, R. B., Devereaux, P. J., & Guyatt, G. H. (2002). Clinical expertise in the era of evidence-based medicine and patient choice. *Evidence-Based Medicine*, 7(2), 36–38.

NASW (1999). Code of ethics of the National Association of Social Workers. Washington, DC: NASW Press.

NASW (2017). NASW practice snapshot: Evidence-based practices—for social workers. Washington, DC: NASW Press.

Sackett, D. L. (1997). Evidence-based medicine. *Seminars in Perinatology* 21(1), 3–5.

Credit

CHAPTER 1

The Context of Evidence-based Social Work Practice with Older Adults

Introduction

This chapter provides an overview of key domains relevant to the context of evidence-based social work practice with older adults. It begins with a description of the Council on Social Work Education (CSWE) Gero Competencies. It is followed by an introduction to key domains for clinical practice with older adults that include: professional competencies, assessing context, bio-psychosocial/spiritual assessment, diversity, interdisciplinary team roles and planning, evidence-based interventions and best practices, assessing/monitoring treatment outcomes, community resources and interagency coordination, transference and countertransference, technological resources, and legal/ethical issues. Each of these will serve as a template for subsequent chapters. This chapter also introduces a clinical case vignette that illustrates the context of practice with an older adult client experiencing elder abuse and neglect, and strategies for identifying and managing clinician responses follow. This chapter ends with a discussion on clinician responses—specifically compassion fatigue and vicarious trauma—and a recommended self-administered questionnaire that clinicians can use to assess their own levels of compassion satisfaction, compassion fatigue, and vicarious trauma.

Council for Social Work Education (CSWE) Gero Competencies

Professional standards such as the National Association of Social Workers (NASW) Code of Ethics and Geriatric Competencies provide guidelines for professional knowledge, skills, and behavior for social workers. In 2004, the CSWE Gero Competencies provided key guidelines and skills required of social workers entering the field of geriatric social work. In 2015, CSWE updated the competencies—reducing the number from 10 to 9—which now include the following (Council on Social Work Education, 2017):

- Competency 1: Demonstrate ethical and professional behavior
- Competency 2: Engage diversity and difference in practice
- Competency 3: Advance human rights and social, economic, and environmental justice
- Competency 4: Engage in practice-informed research and research-informed practice
- Competency 5: Engage in policy practice curricular resources
- Competency 6: Engage with individuals, families, groups, organizations, and communities
- Competency 7: Assess with individuals, families, groups, organizations, and communities
- Competency 8: Intervene with individuals, families, groups, organizations, and communities
- Competency 9: Evaluate practice with individuals, families, groups, organizations, and communities

For each subsequent chapter, key competencies and respective gero social work competencies will be introduced, highlighted, and applied as appropriate. The next key domain for micro, mezzo, and macro practice with older adults is assessing context.

Assessing Context

Assessing context is a key domain in providing evidence-based practice as it enables the clinician to gain a full understanding of the intersecting factors that may impact and influence a client's treatment choices, preferences, and decision making. It includes assessing and identifying multiple factors that intersect with the client's clinical state and circumstances; preferences and actions; past experiences with services; the service delivery context, including insurance and geographic proximity of service providers and resources; as well as biological, psychological, social, and cultural/spiritual factors. An assessment of context matters because in many cases, the treatment options available to a client may be limited by constraints, such as insurance not covering the best treatment or service or the treatment or resource being far from a client geographically. It includes the setting in which care is provided by the social worker to the client: in a private home, assisted living, board and care; in a community setting, community center, adult day care, adult day health care; in an outpatient setting, doctor's office, partial hospitalization program, intensive outpatient program; in an institution (hospital, nursing home, or forensic setting); or in a private practice office. There may be cultural and spiritual beliefs, values, customs, and rituals that influence the preferences of a client regarding treatment. For some, there may be a range of options available because of insurance, geographical location, and/or financial resources. For all, it is helpful to engage in decisional balance exercises to explore the range of treatment options available, the pros and cons of each, the contextual factors that limit or facilitate access, and the clinical recommendation as to which option provides the best fit for the client based on the clinician's expertise and experience in the field as well as best research evidence. Chapters 3 through 12 explore contextual factors that may impact treatment decision making. Chapters 13 and 14 consider context for mezzo- and macro-level practice with older adults. A comprehensive biopsychosocial/spiritual assessment, informed by context, is critical to developing an understanding of presenting issues for treatment, treatment planning, and interventions appropriate and available for treating older adults and their families.

Biopsychosocial/Spiritual Assessment

A thorough biopsychosocial/spiritual assessment is a key domain for effective social work practice with older adults. According to the NASW (2016), the biopsychosocial/spiritual perspective "recognizes the importance of whole person care and takes into account a client's physical or medical condition; emotional or psychological state; socioeconomic, sociocultural, and sociopolitical status; and spiritual needs and concerns" (p. 10). It is through this kind of assessment that a clinician becomes aware of the strengths and unmet biopsychosocial/spiritual needs of the client, including preferences, values, past experiences, and circumstances. In evidence-based practice, the clinician applies their expertise to the assessment results to understand the nature of the client's presenting problem and identify the best interventions to present to the client that both address these problem(s) with a goodness of fit that are both valued and preferred by the client. In Chapter 2, a template that can be used to guide clinicians in conducting a geriatric biopsychosocial/spiritual assessment is presented. In Chapters 3 through 12, the biopsychosocial/spiritual assessment is applied to working with an older adult or caregiver. Supplemental standardized screening tools and their use with an older adult are presented in select chapters.

The risk for abuse, neglect, and suicide are key aspects of the context of clinical practice with older adults as well. They must simultaneously be addressed along with other issues that the client needs treatment for. Social workers require skills to appropriately triage presenting issues. For example, if a social worker is completing a biopsychosocial/spiritual assessment and the clinician discovers that the client is endorsing suicidal ideations and has intent and means, the clinician shifts attention to the presenting high-risk situation and intervenes immediately to ensure the client's safety. A discussion of the context, assessment, and assessment tools for elder abuse/neglect and suicide follows, along with a discussion of treatment for imminent risk.

Abuse/Neglect

Assessing elder abuse and neglect are important mandated responsibilities for health-care providers and clinicians. An understanding of the national context for abuse and neglect needs to be considered by the clinician working with older adults in the United States. According to the National Center on Elder Abuse, which examined data collection of elder abuse from multiple sources—including Adult Protective Services; International Classification of Diseases (ICD) coding on abuse; Centers for Disease Control and Prevention (CDC); Medicare Claims Data; Agency for Healthcare Research and Quality (AHRQ);

Department of Health and Human Services Office of the Inspector General (OIG) Report on State Medicaid Fraud Control Units (MFCUs); Nursing Home Enforcement data; Online Survey, Certification, and Reporting System (OSCAR); suspicious activity reports; Bureau of Justice Statistics National Survey of Prosecutors; National Domestic Violence Hotline; Social Security Representative Payee System; U.S. Department of Veterans Affairs (VA) Fiduciary Program; guardianship and conservatorship data; Legal Hotlines of Elderly Data; and National Ombudsman Reporting System (NORS)—"there is a wide consensus that currently a clear picture of elder abuse in the United States is sadly lacking" (2006, p. 20). The National Center for Elder Abuse concluded that a clear understanding of prevalence and incidence rates of abuse and neglect among older adults is due to lack of training for detection by providers, difficulty identifying it nationally because of the lack of incentives for ICD coding of elder abuse (which is often a secondary rather than primary ICD-coded condition among health and behavioral health providers), and difficulty yielding data for existing ICD codes elder maltreatment codes (2006).

Using the National Crime Victimization Survey (NCVS), investigators report that the ratio of violent to property crimes in the United States from 2003 to 2013 against adults ages 65 and older was higher (13:1) than those for adults ages 50 to 64 (5:1) and adults ages 25 to 49 (3:1) (Morgan & Mason, 2014). Although homicide rates for older adults declined during the same period by 44%, reports of violent crimes against older adults revealed 59% becoming victims in their homes or close to it (Morgan & Mason, 2014). Older adults are more likely (56%) to report violent crimes perpetrated against them than those ages 12 to 24 years (38%) (Morgan & Mason, 2014). According to the World Health Organization (2017), 1 in 6 older adults were victims of elder abuse and neglect in 2016 internationally, with the type of abuse classified as psychological (11.6%), financial (6.8%), neglect (4.2%), physical (2.6%), and sexual (0.9%). Finally, according to the Administration on Community Living (2017), in the United States, the incidence of elder abuse is approximately 5 million per year at a cost of $2.6 billion per year.

The Centers for Disease Control and Prevention (2018) defines elder abuse as "an intentional act, or failure to act, by a caregiver or another person in a relationship involving an expectation of trust that causes or creates a risk of harm to an older adult" (p. 1). Familiarity with the definitions and forms of elder abuse and neglect, as defined by the CDC (Box 1.1), are essential for the clinician's role in preventing, detecting, treating, and reporting when working with older adults.

Assessing abuse/neglect. When engaging, assessing, intervening, and evaluating treatment interventions with older adults, it is important to understand both client protective factors that prevent abuse and perpetrator risk factors that contribute to elder abuse, whether at the individual, relationship, community, and/or societal level (or some combination of these) (Centers for Disease Control and Prevention, 2017b). Protective factors for the older adult client at the relationship level include strong social support networks and at the community level, coordinated services for older adults by organizations serving older adults, a sense of community cohesion, and collective functioning (Centers for Disease Control and Prevention, 2017). Among organizations, protective factors include

Box 1.1

CDC Elder Abuse Definitions

"**Physical Abuse:** the intentional use of physical force that results in acute or chronic illness, bodily injury, physical pain, functional impairment, distress, or death. Physical abuse may include, but is not limited to, violent acts such as striking (with or without an object or weapon), hitting, beating, scratching, biting, choking, suffocation, pushing, shoving, shaking, slapping, kicking, stomping, pinching, and burning" (Centers for Disease Control 2018, para.1).

"**Sexual Abuse or Abusive Sexual Contact:** forced or unwanted sexual interaction (touching and non-touching acts) of any kind with an older adult. This may include but is not limited to forced or unwanted: completed or attempted contact between the penis and the vulva or the penis and the anus involving penetration; contact between the mouth and the penis, vulva, or anus; penetration of the anal or genital opening of another person by a hand, finger, or other object; intentional touching, either directly or through the clothing, of the genitalia, anus, groin, breast, inner thigh, or buttocks. These acts also qualify as sexual abuse if they are committed against a person who is not competent to give informal approval" (Centers for Disease Control 2018, para. 2).

"**Emotional or Psychological Abuse:** verbal or nonverbal behavior that results in the infliction of anguish, mental pain, fear, or distress. Examples include behaviors intended to humiliate (e.g., calling names or insults), threaten (e.g., expressing an intent to initiate nursing home placement), isolate (e.g., seclusion from family or friends), or control (e.g., prohibiting or limiting access to transportation, telephone, money or other resources)" (Centers for Disease Control 2018, para. 3).

"**Neglect:** failure by a caregiver or other responsible person to protect an elder from harm, or the failure to meet needs for essential medical care, nutrition, hydration, hygiene, clothing, basic activities of daily living or shelter, which results in a serious risk of compromised health and safety. Examples include not providing adequate nutrition, hygiene, clothing, shelter, or access to necessary health care; or failure to prevent exposure to unsafe activities and environments" (Centers for Disease Control 2018, para. 4).

"**Financial Abuse or Exploitation:** the illegal, unauthorized, or improper use of an older individual's resources by a caregiver or other person in a trusting relationship, for the benefit of someone other than the older individual. This includes depriving an older person of rightful access to, information about, or use of, personal benefits, resources, belongings, or assets. Examples include forgery, misuse or theft of money or possessions; use of coercion or deception to surrender finances or property; or improper use of guardianship or power of attorney. (Centers for Disease Control 2018, para. 4).

Source: www.cdc.gov/violenceprevention/elderabuse/definitions.html.

monitoring abuse/neglect, procedures and protocols outlined in policies, protocols for power of attorney and how it is enacted, and frequent visits by social workers, friends, family, and volunteers (Centers for Disease Control and Prevention, 2017).

Risk factors for elder abuse perpetrators at the individual level include: a mental health diagnosis, alcohol abuse, anger, being ill-equipped for caregiving, assuming caregiving responsibility at a young age, poor coping skills, and early childhood abuse (Centers for Disease Control and Prevention, 2017b). At the relationship level, they include being emotionally or financially dependent on the older adult, no support socially, and prior behavior issues (Centers for Disease Control and Prevention, 2017b). The sole community-level risk factor is the lack of formal caregiver support for caregivers of older adults (Centers for Disease Control and Prevention, 2017b). At the societal level, risk factors include cultures with socially acceptable and tolerated aggression, where routine screening is not provided by providers due to provider discretion to screen or not, reluctance of families to accept formal and informal care outside of the family, negative stereotypes about older adults, and where there is silencing of pain and suffering (Centers for Disease Control and Prevention, 2017b).

Screening tools to detect elder abuse/neglect. There are several elder abuse screening tools that a clinician can use in primary care, dental offices, home health settings, emergency departments, OB/GYN offices, and long-term care settings (National Center on Elder Abuse, 2016). In health care settings, there is the Elder Abuse Suspicion Index (EASI), a six-item provider-administered screening that takes two minutes to complete and detects abuse and neglect over the past 12 months, or the six-item self- or provider-reported Hwalek-Sengstock Elder Abuse Screening Test (National Center on Elder Abuse, 2016). A 12-item client self-report that detects vulnerability for abuse is the Vulnerability to Abuse Screening Scale (VASS) (National Center on Elder Abuse, 2016).

Suicide

Multiple contextual factors for suicide prevention, risk, survivorship, safety, and recovery/aftercare must be considered by clinicians working with older adults with high-risk factors for suicide. In terms of causes of death in the United States in 2015, suicide ranked 10th at an annual cost of $51 billion (American Foundation for Suicide Prevention, 2017). In 2014, the highest completed suicide rates in the United States for males were among older adults ages 75 and older (rate of 38.8 per 100,000) (Curtin, Warner, & Hedegaard, 2016). The oldest adults, ages 85 and older, have the second highest rate of suicide at 19.4%, compared to 19.6% for adults ages 45 to 64 (American Foundation for Suicide Prevention, 2017). Suicide attempts occur at a ratio of 4:1 among older adults in comparison to 25:1 among youth; the most commonly used method for completed suicide is firearms (49.8%), followed by suffocation (26.8%), poisoning (15.4%), and other methods (7.9%) (American Foundation for Suicide Prevention, 2017). In 2015, men were 3.5 times more likely to die from suicide than women (American Foundation for Suicide Prevention, 2017).

Suicide is defined by the Centers for Disease Control (2017) as "death caused by self-directed injurious behavior with an intent to die as a result of the behavior" (p. 1). A suicide attempt is defined as "a non-fatal, self-directed, potentially injurious behavior with an intent to die as a result of the behavior" that "might not result in injury," and a suicidal ideation is defined as "thinking about, considering, or planning suicide" (Centers for Disease Control, 2017, p. 1). In comparison to younger adults, older adults are more likely to develop a plan using a lethal method (Karlin, 2014). Although sadness is a key characteristic of depression among adults, in older adults, key characteristics include changes in sleep patterns, diminished interest in activities that were pleasurable before, and appetite changes (Karlin, 2014).

Assessing suicide risk. Awareness and knowledge of how to screen older adults for warning signs and risk factors of suicide is a key skill for clinicians. Contextual risk factors for suicide among older adults include the following (Box 1.2):

Box 1.2

- Depression
- Prior suicide attempts
- Marked feelings of hopelessness; lack of interest in future plans
- Feelings of loss of independence or sense of purpose
- Medical conditions that significantly limit functioning or life expectancy
- Impulsivity due to cognitive impairment
- Social isolation
- Family discord or losses (i.e., recent death of a loved one)
- Inflexible personality or marked difficulty adapting to change
- Access to lethal means (i.e., firearms, other weapons, etc.)
- Daring or risk-taking behavior
- Sudden personality changes
- Alcohol or medication misuse or abuse
- Verbal suicide threats such as, "You'd be better off without me" or "Maybe I won't be around"
- Giving away prized possessions

Source: http://www.mentalhealthamerica.net/preventing-suicide-older-adults.

Screening tools to detect suicide. There are several screening tools clinicians can use to assess suicide risk among older adults. The most commonly used suicide risk screening tool, available in more than 114 languages and used in inpatient, outpatient, and community settings, is the Columbia-Suicide Severity Rating Scale (C-SSRS) (Posner, 2008). The clinician-administered screening tool contains six questions, and clients answer "yes" or "no" to each. If clients answer "yes" to question 2, the clinician is instructed to ask questions 3 through 6; if they answer "no" to question 2, the clinician asks question 6 (Posner, 2008). This list of questions follow: (1) "Have you ever wished you were dead or wished you could go to sleep and not wake up?," (2) "Have you actually had any thoughts of killing yourself?," (3) "Have you been thinking about how you might kill yourself?," (4) "Have you had these thoughts and had some intention on acting on them?," (5) "Have you started to work out or worked out the details of how to kill yourself? Do you intend to carry out this plan?," and (6) "Have you ever done anything, started to do anything, or prepared to end your life?" (Posner, 2008, p. 1). If the client answers "yes," the clinician is prompted to ask "How long ago did you do any of these?" (Posner, 2008, p. 1).

In the National Institute for Mental Health toolkit, one brief screening tool that can be used in a variety of settings with older adults is the Ask Suicide-Screening Questions (ASQ), which has five questions clinicians use to assess risk, each with a "yes" or "no" answer (National Institute of Mental Health, 2017). A positive screen is considered for an answer of yes to any of the following four questions: (1) "In the past few weeks, have you wished you were dead?"; (2) "In the past few weeks, have you felt that you or your family would be better off if you were dead?"; (3) "In the past week, have you been having thoughts about killing yourself?;" and (4) Have you ever tried to kill yourself" (National Institute of Mental Health, 2017, p. 1). A fifth question is asked to assess acuity of risk for a client who answers "yes" to any of the prior questions: "Are you having thoughts of killing yourself right now?" A "yes" answer to question 5 is considered an acute positive screen (National Institute of Mental Health, 2017, p. 1).

Intervention for Imminent Risk

Clients with an imminent risk require a crisis intervention approach, and older adults with an imminent risk require an immediate intervention to include a plan to contract for safety. Clinicians engage in further screening for mental health/safety and determine whether the client needs to be placed on a psychiatric hold or a less restrictive plan is appropriate to ensure safety. For older adults experiencing neglect or abuse, clinicians must follow the state and local reporting procedures and protocols and provide a safety plan for the older adult. In addition to crisis intervention and primary prevention for older adults at risk of suicide, clinicians can address social risk factors by including psychosocial interventions to promote connectedness between the older adult, family members, and others in their social support networks (Karlin, 2014). Because declining functional and physical health are risk factors for suicide among older adults, clinicians should address the client's perception of "being a burden on others" in the context of both physical and functional health declines (Karlin, 2014, p.1). Cognitive behavioral therapy and pharmacotherapy are also evidence-based interventions that lower depression and suicidal ideations among older adults (Karlin, 2014).

Case Study and Intervention Application

Mrs. Hansen is an 83-year-old female living in a large estate with a 24-hour live-in caregiver. Her husband died three years prior; For 10 years, he was her primary caregiver once she was diagnosed with Alzheimer's disease at the age of 70. She was a homemaker, she never worked, and she and her husband never had children. Although she was once socially active, playing bridge and participating in the local Women's Auxiliary Club, she stopped once her Alzheimer's disease progressed to a moderate level at the age of 77. Her husband was an attorney at a large firm in Los Angeles County, California, and worked 70 hours per week up until the time he became Mrs. Hansen's caregiver. Their nephew, who lives out of state, was the executor of his will and became the Power of Attorney over person, estate, health, and finances once Mr. Hansen died. The nephew, unprepared to become his aunt's caregiver, hired a 24-hour live-in caregiver. The social worker was referred to do a home evaluation with the nurse after Mrs. Hansen was brought into the emergency room by the caregiver and treated for dehydration and malnutrition. The emergency room report indicated Mrs. Hansen had friction burns on her wrists, was unkempt, and had a strong odor. The attending physician filed a suspected Adult Protective Services report.

The biopsychosocial/spiritual assessment narrative, presenting problems, and treatment plan for Mrs. Hansen from the social worker is as follows:

> Mrs. Hansen is an 83-year-old female, non-Hispanic white, English speaking, widow, with a high school education. She presented to the emergency department with dehydration and malnutrition—referral source: attending physician in ED. Her religious preference is Catholic per nephew report; no use of complementary or alternative medicines per nephew report. Her personal and family history includes: current contact with family and friends, was a homemaker, has no children, was socially active in Women's Auxiliary Club previously, is currently socially isolated, and her caregiver is overwhelmed and untrained to care for older adult with Alzheimer's disease; her nephew has maintained contact by phone; no other family or friends. Her financial resources include: an ability to provide basic needs with her power of attorney, nephew, in charge of securing basic needs for housing, food, shelter, clothing; her health insurance is adequate—she has Medicare and AARP supplemental insurance; and her income sources are also adequate—she has Social Security, pension, savings, and investments managed by her nephew. An assessment of her environment for personal safety, maintenance of residence, and safety of community revealed the following: Her current social context/environmental is living at home with 24-hour caregiver; the neighborhood safety is adequate; home safety slip rugs were removed, and there are stairs to front door with handrail; there are no guns or access to guns in the home; and the screen for abuse or neglect by self or perpetrated by others (APS SOC341 report if suspected) resulted in an additional immediate report filed upon first assessment due to caregiver report of barricading client in her room with a dresser at night and using soft wrist restraints to tie patient's wrists to the bed at night to prevent wandering. Mrs. Hansen's health literacy and self-rated health were compromised as she presented with moderate dementia, lacks insight, and was unable to verbalize; an advance directive is in place, and her nephew is the power of attorney over person, finances, place, and estate; her diagnoses are moderate Alzheimer's disease, dehydration, and malnutrition; her medications include Aricept

and Namenda for dementia; an assessment of her functional health (ADLs, IADLs) revealed she requires full assist with IADLs and moderate to full assist with supervision of ADLs; she has no other chronic or life-threatening illnesses; and sexual health is inactive. Assessment of her mental status included administering the mini mental status exam—she scored 13, at the lower end of the scale of moderate dementia; no indicators were present for suicide, homicide, or substance use risk. The presenting problems and needs include: appropriate supervision and 24-hour care; immediate Adult Protective Services report for additional findings that caregiver was using wrist restraints to tie patient down to the bed at night to prevent her from wandering and caregiver also used a dresser to barricade client in her room at night. The treatment plan included advocacy for appropriate long-term care options presented to nephew to ensure safety, collaboration with physician and nurse for treatment plans and goals of care, two additional follow-up visits by the social worker, and ongoing nursing visits per MD order as nephew selected board and care placement as the best option for Mrs. Hansen; the social worker assisted with transfer to board and care and transferred home health services there for two additional follow-up visits by the social worker and ongoing nursing visits per MD order.

When engaging, assessing, intervening, evaluating, and providing advocacy with or on behalf of older adults and their families, clinicians must consider the next key domain—diversity factors—when working with older adult clients and their families.

Diversity–Cultural Competence/Spirituality/LGBT/Sexuality

Chapters 3 through 12 will explore areas pertaining to diversity, a key domain of evidence-based practice with older adults and caregivers. Holistic treatment approaches with clients at the micro, mezzo, and macro levels factor in the multiple aspects of diversity in clients and the clinician's practice of cultural humility (NASW, 2015). Diversity, according to the NASW, "includes the sociocultural experiences of people inclusive of, but not limited to, national origin, color, social class, religious and spiritual beliefs, immigration status, sexual orientation, gender identity or expression, age, marital status, and physical or mental disabilities" (2015, p. 9). The NASW outlines 10 standards for culturally competent social work practice that include: ethics and values, self-awareness, cross-cultural knowledge, cross-cultural skills, service delivery, empowerment and advocacy, diverse workforce, professional education, language and communication, and leadership to advance cultural competence (2015).

Cultural humility, or an attitude of humility in working with clients, ensures that cultural competence skills and knowledge are applied effectively in practice through recognition of "the dynamic quality of culture" and "[commitment] to the practice of cultural humility…an important facet of professional identity that encourages self-evolvement and evolvement of self through one's professional life" (NASW, p. 16). The NASW underscores the body of literature in health and human services that support culturally tailored and appropriate interventions in:

addressing racial identity formation for people of color as well as for white people; the interrelationship among class, race, ethnicity, and gender; working with low-income families; working with older adults; the importance of religion and spirituality in the lives of clients; the development of gender identity and sexual orientation; immigration, acculturation, and assimilation stressors; biculturalism; working with people with disabilities; empowerment skills; community building; reaching out to new populations of color; conscious and unconscious bias; cultural humility, culture-specific and culturally adapted interventions; and training in culturally competent models of practice (2015, pp. 9–10)

Clinicians play an instrumental role in bringing diversity of the older adult client and culturally preferred practices to the interdisciplinary team, the next key domain for effective social work practice with older adults.

Interdisciplinary Team Roles and Planning

Interdisciplinary team roles, approaches, and care planning strategies will be emphasized as a key domain of effective social work practice with older adults and caregivers in Chapters 3 through 12. Interdisciplinary teamwork involves "a complex process in which different types of staff work together to share expertise, knowledge, and skills to impact on patient care" (Nancarrow et al., 2013, p. 1). Multidisciplinary teams differ from interdisciplinary teams in two key ways: In the former, each team member implements a specialized part of the patient care plan and a consultative approach is often used with one practitioner (oftentimes, the doctor or psychiatrist) assuming central responsibility and consulting with other disciplines as needed. In contrast, in the latter, each member of the team (social worker, nurse, doctor, psychiatrist, physical therapist, occupational therapist, dietician, pharmacist, dentist, etc.) shares individual knowledge about the patient, and they collectively create a treatment plan. They understand the roles of each discipline in providing holistic and comprehensive patient care, and they seek to understand the perspectives of other disciplines on the team. Effective interdisciplinary teams can be transdisciplinary when they share the responsibility of implementing an integrated treatment plan—this is often seen in patient-centered and integrated care practice settings. Evidence-based interdisciplinary practice requires all team members to "learn to communicate, understand each other's language, ideally develop a shared language, and learn to coordinate their actions as a team" (Newhouse & Spring, 2010, p. 9).

The interdisciplinary team for Mrs. Hansen was composed of the nurse, social worker, and physician. Together, the treatment team developed a treatment recommendation, and per the nephew's request, Mrs. Hansen was transferred to a board and care home. The social worker provided two additional visits. During the second visit, which was the first that took place at the board and care, Mrs. Hansen was observed after lunch sitting in a reclining chair singing a song she was familiar with, following the text on a large projection television in front of her. The caregivers at the board and care reported Mrs.

Hansen was adjusting well to the placement, her appetite was good, and she accepted care from the caregivers. The nephew decided to keep Mrs. Hansen at the board and care.

Social workers are key members of the interdisciplinary team. They respond rapidly to issues concerning imminent risk and safety of older adults and work collaboratively with the rest of the team, the client, and/or the family/conservator in identifying best practices and evidence-based interventions appropriate for the client, the next key domain for effective social work practice with older adults.

Evidence-based Interventions

A survey of evidence-based interventions to address older adult patient and caregiver issues will be presented in Chapters 3 through 12. The Social Work Policy Institute (2008) notes that the terms *evidence-based interventions*, *evidence-based practices*, *evidence-informed interventions*, and *evidence-based treatments* are used interchangeably frequently in literature, as well as, in practice settings. The gold standard for an evidence-based intervention is that it has undergone randomized controlled trials (RCTs). Evidence-based practices "are interventions for which there is consistent scientific evidence showing that they improve client outcomes" (Drake et al., 2001, p 179). Evidence-based interventions that have been tested with RCTs, meta-analyses, or systematic reviews will be emphasized. Experimental, quasiexperimental, and pre-experimental studies that provide emerging practices to address diversity (where RCTs or systematic reviews are not available) will be drawn upon as well.

When applied to suicide prevention, clinicians can use effective models for prevention such as the Comprehensive Approach to Suicide Prevention, which involves identifying and assisting an older adult client at risk; increasing help-seeking behaviors of the client; providing rapid access to mental health and suicide care and treatments that are evidence based and provided by trained professionals; assisting with linkages to organizations to ensure safe transition of care for older adults; responding with a full continuum of care options for the older adult in crisis, including emergency, peer, clinic, and emergency hotline options; providing postintervention services for survivors of suicide; working with the older adult client to reduce lethal means for self-harm/suicide; enhancing resilience and coping skills; and promoting social support and connections with community resources and support (Suicide Prevention Resource Center, 2017).

With all interventions, clinicians are responsible for assessing and monitoring the effects on desirable outcomes with older adults, the next key domain of effective social work practice with older adults.

Assessing/Monitoring Evidence-based Treatment Outcomes

A key domain of clinical practice with older adults involves assessing and monitoring the evidence-based intervention treatment on key patient outcomes. In Chapters 3 through 12, strategies for assessing and monitoring the impact of an evidence-based intervention on improving desirable client outcome(s) are explored. Begin with identifying standardized outcome measures and assessing the outcomes before the evidence-based intervention is delivered in treatment—this establishes a baseline. RCTs generally provide a description of standardized assessment tools used when testing the evidence-based intervention. The National Registry of Evidence-based Practices and Programs (NREPP) is a reliable source for identifying evidence-based interventions. Process, or subjective outcomes or indicators of well-being and quality of life, should also be assessed and monitored. In clinical practice, monitoring of the evidence-based intervention occurs with each delivery of treatment where the clinician administers the standardized assessment tool and gathers other indicators of subjective well-being from the client. This allows the clinician to identify whether desired client outcomes are improving or worsening. As desired outcomes approach attainment, the clinician can begin preparing the client for termination. If the outcomes get worse, the clinician and client explore other options: stopping the treatment, consulting with members of the interdisciplinary team, and/or identifying alternative evidence-based interventions. Monitoring of the evidence-based interventions on patient outcomes ensures that the clinician avoids harm to the patient; it allows the client and clinician to engage in discussion on the effectiveness or ineffectiveness of the treatment.

The use of appropriate community resources and interagency coordination of services and programs to meet the biopsychosocial/spiritual needs of older adult clients is another key domain of effective practice with older adults. Referral to and coordination of services with other service providers is essential for ensuring continuity of care from one treatment setting to another as well as when the older adult client returns back to a community setting.

Community Resources/Interagency Coordination

A central area of expertise among social workers is that of community resource knowledge and referral, as well as, communication and coordination of services and client care with agencies. In Chapters 3 through 12, possible community resources and interagency collaborations for coordinated care will be discussed. Clinicians use case management skills to identify appropriate community-based services, such as transportation, senior centers, home and congregate meals, and support groups to meet the biopsychosocial/spiritual needs of an older adult client. According to the NASW (2016), case management "is a collaborative process to plan, seek, advocate for, and monitor services, resources, and supports on behalf of a client. [It] enables a health care social worker to serve clients who may require the services of various health care providers and facilities, community-based organizations, social services agencies, and other programs. [It] limits problems arising from fragmentation of services, staff turnover, and inadequate coordination among providers" (p. 11).

Community resources and interagency coordination/collaboration are increasingly important in preventing recidivism, complications, or unmet biopsychosocial/spiritual needs for an older adult client. Clinicians help educate an older adult client and caregiver on how to navigate systems that include the health care system, integrated care, public social services, legal services, community-based care, and long-term care planning and financing.

In working with older adult clients and their families, clinicians may experience transference and/or countertransference issues that may present in the therapeutic relationship—the next domain of clinical practice. Clinicians must develop skills to identify and manage both transference and countertransference to prevent interference with the treatments and ultimately outcomes of treatment with older adult clients and families.

Transference/Countertransference

Another key domain of effective social work practice with older adult clients and caregivers is the identification and management of both transference and countertransference as it presents in therapeutic relations. Potential transference and countertransference issues and how to manage them will be explored in Chapters 3 through 12. Transference is defined as "a phenomenon in psychoanalysis characterized by unconscious redirection of feelings from one person to another, in the case of psychotherapy from patient to therapist," whereas countertransference is defined as the "transference of feelings from therapist to patient," both of which are "based on the human ability to recognize the outside world" by comparing the "present perception with past experience" (Prasko et al., 2010, p. 1). Transference with an older adult client may involve the client transferring feelings about adult children or grandchildren onto the therapist or feelings toward past helping professionals onto the current clinician. Friedman and Goldbaum note two common areas of countertransference when working with older adult clients: "tendencies (a) to act with enormous compassion, advocacy, and altruism, sometimes ignoring the wishes of the client or becoming more invested in the outcome than in the relationship with the client; and (b) to avoid contact because of feelings of powerlessness, inadequacy, denial, fear, or cowardice" (2016, p. 188). Both issues should be explored and reflected on by the clinician; options and strategies for identifying and managing them will be discussed.

Technological resources, the next key domain of effective practice with older adults, plays a large role in education, support, and management /maintenance of desirable treatment outcomes with older adults.

Technological Resources

Technological resources are an important domain of effective social work practice with older adults. Resources may range from websites for health, mental health, substance use, legal, and supportive resources to applications for smartphones for self-management, medication reminders, and/or online support group, telehealth services, or computer-based biofeedback for self-management and provider monitoring. Clinicians can refer and link older adult clients to organizations specific to a client's presenting condition, which can provide further education and support to the client. For example, if a client has been diagnosed with diabetes, the American Diabetes Association is an appropriate resource because they provide psychoeducation about the health condition and skills for managing various facets of diabetes, as well as other sources of support. Chapters 3 through 14 will present potential technological resources an older adult and caregiver may use to improve well-being. Technological resources for elder abuse and neglect, as well as suicide, are as follows.

Abuse/Neglect

Clearinghouse on Neglect and Abuse of the Elderly: https://www.elderabusecenter.org/default.cfm_p_cane.html

Frameworks Institute Talking Elder Abuse Toolkit: http://www.frameworksinstitute.org/toolkits/elderabuse/

National Adult Protective Services Association (NAPSA): http://www.napsa-now.org/

NAPSA Get Help: http://www.napsa-now.org/get-help/how-aps-helps/

NAPSA Get Informed: http://www.napsa-now.org/get-informed/

National Center on Elder Abuse state information: https://ncea.acl.gov/resources/state.html

National Consumer Voice for Quality Long-Term Care: www.theconsumervoice.org

National Long-Term Care Ombudsman Resource Center: www.ltcombudsman.org

National Organization for Victim Assistance: http://www.trynova.org/

Prevention of elder abuse, neglect, and exploitation: https://www.acl.gov/node/10

Tools and tips: http://eldermistreatment.usc.edu/weaad-home/tools-and-tips/

University of Southern California (USC) Center on Elder Mistreatment: http://eldermistreatment.usc.edu/

USC Training Resources on Elder Abuse: http://trea.usc.edu/

U.S. Department of Health and Human Services, Administration for Community Living: https://acl.gov/

World Elder Abuse Awareness Day: http://eldermistreatment.usc.edu/weaad-home/

Suicide

ASQ Suicide Risk Screening Tool: https://www.nimh.nih.gov/labs-at-nimh/asq-toolkit-materials/index.shtml

Best practices: https://suicidepreventionlifeline.org/best-practices/

Columbia-Suicide Severity Rating Scale (C-SSRS): https://www.integration.samhsa.gov/clinical-practice/Columbia_Suicide_Severity_Rating_Scale.pdf

National Institute of Mental Health: https://www.nimh.nih.gov/health/topics/suicide-prevention/index.shtml

National Suicide Prevention Lifeline: https://suicidepreventionlifeline.org/

Suicide Assistant Five-Step Evaluation and Triage (SAFE-T): https://www.integration.samhsa.gov/images/res/SAFE_T.pdf

Substance Abuse and Mental Health Services Administration: https://www.integration.samhsa.gov/clinical-practice/screening-tools#suicide

Suicide Prevention Resource Center: https://www.sprc.org/

Clinicians must also have knowledge and skills to identify legal and ethical issues that may present when working with older adult clients and their families, the next key domain, as well as strategies for addressing such issues.

Legal/Ethical Considerations

Chapters 3 through 12 will present key legal and ethical considerations that a clinician may consider when working with an older adult client and caregiver, including legal mandates and laws that inform practice as well as ethical dilemmas and how to identify and address legal and/or ethical issues that present. For example, legal requirements for mandated reporting as well as considerations for estate planning and conservatorship will be discussed. Ethical considerations include ethical dilemmas, end-of-life decision making and options, and contextual ethical issues. The clinician should be familiar with reporting procedures and protocols at the state, local, and organizational levels. For older adults presenting with suicide risk factors, clinicians should be aware of procedures and protocols within their state and organization for initiating psychiatric holds for clients at imminent risk for suicide. The same follows for self-neglect and/or abuse/neglect perpetrated by others.

Clinicians working with older adults may experience great satisfaction in providing interventions that improve the quality of life and well-being of older adult clients, referred to as compassion satisfaction. They may experience compassion fatigue, however, in some instances where system issues create barriers for improving the well-being of older adults, or they may experience vicarious trauma when working with older adults experiencing trauma presently or previously. Ethically, clinicians must manage these responses so that they do not interfere with the treatment of and outcomes of treatment for older adults.

Clinician Responses

Engagement in self-care is key to clinical practice with older adults and caregivers. Self-care and coping skills can be sources of strength and resiliency for clinicians when they are working with complex patients, situations, and trauma. Clinicians can assess their current use of various categories of self-care using the Self-Care Assessment developed by Saakvitne, Pearlman, and Abrahamson (1996). The Self-Care Assessment allows clinicians to rate on a scale from 1 (i.e., it never occurred to me to use this self-care strategy) to 5 (i.e., frequent use of the self-care strategy) for 15 types of physical self-care, 14 types of psychological self-care, 11 types of emotional self-care, 17 types of spiritual self-care, 12 types of workplace or professional self-care, and 2 types of balance self-care (Saakvitne, Pearlman, & Abrahamson, 1996). Respondents are prompted to identify one area from each category of self-care to work on (Saakvitne, Pearlman, & Abrahamson, 1996). Empathy has been identified as a tool to prevent both compassion fatigue and vicarious or secondary trauma/stress among social workers (Wagaman, Geiger, Shockley, & Segal, 2015). Additionally, compassion satisfaction, or positive feelings on the part of the social worker to engage in the helping process, can be enhanced by empathy (Wagaman, Geiger, Shockley, & Segal, 2015).

Compassion Fatigue

Compassion fatigue is defined as the clinician's "reduced capacity or interest in being empathic" and natural emotions and behavioral consequences to bearing witness and becoming knowledgeable about the pain and suffering of an older adult client who has experienced trauma; as such, it is a "hazard associated primarily with the clinical setting and with first responders to traumatic events" (Adams, Boscarino, & Figley, 2006, p. 2). Clinician awareness of compassion fatigue and exploration of strategies for preventing burnout are an ongoing component of clinical practice with older adults and their families.

Vicarious and Secondary Trauma

Vicarious trauma and secondary trauma or stress occur when a clinician's "empathic engagement with traumatized clients often requires the professional to discuss details of the traumatic experience, including role playing and dramatic reenactment of the events, which are thought to be vital to the therapeutic process but can have an adverse emotional impact on the caregiver" (Adams, Boscarino, & Figley, 2006, p. 2). One strategy for addressing vicarious or secondary trauma/stress is to process the case with a colleague or supervisor so that the clinician does not hold the trauma.

Strategies for addressing both compassion fatigue and vicarious and secondary trauma include: setting good personal and work boundaries; having healthy personal networks professionally, socially, and recreationally; managing work challenges; and maintaining good physical, nutritional, and spiritual practices (Wagaman, Geiger, Shockley, & Segal, 2015). Clinicians can also use the 30-item Professional Quality of Life Scale (PROQOL) to assess their scores on three different subscales in the past 30 days at work (i.e., compassion satisfaction, burnout, and secondary traumatic stress) (Stamm, 2010).

Discussion Questions

1. What is your understanding of what evidence-based practice is?
2. Identify the evidence-based practices in your field placement or work setting.
   a. For what populations were the evidence-based practices developed?
   b. Are there any cultural adaptations made to the evidence-based intervention for diverse populations?
3. Are there any barriers to bringing evidence-based practices into your field placement or work setting?
4. How might you introduce new evidence-based practices into your field placement or work setting?
5. How are older adults with high-risk factors for neglect/abuse screened in your agency or community?
   a. What treatments and interventions are typically provided to organizations at your agency, in the local community, or in the state where you work with older adults?
   b. What resources are available?
   c. What legal/ethical issues have occurred that you are aware of, and how were they addressed?
6. How are older adults with high-risk factors for suicide screened in your agency or community?
   a. What treatments and interventions are typically provided to organizations at your agency, in the local community, or in the state where you work with older adults?
   b. What resources are available?
   c. What legal/ethical issues have occurred that you are aware of and how were they addressed?

Self-Reflection Exercises

1. Think of an older adult client you have recently seen, or anticipate your first visit with an older adult client.
   a. What transference issues presented or do you anticipate may present?
   b. What countertransference issues presented or do you anticipate may present?
2. Complete the PROQOL.
   a. What is your score on the compassion satisfaction scale?
   b. What is your score on the burnout scale?
   c. What is your score on the secondary traumatic stress subscale?
   d. What new insights do you have?

3. Complete the Self-Care Assessment.
    a. What new insights do you have about the types of self-care you engage in the most? The least?
    b. Which new self-care activities do you want to work on?

References

Adams, R. E., Boscarino, J. A., & Figley, C. R. (2006). Compassion fatigue and psychological distress among social workers: A validation study. *The American Journal of Orthopsychiatry*, 76(1), 103–108.

Administration on Community Living. (2017). National Center on Elder Abuse. Retrieved from https://www.acl.gov/index.php/grants/national-center-elder-abuse-ncea-0

American Foundation for Suicide Prevention. (2017). Suicide statistics. Retrieved from https://afsp.org/about-suicide/suicide-statistics/

Centers for Disease Control. (2017). Definitions: Self-directed violence. Retrieved from https://www.cdc.gov/violenceprevention/suicide/definitions.html

Centers for Disease Control. (2018). Elder abuse: Definitions. Retrieved from www.cdc.gov/violenceprevention/elderabuse/definitions.html

Council on Social Work Education. (2017). EPAS Handbook. Council on Social Work Education. Retrieved from https://www.cswe.org/Accreditation/Standards-and-Policies/EPAS-Handbook

Curtin, S. C., Warner, M., & Hedegaard, H. (2016). Increase in suicide in the United Sates, 1994–2014. NCHS Data Brief No. 241, April 2016. Centers for Disease Control/National Center for Health Statistics. Retrieved from https://www.cdc.gov/nchs/products/databriefs/db241.htm

Drake, R. E., Goldman, H. H., Leff, H. S., Lehman, A. F., Dixon, L., Mueser, K. T., & Torrey, W. C. (2001). Implementing evidence-based practices in routine mental health service settings. *Psychiatric Services*, 52(2), 179–182.

Friedman, F. B., & Goldbaum, C. S. (2016). Experiential learning: Developing insights about working with older adults. *Clinical Social Work Journal, 44*(2), 186–197.

Karlin, B. E. (2014). Suicide in late life: Unique factors and enduring treatment gaps. Suicide Prevention Resource Center. Retrieved from http://www.sprc.org/news/suicide-late-life-unique-factors-enduring-treatment-gaps

Mental Health America & National Council on Aging. (2017). Preventing suicide in older adults: Mental health in older adults (Fact Sheet). Retrieved from http://www.mentalhealthamerica.net/preventing-suicide-older-adults

Morgan, R. E., & Mason, B. J. (2014). Crimes against the elderly. Bureau of Justice Statistics. Retrieved from www.bjs.gov/index.cfm?ty=pbdetail&iid=5136

Nancarrow, S. A., Booth, A., Ariss, S., Smith, T., Enderby, P., & Roots, A. (2013). Ten principles of good interdisciplinary team work. *Human Resources for Health, 11*, 19.

NASW. (2015). Standards and indicators for cultural competence in social work practice. Washington, DC: NASW Press.

NASW. (2016). NASW standards for social work practice in health settings. Washington, DC: NASW Press.

National Center on Elder Abuse. (2006). The availability and utility of interdisciplinary data on elder abuse: A white paper for the National Center on Elder Abuse. American Bar Association on Law and Aging. Washington, DC. Retrieved from https://ncea.acl.gov/resources/docs/archive/Availability-Utility-Interdisciplinary-Data-EA-WhitePaper-NCEA-2006.pdf

National Center on Elder Abuse. (2016). Elder abuse screening tools for healthcare professionals. Retrieved from http://eldermistreatment.usc.edu/wp-content/uploads/2016/10/Elder-Abuse-Screening-Tools-for-Healthcare-Professionals.pdf

National Institute of Mental Health. (2017). NIMH Toolkit: Suicide Risk Screening Tool. Retrieved from https://www.nimh.nih.gov/news/science-news/2013/file_143902.pdf

Newhouse, R. P., & Spring, B. (2010). Interdisciplinary evidence-based practice: Moving from silos to synergy. *Nursing Outlook, 58*(6), 309–317.

Posner, K. (2008). Columbia-Suicide Severity Rating Scale. The Research Foundation for Mental Hygiene, Inc. Retrieved from https://www.integration.samhsa.gov/clinicalpractice/Columbia_Suicide_Severity_Rating_Scale.pdf

Prasko, J., Diveky, T., Grambal, A., Kamaradova, D., Mozny, P., Sigmundova, Z., ... & Vyskocilova, J. (2010). Transference and countertransference in cognitive behavioral therapy. *Biomedical Papers, 154*(3), 189–197.

Saakvitne, K. W., Pearlman, L. A., & Abrahamson, D. J. (1996). *Transforming the pain: A workbook on vicarious traumatization.* New York: WW Norton.

Social Work Policy Institute. (2008). Research: Evidence-based practice. Retrieved from http://www.socialworkpolicy.org/research/evidence-based-practice.html

Stamm, B. H. (2010). The Concise ProQOL Manual (2nd ed.). Pocatello, ID: ProQOL.org.

Suicide Prevention Resource Center. (2017). A comprehensive approach to suicide prevention. Retrieved from https://www.sprc.org/effective-prevention/comprehensive-approach

Wagaman, M. A., Geiger, J. M., Shockley, C., & Segal, E. A. (2015). The role of empathy in burnout, compassion satisfaction, and secondary traumatic stress among social workers. *Social Work, 60*(3), 201–209.

World Health Organization. (2017). Elder abuse. Retrieved from www.who.int/mediacentre/factsheets/fs357/en/

CHAPTER 2

Theoretical and Assessment Approaches

T his chapter highlights key theories that inform assessment and interventions with older adults and provides suggestions on how to apply each theory to an older adult client. It reviews assessment and screening approaches with older adults and provides case examples to illustrate their use in clinical practice.

Competency 7: Assess Individuals, Families, Groups, Organizations, and Communities

The specific Council for Social Work Education (CSWE) competency from the curriculum guide for specialized practice with older adults highlighted in this chapter is Competency 7: Assess individuals, families, groups, organizations, and communities. The competency description and specific behaviors of practitioners that demonstrate competency with this population follow:

> **Specialized Practice Competency Description:** Practitioners in aging utilize ecological-systems theory, a strengths-based and person/family-centered framework to conduct assessments that value the resilience of diverse older adults, families, and caregivers. They select appropriate assessment tools, methods and technology, and evaluate, adapt, and modify them, as needed, to enhance their validity in working with diverse, vulnerable and at-risk groups. The comprehensive biopsychosocial assessment takes into account the multiple factors of physical, mental and social well-being needed for treatment planning for older adults and their families. They develop skills in interprofessional assessment and communication with key constituencies to choose the most effective practice strategies. Gero social workers understand how their own experiences and affective reactions about aging, quality of life, loss and grief may affect their assessment and resultant decision-making.

Competency Behaviors: (1) Conduct assessments that incorporate a strengths-based perspective, person/family-centered focus, and resilience while recognizing aging related risk, (2) Develop, select, and adapt assessment methods and tools that optimize practice with older adults, their families, caregivers, and communities, and (3) Use and integrate multiple domains and sources of assessment information and communicate with other professionals to inform a comprehensive plan for intervention. (Council for Social Work Education, 2017, pp. 89–90)

Case Study

Mr. Kahale is a 68-year-old Hawaiian American who moved with his spouse to the mainland after retiring from his general manager position in transportation to be closer to his 33-year-old daughter, 35-year-old son-in-law, and two grandchildren, ages 10 and 13. Mr. Kahale developed heart disease at the age of 55 and was hospitalized for a heart attack at the age of 68; he underwent coronary artery bypass surgery during the hospital stay and was discharged by the hospitalist with an order for home health services as Mr. Kahale had a skilled need for both a nurse and physical therapist. The order for the nurse included chronic disease self-management training for heart disease, medication management, and physical health assessment. The order for the physical therapist included functional health, home safety, and durable medical equipment assessment and treatment. One week after Mr. Kahale returned home and began home health services, his spouse had a massive heart attack while gardening in the front yard and died. Mr. Kahale's daughter reported to the nurse that Mr. Kahale seemed depressed and that she was worried about his mental health. The nurse contacted Mr. Kahale's primary care physician for a social work consultation.

Part I. Key Theories

Part I identifies key theories relevant to practice with older adults. Application of each theory to the case study and older adults in various practice settings illustrates the use of the theory in practice. The key theories that follow include the life course theory, strengths perspective, activity theory, developmental theory, cognitive behavioral theory, intersectionality theory, transtheoretical model and stages of change, and health belief model.

Life Course Theory

Life course theory (LCT) is an approach that recognizes the influence on human development and life pathways by both historical and life course changes (Elder, Johnson, & Crosnoe, 2003). The life course is defined as "an age-graded sequence of socially defined roles and events that are enacted over historical time and place" (Elder, Johnson, & Crosnoe, 2003, p. 15). There are five key principles that guide life course inquiries that consider social change, development, and pathways (Elder, Johnson, & Crosnoe, 2003). The first, the principle of life-span development, recognizes that "human development and aging are lifelong processes" (Elder, Johnson, & Crosnoe, 2003, p. 11). Under this principle, the biopsychosocial changes that individuals undergo may be viewed as adaptive or positive experiences that impact life course development (Elder, Johnson, & Crosnoe, 2003). Mr. Kahale, from the case study, developed heart disease during his last five years of work, and he also had grandchildren on the mainland he wanted to be closer to—both factors influenced his decision to relocate to the mainland, a decision he was content with. The second, the principle of agency, considers that "individuals construct their own life course through the choices and actions they take within the opportunities and constraints of history and social circumstance" (Elder, Johnson, & Crosnoe, 2003, p. 11). This principle recognizes the strengths of individuals to be active rather than passive decision makers based on either opportunities presented to them or contextual constraints that may limit their ability to act on such opportunities (Elder, Johnson, & Crosnoe, 2003). Mr. Kahale came from an upper–middle-class family, and he had financial resources available to allow him to attend college and focus on his education, allowing him to complete his goal of higher education in a shorter time frame than if he had to work while pursuing his education. He and his spouse made the decision to wait to have children until his career became established around the age of 35; although he and Mrs. Kahale wanted to have more than one child, she had difficulty conceiving due to this delay.

The third, the principle of time and place, posits that the "life course of individuals is embedded and shaped by the historical times and places they experience over their life-time" (Elder, Johnson, & Crosnoe, 2003, p. 12). This principle specifically considers the impacts of history, geographical location, culture, and values on an individual's life course (Elder, Johnson, & Crosnoe, 2003). The fourth, the principle of timing, recognizes that "the developmental antecedent and consequences of life transitions, events, and behavioral patterns vary according to their timing in a person's life" (Elder, Johnson, & Crosnoe, 2003, p. 12). Essentially, this means that the impact and/or perception of an event or experience depends on the developmental stage the individual is in (Elder, Johnson, & Crosnoe, 2003). Returning back to the case study, Mr. Kahale became a grandparent at the age of 55—the developmental stage of generativity versus stagnation, where a middle-aged adult seeks to mentor the next generation. The geographical distance between his grandchildren and himself created challenges for resolving this psychosocial crisis. However, he had nieces and nephews from his siblings in Hawaii to spend time with and mentor, and he traveled frequently to the mainland. The fifth, the principle of linked lives, factors in interdependence and the influence of macro events on social relationships: "Lives are lived interdependently and socio-historical influences are expressed through this network of shared relationships" (Elder, Johnson, & Crosnoe, 2003, p. 12). This principle recognizes that changes in the life of one individual may create subsequent transitions for others in his or her social network. In regard to Mr. Kahale from the case study, his sudden transition into widowhood, after retirement and relocation, meant that his daughter would in turn transition into the sandwich generation, caring for an older adult parent and young children simultaneously.

The life course theory, also commonly referred to as the life course perspective, provides a conceptual framework for the clinician to gain an understanding of a client by considering key transitions and events in the client's life to date that have been influenced by social, historical, sociopolitical, environmental, financial, health, societal, and financial contextual factors. In clinical practice, the life course, or path, of the client is used to gain an understanding about continuity and alterations in expected pathways (Hutchinson, 2013). In LCT, commonly used biographical and historical concepts that capture the context of movement and time in an individual's life course include: social pathways, "the trajectories of education and work, family and residences that are followed by individuals and groups through society;" trajectories, which are "sequences of roles and experiences" that are composed of transitions; transitions, the "changes in state or role"; duration, which refers to the "time between transitions;" and turning points, or "substantial changes in the direction of one's life" (Elder, Johnson, & Crosnoe, 2003, p. 8). Finally, a commonly used concept that signifies age and time contexts in the life course is a cohort. A cohort refers to similar experiences, due to the sociohistorical and cultural context of change, for a group of individuals from the same generation or time period (Hutchinson, 2013).

For further thought: Consider how the formerly defined terms social pathways, trajectories, duration, turning points, and/or cohort might apply to Mr. Kahale, older adults in your own life, or clients that you are working with.

Strengths Perspective

The strengths perspective is an empowerment and human strength approach used to understand the ways that human beings have the capacity for strength, resilience, and creativity to overcome adversity and respond effectively during challenging times in their lives in order to achieve aspirations and goals through their personal and social capital resources (Robbins, Chatterjee, & Canda, 2012). Rather than focusing on deficits, pathology, limitations, or weaknesses of a client, the strengths perspective emphasizes the positive attributes of human beings and their innate ability to identify and reduce problems in their lives to achieve desirable levels of well-being and quality of life. In this way, it is an empowering model that clinicians use to reconnect clients during challenging periods in their lives to the inner strengths, resiliency, and approaches to addressing problems in the past that could be drawn upon to address a current problem, challenge, or issue. The strengths perspective does not ignore that illness or real problems exist for individuals, but rather it focuses on identifying and building on the strengths and resiliency of the client to further assist and empower the client (Simmons, Shapiro, Accomazzo, & Manthey, 2016). The assumption is that when a clinician supports and recognizes a client's strengths, it increases the client's ability to learn, overcome, develop, and grow through the current challenge or issue (Robbins, Chatterjee, & Canda, 2012).

Key constructs from the strengths perspective include: empowerment, resilience, self-determination, and hope (Simmons, Shapiro, Accomazzo, & Manthey, 2016). Empowerment is "a means by which a person creatively uses his or her resources to gain and use power to achieve goals, improve and control life circumstances, and positively contribute to one's community" (Simmons, Shapiro, Accomazzo, & Manthey, 2016, p. 41). Meetings with Mr. Kahale for several visits after the death of his spouse showed that once he had time to process his grief, accept the loss, and reinvest in himself, he recognized how important it was to return back to his Hawaiian Club to seek support and socialization after the death of his spouse. Resilience refers to the ability to rebound from life-challenging circumstances; it involves both internal (i.e., coping skills) and external (i.e., social capital and support networks) protective factors that reduce risk (Simmons, Shapiro, Accomazzo, & Manthey, 2016). For Mr. Kahale, his faith and cultural community, as well as family and neighbor support, were important external protective factors; he was not socially isolated after the death of his spouse and had a great amount of support available to him. Mr. Kahale's internal factors included a sense of optimism and hope for his future and use of coping skills (i.e., spirituality and increasing his participation in his diversity and faith communities).

Self-determination involves the client's right to engage in decision making, participate in, and make their preferences for treatment known throughout the episode of care/treatment, as well as the right to exercise autonomy in their ability to choose the course of their own life (Simmons, Shapiro, Accomazzo, & Manthey, 2016). With the initial referral for Mr. Kahale, there was great concern by his daughter that his grief reactions were abnormal; she was concerned he was depressed and needed medication because he was crying and having visual and olfactory hallucinations of his spouse in the home the first week after her death. Mr. Kahale was screened for depression using the Patient Health Questionnaire (PHQ-9) and Geriatric Depression Scale (GDS); his symptoms were more indicative of normal uncomplicated grief. Mr. Kahale was concerned about the side effects of antidepressant medications and was very distressed by the social worker's initial visit, where he was assessed for depression and psychosis; he shared a fear of being sent off to a nursing home and being removed from his home. Mr. Kahale was provided with psychoeducation about his normal grief reactions, of which crying and hallucinations are both common and normal. His goals and preferences were incorporated into in the plan of care and treatment with the social worker. He was provided with grief counseling and symptom monitoring for four weeks; he developed goals for becoming for active in his Hawaiian and faith communities; psychotropic medications were not indicated; and he was able to remain in his home, his preference. Hope refers to the "belief that good things, rather than bad things, will happen … when people can identify goals and see potential pathways to these goals" in different situations over time (Simmons, Shapiro, Accomazzo, & Manthey, 2016, p. 41). Mr. Kahale was initially fearful that a visit by the social worker would result in his removal from his home because he felt like he was "going crazy" with his hallucinations. Once his grief symptoms were addressed and the social worker explained her role to preserve autonomy, self-determination, dignity, and respect in his care and treatment while ensuring his safety and well-being, his perspective shifted, and hope became activated for him in his transition to widowhood. He began to see the possibilities and ways to adjust to his new identity, maintain a continuing bond with his spouse, and reinvest in his family, cultural, and faith communities.

There are eight major tenants that guide clinical practice using the strengths perspective:

1. *It is goal oriented.* Clinicians work with clients to identify and establish goals based informed by the client's values, preferences, and hopes for his or her life and future (Simmons, Shapiro, Accomazzo, & Manthey, 2016). Clinicians can assist the client with establishing SMART goals—goals that are specific, measurable, attainable, realistic, and have a time frame. Mr. Kahale's SMART goal, for example, was: S—Hawaiian club for support, M—attendance once a week, A—it was a goal Mr. Kahale could attain, R—it was both a realistic and desirable goal, and T—within 2 weeks from the social worker's first visit, he would start attending the Hawaiian Club.

2. *The client's strengths are assessed systematically.* The internal and external resources of the client that can be drawn upon to assist the client in addressing or overcoming an issue or challenge are explored (Simmons, Shapiro, Accomazzo, & Manthey, 2016). For example, systematic assessment of strengths can include identifying past and current coping strategies to address similar issues or challenges, looking for exceptions when the issue or problem is not present or is better, and identifying which external or environmental resources were helpful in past situations that may help the client with overcoming the presenting issue or challenge (Simmons, Shapiro, Accomazzo, & Manthey, 2016).

3. The strengths perspective *views the "environment as rich in resources and explicit methods are used to leverage client and environmental strengths for goal attainment"* (Simmons, Shapiro, Accomazzo, & Manthey, 2016, p. 144). In other words, the external resources of the client (i.e., social support network, community, diversity, faith, social, recreational, etc.) are identified and the clinician encourages the client to activate and utilize the external resources to assist the client in achieving desirable goals. For Mr. Kahale, increasing attendance at both his faith and diversity external resources were important specific goals he established for himself after the death of his spouse. The clinician explored with Mr. Kahale the actions he needed to complete in order to accomplish the established goals.

4. *The therapeutic relationship between the client and clinician is "hope inducing"* in that the clinician focuses on the strengths of the client rather than deficits, strives to instill empowerment and hope in the client, and strives for the client to begin to have more "positive self-perceptions about his or her abilities, resources, choices, strengths, interests, knowledge, and capacities" (Simmons, Shapiro, Accomazzo, & Manthey, 2016, p. 145). Mr. Kahale had forgotten his internal and external resources after the death of his spouse; he questioned his grief reactions. The social worker guided Mr. Kahale back to his inner and external strengths, resiliency, and skills and what he hoped for changed in the direction of new goals and aspirations for himself.

5. In strengths-based practice, *"the provision of meaningful choices is central and individuals have the authority to choose"* (Simmons, Shapiro, Accomazzo, & Manthey, 2016, p. 145). In times of crisis or change, clients oftentimes feel that their

choices to address an issue may be limited or that they do not have control over the situation or decisions about it. As such, by using a strengths-based approach, the clinician ensures that the autonomy of the client to choose and engage in all aspects of decision making for treatment and options is emphasized. Mr. Kahale had a fear about the initial social work visit; he also shared with his daughter that he was having hallucinations after the death of his spouse. Mr. Kahale was worried that his daughter and the social worker might force him out of his home and into an institution. The social worker assured Mr. Kahale that he had the authority to participate in the decision making and choose options consistent with his values and preferences.

6. *"Strengths-based practice assumes that we best serve clients by collaborating with them"* (Simmons, Shapiro, Accomazzo, & Manthey, 2016, p. 145). What this means is that clinicians meet the client where they are, allowing them to be the expert of their own lives. Establishing the therapeutic relationship for this to take place involves engaging a client, establishing trust, and confidence by the client that the clinician is there to come alongside the client and work collaboratively to explore options meaningful to the client. When Mr. Kahale was provided this message and understood that that the social worker was not there to remove him from his home, his tension and fear immediately subsided. He was then able to understand the role of the social worker and his role in partnering together to explore options to address his presenting challenge and desirable goals for treatment.

7. Strengths-based practice *"assumes that trauma, abuse, illness, and struggle may be harmful but they may also be sources of challenge and opportunity"* as the clinician can explore with the client how they have overcome prior challenges and activate those same sources of strength and resiliency for overcoming the presenting challenge (Simmons, Shapiro, Accomazzo, & Manthey, 2016, p. 146). The social worker asked Mr. Kahale to think of a challenge in the past and identify what he did to get through it. Mr. Kahale talked about the death of his father; he stated what helped him the most was the support from family, his faith, and cultural communities. He was asked whether those same external and internal resources could help him in adjusting to the death of his spouse. Mr. Kahale responded that he thought it would be helpful, and he considered how to activate those similar resources to help him through his grief and adjustment to the death of his spouse.

8. Strength-based practice *"assumes that the worker does not know the upper limits of individuals' capacity to grow and change;"* in other words, the clinician avoids making assumptions about whether a client has the capacity to engage in change behaviors and assists the client with overcoming his or her own presuppositions about helping professionals based on assumptions or previous experiences (Simmons, Shapiro, Accomazzo, & Manthey, 2016, p. 146). Mr. Kahale had an assumption about the social worker that she would have him removed from his home; this was based on his own understanding of child protective social work services. The social worker processed these assumptions and provided psychoeducation on the role of the social worker.

Activity Theory

A major premise of activity theory, introduced in 1953 by Havighurst and Albrecht, is that to achieve life satisfaction, successful aging, and psychological well-being in older adulthood, one should continue to engage in desirable activities (Lange & Grossman, 2010) to maintain physical and mental health. Activity theory posits that an older adult should remain occupied to attain life satisfaction (Lange & Grossman, 2010) and that such activity delays when continuing from middle to older adult. The positive aspects of socialization and social support on health and well-being are emphasized in this theory. The activity theory was initially critiqued for overlooking challenges to engage in activity due to functional health declines or inadequate social resources. It was also critiqued for not defining the range of activities an individual may perceive as pleasurable that promote life satisfaction (i.e., solitary activities such as reading, journaling, or gardening; physical activities including exercise and fitness; and social activities).

The theoretical underpinnings of the activity theory have been used in the development of programs for older adults (Bengston & DiLiema, 2016), emphasizing activity in community centers, senior centers, adult day care centers, adult day health-care centers, retirement communities, and skilled nursing homes. The benefits of activity and social support on well-being among older adults is well documented in the literature. Well-being is enhanced by friendships (Huxhold, Miche, & Schüz, 2013). Activities such as volunteering reduce risks for functional declines and dementia (Anderson et al., 2014). High levels of exercise reduce cognitive decline risks (Kelly, Loughrey, Lawlor, Robertson, Walsh, & Brennan, 2014), and high levels of social engagement are predictors of both life satisfaction maintenance and increases (Huxhold, Fiori, & Windsor, 2013). For clinicians, activity theory informs interventions to assess, identify, and promote socialization and activity opportunities for older adults to enhance life satisfaction.

For further thought: Consider how activity theory applies to Mr. Kahale, older adults in your own life, or clients that you are working with. What positive benefits have you observed among older adults who engage in meaningful activities? In what ways has your client noticed that the forms of meaningful activities have changed or remained the same?

Developmental Theory

Erik Erikson's lifespan developmental theory—the eight stages of man—outlines the key psychosocial crisis in older adulthood: integrity versus despair. A developmental crisis refers to a change that results in disequilibrium due to events or other circumstances that challenge an individual's problem-solving ability to resolve the stressor or tension with either healthy or unhealthy coping (Hutchinson, 2013). The psychosocial crisis, according to Erikson, involves the resolution of the developmental crisis and mastery in the stage, which is either egodystonic, the state in which the developmental crisis was not resolved successfully, or egosystonic, the state in which the developmental crisis is resolved successfully (Robbins, Chatterjee, & Canda, 2012). When the crisis is resolved successfully, ego qualities referred to as strengths emerge (Robbins, Chatterjee, & Canda, 2012).

Integrity is achieved by the older adult who is able to examine his or her life and accept both the unanticipated and unfulfilled goals, aspirations, and events, along with the sense of contentment and meaning in life lived to date, as well as choices (Robbins, Chatterjee, & Canda, 2012). An older adult who achieves integrity has successfully adapted to changes and losses throughout the life course and is satisfied overall with life. The older adult who achieves integrity approaches the end of life without the complications that accompany regret, which may interfere with life satisfaction. Despair is described as a state in which the older adult lives with regrets and may experience anger, depression, and self-contempt (Robbins, Chatterjee, & Canda, 2012). The developmental stage of the client and the resolution of the psychosocial crisis is an important area to assess. If a goal of the client is to achieve integrity, interventions can be targeted toward processes and activities that promote such resolution through reminiscence therapy, dignity therapy, life review, and/or support groups.

For further thought: Consider Mr. Kahale: How would you assess his resolution of the psychosocial crisis of integrity versus despair in stage 8? Consider your own older adult clients or older adults in your life: To what extent is integrity versus despair resolved? How does your assessment of the resolution of the psychosocial crisis inform your approaches to treatment?

Cognitive Behavioral Theory

Cognitive behavioral treatment is informed by both cognitive and behavioral theoretical contributions of Beck, Ellis, and Meichenbaum in the 1970 to 1980s that draw from behaviorism, as well as classical behavioral approaches from Pavlov (1900 to 1930s) and Skinner (1930 to1970s) (Thomlison & Thomlison, 2017). Cognitive behavioral treatment approaches emphasize the connection between events, automatic thoughts, emotions, and behaviors of an individual. Drawing from behavioral theory, one assumption of cognitive behavioral treatment approaches is that overt and covert behaviors are learned through modeling or operant conditioning involving reinforcement of behavior with positive or negative stimuli that serve to increase or decrease behaviors (Cobb, 2016). Take a 67-year-old female client who has been struggling with depression after retirement from a corporate accounting firm. The client reports that the depression is causing behaviors of self-isolation and that she has stopped engaging in pleasurable activities with friends and family members. In clinical practice, this would involve a client identifying sources in the environment that serve to reinforce or maintain a problematic behavior (Cobb, 2016). The client reports that she watches a lot of television and then loses motivation to do anything else—the television watching is influencing and serving to maintain the behavior of self-isolating. A clinician working with this client would work with the client to determine treatment goals that are specific, measurable, attainable, realistic, and have a time frame for completing actions and activities to accomplish the goal. The client's goal is to reduce self-isolating behaviors. The television watching is modified, so rather than watching television all day, she contracts to watch television at the end of the day between 8 and 10 p.m. She then creates goals for engagements with family and friends and lists actions and time frames for completing them. Engagement in positive, pleasurable, and meaningful activities replaces problematic behaviors. This approach is common in behavioral activation therapy, which is an effective intervention that uses activity scheduling to target and replace problem behaviors related to depression and uses self-monitoring homework to track and monitor mood and activities (Cuijpers, Van Straten, & Warmerdam, 2007).

Cognitive behavioral approaches do not, however, rely exclusively on external sources that maintain or influence behavior. Rather, they recognize that internal sources or cognitive processes interact with external sources and, thus, together influence and maintain behaviors. The cognitive behavioral model is enhanced by cognitive therapy approaches that recognize that it is "the way that individuals perceive a situation is more closely connected to their reaction than the situation itself" and that changes in "unhelpful thinking and behavior" can "lead to enduring improvement in their mood and functioning" (Beck Institute for Cognitive Behavioral therapy, 2016, para. 1). The key assertions of the model include: (1) "maladaptive cognitions contribute to the maintenance of emotional distress and behavioral problems," (2) "maladaptive cognitions include general beliefs, or schemas, about the world, the self, and the future, giving rise to specific and automatic thoughts in particular situations;" and (3) "therapeutic strategies to change these maladaptive cognitions lead to changes in emotional distress" (Hoffman, Asnaani, Vonk, Sawyer, & Fang, 2012, p. 427). Creed, Wolk, Feinberg, Evans, & Beck, 2016). In clinical practice, a client who is expressing bothersome moods and feelings can be directed to identify the automatic thoughts and cognitive distortions that are maintaining and influencing them (Cobb, 2016). In addition to recording and tracking depressed moods and feelings for the 67-year-old client, for example, the clinician could explore with the client the internal sources that reinforce and maintain those feelings and moods and work on restructuring those cognitions to be more accurate. There are three levels of cognition Beck outlines in the cognitive model: core beliefs or schemas, which are "deeply held beliefs about self, others and the world;" dysfunctional assumptions, which are "rigid conditional rules for living that people adopt … (that may be) unrealistic and therefore maladaptive;" and negative automatic thoughts, which are "involuntarily activated in certain situations" (Fenn & Byrne, 2013, p. 579).

For further thought: Consider your own older adult clients or older adults in your life: To what extent are core beliefs, dysfunctional assumptions, or negative automatic thoughts influencing their behaviors and emotions? Apply the cognitive behavioral model to Mr. Kahale.

Intersectionality Theory

Intersectionality is a theoretical perspective that helps provide the clinician with a framework for understanding social inequality in the context of factors that mutually influence a client's lived experience (Collins & Bilge, 2016). It enables the clinician to understand and frame interventions for empowerment and social justice that consider the person in the environment and the context of inequality as it relates to multiple layers and interacting factors that influence the individual and presenting problems or issues, including, for example, social/interpersonal, societal, socioeconomical, racial/ethnic, gender, political, geographical, cultural, generational, physical, and organizational/institutional contexts. Intersectionality allows the clinician to frame interventions that ensure equity and social justice informed by the client's perspective on the culmination of barriers experienced in the life course that prevent opportunity and equality that lead to upward mobility and influence presenting issues and challenges. The key concepts of intersectionality include considering multiple aspects of diversity for clients, considering these aspects simultaneously and considering the context for aspects of diversity. Intersectionality is eloquently described by Collins and Bilge as:

> A way of understanding and analyzing the complexity in the world, in people, and in human experiences. The events and conditions of social and political life and the self can seldom be understood or shaped by one factor. They are generally shaped by many factors in diverse and mutually influencing ways. When it comes to social inequality, people's lives and the organization of power in a given society are better understood as being shaped by not a single axis of social division, be it race or gender or class, but by many axes that work together and influence each other. Intersectionality as an analytic tool gives people better access to the complexity of the world and of themselves. (2016, p. 2)

For further thought: Consider your own older adult clients or older adults in your life: To what extent does intersectionality help you understand issues of social justice, equity, discrimination, and barriers experienced in the life course? Apply intersectionality to Mr. Kahale, an older adult client, or an older adult in your life.

Transtheoretical Model and Stages of Change

The transtheoretical model of behavior change provides clinicians with a framework and guide for interventions targeting health and behavioral health-related changes. The model recognizes that health and behavioral health changes occur in stages over time. The time spent in any one of the stages varies according to the client's motivation to engage in change behaviors, and there are tasks the client must complete before he or she moves onto the next stage. The first stage of change, precontemplation, is a stage where the client has "no intention to take action within the next 6 months" (Prochaska, Redding, & Evers, 2013, p. 98). In precontemplation, there is a tendency for the client to be unaware of, minimize, be in denial of a problem behavior, and have no motivation or intention of changing behavior in the immediate or near future. Clients in precontemplation oftentimes present for treatment at the recommendation of someone else. Take the example of an insulin-dependent diabetic client who sees no correlation between dietary and medication compliance and managing symptoms to prevent hospitalization and reduce risks for harmful complications such as neuropathy, blindness, and or amputation.

The second stage of change, contemplation, is described as the stage when the client "intends to take action within the next 6 months" (Prochaska, Redding, & Evers, 2013, p. 98). In this stage, a client is no longer in denial about a health or behavioral health problem, and they have contemplated or thought seriously about making a commitment to engage in change behaviors to overcome the problem. This client has engaged in decisional balance where the benefits (pros) and costs (cons) of change have been considered, and it is not common for a client to experience ambivalence to engage in change behaviors and delay behavior change actions (Prochaska, Redding, & Evers, 2013). Return to the example of the insulin-diabetic client who now reports an interest to become compliant with medication and diet within the next six months but contemplates the time it will take to regularly test and record their blood sugar, take the correct dosage of insulin, and give up a food they enjoy eating such as desserts, fast food, or soda. There may be procrastination with engaging in all desirable behaviors. For example, the client may feel more committed to blood sugar testing and begin engaging in the behaviors of regular blood sugar testing and taking the appropriate insulin dosage, however, the client may still be less committed to delay giving up foods with high sugar content.

In the third stage of change, preparation, a client "intends to take action within the next 30 days and has taken some behavioral steps in this direction" (Prochaska, Redding & Evers, 2013, p. 98). In the preparation stage, it is common for a client to begin taking actions to engage in change behaviors but without full success in carrying out the change behavior consistently. In the example of the insulin-dependent diabetic client, the client reports efforts to try to stop eating sugary foods but also reports difficulty in maintaining dietary compliance successfully.

In the fourth stage of change, action, the client has "changed overt behavior for less than 6 months" (Prochaska, Redding, & Evers, 2013, p. 98). In this stage, a client begins making overt modifications in their environment, behavior, and experiences to overcome the presenting health or behavioral health problem. The client successfully changes such behavior(s) between one day and six months. In the example of the insulin-diabetic client, the client reports successfully eating healthy foods, regularly tests blood sugar, and takes all required dosages of insulin.

In the fifth stage of change, maintenance, the client has "changed overt behavior for more than 6 months" (Prochaska, Redding, & Evers, 2013, p. 98). In the maintenance stage, the client continues to maintain motivation and engage in change behaviors consistent with recovery, therefore avoiding relapse. The client has successfully substituted problematic behaviors with healthy ones in his or her lifestyle. Clients in the maintenance stage have successfully applied and incorporated behavior modifications into their lives between six months to five years (Prochaska, Redding, & Evers, 2013). Returning to the insulin-dependent diabetic client, the client reports successful maintenance of both dietary and medication/blood sugar-testing compliance. To prevent relapse of dietary noncompliance, the client exercises when feeling stressed, rather than eating sugary foods, and makes a modification to the driving route home after work to avoid fast food restaurants.

And finally, the last stage, termination, occurs when the client has "no temptation to relapse and 100% confidence" (Prochaska, Redding, & Evers, 2013, p. 98). This is the client who has certainty and confidence that he or she will not return to the former unhealthy problematic health or behavioral health behaviors. This client has internalized the new behaviors into his or her lifestyle and is able to resist the temptations that lead to relapse. Returning to the insulin-dependent diabetic client, the client tests his or her blood sugar at the same time every day, monitors his or her diet, and engages in routine exercise for well-being.

For further thought: Consider your own older adult clients or older adults in your life: To what extent do you see how the stages of change apply to their motivation to engage in change behaviors at various stages?

Health Belief Model

The Health Belief Model was developed in the 1950s by social psychologists to inform disease prevention programs in public health (Champion & Skinner, 2013). The model initially informed simple preventive health behaviors such as getting an immunization. It is commonly used today to inform interventions to change and maintain healthy behaviors (Champion & Skinner, 2013). The key constructs of the theory are perceived susceptibility, which "refers to beliefs about the likelihood of getting a disease or condition," and perceived severity, or the "feelings about the seriousness of contracting an illness or of leaving it untreated," which includes the perception of the consequences, medical, clinical, and/or social (i.e., death, pain, changes in functional health, effects on family and work) (Champion & Skinner, 2013, p. 47). Perceived benefits pertain to perception of the client that the health threat can be reduced through the means and actions available to the client to address the threat (Champion & Skinner, 2013). Perceived barriers are the client's "belief about the tangible and psychological costs of the advised action plan;" cues to action are the "strategies to activate readiness" to engage in change behavior; and finally, self-efficacy, or the client's "confidence in one's ability to take action" (Champion & Skinner, 2013, p. 48).

The health belief model hypothesizes that a decision to undertake a health action will not be made unless the client is psychologically ready to take action relative to a particular health threat or condition. For example, a client diagnosed with cardiovascular disease decides to take medication prescribed by a physician to prevent a heart attack or stroke. The extent to which a client demonstrates readiness to engage in change behavior or health-related actions is thought to be influenced by the extent to which the following conditions occur simultaneously: (1) the existence of sufficient motivation and confidence by the client to carry out an action to address a health issue that is relevant or salient (self-efficacy), (2) the belief that the client is susceptible or vulnerable to a serious health problem or to the threats of that illness or condition (perceived susceptibility and perceived severity), and (3) the belief that following a particular health recommendation would be beneficial in reducing the perceived threat, and at a subjectively low cost (perceived benefits and perceived barriers).

Returning to the case study, Mr. Kahale, after his coronary artery bypass surgery, received instruction from the home health nurse on chronic disease management. This included medication and dietary and exercise instruction to prevent future heart attacks. Although he was diagnosed with heart disease at the age of 55, it was not until the heart attack and bypass surgery at the age of 68 that Mr. Kahale became motivated to engage in the health behaviors and actions necessary to prevent a future heart attack. At this point, Mr. Kahale was confident in his ability to carry out the health actions (self-efficacy); he had a salient awareness of the seriousness of not managing his chronic illness (perceived susceptibility), as well as the potential risks or threat, such as, another heart attack or death (perceived severity). Mr. Kahale was confident in the benefits of the chronic disease management actions he learned would help prevent a future heart attack (perceived benefits). He was aware of the potential risks to his health, family, and ability to engage in social activities if he did not follow the chronic disease management regime (perceived barriers).

For further thought: Consider your own older adult clients or older adults in your life: To what extent do you see how the constructs from the health belief model influence their readiness to engage in health behaviors and actions.

Part II. Assessment and Screening

In this section, assessment and screening approaches that clinicians can consider when working with older adults are presented. It begins with an introduction to biopsychosocial/spiritual assessment and presents a geriatric biopsychosocial/spiritual assessment template that considers key domains of assessment for older adults. The template is applied to a case study to illustrate use of the template with an older adult. Common screening tools used with older adults are also presented. This section concludes with a discussion about the multidisciplinary comprehensive geriatric assessment.

Biopsychosocial/Spiritual Assessment

A thorough biopsychosocial/spiritual assessment enables the clinician to: gather relevant information from the client, make informed clinical impressions, and better formulate a treatment plan and interventions that provide the best fit for the client. Assessment is done to gain an understanding from the client as to the presenting issues they seek treatment for and helps frame dialogue when the client is referred by other providers or service delivery systems. The quality of a biopsychosocial/spiritual assessment is dependent in part on the establishment of good rapport in the therapeutic relationship during the engagement stage with the client. Clinician practices that lead to good rapport in the engagement stage include, but are not limited to, unconditional regard, a nonjudgmental stance, cultural humility, establishing a safe environment in which the client gains trust in the clinician, and discussing the limits to confidentiality. Among the 13 standards outlined by the NASW (2016) for social work practice in health-care settings, standard 5 underscores assessment and screening as a process which occurs on an ongoing basis when engaging and intervening with client and family systems. Assessment is used to formulate evidence-based and informed treatment plans.

Criteria for a biopsychosocial spiritual assessment outlined by the NASW (2016) include: mental, physical, and behavioral health; risk factors (i.e., suicide, homicide, neglect/abuse, and drug and alcohol use); well-being and functioning (i.e., cognitive, psychosocial, spiritual); culture; resilience and protective factors; employment history; financial resources; family composition; social support and status; language(s); education; barriers and ability to navigate health and community resources; the need for long-term and advance care planning; patient's perceived needs; and ability for treatment adherence.

A comprehensive geriatric biopsychosocial/spiritual assessment includes the following domains: basic demographic information, referral information, social, financial, environmental, physical, mental, cultural/spiritual, strengths, formulation and evaluation of presenting needs, treatment plan, and community resources (Box 2.1). Each domain allows the clinician to gather important information about the client used for treatment planning and interventions. Basic demographic information of clients helps the clinician understand client self-identification (i.e., gender identity, names and pronouns, marital status) and the client's preference for how the clinician should address the client (i.e., he/she, him/her, his/her, etc.). Demographic information is used in part for screening/eligibility criteria for programs/services (i.e., Supplemental Security Income (SSI), veteran benefits, other community-based waiver programs, etc.), language preference, and whether interpreter services are needed. The education level of the client informs the clinician's approach regarding the tailoring of information and interventions to the educational level of the client.

An assessment of the domain referral information allows the clinician to gain an understanding from the client about their level of insight into the presenting issues and problems the client has been referred to work with the clinician on. The assessment sets the stage for communication between the clinician and the client about the nature of the self-referral, provider referral, or mandated referral sources (i.e., psychiatric hold, court-mandated therapy). Creating a safe space for the client to process presenting issues is crucial and further enhances the rapport between the client and clinician. An assessment of the client's cultural and spiritual practices, beliefs, and values allows the clinician to further understand the approaches to treatment the client may prefer and thus informs treatment planning to ensure goodness of fit. The intersection of culture and spirituality provides a lens or perspective for the client that often frames the meaning of both disease and pain as well as appropriate pathways to wellness and/or recovery, thus further informing treatment planning and clinical interventions for their goodness of fit to ensure they are preferred, meaningful, and relevant to the client.

Assessment of the social domain allows the clinician to gain an understanding of the availability and extent of social support networks and social capital of the client. It includes an examination of the client's personal history (i.e., work, military service, immigration

Box 2.1

Geriatric Biopsychosocial/Spiritual Assessment

Basic Demographic: Age; gender identity, names, and pronouns; ethnicity/race, language(s), marital status, educational background

Referral Information: Presenting problem and reason for referral

Cultural/Spiritual: Understanding of disease and illness, complementary and alternative medicine, spiritual beliefs and values; FICA assessment

Social: Relationships within family, social/diversity groups, and community

- Personal and family history: work history, military service, immigration; family background: children, family of origin, family of choice

- Current relationships and contact with family, friends, social/diversity groups, community, caregiver stress; Zarit Burden Interview

Financial: Ability to provide basic needs and access health services

- Ability to provide basic needs: housing, food, shelter, clothing
- Health insurance: does it provide essential benefits, is the coverage adequate (i.e., are there any gaps in coverage, are co-pays and any out-of-network fees manageable), medication coverage
- Income sources: Social Security, pension, Social Security Disability Insurance (SSDI), Supplemental Security Income (SSI), savings, investments, family support, employment, general relief, food stamps

Environmental: Personal safety, maintenance of residence, and safety of community

- Current social context/environmental
- Neighborhood safety
- Home safety: smoke and carbon monoxide detectors, fire extinguisher, lighting, removal of slip rugs, shower- and toilet-accessible, elevators, stairs, ramps to access home
- Access to guns: are guns locked in a safe
- Screen for abuse or neglect by self or perpetrated by others, complete APS SOC341 report if suspected, mandated reporting

Physical: Individual function and disease morbidity

- Health literacy, self-rated health, and advance directive (is there a document, when was it last updated), knowledge on diagnosis(es), medications and adherence, functional health (Activities of Daily Living, Instrumental Activities of Daily Living), current treatment(s) for chronic or life-threatening illnesses, sexual health

Mental: Mental status, depression, anxiety, and substance abuse

- Standardized screening instruments: Mini-Mental State Examination, SLUMS, Montreal Cognitive Assessment, Geriatric Depression Scale, GAD-7 (anxiety), PHQ-9 (depression)
- Suicide risk assessment: client does or does not endorse suicidal ideations, consider intent, plan, and means (Columbia-Suicide Severity Rating Scale)
- Homicidal ideations: rule out or initiate Tarasoff duty to warn, mandated reporting-Substance use: WHO ASSIST V3 assessment, alcohol: AUDIT assessment

Formulation/Evaluation: Identified biopsychosocial/spiritual needs

Treatment Planning: In consult with interprofessional team

Community Resource Needs: Appropriate home and community-based services to meet identified needs

experiences, etc.), family history (i.e., number of children, grandchildren, great-grandchildren; siblings and extended family; marriages and divorces) and family of origin versus family of choice. The social domain also includes assessing the quality and frequency of contact with friends and engagement in spiritual, diversity, social, and community groups. If the client has a primary caregiver assisting with day-to-day or other activities, it is important to assess for caregiver stress and the need for respite care. The Zarit Burden Interview, a standardized instrument with strong reliability and validity, is commonly used to assess caregiver stress or burden in a self-administered 22-item questionnaire with respondent responses ranging from 0 (never) to 4 (nearly always) (Zarit, Reever, & Back-Peterson, 1980). Along with a client's personal history, the availability, extent, and quality of a client's social support network informs decision making with the client when formulating a treatment plan and making recommendations for community-based services such as caregiver assistance, respite care, and/or programs for socialization.

An assessment of the financial domain allows the clinician to screen the client using eligibility criteria for public and social service programs to meet basic, health and behavioral health, and income security needs. For example, a single client who is older than age 65, who is low-income (i.e., $500 monthly Social Security, savings of less than $2,000), does not own a home, and has one car is eligible for food stamps (until SSI is approved), section 8 subsidized housing, in-home assistance or Medicaid waiver programs, SSI, and/or Medicaid insurance as a supplement to Medicare or primary coverage. Assessment of contextual factors for the environmental domain informs the direction of the clinician's immediate crisis intervention and safety planning with the client. Factors to assess include: neighborhood safety, home safety (i.e., lighting, stairs, access to a tub or shower, slip rugs), gun ownership, and/or access to guns, as well as mandated reporting responsibilities for abuse perpetrated by others or self-neglect.

Assessment of the client's physical domain includes factors that inform interventions related to the individual functioning and disease morbidity. The client's health literacy, self-rated overall health (i.e., excellent, very good, good, fair, or poor), knowledge about health diagnoses, treatments, and medications prescribed to manage the symptoms of chronic and/or life-threatening illnesses informs treatment planning for interventions such as crisis, psychoeducation, medication adherence, and chronic disease management interventions.

An assessment by the clinician of whether a client has an advance directive, living will, or trust and when the documents were last updated inform both advance care planning by the clinician with the client and legal referrals. Sexual health assessment includes a brief sexual health history using the five P's: partners, past STD history, pregnancy, practices, and protection from STDs to inform prevention counseling and risk reduction strategies (Centers for Disease Control and Prevention, 2011).

Measures of functional health to assess include both activities of daily living (ADLs) (i.e., bathing; toileting; transferring into or out of the bed, chair, or car; eating; dressing; bowel and bladder continence) and instrumental activities of daily living (IADLs) (i.e., communication with phone or internet; shopping, transportation, meal preparation, housekeeping, managing medications, and managing finances). An assessment of functional health and whether the client is independent needs minimal, moderate, or full assistance with ADLs and IADLs informs treatment planning and resource coordination for formal and informal care, as well as home and community-based resource coordination.

The mental domain includes assessment of factors such as the client's mental status, the presence or absence of mental health and substance use disorders, suicide risk, and homicidal ideations. The mental status of a client informs the clinician's approach to treatment planning; for example, the power of attorney or surrogate decision maker of a client with diminished capacity would be consulted for consent to treatment, intervention, and provider referral recommendations. Assessment of mental health disorders includes past and current diagnoses, screening and referral for differential diagnosis and/or medication consult, and the use of screening tools to establish a baseline measure that can be monitored during each subsequent session with the client. The mental domain also considers immediate mandated reporting responsibilities of the clinician when criteria are met for the state's Tarasoff duty-to-warn laws when a client presents with active homicidal ideations. It also includes mandated responsibilities following the state's welfare and institution codes for initiating psychiatric holds for a client with suicidal or homicidal ideations and/or meets criteria for grave disability. Lastly, the mental domain addresses assessment of mental health and substance use disorders using brief screening tools such as the Patient Health Questionnaire 9-item (PHQ-9) for depression; Generalized Anxiety Disorder 7-item (GAD-7); World Health Organization Alcohol, Smoking and Substance Involvement Screening Test (WHO ASSIST v3) for substance use; and World Health Organization Alcohol Use Disorders Identification Test (AUDIT) for alcohol abuse.

The formulation and evaluation domain considers the initial diagnostic impression of the clinician for the presenting biopsychosocial/spiritual needs of the client as well as the strengths, resiliency, and protective factors of the client. This informs treatment planning that is done to address the presenting biopsychosocial/spiritual needs in consultation with the client and interprofessional team. The community resource needs of the client are often identified at the time of the first meeting with the client and reassessed throughout the duration of treatment to ensure that the client gains access to appropriate home and community-based services to meet biopsychosocial/spiritual needs. An application of the biopsychosocial/spiritual assessment template to study presented at the beginning of the chapter follows.

Case Study Application

Following is the social worker's biopsychosocial/spiritual assessment of Mr. Kahale:

Box 2.2

Geriatric Biopsychosocial Spiritual Assessment

Basic Demographic: 68-year-old male, Hawaiian native, married 50 years, speaks Hawaiian and English fluently, has a bachelor and master's degree

Referral Information: Unexpected death of spouse

Cultural/Spiritual: Mr. Kahale is a member of the Roman Catholic Church; he believes his spouse and he will be reunited in the afterlife; cultural beliefs surrounding death include recognizing death as a sad, not a happy time; Mr. Kahale reported that although his extended family has traditional native Hawaiian burials at sea, his spouse preferred a Catholic burial and ceremony at the Hawaiian ceremony; he does not use complementary and alternative medicine

Social: [Relationships within family, social/diversity groups, and community]

- General manager in transportation 40 years, no military service, born in Hawaii and moved to mainland after retirement at age 65, one daughter and two grandchildren, two brothers and two sisters live in Hawaii.

- Mr. Kahale sees his daughter, son-in-law and grandchildren daily; he has friendships with neighbors; he attends a local Catholic church and has participated in activities, until his hospitalization, weekly at a local Hawaiian cultural center; his daughter is experiencing caregiver stress

Financial: [Ability to provide basic needs and access health services]

- All basic needs are met: Mr. Kahale owns his own home, and his daughter, church members, and neighbors are assisting with meals currently

- Health insurance: Mr. Kahale has both Medicare and private insurance; he reports he is able to manage all co-pays and deductibles for health care and medications

- Income sources: Social Security, pension, savings, and investments

---

Environmental: [Personal safety, maintenance of residence, and safety of community]

- Current social context/environmental: Mr. Kahale lives in a two-story home; his daughter, son-in-law, and two grandchildren live one block away
- Neighborhood safety: Mr. Kahale lives in a suburban neighborhood with low crime and lighting
- Home safety: Mr. Kahale has smoke and carbon monoxide detectors, a fire extinguisher, and proper lighting; removal of slip rugs occurred during the physical therapy evaluation; grab bars have been installed for shower and toilet safety; there is a handrail for stairs upstairs and two steps leading to front door
- Access to guns: Mr. Kahale has no guns
- There are no reports or suspicion of abuse or neglect by self or perpetrated by others

Physical: [Individual function and disease morbidity]

- Patient has high health literacy, understands his chronic illnesses and medications, and rates his health as "good;" he has an advanced directive and living will; his daughter is his agent and executor of the will; he is compliant with medications; he needs assistance with transportation and shopping currently; he is independent with ADLs; he reports monthly sexual intercourse with spouse prior to her death

Mental: [Mental status, depression, anxiety, and substance abuse]

- Standardized screening instruments: Mr. Kahale was assessed with the Geriatric Depression Scale—low level of depression detected; depression more indicative of normal uncomplicated grief in differential diagnosis using DSM-V
- Suicide risk assessment: Mr. Kahale does not endorse suicidal ideations
- Homicidal ideations: Mr. Kahale does not endorse homicidal ideations [rule out or initiate Tarasoff duty to warn, mandated reporting]
- Substance use: Mr. Kahale does not drink alcohol or use substances

Formulation/Evaluation: [Identified biopsychosocial/spiritual needs] Psychoeducation on grief; grief and loss counseling; monitor depression; rule out medication consult for antidepressant at first visit

Treatment Planning: [In consult with interprofessional team] Grief counseling weekly for four weeks; reassessment each visit of depression to rule out major depressive disorder and medication; community resource coordination

Community Resource Needs: [Appropriate home and community-based services to meet identified needs] Transportation services, caregiver agencies, Meals on Wheels, and congregate meal sites; local grief and bereavement counseling center after home health bereavement counseling and resource coordination

Clinicians can use screening tools to further diagnose presenting issues and concerns requiring treatment for older adults. The screening tools are used as baseline measures of target symptoms or a condition that clinicians can administer during the first visits and readminister during subsequent visits to assess and monitor the impact of treatment on outcomes—for example, depression or anxiety.

Screening Tools

Screening tools with high validity and reliability should be used to establish a baseline measure of an older adult's cognitive and mental status, depression, and anxiety. The screening tool should be readministered throughout treatment to monitor the effect of treatment on desirable client outcomes. Screening tools help clinicians and clients determine the extent to which the intervention is effective in reducing symptoms. The scores can be used to determine whether an intervention should be discontinued or whether a consult with a medical doctor or psychiatrist should be sought (i.e., in the event client outcomes worsen). The scores can also be used to monitor when the client is reaching desirable target goals for the outcome and inform decisions on preparation for termination. A review of common screening tools to assess the cognitive/mental status of older adults and detect depression and anxiety follow.

Cognitive/Mental Status

Mini-Mental State Examination

The most commonly used standardized screening tool to assess cognitive function of older adults is the Mini-Mental State Examination (MMSE) (O'Bryant et al., 2008). The MMSE contains 11 items that allow detection of severe, moderate, mild, and questionably significant impairment as well as implications for further psychometric assessment and the expected impact on the day-to-day functioning of a client's ability to perform activities of daily living (Folstein, Folstein, & McHugh, 1975). The 11 items include: orientation (i.e., person, place, time, situation), registration (i.e., ability to name three objects), attention and calculation (i.e., ability to subtract a number backward from 100 or spell a word backward), recall (i.e., remembering the three objects named in registration item of exam), and language (i.e., naming, repetition, and three-stage command, reading, writing, and copying) (Folstein, Folstein, & McHugh, 1975). Scores range from 0 to 30: Scores of 0 to 17 are indicative of severe cognitive impairment, scores of 18 to 23 are indicative of mild cognitive impairment, and scores of 24 to 30 are indicative of no cognitive impairment (Folstein, Folstein, & McHugh, 1975). The MMSE is easy to administer and score. It has been produced in many languages and tested cross-culturally with high sensitivity (McDowell, 2006). However, it has been criticized for showing bias "in assessing non-English speakers by consistently providing lower scores to those who are not Caucasian" (Buckingham et al., 2013, p. 2). It has been critiqued regarding the educational level of respondents, with studies suggesting that those with lower education levels often score lower on the MMSE (McDowell, 2006). The MMSE has also been criticized for assessing only "certain aspects of cognitive function, while dismissing other important factors, such as mood and a more complete assessment of executive function" (Buckingham et al., 2013, p. 1). Additionally, items on the MMSE require some adaption to the cultural context of respondents when translated into forms with different languages (McDowell, 2006) as some words from the original English version mean different things in different cultures.

SLUMS

A second screening tool for assessing cognitive function of older adults is the Saint Louis University Mental Status Examination (SLUMS). It is most commonly administered by primary care physicians to older adults and adults to screen for dementia and Alzheimer's dementia and is considered to be more sensitive at detecting mild neurocognitive disorder (Tariq, Tumosa, Chibnall, Perry, & Morley, 2006). Like the MMSE, the SLUMS is an 11-item questionnaire that assesses orientation, attention, executive function, and memory (Tariq, Tumosa, Chibnall, Perry, & Morley, 2006). Scores range from 1 to 30, and there is differentiation of scores for dementia, mild neurocognitive disorder, and normal cognitive functioning based on whether the client has less than a high school education or a high school education. Scores for dementia range from 1 to 20 for a client with a high school education and 1 to 19 if the client has less than a high school education (Tariq, Tumosa, Chibnall, Perry, & Morley, 2006). Scores for mild neurocognitive disorder range from 21 to 26 with a high school education and 20 to 24 if the client has less than a high school education (Tariq, Tumosa, Chibnall, Perry, & Morley, 2006). The scores for normal cognitive functioning are 27 to 30 for a client with a high school education and 25 to 30 for if the client has less than a high school education (Tariq, Tumosa, Chibnall, Perry, & Morley, 2006). In comparison to the MMSE, the SLUMS is perceived as having "a greater range in possible scores and potentially greater discrimination in measuring one's ability to remember information after a short delay," and it may be better in detecting "aphasia (i.e., language impairment) than the MMSE by providing a possible score of three (zero, one, two, or three points), whereas the MMSE only asks a participant to identify two simple objects, such as a paperclip or pencil" (Buckingham et al., 2013, p. 2). The SLUMS has also been translated successfully into several languages and is easy to administer, taking six to eight minutes (Malmstrom et al., 2015).

Montreal Cognitive Assessment

The Montreal Cognitive Assessment (MoCA) detects mild cognitive impairment through the administration of 11 items that assess:

+ visuospatial/executive functions (i.e., trail-making test involving shifting between letters and numbers in ascending order and the clock-drawing test involving drawing a clock with the time of 10 past11),
+ naming (i.e., of three animals),
+ attention (i.e., the digit span forward involving repeating back of five numbers in order, the digit span backward involving repeating five new numbers in backward order)

- vigilance involving tapping of the hand when a word with the letter A is announced, and serial 7's involving subtracting 7 from 100 backward,
- sentence repetition,
- verbal fluency (i.e., involving naming of words that begin with a certain letter that are not nouns or numbers),
- abstracting (i.e., involving identifying what two words have in common),
- delayed recall (i.e., involving recalling the five words announced earlier in the memory item), and
- orientation (Julayanont & Nasreddine, 2017).

For patients without impairments in ADLs, the MoCA is the recommended first psychometric test for detecting mild cognitive impairment (Julayanont & Nasreddine, 2017). Alternatively, if the older adult client has an impairment with ADLs, the recommendation is to first start with the MMSE and then use the MoCA if the client has a score in the normal range on the MMSE (Julayanont & Nasreddine, 2017). The MoCA has a total score of 30 points, with a score of 26 or higher indicative of normal cognitive functioning (Julayanont & Nasreddine, 2017). An advantage of the MoCA in comparison to the MMSE is that "it is less susceptible to educational and cultural artifacts and it eliminates most ceiling effects in normal control groups" (Gluhm et al., 2013, p. 1).

Screening tools to detect depression among older adults are equally important to those for detecting mild cognitive impairments and dementia. Clinical depression left untreated may alter the scores of an older adult client on a cognitive/mental status screen. Additionally, comorbid health conditions may also overlap in symptoms, making a differential diagnosis more challenging. For example, among older adults with Parkinson's disease (PD), "depression can be difficult to assess in patients with PD due to overlapping symptoms and difficulties in the assessment of depression in cognitively impaired patients" (Schrag et al., 2007, p. 1077). Therefore, it is recommended that clinicians factor in comorbid conditions as well as depression when considering the end result and implications of a mental status/cognitive screen.

Depression

The prevalence of major depression among older adults in the United States ranges from 1% to 5% for community-dwelling older adults, 13.5% for community-dwelling older adults who receive home health-care services, and 11.5% for older adults in acute hospital settings (Centers for Disease Control, 2017). Both health-care providers and older adults often perceive depression as a common experience of aging, thus leading to the misdiagnosis and undertreatment of depression in older adults (Centers for Disease Control, 2017). Depression is more common among older adults with chronic illnesses and functional health declines (Centers for Disease Control, 2017). Older adults are at an increased risk for depression due to this comorbidity as prevalence rates of chronic illnesses among older adults in the United States for one or two or more chronic illnesses is 80% and 50%, respectively (Centers for Disease Control, 2017). Two of the most commonly administered depression screening tools are the Geriatric Depression Scale and the PHQ-9.

Geriatric Depression Scale

The first screening tool for depression, the Geriatric Depression Scale (GDS), is a 15-item self- or clinician-administered questionnaire used to screen older adults for depression in community, long-term, and acute care settings and establish a baseline measure of depression in an older adult client (Greenberg, 2012). It can be administered among older adults who have mild cognitive impairments or chronic illness, or among those who are healthy without comorbid or chronic health conditions (Greenberg, 2012). Scores range from 0 to 15: A normal score is 0 to 4, the range for mild depression is 5 to 8, moderate depression scores range from 9 to 11, and a score between 12 and 15 is indicative of severe depression (Greenberg, 2012). According to McDowell (2006), research suggests the GDS has low validity in discriminating between cognitive impairment and depression; research shows higher sensitivity (75%) for older adults without cognitive impairment and lower sensitivity (25%) for older adults in long-term care settings. However, research also suggests the GDS has strong reliability and validity for detecting depression among older adults, and it has been found to be easy for older adults to complete (McDowell, 2006).

PHQ-9

The second screening tool, the Patient Health Questionnaire (PHQ-9), is a reliable and valid nine-item self-administered questionnaire used to detect severity of depression in adult populations (Kroenke, Spitzer, & Williams, 2001). The PHQ-9 has been found to be an effective tool for detecting depression among older adults in primary care settings (Phelan et al., 2010). It is recommended as an evidence-based guideline for screening and detecting depression in older adults (Smith, Haedtke, & Shibley, 2015). The PHQ-9 includes major criteria from the DSM-V for major depressive disorder (Smith, Haedtke, & Shibley, 2015). Respondents rate each of the nine items from 0 (not at all) to 3 (nearly every day): A score of 0 to 5 is normal, 5 to 9 is indicative of mild depression, 10 to 14 is indicative of moderate levels of depression, 15 to 20 is indicative of moderately severe depression, and 20 to 27 is indicative of high levels of depression (Smith, Haedtke, & Shibley, 2015).

For older adult clients presenting with symptoms of anxiety, the GAD-7 is a commonly used screening tool to detect anxiety and inform interdisciplinary team treatment planning.

Anxiety

The prevalence of older adults who meet the criteria for an anxiety disorder is estimated at 3% to 14% (Substance Abuse and Mental Health Services Administration/Administration on Aging, 2013). Risk factors for older adults with anxiety include impacts on quality of life, functional health, comorbid chronic illness, life satisfaction, and higher rates of hospitalizations (i.e., three to 10 times higher) in comparison to adults with anxiety who are younger than age 65 (Bassil, Ghandour, & Grossberg, 2011). Additional risk factors associated with older adults with anxiety include: disruptions in sleep, poor self-rated general health, and medication and alcohol abuse or misuse (Substance Abuse and Mental Health Services Administration/Administration on Aging, 2013).

GAD-7

The Generalized Anxiety Disorder 7-item (GAD-7) is a valid seven-item self-administered screening tool used to detect severity of generalized anxiety disorder (Spitzer, Kroenke, Williams, & Löwe, 2006). For each of the seven items, respondents rate the extent to which their symptoms over the past two weeks have been bothersome (i.e., 0 = not all, 1 = several days, 2 = more than half the days, or 3 = nearly every day) (Spitzer, Kroenke, Williams, & Löwe, 2006). Scores range from 0 to 21, and the level of severity may be minimal (a score of 0 to 4), mild (a score of 5 to 9), moderate (a score of 10 to 14), or severe (a score of 15 to 21) (Spitzer, Kroenke, Williams, & Löwe, 2006).

The next form of assessment involves a multidisciplinary team approach using the comprehensive geriatric assessment—this is most commonly conducted by multidisciplinary teams led by a geriatrician specialist.

Comprehensive Geriatric Assessment

A comprehensive geriatric assessment involves a multidisciplinary team assessment, treatment plan, coordination, management, and follow-up on care of an older adult organized under three key areas: medical, functional, and psychosocial (Eamer et al., 2017). Areas assessed, treated, and managed under the medical category include: the client's primary medical diagnoses, monitoring the episode of care by a geriatrician, medication management by the geriatrician, and review by the pharmacist to minimize complications from medication with older adults such as delirium or functional health changes (Eamer et al., 2017). The physical assessment also includes a traditional medical history: presenting issue, past and current medical diagnoses, demographic information, the client's social as well as family history, nutrition, hearing, continence, and vision (Bassem & Higgins, 2011). Areas assessed, treated, and managed under the functional category include: fall prevention, physical and occupational therapist interventions, and modifications to the environment to prevent falls and reduce risks for both symptoms of confusion and delirium (Eamer et al., 2017). The functional category also considers assessment of functional health: activities of daily living and instrumental activities of daily living (Bassem & Higgins, 2011).

Psychosocial and environmental areas assessed on the Stanford PCC Comprehensive Elder Exam (HIS-865), a guide and form for interdisciplinary comprehensive geriatric assessment, includes: alcohol and tobacco use, work history, exercise, caregiving status of the client, key family and support of the client, community services, home equipment, and assistive devices; and under review of systems: substance abuse, neglect, and abuse (Periyakoil, 2010). Other psychosocial areas include: mental health (i.e., mood, cognition, anxiety, and client fears), social circumstances (i.e., social networks, formal and informal care, and finances), and environment (i.e., housing, safety, access to community resources, transportation, and use of technology such as telehealth) (Welsh, Gordon, & Gladman, 2014).

When comparing mortality and functional health outcomes among older adults who receive comprehensive geriatric assessment to those who receive standard or usual geriatric care, there are fewer deaths and improvements in independence among older adults who receive comprehensive geriatric assessment (Welsh, Gordon, & Gladman, 2014). The use of a comprehensive geriatric assessment, identified in a Cochrane systematic review of 29 trials in nine countries, is associated with a likelihood for survival among older adults at three- and nine-month follow-ups after discharge from a hospital (Ellis et al., 2017). The efficacy of the comprehensive geriatric assessment has not only been established for inpatient and outpatient community-based care but also internationally for reducing mortality and improving both functional health and quality of life among older adults. In a review of trials using comprehensive geriatric assessment internationally, in six countries with 10,315 older adults, in comparison to older adults who received regular medical care, among those who received comprehensive geriatric assessment: There were fewer deaths and institutionalizations, and more remained living at home at six- and 12-month follow-ups and had cognitive improvements (Ellis, Whitehead, O'Neill, Langhorne, & Robinson, 2011).

Comprehensive geriatric assessment is an effective way to formulate, treat, and manage functional and physical health of older adult populations that promotes quality of life through a multidisciplinary approach that integrates environmental, social, mental, physical health, and functional health of older adults (Jiang & Li, 2016). Appropriate referrals for an older adult for a comprehensive geriatric assessment include: comorbid medical conditions, psychosocial issues, isolation, depression, functional health limitations, dementia, falls or fall risk, frequent use of health-care services, age, and when a change in the level of care for living arrangement is being considered (i.e., home, assisted living, board and care, custodial care, or in-home care) (Ward & Reuben, 2017).

References

Anderson, N. D., Damianakis, T., Kröger, E., Wagner, L. M., Dawson, D. R., Binns, M. A., ... & Cook, S. L. (2014). The benefits associated with volunteering among seniors: A critical review and recommendations for future research. *Psychological Bulletin, 140*(6), 1505.

Bassem, E., & Higgins, K. (2011). The geriatric assessment. *American Family Physician, 83*(1), 48–56.

Bassil, N., Ghandour, A., & Grossberg, G.T. (2011). How anxiety presents differently in older adults. *Current Psychiatry, 3*(10), 65–71.

Beck Institute for Cognitive Behavioral Therapy. (2016). What is Cognitive Behavioral Therapy (CBT)? Retrieved from https://beckinstitute.org/get-informed/what-is-cognitive-therapy/

Bengston, V. L., & DiLiema, M. (2016). In M. H. Meyer & E. Daniele (Eds.), *Gerontology: Changes, Challenges and Solutions Theoretical Perspectives for Direct Social Work Practice* (3rd ed., pp. 25–56). Santa Barbara, CA: Praeger.

Buckingham, D. N., Mackor, K. M., Miller, R. M., Pullam, N. N., Molloy, K. N., Grigsby, C. C., ... & Winningham, R. G. (2013). Comparing the cognitive screening tools: MMSE and SLUMS. *Pure Insights, 2*(1), 3.

Centers for Disease Control and Prevention. (2011). Clinical prevention guidance. Retrieved from https://www.cdc.gov/std/treatment/2010/clinical.htm

Centers for Disease Control and Prevention. (2017). Healthy aging. Retrieved from https://www.cdc.gov/aging/mentalhealth/depression.htm

Champion, V., & Skinner, C. S. (2013). The health belief model. In K. Glanz, B. K. Rimer, & K. Viswanath (Eds.), *Health behavior and health education theory, research and practice* (4th ed., pp. 45–65). San Francisco: John Wiley & Sons, Inc.

Cobb, N. H. (2016). Cognitive behavioral theory and treatment. In N. Coady & P. Lehmann (Eds.), *Theoretical perspectives for direct social work practice: A generalist-eclectic approach* (3rd ed., pp. 223–248). New York: Springer Publishing Company.

Collins, P. H. & Bilge, S. (2016). What is intersectionality? In P. H. Collins & S. Bilge (Eds.), *Intersectionality: Key concepts* (pp. 1–30). Malden, MS: Polity Press.

Council for Social Work Education. (2017). Specialized practice curricular guide for gero social work practice. Alexandria, VA: Council on Social Work Education.

Creed, T. A., Wolk, C. B., Feinberg, B., Evans, A. C., & Beck, A. T. (2016). Beyond the label: Relationship between community therapists' self-report of a cognitive behavioral therapy orientation and observed skills. *Administration and Policy in Mental Health and Mental Health Services Research*, 43(1), 36–43.

Cuijpers, P., Van Straten, A., & Warmerdam, L. (2007). Behavioral activation treatments of depression: A meta-analysis. *Clinical Psychology Review*, 27(3), 318–326.

Eamer, G., Taheri, A., Chen, S. S., Daviduck, Q., Chambers, T., Shi, X., Khadaroo, R. G. (2017). Comprehensive geriatric assessment for improving outcomes in elderly patients admitted to a surgical service (Protocol). *The Cochrane Database of Systematic Reviews* (1), CD012485.

Elder, G. H., Jr., Johnson, M. K., & Crosnoe, R. (2003). The emergence and development of life course theory. In J. T. Mortimer & M.J. Shanahan (Eds.) *Handbook of the life course* (pp. 3–19). New York: Klewer Academic Publishers.

Ellis, G., Gardner, M., Tsiachristas, A., Langhorne, P., Burke, O., Harwood, R. H., ... & Wald, H. (2017). Comprehensive geriatric assessment for older adults admitted to hospital. *The Cochrane Library*.

Ellis, G., Whitehead, M. A., O'Neill, D., Langhorne, P., & Robinson, D. (2011). Comprehensive geriatric assessment for older adults admitted to hospital. *The Cochrane Database of Systematic Reviews* (7), CD006211.

Fenn, K., & Byrne, M. (2013). The key principles of cognitive behavioral therapy. *InnovAit*, 6(9), 579–585.

Folstein, M. F., Folstein, S. E., & McHugh, P. R. (1975). "Mini-mental state:" A practical method for grading the cognitive state of patients for the clinician. *Journal of Psychiatric Research*, 12(3), 189–198.

Gluhm, S., Goldstein, J., Loc, K., Colt, A., Van Liew, C., & Corey-Bloom, J. (2013). Cognitive performance on the Mini-Mental State Examination and the Montreal Cognitive Assessment across the healthy adult lifespan. *Cognitive and Behavioral Neurology: Official Journal of the Society for Behavioral and Cognitive Neurology*, 26(1), 1.

Greenberg, S.A. (2012). The Geriatric Depression Scale (GDS). Hartford Institute for Geriatric Nursing, NYU College of Nursing. Retrieved from https://consultgeri.org/try-this/general-assessment/issue-4.pdf

Hofmann, S. G., Asnaani, A., Vonk, I. J., Sawyer, A. T., & Fang, A. (2012). The efficacy of cognitive behavioral therapy: A review of meta-analyses. *Cognitive therapy and research*, 36(5), 427–440.

Hutchinson, E. D. (2013). Essentials of human behavior: Integrating person, environment, and the life course. Los Angeles: Sage.

Huxhold, O., Fiori, K. L., & Windsor, T. D. (2013). The dynamic interplay of social network characteristics, subjective well-being, and health: The costs and benefits of socio-emotional selectivity. *Psychology and Aging*, 28(1), 3.

Huxhold, O., Miche, M., & Schüz, B. (2013). Benefits of having friends in older ages: Differential effects of informal social activities on well-being in middle-aged and older adults. *Journals of Gerontology Series B: Psychological Sciences and Social Sciences*, 69(3), 366–375.

Jiang, S., & Li, P. (2016). Current Development in Elderly Comprehensive Assessment and Research Methods. *BioMed Research International*, Volume 2016, Article ID 3528248, 10 pages. http://dx.doi.org/10.1155/2016/3528248

Julayanont, P., & Nasreddine, Z. S. (2017). Montreal Cognitive Assessment (MoCA): Concept and clinical review. In *Cognitive Screening Instruments* (pp. 139–195). Switzerland: Springer International Publishing.

Kelly, M. E., Loughrey, D., Lawlor, B. A., Robertson, I. H., Walsh, C., & Brennan, S. (2014). The impact of exercise on the cognitive functioning of healthy older adults: A systematic review and meta-analysis. *Ageing Research Reviews*, 16, 12-31.

Kroenke, K., Spitzer, R. L., & Williams, J. B. W. (2001). The PHQ-9: Validity of a brief depression severity measure. *Journal of General Internal Medicine*, 16(9), 606–613.

Lange, J., & Grossman, S. (2010). Theories of aging. *Gerontological Nursing Competencies for Care*, 50–73. Retrieved from http://samples.jbpub.com/9781284104479/Chapter_3.pdf

Malmstrom, T. K., Voss, V. B., Cruz-Oliver, D. M., Cummings-Vaughn, L. A., Tumosa, N., Grossberg, G. T., & Morley, J. E. (2015). The Rapid Cognitive Screen (RCS): A point-of-care screening for dementia and mild cognitive impairment. *The Journal of Nutrition, Health & Aging*, 19(7), 741–744.

McDowell, I. (2006). *Measuring health: A guide to rating scales and questionnaires*. New York: Oxford University Press.

NASW (2016). NASW standards for social work practice in health settings. Washington, DC: NASW Press.

O'Bryant, S. E., Humphreys, J. D., Smith, G. E., Ivnik, R. J., Graff-Radford, N. R., Petersen, R. C., & Lucas, J. A. (2008). Detecting dementia with the Mini-Mental State Examination in highly educated individuals. *Archives of Neurology*, 65(7), 963–967.

Periyakoil, V. J. (2010). PCC Comprehensive Elder Exam (HIS-865). Retrieved from http://geriatrics.stanford.edu/wp-content/uploads/downloads/culturemed/overview/assessment/downloads/pcc_elder_exam.pdf

Phelan, E., Williams, B., Meeker, K., Bonn, K., Frederick, J., LoGerfo, J., & Snowden, M. (2010). A study of the diagnostic accuracy of the PHQ-9 in primary care elderly. *BMC Family Practice*, 11(63).

Prochaska, J. O., Redding, C.A., & Evers, K. E. (2013). Transtheoretical model of behavior change. In K. Glanz, B. K. Rimer, & K. Viswanath (Eds.), *Health behavior and health education theory, research and practice* (4th ed., pp. 87–121). San Francisco: John Wiley & Sons, Inc.

Robbins, S. P., Chatterjee, P., & Canda, E. R. (2012). Contemporary human behavior theory: A critical perspective for social work. Upper Saddle River, NJ: Pearson Education, Inc.

Schrag, A., Barone, P., Brown, R. G., Leentjens, A. F., McDonald, W. M., Starkstein, S., ... & Stebbins, G. T. (2007). Depression rating scales in Parkinson's disease: Cand recommendations. *Movement Disorders*, 22(8), 1077–1092.

Simmons, C. A., Shapiro, V. B., Accomazzo, S., & Manthey, T. J. (2016). Strengths-based social work: A meta-theory to guide social work research and practice. In N. Coady & P. Lehmann (Eds.), *Theoretical perspectives for direct social work practice* (3rd ed., pp. 131–154). New York: Springer Publishing Company.

Smith, M., Haedtke, C., & Shibley, D. (2015). Late life depression detection: An evidence-based guideline. *Journal of Gerontological Nursing*, 41(2), 18–25.

Spitzer, R. L., Kroenke, K., Williams, J. B., & Löwe, B. (2006). A brief measure for assessing generalized anxiety disorder: The GAD-7. *Archives of Internal Medicine*, 166(10), 1092–1097.

Substance Abuse and Mental Health Services Administration/Administration on Aging. (2013). *Older Americans behavioral health issue brief 6: Depression and anxiety: Screening and intervention.* Retrieved from https://www.ncoa.org/wp-content/uploads/IssueBrief_6_DepressionAnxiety_Color.pdf

Tariq, S. H., Tumosa, N., Chibnall, J. T., Perry III, H. M., & Morley, J. E. (2006). The Saint Louis University Mental Status (SLUMS) examination for detecting mild cognitive impairment and dementia is more sensitive than the Mini-Mental State Examination (MMSE): A pilot study. *American Journal of Geriatric Psychiatry*, 14(11), 900–910.

Thomlison, R. J., & Thomlison, B. (2017). Cognitive behavior theory and social work treatment. In F. J. Turner (Ed.), *Social work treatment: Theoretical approaches* (6th ed., pp. 54–79). New York: Oxford University Press.

Ward, K. T., & Reuben, D.B. (2017). Comprehensive geriatric assessment. Retrieved from https://www.uptodate.com/contents/comprehensive-geriatric-assessment

Welsh, T. J., Gordon, A. L., & Gladman, J. R. (2014). Comprehensive geriatric assessment: A guide for the non-specialist. *International Journal of Clinical Practice*, 68(3), 290–293.

Yesavage, J. A., Brink, T. L., Rose, T. L., Lum, O., Huang, V., Adey, M., & Leirer, V. O. (1983). Development and validation of a geriatric depression screening scale: A preliminary report. *Journal of Psychiatric Research*, 17(1), 37–49.

Zarit, S. H., Reever, K. E., & Back-Peterson, J. (1980). Relatives of the impaired elderly: Correlates of feelings of burden. *The Gerontologist*, 20, 649–655.

CHAPTER 3

Assessing Risk Factors

Sexual Health (HIV, STI, STDs) and Homelessness

This chapter identifies risk factors related to sexual health and homelessness among older adults, presents evidence-based interventions for addressing risk factors, and explores key domains to promote both effective clinical practice with older adults and optimal client outcomes.

CSWE Gero Competencies Highlighted

Competency 1: Demonstrate Ethical and Professional Behavior

Specialized Practice Competency Description: Social workers understand the value base of the profession and its ethical standards, as well as relevant laws and regulations that may impact practice at the micro, mezzo, and macro levels. Social workers understand frameworks of ethical decision-making and how to apply principles of critical thinking to those frameworks in practice, research, and policy arenas. Social workers recognize personal values and the distinction between personal and professional values. They also understand how their personal experiences and affective reactions influence their professional judgment and behavior. Social workers understand the profession's history, its mission, and the roles and responsibilities of the profession. Social workers also understand the role of other professions when engaged in inter-professional teams. Social workers recognize the importance of lifelong learning and are committed to continually updating their skills to ensure they are relevant and effective. Social workers also understand emerging forms of technology and the ethical use of technology in social work practice.

Competency Behaviors: (1) Guided by ethical reasoning and self-reflection, demonstrate adherence to ethical frameworks and key laws, policies, and procedures related to aging, and the rights of older adults. (2) Engage in active dialogue with field faculty/

instructors regarding aging field placement agency policies and culture around behavior, appearance, communication, and the use of supervision. (3) Develop and sustain effective collaborative relationships that respect older adults' needs for protection, self-determination, and the provision of services in the least restrictive environment possible with colleagues and community stakeholders, including older adults, their family members, other care providers, and Tribes. (4) Effectively manage professional boundary issues and other challenges arising in the course of aging-related work, particularly ambiguities presented by home visits, personal loss, trauma, and other highly involved and potentially emotionally triggering aspects of the work. (5) Develop and sustain relationships with members of interdisciplinary and integrated health care teams, including social workers, primary care providers, hospital staff, home health care providers, psychiatrists, psychologists, substance use disorder treatment staff, Tribal service providers, and others, that reflect clear understanding of their roles in providing care to older adults. (6) Demonstrate both knowledge of the history and evolution of social work practice related to aging and older adults in the United States and California, and a commitment to lifelong learning around this practice. (7) Follow all ethical guidelines and legal mandates in the use of technology in order to maintain the confidentiality of all personal, behavioral health, and health-related information. (CalSWEC, 2017, pp. 1–2)

Competency 2: Engage Diversity and Difference in Practice

Specialized Practice Competency Description: Social workers understand how diversity and difference characterize and shape the human experience and are critical to the formation of identity. The dimensions of diversity are understood as the intersectionality of multiple factors, including, but not limited to, age, class, color, culture, disability and ability, ethnicity, gender, gender identity and expression, immigration status, marital status, political ideology, race, religion/spirituality, sex, sexual orientation, and Tribal sovereign status. Social workers understand that, as a consequence of difference, a person's life experiences may include oppression, poverty, marginalization, and alienation as well as privilege, power, and acclaim. Social workers also understand the forms and mechanisms of oppression and discrimination and recognize the extent to which a culture's structures and values, including social, economic, political, and cultural exclusions, may oppress, marginalize, alienate, or create privilege and power.

Competency Behaviors: (1) Engage in critical analysis of the interpersonal, community, and social structural causes and effects of disproportionality, disparities, and inequities in the incidence and trajectory of aging-related care needs, housing, transportation, and resource access among older adults, their families, and their communities. (2) Evidence respectful awareness and understanding of the impact of being a member of a marginalized group on aging experiences, and accurately identify differences in access to and quality of available services for members of different communities and populations. (3) Demonstrate knowledge of diverse cultural norms and traditional methods of providing care to older adults, as well as an applied understanding of how these realities affect work with older adults from diverse backgrounds, their families, and their communities. (4) Develop and use practice methods that acknowledge, respect, and address how individual and cultural values, norms, and differences impact the various systems with which older adults interact, including, but not limited to, families, communities, primary care systems, mental and behavioral health care systems, and integrated care systems. (CalSWEC, 2017, pp. 3–4)

Competency 3: Advance Human Rights and Social, Economic, and Environmental Justice

Specialized Practice Competency Description: Social workers understand that every person regardless of position in society has fundamental human rights such as freedom, safety, privacy, an adequate standard of living, health care, and education. Social workers understand the global interconnections of oppression and human rights violations, and are knowledgeable about theories of human need and social justice and strategies to promote social and economic justice and human rights. Social workers understand strategies designed to eliminate oppressive structural barriers to ensure that social goods, rights, and responsibilities are distributed equitably and that civil, political, environmental, economic, social, and cultural human rights are protected.

Competency Behaviors: (1) Clearly articulate the systematic effects of discrimination, oppression, and stigma on the needs and experiences of older adults and on the quality and delivery of services available to them, and identify and advocate for policy changes needed to address these issues. (2) Advocate for changes in policies and programs that reflect a social justice practice framework for facilitating access and providing services to older adults, their families, and care providers, especially among underserved groups and communities. (3) Demonstrate the ability to work effectively in cross-disciplinary collaboration to develop and provide interventions that explicitly address the specific needs of diverse older adults, their families, and care providers. (4) Integrate into all aspects of policy and practice sensitivity to the reality that fundamental rights, including freedom and privacy, may be compromised for older adults engaged in care, and the goal that services should be provided in the least restrictive environment possible. (CalSWEC, 2017, pp. 4–5)

Competency 4: Engage in Practice-informed Research and Research-informed Practice

Specialized Practice Competency Description: Social workers understand quantitative and qualitative research methods and their respective roles in advancing a science of social work and in evaluating their practice. Social workers know the principles of logic, scientific inquiry, and culturally informed and ethical approaches to building knowledge. Social workers understand that evidence that informs practice derives from multidisciplinary sources and multiple ways of knowing. They also understand the processes for translating research findings into effective practice.

Competency Behaviors: (1) Demonstrate the ability to understand, interpret, and evaluate the benefits and limitations of various evidence-based and evidence-informed treatment models as they influence practice with older adults. (2) Engage in critical analysis of research findings, practice models, and practice wisdom as they inform aging related practice, including how research practices have historically failed to address the needs and realities of exploited and/or disadvantaged communities, and how cross-cultural research practices can be used to enhance equity. (3) Clearly communicate research findings, conclusions, and implications, as well as their applications to aging practice, across a variety of professional interactions with consumers, families, and multidisciplinary service providers. (4) Apply research findings to aging-related practice with individuals, families, and communities and to the development of professional knowledge about the needs, experiences, and well-being of older adults. (CalSWEC, 2017, pp. 5–6)

Competency 6: Engage With Individuals, Families, Groups, Organizations, and Communities

Specialized Practice Competency Description: Social workers understand that engagement is an ongoing component of the dynamic and interactive process of social work practice with, and on behalf of, diverse individuals, families, groups, organizations, and communities. Social workers value the importance of human relationships. Social workers understand theories of human behavior and the social environment, and critically evaluate and apply this knowledge to facilitate engagement with clients and constituencies, including individuals, families, groups, organizations, and communities. Social workers understand strategies to engage diverse clients and constituencies to advance practice effectiveness. Social workers understand how their personal experiences and affective reactions may impact their ability to effectively engage with diverse clients and constituencies. Social workers value principles of relationship-building and inter-professional collaboration to facilitate engagement with clients, constituencies, and other professionals as appropriate.

Competency Behaviors: (1) Appropriately engage and activate older adults, their families, and other care providers in the development and coordination of care plans that reflect relevant theoretical models and balance older adults' needs for care with respect for autonomy and independence. (2) Effectively utilize interpersonal skills to engage older adults, their families, and other care providers in culturally responsive, consumer-driven, and trauma-informed integrated care that addresses mutually agreed upon service goals and balances needs for care, protection, autonomy, and independence. (3) Establish effective and appropriate communication, coordination, and advocacy planning with other care providers and interdisciplinary care teams as needed to address mutually agreed upon service goals. Recognizing the complex nature of service engagement, ensure that communications with consumers and their families regarding service goals are both sensitive and transparent. (4) Manage affective responses and exercise good judgment around engaging with resistance, trauma responses, and other potentially triggering situations with older adults, their families, and other care providers (CalSWEC, 2017, pp. 9–10).

Competency 7: Assess Individuals, Families, Groups, Organizations, and Communities

Specialized Practice Competency Description: Practitioners in aging utilize ecological-systems theory, a strengths-based and person/family-centered framework to conduct assessments that value the resilience of diverse older adults, families, and caregivers. They select appropriate assessment tools, methods and technology, and evaluate, adapt, and modify them, as needed, to enhance their validity in working with diverse, vulnerable and at-risk groups. The comprehensive biopsychosocial assessment takes into account the multiple factors of physical, mental and social well-being needed for treatment planning for older adults and their families. They develop skills in interprofessional assessment and communication with key constituencies to choose the most effective practice strategies. Gero social workers understand how their own experiences and affective reactions about aging, quality of life, loss and grief may affect their assessment and resultant decision-making.

Competency Behaviors: (1) Conduct assessments that incorporate a strengths-based perspective, person/family-centered focus, and resilience while recognizing aging related risk, (2) Develop, select, and adapt assessment methods and tools that optimize practice with older adults, their families, caregivers, and communities, and (3) Use and integrate multiple domains and sources of assessment information and communicate with other professionals to inform a comprehensive plan for intervention. (Council for Social Work Education, 2017, pp. 89–90)

Competency 8: Intervene With Individuals, Families, Groups, Organizations, and Communities

Specialized Practice Competency Description: Social workers understand that intervention is an ongoing component of the dynamic and interactive process of social work practice with, and on behalf of, diverse individuals, families, groups, organizations, and communities. Social workers are knowledgeable about evidence-informed interventions to achieve the goals of clients and constituencies, including individuals, families, groups, organizations, and communities. Social workers understand theories of human behavior and the social environment, and critically evaluate and apply this knowledge to effectively intervene with clients and constituencies. Social workers understand methods of identifying, analyzing, and implementing evidence-informed interventions to achieve client and constituency goals. Social workers value the importance of inter-professional teamwork and communication in interventions, recognizing that beneficial outcomes may require interdisciplinary, inter-professional, and inter-organizational collaboration.

Competency Behaviors: (1) In partnership with older adults and their families, develop appropriate intervention plans that reflect respect for autonomy and independence, as well as contemporary theories and models for interventions with older adults. Plans should:

- Reflect cultural humility and acknowledgement of individualized needs;
- Incorporate consumer and family strengths;
- Utilize community resources and natural supports;
- Incorporate multidisciplinary team supports and interventions;
- Include non-pharmacological interventions; and
- Demonstrate knowledge of poly-pharmacy needs and issues specific to older adults.

(2) Apply the principles of teaming, engagement, inquiry, advocacy, and facilitation within interdisciplinary teams and care coordination to the work of supporting older adults, family members, and other care providers to accomplish intervention goals and satisfy advanced care planning needs. (3) Effectively implement evidence-based interventions in the context of providing emergency response, triage, brief treatment, and longer-term care, and in the course of addressing a range of issues presented in primary care, specialty care, community agency, inpatient, and palliative care settings. Interventions should be guided by respect for older adults' autonomy and independence and should include components such as psychoeducation, problem-solving treatment skills, symptom tracking, medication therapies, follow-up, and planning for evolving care needs. (4) Effectively plan for interventions in ways that incorporate thoughtfully executed

transitions during time-limited internships, recognizing that consumer needs for support may continue beyond these time periods. (CalSWEC, 2017, pp. 12–14)

Specialized Practice Competency Description: Social workers understand that evaluation is an ongoing component of the dynamic and interactive process of social work practice with, and on behalf of, diverse individuals, families, groups, organizations and communities. Social workers recognize the importance of evaluating processes and outcomes to advance practice, policy, and service delivery effectiveness. Social workers understand theories of human behavior and the social environment, and critically evaluate and apply this knowledge in evaluating outcomes. Social workers understand qualitative and quantitative methods for evaluating outcomes and practice effectiveness.

Competency Behaviors: (1) Record, track, and monitor consumer engagement, assessment, and intervention data in practice with older adults, their families, and other care providers accurately and according to field education agency policies and guidelines. (2) Conduct accurate process and outcome analysis of engagement, assessment, and intervention data in practice with older adults, their families, and other care providers that incorporates consumer perspectives and reflects respect for older adults' autonomy and independence. (3) Use findings to evaluate intervention effectiveness, develop recommendations for adapting service plans and approaches as needed, improve interdisciplinary team coordination and care integration, and help agency and community policies better support older adults, their families, and their formal and informal care systems. (4) Share both the purposes of such data collection and the overall results of data analysis with older adults, their families, and communities whenever possible, with the goal of engaging them more meaningfully in the evaluation process. (CalSWEC, 2017, pp. 14–15)

Learning Objectives

1. Learners will become aware of contextual and diversity factors to consider when engaging, assessing, intervening, and evaluating outcomes with older adults with risk factors for sexual health and homelessness.
2. Learners will identify screening tools for assessing high-risk factors among older adults.
3. Learners will identify appropriate evidence-based interventions.
4. Learners will understand the importance of referring older adult clients to appropriate technological and community resources and when to assist with coordination.
5. Learners will identify sources of transference and countertransference when working with older adults with high-risk factors.

Case Study

Mr. Peters, a 70-year-old, single, non-Hispanic White male, who resides in California, had just been discharged from the hospital to a board and care. Mr. Peters's diagnoses were PTSD, depression, high blood pressure, and an alcohol-related substance use disorder; he was discharged with a walker due to his recovery from a hip replacement. The hip replacement was required due to injuries he sustained from a hit-and-run driver; the crime had been reported by the emergency department to the police and Adult Protective Services. Mr. Peters medically detoxed from alcohol during his hospitalization. He reported he had been homeless for the past two months after being evicted from an apartment; he also reported he has had difficulty with securing another apartment since his eviction. Mr. Peters was evicted from his apartment due to disruptions with neighbors and the police being called out several times while he was intoxicated. He was socially isolated with no friends or community contacts for socialization and support. Mr. Peters was never married and had no children. He reported he was estranged from his family members, who live in Texas, after returning from his four-year service in the Vietnam War. He reported he did not qualify for a service-connected disability from the Veterans Administration for his PTSD. His sole income source was Social Security, in the amount of $1,450 per month. He worked in construction for 35 years prior to retiring and collecting Social Security. His insurance was Medicare primary and AARP. Mr. Peters reported he had no place to go from the board and care.

Assessing Context

Sexuality

Influential contextual factors to consider when engaging, assessing, intervening, and evaluating interventions with older adults about healthy sexuality are policy and societal contexts in the United States. Similar to countries such as Australia, the United Kingdom, Scotland, Wales, and Northern Ireland, the United States lacks a nationwide policy on sexual health explicitly addressing sexual health prevention and promotion that supports healthy sexuality among older adults (Kirkman, Fox, & Dickson-Swift, 2016). In the United States, sexual health policies emphasize reproductive health and prevention of sexually transmitted diseases (STDs), sexually transmitted infections (STIs), and human immunodeficiency virus (HIV) among youth and younger adult populations and, thus, overlook detection and prevention of STDs, STIs, and HIV among older adults as well as education targeting older adults and providers on sexual health promotion. The definition of sexual health adopted by the Centers for Disease Control (CDC) reflects the World Health Organization's definition:

> A state of physical, emotional, mental and social well-being in relation to sexuality; it is not merely the absence of disease, dysfunction or infirmity. Sexual health requires a positive and respectful approach to sexuality and sexual relationships, as well as the possibility of having pleasurable and safe sexual experiences, free of coercion, discrimination and violence. (World Health Organization, 2006, p. 5)

The sociocultural context is equally important to understand. In many cultures, sexuality continues to be a taboo topic as well as the myth that sexual activity and desire decline with age (Lusti-Narasimham & Beard, 2013). For older women, healthy sexual functioning and intimacy are predictors of relational satisfaction (Lusti-Narasimham & Beard, 2013). Globally, women comprise 50% to 60% of HIV infections; the rates of STIs and HIV among older adults internationally are underreported, as well as internationally; and screening targets younger adults (Lusti-Narasimham & Beard, 2013). Older women—widows in particular—are at a higher risk for sexual violence and harassment due to their dependency financially and socially on families and others (Lusti-Narasimham & Beard, 2013). The most commonly reported STIs among older adults include syphilis, gonorrhea, chlamydia, and HIV (Johnson, 2013). Physical aging and issues affecting healthy sexual functioning are other contextual factors to consider when assessing the sexual health of older adults. Normal changes for females include thinning of vaginal walls and decreases in lubrication while normal changes for men include erectile dysfunction (National Institute on Aging, 2013). In an international study examining sexual functioning among older adult females in 29 countries, the highest reported concerns were low desire, issues with vaginal lubrication, and difficulty with orgasm (Lusti-Narasimham & Beard, 2013). Sexual health and functioning are affected by chronic diseases, such as cardiovascular disease, cancer, diabetes, pulmonary disease (Aboderin, 2014), arthritis, chronic pain, stroke, depression, and incontinence (National Institute on Aging, 2013). Sexual functioning is also affected by alcohol—too much alcohol leads to orgasm difficulties in women and erectile issues for men (National Institute on Aging, 2013). Health status affects sexual health and activity of older adults (Lindau & Gavrilova, 2010). With increasing age, sexual activity, interest, and quality of sexual experiences have been found in one cross-sectional study to be greater for men than women in the United States; however, poor health affects sexual activity more for men than women in middle and older adulthood (Lindau & Gavrilova, 2010).

Homelessness

The U.S. Department of Housing and Urban Development (HUD) defines four federal categories for homelessness: The first, "literally homeless" (2017b, p. 1), refers to individuals who live in a place not meant for habitation by humans, reside in a shelter or transitional housing, or are exiting an institution they lived at for 90 days (but were in a shelter or at an inhabitable site prior to admission) (National Alliance to End Homelessness, 2017a). The second federal category for homeless is "imminent risk of homelessness" (U.S. Department of Housing and Urban Development, 2017b, p. 1), which includes those who are at risk of losing their residence within 14 days (including those in hotels or living with a friend, doubled up) (National Alliance to End Homelessness, 2017a). The third federal category of homeless is "homeless under other Federal statutes" (U.S. Department of Housing and Urban Development, 2017b, p. 1), which is a category for families with children who have moved two or more times in the past 60 days or do not have a lease or ownership for housing for 60 or greater days (National Alliance to End Homelessness, 2017a). The fourth federal category for homeless is "fleeing/attempting to flee domestic violence"

(U.S. Department of Housing and Urban Development, 2017b, p. 1), which includes those who do not have resources for housing or support to secure it (National Alliance to End Homelessness, 2017a). Chronic homelessness is defined as homelessness among individuals who "have a disability—including serious mental illness, chronic substance use disorders, or chronic medical conditions—and who are homeless repeatedly or for long periods of time" (National Alliance to End Homelessness, 2016, p. 21).

According to a report by the National Alliance to End Homelessness (2016), in 2015 on any given night, there were approximately 564,709 individuals homeless. Financial restraints and the high cost of housing attribute to the majority of homelessness among individuals (National Alliance to End Homelessness, 2016). This reality provides a context for many older adults living in poverty being at risk for homelessness or premature institutionalization to avoid it. According to the National Health Care for the Homeless Council (2013), with the rapid growth of the aging population, it is anticipated that by 2050, the homeless aging population will have more than doubled in size from 44,172 in 2010 to 92,572. In 2013, roughly 5% of older adults ages 65 and older had unstable housing (National Health Care for the Homeless Council, 2013). Older adults with unstable housing account for more than 33% of emergency department visits (National Health Care for the Homeless Council, 2013). Older adults living in poverty at risk of homelessness often experience high levels of stress over long periods of time, leading to premature aging also referred to as weather, which shortens life expectancy by 10 to 20 years (National Health Care for the Homeless Council, 2013). Older adults without stable housing also experience higher rates of geriatric syndromes (i.e., mild cognitive impairment, falls, major depression, bladder incontinence, and impairments in senses) (National Health Care for the Homeless Council, 2013).

Clinicians should be familiar with best practices for assessing sexual health and homeless risk and protective factors of older adults when conducting biopsychosocial/spiritual assessments.

Biopsychosocial/Spiritual Assessment

Assessing Sexual Health

Clinicians can routinely assess sexual health of older adults using the Centers for Disease Control's five P's of sexual health (i.e., partners, practices, protection from STDs, past history of STDs, and prevention of pregnancy) or other models such as the Permission, Limited Information, Specific Suggestions, and Intensive Therapy (PLISSIT) model (reviewed later in this chapter). Protective factors include education, health literacy, self-efficacy, social support, availability of health insurance, preventive health screenings, resiliency, spirituality, and socioeconomic resources. Clinicians who identify risk or issues with healthy sexual functioning should provide harm reduction psychoeducation (reviewed later in this chapter) and referral for older adults to physicians for physical evaluations to rule out treatable medical conditions and to therapists for assistance with mental health disorders impacting sexual functioning.

Assessing Homelessness

Clinicians should assess all older adults for socioeconomic, poverty, and social risks that predispose them to homelessness. The lack of availability of affordable housing for older adults places older adults living in poverty at risk. For every affordable housing unit in the United States, there is a minimum of nine older adults on the waiting list for a housing unit (National Coalition for the Homeless, 2009). Isolation is another risk factor for homelessness; among older adults receiving Supplemental Security Income (SSI), placing them at the poverty level, approximately 50% lost their housing that lived alone (National Coalition for the Homeless, 2009). Protective factors include social support; self-efficacy; skill in navigating health services; health insurance; knowledge about and use of home and community-based services to meet needs for shelter, food, and clothing; spirituality; a positive outlook on the future; and resiliency.

Case Study Application

Following is an application of the Geriatric Biopsychosocial/Spiritual Assessment conducted by Mr. Peter's social worker.

Box 3.1

Geriatric Biopsychosocial/Spiritual Assessment

Basic Demographic: 70-year-old, single, non-Hispanic White male, English language, high school education

Referral Information: Client referred to social work for assistance with housing options

Cultural/Spiritual: Client has no religious preference; no use of complementary or alternative medicines

Social: Relationships within family, social/diversity groups, and community

- Personal and family history: Estranged from family; no friends or community affiliations

Financial: Ability to provide basic needs and access health services

- Ability to provide basic needs: No power of attorney; was evicted from apartment and unable to currently secure housing but able to secure food and clothing needs through local community-based agencies serving homeless
- Health insurance: Adequate—Medicare and AARP
- Income sources: Adequate per client report—$1,450 in Social Security monthly

Environmental: Personal safety, maintenance of residence, and safety of community

---

- Current social context/environmental: At board and care facility with 24-hour assistance
- Neighborhood safety: Adequate
- Home safety: Slip rugs are absent at the board and care, there is a wheelchair ramp to access the board and care
- Access to guns: No guns or access to guns in the board and care
- Screen for abuse or neglect by self or perpetrated by others (APS SOC341 report if suspected): APS and police reports filed at the emergency department; no further abuse/neglect identified

Physical: Individual function and disease morbidity

- Health literacy and self-rated health: Client with adequate health literacy and low self-rated health; no advance directive; diagnoses are PTSD, depression, high blood pressure, and substance use disorder; client ambulates with a walker; no other chronic or life-threatening illnesses; sexual health: inactive

Mental: Mental status, depression, anxiety, and substance abuse

- Standardized screening instruments: Score of 11 for moderate depression on Geriatric Depression Scale; Mini-Mental State Examination: client scored 25, an indicator of no cognitive impairment
- Suicide risk assessment: Ruled out
- Homicidal ideations: Ruled out
- Substance use: High risk, was drinking more than 14 alcoholic beverages per week prior to medical detox

Formulation/Evaluation: Comorbid substance use and depression; assistance needed with discharge planning for housing options; high risk for homelessness

Treatment Planning: Appropriate housing options (sober living or residential treatment for co-occurring disorder vs. independent, senior housing with instrumental activities of daily living assistance, assisted living); medication consult for depression; outpatient substance use and co-occurring disorder treatment options; social worker evaluation plus two follow-up case management visits per medical doctor's order

Community Resource Needs: Intensive outpatient program or partial hospitalization programs for co-occurring PTSD, depression, and substance use disorder (depending upon place of residence discharged from board and care to) vs. residential treatment

Screening Tools for High-Risk Factors

Sexual Health

The Centers for Disease Control (2005) guide for taking a sexual health history can be used by clinicians to assess the sexual health of older adult clients; it includes a dialogue or script for the clinician to follow. The first P, partners, has four questions that allow providers to assess the risk of the client for STDs with questions assessing current sexual activity and sex partners during the past 12 months (Centers for Disease Control, 2005). The second P, practices, allows the clinician to assess the kind of sex the client has been engaged in during the past 12 months to assess risk for STDs (i.e., genital, anal, oral) (Centers for Disease Control, 2005). The third P, protection, allows the clinician to assess the type(s) of protection from STDs and the frequency of the usage of protection the client is or is not using (Centers for Disease Control, 2005). The fourth P, past history, allows the clinician to assess the client's past testing, diagnostic history, and treatment of STDs of the client and his or her partners (Centers for Disease Control, 2005). And the last P, prevention of pregnancy, assesses the client who may be trying to "conceive or father a child," pregnancy concerns, and the use of contraception/condoms (Centers for Disease Control, 2005, p. 17).

The PLISSIT model was modified in 2012 for use with discussion about sexuality with older adults in various settings for older adults (Kazer, 2012). P refers to "obtaining permission from the client to initiate sexual discussion," LI refers to "providing limited information needed to function sexually," SS refers to "giving specific suggestions for the individual to proceed with sexual relations," and IT refers to "providing intensive therapy surrounding issues of sexuality for that client" (Kazer, 2012, p. 1). The modified PLISSIT model includes questions for the clinician for discussion with the older adult that include: (1) "Can you tell me how you express your sexuality?" (2) "What concerns or questions do you have about fulfilling your continual sexual needs?" (3) "In what ways has your sexual relationship with your partner changed as you have aged?" and (4) "What interventions or information can I provide to help fulfill your sexuality?" (Kazer, 2012, p. 2). Screening tools can also be used by clinicians to assess an older adults risk for homelessness.

Homelessness

The National Alliance to End Homelessness developed a toolkit (2017b) for use by Continuum of Care (CoC) programs that are required by HUD to have coordinated entry systems for geographical areas covered by their respective programs across the United States. Within this toolkit are a variety of screening tools, documents, and products created by programs across the United States that address access, assessment, prioritization, and housing referrals for individuals and families (National Alliance to End Homelessness, 2017b). HUD (2017a) also has a Coordinated Entry Community Samples Toolkit available that is more comprehensive and includes screening tools; documents; products to address access, assessment, prioritization, and housing referrals; and planning, management and oversight, data management, and evaluation similar to the National Alliance to End Homelessness toolkit.

To inform formulation of the issues for treatment and treatment planning, clinicians assess the domain of diversity to ensure that the cultural and diversity context and preferences of the older adult client inform the identification of options for treatment for older adults who clinicians detect are at risk for sexual health and/or homelessness.

Diversity–Cultural Competence/Spirituality/LGBT/Sexuality

Cultural competence and humility are required by clinicians working with older adults with risk factors for sexual health and homelessness. According to the Centers for Disease Control (2017), in 2015, African Americans ages 50 and older had a higher incidence of HIV diagnosis (43%) in comparison to non-Hispanic Whites (36%) and Hispanics/Latinos (17%). In 2014, adults ages 50 and older accounted for 45% of all people living with a HIV diagnosis in the United States (Centers for Disease Control, 2017). Although HIV is now a manageable chronic health condition and no longer a death sentence, older adults are diagnosed at later stages in the disease in comparison to younger adults (Centers for Disease Control, 2017). When working with lesbian, gay, bisexual, and transgender (LGBT) older adults, using a strengths-based approach, clinicians should recognize the resiliency and community-building and social network capacity. Clinicians should be aware that several older LGBT adults were and continue to be impacted by the HIV/AIDS epidemic (Fredriksen-Goldsen, Kim, Goldsen, & Emlet, 2014). By 2016, it was estimated that approximately 50% of individuals living with HIV were ages 50 and older (Fredriksen-Goldsen, Kim, Goldsen, & Emlet, 2014). Screening LGBT older adults for sexual health may trigger memories and experiences that may be stigmatizing and traumatizing from the AIDS epidemic of the 1980s. Clinicians should be prepared to address any survivor's guilt and losses of friends, family, and loved ones that resulted from the AIDs epidemic (Fredriksen-Goldsen, Kim, Goldsen, & Emlet, 2014). Clinicians should follow the CSWE Gero Competency 2: Engage Diversity and Difference in Practice and ensure that all practice behaviors 1–4 are adhered to for competent practice with diverse older adults. Clinicians should seek training in best practices for attitudes, knowledge, and skills to work effectively with diverse older adults with risk factors for sexual health and homelessness. Clinicians inform the interdisciplinary treatment team with the diversity context relevant to the older adult client and, using a strengths perspective, present the risk and protective factors of the client to inform interdisciplinary team treatment planning.

Interdisciplinary Team Roles and Planning

Clinicians working with older adults with risk factors for sexual health and homelessness work collaboratively with other disciplines on the interdisciplinary team and seek consultation from and engage in collaborative treatment planning to address presenting issues of the older adult client. Consistent with the CSWE Gero Competency 1: Demonstrate Ethical and Professional Behavior, clinicians should engage in the following competency behavior 5: "Develop and sustain relationships with members of interdisciplinary and integrated health care teams, including social workers, primary care providers, hospital staff, home health care providers, psychiatrists, psychologists, substance use disorder treatment staff, Tribal service providers, and others, that reflect clear understanding of their roles in providing care to older adults" (CalSWEC, 2017, pp. 1–2). Clinicians should also follow CSWE Gero Competency 6: Engage With Individuals, Families, Groups, Organizations, and Communities behaviors 1–4. Clinicians follow CSWE Gero Competency 7: Assess Individuals, Families, Groups, Organizations, and Communities competency behavior 3: "Use and integrate multiple domains and sources of assessment information and communicate with other professionals to inform a comprehensive plan for intervention" (CalSWEC, 2017, pp. 89–90). Competency 8: Intervene With Individuals, Families, Groups, Organizations, and Communities should be adhered to with treatment planning with the interdisciplinary team under behavior 2: "Apply the principles of teaming, engagement, inquiry, advocacy, and facilitation within interdisciplinary teams and care coordination to the work of supporting older adults, family members, and other care providers to accomplish intervention goals and satisfy advanced care planning needs" (CalSWEC, 2017, pp. 12–14).

Mr. Peters's social worker, after the first visit at the board and care, met with the physician, nurse, and physical therapist to develop a treatment plan that would address Mr. Peters's co-occurring PTSD, depression, and substance use disorder while addressing housing needs and support simultaneously. Mr. Peters elected to discharge to a residential treatment center with a program designed for older adults. The program had accommodations for his walker and provided case management for permanent housing and recovery services. Clinicians work with the older adult client and interdisciplinary team to present options for evidence-based treatment and best practices with older adults who present with risk for sexual health and/or homelessness.

Evidence-based Interventions

Crisis Intervention

One intervention that can be used by clinicians when working with an older adult in crisis due to high-risk factors for sexual health or homelessness is crisis intervention. Roberts and Ottens define a crisis as "an acute disruption of psychological homeostasis in which one's usual coping mechanisms fail and there exists evidence of distress and functional impairment" (2005, p. 331). Two conditions are necessary: (1) "the individual's perception of the event as the cause of considerable upset and/or disruption" and (2) "the individual's inability to resolve the disruption by previously used coping mechanisms" (Roberts & Ottens, 2005, p. 331). Roberts's seven-stage crisis intervention model is used to understand and intervene with clients to achieve stabilization of the crisis, resolution of the crisis, and mastery (Roberts & Ottens, 2005). Stage one, psychosocial and lethality assessment, involves a rapid biopsychosocial/spiritual assessment that assesses: suicidal feelings and thoughts, client strengths, suicide plan lethality and history, and other contextual risk factors (i.e., depression; social isolation; loss of a job, home, or divorce) (Roberts & Ottens, 2005). Stage two, rapidly establish rapport, involves the clinicians using unconditional regard, acceptance, genuineness, and respect to establish trust and rapport in the therapeutic relationship (Roberts & Ottens, 2005). Stage three, identify the major problems or crisis precipitants, allows the clinician to hear from the client the precipitating events to the crisis and the client's coping style(s), and it provides a point for establishing and triaging priorities to address (Roberts & Ottens, 2005).

Stage four, deal with feelings and emotions, involves two processes: expression of feelings and emotions and challenging of responses (Roberts & Ottens, 2005). In the first process, the clinician invites and allows the client to tell their story about the precipitating events leading to the crisis; here, the client is allowed to express their thoughts, emotions, and feelings (Roberts & Ottens, 2005). The clinician uses a key skill from motivational interviewing—active listening—that involves simple reflections of feelings, paraphrasing, and summarizing, as well as probing (Roberts & Ottens, 2005). In the second process, the clinician also uses a key skill from motivational interviewing—rolling with resistance—to challenge cognitive distortions and beliefs of the client interfering with reality-based interpretations. Here, the clinician uses interpretation and reframing and challenges client responses to facilitate readiness for options for behavior for the client to engage in (Roberts & Ottens, 2005).

In stage five, generate and explore alternatives, the clinician begins to explore options to promote stabilization of the crisis, considering what has and has not worked in the past for the client, as well as recommendations from the clinician to stabilize the crisis (Roberts & Ottens, 2005). The key is that this is a collaborative process between the clinician and client. Stage six, implement an action plan, involves generating and implementing an action plan geared toward restoring equilibrium and homeostasis of the client (Roberts & Ottens, 2005). This plan should be specific to address the nature of the crisis, contextual factors, and best evidence for treatment for older adults with high-risk factors or crisis pertaining to sexual health, abuse/neglect, suicide, or homelessness. Stage seven, follow-up, involves a check-in by the clinician to monitor the implementation and effectiveness of the action plan established in stage seven (Roberts & Ottens, 2005). The post-crisis evaluation should include: the current physical state of the client (i.e., meeting basic needs), improvements with cognitive mastery over the precipitating events leading to the crisis, overall functioning assessment, treatment satisfaction, the use of coping skills and management of any stressors, and the needs for any additional referrals (Roberts & Ottens, 2005).

Crisis intervention was an appropriate intervention to use with Mr. Peters as he was motivated to secure permanent housing as well as treatment for his co-occurring PTSD, depression, and substance use disorder. The seven-stage crisis intervention model was implemented during three visits with Mr. Peters. During the initial visits at the board and care, the social worker engaged in the first four stages with Mr. Peters. The social worker completed a biopsychosocial/spiritual and lethality assessment (stage one); rapidly established rapport with the client using motivational interviewing techniques and empathic responses (stage two); identified the major problems and precipitants, such as homelessness, victim of a crime, and a co-occurring substance use disorder (stage three); and created an environment where the client could openly express his feelings about his circumstances and ambiguity about his future (stage four). In the second visit, after the interdisciplinary treatment team meeting, Mr. Peters and the social worker collaborated on options for treatment and a safe discharge plan for him. Mr. Peters identified pros and cons for each option and made an informed decision to select a residential treatment facility with a program for older adults (stage five). The preferred option was then implemented and a plan was secured for his discharge to the residential treatment facility once home health was discharged. Transportation arrangements were made to transport Mr. Peters to the residential treatment facility as well (stage six). In the third visit, the social worker followed up with Mr. Peters on the discharge plan, and Mr. Peters maintained satisfaction with the discharge plan and reported a decrease in his depressive symptoms. He was engaging in coping skills to improve his outlook for his future and maintained motivation for residential treatment (stage seven).

Primary prevention is a second evidence-based intervention that can be used effectively with older adults with sexual health risk factors and homeless risk.

Primary Prevention

Primary prevention is defined by the World Health Organization as "actions aimed at avoiding the manifestation of a disease," which includes services and activities such as vaccination (i.e., against diseases and STDs), "provision of information on behavioral and medical health risks, and measures to reduce risks at individual and population levels" (which include sexual health) (2017). Primary prevention can be used as a principle for screening, assessing, and treating older adults with high-risk factors for sexual health, abuse/neglect, suicide, and homelessness. When applied to sexual health of older adults, clinicians can use the Centers for Disease Control (2005) guide for taking a sexual health history using the five P's (i.e., partners, practices, protection from STDs, past history of STDs, and prevention of pregnancy) to assess risk for STDs, provide education on protection from STDs, and refer for testing and treatment of STDs. When applied to elder abuse/neglect, it involves the prevention of elder abuse and neglect through psychoeducation prevention programs, such as the WISE & Healthy Aging Prevention Program, which educate older adults about forms of abuse perpetrated by others (i.e., emotional, physical, financial, sexual) and provide them with skills and resources to prevent themselves from becoming a victim (WISE & Healthy Aging, 2017).

When working to prevent homelessness among older adults, the following solutions recommended by *Justice in Aging* (2016) can be incorporated into clinician interventions with older adults with high-risk factors for homelessness: *Increase income supports* (by identifying and assisting the older adult with applying for all safety net programs he or she is eligible for: Social Security, SSI, food/stamps, general relief/cash aid). A second solution, *make health care affordable and accessible*, includes advocacy by clinicians for accessible and affordable health care, particularly lower out-of-pocket expenses for health care under Medicaid and Medicare programs (Justice in Aging, 2016) and any potential charity programs available to help subsidize expenses for health care through charitable, nonprofit, and community-based organizations. A third solution, *target health-care programs and supportive services to the unique needs of homeless older adults*, involves advocating for more preventive health care to avoid emergency room visits and risk for premature institutionalization, advocating for and identifying transitional care and recuperative housing for older adults discharged from an acute care setting, advocating for the use of Medicaid expansion programs to support housing services for older adults at risk of homelessness, and ensuring that systems of care coordination are in place and strengthened so that older adults receive the necessary referrals and case management services to secure appropriate housing (Justice in Aging, 2016). The fourth solution, *expand the availability of low-cost legal services that serve seniors,* can ensure timely access by older adults at risk of homelessness to legal assistance with foreclosures, evictions, financial abuse, and applying for safety net programs such as Medicaid and Medicare (Justice in Aging, 2016).

CSWE Gero Competency 8: Intervene With Individuals, Families, Groups, Organizations, and Communities should be adhered for all behaviors for all specialized practice behaviors 1–4 when intervening with older adults with high-risk factors for sexual health, abuse/neglect, suicide, and homelessness (CalSWEC, 2017, pp. 12–14). CSWE Gero Competency 3: Advance Human Rights and Social, Economic, and Environmental Justice specialized practice behaviors 1–4 should also be incorporated into interventions to improve access and address barriers to treatment (CalSWEC, 2017, pp. 13–14).

Clinicians also assess and monitor the impact of treatment on the desired outcomes for older adults with risk factors.

Assessing/Monitoring Evidence-based Treatment Outcomes

An important part of clinical practice is to evaluate the effectiveness of interventions with older adults presenting with high-risk factors for sexual health and homelessness. Clinicians have an ethical responsibility to monitor and evaluate the treatment effectiveness of their interventions with an older adult. This ensures that the clinician is providing no harm to the client, allows the clinician to assess the satisfaction with and progress of the intervention for addressing the desirable outcomes, and allows the clinician to gauge whether an intervention is not effective, should be changed, or should be discontinued. The treatment modality for high-risk and crisis interventions are often brief, occurring in one to six sessions. During this time, the clinician can assess the client's motivation to engage in and implement the action plan (for a single session) and determine if case management and care coordination are needed to assist the client with implementing the action plan. For brief crisis and prevention interventions of more than one session, the clinician monitors client progress toward resolving a crisis and restoring homeostasis and revisits and revises action plans appropriate to changing or improving needs of the client. Once desirable treatment outcomes are attained, the client should be prepared for termination, and other referrals provided for treatment if needed, or a clear statement on how to re-engage with the clinician if allowable by the organization should be provided to the older adult client. The clinicians monitoring and evaluating practices should be consistent with CSWE specialized practice Gero Competency 9: Evaluate Practice With Individuals, Families, Groups, Organizations, and Communities behaviors 1–4 (CalSWEC, 2017, pp. 14–15).

When intervening with older adults with high-risk factors, clinicians should be aware of myriad home and community-based services and programs to address the presenting needs of the older adult and provide advocacy and assistance with coordinating services between systems and providers to ensure that their needs are addressed in a timely manner.

Community Resources/Interagency Coordination

Community resource coordination and interagency coordination are a key component of interventions with older adults presenting with high-risk factors for sexual health, abuse/neglect, suicide, and homelessness. Knowledge of local community, organizational, county, state, and national resources to address high-risk factors of older adults is an essential skill for clinicians. Clinicians should be familiar with eligibility requirements, fees, application processes, and anticipated wait lists for services. Knowledge, awareness, and skills to provide appropriate and timely community resources and coordination of services among agencies and providers is consistent with CSWE Gero Competency 8: Intervene With Individuals, Families, Groups, Organizations, and Communities specialized practice behaviors 1–4 (CalSWEC, 2017, pp. 12–14). Clinicians should be aware of potential transference and countertransference issues that may present when working with older adults with sexual health and/or homeless risk factors.

Transference/Countertransference

Clinicians working with older adults with risk factors for sexual health and/or homelessness should be aware of the potential triggering of transference on the part of the client toward the clinician, countertransference, and how to manage it if it surfaces in the therapeutic relationship. A client may overidentify or disengage from the clinician if he or she reminds the client of someone with whom they may have had a positive or negative experience with in the past. For countertransference, the clinician who learned particular sexual health practices from their parents, family, or culture may overidentify or disengage from a client who has similar or very different views, beliefs, and attitudes about sexual health and practices. The same may follow with personal attitudes and experiences triggered surrounding older adults experiencing discrimination or oppression and/or who are victims of a crime. The clinician may have personal, cultural, spiritual, and/or philosophical views and beliefs about sexual health and/or homelessness; they may know or have worked with an older adult diagnosed with an STD or experiencing or at risk of homelessness. These scenarios could trigger countertransference. Similarly, countertransference may present for the clinician who may have personally experienced homelessness or who knows someone or has attitudes and beliefs about homelessness that may interfere with their ability to be effective in working with an older adult at risk of homelessness. When working with older adults with high-risk factors for sexual health and/or homelessness, CSWE Gero Competency 1: Demonstrate Ethical and Professional Behavior specialized practice behaviors 1–6 should be adhered to to ensure both ethical and professional practices around transference/countertransference issues (CalSWEC, 2017, pp. 1–2). Clinicians can use technological resources to gain more knowledge and skills to work effectively with older adults and can refer clients and their family members to appropriate technological resources as well.

Technological Resources

Sexual Health

A Guide to Taking a Sexual Health Assessment: The Five P's: https://www.cdc.gov/std/treatment/sexualhistory.pdf

Centers for Disease Control and Prevention: https://www.cdc.gov/sexualhealth/Default.html

Diseases and related conditions: https://www.cdc.gov/std/general/default.htm

Gay, bisexual, and other men who have sex with men (MSM): https://www.cdc.gov/std/life-stages-populations/msm.htm

How you can prevent sexually transmitted diseases: https://www.cdc.gov/std/prevention/default.htm

Program management and evaluation tools: https://www.cdc.gov/std/program/default.htm

Sexual health: https://www.cdc.gov/sexualhealth/Default.html

Sexually transmitted diseases: https://www.cdc.gov/STD/

Tools and materials: https://www.cdc.gov/std/products/default.htm

Training: https://www.cdc.gov/std/training/default.htm

Homelessness

National Alliance to End Homelessness: https://endhomelessness.org/resource/coordinated-entry-toolkit-core-elements/

National Alliance to End Homelessness. Coordinated entry toolkit: Core elements:

Samples toolkit: https://www.hudexchange.info/programs/coc/toolkit/responsibilities-and-duties/coordinated-entry-samples-toolkit/#referral

U.S. Department of Housing and Urban Development Coordinated Entry Community https://endhomelessness.org/resource/coordinated-entry-community-samples-resource-library/

Legal/Ethical Considerations

Clinicians must also consider potential legal and/or ethical issues that present when working with older adults with sexual and homeless risk and how to respond ethically to them. For sexual health, in institutional settings, older adult females are vulnerable and in need of protection from sexual abuse and harassment. Particularly among females with mild cognitive impairments or dementia, ethical dilemmas can arise (Lusti-Narasimham & Beard, 2013). Older adults experiencing intimate partner or domestic violence should be provided with psychoeducation and safety treatment plans, and appropriate reporting should be made to Adult Protective Services and/or police, according to state laws. Clinicians should also be advocates for less restrictive measures when clients can contract for safety. When working with all clients with high-risk factors, the client's right to self-determination is an ethical standard that clinicians must balance with safety and protection of the individual. When working with older adults at high risk for homelessness, clinicians ethically maintain the role of advocate to ensure all possible options are identified and explored with the client to ensure the client's participation in decision making and to prevent premature institutionalization if it is not consistent with the client's preference. CSWE Gero Competency 1: Demonstrate Ethical and Professional Behavior specialized practice behaviors 1 through 6 should be adhered to ensure both ethical and professional practices with older adults presenting with high-risk factors for sexual health, abuse/neglect, suicide, and homelessness (CalSWEC, 2017, pp. 1–2).

Critical Thinking Activity/Discussion Questions

1. How are older adults with high-risk factors for sexual health screened in your agency or community?
   a. What treatments and interventions are typically provided to organizations at your agency, in the local community, or in the state where you work with older adults?
   b. What resources are available?
   c. What legal/ethical issues have occurred that you are aware of, and how were they addressed?

2. How are older adults with high-risk factors for homelessness screened in your agency or community?
   a. What treatments and interventions are typically provided to organizations at your agency, in the local community, or in the state where you work with older adults?

b. What resources are available?

c. What legal/ethical issues have occurred that you are aware of, and how were they addressed?

3. Conduct a brief search for protective factors and risk factors for sexual health of older adults.
   a. Summarize the protective factors of older adults.
   b. Summarize the risk factors.
   c. How can this new knowledge inform your practice with older adults in whom you detect sexual health risk or who currently have a sexually transmitted disease?

4. Conduct a brief search for protective factors and risk factors for homelessness of older adults.
   a. Summarize the protective factors of older adults.
   b. Summarize the risk factors.
   c. How can this new knowledge inform your practice with older adults in whom you detect homeless risk or who are currently homeless?

Self-Reflection Exercises

1. Critically examine your own attitudes and beliefs about sexual health.
   a. What did you learn about sexual health growing up?
   b. From whom did you learn it?
   c. How do those beliefs influence your sexual health today?
   d. How might those beliefs affect your ability to engage, assess, and intervene with older adults with high-risk factors for sexual health?

2. Critically examine your own attitudes and beliefs about homelessness.
   a. What did you learn about homelessness growing up?
   b. From whom did you learn it?
   c. How do those beliefs influence your attitudes about suicide today?
   d. How might those beliefs affect your ability to engage, assess, and intervene with older adults with high-risk factors for homelessness?

References

Aboderin, I. (2014). Sexual and reproductive health and rights of older men and women: Addressing a policy blind spot. *Reproductive Health Matters, 22*(44), 185–190.

CalSWEC. (2017). CalSWEC curriculum competencies for public child welfare, behavioral health, and aging in California. Retrieved from https://calswec.berkeley.edu/sites/default/files/2017_calswec_curriculum_competencies_0.pdf

Centers for Disease Control. (2005). A guide to taking a sexual history. Retrieved from https://www.cdc.gov/std/treatment/sexualhistory.pdf

Centers for Disease Control. (2017). HIV among people aged 50 or over. Retrieved from www.cdc.gov/hiv/group/age/olderamericans/index.html

Fredriksen-Goldsen, K. I., Kim, H. J., Goldsen, J., & Emlet, C. A. (2014). Successful aging among LGBT older adults: Physical and mental health-related quality of life by age group. *The Gerontologist*, 55(1), 154–168.

Johnson, B. K. (2013). Sexually transmitted infections and older adults. *Journal of Gerontological Nursing*, 39(11), 53–60.

Justice in Aging. (2016). How to prevent and end homelessness among older adults. Retrieved from http://www.justiceinaging.org/wp-content/uploads/2016/04/Homelessness-Older-Adults.pdf

Kazer, M. W. (2012). Sexuality assessment for older adults. *Hartford Institute for Geriatric Nursing* (10). Retrieved from https://consultgeri.org/try-this/general-assessment/issue-10.pdf

Kirkman, L., Fox, C., & Dickson-Swift, V. (2016). A case for sexual health policy that includes midlife and older adult sexuality and sexual health. *The International Journal of Aging and Society*, 6(2), 17–27.

Lindau, S. T., & Gavrilova, N. (2010). Sex, health, and years of sexually active life gained due to good health: Evidence from two U.S. population-based cross-sectional surveys of ageing. *BMJ*, 230, c810.s doi: 10.1136/bmj.c810

Lusti-Narasimham, M., & Beard, J.R. (2013). Sexual health in older women. *Bulletin of World Health Organization*, 91(9), 707–709.

National Alliance to End Homelessness. (2016). The state of homelessness in America: 2016. Retrieved from https://endhomelessness.org/homelessness-in-america/homelessness-statistics/state-of-homelessness-report/

National Alliance to End Homelessness. (2017a). Changes in the HUD definition of "homeless." Retrieved from https://endhomelessness.org/resource/changes-in-the-hud-definition-of-homeless/

National Alliance to End Homelessness. (2017b). Coordinated entry toolkit: Core elements. Retrieved from https://endhomelessness.org/resource/coordinated-entry-toolkit-core-elements/

National Coalition for the Homeless. (2009). Homelessness among elderly persons. Retrieved from www.nationalhomeless.org/factsheets/Elderly.pdf

National Health Care for the Homeless Council. (2013). Aging and housing instability: Homelessness among older and elderly adults. *Focus: A Quarterly Research Review of the National HCH Council*, 2(1). Retrieved from www.nhchc.org/wp-content/uploads/2011/09/infocus-september2013.pdf

National Institute on Aging, 2013. Sexuality in later life. Retrieved from www.nia.nih.gov/health/sexuality-later-life

Roberts, A. R., & Ottens, A. J. (2005). The seven-stage crisis intervention model: A road map to goal attainment, problem solving, and crisis resolution. *Brief Treatment and Crisis Intervention*, 5(4), 329–339.

U.S. Department of Housing and Urban Development. (2017a). Coordinated entry community samples toolkit. Retrieved from https://www.hudexchange.info/programs/coc/toolkit/responsibilities-and-duties/coordinated-entry-samples-toolkit/#referral

U.S. Department of Housing and Urban Development. (2017b). Homeless assistance. Retrieved from www.hud.gov/program_offices/comm_planning/homeless

WISE & Healthy Aging. (2017). About WISE & Health Aging. Retrieved from http://www.wiseandhealthyaging.org/about

World Health Organization. (2006). Defining sexual health: Report of a technical consultation on sexual health. 28–31 January, 2002, Geneva. Retrieved from file:///C:/Users/joosten/Documents/COGNELLA%20PUBLISHING/References/Chapter%203/defining_sexual_health%20WHO.pdf

World Health Organization. (2017). Disease prevention. Retrieved from http://www.emro.who.int/about-who/public-health-functions/health-promotion-disease-prevention.html

CHAPTER 4

Aging in Place

Health Promotion, Prevention, and Wellness

Chapter Overview

This chapter addresses evidence-based approaches for health promotion, prevention, and wellness with older adults and explores key domains to promote both effective clinical practice with older adults and optimal health and wellness outcomes for older adults.

CSWE Gero Competencies Highlighted

Competency 1: Demonstrate Ethical and Professional Behavior

Specialized Practice Competency Description: Social workers understand the value base of the profession and its ethical standards, as well as relevant laws and regulations that may impact practice at the micro, mezzo, and macro levels. Social workers understand frameworks of ethical decision-making and how to apply principles of critical thinking to those frameworks in practice, research, and policy arenas. Social workers recognize personal values and the distinction between personal and professional values. They also understand how their personal experiences and affective reactions influence their professional judgment and behavior. Social workers understand the profession's history, its mission, and the roles and responsibilities of the profession. Social workers also understand the role of other professions when engaged in inter-professional teams. Social workers recognize the importance of lifelong learning and are committed to continually updating their skills to ensure they are relevant and effective. Social workers also understand emerging forms of technology and the ethical use of technology in social work practice.

Competency Behaviors: (1) Guided by ethical reasoning and self-reflection, demonstrate adherence to ethical frameworks and key laws, policies, and procedures related to aging, and the rights of older adults. (2) Engage in active dialogue with field faculty/

instructors regarding aging field placement agency policies and culture around behavior, appearance, communication, and the use of supervision. (3) Develop and sustain effective collaborative relationships that respect older adults' needs for protection, self-determination, and the provision of services in the least restrictive environment possible with colleagues and community stakeholders, including older adults, their family members, other care providers, and Tribes. (4) Effectively manage professional boundary issues and other challenges arising in the course of aging-related work, particularly ambiguities presented by home visits, personal loss, trauma, and other highly involved and potentially emotionally triggering aspects of the work. (5) Develop and sustain relationships with members of interdisciplinary and integrated health care teams, including social workers, primary care providers, hospital staff, home health care providers, psychiatrists, psychologists, substance use disorder treatment staff, Tribal service providers, and others, that reflect clear understanding of their roles in providing care to older adults. (6) Demonstrate both knowledge of the history and evolution of social work practice related to aging and older adults in the United States and California, and a commitment to lifelong learning around this practice. (7) Follow all ethical guidelines and legal mandates in the use of technology in order to maintain the confidentiality of all personal, behavioral health, and health-related information. (CalSWEC, 2017, pp. 1–2)

Competency 2: Engage Diversity and Difference in Practice

Specialized Practice Competency Description: Social workers understand how diversity and difference characterize and shape the human experience and are critical to the formation of identity. The dimensions of diversity are understood as the intersectionality of multiple factors, including, but not limited to, age, class, color, culture, disability and ability, ethnicity, gender, gender identity and expression, immigration status, marital status, political ideology, race, religion/spirituality, sex, sexual orientation, and Tribal sovereign status. Social workers understand that, as a consequence of difference, a person's life experiences may include oppression, poverty, marginalization, and alienation as well as privilege, power, and acclaim. Social workers also understand the forms and mechanisms of oppression and discrimination and recognize the extent to which a culture's structures and values, including social, economic, political, and cultural exclusions, may oppress, marginalize, alienate, or create privilege and power.

Competency Behaviors: (1) Engage in critical analysis of the interpersonal, community, and social structural causes and effects of disproportionality, disparities, and inequities in the incidence and trajectory of aging-related care needs, housing, transportation, and resource access among older adults,

their families, and their communities. (2) Evidence respectful awareness and understanding of the impact of being a member of a marginalized group on aging experiences, and accurately identify differences in access to and quality of available services for members of different communities and populations. (3) Demonstrate knowledge of diverse cultural norms and traditional methods of providing care to older adults, as well as an applied understanding of how these realities affect work with older adults from diverse backgrounds, their families, and their communities. (4) Develop and use practice methods that acknowledge, respect, and address how individual and cultural values, norms, and differences impact the various systems with which older adults interact, including, but not limited to, families, communities, primary care systems, mental and behavioral health care systems, and integrated care systems. (CalSWEC, 2017, pp. 3–4)

Competency 3: Advance Human Rights and Social, Economic, and Environmental Justice

Specialized Practice Competency Description: Social workers understand that every person regardless of position in society has fundamental human rights such as freedom, safety, privacy, an adequate standard of living, health care, and education. Social workers understand the global interconnections of oppression and human rights violations, and are knowledgeable about theories of human need and social justice and strategies to promote social and economic justice and human rights. Social workers understand strategies designed to eliminate oppressive structural barriers to ensure that social goods, rights, and responsibilities are distributed equitably and that civil, political, environmental, economic, social, and cultural human rights are protected.

Competency Behaviors: (1) Clearly articulate the systematic effects of discrimination, oppression, and stigma on the needs and experiences of older adults and on the quality and delivery of services available to them, and identify and advocate for policy changes needed to address these issues. (2) Advocate for changes in policies and programs that reflect a social justice practice framework for facilitating access and providing services to older adults, their families, and care providers, especially among underserved groups and communities. (3) Demonstrate the ability to work effectively in cross-disciplinary collaboration to develop and provide interventions that explicitly address the specific needs of diverse older adults, their families, and care providers. (4) Integrate into all aspects of policy and practice sensitivity to the reality that fundamental rights, including freedom and privacy, may be compromised for older adults engaged in care, and the goal that services should be provided in the least restrictive environment possible. (CalSWEC, 2017, pp. 4–5)

Competency 4: Engage in Practice-informed Research and Research-informed Practice

Specialized Practice Competency Description: Social workers understand quantitative and qualitative research methods and their respective roles in advancing a science of social work and in evaluating their practice. Social workers know the principles of logic, scientific inquiry, and culturally informed and ethical approaches to building knowledge. Social workers understand that evidence that informs practice derives from multidisciplinary sources and multiple ways of knowing. They also understand the processes for translating research findings into effective practice.

Competency Behaviors: (1) Demonstrate the ability to understand, interpret, and evaluate the benefits and limitations of various evidence-based and evidence-informed treatment models as they influence practice with older adults. (2) Engage in critical analysis of research findings, practice models, and practice wisdom as they inform aging related practice, including how research practices have historically failed to address the needs and realities of exploited and/or disadvantaged communities, and how cross-cultural research practices can be used to enhance equity. (3) Clearly communicate research findings, conclusions, and implications, as well as their applications to aging practice, across a variety of professional interactions with consumers, families, and multidisciplinary service providers. (4) Apply research findings to aging-related practice with individuals, families, and communities and to the development of professional knowledge about the needs, experiences, and well-being of older adults. (CalSWEC, 2017, pp. 5–6)

Competency 6: Engage With Individuals, Families, Groups, Organizations, and Communities

Specialized Practice Competency Description: Social workers understand that engagement is an ongoing component of the dynamic and interactive process of social work practice with, and on behalf of, diverse individuals, families, groups, organizations, and communities. Social workers value the importance of human relationships. Social workers understand theories of human behavior and the social environment, and critically evaluate and apply this knowledge to facilitate engagement with clients and constituencies, including individuals, families, groups, organizations, and communities. Social workers understand strategies to engage diverse clients and constituencies to advance practice effectiveness. Social workers understand how their personal experiences and affective reactions may impact their ability to effectively engage with diverse clients and constituencies. Social workers value principles of relationship-building and inter-professional collaboration to facilitate engagement with clients, constituencies, and other professionals as appropriate.

Competency Behaviors: (1) Appropriately engage and activate older adults, their families, and other care providers in the development and coordination of care plans that reflect relevant theoretical models and balance older adults' needs for care with respect for autonomy and independence. (2) Effectively utilize interpersonal skills to engage older adults, their families, and other care providers in culturally responsive, consumer-driven, and trauma-informed integrated care that addresses mutually agreed upon service goals and balances needs for care, protection, autonomy, and independence. (3) Establish effective and appropriate communication, coordination, and advocacy planning with other care providers and interdisciplinary care teams as needed to address mutually agreed upon service goals. Recognizing the complex nature of service engagement, ensure that communications with consumers and their families regarding service goals are both sensitive and transparent. (4) Manage affective responses and exercise good judgment around engaging with resistance, trauma responses, and other potentially triggering situations with older adults, their families, and other care providers. (CalSWEC, 2017, pp. 9–10)

Competency 7: Assess Individuals, Families, Groups, Organizations, and Communities

Specialized Practice Competency Description: Practitioners in aging utilize ecological-systems theory, a strengths-based and person/family-centered framework to conduct assessments that value the resilience of diverse older adults, families, and caregivers. They select appropriate assessment tools, methods and technology, and evaluate, adapt, and modify them, as needed, to enhance their validity in working with diverse, vulnerable and at-risk groups. The comprehensive biopsychosocial assessment takes into account the multiple factors of physical, mental and social well-being needed for treatment planning for older adults and their families. They develop skills in interprofessional assessment and communication with key constituencies to choose the most effective practice strategies. Gero social workers understand how their own experiences and affective reactions about aging, quality of life, loss and grief may affect their assessment and resultant decision-making.

Competency Behaviors: (1) Conduct assessments that incorporate a strengths-based perspective, person/family-centered focus, and resilience while recognizing aging related risk, (2) Develop, select, and adapt assessment methods and tools that optimize practice with older adults, their families, caregivers, and communities, and (3) Use and integrate multiple domains and sources of assessment information and communicate with other professionals to inform a comprehensive plan for intervention. (Council for Social Work Education, 2017, pp. 89–90)

Competency 8: Intervene With Individuals, Families, Groups, Organizations, and Communities

Specialized Practice Competency Description: Social workers understand that intervention is an ongoing component of the dynamic and interactive process of social work practice with, and on behalf of, diverse individuals, families, groups, organizations, and communities. Social workers are knowledgeable about evidence-informed interventions to achieve the goals of clients and constituencies, including individuals, families, groups, organizations, and communities. Social workers understand theories of human behavior and the social environment, and critically evaluate and apply this knowledge to effectively intervene with clients and constituencies. Social workers understand methods of identifying, analyzing, and implementing evidence-informed interventions to achieve client and constituency goals. Social workers value the importance of interprofessional teamwork and communication in interventions, recognizing that beneficial outcomes may require interdisciplinary, inter-professional, and inter-organizational collaboration.

Competency Behaviors: (1) In partnership with older adults and their families, develop appropriate intervention plans that reflect respect for autonomy and independence, as well as contemporary theories and models for interventions with older adults. Plans should:

- Reflect cultural humility and acknowledgement of individualized needs;
- Incorporate consumer and family strengths;
- Utilize community resources and natural supports;
- Incorporate multidisciplinary team supports and interventions;
- Include non-pharmacological interventions; and
- Demonstrate knowledge of poly-pharmacy needs and issues specific to older adults.

(2) Apply the principles of teaming, engagement, inquiry, advocacy, and facilitation within interdisciplinary teams and care coordination to the work of supporting older adults, family members, and other care providers to accomplish intervention goals and satisfy advanced care planning needs. (3) Effectively implement evidence-based interventions in the context of providing emergency response, triage, brief treatment, and longer-term care, and in the course of addressing a range of issues presented in primary care, specialty care, community agency, inpatient, and palliative care settings. Interventions should be guided by respect for older adults' autonomy and independence and should include components such as psychoeducation, problem-solving treatment skills, symptom tracking, medication therapies, follow-up, and planning for evolving care needs. (4) Effectively plan for interventions in ways that incorporate

thoughtfully executed transitions during time-limited internships, recognizing that consumer needs for support may continue beyond these time periods. (CalSWEC, 2017, pp. 12–14)

Competency 9: Evaluate Practice With Individuals, Families, Groups, Organizations, and Communities

Specialized Practice Competency Description: Social workers understand that evaluation is an ongoing component of the dynamic and interactive process of social work practice with, and on behalf of, diverse individuals, families, groups, organizations and communities. Social workers recognize the importance of evaluating processes and outcomes to advance practice, policy, and service delivery effectiveness. Social workers understand theories of human behavior and the social environment, and critically evaluate and apply this knowledge in evaluating outcomes. Social workers understand qualitative and quantitative methods for evaluating outcomes and practice effectiveness.

Competency Behaviors: (1) Record, track, and monitor consumer engagement, assessment, and intervention data in practice with older adults, their families, and other care providers accurately and according to field education agency policies and guidelines. (2) Conduct accurate process and outcome analysis of engagement, assessment, and intervention data in practice with older adults, their families, and other care providers that incorporates consumer perspectives and reflects respect for older adults' autonomy and independence. (3) Use findings to evaluate intervention effectiveness, develop recommendations for adapting service plans and approaches as needed, improve interdisciplinary team coordination and care integration, and help agency and community policies better support older adults, their families, and their formal and informal care systems. (4) Share both the purposes of such data collection and the overall results of data analysis with older adults, their families, and communities whenever possible, with the goal of engaging them more meaningfully in the evaluation process. (CalSWEC, 2017, pp. 14–15)

Learning Objectives

1. Learners will understand the context for aging in place in the United States and internationally.
2. Learners will identify screening tools to prevent and promote healthy aging and wellness among older adults.
3. Learners will identify appropriate evidence-based interventions.

4. Learners will understand the importance of referring older adult clients to appropriate technological and community resources and when to assist with coordination.
5. Learners will identify sources of transference and countertransference when workers with older adults to promote aging in place, health promotion, and wellness.

Case Study

Mr. Kaplan is a 91-year-old male who resides in a single-story home with his spouse. He has been married for 70 years. He retired from an electronics engineer position from aerospace at the age of 85. He served in the Navy for four years. He has three sons and eight grandchildren, and all live within 30 minutes from him and his spouse. He attends the local health club daily, swims for 30 minutes, and uses the weight machines 30 minutes each day. Mr. Kaplan drives and has been independent with all activities of daily living (ADLs) and instrumental activities of daily living (IADLs). His only health condition is osteoarthritis. One day while at the health club, Mr. Kaplan tripped on a floor mat in the weight room and fell on his left side; the X-ray at the hospital revealed a small fracture, so he underwent surgery to have metal screws inserted and was discharged home with a home health physical and occupational therapist. Mr. Kaplan was started on bisphosphonate therapy to prevent a future hip fracture. Mr. Kaplan was sent home using a walker and was instructed by his physician to continue using it throughout his hip fracture rehabilitation for four to six weeks. Upon the admission to home health, the physical therapist discovered that Mrs. Kaplan does not drive; the physical therapist received an order from the primary physician for a social worker to evaluate and assist with psychosocial needs, primarily transportation, and other community resources while Mr. Kaplan underwent rehabilitation. After four weeks of physical therapy at home, Mr. Kaplan was ready to discharge to outpatient rehabilitation for two more weeks.

Assessing Context

The Centers for Disease Control and Prevention (CDC) defines *aging in place* as "the ability to live in one's home and community safely, independently, and comfortably, regardless of age, income, or ability level" (2013a, p. 1). Aging in place "supports older adults in their homes and makes it possible for them to get out into the community" (Ball, 2017, p. 3). Aging in place is an internationally recognized concept; the World Health Organization promotes an *age-friendly world* as one that "enables people of all ages to actively participate in communities and treats everyone with respect, regardless of their age" (2017, p. 1). The World Health Organization definition emphasizes social support and networks specifically for older adults as illustrated in the following statement describing characteristics of an *age-friendly world*: "it is a place that makes it easy for older people to stay connected to people that are important to them" (2017, p. 1). The World Health Organization definition also underscores the importance of opportunities for health and activity as well as ensuring necessary support is available for those who need it—"it helps people stay healthy and active even at the oldest ages and provides appropriate support to those who can no longer look after themselves" (2017, p. 1).

Research on aging in place is not unique to the United States—it is of global importance. In a meta-analysis of studies conducted internationally on aging in place over a 30-year period (1980–2010), it was discovered that multiple studies were conducted within the following countries: Australia, China, Japan, Malaysia, New Zealand, Taiwan, and the United Kingdom (Vasunilashorn, Steinman, Liebig, & Pynoos, 2012). Within international research to date, contextual factors that impact the opportunities for, or lack thereof, an older adult to age in place or make choices to age in place include health factors and preferences of older adults, technology, and service-based and environmental factors (Vasunilashorn, Steinman, Liebig, & Pynoos, 2012). Some studies focused on aging communities and preferences of older adults to age in place, whereas other studies focused on specific services used by older adults to age in place such as palliative care, social support, housing support, and health monitoring (Vasunilashorn, Steinman, Liebig, & Pynoos, 2012).

With regard to the environment, studies examined the "home" in the context of community and home structures promoting community care (Vasunilashorn, Steinman, Liebig, & Pynoos, 2012). With regard to the preferences for older adults to access home and community-based services, the study found great diversity in accessing preferences pertaining to urban- versus rural-residing older adults, sexual orientation (LGBT), older adults with cognitive impairments, older adults who are parenting grandchildren, perceptions of Western versus Eastern attitudes and beliefs about what aging in place is and looks like, financial resources, and whether an older adult is incarcerated (Vasunilashorn, Steinman, Liebig, & Pynoos, 2012). Lastly, the availability and use of technology impacts an older adult's ability to age in place. Telehealth, e-communication, and mobile and interactive technologies, as well as the access, or lack thereof, impact an older adult's ability to successfully age in place. Barriers to aging in place include limited programs for home modifications to make homes accessible, training issues for care, consumer awareness, access to services, fragmented care, and communication among agencies that coordinate services, health, and housing resources for older adults with functional health impairments (Vasunilashorn, Steinman, Liebig, & Pynoos, 2012).

In the United States, according to a survey conducted by the American Association of Retired Persons (AARP) in 2014, in a sample of 1,014 adults ages 45 and older with non-Hispanic White, Hispanic, and African American respondents, 78% agreed with the statement "what I'd really like to do is stay in my current residence for as long as possible," and 80% agreed "what I'd really like to do is remain in my local community as long as possible" (Barrett, 2014, p. 2). Among adults 65 and older, 75% agreed with the statement "I want to stay in my home because I like what my community has to offer" (Barrett, 2014, p. 10). Specific characteristics identified by older adults ages 65 and older for staying in their home because of the community included: "being near family and friends" (74%); "being near where you want to go" (72%), "easy to walk" (64%), "being near church/social events" (57%), "living with different age groups" (50%), "being near good schools" (42%), "housing for different income levels" (39%), "being near transit" (34%), "being near work" (30%), and "being near a park" (28%) (Barrett, 2014, p. 10).

If older adults prefer to stay in their homes and within communities because of characteristics and preferences for the community that are desirable to them, what does it take? The Community Housing Resource Center developed a toolkit for local governments, funded by the Robert Wood Johnson Foundation and Quality Growth Partnership, to provide the context for successful aging in place within an aging community (Ball, 2017). Specifically within the toolkit, five key components or contextual factors to successful aging in place in communities were identified: choice, flexibility, entrepreneurship, mixed generations, and smart growth (Ball, 2017). Choice refers to "providing both healthcare and housing options that meet the diverse needs of individuals as they move through the later third of their lives"—this includes affordable options for older adults to choose from based on their preferences for services to meet their housing and health needs (Ball, 2017, p. 3). The second component, flexibility, "requires that levels of health and housing supports be adjustable whether an individual lives in a single family home, rents a privately or publicly managed apartment or lives in an assisted living facility"—this component ensure appropriate tailoring of services to meet the preferences of the older adults and their specific housing and health needs (Ball, 2017, p. 3). The third component, entrepreneurship, involves service planners' and entrepreneurs' recognition of opportunities due to the strengths and contributions of older adults to sustain and contribute to communities—"new economies of scale exists as the percentage of older adults in a community grow, presenting new opportunities for affordable service delivery" (Ball, 2017, p. 3).The fourth component, mixed generations, also emphasizes the strengths and contributions of older adults to communities in "maintaining mixed-generation communities in order to maximize older adults' capacity for self-help and community contribution" and assures that there are "valuable links to be made between the needs and skills of different age groups" (Ball, 2017, p. 3). Lastly, the fifth component, smart growth, considers the design of new communities that are accessible with mixed generations, the combined benefits to members of all ages in the community, and shared communal spaces as "for many older adults good community design is a fundamental necessity, not just an amenity" (Ball, 2017, p. 3).

The availability of financial resources is a clear contextual reality that impacts the ability of an older adult to age in place. Home and community-based services provided in the private, public, and nonprofit sectors are associated with out-of-pocket expenses, co-insurances and co-payments, and/or specific eligibility criteria associated with receiving services or qualifying for services at reduced or no cost. For example, financial resources impact eligibility for programs such as nutrition (i.e., whether an older adult will pay full or reduced costs for congregate or home-delivered meals); transportation (i.e., whether an older adult pays full or reduced costs for transportation services); and caregiver assistance (i.e., whether assistance can be fully financed out of pocket, through long-term care insurance, low-cost Medicaid waiver programs, or county/state programs or whether an older adult neither has financial resources nor qualifies for reduced cost/subsidized services).

Many older adults without the financial resources to pay full price for services when they have functional health needs, and who do not qualify for subsidized programs due to exclusion based on financial eligibility (i.e., being overqualified), often have unmet needs as they attempt to age in place. Vulnerable, low-income older adults may not be aware of services available to them or how to access them, or they may experience barriers in accessing services. These scenarios present both challenges and opportunities for clinicians to be aware of many home and community-based programs available to older adults in the private, public, and nonprofit sectors as well as the eligibility criteria and any associated costs. Financial screening during biopsychosocial/spiritual assessment is important to ensuring that older adult clients receive education and information about home and community-based programs that can assist them to age in place in the environment of their choice.

Biopsychosocial/Spiritual Assessment

This section applies the biopsychosocial/spiritual assessment template from Chapter 2 to the case study presented at the beginning of the chapter (Box 4.1). Two screening tools that can be used by clinicians to assess overall health and well-being (SF-36) and global functioning (PROMIS) are also described. The scores from both tools can be used by clinicians to engage older adults in discussion about their goals and needs for aging in place, informing both treatment planning and interventions.

Box 4.1

Geriatric Biopsychosocial Spiritual Assessment

Basic Demographic: Mr. Kaplan is a 91-year-old male, married; English is primary language; non-Hispanic White; has a bachelor degree in electronics

Referral Information: Post-hip fracture rehabilitation at home; primary physician referral for community resources and transportation for outpatient physical therapy

Cultural/Spiritual: High literacy and knowledge about osteoarthritis and hip fracture procedure and rehabilitation; practices no complementary and alternative medicine; Jewish faith

Social: [Relationships within family, social/diversity groups, and community]

- Worked in electronics in aerospace, retired at age 85; served in the Navy for four years; born in Chicago; has three sons and eight grandchildren (all live locally)
- Has several friends from the health club, neighbors, and members of his synagogue and attended a community reading club at the senior center in his community weekly. Spouse is supportive and coping well with changes in functional health of patient and is socially active; she no longer drives and ambulates with a cane.

Financial: [Ability to provide basic needs and access health services]

- Basic needs for housing, food, clothing are met. Mr. Kaplan owns his own home; his sons are assisting with grocery shopping and errands.
- Mr. Kaplan has Medicare primary and Blue Cross/Blue Shield secondary for insurances; co-pays and fees are manageable
- Income sources: Social Security, pension, savings, and investments

Environmental: [Personal safety, maintenance of residence, and safety of community]

- Lives with spouse in a single-story home
- Lighting on the streets, neighborhood watch, low crime
- Home safety: Smoke and carbon monoxide detectors and fire extinguisher are operable; adequate lighting throughout the home; physical therapist recommended removal of slip rugs in the kitchen, which patient complied with and removed; shower and toilet accessibility—a shower bench was ordered and a detachable shower head was already in place in in walk-in shower; no elevators; two stairs to front door with handrail; no ramps to access home
- No guns in the home
- Screen for abuse or neglect by self or perpetrated by others: No evidence or suspicion of abuse or neglect by self or others

Physical: [Individual function and disease morbidity]

- Mr. Kaplan has a high level of health literacy; his self-rated health is "very good;" he has an updated advance directive from the recent hospitalization; he is knowledgeable about his diagnosis of osteoarthritis and hip surgery procedure and recovery; he is compliant with bisphosphonate medication and takes Tylenol for pain as needed; functional health—he ambulated with a walker and performs ADLs independently; currently receiving assistance with shopping and errands; no other treatments for chronic or life-threatening illnesses; he reports he and spouse have been inactive sexually for the past two years

Mental: [Mental status, depression, anxiety, and substance abuse]

- Standardized screening instruments: No indicators of mild cognitive impairment; score of 27 on Mini-Mental State Examination; no indicators of depression or anxiety; scores in normal range for both screenings
- Suicide risk assessment: Ruled out—does not endorse suicidal ideations and no history of suicide attempts or plans
- Homicidal ideations: Ruled out—does not endorse homicidal ideations and no history of homicidal ideations
- Substance use: Does not drink alcohol or use drugs

> **Formulation/Evaluation:** Transportation to outpatient physical therapy and for personal use until he resumes driving
>
> **Treatment Planning:** Consultation with physical therapist—physical therapy and social work to discharge; transportation application completed by social worker and taxi card to arrive by mail in one to three business days; patient's outpatient physical therapy appointment confirmed; no further psychosocial needs at this time
>
> **Community Resource Needs:** Local senior dial-a-taxi program for patient and spouse

Screening Tools

SF-36

The first screening tool, the SF-36, a 36-item short-form health survey, was developed by RAND as part of the Medical Outcomes Study to assess and survey health status through eight key concepts for health and 36 questions total: (1) "physical functioning" (10 questions), (2) "role limitations because of physical health problems" (four questions), (3) "bodily pain" (two questions), (4) "social functioning" (two questions), (5) "general mental health (psychological distress and psychological well-being)" (five questions), (6) "role limitations because of emotional problems" (three questions), (7) "vitality (energy/fatigue)" (four questions), and (8) "general health perceptions" (five questions) (Ware & Sherbourne, 1992, p. 474). The SF-36 is used in clinical, research, and community settings (Ware & Sherbourne, 1992). It has been tested as a self-completion tool with older adults and found to be suitable for self-completion in older adults ages 65 and older in outpatient and primary care settings (Hayes, Morris, Wolfe, & Morgan, 1995). It has been tested for validity and reliability in measuring health perceptions of older adults up to the age of 74 in general practice settings (Brazier et al., 1992) as well as among older adults living in community settings (Walters, Munro, & Brazier, 2001).

PROMIS

The second screening tool clinicians can administer with an older adult, the Patient-Reported Outcomes Measurement Information System (PROMIS), was funded by the National Institute of Health and measures health status in adult populations in similar categories of the SF-36: "emotional distress (depression), anxiety, pain, fatigue, sleep disturbance, physical functioning, and social participation" (Tatsuoka et al., 2016, p. 1). The PROMIS system provides global measures of physical, mental, and social health of adult populations (Northwestern University, 2017).

An important domain for clinicians to assess in addition to a consideration of contextual factors, a formal biopsychosocial/spiritual assessment, and relevant screening tools is that of diversity; along with the former domains, it informs treatment planning and interventions for older adults to age in place.

Diversity–Cultural Competence/Spirituality/LGBT/Sexuality

When engaging, assessing, and intervening with older adult clients who prefer to age in place, the clinician should follow CSWE Competency 2: Engage Diversity and Difference in Practice to ensure that the life histories, experiences, preferences, opportunities, and barriers are fully understood and factored in to treatment planning with the client for successful aging in place that is valued and preferred by the client (specialized practice competency 2, behavior 3). For example, when developing treatment plans and interventions, clinicians seek to identify the specific cultural and diversity preferences for older adults to age in place, whether that is independently; with or without private, public, or subsidized assistance; or in the context of an intergenerational or extended family or cultural/faith community. Clinicians seek to gain knowledge and understand from the client his or her experiences and intersections with disparities and inequities that may have impacted opportunities to achieve healthy aging in place as they define it through resources including health, housing, and services (specialized practice competency 2, behavior 1). In the United States in 2015, disparities were evident in life expectancy rates at birth between both male non-Hispanic Whites and African Americans, 76.3 years and 71.8 years, and females, 81.1 years and 78.1 years, respectively (National Center for Health Statistics, 2016). Hispanic males and females had the highest life expectancy at birth in 2015, 79.3 years and 84.3 years (National Center for Health Statistics, 2016).

Across all ages in the United States, health disparities for African Americans, Asian Americans, Hispanics, American Indian/Alaskan Natives, and Native Hawaiians/Pacific Islanders are evident when comparing health status to non-Hispanic Whites (Centers for Disease Control and Prevention, 2013b). A report titled *The State of Aging and Health in America 2013* underscored challenges to healthy aging for diverse older adults: "language barriers, reduced access to health care, low socioeconomic status, and differing cultural norms" (Centers for Disease Control and Prevention, 2013b, p. 10). Clinicians seek to understand such impacts on access to health promotion opportunities for diverse older adults (specialized practice competency 2, behavior 2). Disparities for health and service access present in the lesbian, gay, bisexual, and transgender (LGBT) older adult population as well. In a population-based study in California that used the California Health Interview Study, LGB adults ages 50 to 70 reported higher rates of physical health conditions in comparison to heterosexual adults (Wallace, Cochran, Durazo, & Ford, 2011). Delays were higher in receiving needed service care for lesbian and bisexual females in comparison to heterosexual females (Wallace, Cochran, Durazo, & Ford, 2011). In a separate cross-sectional population-based study of 96,992 adults ages 50 and older using the Washington State Behavioral Risk Factor Surveillance System, in comparison to heterosexual adults, older LGB adults had greater risks for mental health needs, disability, and modifiable risk factors of smoking and consumption of excessive alcohol (Fredriksen-Goldsen, Hyun-Jun, Barkan, Muraco, & Hoy-Ellis, 2013). When engaging, assessing, intervening, and evaluating practice with diverse older adult populations, clinicians demonstrate respect of the cultural norms, beliefs, and practices of diverse older adults and the influence on interactions of the older adult with various micro, mezzo, and macro systems (specialized practice competency 2, behavior 4). Clinicians further bring contextual, assessment, screening, and diversity information into interdisciplinary team meetings to inform treatment planning and interventions.

Interdisciplinary Team Roles and Planning

To promote wellness, health promotion, and aging in place among older adults, interdisciplinary teams play a vital role when engaging, assessing, and intervening with older adults and their families for options to age in place, promote health, and achieve wellness as it is defined by the older adult. Physical and occupational therapists play a large role in ensuring the environments that older adults age in place in are accessible, functional, and modified to ensure safety and physical functioning. Nurses and physicians play a role in prevention, screening, treatment, and management of chronic and life-threatening illnesses that may impact the ability of and preferences for aging in place by an older adult. Geriatric psychiatrists play a key role in assessing and treating mental health conditions that present for older adults to enable them to age in place and prevent premature institutionalization. Clinicians and social workers, as global assessors, and members of the interdisciplinary team help to engage, assess, intervene, and evaluate best practices to ensure that older adults have the range of biopsychosocial/spiritual needs addressed and met to enable aging in place successfully and safely according to their preferences, values, and culture to ensure self-determination (CSWE Gero Competency 1: Demonstrate Ethical and Professional Behavior, specialized practice behavior 5; CSWE Gero Competency 2: Engage Diversity and Difference in Practice, specialized practice behavior 4; CSWE Gero Competency 4: Engage in Practice-informed Research and Research-informed Practice, specialized practice behavior 3; CSWE Gero Competency 6: Engage With Individuals, Families, Groups, Organizations, and Communities, specialized practice behaviors 1–4; CSWE Gero Competency 7: Assess Individuals, Families, Groups, Organizations, and Communities, specialized practice behavior 3; CSWE Gero Competency 8: Intervene With Individuals, Families, Groups, Organizations, and Communities, specialized practice behaviors 1–3; and CSWE Gero Competency 9: Evaluate Practice With Individuals, Families, Groups, Organizations, and Communities, specialized practice behaviors 1–3). Clinicians provide advocacy and work collaboratively across disciplines to ensure access to health promotion, wellness, and opportunities for aging in place (CSWE Gero Competency 3: Advance Human Rights and Social, Economic, and Environmental Justice, specialized practice behaviors 2–4). Together, the interdisciplinary team engages in treatment planning with the older adult client to present options for evidence-based interventions.

Evidence-based Interventions

Primary Prevention

A key intervention, primary prevention approaches seek to control all risk factors of an individual that are modifiable to prevent disease (Yong, Saunders, & Olsen, 2010). For clinical prevention, primary prevention includes "behavioral counseling by clinicians" and immunizations (Yong, Saunders, & Olsen, 2010, p. 222). For community- or population-based prevention, it includes "altering the community environment to promote healthy lifestyles and reduce risks for disease and injuries" (Yong, Saunders, & Olsen, 2010, p. 222). For clinical prevention of alcohol misuse among older adults, the U.S. Preventive Services Task Force recommends brief behavioral counseling in primary care to improve outcomes such as reducing risky, hazardous, or heavy drinking and hospitalizations with a goal of reducing, not abstinence (Jonas et al., 2012). It is recommended that adult females who screen positive for BRCA cancer risk receive genetic counseling (Nelson et al., 2013). To prevent falls among older adults ages 65 and older, it is recommended by the U.S. Preventive Services Task Force that they take vitamin D supplements and engage in physical exercise or physical therapy (Michael et al., 2010).

The U.S. Preventive Services Task Force recommends selective individualized decisions by primary care providers to recommend behavioral counseling for promoting healthy diet and exercise behaviors to adults without obesity and risk factors for cardiovascular disease (i.e., diabetes, glucose levels that are abnormal, hypertension, and dyslipidemia) or diet and exercise behavior (Patnode, Evans, Senger, Redmond, & Lin, 2017). Healthy dietary recommendations include diets that promote heart health (i.e., "increased consumption of fruits, vegetables, fibers, and whole grains; decreased consumption of salt, fat, and red and processed meats") (U.S. Preventive Services Task Force, 2017, p.1). Healthy physical activities include promoting walking and appropriate aerobic activities increased over time to desirable levels (U.S. Preventive Services Task Force, 2017, p.1). Behavioral counseling for diet and exercise ranged from low intensity (i.e., web-based feedback tools that are printed or on the internet that tailor diet and exercise) to medium or high intensity (i.e., in-person individual, or group counseling, or both; all followed up with text messages, phone calls, or emails) (U.S. Preventive Services Task Force, 2017).

For adults with body mass indexes (BMIs) of 30 kg/m² or higher, multicomponent intense behavioral interventions recommended to prevent risks to health of adults include "behavioral management activities, such as weight-loss goals, improving diet or nutrition and increasing physical activity; addressing barriers to change; self-monitoring; and strategizing how to maintain lifestyle changes" (U.S. Preventive Services Task Force, 2014). Effective smoking cessation interventions include behavioral counseling interventions such as face-to-face counseling, printed materials for self-help, and phone counseling; and/or medications, such as nicotine replacement therapy, and varenicline (U.S. Preventive Services Task Force, 2015).

Medications may be prescribed as primary prevention of specific diseases in older adults. The use of low-dose aspirin for older adults ages 60 to 69 with a 10-year risk for cardiovascular disease is recommended to be offered selectively to older adults who can benefit from it; there are no recommendations for older adults ages 70 and older (Guirguis-Blake et al., 2015). Clinical trials of menopausal and older female adults without a history of breast cancer but with increased risks for breast cancer had reduced incidence of invasive breast cancers by 30% to 68% in those who were prescribed tamoxifen, tibolone, or raloxifene (Nelson et al., 2009). The use of low-dose statin medications for prevention of cardiovascular disease events in adults ages 40 to 75 is recommended for those who: (1) "have 1 or more CVD risk (i.e., dyslipidemia, diabetes, hypertension, or smoking" and (2) "have a calculated 10-year risk of a cardiovascular event of 10% or greater" (U.S. Preventive Services Task Force, 2016, p. 1). Pharmacotherapy (i.e., nicotine replacement therapy, varenicline, bupropion SR) alone or with behavioral counseling interventions is effective for tobacco cessation (U.S. Preventive Services Task Force, 2015).

Among evidence-based wellness and prevention programs for older adults, the Substance Abuse and Mental Health Services Administration (SAMHSA) National Registry of Evidence-based Programs and Practices (NREPP, 2017a) reports the Wellness Initiative for Senior Education (WISE) program has evidence for improving the well-being and general functioning of older adults as well as beliefs, knowledge, and attitudes about substance use. The WISE program provides education regarding high-risk behaviors to promote health and well-being of older adults in a brief group format for two hours for six consecutive weeks; the curriculum includes: (1) "understanding the changes associated with aging, (2) "ageing sensitivity," (3) "valuing cultural and generational diversity," (4) "medication and the older adult," (5) "addiction, ATOD (alcohol, tobacco, and other drugs) and the older adult," and (6) "an enhanced quality of life" (NREPP, 2017a, p. 1). A second evidence-based program effective for improving well-being, general functioning, and health-care access/receipt among older adults is the PEARLS program (NREPP, 2017b). The PEARLS program, or Program to Encourage Active, Rewarding Lives, is a one-on-one, individually delivered program to an older adult in six to eight sessions, emphasizing three key components: (1) "problem-solving treatment (PST), a 7-step approach for gaining control over stressful issues," (2) behavioral activation (BA), "which encourages social-activity planning," and (3) "scheduling physical activities and pleasant activities to increase mood and energy to better tackle life's problems" (NREPP, 2017b, p. 1).

Evidence-based fall prevention programs funded by the Administration for Community Living (2017) National Falls Prevention Resource Center reduced the fear of falls among 89% of the more than 48,000 older adults who have participated in fall prevention programs such as Moving for Better Balance, Stepping On, Tai Ji Quan, and A Matter of Balance. Rates of fall prevention actions undertaken by older adults who participated in the formed evidence-based falls prevention programs follow: (1) "77 percent did exercises they learned in the program at home," (2) "53 percent made changes in their home," (3) "43 percent talked to a family member or friend about how they can reduce their fall risk," (4) "27 percent had their vision checked," (5) "26 percent had their medications reviewed by a health care provider or pharmacist," and (7) "21 percent talked to a health care provider or pharmacist" (Administration for Community Living, 2017, p. 1). Interdisciplinary teams also consider secondary prevention options with older adults to assist the older adult with achieving goals for aging in place.

Secondary Prevention

Secondary prevention approaches involve the "early detection of disease before it manifests clinical symptoms" (Yong, Saunders, & Olsen, 2010, p. 221). Clinical prevention for secondary prevention includes "testing by clinicians for early detection of cancer, heart disease, and other conditions" (Yong, Saunders, & Olsen, 2010, p. 222). Community- and population-based secondary prevention often involves "screening fairs and other community venues for disease testing" (Yong, Saunders, & Olsen, 2010, p. 222). Screening is an important component of prevention, wellness, and health promotion of older adults who prefer to age in place. Screening ensures early detection of disease. It also ensures that treatment can be provided early enough to both prevent and delay symptoms of the disease that may affect functional health and wellness of older adults aging in place.

The recommended CDC clinical screening for secondary prevention services for older adults is based on systematic reviews conducted for the U.S. Preventive Services Task Force. Abdominal aortic aneurysm screening is recommended for males ages 65 to 75 with a history of smoking (Guirguis-Blake, Beil, Sun, Senger, & Whitlock, 2014). Abnormal blood glucose and type 2 diabetes mellitus screening is recommended for adults ages 40 to 70 who are obese or overweight (Selph et al., 2015). Alcohol misuse screening and behavioral counseling intervention in primary care is recommended for all adults ages 18 and older (Jonas et al., 2012). BRCA-related cancer screenings are recommended for all women with a family history of tubal, breast, ovarian, or peritoneal cancer (Nelson et al., 2013). Breast cancer screenings for women are recommended every other year for women between the ages of 50 to 74 (Nelson et al., 2016). Chlamydia and gonorrhea screening is recommended for older adult females with an infection risk (Nelson, Zakher, Cantor, Deagas, & Pappas, 2014). Colorectal cancer screening is recommended for all adults ages 50 to 75 and selectively for adults ages 76 to 85 (Lin et al., 2016).

Recommended hepatitis screenings include screening for high-risk populations for hepatitis B (i.e., people born in regions to countries with high rates of hepatitis B and their children born in the United States, HIV-positive, injection drug use, men who have sex with men, sexual partners or contact with hepatitis B) (Chou et al., 2014) and hepatitis C screening for high-risk populations (i.e., drug injectors and intranasal users, receiving blood transfusion before 1992, a hepatitis C virus-infected mother, tattoos that are unregulated or incarcerated), and adults born between the years of 1945 and 1965 (Chou, Cottrell, Wasson, Rahman, & Guise, 2012). Annual screenings for high blood pressure are recommended (Piper et al., 2014). Latent tuberculosis screening is recommended for high-risk populations (i.e., those born in countries with high TB prevalence, homeless shelters, or incarceration) (Kahwati et al., 2016). Lung cancer screening is recommended for adults ages 55 to 80 years with a history of smoking 30 packs of cigarettes per year, who stopped smoking within the past 15 years, or are currently smoking (Humphrey et al., 2013). It is recommended for adults of all ages to be screened for obesity, which is a body mass index (BMI) of 30 kg/m^2 or higher (LeBlanc, O'Connor, Whitlock, Patnode, & Kapka, 2011). Osteoporosis screening is recommended for women ages 65 and older (Nelson et al., 2010). Screening for syphilis is also recommended for adults asymptomatic but at risk of infection (Cantor, Nelson, Daeges, & Pappas, 2016). Tertiary prevention is a third level of prevention interdisciplinary teams can present as intervention options to older adults seeking to age in place.

Tertiary Prevention

Tertiary prevention approaches involve "the control of existing diseases to prevent more serious complications" (Yong, Saunders, & Olsen, 2010, p. 221). Clinical prevention for tertiary prevention includes "chronic illness care and disease management administered by clinicians" (Yong, Saunders, & Olsen, 2010, p. 222). Community- and population-based tertiary prevention includes "self-care, disease management at home, work, school" (Yong, Saunders, & Olsen, 2010, p. 222). The Chronic Disease Self-Management Program (CDSMP) is an evidence-based program proved to be effective for maintaining healthy and active aging lifestyles by improving participants' ability and confidence to manage their chronic illnesses (Self-Management Resource Center, 2017). The programs are brief—six sessions that last two and a half hours each—and are conducted in community settings with two leaders (both of whom are certified Master Trainers and one of whom is a peer living with a chronic disease), include 12 to 16 older adults, and include teaching participants the following subjects, which are modified depending upon the chronic disease, to promote participant self-management skills: (1) "techniques to deal with problems such as frustration, fatigue, pain, and isolation," (2) "appropriate exercise for maintaining and improving strength, flexibility, and endurance," (3) "appropriate use of medications," (4) "communicating effectively with family, friends, and health professionals," (5) "nutrition," (6) "decision-making," and (7) "how to evaluate new treatments" (Self-Management Resource Center, 2017). The CDSMP also include evidence-based workshop materials for Diabetes Self-Management Program (DSMP), Chronic Pain Self-Management Program (CPSMP), Positive Self-Management Program (PSMP), and the Cancer Thriving and Surviving (CTS) program (Self-Management Resource Center, 2016).

Whether primary, secondary, or tertiary prevention interventions or a combination, clinicians assess and monitor the impact of interventions on desirable treatment outcomes that facilitate an older adults goal to age in place.

Assessing/Monitoring Evidence-based Treatment Outcomes

The RE-AIM model (reach, efficacy, adoption, implementation, and maintenance) is a commonly used evaluation tool for determining the immediate short-term, intermediate, and long-term impacts of evidence-based primary, secondary, and tertiary intervention programs implemented and adopted by organizations to address chronic disease management and efficacy (Self-Management Resource Center, 2016). The RE-AIM model allows clinicians and program administrators to assess the extent to which the CDSMP reaches the intended target population, is effective, can be adopted by the organization and other desirable institutions, is implemented with consistent delivery of the intervention, and demonstrates maintenance of the intervention effects for program participants and settings over time. Clinicians adhere to CSWE Competency 9: Evaluate Practice With Individuals, Families, Groups, Organizations, and Communities to engage, assess, track, and monitor data for health promotion, wellness, and interventions for aging in place with older adults and their families that promotes self-determination and independence of older adults (specialized practice behaviors 1–2). Clinicians use the outcomes from evaluations to improve interdisciplinary care planning, treatment, and evaluation of interventions with older adults and their families and to engage them in processes related to wellness, health promotion, and aging in place (specialized practice behaviors 3–4). Clinicians further engage older adults in discussions, education, referral to, and coordination of home and community-based services across agencies to ensure older adults have services to allow them to meet their goals to age in place.

Community Resources/Interagency Coordination

Clinicians working with older adults and their families to promote wellness, prevention, and aging in place should be aware of myriad resources that an older adult can utilize to achieve desired goals. With all resource referrals and interagency collaborations, clinicians adhere to CSWE Gero Competency 1: Demonstrates Ethical and Professional Behavior, specialized practice behaviors 3, 5, and 7. Clinicians adhere to the standards for advancing human rights and advocating for access to necessary services and information to enable older adults to age in place in the least restrictive environment and have access to and maintain wellness and prevention of disease (CSWE Competency 3: Advance Human Rights and Social, Economic, and Environmental Justice, specialized practice behaviors 2–4). Clinicians engage in research-informed practice (CSWE Gero Competency 4) by communicating and collaborating with interdisciplinary and agency provider systems on best practices to meet the needs of the older adult (specialized practice behaviors 3–4). When working with older adults to promote aging in place, wellness, and preventive services, clinicians adhere to CSWE Gero Competencies in all phases of treatment:

+ engagement (CSWE Competency 6: Engage With Individuals, Families, Groups, Organizations, and Communities, specialized practice behaviors 1–4) by ensuring self-determination and participation in the decision making of older adults;
+ assessment (CSWE Gero Competency 7: Assess Individuals, Families, Groups, Organizations, and Communities, specialized practice behaviors 1–3) by using a strengths-perspective that emphasizes resilience of the client; when using assessment tools and purposively informing plans by eliciting interdisciplinary communication;
+ intervention (CSWE Gero Competency 8: Intervene With Individuals, Families, Groups, Organizations, and Communities, specialized practice behaviors 1–4) by developing and implementing evidence-based treatments that are client preferred and provide goodness of fit for the client and the presenting issue, communicating and coordinating treatment with the interdisciplinary team; and

+ evaluation (CSWE Gero Competency 9: Evaluate Practice With Individuals, Families, Groups, Organizations, and Communities, specialized practice behaviors 1–4) to ensure that older adults obtain and have access to home and community-based and interagency resources to meet their needs, to determine the effectiveness of the intervention and inform future practice and service delivery to ensure older adults have optimal opportunities to age in place successfully.

Referrals and coordination of care to primary care for annual preventive screenings, detection of disease, and treatment are essential. Clinicians should be aware of and maintain updated lists of local and county community-based wellness programs administered by county-level area agencies on aging and municipal, private, nonprofit, and faith-based agencies for: evidence-based fitness programs (i.e., enhance fitness) and senior fitness programs, healthy living, dietary, legal resources, fall prevention, mental health, substance use, and social and recreational programs to refer clients to in geographical areas in which the client resides. Clinicians must be knowledgeable in eligibility criteria for all programs they refer older adult clients to, such as financial, functional health, veteran status, and/or health/mental health criteria. To assist older adults with aging in place, clinicians maintain up-to-date lists of all home and community-based services a client may need as their functional health and/or support networks and assistance available change, including: transportation; home-delivered and congregate meals; options for temporary or permanent caregiver assistance with ADLS and IADLS (i.e., county Medicaid waiver programs such as in-home supportive services, private pay, nonprofit, veterans' aid, and attendant services, etc.); and comprehensive case management services through subsidized, private, or nonprofit organizations to assist an older adult with accessing and coordinating care among the multiple aging networks. Clinicians maintain comprehensive referral lists and knowledge about web-based organizations for psychoeducation on prevention of disease, understanding and managing risk factors, and living with and managing a chronic or life-threatening disease among those in whom it has been detected. Organizations such as the American Heart Association, American Diabetes Association, Parkinson's Association, Stroke Association, and American Cancer Society have prevention education, as well as resources, programs, and support services, for those living with a chronic or life-threatening condition. Clinicians also consider potential areas of transference and countertransference that may present when engaging, assessing, intervening, and evaluating outcomes with older adults who seek to age in place.

Transference/Countertransference

When working with older adults to promote wellness, prevention, and aging in place, clinicians can manage transference and countertransference that may present in the therapeutic relationship through strategies such as supervision, consultations, and adherence to the CSWE Gero Competency 1: Demonstrate Ethical and Professional Behavior, specialized practice behaviors 1–6 to ensure both ethical and professional practices (CalSWEC,

2017, pp. 1–2). Clinicians manage triggers for transference and countertransference when resistance to interventions or other situations present when engaging with the client, family, and caregiver systems on wellness and prevention strategies as well as options for aging in place (CSWE Gero Competency 6: Engage With Individuals, Families, Groups, Organizations, and Communities, specialized practice behavior 4). Clinicians working with older adults should be aware of the potential triggering of transference on the part of the client toward the clinician when recommending prevention, wellness, and options for aging in place based on their potential positive or negative experiences with other providers' recommendations. Clinicians manage countertransference reactions equally when working with older adult clients whose learned preventive health and wellness practices or preferences differ from the preventive health and wellness practices clinicians learned from their parents, family, or culture. This may cause the clinician to overinvest or withdraw from a client who has similar or very different values and beliefs about preventive and wellness practices. Clinicians also consider technological resources that may be useful to assist older adults with aging in place as well as potential legal and/ or ethical issues that may present.

Technological Resources

Administration on Aging: Community living programs: https://www.acl.gov/about-acl/administration-aging

American Cancer Society: Stay healthy: https://www.cancer.org/healthy.html

American Diabetes Association: Older adults awareness programs: http://www.diabetes.org/in-my-community/awareness-programs/older-adults/?loc=imc-slabnav?referrer=http://diabetes.org/

American Heart Association: Healthy eating: http://www.heart.org/HEARTORG/HealthyLiving/HealthyEating/Healthy-Eating_UCM_001188_SubHomePage.jsp

American Heart Association: Healthy living: http://www.heart.org/HEARTORG/HealthyLiving/How-to-Help-Prevent-Heart-Disease---At-Any-Age_UCM_442925_Article.jsp#

American Heart Association: Physical activity: http://www.heart.org/HEARTORG/HealthyLiving/PhysicalActivity/Physical-Activity_UCM_001080_SubHomePage.jsp

American Heart Association: Quit smoking: http://www.heart.org/HEARTORG/HealthyLiving/QuitSmoking/Quit-Smoking_UCM_001085_SubHomePage.jsp

American Heart Association: Stress management: http://www.heart.org/HEARTORG/HealthyLiving/StressManagement/Stress-Management_UCM_001082_SubHomePage.jsp

American Heart Association: Weight management: http://www.heart.org/HEARTORG/HealthyLiving/WeightManagement/Weight-Management_UCM_001081_SubHomePage.jsp

American Stroke Association: Stroke prevention and brain health: https://brainhealth.strokeassociation.org/

American Stroke Association: Understanding risk: https://www.strokeassociation.org/STROKEORG/AboutStroke/UnderstandingRisk/Understanding-Stroke-Risk_UCM_308539_SubHomePage.jsp

Office of Disease Prevention and Health Promotion: HealthyPeople2020: https://www.healthypeople.gov/

Parkinson's Foundation: http://www.parkinson.org/?_ga=2.149682166.1317723251.1513366242-942283842.1513366242&_gac=1.182634002.1513366242.EAIaIQobChMIn-m6xuCM2AIVhaDsCh2l2wGJEAAYAiAAEgKakfD_BwE

World Health Organization: Ageing and the life course: http://www.who.int/ageing/en/

World Health Organization: Age-friendly environments: http://www.who.int/ageing/age-friendly-environments/en/

Legal/Ethical Considerations

When communicating with older adults, family, care providers, interdisciplinary team members, and home and community-based and interagency providers, clinicians adhere to federal and state laws to protect the privacy and confidentiality of the older adults' electronic health and medical records and communications (CSWE Gero Competency 1: Demonstrate Ethical and Professional Behavior, specialized practice behaviors 1, 3, and 7). Clinicians follow the regulations of the Health Insurance Portability and Accountability Act of 1996 (HIPAA) to protect the security and privacy of protected health information of older adults (Schulz & Eden, 2016). This includes communications about where electronic health information and medical records by phone conversation, emails, faxes, and mail. There are two mandatory disclosures under HIPAA's privacy rule's where protected health information is permitted for: (1) "disclosure to the individual (and certain representatives authorized by the individual)" and (2) "disclosure to the Secretary of HHS for purposes of investigating compliance" (Schulz & Eden, 2016, pp. 339–340). When engaging in planning with older adults for options to age in place, clinicians advocate for plans that ensure self-determination and promote tailoring to meet cultural and diversity preferences (CSWE Gero Competency 1: Demonstrate Ethical and Professional Behavior, specialized practice behavior 3 and CSWE Gero Competency 2: Engage Difference in Practice, specialized practice behaviors 3–4).

Critical Thinking Activity/Discussion Questions

1. How are older adults screened in your agency or community for wellness and health promotion?
   a. What treatments and interventions are typically provided to organizations at your agency, in the local community, or in the state where you work with older adults?
   b. What resources are available?
   c. What legal/ethical issues have occurred that you are aware of, and how were they addressed?

2. How are older adults screened in your agency or community for options, opportunities, and/or preferences for aging in place?
   a. What treatments and interventions are typically provided to organizations at your agency, in the local community, or in the state where you work with older adults?
   b. What resources are available?
   c. What legal/ethical issues have occurred that you are aware of, and how were they addressed?

Self-Reflection Exercises

1. Critically examine your own attitudes and beliefs about wellness.
   a. What did you learn about wellness growing up?
   b. From whom did you learn it?
   c. How do those beliefs influence your wellness today?
   d. How might those beliefs affect your ability to engage, assess, and intervene with older adults to promote and understand wellness?

2. Critically examine your own attitudes and beliefs about health promotion.
   a. What did you learn about health promotion growing up?
   b. From whom did you learn it?
   c. How do those beliefs influence your attitudes about health promotion today?
   d. How might those beliefs affect your ability to engage, assess, and intervene with older adults for health promotion?

3. Critically examine your own attitudes and beliefs about aging in place.
   a. What did you learn about aging in place?
   b. From whom did you learn it?
   c. How do those beliefs influence your attitudes about aging in place today?
   d. How might those beliefs affect your ability to engage, assess, and intervene with older adults who prefer to age in place?

References

Administration for Community Living. (2017). Falls prevention. Retrieved from https://www.acl.gov/node/506

Ball, M. S. (2017). Aging in place: A toolkit for local governments. Retrieved from https://www.aarp.org/livable-communities/Plan/planning/info-12-2012/aging-in-place-a-toolkit-for-local-governments.html

Barrett, L. (2014). Home and community preferences of the 45+ population 2014. Retrieved from www.aarp.org/content/dam/aarp/research/surveys_statistics/il/2015/2014-Home-Community-45plus-res-il.pdf

Brazier, J. E., Harper, R., Jones, N. M., O'Cathain, A., Thomas, K. J., Usherwood, T., & Westlake, L. (1992). Validating the SF-36 health survey questionnaire: New outcome measure for primary care. *BMJ*, *305*(6846), 160–164.

CalSWEC. (2017). CalSWEC curriculum competencies for public child welfare, behavioral health, and aging in California. Retrieved from https://calswec.berkeley.edu/sites/default/files/2017_calswec_curriculum_competencies_0.pdf

Cantor A., Nelson, H. D., Daeges, M., & Pappas, M. (2016). *Screening for syphilis in nonpregnant adolescents and adults: Systematic review to update the 2004 U.S. Preventive Services Task Force Recommendation* (Evidence Synthesis, No. 136). Rockville, MD: Agency for Healthcare Research and Quality.

Centers for Disease Control and Prevention. (2013a). Health places terminology. Retrieved from www.cdc.gov/healthyplaces/terminology.htm

Centers for Disease Control and Prevention. (2013b). *The state of aging and health in America 2013*. Atlanta, GA: Centers for Disease Control and Prevention, U.S. Department of Health and Human Services.

Chou, R., Cottrell, E. B., Wasson, N., Rahman, B., & Guise, J. M. (2012). Screening for hepatitis C virus infection in adults. Comparative effectiveness review No. 69.(Prepared by the Oregon Evidence-based Practice Center under Contract No. 290-2007-10057-I.). *AHRQ-Agency Healthcare Research Quality*, *12*(13). Retrieved from https://www.uspreventiveservicestaskforce.org/Page/Document/final-evidence-review49/hepatitis-c-screening

Chou, R., Dana, T., Bougatsos, C., Blazina, I., Zakher, B., & Khangura, J. (2014). *Screening for hepatitis B virus infection in nonpregnant adolescents and adults: Systematic review to update the 2004 U.S. Preventive Services Task Force recommendation* (Evidence Synthesis, No. 110). Rockville, MD: Agency for Healthcare Research and Quality.

Fredriksen-Goldsen, K. I., Kim, H. J., Barkan, S. E., Muraco, A., & Hoy-Ellis, C. P. (2013). Health disparities among lesbian, gay, and bisexual older adults: Results from a population-based study. *American journal of public health*, *103*(10), 1802-1809.

Guirguis-Blake, J. M., Beil T. L., Sun, X., Senger, C. A., & Whitlock, E. P. (2014). *Primary care screening for abdominal aortic aneurysm: A systematic evidence review for the U.S. Preventive Services Task Force* (Evidence Syntheses, No. 109). Rockville, MD: Agency for Healthcare Research and Quality.

Guirguis-Blake, J. M., Evans, C. V., Senger, C. A., Rowland, M. G., O'Connor, E., & Whitlock, E. P. (2015). *Primary prevention of cardiovascular events: A systematic evidence review for the U.S. Preventive Services Task Force* (Evidence Syntheses, No. 131). Rockville, MD: Agency for Healthcare Research and Quality.

Hayes, V., Morris, J., Wolfe, C., & Morgan, M. (1995). The SF-36 health survey questionnaire: Is it suitable for use with older adults? *Age and Ageing, 24*(2), 120–125.

Humphrey, L., Deffebach, M., Pappas, M., Baumann, C., Artis, K., Mitchell, J.P., … & Slatore, C. (2013). *Screening for lung cancer: Systematic review to update the U.S. Preventive Services Task Force Recommendation* (Evidence Syntheses, No. 105). Rockville, MD: Agency for Healthcare Research and Quality.

Jonas, D. E., Garbutt, J. C., Brown, J. M., Amick, H. R., Brownley, K. A., Council, C. L., … & Harris, R. P. (2012). *Screening, behavioral counseling, and referral in primary care to reduce alcohol misuse* (Comparative Effectiveness Reviews, No. 64). Rockville, MD: Agency for Healthcare Research and Quality.

Kahwati, L. C., Feltner, C., Halpern, M., Woodell, C. L., Boland, E., Amick, H. R., … & Jonas, D. E. (2016). *Screening for latent tuberculosis infection in adults: An evidence review for the U.S. Preventive Services Task Force* (Evidence Syntheses, No. 142). Rockville, MD: Agency for Healthcare Research and Quality.

LeBlanc, E., O'Connor, E., Whitlock, E. P., Patnode, C., & Kapka, T. (2011). *Screening for and management of obesity and overweight in adults* (Evidence Syntheses, No. 89). Rockville, MD: Agency for Healthcare Research and Quality.

Lin, J. S., Piper, M. A., Perdue, L. A., Perdue, L. A., Rutter, C. M., Webber, E. M., … & Whitlock, E. P. (2016). *Screening for colorectal cancer: A systematic evidence review for the U.S. Preventive Services Task Force* (Evidence Syntheses, No. 135). Rockville, MD: Agency for Healthcare Research and Quality.

Michael, Y. L., Lin, J. S., Whitlock, E. P., Gold, R., Fu, R., O'Connor, E. A., … & Lutz, K. W. (2010). *Interventions to prevent falls in older adults: An updated systematic review* (Evidence Syntheses, No. 80). Rockville, MD: Agency for Healthcare Research and Quality.

National Center for Health Statistics (2016). *Health, United States, 2015: With special feature on racial and ethnic disparities.* Hyattsville, MD: U.S. Department of Health and Human Services, Centers for Disease Control and Prevention.

Nelson, H. D., Cantor, A., Humphrey, L., Fu, R., Pappas, M., Daeges, M., & Griffin, J. (2016). *Screening for breast cancer: A systematic review to update the 2009 U.S. Preventive Services Task Force Recommendation* (Evidence Syntheses, No. 124). Hyattsville, MD: Centers for Disease Control and Prevention.

Nelson, H. D. Fu, R., Goddard, K., Mitchell, J. P., Okinaka-Hu, L., Pappas, M., & Zakher, B. (2013). *Risk assessment, genetic counseling, and genetic testing for BRCA-related cancer: Systematic review to update the U.S. Preventive Services Task Force Recommendation* (Evidence Syntheses, No. 101). Hyattsville, MD: Centers for Disease Control and Prevention.

Nelson, H. D., Fu, R., Humphrey, L., Smith, B., Griffin, J. C., & Nygren, P. (2009). *Comparative effectiveness of medications to reduce risk of primary breast cancer in women* (Comparative Effectiveness Review, No. 17). Rockville, MD: Agency for Healthcare Research and Quality.

Nelson, H. D., Haney, E. M., Chou, R., Dana, T., Fu, R., & Bougatos, C. (2010). *Screening for osteoporosis: Systematic review to update the 2002 U.S. Preventive Services Task Force Recommendation* (Evidence Syntheses, No. 77). Rockville, MD: Agency for Healthcare Research and Quality.

Nelson, H. D., Zakher, B., Cantor, A., Deagas, M., & Pappas, M. (2014). *Screening for gonorrhea and chlamydia: Systematic review to update the U.S. Preventive Services Task Force Recommendations* (Evidence Syntheses, No. 115). Hyattsville, MD: Centers for Disease Control and Prevention.

Northwestern University. (2017). PROMIS. Retrieved from http://www.healthmeasures.net/index.php?option=com_content&view=category&layout=blog&id=147&Itemid=806

NREPP. (2017a). Wellness Initiative for Senior Education (WISE). Retrieved from https://nrepp.samhsa.gov/ProgramProfile.aspx?id=1279#hide2

NREPP (2017b). Program to Encourage Active, Rewarding Lives (PEARLS). Retrieved from https://nrepp.samhsa.gov/ProgramProfile.aspx?id=1237#hide1

Patnode, C. D., Evans, C. V., Senger, C. A., Redmond, N., & Lin, J. S. (2017). *Final evidence review: Healthful diet and physical activity for cardiovascular disease prevention in adults without known risk factors: Behavioral counseling.* Rockville, MD: U.S. Preventive Services Task Force.

Piper, M. A., Evans, C. V., Burda, B. U., Margolis, K. L., O'Connor, E., & Whitlock, E. P. (2014). *Screening for high blood pressure in adults: A systematic evidence review for the U.S. Preventive Services Task Force* (Evidence Syntheses, No. 121). Hyattsville, MD: Centers for Disease Control and Prevention.

Schulz, R., Eden, J., & National Academies of Sciences, Engineering, and Medicine. (2016). Older Adults Who Need Caregiving and the Family Caregivers Who Help Them. Retrieved from https://www.ncbi.nlm.nih.gov/books/NBK396397/

Self-Management Resource Center. (2016). Evidence-based self-management programs. *Administrative/Implementation Manual.* Retrieved from www.slefmanagementresource.com/docs/pdfs/Admin_Manual_2016.pdf

Self-Management Resource Center. (2017). Chronic disease self-management (CDSMP). Retrieved from https://www.selfmanagementresource.com/

Selph, S., Dana, T., Bougatsos, C., Blazina, I., Patel, H., & Chou, R. (2015). *Screening for abnormal glucose and type 2 diabetes mellitus: A systematic review to update the 2008 U.S. Preventive Services Task Force Recommendation* (Evidence Synthesis, No. 117). Rockville, MD: U.S. Department of Health and Human Services, Agency for Healthcare Research and Quality.

Tatsuoka, C., DeMarco, L., Smyth, K. A., Wilkes, S., Howland, M., Lerner, A. J., & Sajatovic, M. (2016). Evaluating PROMIS physical function measures in older adults at risk for Alzheimer's disease. *Gerontology and Geriatric Medicine, 2,* 1–8.

U.S. Preventive Services Task Force. (2014). Clinical summary: Obesity in adults: Screening and management. Retrieved from https://www.uspreventiveservicestaskforce.org/Page/Document/ClinicalSummaryFinal/obesity-in-adults-screening-and-management

U.S. Preventive Services Task Force. (2015). Clinical summary: Tobacco smoking cessation in adults, including pregnant women: Behavioral and pharmacotherapy interventions. Retrieved from https://www.uspreventiveservicestaskforce.org/Page/Document/ClinicalSummaryFinal/tobacco-use-in-adults-and-pregnant-women-counseling-and-interventions1

U.S. Preventive Services Task Force. (2016). Final update summary: Statin use for the primary prevention of cardiovascular disease in adults: Preventive medication. Retrieved from https://www.uspreventiveservicestaskforce.org/Page/Document/UpdateSummaryFinal/statin-use-in-adults-preventive-medication1

U.S. Preventive Services Task Force. (2017). Clinical summary: Healthful diet and physical activity for cardiovascular disease prevention in adults without known risk factors: behavioral counseling. Retrieved from https://www.uspreventiveservicestaskforce.org/Page/Document/ClinicalSummaryFinal/healthful-diet-and-physical-activity-for-cardiovascular-disease-prevention-in-adults-without-known-risk-factors-behavioral-counseling

Vasunilashorn, S., Steinman, B. A., Liebig, P. S., & Pynoos, J. 2012). Aging in place: Evolution of a research topic whose time has come. *Journal of Aging Research,* 1–7.

Wallace, S. P., Cochran, S. D., Durazo, E. M., & Ford, C. L. (2011). The health of aging lesbian, gay and bisexual adults in California. *Policy Brief UCLA Center for Health Policy Research,* 1.

Walters, S. J., Munro, J. F., & Brazier, J. E. (2001). Using the SF-36 with older adults: A cross-sectional community-based survey. *Age and ageing, 30*(4), 337–343.

Ware, J. E., & Sherbourne, C. D. (1992). The MOS 36-item Short-Form Health Survey (SF-36): I. Conceptual framework and item selection. *Medical Care, 30*(6), 473–483.

World Health Organization. (2017). Towards an Age-friendly world. Retrieved from https://www.who.int/ageing/age-friendly-world/en/

Yong, Saunders, & Olsen. (2010). The healthcare imperative. Retrieved from https://www.ncbi.nlm.nih.gov/books/NBK53944/

CHAPTER 5

Aging in Institutions

Long-Term Care and Prison Settings

This chapter identifies issues, strategies, and evidence-based interventions for working with older adults aging in long-term skilled nursing and prison institutional settings. Key domains to promote both effective clinical practice with older adults and optimal client outcomes are presented.

CSWE Gero Competencies Highlighted

Competency 1: Demonstrate Ethical and Professional Behavior

Specialized Practice Competency Description: Social workers understand the value base of the profession and its ethical standards, as well as relevant laws and regulations that may impact practice at the micro, mezzo, and macro levels. Social workers understand frameworks of ethical decision-making and how to apply principles of critical thinking to those frameworks in practice, research, and policy arenas. Social workers recognize personal values and the distinction between personal and professional values. They also understand how their personal experiences and affective reactions influence their professional judgment and behavior. Social workers understand the profession's history, its mission, and the roles and responsibilities of the profession. Social workers also understand the role of other professions when engaged in inter-professional teams. Social workers recognize the importance of lifelong learning and are committed to continually updating their skills to ensure they are relevant and effective. Social workers also understand emerging forms of technology and the ethical use of technology in social work practice.

Competency Behaviors: (1) Guided by ethical reasoning and self-reflection, demonstrate adherence to ethical frameworks and key laws, policies, and procedures related to aging, and the rights of older adults. (2) Engage in active dialogue with field faculty/

instructors regarding aging field placement agency policies and culture around behavior, appearance, communication, and the use of supervision. (3) Develop and sustain effective collaborative relationships that respect older adults' needs for protection, self-determination, and the provision of services in the least restrictive environment possible with colleagues and community stakeholders, including older adults, their family members, other care providers, and Tribes. (4) Effectively manage professional boundary issues and other challenges arising in the course of aging-related work, particularly ambiguities presented by home visits, personal loss, trauma, and other highly involved and potentially emotionally triggering aspects of the work. (5) Develop and sustain relationships with members of interdisciplinary and integrated health care teams, including social workers, primary care providers, hospital staff, home health care providers, psychiatrists, psychologists, substance use disorder treatment staff, Tribal service providers, and others, that reflect clear understanding of their roles in providing care to older adults. (6) Demonstrate both knowledge of the history and evolution of social work practice related to aging and older adults in the United States and California, and a commitment to lifelong learning around this practice. (7) Follow all ethical guidelines and legal mandates in the use of technology in order to maintain the confidentiality of all personal, behavioral health, and health-related information. (CalSWEC, 2017, pp. 1–2)

Competency 2: Engage Diversity and Difference in Practice

Specialized Practice Competency Description: Social workers understand how diversity and difference characterize and shape the human experience and are critical to the formation of identity. The dimensions of diversity are understood as the intersectionality of multiple factors, including, but not limited to, age, class, color, culture, disability and ability, ethnicity, gender, gender identity and expression, immigration status, marital status, political ideology, race, religion/spirituality, sex, sexual orientation, and Tribal sovereign status. Social workers understand that, as a consequence of difference, a person's life experiences may include oppression, poverty, marginalization, and alienation as well as privilege, power, and acclaim. Social workers also understand the forms and mechanisms of oppression and discrimination and recognize the extent to which a culture's structures and values, including social, economic, political, and cultural exclusions, may oppress, marginalize, alienate, or create privilege and power.

Competency Behaviors: (1) Engage in critical analysis of the interpersonal, community, and social structural causes and effects of disproportionality, disparities, and inequities in the incidence and trajectory of aging-related care needs, housing, transportation, and resource access among older adults,

their families, and their communities. (2) Evidence respectful awareness and understanding of the impact of being a member of a marginalized group on aging experiences, and accurately identify differences in access to and quality of available services for members of different communities and populations. (3) Demonstrate knowledge of diverse cultural norms and traditional methods of providing care to older adults, as well as an applied understanding of how these realities affect work with older adults from diverse backgrounds, their families, and their communities. (4) Develop and use practice methods that acknowledge, respect, and address how individual and cultural values, norms, and differences impact the various systems with which older adults interact, including, but not limited to, families, communities, primary care systems, mental and behavioral health care systems, and integrated care systems. (CalSWEC, 2017, pp. 3–4)

Competency 3: Advance Human Rights and Social, Economic, and Environmental Justice

Specialized Practice Competency Description: Social workers understand that every person regardless of position in society has fundamental human rights such as freedom, safety, privacy, an adequate standard of living, health care, and education. Social workers understand the global interconnections of oppression and human rights violations, and are knowledgeable about theories of human need and social justice and strategies to promote social and economic justice and human rights. Social workers understand strategies designed to eliminate oppressive structural barriers to ensure that social goods, rights, and responsibilities are distributed equitably and that civil, political, environmental, economic, social, and cultural human rights are protected.

Competency Behaviors: (1) Clearly articulate the systematic effects of discrimination, oppression, and stigma on the needs and experiences of older adults and on the quality and delivery of services available to them, and identify and advocate for policy changes needed to address these issues. (2) Advocate for changes in policies and programs that reflect a social justice practice framework for facilitating access and providing services to older adults, their families, and care providers, especially among underserved groups and communities. (3) Demonstrate the ability to work effectively in cross-disciplinary collaboration to develop and provide interventions that explicitly address the specific needs of diverse older adults, their families, and care providers. (4) Integrate into all aspects of policy and practice sensitivity to the reality that fundamental rights, including freedom and privacy, may be compromised for older adults engaged in care, and the goal that services should be provided in the least restrictive environment possible. (CalSWEC, 2017, pp. 4–5)

Competency 4: Engage in Practice-informed Research and Research-informed Practice

Specialized Practice Competency Description: Social workers understand quantitative and qualitative research methods and their respective roles in advancing a science of social work and in evaluating their practice. Social workers know the principles of logic, scientific inquiry, and culturally informed and ethical approaches to building knowledge. Social workers understand that evidence that informs practice derives from multidisciplinary sources and multiple ways of knowing. They also understand the processes for translating research findings into effective practice.

Competency Behaviors: (1) Demonstrate the ability to understand, interpret, and evaluate the benefits and limitations of various evidence-based and evidence-informed treatment models as they influence practice with older adults. (2) Engage in critical analysis of research findings, practice models, and practice wisdom as they inform aging related practice, including how research practices have historically failed to address the needs and realities of exploited and/or disadvantaged communities, and how cross-cultural research practices can be used to enhance equity. (3) Clearly communicate research findings, conclusions, and implications, as well as their applications to aging practice, across a variety of professional interactions with consumers, families, and multidisciplinary service providers. (4) Apply research findings to aging-related practice with individuals, families, and communities and to the development of professional knowledge about the needs, experiences, and well-being of older adults. (CalSWEC, 2017, pp. 5–6)

Competency 6: Engage With Individuals, Families, Groups, Organizations, and Communities

Specialized Practice Competency Description: Social workers understand that engagement is an ongoing component of the dynamic and interactive process of social work practice with, and on behalf of, diverse individuals, families, groups, organizations, and communities. Social workers value the importance of human relationships. Social workers understand theories of human behavior and the social environment, and critically evaluate and apply this knowledge to facilitate engagement with clients and constituencies, including individuals, families, groups, organizations, and communities. Social workers understand strategies to engage diverse clients and constituencies to advance practice effectiveness. Social workers understand how their personal experiences and affective reactions may impact their ability to effectively engage with diverse clients and constituencies. Social workers value principles of relationship-building and inter-professional collaboration to facilitate engagement with clients, constituencies, and other professionals as appropriate.

Competency Behaviors: (1) Appropriately engage and activate older adults, their families, and other care providers in the development and coordination of care plans that reflect relevant theoretical models and balance older adults' needs for care with respect for autonomy and independence. (2) Effectively utilize interpersonal skills to engage older adults, their families, and other care providers in culturally responsive, consumer-driven, and trauma-informed integrated care that addresses mutually agreed upon service goals and balances needs for care, protection, autonomy, and independence. (3) Establish effective and appropriate communication, coordination, and advocacy planning with other care providers and interdisciplinary care teams as needed to address mutually agreed upon service goals. Recognizing the complex nature of service engagement, ensure that communications with consumers and their families regarding service goals are both sensitive and transparent. (4) Manage affective responses and exercise good judgment around engaging with resistance, trauma responses, and other potentially triggering situations with older adults, their families, and other care providers. (CalSWEC, 2017, pp. 9–10)

Competency 7: Assess Individuals, Families, Groups, Organizations, and Communities

Specialized Practice Competency Description: Practitioners in aging utilize ecological-systems theory, a strengths-based and person/family-centered framework to conduct assessments that value the resilience of diverse older adults, families, and caregivers. They select appropriate assessment tools, methods and technology, and evaluate, adapt, and modify them, as needed, to enhance their validity in working with diverse, vulnerable and at-risk groups. The comprehensive biopsychosocial assessment takes into account the multiple factors of physical, mental and social well-being needed for treatment planning for older adults and their families. They develop skills in interprofessional assessment and communication with key constituencies to choose the most effective practice strategies. Gero social workers understand how their own experiences and affective reactions about aging, quality of life, loss and grief may affect their assessment and resultant decision-making.

Competency Behaviors: (1) Conduct assessments that incorporate a strengths-based perspective, person/family-centered focus, and resilience while recognizing aging related risk, (2) Develop, select, and adapt assessment methods and tools that optimize practice with older adults, their families, caregivers, and communities, and (3) Use and integrate multiple domains and sources of assessment information and communicate with other professionals to inform a comprehensive plan for intervention. (Council for Social Work Education, 2017, pp. 89–90)

Competency 8: Intervene With Individuals, Families, Groups, Organizations, and Communities

Specialized Practice Competency Description: Social workers understand that intervention is an ongoing component of the dynamic and interactive process of social work practice with, and on behalf of, diverse individuals, families, groups, organizations, and communities. Social workers are knowledgeable about evidence-informed interventions to achieve the goals of clients and constituencies, including individuals, families, groups, organizations, and communities. Social workers understand theories of human behavior and the social environment, and critically evaluate and apply this knowledge to effectively intervene with clients and constituencies. Social workers understand methods of identifying, analyzing, and implementing evidence-informed interventions to achieve client and constituency goals. Social workers value the importance of interprofessional teamwork and communication in interventions, recognizing that beneficial outcomes may require interdisciplinary, inter-professional, and inter-organizational collaboration.

Competency Behaviors: (1) In partnership with older adults and their families, develop appropriate intervention plans that reflect respect for autonomy and independence, as well as contemporary theories and models for interventions with older adults. Plans should:

- Reflect cultural humility and acknowledgement of individualized needs;
- Incorporate consumer and family strengths;
- Utilize community resources and natural supports;
- Incorporate multidisciplinary team supports and interventions;
- Include non-pharmacological interventions; and
- Demonstrate knowledge of poly-pharmacy needs and issues specific to older adults.

(2) Apply the principles of teaming, engagement, inquiry, advocacy, and facilitation within interdisciplinary teams and care coordination to the work of supporting older adults, family members, and other care providers to accomplish intervention goals and satisfy advanced care planning needs. (3) Effectively implement evidence-based interventions in the context of providing emergency response, triage, brief treatment, and longer-term care, and in the course of addressing a range of issues presented in primary care, specialty care, community agency, inpatient, and palliative care settings. Interventions should be guided by respect for older adults' autonomy and independence and should include components such as psychoeducation, problem-solving treatment skills, symptom tracking, medication therapies, follow-up, and planning for evolving care needs. (4) Effectively plan for interventions in ways that incorporate

thoughtfully executed transitions during time-limited internships, recognizing that consumer needs for support may continue beyond these time periods. (CalSWEC, 2017, pp. 12–14)

Competency 9: Evaluate Practice With Individuals, Families, Groups, Organizations, and Communities

Specialized Practice Competency Description: Social workers understand that evaluation is an ongoing component of the dynamic and interactive process of social work practice with, and on behalf of, diverse individuals, families, groups, organizations and communities. Social workers recognize the importance of evaluating processes and outcomes to advance practice, policy, and service delivery effectiveness. Social workers understand theories of human behavior and the social environment, and critically evaluate and apply this knowledge in evaluating outcomes. Social workers understand qualitative and quantitative methods for evaluating outcomes and practice effectiveness.

Competency Behaviors: (1) Record, track, and monitor consumer engagement, assessment, and intervention data in practice with older adults, their families, and other care providers accurately and according to field education agency policies and guidelines. (2) Conduct accurate process and outcome analysis of engagement, assessment, and intervention data in practice with older adults, their families, and other care providers that incorporates consumer perspectives and reflects respect for older adults' autonomy and independence. (3) Use findings to evaluate intervention effectiveness, develop recommendations for adapting service plans and approaches as needed, improve interdisciplinary team coordination and care integration, and help agency and community policies better support older adults, their families, and their formal and informal care systems. (4) Share both the purposes of such data collection and the overall results of data analysis with older adults, their families, and communities whenever possible, with the goal of engaging them more meaningfully in the evaluation process. (CalSWEC, 2017, pp. 14–15)

Learning Objectives

1. Learners will understand the context for aging in long-term skilled nursing and prison institutional settings in the United States.
2. Learners will identify screening tools to inform treatment planning with older adults in skilled nursing and prison institutions.
3. Learners will identify appropriate evidence-based interventions for use with adults aging in skilled nursing and prison institutional settings.

4.   Learners will understand the importance of referring older adult clients and their family members to appropriate technological and community resources and when to assist with coordination.

5.   Learners will identify sources of transference and countertransference when workers with older adults aging in skilled nursing or prison institutional settings.

Part I. Aging in Long-Term Skilled Nursing Facility Settings

Case Study

Mr. Chou is a 70-year-old male, newly admitted to a skilled nursing facility after becoming bedbound; his spouse and oldest son were no longer able to provide 24-hour care at home. Mr. Chou's eldest son was his in-home supportive services caregiver; Mr. Chou received 124 hours per month of paid assistance but required total assistance with activities of daily living (ADLs) and instrumental activities of daily living (IADLs) three months into his diagnosis of stage 4 metastatic lung cancer. He received radiation and chemotherapy for treatment and had home health services consisting of a nurse, physical therapist, and social worker. He was independent with ADLs and IADLs prior to his diagnosis and at the time of his admission to the skilled nursing facility required gurney transportation for medical appointments; he had to have drainage (i.e., thoracentesis) twice a week due to pleural effusion from the cancer treatments and required the use of oxygen. Mr. Chou, his spouse, and eldest son lived in a two-bedroom apartment on the second floor with no elevator; his other two sons lived out of state, and there were no other family or friends to assist with care. Despite his spouse's and son's efforts and cultural values to keep him in the home and provide care for him, Mr. Chou and his family agreed that it was in his best interest to have 24-hour care in a skilled nursing facility at the recommendation of his primary care physician and oncologist.

Assessing Context

Institutional long-term care. Institutional long-term care is defined by the Centers for Medicare and Medicaid Services as an institution or residential facility that provides services authorized under the Social Security Act that "assume total care of the individuals who are admitted," include comprehensive care with "room and board" that are billable in "bundle payment," are "licensed and certified by the state, according to federal standards," and are "subject to survey at regular intervals to maintain their certification and license to operate" (2017, p. 1). For adults ages 65 and older, skilled nursing facilities and institutions for adults 65 and older with mental diseases (IMDs) (i.e., institutions for mental disorders that meet skilled nursing and hospital requirements) fall under this definition of institutional long-term care. In terms of the continuum of long-term care, skilled nursing facilities and psychiatric long-term care settings (IMD over 65) are the most restrictive institutional environments for vulnerable older adults. Although the population of older adults ages 65 and older is increasing, between 1977 to 2014, the number of adult residents ages 65 and older in nursing homes per 1,000 adults 65 in the population decreased by nearly 50%, from 47.1 in 1977 to 25.2 in 2014 (National Center for Health Statistics, 2017).

Among adults residing in nursing homes in 2011 and 2012, 85.1% and 48.5% were ages 65 and older, respectively, who had a diagnosis of depression, Alzheimer's disease, or other dementia (Harris-Kojetin, Sengupta, Park-Lee, & Valverde, 2013). In 2017, approximately 5.3 million adults ages 65 and older were living with a diagnosis of Alzheimer's dementia, or roughly 10 percent of adults 65 and older (Alzheimer's Association, 2017). The estimates for mental health disorders for residents of skilled nursing facilities in the 1990s was 65% to 91% (Grabowski, Aschbrenner, Rome, & Bartels, 2010). Among institutionalized older adults ages 65 and older with mental health conditions including dementia, the skilled nursing facility setting is the most common care setting. This is in part due to deinstitutionalization policies from the 1960s to the 1970s that shifted long-term institutional care in psychiatric settings to skilled nursing settings as during that time frame, there was a 40% decrease for IMD settings over 65 and a 100% increase in skilled nursing facilities observed (Grabowski, Aschbrenner, Rome, & Bartels, 2010). As a result, nursing homes "became the de facto destination for individuals with mental illness" (Grabowski, Aschbrenner, Rome, & Bartels, 2010, p. 2). Funding is yet another factor, with long-term Medicaid providing funding for skilled nursing care for both physical and psychiatric disability (Grabowski, Aschbrenner, Rome, & Bartels, 2010).

After deinstitutionalization, skilled nursing facilities were ill prepared to care for older adults with mental health needs, and deficiencies were identified in the use of physical restraints and antipsychotic medications, resulting in the Federal Nursing Home Reform Act of 1987 under the Omnibus Budget Reconciliation Act (OBRA) of 1987 (Grabowski, Aschbrenner, Rome, & Bartels, 2010). As part of OBRA, a preadmission screening and annual resident review (PASRR) requires skilled nursing facilities to be deemed appropriate for care by state mental health authorities for any resident with a mental health condition or prospective applicants (Grabowski, Aschbrenner, Rome, & Bartels, 2010). Quality measures for nursing home residents outlined by the Centers for Medicare and Medicaid Services (2017) with short-term stays (i.e., transitional care) include the percentage of residents with: moderate to severe self-rated pain, new or worsened pressure ulcers, assessment and administration of the influenza vaccination, assessment and administration of the pneumococcal vaccine, and receipt of new antipsychotic medications. For nursing home residents with long-term stays or custodial stays, quality measures outlined by the Centers for Medicare and Medicaid Services (2017) include the percent of residents with: injury from one or more falls, moderate to severe self-rated pain, pressure ulcers among those at high risk, assessment and administration of the influenza vaccination, assessment and administration of the pneumococcal vaccine, urinary tract infection, bowel and bladder incontinence among those at low risk, catheter insertions, physical restraints, increases in assistance with ADLs, weight gain or loss, depression symptoms, and use of antipsychotic medication. These quality measures are gathered on the Minimum Data Set (MDS), a "powerful tool for implementing standardized assessment and for facilitating care management" required by all Medicare and Medicaid certified skilled nursing facilities (Centers for Medicare and Medicaid Services, 2015).

Older adults residing in nursing homes without access to social support and spiritual, social, and recreational activities are at risk for isolation as the average time a resident spends with providers per day over a 24-hour period is low. In 2012, the average hours spent for long-term care services with a resident of a skilled nursing home by provider type follow: 2.46 hours with aides, 0.85 hours with a licensed practical or vocational nurse (LVN), 0.52 hours with a registered nurse (RN), and 0.08 hours with a social worker (Harris-Kojetin, Sengupta, Park-Lee, & Valverde, 2013). Older adults without access to these long-term care services living with mental health and unmet biopsychosocial/ spiritual needs are especially vulnerable. Among nursing facilities in the United States in 2012, 86.6% provided mental health or counseling services and 88.9% provided social work services (Harris-Kojetin, Sengupta, Park-Lee, & Valverde, 2013). In 2011 and 2012, a large proportion of older adults required assistance with ADLs, 96.1% required assistance with bathing, 90.9% with dressing, 86.6% with toileting, and 56% with eating (Harris-Kojetin, Sengupta, Park-Lee, & Valverde, 2013). Disability is a predictor of mortality in older adults—mortality risk for older adults in need of assistance with one or two ADLs increases by 20.7%; for three to four ADLs, risk increases by 24%; and for five or six ADLs, mortality risk increases by 37.2% (Guralnik, Fried, & Salive, 1996).

A thorough biopsychosocial/spiritual assessment informs the identification of issues to address as well as appropriate interventions they bring into interdisciplinary treatment planning and decision-making discussions with the client for preferred options and treatment. Clinicians can use screening tools to further inform treatment planning and interventions with older adults in skilled nursing institutional settings.

Biopsychosocial/Spiritual Assessment

Following is an application of the Geriatric Biopsychosocial/Spiritual Assessment conducted by Mr. Chou's social worker.

Box 5.1

Geriatric Biopsychosocial/Spiritual Assessment

Basic Demographic: Mr. Chou is a 70-year-old Chinese American, married, male; he speaks Mandarin Chinese and English as a second language; he has a high school education

Referral Information: New admission to a skilled nursing facility

Cultural/Spiritual: Mr. Chou is able to verbalize understanding of his life-threatening illness and treatment for it; he does not engage in complementary or alternative medicine practices and has no organized religious or spiritual beliefs/values

Social: [Relationships within family, social/diversity groups, and community]

- Mr. Chou worked in the garment and textile industry in Los Angeles, CA; he has no military service record or experience; he immigrated to the United States at the age of 40; he has three adult sons (one local and two out-of-state) and three grandchildren
- Mr. Chou's spouse and son visit him daily at the skilled nursing facility; he speaks by phone weekly to his two sons who live out of state; he has no friends, family, or cultural/diversity members visiting him; his spouse and son are adjusting to his placement in the skilled nursing facility

Financial: [Ability to provide basic needs and access health services]

- Basic needs met at the skilled nursing facility for housing, food, and shelter; his family provides clothing
- Health insurance: Medicare and Medicaid; all deductibles and co-pays currently paid 100%
- Income sources: Social Security, family support

Environmental: [Personal safety, maintenance of residence, and safety of community]

- Skilled nursing facility within 3 miles from spouse and son and next-door to hospital
- Neighborhood safety: Mr. Chou is leaving the facility attended during the day; the crime level is low in the neighborhood
- Home safety: Controlled in nursing home environment
- No access to guns or gun ownership
- No indicators of abuse or neglect by self or perpetrated by others

Physical: [Individual function and disease morbidity]

- Moderate health literacy; poor self-rated health; advance directive in place with CPR but ventilator, respirator, tracheotomy, or feeding tubes preferred; advance directive initiated during home health four months prior to admission; Mr. Chou has knowledge of his diagnosis and medications and is compliant with treatment; he is dependent with ADLs and IADLs, requires oxygen 24 hours a day, and is currently receiving radiation twice a month and thoracentesis twice weekly; Mr. Chou reports no sexual activity over the past three years with his spouse; no concerns verbalized

Mental: [Mental status, depression, anxiety, and substance abuse]

- No indicators of depression or anxiety; Mr. Chou is alert and oriented and competent to engage in decision making
- Suicide risk assessment: Mr. Chou does not endorse suicidal ideations, and no history is reported
- Homicidal ideations: Ruled out—no history of homicidal ideations

- Mr. Chou smoked one pack of cigarettes per day since the age of 17, but he is no longer smoking; he consumed two to three alcoholic beverages per week prior to his lung cancer diagnosis, but he stopped drinking alcohol after his diagnosis

Formulation/Evaluation: Socialization and palliative care, monitor for hospice needs depending on prognosis, continued daily visits and support from family

Treatment Planning: Social worker, nurse, and physician in agreement on a palliative care consultation for symptom management; social worker to engage Mr. Chou in advance care planning and life review therapy; assistance for Mr. Chou daily outside of the room for planned social activities

Community Resource Needs: Transportation secured for ambulance transport for treatments; support groups for spouse and son

Screening tools in long-term care settings. The Centers for Medicare and Medicaid Services (2017) requires skilled nursing facilities to assess all residents at admission and quarterly with the MDS on domains such as: hearing, speech, and vision; cognitive patterns with the Brief Interview for Mental Status, which includes repetition of three words, temporal orientation, recall, short-term memory, long-term memory, memory recall/ability, and cognitive skills for daily decision making; signs and symptoms of delirium, which includes evidence of change in mental status, inattention, disorganized thinking, and altered level of consciousness; mood with the Resident Mood Interview (PHQ-9) or the Staff Assessment of Resident Mood (PHQ-9-OV); potential for self-harm by the resident; behavior including potential indicators of psychosis, behavioral symptom presence and frequency, overall presence of behavioral symptoms, impact on resident, impact on others, rejection of care presence and frequency, wandering presence and frequency, wandering impact, and change in behavior or other symptoms.

The MDS also includes assessment of resident preferences for customary routines, which includes daily preferences such as clothing choice, care of personal belongings, bathing preferences, snacks, bedtime choice, involvement of family or others in care, use of private phone, and space to lock up belongings (Centers for Medicare and Medicaid Services, 2017). Preferences for activities are assessed for reading materials, music, animals, news, activities with groups, favorable activities, getting outside, and spiritual practices (Centers for Medicare and Medicaid Services, 2017). Resident or family as well as staff assessments are completed for both preferences for customary routine and activities (Centers for Medicare and Medicaid Services, 2017). Functional status is assessed for ADLs, balance during walking and transferring, range of motion, assistive devices, and potential for functional rehabilitation, functional abilities, and goals (Centers for Medicare and Medicaid Services, 2017).

Bladder and bowel continence, appliances, and toileting programs are assessed as active diagnoses (Centers for Medicare and Medicaid Services, 2017). A pain management assessment is completed, and a pain assessment interview is conducted, which includes pain presence, frequency, effect on function, intensity by numeric rating on a scale of 0 to 10, and a verbal descriptor from mild to very severe (Centers for Medicare and Medicaid Services, 2017). A staff pain assessment includes assessing nonverbal sounds, verbalized complaints of pain, facial expressions, and body movements that are protective (Centers for Medicare and Medicaid Services, 2017). Other assessed health conditions include shortness of breath, tobacco use, prognosis, and problem conditions (Centers for Medicare and Medicaid Services, 2017). Fall history in the past 30 days, two months, and six months and injuries from a fall in the past six months are assessed (Centers for Medicare and Medicaid Services, 2017). Additional assessment domains include swallowing/nutritional status; oral/dental status; skin conditions; medications; special treatments, procedures, and programs; restraints and alarms; and participation in assessment and goal setting (Centers for Medicare and Medicaid Services, 2017). Clinicians can access and use data from the MDS when engaging, assessing, intervening, and evaluating outcomes of older adults in skilled nursing settings.

Following is an application of the Geriatric Biopsychosocial/Spiritual Assessment presented in Chapter 2 to the case study introduced in the beginning of this chapter. Clinicians must also consider diversity of an older adult when preparing for treatment planning with the interdisciplinary team for older adults in long-term skilled nursing settings.

Diversity–Cultural Competence/Spirituality/LGBT/Sexuality

Clinicians have knowledge and skill in assessing the context of diversity for older adults in skilled nursing settings. Although Mr. Chou and his family preferred that he remain at home, the complexity of his care and his caregivers' acknowledgement in being overwhelmed with the demands of caring for him resulted in the decision to pursue long-term care in a skilled nursing facility for him. Clinicians can assist clients like Mr. Chou and his caregivers with processing the range of reactions, feelings, and emotions surrounding decision making for long-term care that goes against their cultural preferences and practices. Among adults residing in nursing homes in 2011 and 2012, 85.1% were ages 65 and older; 67.7% women; 78.7% non-Hispanic White, 14% African American, 5.1% Hispanic, and 2.3% other race; and 48.5% had a diagnosis of depression or Alzheimer's disease or other dementia (Harris-Kojetin, Sengupta, Park-Lee, & Valverde, 2013). In engaging diversity in practice (CSWE Competency 2) clinicians adhere to specialized practice behaviors 1–4 to ensure that all care planning and treatments are culturally preferred and valued by the older adult and involve decision makers according to the older adult's preferences (CalSWEC, 2017). Clinicians provide appropriate support for older adult clients and their families, paying special attention to cultural preferences and potential ambiguities, such as regret about placement and not providing care to the older adult outside of an institutional setting, and/or conflicts such as disagreements among extended family members about placement that may arise as a result of an older adult residing in a skilled nursing setting. Clinicians provide the context of diversity and preferences as well as familial/cultural contexts and preferences into interdisciplinary treatment planning meetings to inform appropriate interventions with older adults in skilled nursing facilities.

Interdisciplinary Team Roles and Planning

Interdisciplinary team planning and care improves impacts on outcomes for older adults aging in skilled nursing settings. Interdisciplinary teams play an important role in providing holistic interventions that impact nursing home resident outcomes positively. In a meta-analysis of 27 randomized clinical trials conducted between 1990 to 2011 that tested the effectiveness of interdisciplinary team interventions on nursing home resident outcomes, 18 demonstrated positive outcomes (Nazir et al., 2013). Common features of studies demonstrating a positive impact on nursing home resident outcomes included the primary physician or pharmacist on the interdisciplinary team, interdisciplinary communication, coordination, resolution of conflicts, and leadership (Nazir et al., 2013). Clinicians suggest appropriate evidence-based interventions as treatment options during interdisciplinary team meetings that then is presented to and informs treatment option decision making of older adults and/or their legal guardians/conservators. When presenting the assessment of biopsychosocial/spiritual and diversity factors for Mr. Chou during the initial treatment plan team meeting with the interdisciplinary team, the social worker was able to provide a context for what was perceived previously by providers as reluctance, denial, combativeness, and/or borderline neglect surrounding the care and recommended placement of Mr. Chou. Although other disciplines brought the social worker in for observations (i.e., that he had unmet physical/health needs), the context of culture and diversity shed light on the context that despite his caregivers' best attempts and efforts to provide care for him, consistent with their cultural preferences and practices to care for family and elders, they realized they could not provide the care he needed, and together, they decided placement was indeed his best option for appropriate care.

Evidence-based Interventions

Best practices in skilled nursing settings. There are several evidence-informed and evidence-based practices that can improve the well-being of older adults residing in nursing homes. A goal to ensure higher functioning and well-being for an older adult resident prescribed psychotropic medications is for the resident to have the least restrictive chemical restraints to control mood and behavior to maximize optimal functioning of the resident. Mood and behavior tracking on the Medication Administration records allows the interdisciplinary team to monitor the effectiveness of a psychotropic medication and establish a baseline. Psychotropic medications should not be the only means for alleviating mood and behavioral symptoms. The reduction of symptoms can be approached with nonpharmacological interventions that focus on socialization, exercise, person-centered care, and antipsychotic medication reduction to improve the well-being and health of older adults residing in nursing homes. Among older adults prescribed psychotropic medications to reduce mood and behavior symptoms of depression and dementia, a growing body of evidence demonstrates the effectiveness of nonpharmacologic and patient-centered care interventions for symptom management (Ballard et al., 2015).

In the United Kingdom, a randomized clinical trial conducted in 16 nursing homes using the Well-being and Health for People with Dementia (WHELD) program provided antipsychotic review, person-centered care, exercise, and social interaction with pleasant activities interventions with 277 older adults diagnosed with dementia over a nine-month period. The antipsychotic review intervention focused on working with psychiatrists and primary physicians to review psychotropic medications prescribed, seminars with toolkits for best practices for prescription, review, monitoring, and trial discontinuations (Ballard et al., 2015). The person-centered care intervention consisted of use of evidence-based tools from the Focused Intervention for Training of Staff (FITS) program and emphasized five key areas: (1) "embedding an understanding of dementia and person-centered care," (2) "assessing how each home personalizes care in terms of plans and provision of opportunities for individual's person-centered care," (3) developing the staff's understanding of the relationship between an individual resident's experience, behavior, and well-being through the use of his or her life story and the principles of functional analysis to understand challenging behavior," (4) "recognizing the impact of staff-resident interactions on the care experience by using cognitive-behavioral principles," and (5) "implementing person-centered care planning based on these principles" (Ballard et al., 2015, p. 254). The social interaction with pleasant activities intervention included a manual based on three evidence-based approaches for social interactions and communication: "the Positive Events Schedule; a social interaction intervention; and the Needs, Environment, Stimulation, and Techniques (NEST) program" with a goal of "1 hour a week of social interactions to increase social interactions by 20 percent" (Ballard et al., 2015, p. 254). The exercise intervention consisted of physical activities that are enjoyable from the NEST program and Seattle protocols and included: walking routinely and dancing, exercise with music, and playing volleyball in a chair where appropriate with a goal of one hour per week (Ballard et al., 2015). The WHELD program resulted in reduced psychotropic medication use by 50%; reduced mortality and neuropsychiatric symptoms for residents who received both social interaction and antipsychotic review interventions; and improvements in neuropsychiatric symptoms among residents who received the exercise intervention (Ballard et al., 2015).

In an experimental study conducted in Taipei, Taiwan, testing the effectiveness of reminiscence therapy on loneliness, depression, and psychological well-being among 92 older adults residing in institutional settings, participants at three months had improved depression, loneliness, and psychological well-being with positive impacts on socialization and residents' sense of accomplishment (Chiang et al., 2010). In a randomized control study comparing the effectiveness of supportive manualized therapy versus problem-solving therapy for 12 individual sessions with 221 noninstitutionalized adults ages 60 and over, adults who received problem-solving therapy had improvements in symptom severity for major depression and executive dysfunction in comparison to those who received supportive manualized psychotherapy (Alexopoulos et al., 2011).

On-Time Falls Prevention (On-Time) is an evidence-based prevention program for older adults residing in skilled nursing settings developed by the Agency for Healthcare Research and Quality to assist with clinical decision making with high-risk residents to prevent four sentinel events: "pressure ulcers, pressure ulcers that are not healing appropriately, avoidable hospitalizations, and falls" (Agency for Healthcare Research and Quality, 2017, p. 1). On-Time provides clinical tools for each of the four sentinel events that includes: (1) "a set of electronic clinical reports that is updated weekly … [that] identify who is experiencing increasing risks and provides easy access to important clinical information that is needed to help clinical staff make timely adjustments to care plans," (2) "functional specifications for EMR vendors to program the reports," (3) "implementation materials to help a multidisciplinary change team integrate the reports into the nursing home's care planning processes," and (4) "training for On-Time facilitators" (Agency for Healthcare Research and Quality, 2017, p. 1).

When working with older adults in nursing home institutions, clinicians adhere to CSWE Gero Competency 1: Demonstrate Ethical and Professional Behavior to ensure that at the micro, mezzo, and macro levels, professional, ethical, and legal standards are followed when engaging diversity and difference in practice (CSWE Gero Competency 2) and when engaging in advocacy to ensure human and civil rights of the older adult socially, economically, and environmentally (CSWE Gero Competency 3) (CalSWEC, 2017). In all phases of practice with older adults in institutional settings, clinicians adhere to CSWE Gero Competency 4 to engage in research- and evidence-informed practice when engaging, assessing, intervening, and evaluating interventions and outcomes (CSWE Gero Competencies 6–9) (CalSWEC, 2017).

Assessing/Monitoring Evidence-based Treatment Outcomes

In skilled nursing facilities, Medication Administration Records (MARS) are used to record all medication prescribed to a resident; psychotropic medications are accompanied by behavior/side effects records to allow clinicians to monitor the effectiveness of psychotropic medications on reducing mood and behavior symptoms. In following CSWE Gero Competency 9: Evaluate Practice With Individuals, Families, Groups, Organizations, and Communities, clinicians working with older adults residing in skilled nursing settings adhere to agency, state, and federal guidelines for practice in such settings and "record, track and monitor their engagement, assessment, and intervention data in practice" (specialized competency behavior 1), uphold self-determination of the older adult and relevant consumers in analyzing outcomes and processes (specialized competency behavior 2), use intervention findings to improve best practices and interdisciplinary and interagency coordination of services and policies (specialized competency behavior 3), and engage older adults and other stakeholders in the evaluation process and share outcomes with them (specialized competency behavior 4) (CalSWEC, 2017, pp. 14–15). To ensure further protection of frail older adults aging in nursing home settings, ethically, a strengths-based approach versus pathology approach is more consistent with social justice, dignity, integrity, and the worth and value of the individual when interpreting processes and outcomes of interventions with vulnerable older adults in nursing home settings. Clinicians also consider community resources appropriate for older adults as well as interagency coordination of services and programs to meet the needs of older adults in long-term care skilled nursing facility institutional settings.

Community Resources/Interagency Coordination

In working with older adults aging in skilled nursing settings, clinicians should seek to become knowledgeable of the range of health, mental health, hospice and palliative care, social and physical health programs, services, and opportunities, as well as the procedures and protocols for referral and access of such services in both institutional settings. For older adults planning for release from a prison system, awareness of re-entry programs for case management to plan for and assist with accessing the specialized care needs for housing, physical, financial, cognitive, mental health, social, and recreational needs are essential to prevent recidivism and homelessness. Clinicians should be aware of the range of the agency and community-based programs and services available to older adults aging in skilled nursing facilities that can be accessed in the setting they live in, out in the community, or both to promote well-being. Clinicians adhere to the standards for advancing human rights and advocating for access to necessary services and information to enable older adults living in institutions to receive necessary social, spiritual, legal/ethical, physical, and psychological services to ensure their well-being, safety, and quality of life (CSWE Competency 3: Advance Human Rights and Social, Economic, and Environmental Justice, specialized practice behaviors 2–4). Clinicians must also recognize and manage potential transference and countertransference issues that may present when engaging, assessing, intervening, and evaluating practice with older adults in skilled nursing facilities.

Transference/Countertransference

In working with older adults aging in long-term care systems, clinicians should be aware of potential transference and countertransference issues that may present in the therapeutic relationship and how to manage them. Clinicians working with older adults in long-term care settings should be aware of potential transference reactions from their older adult clients toward them. For example, the clinician may remind the client of a child or grandchild, he or she may see the visit as demeaning if the clinician is seen as a competitor "with whom they can no longer compete," a frail client "may see the therapist as a rescuer," and a healthy older adult may see the clinician as an authority figure such as an educator or parent and may "sell short his or her own abilities" (Morgan, 2003, pp. 1592–1593). In terms of countertransference, an older adult residing in a long-term care setting may trigger fears within the clinician about their own aging in a long-term care setting or fears related to their own mortality. Countertransference may be triggered by "memories of parent or grandparents;" perceptions that a resistant client is helpless may interfere with the clinician's ability to see "how the patient's aggression and self-absorption pushes away the very help the patient so desperately needs" (Morgan, 2003, p. 1593). Additionally, if the clinician does not understand the vulnerability of a resistant older adult client, "the therapist may become excessively punitive and withdraw the help the patient needs" (Morgan, 2003, p. 1593). Clinicians should be familiar with technological resources to assist older adults residing in skilled nursing facilities and their families. They should also be able to detect and intervene when ethical and legal issues present.

Technological Resources

American Health Care Association: https://www.ahcancal.org/advocacy/Pages/default.aspx

California Advocates for Nursing Home Reform: Nursing home care standards: http://www.canhr.org/factsheets/nh_fs/html/fs_CareStandards.html

Centers for Disease Control: Nursing homes and assisted living (long-term care facilities): https://www.cdc.gov/longtermcare/index.html

Long-Term Care Community Coalition: http://nursinghome411.org/

National Consumer Voice for Quality Long-Term Care: Advocacy toolkit: http://the-consumervoice.org/issues/for-advocates/advocacy-toolkit

National Consumer Voice for Quality Long-Term Care: Long-term care issues and resources: http://theconsumervoice.org/issues/other-issues-and-resources

National Consumer Voice for Quality Long-Term Care: Ombudsman Resource Center: http://theconsumervoice.org/

U.S. Department of Health and Human Services: Long-term care: The basics: https://longtermcare.acl.gov/the-basics/

Legal/Ethical Considerations

In considering ethical issues for older adults in skilled nursing facilities, some of the most commonly experienced ethical issues include: "advance directives, competence and decision-making capacity, decisions about life-sustaining treatment, resident abuse, restraints, psychotropic medications, risk management, participation in research, and ethics committees" (Hayley, Cassel, Snyder, & Rudberg, 1996, p. 249). With high rates of dementia among residents in nursing homes, competency to engage in treatment decisions pertaining to end-of-life decision making is a common ethical dilemma pertaining to issues such as withdrawal and withholding of care, whether a power of attorney is following the wishes of the resident, and care that may be determined as futile by the attending physician. The long-term care ombudsman is the appropriate resident advocate for issues pertaining to abuse or neglect by the older adult resident. The use of physical and chemical restraints requires continual monitoring and interdisciplinary care and coordination to prevent ethical dilemmas from occurring and to ensure safety, protection, well-being, and quality of care. Consider the scenario, for example, of a resident with dementia with a nasal or gastric feeding tube who continues to attempt to pull the NG-tube or G-tube out who is prescribed sedating psychotropic medications and soft wrist restraints to prevent pulling the tubes: What are the resident's wishes? Is the power of attorney or health-care agent following the wishes of the resident? Is the resident at risk for developing pressure sores? In what ways does the resident have access to socialization and stimulation? Clinicians have an ethical obligation to advocate for the least restrictive chemical and physical restraints for reducing mood and behavior symptoms of residents in nursing homes. Clinicians working with older adults in prison or nursing home institutions adhere to CSWE Gero Competency 1: Demonstrate Ethical and Professional Behavior specialized practice behaviors 1–7 to ensure micro-, mezzo-, and macro-practice professional, ethical, and legal standards are followed (CalSWEC, 2017).

Part II. Aging in Prison Settings

Case Study

Mr. Adams, a 72-year-old Caucasian male with a life sentence after being convicted at the age of 40 for killing a security guard and a bystander within a bank during an armed robbery, was diagnosed with stage 4 metastatic lung cancer. Mr. Adams, estranged from his girlfriend and three biological children, had no social support outside of the prison. He sought educational and spiritual resources while in prison. Mr. Adams was referred to the social worker due to symptoms of depression and anxiety. Mr. Adams was also referred to Hospice Care since he was especially interested in pain and symptom management as well as spiritual support from a chaplain. Mr. Adams subsequently signed up for hospice services and reported satisfaction with his decision to the social worker. The prison he was in had a hospice program where other inmates could serve as caregivers for him under the hospice program.

Assessing Context

Prisons. Increasingly, older adults are aging in state and federal prison systems. Between 1995 and 2010, the state and federal prison population of adults ages 65 and older grew by 63% in comparison to the overall prisoner sentencing in prisons of 0.7% (Human Rights Watch, 2012). For that same period, the rates of adults ages 55 and older in state and federal prisons increased by 282% (Human Rights Watch, 2012). Within states between 1993 and 2013, the population of adults ages 55 and older doubled (Carson & Sabol, 2016). The admission of adults ages 55 and older to prison increased 82% between the period of 2003 to 2013, whereas rates declined by 11% and 12% for those ages 40 to 54 and 39 and younger, respectively (Carson & Sabol, 2016). In examining trends of sentencing among inmates ages 18 to 39, 40 to 54, and 55 or older for 1993, 2003, and

2013, inmates ages 55 and older were "sentenced to-and were expected to serve-more time on average than younger inmates" (Carson & Sabol, 2016, p. 21).

Males accounted for 97% of the state prison population in 2013 for adults ages 65 and older, with rates of 61% for non-Hispanic Whites, 23% for African Americans, and 15% for Hispanics (Carson & Sabol, 2016). Among females ages 65 and older, 73% were non-Hispanic White, 18% African American, and 8% Hispanic (Carson & Sabol, 2016). The number of both African American and Hispanics in state prisons increased by 164% and 125%, respectively (Carson & Sabol, 2016). In 2013, among older adults ages 65 and older in state prisons, 31% served life or death sentences (Carson & Sabol, 2016). In 2013, adults ages 55 and older sentenced for violent crimes were higher than adults ages 24 and younger, 25 to 34, 35 to 44, and 45 to 54, reflecting a similar trend for both 1993 and 2003 (Carson & Sabol, 2016). Sources for the growth of the aging state prison population, according to the Department of Justice, include "increased admissions of older persons, longer time spent serving sentences that permit prisoners to age into the older age categories, or a combination of the two" (Carson & Sabol, 2016, p. 12). Rates of new property and public order offenses among adults ages 55 and older increased between 1993 to 2013, from 16.3% in 1993 to 22% for property offenses and 17.4% to 24.3% for public order offenses (i.e., weapons, DUIs, liquor law, commercialized, and other public order offenses) (Carson & Sabol, 2016).

For older adults with life and death sentences, aging in a prison system presents challenges for meeting their biopsychosocial/spiritual needs. Chronic and life-threatening illnesses, cognitive, and functional health changes contribute to needs for assistance with ADLs and IADLs at a skilled nursing or assisted living level (Human Rights Watch, 2012). Some may require hospice care, bathing assistance, assistance with ambulating, getting meals, and medications (Human Rights Watch, 2012). There are 75 prison hospice programs in the United States, six of which are federal, and roughly 3,300 inmates die each year from natural causes of death (National Hospice and Palliative Care Organization, 2017). In 2011, Human Rights Watch (2012) conducted a study to understand aging and human rights in prison systems and conducted site visits and interviews at 20 prisons in nine states with older adult inmates, correctional officers, senior correctional medical personnel, state officials, and aging experts. They identified several challenges in meeting the needs of older adults aging in prison and concluded that many experience human rights violations (Human Rights Watch, 2012). Prison systems mainstream older adults with the general population as long as possible, creating safety concerns for older adults (Human Rights Watch, 2012). As the older adults' functional health changes, challenges for safety present in the environment, such as "top bunk assignment and crowds of quickly moving young inmates oblivious to the slower, more fragile inmates among them" (Human Rights Watch, 2012, p. 46). Incontinence of bowel and bladder places older adult inmates at risk for "social isolation, depression, diminished dependence, and even harassment and physical confrontations from inmates offended when an older adult urinates or defecates in her clothes" (Human Rights Watch, 2012, p. 47). The medical costs for older adults in prison systems are three to eight times higher than other populations, with states paying for expenses and providing prison-based health care due to noncoverage by federal health insurance programs (Human Rights Watch, 2012) such as Medicare and Medicaid that stop upon incarceration. Inmates are entitled to timely health care services required under the Eighth Amendment of the U.S. Constitution (Williams, Stern, Mellow, Safer, & Greifinger, 2012).

In a report prepared by the Office of Legislative Research in 2013, initiatives at state levels to address the growing aging population in prisons vary according to state policy. A summary of initiatives by state follow:

> California law allows the Department of Corrections and Rehabilitation to contract with public or private entities to establish and operate skilled nursing facilities to incarcerate and care for inmates. But, it appears that California has not used this law to date. Instead, the state is building a 1,722-bed prison in Stockton to house medically infirm prisoners, including those with Alzheimer's disease and mental illnesses. California also has a program where convicted murderers serve as aides to other inmates who have dementia.

> Florida has four facilities that house large numbers of elderly prisoners, with varying eligibility criteria. Louisiana's state penitentiary has a hospice for prisoners near the end of their life, as do at least 75 prisons in 40 states. ... Nevada and other states have a wide range of programs for elderly prisoners that address rehabilitation and diseases of the elderly. New York's Unit for the Cognitively Impaired, located in the Fishkill Correctional Facility, primarily serves prisoners with dementia. In Pennsylvania, the Laurel Highlands facility serves sick and elderly inmates. A minimum security facility, it houses nearly 1,400 inmates, approximately 400 of whom are over 50.

> Most older prisoners in Virginia are housed at the Deerfield Correctional Center. In 2009, Virginia compared the costs and benefits of contracting for privately operated assisted living or nursing facilities for geriatric offenders, compared to the state operating such facilities. It found that the center is less costly than caring for these prisoners at private nursing homes in the same area would be.

> To address the needs of prisoners 50 and older, Washington created an assisted-living unit at the Coyote Ridge correctional facility. The unit, which has a capacity of 74 inmates, is inside the fence of a regular prison but is segregated from other units. (McCarthy, 2013, p. 1)

Clinicians working with older adults aging in prison systems can utilize screening tools to inform and supplement their biopsychosocial/spiritual assessments with older adults, informing treatment planning and interventions.

Biopsychosocial/Spiritual Assessment

Following is an application of the Geriatric Biopsychosocial/Spiritual Assessment conducted by Mr. Adam's social worker.

Box 5.2

Geriatric Biopsychosocial/Spiritual Assessment

Basic Demographic: Mr. Adams is a 72-year-old Caucasian male, he speaks English, and he has a high school education

Referral Information: Consult for depression and anxiety

Cultural/Spiritual: Mr. Adams is able to verbalize understanding of his life-threatening illness and treatment for it, he engages in no complementary or alternative medicine practices, and he has no organized religious or spiritual beliefs/values

Social: [Relationships within family, social/diversity groups, and community]

- Mr. Adams worked in the fast food industry; he has no military service record or experience; he has three children from whom he is estranged and who live in separate states from the prison he is institutionalized in
- Mr. Adam's girlfriend and children do not visit him; he has no friends, family, or other cultural/diversity members who visit him

Financial: [Ability to provide basic needs and access health services]

- Basic needs met at the prison for housing, food and shelter, and clothing
- Health insurance: Prison insurance; not eligible for Medicare or Medicaid due to prison institutional setting
- Income sources: None

Environmental: [Personal safety, maintenance of residence, and safety of community]

- Controlled environment in prison setting
- No indicators of abuse or neglect by self or perpetrated by others

Physical: [Individual function and disease morbidity]

- Moderate health literacy; poor self-rated health; no advance directive in place; Mr. Adams has knowledge of his diagnosis and medications and is realistic about

---

his options for comfort vs. cure; he requires bathing, transferring, and toileting assistance; Mr. Adams reports no sexual activity since his incarceration

Mental: [Mental status, depression, anxiety, and substance abuse]

- No indicators of depression or anxiety; Mr. Adams presents with moderate depression and anxiety as revealed by his PHQ-9 and GAD-7 scores
- Suicide risk assessment: Mr. Adams does not endorse suicidal ideations and no history reported
- Homicidal ideations: Ruled out—no history of homicidal ideations
- Mr. Adams does not smoke cigarettes or drink alcohol presently; he reports he drank heavily and smoked one pack of cigarettes per day prior to his confinement in a prison setting

Formulation/Evaluation: Hospice consultation for end-of-life care

Treatment Planning: Social worker and physician in agreement of hospice care for symptom management; social worker to engage Mr. Adams in advance care planning and life review therapy; assistance for Mr. Adams with ADLs and IADLs for desirable social activities

Community Resource Needs: Hospice services

Screening tools in prisons. A round table of 29 experts in correctional facilities, nursing, academic medicine, and civil rights across the United States convened in 2011 to identify health-care policy recommendations and knowledge gaps for serving older adults in prisons (Williams, Stern, Mellow, Safer, & Greifinger, 2012). They recommended cognitive screenings for all adults ages 55 and older and noted that cognitive impairment screening tools such as the Mini-Mental State Examination (MMSE) and Montreal Cognitive Assessment (MoCA) used traditionally with older adults may not be appropriate for older adults in prisons due to "lower educational attainment and lower literacy among prisoners than among the general U.S. population" (Williams, Stern, Mellow, Safer, & Greifinger, 2012, p. 1478). They note that screening tools to assess cognition that incorporate IADLs may also may make it harder to detect mild cognitive impairments as many tasks such as cooking, laundry, and managing finances are either done for the older adult or not relevant due to the settings (Williams, Stern, Mellow, Safer, & Greifinger, 2012). The experts further note that though standardized screening tools for older adults for ADLs are similar to activities performed in the general population, IADL tasks may look different from the general population and include activities such as "the ability to get from one's cell to the dining hall in time for meals, to climb on and off one's assigned bunk, to hear orders from staff, or to get down on the floor for alarms" (Williams, Stern, Mellow, Safer, & Greifinger, 2012, p. 1477).

Comorbid health and mental health conditions of older adults in prison systems require specialized expertise by the clinician in screening, assessment, and treatment. Between 16% and 36% of older adults in prison systems have mental health disorders (Maschi, Viola, & Morgen, 2014). The 53-item Brief Symptom Inventory has been used successfully with adults and older adults in correctional settings to assess psychological symptoms across nine dimensions: "somatization, obsession-compulsion, interpersonal sensitivity, depression, anxiety, hostility, phobic anxiety, paranoid ideation and psychoticism" (Maschi, Viola, & Morgen, 2014, p. 862).

Clinicians assess diversity factors of the client as well to inform problem formulation, treatment planning, and interventions with the older adult and interdisciplinary treatment team.

Diversity–Cultural Competence/Spirituality/LGBT/Sexuality

To date, little is known about the issues related to women aging in prisons; what is known is that older adult females in prison systems report poorer self-rated health in comparison to their male counterparts, and they have higher rates of health-care utilization than males among those with advanced age in prisons (Williams, Stern, Mellow, Safer, & Greifinger, 2012). In addressing culturally diverse prison populations with acute trauma symptoms, the PTSD treatment model has been used among diverse older adults in stages to reduce acute symptoms first, followed by the use of treatment interventions that strengthen coping resources of older adults externally and internally, with an emphasis on social support maintenance (Maschi, Viola, & Morgen, 2014). In engaging diversity in practice (CSWE Competency 2), clinicians adhere to specialized practice behaviors 1–4 to ensure that all care planning and treatments are culturally preferred and valued by the older adult and involve decision makers according to the older adult's preferences (CalSWEC, 2017). Clinicians bring findings from biopsychosocial/spiritual assessments, screening tools, and diversity into interdisciplinary treatment team meetings to inform treatment planning and appropriate interventions with older adults residing in prison systems.

Interdisciplinary Team Roles and Planning

Interdisciplinary team planning and care improves impacts on outcomes for older adults aging in prison settings. In a qualitative study of prison hospice programs across 11 states at 14 prisons, themes from interviews with coordinators emerged reflecting high levels of collaboration evident in five key themes: (1) prison wardens and administrators were supportive of collaborative processes, (2) collaboration with providers outside of the prison was evident, (3) collaboration had a "positive impact on dying prisoners," (4) collaboration also had a "positive impact on prisoner volunteers," and (5) "collaboration through the hospice program had a positive impact on the entre culture of the prison" (Bronstein & Wright, 2007, p. 85). In a separate qualitative study of the Louisiana State Penitentiary (Angola) prison hospice program, one key contributing factor leading to the longevity of the program identified was that of teamwork (Cloyes et al., 2016). The social worker who assessed Mr. Adams collaborated with the physician, together with Mr. Adams, and a request for hospice services was ordered and implemented. Clinicians can incorporate these best practices when formulating treatment plans and best practices for older adults aging in prison systems.

Evidence-based Interventions

Best practices for older adults aging in state and federal prison systems. For older adults who will be released from a state or federal prison system, there is a need for transitional health post-release programs that assist with access to health and medical services (Williams, Stern, Mellow, Safer, & Greifinger, 2012). In a study of 360 older adult males ages 55 to 84 scheduled for release from a California prison, about 80% had one or more chronic illness, 45% had a substance use disorder, 31% had a functional health disability, and 13% had a mental health condition (Williams et al., 2010). The comorbid health and mental health disorders, as well as risk for homelessness, suggest a need for re-entry programs coordinating physical, mental health, and social/housing support services prior to release. A large proportion of re-entry programs to date in the United States focus on male and females younger than age 18 or between ages 18 and 54. In a search for effective re-entry programs for adults ages 55 and older, none were identified with an evidence rating of effective overall (National Institute of Justice, 2016). Among re-entry programs for adults ages 55 and older with promising results (i.e., some outcomes indicating recidivism), 13 of the 14 promising re-entry programs included both corrections and re-entry as well as drugs and substance abuse program services, resulting in lower recidivism across all programs (National Institute of Justice, 2016). One program, the Minnesota Comprehensive Offender Reentry Plan (MCORP), provided case management wrap around services, motivational interviewing, and SMART planning incorporating a needs–risk assessment in planning for release (National Institute of Justice, 2016). Specific case management activities from MCORP focused on the phases of re-entry (i.e., institutional, transitional, and community) with connection of participants to financial, educational, mentorship, faith-based, housing, health, employment, and vocational services (National Institute of Justice, 2016). The MCORP pilot program was a randomized clinical trial of 689 males and females in five counties of Minnesota, which resulted in fewer rearrests, reconvictions, technical violations, and reincarcerations among program participants at a cost savings of $1.8 million (Duwe, 2013).

Interventions to address and treat trauma symptoms of older adults aging in prison systems is equally important. In a study of 677 adults ages 50 and older, 70% indicated they had experienced a traumatic experience in their lifetime (Maschi, Viola, & Morgen, 2014). Specifically, before the age of 16, respondents reported they experienced interpersonal traumas, such as "witnessing family violence (48%), being physically attacked (21%), sexual assault (9%) and foster care or adoption (10 %)" (Maschi, Viola, & Morgen, 2014, p. 862). Other traumas and stressors included: "being diagnosed with a serious physical (41 percent) or mental illness (27%), unexpected death of someone close (60%), forced separation from a child (28%), and being a caregiver of a person with serious illness (28%)" (Maschi, Viola, & Morgen, 2014, p. 862). Interventions that focus on enhancing internal and external coping resources (i.e., physical, emotional, social, spiritual, cognitive) can be beneficial in promoting well-being among older adults aging in prison systems (Maschi, Viola, & Morgen, 2014). Additional recommended interventions include holistic prevention and treatments that emphasize: "empowerment-based and cognitive-based interventions that target negative cognitions, building an internal sense of safety, improving self-esteem, and self-help and advocacy efforts," and yoga and mindfulness interventions to improve regulation of emotions, grief and loss, peer-led support groups, art therapy, exercise, and management of stress (Maschi, Viola, & Morgen, 2014, p. 865).

For older adults receiving hospice services, the Louisiana State Penitentiary (Angola) prison hospice program has a model on par with community-based standards established by the National Hospice and Palliative Care Organization (Evans, Herzog, & Tillman, 2002). The Louisiana State Penitentiary (Angola) prison hospice program prepared this program to respond to the reality that 85% of its more than 5,000 inmates serve life sentences and will die in an institutional prison setting (Evans, Herzog, & Tillman, 2002). In a qualitative study using observation and interviews with hospice volunteers, staff, and correctional officers of the Louisiana State Penitentiary (Angola) prison hospice program, five elements that have led to the success of this program include "patient-centered care, an inmate volunteer model, safety and security, shared values, and teamwork" (Cloyes et al., 2016, p. 390). Clinicians assess and monitor treatment outcomes with older adults in prison systems.

Assessing/Monitoring Evidence-based Treatment Outcomes

In following CSWE Gero Competency 9: Evaluate Practice With Individuals, Families, Groups, Organizations, and Communities, clinicians working with older adults residing in prison settings keep accurate records, track, continually monitor, and evaluate their interventions with older adults in prison systems (specialized competency behavior 1); they ensure client self-determination with this vulnerable population in all analyses (specialized competency behavior 2); and they ethically use findings to improve practices with older adults in prison systems (specialized competency behavior 3) (CalSWEC, 2017, pp. 14–15). To ensure further protection of frail older adults aging in prison settings, ethically, a strengths-based approach versus pathology approach is more consistent with social justice, dignity, integrity, and the worth and value of the individual when interpreting processes and outcomes of interventions with vulnerable older adults in prison and nursing home settings. Clinicians also consider community and interagency coordination when working with older adults aging in prison systems. The social worker provided weekly visits to Mr. Adams to assess his satisfaction with hospice services, and Mr. Adams reported his symptoms were controlled and his psychosocial needs were met—he was able to request that two inmates receive caregiver training and assist him with ADLs through the hospice program at his prison.

Community Resources/Interagency Coordination

In working with older adults aging in prison settings, clinicians should seek to become knowledgeable of the range of health, mental health, hospice and palliative care, social and physical health programs, services, and opportunities, as well as the procedures and protocols for referral and access of such services in both institutional settings. For older adults planning for release from a prison system, awareness of re-entry programs for case management to plan for and assist with accessing the specialized care needs for housing, physical, financial, cognitive, mental health, social, and recreational services to prevent recidivism and homelessness. Clinicians adhere to the standards for advancing human rights and advocating for access to necessary services and information to enable older adults living in institutions to receive necessary, social, spiritual, legal/ethical, physical, and psychological services to ensure their well-being, safety, and quality of life (CSWE Competency 3: Advance Human Rights and Social, Economic, and Environmental Justice, specialized practice behaviors 2–4). Clinicians should be aware of potential transference and countertransference issues that may present in the therapeutic relationship when working with older adults in prison systems.

Transference/Countertransference

In working with older adults aging in prison systems, clinicians should be aware of potential transference and countertransference issues that may present in the therapeutic relationship and how to manage them. Consider some of the trauma experiences and triggers identified by older adults in prison systems and how experiences with clinicians during those events may trigger transference toward the clinician: when they experienced family violence or physical or sexual assault, when they were placed in the foster care or adoption system, when they were diagnosed with a chronic or mental health condition, or when one of their loved ones died. In turn, clinicians must consider their own countertransference reactions if they have experienced or know someone who has experienced any of the trauma experiences identified by an older adult aging in a prison system and work toward managing those countertransference reactions to engage in ethical and professional practice with the client (CSWE Gero Competency 1, specialized practice behaviors 1–7). Clinicians are aware of possible technological resources as well as legal and ethical issues that may present when working with older adults in prison systems.

Technological Resources

American Civil Liberties Union (ACLU): Prisoners' Rights: https://www.aclu.org/issues/prisoners-rights

The Center for Prisoner Health and Human Rights: http://www.prisonerhealth.org/resources-for-prisoners-families-and-advocates/resources-by-state/

Center for Prison Reform: https://centerforprisonreform.org/prison-reform-organizations/

Legal/Ethical Considerations

Older adults released from prison systems are a vulnerable population with comorbid mental health, physical health, cognitive, social, and housing needs. The former bio-psychosocial/spiritual needs put them at risk for homelessness, mortality, emergency room use, and reincarceration (Williams, Stern, Mellow, Safer, & Greifinger, 2012). Clinicians should be aware of re-entry challenges older adults are subject to and provide advocacy for interventions to link older adults to health and other necessary resources or programs before release. Such advocacy includes ethical and legal considerations related to advocacy and treatment for older adults released without transitional services in place and/or with cognitive deficits. Clinicians can be involved in policy efforts to develop national medical criteria for release eligibility, improvements in palliative care (pain and symptom management), and the development of policies outlining appropriate continuums of care for geriatric housing units within prison systems (Williams, Stern, Mellow, Safer, & Greifinger, 2012).

Critical Thinking Activity/Discussion Questions

1. What screenings and treatments for older adults aging in prison systems or being released from prison systems do you think are needed?
   a. What treatments and interventions are typically provided to organizations at your agency, in the local community, or in the state where you work with older adults?
   b. What resources are available?
   c. What legal/ethical issues have occurred that you are aware of, and how were they addressed?
   d. How might you engage in advocacy to address any unmet needs of older adults in prison systems?

Self-Reflection Exercises

1. What screenings and treatments for older adults aging in long-term care settings do you think are needed?
    a. What treatments and interventions are typically provided to organizations at your agency, in the local community, or in the state where you work with older adults in long-term care settings?
    b. What resources are available?
    c. What legal/ethical issues have occurred that you are aware of, and how were they addressed? How should they have been addressed?
    d. How are older adults residing in long-term care settings engaged in decision making in your agency or community? What role can clinicians play in ensuring their participation in decision making?

2. Critically examine your own attitudes and beliefs about aging in prison systems.
    a. What attitudes and beliefs do you have about individuals in prison systems?
    b. From what sources did these attitudes and beliefs develop?
    c. How do those beliefs influence your perception on programs and services for re-entry and aging in prison systems today?
    d. How might those beliefs affect your ability to engage, assess, and intervene with older adults in prison systems or preparing to be released?

3. Critically examine your own attitudes and beliefs about aging in long-term care settings.
    a. What did you learn about long-term care settings growing up?
    b. From what sources did you learn it?
    c. How do those beliefs influence your attitudes about care for older adults in long-term care settings today?
    d. How might those beliefs affect your ability to engage, assess, and intervene with older adults aging in long-term care settings?

References

Agency for Healthcare Research and Quality. (2017). AHRQ's safety program for nursing homes: On-time prevention. Retrieved from https://www.ahrq.gov/professionals/systems/long-term-care/resources/ontime/ontimeovervw.html

Alexopoulos, G. S., Raue, P. J., Kiosses, D. N., Mackin, R. S., Kanellopoulos, D., McCulloch, C., & Areán, P. A. (2011). Problem-solving therapy and supportive therapy in older adults with major depression and executive dysfunction: Effect on disability. *Archives of General Psychiatry, 68*(1), 33–41.

Alzheimer's Association. (2017). 2017 Alzheimer's disease facts and figures. Retrieved from https://www.alz.org/facts/

Ballard, C., Orrell, M., YongZhong, S., Moniz-Cook, E., Stafford, J., Whittaker, R., ... & Woodward-Carlton, B. (2015). Impact of antipsychotic review and nonpharmacological intervention on antipsychotic use, neuropsychiatric symptoms, and mortality in people with dementia living in nursing homes: A factorial cluster-randomized controlled trial by the Well-Being and Health for People With Dementia (WHELD) program. *American Journal of Psychiatry, 173*(3), 252–262.

Bronstein, L. R., & Wright, K. (2007). The impact of prison hospice: Collaboration among social workers and other professionals in a criminal justice setting that promotes care for the dying. *Journal of Social Work in End-of-Life & Palliative Care, 2*(4), 85–102.

CalSWEC. (2017). CalSWEC curriculum competencies for public child welfare, behavioral health, and aging in California. Retrieved from https://calswec.berkeley.edu/sites/default/files/2017_calswec_curriculum_competencies_0.pdf

Carson, E. A., & Sabol, W. J. (2016). Aging of the state prison population, 1993–2013. NCJ 248766. U.S. Department of Justice, Bureau of Justice Statistics. Retrieved from https://www.bjs.gov/content/pub/pdf/aspp9313.pdf

Centers for Medicare and Medicaid Services. (2015). MDS 3.0 for nursing homes and swing bed providers. Retrieved from https://www.cms.gov/Medicare/Quality-Initiatives-Patient-Assessment-Instruments/NursingHomeQualityInits/NHQIMDS30.html

Centers for Medicare and Medicaid Services. (2017). Institutional Long Term Care. Retrieved from https://www.medicaid.gov/medicaid/ltss/institutional/index.html

Chiang, K. J., Chu, H., Chang, H. J., Chung, M. H., Chen, C. H., Chiou, H. Y., & Chou, K. R. (2010). The effects of reminiscence therapy on psychological well-being, depression, and loneliness among the institutionalized aged. *International Journal of Geriatric Psychiatry, 25*(4), 380–388.

Cloyes, K. G., Rosenkranz, S. J., Berry, P. H., Supiano, K. P., Routt, M., Shannon-Dorcy, K., & Llanque, S. M. (2016). Essential elements of an effective prison hospice program. *American Journal of Hospice and Palliative Medicine, 33*(4), 390–402.

Duwe, G. (2013). *An evaluation of the Minnesota Comprehensive Offender Reentry Plan (MCORP) pilot project: Final report.* St Paul, MN: Minnesota Department of Corrections.

Evans, C., Herzog, R., & Tillman, T. (2002). The Louisiana State Penitentiary: Angola prison hospice. *Journal of Palliative Medicine, 5*(4), 553–558.

Grabowski, D. C., Aschbrenner, K. A., Rome, V. F., & Bartels, S. J. (2010). Quality of mental health care for nursing home residents: A literature review. *Medical Care Research and Review : MCRR, 67*(6), 627–656.

Guralnik, J. M., Fried, L. P., & Salive, M. E. (1996). Disability as a public health outcome in the aging population. *Annual Review of Public Health, 17*(1), 25–46.

Harris-Kojetin, L., Sengupta, M., Park-Lee, E., & Valverde, R. (2013). Long-term care services in the United States: 2013 overview. *Vital Health Statistics, 3*(37).

Hayley, D. C., Cassel, C. K., Snyder, L., & Rudberg, M. A. (1996). Ethical and legal issues in nursing home care. *Archives of Internal Medicine, 156*(3), 249–256.

Human Rights Watch. (2012). Old behind bars: The aging prison population in the United States. Retrieved from www.hrw.org/sites/default/files/reports/usprisons0112webwcover_0.pdf

Maschi, T., Viola, D., & Morgen, K. (2014). Unraveling trauma and stress, coping resources, and mental well-being among older adults in prison: Empirical evidence linking theory and practice. *The Gerontologist, 54*(5), 857–867.

McCarthy, K. E. (2013). *State initiatives to address aging prisons* (Office of Legislative Research Report 2013-R-0166). Retrieved from https://www.cga.ct.gov/2013/rpt/2013-R-0166.htm

Morgan, A. C. (2003). Practical geriatrics: psychodynamic psychotherapy with older adults. *Psychiatric services, 54*(12), 1592–1594.

National Center for Health Statistics. (2017). Health, United States, 2016: With chartbook on long-term trends in health. Retrieved from https://www.cdc.gov/nchs/data/hus/hus16.pdf

National Hospice and Palliative Care Organization. (2017). End of life care in corrections: The facts. Retrieved from https://www.nhpco.org/sites/default/files/public/Access/Corrections/Corrections_The_Facts.pdf

National Institute of Justice. (2016). Program profile: Minnesota Comprehensive Offender Reentry Plan (MCORP). Retrieved from https://www.crimesolutions.gov/ProgramDetails.aspx?ID=486

Nazir, A., Unroe, K., Tegeler, M., Khan, B., Azar, J., & Boustani, M. (2013). Systematic review of interdisciplinary interventions in nursing homes. *Journal of the American Medical Directors Association, 14*(7), 456–458.

Williams, B. A., McGuire, J., Lindsay, R. G., Baillargeon, J., Cenzer, I. S., Lee, S. J., & Kushel, M. (2010). Coming home: Health status and homelessness risk of older pre-release prisoners. *Journal of General Internal Medicine, 25*(10), 1038–1044.

Williams, B. A., Stern, M. F., Mellow, J., Safer, M., & Greifinger, R. B. (2012). Aging in correctional custody: Setting a policy agenda for older prisoner health care. *American Journal of Public Health, 102*(8), 1475–1481.

CHAPTER 6

Employing a Strengths-based Approach to Work, Retirement, and Leisure

This chapter identifies strengths-based approaches to address work, retirement, and leisure among older adults and explores key domains to promote both effective clinical practice with older adults and optimal client outcomes.

CSWE Gero Competencies Highlighted

Competency 1: Demonstrate Ethical and Professional Behavior

Specialized Practice Competency Description: Social workers understand the value base of the profession and its ethical standards, as well as relevant laws and regulations that may impact practice at the micro, mezzo, and macro levels. Social workers understand frameworks of ethical decision-making and how to apply principles of critical thinking to those frameworks in practice, research, and policy arenas. Social workers recognize personal values and the distinction between personal and professional values. They also understand how their personal experiences and affective reactions influence their professional judgment and behavior. Social workers understand the profession's history, its mission, and the roles and responsibilities of the profession. Social workers also understand the role of other professions when engaged in inter-professional teams. Social workers recognize the importance of lifelong learning and are committed to continually updating their skills to ensure they are relevant and effective. Social workers also understand emerging forms of technology and the ethical use of technology in social work practice.

Competency Behaviors: (1) Guided by ethical reasoning and self-reflection, demonstrate adherence to ethical frameworks and key laws, policies, and procedures related to aging, and the rights of older adults. (2) Engage in active dialogue with field faculty/

instructors regarding aging field placement agency policies and culture around behavior, appearance, communication, and the use of supervision. (3) Develop and sustain effective collaborative relationships that respect older adults' needs for protection, self-determination, and the provision of services in the least restrictive environment possible with colleagues and community stakeholders, including older adults, their family members, other care providers, and Tribes. (4) Effectively manage professional boundary issues and other challenges arising in the course of aging-related work, particularly ambiguities presented by home visits, personal loss, trauma, and other highly involved and potentially emotionally triggering aspects of the work. (5) Develop and sustain relationships with members of interdisciplinary and integrated health care teams, including social workers, primary care providers, hospital staff, home health care providers, psychiatrists, psychologists, substance use disorder treatment staff, Tribal service providers, and others, that reflect clear understanding of their roles in providing care to older adults. (6) Demonstrate both knowledge of the history and evolution of social work practice related to aging and older adults in the United States and California, and a commitment to lifelong learning around this practice. (7) Follow all ethical guidelines and legal mandates in the use of technology in order to maintain the confidentiality of all personal, behavioral health, and health-related information. (CalSWEC, 2017, pp. 1–2)

Competency 2: Engage Diversity and Difference in Practice

Specialized Practice Competency Description: Social workers understand how diversity and difference characterize and shape the human experience and are critical to the formation of identity. The dimensions of diversity are understood as the intersectionality of multiple factors, including, but not limited to, age, class, color, culture, disability and ability, ethnicity, gender, gender identity and expression, immigration status, marital status, political ideology, race, religion/spirituality, sex, sexual orientation, and Tribal sovereign status. Social workers understand that, as a consequence of difference, a person's life experiences may include oppression, poverty, marginalization, and alienation as well as privilege, power, and acclaim. Social workers also understand the forms and mechanisms of oppression and discrimination and recognize the extent to which a culture's structures and values, including social, economic, political, and cultural exclusions, may oppress, marginalize, alienate, or create privilege and power.

Competency Behaviors: (1) Engage in critical analysis of the interpersonal, community, and social structural causes and effects of disproportionality, disparities, and inequities in the incidence and trajectory of aging-related care needs, housing, transportation, and resource access among older adults,

their families, and their communities. (2) Evidence respectful awareness and understanding of the impact of being a member of a marginalized group on aging experiences, and accurately identify differences in access to and quality of available services for members of different communities and populations. (3) Demonstrate knowledge of diverse cultural norms and traditional methods of providing care to older adults, as well as an applied understanding of how these realities affect work with older adults from diverse backgrounds, their families, and their communities. (4) Develop and use practice methods that acknowledge, respect, and address how individual and cultural values, norms, and differences impact the various systems with which older adults interact, including, but not limited to, families, communities, primary care systems, mental and behavioral health care systems, and integrated care systems. (CalSWEC, 2017, pp. 3–4)

Competency 3: Advance Human Rights and Social, Economic, and Environmental Justice

Specialized Practice Competency Description: Social workers understand that every person regardless of position in society has fundamental human rights such as freedom, safety, privacy, an adequate standard of living, health care, and education. Social workers understand the global interconnections of oppression and human rights violations, and are knowledgeable about theories of human need and social justice and strategies to promote social and economic justice and human rights. Social workers understand strategies designed to eliminate oppressive structural barriers to ensure that social goods, rights, and responsibilities are distributed equitably and that civil, political, environmental, economic, social, and cultural human rights are protected.

Competency Behaviors: (1) Clearly articulate the systematic effects of discrimination, oppression, and stigma on the needs and experiences of older adults and on the quality and delivery of services available to them, and identify and advocate for policy changes needed to address these issues. (2) Advocate for changes in policies and programs that reflect a social justice practice framework for facilitating access and providing services to older adults, their families, and care providers, especially among underserved groups and communities. (3) Demonstrate the ability to work effectively in cross-disciplinary collaboration to develop and provide interventions that explicitly address the specific needs of diverse older adults, their families, and care providers. (4) Integrate into all aspects of policy and practice sensitivity to the reality that fundamental rights, including freedom and privacy, may be compromised for older adults engaged in care, and the goal that services should be provided in the least restrictive environment possible. (CalSWEC, 2017, pp. 4–5)

Competency 4: Engage in Practice-informed Research and Research-informed Practice

Specialized Practice Competency Description: Social workers understand quantitative and qualitative research methods and their respective roles in advancing a science of social work and in evaluating their practice. Social workers know the principles of logic, scientific inquiry, and culturally informed and ethical approaches to building knowledge. Social workers understand that evidence that informs practice derives from multidisciplinary sources and multiple ways of knowing. They also understand the processes for translating research findings into effective practice.

Competency Behaviors: (1) Demonstrate the ability to understand, interpret, and evaluate the benefits and limitations of various evidence-based and evidence-informed treatment models as they influence practice with older adults. (2) Engage in critical analysis of research findings, practice models, and practice wisdom as they inform aging related practice, including how research practices have historically failed to address the needs and realities of exploited and/or disadvantaged communities, and how cross-cultural research practices can be used to enhance equity. (3) Clearly communicate research findings, conclusions, and implications, as well as their applications to aging practice, across a variety of professional interactions with consumers, families, and multidisciplinary service providers. (4) Apply research findings to aging-related practice with individuals, families, and communities and to the development of professional knowledge about the needs, experiences, and well-being of older adults. (CalSWEC, 2017, pp. 5–6)

Competency 6: Engage With Individuals, Families, Groups, Organizations, and Communities

Specialized Practice Competency Description: Social workers understand that engagement is an ongoing component of the dynamic and interactive process of social work practice with, and on behalf of, diverse individuals, families, groups, organizations, and communities. Social workers value the importance of human relationships. Social workers understand theories of human behavior and the social environment, and critically evaluate and apply this knowledge to facilitate engagement with clients and constituencies, including individuals, families, groups, organizations, and communities. Social workers understand strategies to engage diverse clients and constituencies to advance practice effectiveness. Social workers understand how their personal experiences and affective reactions may impact their ability to effectively engage with diverse clients and constituencies. Social workers value principles of relationship-building and inter-professional collaboration to facilitate engagement with clients, constituencies, and other professionals as appropriate.

Competency Behaviors: (1) Appropriately engage and activate older adults, their families, and other care providers in the development and coordination of care plans that reflect relevant theoretical models and balance older adults' needs for care with respect for autonomy and independence. (2) Effectively utilize interpersonal skills to engage older adults, their families, and other care providers in culturally responsive, consumer-driven, and trauma-informed integrated care that addresses mutually agreed upon service goals and balances needs for care, protection, autonomy, and independence. (3) Establish effective and appropriate communication, coordination, and advocacy planning with other care providers and interdisciplinary care teams as needed to address mutually agreed upon service goals. Recognizing the complex nature of service engagement, ensure that communications with consumers and their families regarding service goals are both sensitive and transparent. (4) Manage affective responses and exercise good judgment around engaging with resistance, trauma responses, and other potentially triggering situations with older adults, their families, and other care providers. (CalSWEC, 2017, pp. 9–10)

Competency 7: Assess Individuals, Families, Groups, Organizations, and Communities

Specialized Practice Competency Description: Practitioners in aging utilize ecological-systems theory, a strengths-based and person/family-centered framework to conduct assessments that value the resilience of diverse older adults, families, and caregivers. They select appropriate assessment tools, methods and technology, and evaluate, adapt, and modify them, as needed, to enhance their validity in working with diverse, vulnerable and at-risk groups. The comprehensive biopsychosocial assessment takes into account the multiple factors of physical, mental and social well-being needed for treatment planning for older adults and their families. They develop skills in interprofessional assessment and communication with key constituencies to choose the most effective practice strategies. Gero social workers understand how their own experiences and affective reactions about aging, quality of life, loss and grief may affect their assessment and resultant decision-making.

Competency Behaviors: (1) Conduct assessments that incorporate a strengths-based perspective, person/family-centered focus, and resilience while recognizing aging related risk, (2) Develop, select, and adapt assessment methods and tools that optimize practice with older adults, their families, caregivers, and communities, and (3) Use and integrate multiple domains and sources of assessment information and communicate with other professionals to inform a comprehensive plan for intervention. (Council for Social Work Education, 2017, pp. 89–90)

Competency 8: Intervene With Individuals, Families, Groups, Organizations, and Communities

Specialized Practice Competency Description: Social workers understand that intervention is an ongoing component of the dynamic and interactive process of social work practice with, and on behalf of, diverse individuals, families, groups, organizations, and communities. Social workers are knowledgeable about evidence-informed interventions to achieve the goals of clients and constituencies, including individuals, families, groups, organizations, and communities. Social workers understand theories of human behavior and the social environment, and critically evaluate and apply this knowledge to effectively intervene with clients and constituencies. Social workers understand methods of identifying, analyzing, and implementing evidence-informed interventions to achieve client and constituency goals. Social workers value the importance of interprofessional teamwork and communication in interventions, recognizing that beneficial outcomes may require interdisciplinary, inter-professional, and inter-organizational collaboration.

Competency Behaviors: (1) In partnership with older adults and their families, develop appropriate intervention plans that reflect respect for autonomy and independence, as well as contemporary theories and models for interventions with older adults. Plans should:

+ Reflect cultural humility and acknowledgement of individualized needs;
+ Incorporate consumer and family strengths;
+ Utilize community resources and natural supports;
+ Incorporate multidisciplinary team supports and interventions;
+ Include non-pharmacological interventions; and
+ Demonstrate knowledge of poly-pharmacy needs and issues specific to older adults.

(2) Apply the principles of teaming, engagement, inquiry, advocacy, and facilitation within interdisciplinary teams and care coordination to the work of supporting older adults, family members, and other care providers to accomplish intervention goals and satisfy advanced care planning needs. (3) Effectively implement evidence-based interventions in the context of providing emergency response, triage, brief treatment, and longer-term care, and in the course of addressing a range of issues presented in primary care, specialty care, community agency, inpatient, and palliative care settings. Interventions should be guided by respect for older adults' autonomy and independence and should

include components such as psychoeducation, problem-solving treatment skills, symptom tracking, medication therapies, follow-up, and planning for evolving care needs. (4) Effectively plan for interventions in ways that incorporate thoughtfully executed transitions during time-limited internships, recognizing that consumer needs for support may continue beyond these time periods. (CalSWEC, 2017, pp. 12–14)

Competency 9: Evaluate Practice With Individuals, Families, Groups, Organizations, and Communities

Specialized Practice Competency Description: Social workers understand that evaluation is an ongoing component of the dynamic and interactive process of social work practice with, and on behalf of, diverse individuals, families, groups, organizations and communities. Social workers recognize the importance of evaluating processes and outcomes to advance practice, policy, and service delivery effectiveness. Social workers understand theories of human behavior and the social environment, and critically evaluate and apply this knowledge in evaluating outcomes. Social workers understand qualitative and quantitative methods for evaluating outcomes and practice effectiveness.

Competency Behaviors: (1) Record, track, and monitor consumer engagement, assessment, and intervention data in practice with older adults, their families, and other care providers accurately and according to field education agency policies and guidelines. (2) Conduct accurate process and outcome analysis of engagement, assessment, and intervention data in practice with older adults, their families, and other care providers that incorporates consumer perspectives and reflects respect for older adults' autonomy and independence. (3) Use findings to evaluate intervention effectiveness, develop recommendations for adapting service plans and approaches as needed, improve interdisciplinary team coordination and care integration, and help agency and community policies better support older adults, their families, and their formal and informal care systems. (4) Share both the purposes of such data collection and the overall results of data analysis with older adults, their families, and communities whenever possible, with the goal of engaging them more meaningfully in the evaluation process. (CalSWEC, 2017, pp. 14–15)

Learning Objectives

1. Learners will understand the context for work, retirement, and leisure in the United States.

2. Learners will identify screening tools to inform treatment planning with older adults in areas of work, retirement, and leisure.

3. Learners will identify appropriate evidence-based interventions for use with adults aging in areas of work, retirement, and leisure.

4. Learners will understand the importance of referring older adult clients and their family members to appropriate technological and community resources and when to assist with coordination.

5. Learners will identify sources of transference and countertransference when workers with older adults to aging in areas of work, retirement, and leisure.

6. Learners will understand how to use a strengths-based approach when engaging, assessing, intervening, and evaluating practice with older adults in areas of work, retirement, and leisure.

Case Study

Mrs. Walsh is a 70-year-old non-Hispanic White, married female who retired from accounting at the age of 65 and re-entered the workforce at the age of 67 to supplement her household income, provide mentorship to younger generations, and allow more income for leisure activities she and her spouse participate in. Mrs. Walsh began working part-time, 20 hours per week, at a local elementary school as a tutor for math students. Mrs. Walsh's husband, a retired accountant from a large firm, retired completely and engaged in several leisure and recreational activities each day, including attending the local fitness club, golfing, and participating in a senior art club at the local senior center. Mrs. Walsh was diagnosed with stage 1 breast cancer in April, had a lumpectomy, and was sent home with home health while she went to outpatient radiation and chemotherapy treatments. She had a good prognosis, with expectations of being able to return back to work after the summer break and resume all leisure activities at the end of treatments, eight weeks after surgery. Mrs. Walsh has five children and 13 grandchildren, all of whom live within 15 minutes from her home. She and her spouse have lived in the same home for 50 years; they have several friends in the community, participate in faith and community programs, and see their family weekly. Mrs. Walsh, her spouse, and their family take annual vacations together during the summer for two weeks.

Assessing Context

Work

In 2014, the U.S. Bureau of Labor Statistics reported the labor force participation rate, or those actively seeking work or working, for adults ages 55 at 40% (Toosey & Torpey, 2017). The U.S. Bureau of Labor Statistics projects that changes among age groups in the entire labor force (ages 16 and older) will be the greatest among older adults ages 65 to 74 and 75 and older (Toosey & Torpey, 2017). Between 2014 and 2024, projected percent increases for the labor force for older adults ages 65 to 74 and 75 and older are 55% and 86%, respectively, while the entire labor force projected percent increase is 5% (Toosey & Torpey, 2017). Explanations for these trends include: (1) in 2014, baby boomers ages 60 to 78 were projected to work even once, qualifying them for Social Security, (2) older adults are experiencing a longer life expectancy and health in comparison to previous cohorts of older adults, (3) their education increases their ability to remain in the labor force, and (4) "changes to Social Security benefits and employee retirement plans, along with the need to save more for retirement, create incentives to keep working" (Toosey & Torpey, 2017, p. 4).

In 2016, the U.S. Bureau of Labor Statistics reported that a higher proportion of the labor force that held jobs in professional, management, and similar positions were among adults ages 55 and older (Toosey & Torpey, 2017). For each of the following occupations, adults ages 55 and older comprised one-third of all positions: "archivists, curators, and museum technicians; bus drivers; clergy; furniture finishers; jewelers and precious stone and metal workers; legislators; medical transcriptionists; proofreaders and copy markers; property, real estate, and community association managers; tax preparers; and travel agents" (Toosey & Torpey, 2017, p. 6). In 2016, self-employment percentages for each age group of the labor force steadily increased with age, with older adults ages 65 and older having the highest percentage of self-employment than all age groups in the labor force. For example, approximate self-employment percentages increased as follows: adults ages 16 to 24 (2%), 25 to 34 (4%), 35 to 44 (6%), 45 to 54 (7%), 55 to 64 (9%), and 65 and older (17%) (Toosey & Torpey, 2017).

In a study using data from the current population survey, a monthly study conducted by the U.S. Census Bureau and U.S. Bureau of Labor Statistics, occupational trends were identified among a sample of 68,000 adults and employment trends of adults ages 45 to 64 in comparison to older adults ages 65 and older in 2014 (Pryor, 2017). The share of food service and preparation jobs was higher among older adults—25.3%—in comparison to 3.1% of adults ages 45 to 64 (Pryor, 2017). For older adult workers ages 65 and older, women had higher ratios of employment in comparison to men in part-time occupations, with low educational attainment (high school degree or less) and lower strenuous activities involved (Pryor, 2017). For example, among older adults ages 65 and older employed in food service occupations, the gender ratio was 1.58 (males were assigned a 1, females a 2) (Pryor, 2017). The civilian occupations included in the current population study include: management; business and financial operations; computer and mathematical science; architecture and engineering; life, physical, and social sciences; community and social services; legal; education, training, and library; arts, design, entertainment, sports, and media; health-care support; protective service; food preparation and serving-related; building, grounds cleaning, and maintenance; personal care and services; sales and related; office and administrative support; farming, fishing, and forestry; production; and transportation and material moving (Pryor, 2017).

In comparison to adults ages 45 to 65, in 2014, older adults ages 65 and older had nearly two to four times or higher percentage rates for all civilian occupations with the exception of installation, maintenance, and repair—5.7% and 1.8%, respectively (Pryor,

2017). The greatest percentage differences between part-time jobs held by adults ages 45 to 64 and older adults ages 65 and older (i.e., with those ages 65 and older having greater percentages) were seen in management (6.3% vs. 31.9%), business and financial operations (10.2% vs. 34.7%), computer and mathematical sciences (4.5% vs. 16.2%), architecture and engineering (2.4% vs. 30.9%), life physical and social sciences (7.8% vs. 30.3%), legal (8% vs. 22%), health-care practitioner and technical (16.8% and 39.3%), protective service (10.2% vs. 46.3%), sales and related (16.7% vs. 38.4%), production (7.1% vs. 29.7%), and transportation and material moving (12.1% vs. 42%) (Pryor, 2017). Similar trends were observed in comparisons of older adults ages 65 and older self-employed in all civilian occupations in comparison to adults ages 45 to 64, though the percentage differences were much smaller. Lastly, in the study, older adult workers with the lowest and highest educational attainment levels increased in comparison to adults ages 45 to 64 (Pryor, 2017). Two untested explanations for this trend include: (1) for older adults with the lowest educational attainment (i.e., high school or less), "we can speculate that they were the lowest paid and chose to work because they needed the money," and (2) for older adults with the highest educational attainment (i.e., master's and doctorate or professional degrees), "they chose to continue working because they enjoyed their jobs and were highly paid" (Pryor, 2017, p.5).

Older adults who have been in the labor force for more than 40 to 60 years may have held a position that was demanding with long hours and frequent travel. Or for older adults who worked in minimum-wage, no-benefits positions, work provides a means to supplement Social Security, Supplemental Security Income (SSI), and subsided programs. Using a strengths-based approach, work can provide a means for older adults to stay connected socially, psychologically, physically, and spiritually with people, community, faith and diversity, and society. Work can provide an opportunity for growth and ease transitions from full time to part time. Work later in life can provide older adults with the opportunity for reinvention when presented with options to seek a job they wanted to try earlier in life but could not because of pressing demands and responsibilities. Work can provide a means for resolving Erikson's psychosocial crisis—integrity versus despair—for the older adult who experiences regret after working in a career where there was low satisfaction and entering a new job with higher satisfaction. These transitions, changes, and adjustments between careers in older adults allow opportunity for older adults to discover who they are in the context of self, family, community, and society. In this way, work can provide a means for an older adult to find meaning and purpose in life through reinvestment in self, attainment and pursuit of satisfaction, and achievement of integrity, all as defined by the older adult. Clinicians recognize the importance of work and its impact on identity and roles throughout the life course as well as the importance of relinquishing such roles when planning for and transitioning into retirement.

Retirement

In the United States, the number of people who turn 65 each day is 9,000 (Johnson & Smith, 2016). Among the 48 million older adults ages 65 and older in the United States in 2015, roughly 80% were retired (Johnson & Smith, 2016). For the month of June in 2017, 42 million retired workers received a total of $57 billion in Social Security benefits, with an average monthly benefit amount of $1,369 (Social Security Administration, 2017). Social Security benefits are, for many older adults, the primary source of income or a major source of income (Social Security Administration, 2017). Roughly nine out of 10 older adults receive Social Security benefits (Social Security Administration, 2017). As an income source, Social Security comprises, on average, 33% of older adults' incomes (Social Security Administration, 2017). The percentage of older adults who rely on Social Security changes with marital status: (1) "50% of married couples and 71% of unmarried persons receive 50% or more of their income from Social Security" and (2) "23% of married couples and about 43% of unmarried persons rely on Social Security for 90% or more of their income" (Social Security Administration, 2017, p. 1). In 2017, the ratio of workers in the labor force paying into Social Security was 2.8 workers per Social Security beneficiary (Social Security Administration, 2017). That rate will lower to 2.2 workers per beneficiary when the older adult population increases from 49 million in 2017 to 79 million in 2035 (Social Security Administration, 2017).

Income sources for older adults are classified in five categories: earnings, Social Security, assets, pensions, and other (Mather, Jacobson, & Pollard, 2015). In comparing higher-income to lower-income households headed by adults ages 65 and older, Social Security comprises 21% of household income for high-income households in comparison to 76% for low-income households (Mather, Jacobson, & Pollard, 2015). Higher-income and middle-income households headed by adults ages 65 and older also have higher percentages of income for pensions, assets, and earnings. Income for pensions among households headed by adults 65 and older were 5% for lower-income households in comparison to 17% and 23% of middle-income and higher-income households, respectively (Mather, Jacobson, & Pollard, 2015). Asset income generated from savings, rental property, and investments was two to six times higher for higher-income households (12%) in comparison to middle-income (4%) and lower-income (2%) households (Mather, Jacobson, & Pollard, 2015). Racial and ethnic minority older adults have fewer pensions, assets, and earnings to draw from as income sources and are, therefore, more reliant upon Social Security as an income source than non-Hispanic Whites (Mather, Jacobson, & Pollard, 2015). For example, in 2013, non-Hispanic Whites that depended solely on Social Security as an income source was 13% in comparison to approximately 20% of Latino and African American older adults (Mather, Jacobson, & Pollard, 2015).

Work remains a key leg of retirement stability for many older adults in the United States. In a health and retirement study conducted by the Bureau of Labor Statistics, bridge jobs, or "jobs that follow full-time career employment and precede complete withdrawal from the labor force," have been a common practice for older adults leaving and re-entering the workforce since the late 1960s (Cahill, Giandrea, & Quinn, 2011, p. 34). Roughly 15% of older adults that retire return to the labor force, and those who do are generally younger, with a "defined-contribution pension plan," and in "better health" (Cahill, Giandrea, & Quinn, 2011, p. 34). The percentage of employer-based defined-contribution plans decreased from 62% in 1983 to 20% in 2004, and the percentage of retirees with both a defined-benefit and defined-contribution pension plan dropped from 26% to 17% during the same period (Cahill, Giandrea, & Quinn, 2011, p. 34). With defined-contribution plans, "workers decide how much to contribute and how to invest their funds," which comes with some risk (Cahill, Giandrea, & Quinn, 2011, p. 35). Re-entry into the workforce after retirement often occurs under one of two circumstances: (1) "first, it can be planned, as a way to move out of career employment gradually by taking a break from paid work for a certain length of time before moving into another job" or (2) workers may reduce consumption expenses based on retirement income, which means re-entry can then "serve as a backup plan in the event that an individual's standard of living in retirement falls short of expectations" (Cahill, Giandrea, & Quinn, 2011, p. 35).

Although to date, older adults in retirement have employer-provided pensions in one form or another, the provision of employer-provided pensions has been reduced during the past two decades due to economic recessions, the Great Recession, corporate downsizing, and takeovers. Among workers ages 18 to 64 in the labor force in 2017, 55 million report they "do not have a way to save for retirement out of their financial security," 90% "wish they had more money saved for their retirement years," 74% report they "are anxious about not having enough money to live comfortably during their retirement," 71% "are somewhat, not too, or not at all confident they will have the means to retire someday," and 93% "think it is important the next generation learn how to manage money and save for retirement at an early age" (Nelson, 2017, p. 1).

An often overlooked contextual factor to consider when working with older adults is the impact of retirement on the relationship of a couple. Research suggests that the meanings and context of retirement differ by gender (Szinovacz & Davey, 2004). Retirement, a transition in the life course, impacts the well-being of older adult couples. Research suggests that when older adult couples do not have joint retirement (i.e., both leaving the workforce at the same time) with the female working longer, there is an association of lower well-being for male spouses, specifically higher-reported depressive symptoms (Szinovacz & Davey, 2004). The former finding has been explained by some as being related to a "timing pattern that undermines the husband's status as the main provider and undermines his power in the marital relationship" (Szinovacz & Davey, 2004, p. 234). Clinicians should also be aware of and assess the extent to which preretirement marital quality may impact postretirement adjustments and general well-being. Research also suggests that those couples with greater marital satisfaction prior to retirement report higher satisfaction postretirement than couples who do not (Kupperbusch, Levenson, & Ebling, 2003). However, emotional qualities of the preretirement marital relationship appear to have a greater impact on postretirement happiness for couples who experienced marital conflict prior to retirement more so for males than females (Kupperbusch, Levenson, & Ebling, 2003). In a study examining the physiological, emotional, and behavioral aspects of marital conflict preretirement with postretirement satisfaction, it was discovered that males who are "physiologically relaxed and affectively positive during marital interaction were happier in their" postretirement than males who were not and emotional aspects of the relationship were not statistically significant predictors for retirement satisfaction for females (Kupperbusch, Levenson, & Ebling, 2003, p. 335). Marital interaction was defined as discussions with a spouse or friends about conflicts in the marriage (Kupperbusch, Levenson, & Ebling, 2003). Post-hoc analyses revealed, however, that the satisfaction by males in retirement was attributed more so to physiological arousal experienced when communicating with their spouse rather than positive emotions. Additionally, for both males and females, health and income were associated with greater retirement satisfaction (Kupperbusch, Levenson, & Ebling, 2003). The former findings have implications for clinicians to assess and examine the marital relationship preretirement and postretirement to provide interventions to address any challenges in the relationship related to the transition to retirement. Clinicians must also consider the context of leisure and factors that contribute to an older adult's ability to engage in desirable leisure activities.

Leisure

As proposed by activity theory, participation in activities promotes well-being among older adults that enhances a sense of purpose or meaning and relationship maintenance (Szanton et al., 2015). In a study conducted in Israel with 383 retired older adults, the association between leisure activities (i.e., behavioral aspects), benefits (i.e., psychological aspects), and life satisfaction were examined after retirement (Nimrod, 2007). A positive association between psychological well-being and activity was found supporting activity theory during retirement (Nimrod, 2007). Among older adults, activity has been positively associated with health, yet little is known to date about the types of activities older adults prefer to participate in (Szanton et al., 2015). Three of the most important factors that mediate the likelihood of an older adult engaging in desirable activities are: (1) "agency/capability of the older adult to choose the activity," (2) "degree of satisfaction/socialization derived from the activity," and (3) "purpose/meaning of the activity for the older adult" (Szanton et al., 2015, p. 131). Using data from the National Health and Aging Trends Study, a sample of 8,245 community-dwelling older adults' activity preferences were examined by living arrangement, age, race, self-rated health, and age cohort (Szanton et al., 2015). More than 25% of older adults ages 65 to 69 and 70 to 74 identified a physical activity as being their favorite (26.5% and 26.3%, respectively), whereas preference for a physical activity as favorite decreased with age (i.e., 21% for ages 75 to 79, 15.7% for ages 80 to 84, 7.6% for ages 85 to 89, and 2.9% for ages 90 and older) (Szanton et al., 2015). Nonphysical activities were identified as a favorite more among older adults ages 80 to 84 (21.4%) and 70 to 74 (21.3%) in comparison to older adults ages 65 to 69 (19.2%), 75 to 79 (21%), 85 to 89 (11.1%), and 90 and older (6%) (Szanton et al., 2015). Among older adults who identified a physical activity as their favorite type of activity, across all age cohorts, more females identified a physical activity as their favorite than males (i.e., 52% vs. 48%) (Szanton et al., 2015). Among older adults who identified a nonphysical activity as their favorite, 66.8% of females identified a nonphysical activity as their favorite activity in comparison to 33.2% of males.

When examining activity preferences by race, 70.7% of non-Hispanic Whites identified a physical activity as a favorite activity in comparison to 20.6% of African Americans, 5% of Hispanics, and 3.8% of other races (Szanton et al., 2015). The same pattern followed for preferred nonphysical activity as being the favorite activity by race. Nonphysical activities were preferred as a favorite activity by 75.5% of non-Hispanic Whites in comparison to 18% of African Americans, 4.3% of Hispanics, and 2.2% of other races (Szanton et al., 2015). Older adults who live with others prefer a physical activity as a favorite activity (71.7%) in comparison to older adults who live alone (28.3%) (Szanton et al., 2015). Among older adults who identify a nonphysical activity as their favorite activity, more older adults who live with others prefer a nonphysical activity (65.4%) in comparison to those who live alone (34.6%) (Szanton et al., 2015). When considering self-rated health, older adults who report very good (32.1%), good (31.2%), and excellent (17.8%) health list a physical activity as a favorite activity in comparison to older adults with fair or poor self-rated health (Szanton et al., 2015). A nonphysical activity was listed as a favorite activity by a larger proportion of older adults with good (34.4%), very good (26.2%), or fair (21.8%) self-rated health in comparison to older adults with excellent (9.9%) or poor (7.7%) self-rated health (Szanton et al., 2015).

A higher proportion of older adults with income levels of $10,000 to $20,000 (18.3%), $20,000 to $30,000 (15.4%), $30,000 to $40,000 (13.5%), and $100,000 or more (10.9%) reported a physical activity as their favorite activity in comparison to older adults with income levels of $10,000 or less (8.6%), $40,000 to $50,000 (9.1%), $50,000 to $60,000 (8%), and $60,000 to $100,000 (5.4% or less) (Szanton et al., 2015). Similar percentages were observed among older adults who prefer nonphysical activities as their favorite activity across all income categories. Nonphysical activities were the favorite for older adults with income levels of $10,000 to $20,000 (23.6%), $20,000 to $30,000 (16.7%), $30,000 to $40,000 (12.7%), less than $10,000 (10.2%), and $40,000 to $50,000 (9.2%), whereas 7.6% or fewer of older adults with income levels of $50,000 or higher preferred a nonphysical activity as their favorite activity (Szanton et al., 2015).

Among all older adults, 14% ranked walking or jogging as their favorite activity, 12.64% ranked outdoor maintenance as their favorite activity, 8.91% ranked playing sports as their favorite activity, and 8.73% and 6.77% of older adults ranked other physical activity and other outdoor activity, respectively, as their favorite activity (Szanton et al., 2015). For nonphysical activities, 8.81% of older adults ranked reading as their favorite activity; 5.50% ranked arts, crafts, and hobbies as their favorite activity; 4.04% ranked puzzles/games not on a computer as their favorite activity; 3.95% ranked socializing in person as their favorite activity; and 2.85% ranked watching TV/movies as their favorite activity (Szanton et al., 2015). Travel for leisure was ranked as a favorite activity by 1.81% of older adults, followed by household chores (1.5%), other shopping (1.23%), going out to eat (1.2%), volunteering (1.09%), food/drink preparation (1.08%), other religious activities (0.99%), attending religious activities (0.9%), gambling at a casino (0.55%), and physical care to others (0.5%) (Szanton et al., 2015). This national sample of adults ages 65 and older dispelled the stereotype some hold that older adults are inactive; rather, when asked their favorite activities they have been able to participate in the past 30 days, they preferred "to walk, jog, garden, or play sports more than they like to watch TV, attend religious services, or travel" (Szanton et al., 2015, p. 134).

Participation in physical activities outside of the home by older adults is influenced by environmental and social factors. Research to date suggests that environmental and neighborhood factors such as crime and violence in a neighborhood, uneven sidewalks, or poor lighting or aesthetics impact older adults' participation in physical activities. In a meta-analysis of 31 qualitative studies conducted in five countries (i.e., North America, Europe, Oceania, South America, and Asia) in urban, suburban, and rural settings examining the association between environment and activity among older adults, five themes and subthemes associated emerged (Moran et al., 2014). The first theme, "pedestrian infrastructure," had two subthemes: (1) sidewalks, and (2) having bike lanes to separate pedestrians (Moran et al., 2014, p. 4). The second theme, "safety," had two subthemes: (1) "crime-related safety" (i.e., where "fear of crime was higher in the absence of street lighting, in areas that were not well-kept" or where there were "vacant houses, overgrown lots and vandalism" and (2) "traffic-related safety" (i.e., "unclear indication of pedestrian crossing, long crossing distances across multiple lanes and inadequate signal times") (Moran et al., 2014, pp. 6-7).

The third theme, "access to facilities," had three subthemes: (1) "access to exercise opportunities" (i.e., small supply of recreation centers for older adults, "having existing facilities located to far from home, and the high costs to use the facilities"), (2) "access to daily destinations" (i.e., being able to walk to places such as stores, post offices, senior centers, or libraries and having public transportation available), and (3) "access to rest areas" (i.e., "benches and public washrooms") (Moran et al., 2014, pp. 7–8). The fourth theme, "aesthetics," had two subthemes: (1) "buildings and streetscapes" and (2) "natural scenery" (Moran et al., 2014, pp. 7–8). For the first subtheme (i.e., "buildings and streetscapes"), older adults liked "streets inhabited by socially responsible residents who took care of their homes and gardens," the presence of "historical buildings and attractive landscapes," and nature; and in "neglected areas," older adults were discouraged to walk and engage in physical activity (Moran et al., 2014, p. 8). The second subtheme (i.e., "natural scenery") included older adults' preferences for forms or bodies of water and trees (Moran et al., 2014, p. 8). The fifth theme, "environmental conditions," had two subthemes: (1) "weather" and (2) "environmental quality" (Moran et al., 2014, p. 8). For the first subtheme, "weather," older adults preferred "warm weather in the spring" and "disliked cold temperatures, wind, ice, snow, rain and early darkness;" they also indicated a barrier to walking and physical activity was high temperatures (Moran et al., 2014, p. 8). For the second subtheme, "environmental quality," older adults reported that they prefer environments that are "quiet and peaceful and provide fresh air" and that they dislike environments with "high levels of traffic exhaust fumes and noise" (Moran et al., 2014, p. 8).

When assessing leisure activity preferences and options with older adults, clinicians must consider also the context by which leisure activities are also influenced by income and wealth disparities. According to a report from McKernan, Ratcliffe, Steuerle, and Zhang from the Urban Institute, "policymakers often focus on income and overlook wealth;" they note that "the racial wealth gap is three times larger than the racial income gap" and that "such great wealth disparities help explain why many middle-income blacks and Hispanics haven't seen much improvement in their relative economic status and, in fact, are at greater risk of sliding backwards" (2013, p. 1). What is wealth? Wealth has to do with assets, such as cars, homes, or assets that can be used as collateral for loans that are accumulated across the life course (McKernan, Ratcliffe, Steuerle, & Zhang, 2013) and/or through inheritance. The inequality of wealth across races is well documented; in fact, in "2010, whites on average had six times the wealth of blacks and Hispanics," meaning that "for every $6.00 whites had in wealth, blacks and Hispanics had $1.00," which reflected an "average wealth of $632,000 versus $103,000)" (McKernan, Ratcliffe, Steuerle, & Zhang, 2013, p. 2). The disparities in income, on the other hand, tend to be lower. For example, in "2010, the average income for whites was twice that of blacks and Hispanics," meaning for an annual income, it was "$89,000 versus $46,000" or, stated in earned dollar amounts, "for every $2.00 whites earned, blacks and Hispanics earned $1.00" (McKernan, Ratcliffe, Steuerle, & Zhang, 2013, p. 2). Recommended solutions to wealth inequality that clinicians can provide microadvocacy for include legislative advocacy for "reforming policies like the mortgage interest tax deduction so it benefits all families, and helping families enroll in automatic savings vehicles, will help improve wealth inequality and promote saving opportunities for all Americans" (McKernan, Ratcliffe, Steuerle, & Zhang, 2013, p. 5). Work, retirement, and leisure factors are all important domains for clinicians to assess when conducting a biopsychosocial/spiritual assessment.

Biopsychosocial/Spiritual Assessment

Clinicians can utilize several screening tools to inform treatment planning and interventions with older adults transitioning to retirement and engaging or contemplating leisure opportunities.

Following is an application of the Geriatric Biopsychosocial/Spiritual Assessment for the case study presented at the beginning of this chapter:

Box 6.1

Geriatric Biopsychosocial/Spiritual Assessment

Basic Demographic: Mrs. Walsh, a 70-year-old, English-speaking non-Hispanic White, married female who has an associate degree in accounting

Referral Information: Physician, nurse, and physical therapist requested social work evaluation for psychosocial support and community resources

Cultural/Spiritual: Client accepts her illness and diagnosis as being part of "God's will in my life;" no cultural or spiritual perspectives noted by client on understanding of disease and illness; no use of complementary and alternative medicine

Social: [Relationships within family, social/diversity groups, and community]

- Personal and family history: Client worked as an accountant until age 65 and re-entered work at age 67 at a local elementary school for 20 hours per week; she and her spouse have five children and 13 grandchildren, friends in the community, and faith organizations
- Client maintains current relationships and contact with family, friends, social/diversity groups, and community groups; no caregiver stress noted

Financial: [Ability to provide basic needs and access health services]

- Client has the ability to provide basic needs for housing, food, shelter, and clothing
- Health insurance: Current primary and secondary insurance provide essential benefits; there is adequate coverage with no gaps in coverage; and client reports co-pays and any out-of-network fees are manageable and medications are covered with no high co-pays
- Income sources: Social Security, pension, savings, investments, and employment

Environmental: [Personal safety, maintenance of residence, and safety of community]

- Current social context/environmental: Client lives in a suburban neighborhood close to stores, recreational activities, faith, health, and community services
- Neighborhood safety: Low crime, street lighting, and paved roads and sidewalks with curb cuts
- Home safety: Client has working smoke and carbon monoxide detectors and fire extinguisher; lighting is adequate; no slip rugs; shower and toilet are accessible; there are no elevators or ramps to access the home and two small steps to front porch with handrail
- Access to guns: No guns or access to guns
- No indicators of abuse or neglect by self or perpetrated by others

Physical: [Individual function and disease morbidity]

- Health literacy is adequate, self-rated health is good, client does not have an advance directive or will, and client is knowledge on diagnosis and medications (and is adherent); functional health—she ambulates independently and performs all ADLs but needs assistance with IADLs while undergoing outpatient radiation and chemotherapy; client reports "good" sexual health with spouse prior to current illness she is treated for and plans to resume sexual activity after treatments

Mental: [Mental status, depression, anxiety, and substance abuse]

- Standardized screening instruments: Client is alert and oriented; no indicators of depression, anxiety, or cognitive deficits
- Suicide risk assessment: Low—client does not endorse suicidal ideations and has no attempted history or history of suicidal ideations
- Homicidal ideations: Ruled out—client does not endorse suicidal ideations
- No substance use or alcohol use reported by client

Formulation/Evaluation: Psychosocial support to process diagnosis and develop plans for rehabilitation and return back to work; client is coping well overall and has support from family, faith, and community groups; client can benefit from advance directive and legal services for will/trust/estate planning

Treatment Planning: In consultation with physician and physical therapist, evaluation and one visit from social work, as well as assistance with advance directive at next visit

Community Resource Needs: American Cancer Society for psychoeducation and support groups; legal referrals for living will/trust and estate planning; national and local volunteer organizations if patient decides to not return back to work

Screening Tools

The Stanford Brief Activity Survey (SBAS) has been validated for use with older adults to assess physical activity levels as well as psychological factors (Taylor-Piliae et al., 2010). In the study, 1,017 male and female older adults ages 60 to 69 enrolled in the Kaiser Permanente Atherosclerotic Disease Vascular Function and Genetic Epidemiology (ADVANCE) study were sent a self-administered questionnaire completed at baseline and after two years containing the SBAS (Taylor-Piliae et al., 2010). The SBAS measures physical activity intensity and the amount an individual engages in daily physical activity (Taylor-Piliae et al., 2006). Both of the items in the SBAS—"on-the-job activity" and "leisure-time activity"—assess different types of activities categorized in five levels: "inactive, light, moderate, hard, and very-hard intensities" (Taylor-Piliae et al., 2010, pp. 3–4). As part of the ADVANCE study, seven psychological health factors were measured at baseline and after two years for perceived stress using the Perceived Stress Scale, anxiety using Spielberger's "State-Trait Anxiety Inventory (STAI)", depression "using the Center for Epidemiological Studies Depression Scale (CES-D) short form," and anger "using Spielberger's (Trait) Anger Expression Inventory (STAXI)" (Taylor-Piliae et al., 2010, p. 4). Trait anger refers to the tendency of an adult's perceptions of a variety of situations as being frustrating or bothersome and the subsequent behavior responses demonstrative of anger (Taylor-Piliae et al., 2010). Another psychological health factor, "cynical distrust," or the "negative view towards others in society," was measured with the Cynical Distrust Scale (Taylor-Piliae et al., 2010, p. 4).

The last psychological health factor in the study, physical and mental well-being, was measured with the "Medical Outcomes Study 12-item Short Form (SF-12)" (Taylor-Piliae et al., 2010, p. 4). Statistically significant relationships were found between physical exercise and psychological health factors. A key finding of the study was that "regular physical exercise is associated with lower levels of negative emotions (e.g., stress, anxiety, and depression)" and higher levels of well-being (e.g., physical and mental health) (Taylor-Piliae et al., 2010, p. 7). A significant finding was that with increasing levels of physical activity among older adults, there were step-wise decreases in depression, anxiety, cynical distrust, well-being, and stress psychological health factors (Taylor-Piliae et al., 2010).

The Retirement Confidence Survey (RCS) measures attitudes and behavior patterns of 1,000 adults ages 25 and older in a representative national sample (Employee Benefit Research Institute, 2018b). The RCS has been conducted annually since 1996 (Employee Benefit Research Institute, 2018b). Similarly, the Annual Transamerica Retirement Survey, conducted annually, has multiple questions that assess current attitudes and perceptions about retirement for adults of all ages (Transamerica Center for Retirement Studies, 2017a). The Annual Transamerica Retirement Survey complies the data using demographics including age cohorts (i.e., baby boomers, millennials, Generation X) and gender (Transamerica Center for Retirement Studies, 2017a). The survey questions and results from national samples can be used to assess the older adult client's attitudes and perceptions about retirement factors, which can inform clinical interventions.

As part of best practices to help employers prepare for the aging workforce, the American Association of Retired Persons (AARP) developed a workforce assessment tool for companies to: (1) "assess how retiring workers will affect their organizations," (2) "address skill shortage challenges due to staff attrition," (3) "create a work environment that attracts qualified workers of all ages, " (4) "manage a multi-generational workforce," and (5) "build an employer brand that attracts and retains top talent" (Tishman, Van Looy, & Bruyere, 2012, p. 7). The assessment tools allow employers to do a comprehensive workplace assessment and use the results to make informed decisions and take actions to recruit, engage in, and retain qualified diverse older adults (Tishman, Van Looy, & Bruyere, 2012).

Clinicians also assess diversity factors as part of the biopsychosocial/spiritual assessment to inform treatment planning and interventions.

Diversity–Cultural Competence/Spirituality/LGBT/Sexuality

With the expansion of Social Security benefits, the poverty rate for older adults decreased from 30% to 10% between 1966 and 2015 (Mather, Jacobson, & Pollard, 2015). However, economic disparities exist for older women and minority subgroups of older adults (Mather, Jacobson, & Pollard, 2015). The percentage of poor older adult females in comparison to males ages 65 and older in 2014 was 12% and 7%, respectively (Mather, Jacobson, & Pollard, 2015). The disparity is amplified among older adults ages 75 and older as 15% of older adult females were poor in 2014 in comparison to 8% of males (Mather, Jacobson, & Pollard, 2015). Among all older adults ages 65 and older in 2014, the poverty rates were higher for minority populations in comparison to non-Hispanic Whites. In 2014, among older adults ages 65 and older, 19% of African Americans and 18% of Latinos lived in poverty in comparison to 8% of non-Hispanic Whites (Mather, Jacobson, & Pollard, 2015).

In the 17th Annual Transamerica Retirement Survey, key influences of ethnicity on readiness for retirement were examined (Transamerica Center for Retirement Studies, 2017b). The 25-minute online survey of 4,161 workers revealed the following ethnic disparity pertaining to retirement: "Hispanic and African American workers are less likely to be saving for retirement and to have emergency savings in the event of a major financial setback, compared to White and Asian workers" (Transamerica Center for Retirement Studies, 2017b, p. 8). In the study, the percentages of workers across ethnicities that reported they expect to have a lifestyle in retirement that was comfortable were 65% among African Americans, 63% for both Hispanics and Asians, and 61% for non-Hispanic Whites (Transamerica Center for Retirement Studies, 2017b). Yet among adults in the labor force ages 18 to 64, African American, Asian American, and Latino adults were more likely to "believe that future generations will be better off" than they are in comparison to non-Hispanic Whites (Nelson, 2017, p. 1).

Clinicians working with older adults that are in the labor force full or part time, in retirement or preparing to retire, and are planning or engaging in leisure activities employ a strengths-based perspective, allowing the inherent strengths, perceptions, and varied lived experiences of the older adult to emerge in order to establish a nonjudgmental therapeutic space and set the context for strengths-based and evidence-informed interventions. Clinicians adhere to the CSWE Gero Competency 2: Engage Diversity and Difference in practice to ensure that all specialized practice behaviors 1–4 are incorporated when engaging, assessing, intervening, evaluating, and advocating for diverse older adults. Clinicians should seek training to become competent in retirement-, leisure-, and work-related areas to work effectively with diverse older adults on work, retirement, and leisure issues in a variety of settings.

Clinicians must also keep in mind when working with older adults surrounding retirement that the definition, rituals, preferences, and practices of retirement vary across cultures. The conceptualization of retirement in Western industrialized nations, for example, is traditionally seen as a transition involving preparing for a time when one leaves the workforce to engage in leisure activities or pursue other meaningful activities such as grandparenting or volunteering. Initially, retirement in the United States was socially constructed within the context of pension plans; today, many older adults do not have jobs that provide pensions. The timing of retirement in the life course varies across cultures—for example, "for the Fulani it is the last child's marriage, for the Hopi it is decrements in physical capability, and for the Americans and Burmese it is the attainment of a certain chronological age;" in addition, "the social implications of the change vary as well: among the Fulani persons are deemed socially dead at old age, in America a second life begins at 65 and among the Thai old age initiates final preparation for the transition to another life course" (Luborsky & LeBlanc, 2003, p. 14). Clinicians inform interdisciplinary treatment planning with findings from contextual, biopsychosocial/ spiritual, and diversity assessments and considerations.

Interdisciplinary Team Roles and Planning

Clinicians working with older adults on work, retirement, and leisure issues work collaboratively with other disciplines on the interdisciplinary team and seek consultation from and engage in collaborative treatment planning to address presenting work, retirement, and leisure issues of the older adult client. For example, the clinician communicates and coordinates care and treatment with the physical and occupational therapist for an older adult who sustained a temporary injury, such as a tear in the rotator cuff, so that they can resume meaningful work or retirement, leisure, and physical activities and understand the timeframe of rehabilitation to resume activities. Consistent with CSWE Gero Competency 1: Demonstrate Ethical and Professional Behavior, clinicians should engage in the following competency behavior 5 to ensure they have the relationships established to communicate with and understand the roles of all members of the interdisciplinary team in caring for the older adult (CalSWEC, 2017). Clinicians working with older adults transitioning from full- to part-time work, work to retirement, or considering options for leisure activity that promote well-being follow CSWE Gero Competency 6: Engage With Individuals, Families, Groups, Organizations, and Communities, competency behaviors 1–4; CSWE Gero Competency 7: Assess Individuals, Families, Groups, Organizations, and Communities, competency behavior 3; and Competency 8: Intervene With Individuals, Families, Groups, Organizations, and Communities to ensure multiple providers' perspectives and assessments are incorporated into care planning and treatment (CalSWEC, 2017). When engaging in treatment planning with the interdisciplinary team and older adult, clinicians are aware of evidence-based and best practices for retirement and leisure.

Evidence-based Interventions

Best Practices for Work

To date, evidence-based clinical trials to examine efficacious interventions for prevention of early retirement among older adults in the United States have not been conducted, yet several studies support prevention of early retirement that focus on "return-to-work after prolonged sick leave, risk/health factors for maintained work ability, and case studies" (Kilbom, 1999, p. 291). In a study that sought to understand whether involvement of the workplace is more effective than interventions that do not involve the workplace for workers with long-term health issues (i.e., back pain leading to sick leave) seeking to return to work, nine clinical trials conducted in Europe and Canada discovered that "interventions involving employees, health practitioners and employers working together, to implement work modifications for the absentee, were more consistently effective than other interventions" as was "early intervention" (Carroll, Rick, Pilgrim, Cameron, & Hillage, 2010, p. 607). The presence of chronic conditions among workers at Dow Chemical Company was attributed to being the "most important determinant of the reported levels of work impairment and absence after adjusting for other factors" as impairment on the job was estimated to be between 17.8% to 36.4% with a loss of productive work hours between one and six hours per month at a cost of nearly 11% of all labor costs (Collins et al., 2005, p. 547). Interventions to assist older adults with managing chronic conditions is clearly critical to ensure they are able to remain in the labor force if they choose to.

In a comprehensive study that sought to understand how best to prepare the workforce for adults and older adults with disabilities, literature was reviewed in academia and public and private sectors, national experts were interviewed with expertise in employment strategies to prepare for an aging workforce, and employers in both the private and public sectors were interviewed (Tishman, Van Looy, & Bruyere, 2012). Workplace accommodations are not only required to comply with the Americans with Disabilities Act (ADA) of 1990, but they are also helpful to retain older adults in the labor force (Tishman, Van Looy, & Bruyere, 2012). Yet many older adults in the labor force do not request accommodations they are entitled to because of perceptions of disabilities as being a natural part of aging; this same perception by employers deters them from providing accommodations and places them in violation of the ADA (Tishman, Van Looy, & Bruyere, 2012). Interdisciplinary teams (i.e., geriatricians, occupational therapists, clinicians, and physical therapists) and interagency collaborations with employers and older workers can help in providing psychoeducation about aging, disability policies, and ways to make the work environment more accessible for an older adult to ensure they remain in the labor force if they choose to.

Modifications for accommodation may include ramps; phones that are customized for hearing or visual needs; tables and desks that adjust to allow wheelchair access; organizing equipment, files, and shelves so they are reachable; computer systems for visual needs and ergonomic chairs, keyboards, and computer mouse; the use of pictures, checklists, or other aids for those with cognitive needs; and environments that do not have clutter to avoid workplace injuries (Ford, 2017). Comprehensive prevention strategies can also aid in the retention of older adults in the labor force through: (1) "ergonomic design to prevent injury/disability," (2) "job analysis examining specific functions that may result in increased injury," (3) "assistive technology devises to increase, maintain, or improve the functional capacity of a worker," (4) "job accommodations involving changes to the work site or work process," (5) "training initiatives to upgrade and maintain skills," and (6) "wellness and integrated health promotions such as smoking cessation, exercise, and weight management" (Tishman, Van Looy, & Bruyere, 2012, p. 9). Another best practice recommended from the study on preparing for an aging labor force includes training, specifically to attract and retain older workers—organizations can use a targeted approach to train older adults tailored to their needs and should ensure that critical skills of older workers are passed on to younger workers and reinforced in older workers—by offering opportunities for skill development and new challenges for older adults to support their career goals using tailoring and train-and-use techniques and by including training in new recruitment to ensure older workers have the knowledge and skills needed to perform the functions of their job (Tishman, Van Looy, & Bruyere, 2012).

Flexibility, in many forms, is yet another best practice recommended to prepare for the aging workforce and retain older workers, especially for older adults who prefer part-time work and are re-entering the labor force after retiring from the traditional 40-hour work week. The Sloan Center on Aging and Work recommends the following aspects of flexibility as best practices for retaining older adults in the workforce: (1) "work hour flexibility (e.g., reduced hours, job sharing, phased retirement, part-year);" (2) "work schedule flexibility (e.g., flex schedule, annualized hours, compressed work week);" (3) "career flexibility (e.g., on/off ramps that include leaves, reduced responsibilities, job change/occupation shift, and phased retirement;" (4) "flexibility of place (e.g., remote work, work from more than a single location);" (5) "flexibility in the employment relationship (e.g., project work, consultant, temporary work);" and (6) "benefit flexibility (e.g., cafeteria plan, benefits during retirement, etc.)" (Tishman, Van Looy, & Bruyere, 2012, pp. 11–12). Clinicians also are aware of best practices for retirement with older adults.

Best Practices for Retirement

The RCS measures six domains with survey questions that fall under each domain: "retirement confidence, changing expectations about retirement, preparing for retirement in America, age comparisons among workers, gender and marital status comparisons among workers, and attitudes about current Social Security and Medicare benefit levels" (Employee Benefit Research Institute, 2018a, p. 1). Clinicians can use questions from these different domains to process their older adult clients' perceptions about retirement and experiences with retirement on a variety of factors. For example, in the 2017 survey for the *retirement confidence* domain, the following question was used for older adult retirees and those in the labor force. The question asks retirees and workers: "Thinking about your current financial situation, how would you describe your level of debt, a major problem, a minor problem or not a problem?" (Employee Benefit Research Institute, 2017a, p. 4). In 2017, debt was not considered to be a problem for 64% of retirees compared to 40% of workers; it was considered a minor problem for 27% of retirees and 41% of workers; and it was considered a major problem among 9% of retirees and 18% of workers (Employee Benefit Research Institute, 2017a). Clinicians can use the survey results to provide psychoeducation on the national representative sample responses in comparison to the clients; this can validate and normalize older adults with similar responses and, in turn, be used to ensure motivation for it entails preparation for retirement and expectations about retirement. Clinicians can use questions to engage in discussions and assess perceptions of their older adult clients about future or current retirement. Clinicians can ask working older adults the following question, for example, from the *expectations about retirement* domain to discuss income source needs for retirement: "Do you expect the following will be/is a major source of income, a minor source of income, or not a source of income in your (and your spouse's) retirement?" from the following sources: "Social Security, employer-sponsored retirement savings plan, employment, individual retirement account or IRA, other personal savings and investment, employer-provided traditional pension or cash balance plan" (Employee Benefit Research Institute, 2017b, p. 3).

Assisting an older adult client to explore volunteerism opportunities and interests can be yet another best practice in working with older adult retirees. Older adults fill important community service needs through volunteerism. The National Association of Area Agencies on Aging highlighted five effective senior volunteer programs that filled important community needs. All programs were funded by the Administration on Community Living; the programs engage older adults and seek to enrich their experiences with the community (Aging Network Volunteer Resource Center, 2016). Three of the five programs are part of the Retired and Senior Volunteer Programs (RSVP) that provide more than 46 million hours of service through volunteerism of 208,000 older adults: the Community Education/Research program, the Vet to Vet program, and the Friendly Caller Program (Aging Network Volunteer Resource Center, 2016). The other two programs, the Bus Buddies program and the Wisconsin Advocacy Team, are sponsored by local Area Agencies on Aging or Office for the Aging (Aging Network Volunteer Resource Center, 2016). Clinicians must also be informed on what the current best practices for leisure with older adults are to inform treatment planning and interventions.

Best Practices for Leisure

Occupational therapists have been successful in improving social participation and leisure activity participation of older adults with low vision. In a systematic review of 13 effective interventions by occupational therapists that sought to improve maintenance, restoration, and performance on both social participation and leisure activities of older adults with impaired vision, among the effective interventions of "using a problem-solving approach, delivering a combination of services, providing skills training, and making home visits and environmental adaptations," the most effective intervention evidence was found to be use of a "problem-solving approach" (Berger, McAteer, Schreier, & Kaldenberg, 2013, p. 303). In a meta-analysis of 43 studies with more than 33,000 older adults, best practices for increasing the physical activity of older adults include: "self-monitoring, intense contact between activity professionals and participants, center-based exercise" that also "focus exclusively on physical behavior and recommend moderate activity, probably walking," as well as "exercise prescription and behavior modification" (Conn, Isaramalai, Banks-Wallace, Ulbrich, & Cochran, 2003, p. 39). An evidence-based program emphasizing older adult behavior changes as well as physical activity is the Fit and Strong! program developed in Chicago at the University of Illinois Center for Research on Health and Aging, which "includes flexibility exercises, aerobic conditioning, strength training, and an educational component on lifestyle change and arthritis disease management" three times per week for eight weeks and also includes education and problem-solving to increase fitness levels of older adults (Belza & PRC-HAN Physical Activity Conference

Planning Workgroup, 2007, p. 7). Clinicians assess and monitor work, retirement, and leisure interventions with older adults.

Assessing/Monitoring Evidence-based Treatment Outcomes

Clinicians working with older adults on issues related to work, retirement, and leisure monitor treatment outcomes. The clinicians monitoring and evaluating practices should be consistent with CSWE Gero Competency 9: Evaluate Practice With Individuals, Families, Groups, Organizations, and Communities, specialized practice behaviors 1–4 (CalSWEC, 2017, pp. 14–15). When working with older adults, families, and collaborators with other providers, employers, or agencies on work-, retirement-, and leisure-related goals and needs, clinicians can monitor and record data in all stages of treatment (i.e., engagement, assessment, and interventions) to ensure that the specific goals and actions required to meet them are implemented and effective in helping older adult clients achieve their goals (specialized practice behavior 1). This type of monitoring and tracking and checking in with the client allows for reflections and dialogues between the clinician and client on whether actions, strategies, or new activities and goals need to be formulated. In all analyses of data and outcomes, clinicians make sure that the client's perspective is incorporated and is reflective of both self-determination and independence of the client (specialized practice behavior 2). Clinicians use the data to improve service delivery between agencies and providers, improve interdisciplinary communication and coordination with other agencies, inform new policy development that incorporates the perspectives of older adults, and improves the coordination of services to ensure that work, retirement, and leisure activity preferences and processes are coordinated (specialized practice behavior 3). Lastly, clinicians disseminate the findings of their analyses and evaluation of treatment to address work, retirement, and leisure interventions to older adults and family and care providers of their choice and relevant providers and agencies to improve the process of evaluation and make it more meaningful (specialized practice behavior 4). Clinicians also are informed of myriad community-based resources to support retirement transitions and options for engaging in leisure activities; when appropriate, they provide interagency referral, communication, and collaboration to ensure desired services are accessed.

Community Resources/Interagency Coordination

An important aspect of treatment and interventions with older adults involves referrals to community-based services and coordination of services with agencies to ensure that older adult clients' work, retirement, and leisure needs and goals are met. This may include referrals to and coordination of services between the client and transportation, legal, informational, recreational, exercise and fitness, vocational counseling, financial/retirement planning, employers and human resources, health and mental health providers, rehabilitation services, recreational therapy, occupational therapy, agencies that make disability modifications to work environments, and community and recreational centers. Clinicians should be knowledgeable about and have the skills to provide access to timely resources and coordinated services consistent with CSWE Gero Competency 8: Intervene With Individuals, Families, Groups, Organizations, and Communities, specialized practice behaviors 1–4 (CalSWEC, 2017, pp. 12–14). Clinicians are aware of and manage both transference and countertransference issues as they present when working with older adults on retirement transitions and leisure options.

Transference/Countertransference

When working with older adults on work, retirement, and leisure activity needs to manage potential transference and countertransference issues, clinicians follow the specialized practice behaviors 1–6 from the CSWE Gero Competency 1: Demonstrate Ethical and Professional Behavior (CalSWEC, 2017). Clinicians may have their own expectations and preferences surrounding work, the age they seek to retire, and how to prepare for retirement, which can be a source of countertransference. Another source of countertransference may include the clinician's own preferences and ideas on how best to spend retirement as well as what types of leisure activities individuals who are retired and/or still working should or should not engage in. Older adult clients may experience transference toward the clinician if they perceive the clinician endorses stereotypes about aging, work, retirement, and leisure activities. Clinicians consider both technological resources to supplement their interventions with older adults with retirement transitions and leisure; they also consider any potential legal or ethical issues that may present and how to respond to and manage them.

Technological Resources

American Association of Retired Persons (AARP): https://www.aarp.org

Corporation for National and Community Service: RSVP program for people ages 55 and older: https://www.nationalservice.gov/programs/senior-corps/senior-corps-programs/rsvp

Employee Benefit Research Institute: https://www.ebri.org/surveys/rcs/

National Association of Area Agencies on Aging: https://www.n4a.org/

National Association of Area Agencies on Aging: Aging and Disability Resource Centers: https://www.n4a.org/adrcs

National Association of Area Agencies on Aging: Volunteerism: https://www.n4a.org/volunteerism

United States Bureau of Labor Statistics: https://www.bls.gov/

United States Department of Labor: Older workers: https://www.dol.gov/odep/topics/OlderWorkers.htm

United States Department of Labor: Senior Community Service Employment Program: https://www.doleta.gov/Seniors/

Legal/Ethical Considerations

CSWE Gero Competency 1: Demonstrate Ethical and Professional Behavior, specialized practice behaviors 1, 3, 4, 5, and 7 should be adhered to to ensure both ethical and professional practices with older adults presenting with work, retirement, and leisure issues and needs (CalSWEC, 2017, pp. 1–2). Clinicians follow all procedures, policies, and laws to work ethically with older adults presenting with work, retirement, and leisure issues and needs and follow confidentiality and privacy laws to protect health and behavioral health information (specialized practice behaviors 1 and 7). Clinicians advocate and build collaborative relationships with older adults, their families, and interdisciplinary providers and agencies to ensure that the older adult's self-determination and safety is respected and the role of providers is understood in all interventions and services pertaining to work, retirement, and leisure, reflective of the standard of the least restricted environment (specialized practice behaviors 3 and 5). Clinicians are aware of professional boundaries and manage any that may emerge between the clinician and client while working on work, retirement, and leisure needs and issues (specialized practice behavior 4).

Critical Thinking Activity/Discussion Questions

1. What screenings and treatments for older adults presenting with work, retirement, and leisure issues and needs do you think are needed?
    a. What treatments and interventions are typically provided to organizations at your agency, in the local community, or in the state where you work with older adults?
    b. What resources are available?
    c. What legal/ethical issues have occurred that you are aware of, and how were they addressed?
    d. How might you engage in advocacy to address any unmet needs or issues of older adults presenting with work, retirement, and leisure issues and needs?

2. How are older adults served by your agency presented with work, retirement, and leisure issues and needs engaged in decision making in your agency or community?
    a. What role can clinicians play in ensuring their participation in decision making?

Self-Reflection Exercises

1. Critically examine your own attitudes and beliefs about work among older adults.
    a. What attitudes and beliefs do you have about work among older adults?
    b. From what sources did these attitudes and beliefs develop?
    c. How do those beliefs influence your perception on programs and services to meet/address work needs and issues among older adults?
    d. How might those beliefs affect your ability to engage, assess, and intervene with older adults presenting with work issues or needs?

2. Critically examine your own attitudes and beliefs about retirement among older adults.
    a. What attitudes and beliefs do you have about retirement among older adults?
    b. From what sources did these attitudes and beliefs develop?
    c. How do those beliefs influence your perception on programs and services to meet/address retirement needs and issues among older adults?
    d. How might those beliefs affect your ability to engage, assess, and intervene with older adults presenting with retirement issues or needs?

3. Critically examine your own attitudes and beliefs about leisure activities among older adults.
    a. What attitudes and beliefs do you have about leisure activities among older adults?
    b. From what sources did these attitudes and beliefs develop?
    c. How do those beliefs influence your perception on programs and services to meet/address leisure activity needs and issues among older adults?
    d. How might those beliefs affect your ability to engage, assess, and intervene with older adults presenting with leisure activity issues or needs?

References

Aging Network Volunteer Resource Center. (2016). Volunteers making a difference in the Lives of Older Adults. Retrieved from https://www.n4a.org/Files/volunteer%20resource%20website/VolunteerCaseStudies_11May2017v2.pdf

Belza, B., & PRC-HAN Physical Activity Conference Planning Workgroup. (2007). *Moving ahead: Strategies and tools to plan, conduct, and maintain effective community-based physical activity programs for older adults.* Atlanta, GA: Centers for Disease Control and Prevention.

Berger, S., McAteer, J., Schreier, K., & Kaldenberg, J. (2013). Occupational therapy interventions to improve leisure and social participation for older adults with low vision: A systematic review. *American Journal of Occupational Therapy, 67*(3), 303–311.

Cahill, K. E., Giandrea, M. D., & Quinn, J. F. (2011). Reentering the labor force after retirement. U.S. Bureau of Labor Statistics. *Monthly Labor Review.*

CalSWEC. (2017). CalSWEC curriculum competencies for public child welfare, behavioral health, and aging in California. Retrieved from https://calswec.berkeley.edu/sites/default/files/2017_calswec_curriculum_competencies_0.pdf

Carroll, C., Rick, J., Pilgrim, H., Cameron, J., & Hillage, J. (2010). Workplace involvement improves return to work rates among employees with back pain on long-term sick leave: A systematic review of the effectiveness and cost-effectiveness of interventions. *Disability and Rehabilitation*, 32(8), 607–621.

Collins, J. J., Baase, C. M., Sharda, C. E., Ozminkowski, R. J., Nicholson, S., Billotti, G. M., ... & Berger, M. L. (2005). The assessment of chronic health conditions on work performance, absence, and total economic impact for employers. *Journal of Occupational and Environmental Medicine*, 47(6), 547–557.

Conn, V. S., Isaramalai, S. A., Banks-Wallace, J., Ulbrich, S., & Cochran, J. (2003). Evidence-based interventions to increase physical activity among older adults. *Activities, Adaptation & Aging*, 27(2), 39–52.

Employee Benefit Research Institute. (2017a). 2017 RCS fact sheet #1: Retirement confidence. Retrieved from https://www.ebri.org/pdf/surveys/rcs/2017/RCS_17.FS-1_Conf.Final.pdf

Employee Benefit Research Institute. (2017b). 2017 RCS fact sheet #2: Expectations about retirement. Retrieved from https://www.ebri.org/pdf/surveys/rcs/2017/RCS_17.FS-2_Expects.Final.pdf

Employee Benefit Research Institute. (2018a). 2017 Retirement Confidence Survey: 2017 results. Retrieved from www.ebri.org/surveys/rcs/2017/

Employee Benefit Research Institute. (2018b). Retirement Confidence Survey (RCS). Retrieved from www.ebri.org/surveys/rcs

Ford, J. (2017). How to prepare your workplace for disabled employees. Intuit QuickBooks Resource Center. Retrieved from https://quickbooks.intuit.com/r/hr-laws-and-regulation/prepare-workplace-disabled-employees/

Johnson, R. W., & Smith, K.E. (2016). How retirement is changing in America. *Urban Institute*. Retrieved from https://www.urban.org/features/how-retirement-changing-america

Kilbom, A. (1999). Evidence-based programs for the prevention of early exit from work. *Experimental Aging Research*, 25(4), 291–299.

Kupperbusch, C., Levenson, R. W., & Ebling, R. (2003). Predicting husbands' and wives' retirement satisfaction from the emotional qualities of marital interaction. *Journal of Social and Personal Relationships*, 20(3), 335–354.

Luborsky, M. R., & LeBlanc, I. M. (2003). Cross-cultural perspectives on the concept of retirement: An analytic redefinition. *Journal of Cross-Cultural Gerontology*, 18(4), 251–271.

Mather, M., Jacobson, L. A., & Pollard, K. M. (2015). Population bulleting: Aging in the United States. Washington, DC: Population Reference Bureau. Retrieved from http://www.prb.org/pdf16/aging-us-population-bulletin.pdf

McKernan, S. M., Ratcliffe, C., Steuerle, C. E., & Zhang, S. (2013). *Less than equal: Racial disparities in wealth accumulation*. Washington, DC: Urban Institute.

Moran, M., Van Cauwenberg, J., Hercky-Linnewiel, R., Cerin, E., Deforche, B., & Plaut, P. (2014). Understanding the relationships between the physical environment and physical activity in older adults: A systematic review of qualitative studies. *International Journal of Behavioral Nutrition and Physical Activity, 11*(1), 79.

Nelson, B. (2017). *2017 AARP retirement security national survey of employed adults ages 18–64.* Washington, DC: AARP Research.

Nimrod, G. (2007). Retirees' leisure: Activities, benefits, and their contribution to life satisfaction. *Leisure Studies, 26*(1), 65–80.

Pryor, F. (2017). Occupational choices of the elderly. U.S. Bureau of Labor Statistics. *Monthly Labor Review.*

Social Security Administration. (2017). Fact sheet: Social Security. Retrieved from https://www.ssa.gov/news/press/factsheets/basicfact-alt.pdf

Szanton, S. L., Walker, R. K., Roberts, L., Thorpe, R. J., Wolff, J., Agree, E., ... & Seplaki, C. (2015). Older adults' favorite activities are resoundingly active: Findings from the NHATS study. *Geriatric Nursing, 36*(2), 131–135.

Szinovacz, M. E., & Davey, A. (2004). Honeymoons and joint lunches: Effects of retirement and spouse's employment on depressive symptoms. *The Journals of Gerontology Series B: Psychological Sciences and Social Sciences, 59*(5), P233–P245.

Taylor-Piliae, R. E., Fair, J. M., Haskell, W. L., Varady, A. N., Iribarren, C., Hlatky, M. A., ... & Fortmann, S. P. (2010). Validation of the Stanford Brief Activity Survey: Examining psychological factors and physical activity levels in older adults. *Journal of Physical Activity and Health, 7*(1), 87–94.

Taylor-Piliae, R. E., Norton, L. C., Haskell, W. L., Mahbouda, M. H., Fair, J. M., Iribarren, C., Hlatky, M.A., & Fortmann, S. P. (2006). Validation of a new brief physical activity survey among men and women aged 60–69 years. *American Journal of Epidemiology, 164*(6), 598–606.

Tishman, F. M., Van Looy, S., & Bruyere, S. M. (2012). *Employer strategies for responding to an aging workforce.* The National Technical Assistance and Research Center to Promote Leadership for Increasing Employment and Economic Independence of Adults with Disabilities. Retrieved from https://www.dol.gov/odep/pdf/NTAR_Employer_Strategies_Report.pdf

Toosey, M., & Torpey, E. (2017). Older workers: Labor force trends and career options. U.S. Bureau of Labor Statistics. *Career Outlook.*

Transamerica Center for Retirement Studies. (2017a). 17th Annual Transamerica Retirement Survey. Retrieved from https://www.transamericacenter.org/retirement-research/17th-annual-retirement-survey

Transamerica Center for Retirement Studies. (2017b). 17th Annual Transamerica Retirement Survey: Influences of ethnicity on retirement readiness. Retrieved from https://www.transamerica-center.org/docs/default-source/retirement-survey-of-workers/tcrs2016_sr_retirement_survey_of_workers_ethnicity.pdf

CHAPTER 7

Mental Health and Substance Use Disorders

Chapter Overview

This chapter explores mental health and substance use disorders among older adults, differential diagnosis, and evidence-based interventions for addressing mental health and substance use disorders, as well as key domains to promote both effective clinical practice with older adults and optimal client outcomes.

CSWE Gero Competencies Highlighted

Competency 1: Demonstrate Ethical and Professional Behavior

Specialized Practice Competency Description: Social workers understand the value base of the profession and its ethical standards, as well as relevant laws and regulations that may impact practice at the micro, mezzo, and macro levels. Social workers understand frameworks of ethical decision-making and how to apply principles of critical thinking to those frameworks in practice, research, and policy arenas. Social workers recognize personal values and the distinction between personal and professional values. They also understand how their personal experiences and affective reactions influence their professional judgment and behavior. Social workers understand the profession's history, its mission, and the roles and responsibilities of the profession. Social workers also understand the role of other professions when engaged in inter-professional teams. Social workers recognize the importance of lifelong learning and are committed to continually updating their skills to ensure they are relevant and effective. Social workers also understand emerging forms of technology and the ethical use of technology in social work practice.

Competency Behaviors: (1) Guided by ethical reasoning and self-reflection, demonstrate adherence to ethical frameworks and key laws, policies, and procedures related to aging, and the rights

of older adults. (2) Engage in active dialogue with field faculty/instructors regarding aging field placement agency policies and culture around behavior, appearance, communication, and the use of supervision. (3) Develop and sustain effective collaborative relationships that respect older adults' needs for protection, self-determination, and the provision of services in the least restrictive environment possible with colleagues and community stakeholders, including older adults, their family members, other care providers, and Tribes. (4) Effectively manage professional boundary issues and other challenges arising in the course of aging-related work, particularly ambiguities presented by home visits, personal loss, trauma, and other highly involved and potentially emotionally triggering aspects of the work. (5) Develop and sustain relationships with members of interdisciplinary and integrated health care teams, including social workers, primary care providers, hospital staff, home health care providers, psychiatrists, psychologists, substance use disorder treatment staff, Tribal service providers, and others, that reflect clear understanding of their roles in providing care to older adults. (6) Demonstrate both knowledge of the history and evolution of social work practice related to aging and older adults in the United States and California, and a commitment to lifelong learning around this practice. (7) Follow all ethical guidelines and legal mandates in the use of technology in order to maintain the confidentiality of all personal, behavioral health, and health-related information. (CalSWEC, 2017, pp. 1–2)

Competency 2: Engage Diversity and Difference in Practice

Specialized Practice Competency Description: Social workers understand how diversity and difference characterize and shape the human experience and are critical to the formation of identity. The dimensions of diversity are understood as the intersectionality of multiple factors, including, but not limited to, age, class, color, culture, disability and ability, ethnicity, gender, gender identity and expression, immigration status, marital status, political ideology, race, religion/spirituality, sex, sexual orientation, and Tribal sovereign status. Social workers understand that, as a consequence of difference, a person's life experiences may include oppression, poverty, marginalization, and alienation as well as privilege, power, and acclaim. Social workers also understand the forms and mechanisms of oppression and discrimination and recognize the extent to which a culture's structures and values, including social, economic, political, and cultural exclusions, may oppress, marginalize, alienate, or create privilege and power.

Competency Behaviors: (1) Engage in critical analysis of the interpersonal, community, and social structural causes and effects of disproportionality, disparities, and inequities in the incidence and trajectory of aging-related care needs, housing, transportation, and resource access among older adults, their families, and their communities. (2) Evidence respectful awareness and understanding of the impact of being a member of a marginalized group on aging experiences, and accurately identify differences in access to and quality of available services for members of different communities and populations. (3) Demonstrate knowledge of diverse cultural norms and traditional methods of providing care to older adults, as well as an applied understanding of how these realities affect work with older adults from diverse backgrounds, their families, and their communities. (4) Develop and use practice methods that acknowledge, respect, and address how individual and cultural values, norms, and differences impact the various systems with which older adults interact, including, but not limited to, families, communities, primary care systems, mental and behavioral health care systems, and integrated care systems. (CalSWEC, 2017, pp. 3–4)

Competency 3: Advance Human Rights and Social, Economic, and Environmental Justice

Specialized Practice Competency Description: Social workers understand that every person regardless of position in society has fundamental human rights such as freedom, safety, privacy, an adequate standard of living, health care, and education. Social workers understand the global interconnections of oppression and human rights violations, and are knowledgeable about theories of human need and social justice and strategies to promote social and economic justice and human rights. Social workers understand strategies designed to eliminate oppressive structural barriers to ensure that social goods, rights, and responsibilities are distributed equitably and that civil, political, environmental, economic, social, and cultural human rights are protected.

Competency Behaviors: (1) Clearly articulate the systematic effects of discrimination, oppression, and stigma on the needs and experiences of older adults and on the quality and delivery of services available to them, and identify and advocate for policy changes needed to address these issues. (2) Advocate for changes in policies and programs that reflect a social justice practice framework for facilitating access and providing services to older adults, their families, and care providers, especially among underserved groups and communities. (3) Demonstrate the ability to work effectively in cross-disciplinary collaboration to develop and provide interventions that explicitly address the specific needs of diverse older adults, their families, and care providers. (4) Integrate into all aspects of policy and practice sensitivity to the reality that fundamental rights, including freedom and privacy, may be compromised for older adults engaged in care, and the goal that services should be provided in the least restrictive environment possible. (CalSWEC, 2017, pp. 4–5)

Competency 4: Engage in Practice-informed Research and Research-informed Practice

Specialized Practice Competency Description: Social workers understand quantitative and qualitative research methods and their respective roles in advancing a science of social work and in evaluating their practice. Social workers know the principles of logic, scientific inquiry, and culturally informed and ethical approaches to building knowledge. Social workers understand that evidence that informs practice derives from multidisciplinary sources and multiple ways of knowing. They also understand the processes for translating research findings into effective practice.

Competency Behaviors: (1) Demonstrate the ability to understand, interpret, and evaluate the benefits and limitations of various evidence-based and evidence-informed treatment models as they influence practice with older adults. (2) Engage in critical analysis of research findings, practice models, and practice wisdom as they inform aging related practice, including how research practices have historically failed to address the needs and realities of exploited and/or disadvantaged communities, and how cross-cultural research practices can be used to enhance equity. (3) Clearly communicate research findings, conclusions, and implications, as well as their applications to aging practice, across a variety of professional interactions with consumers, families, and multidisciplinary service providers. (4) Apply research findings to aging-related practice with individuals, families, and communities and to the development of professional knowledge about the needs, experiences, and well-being of older adults. (CalSWEC, 2017, pp. 5–6)

Competency 6: Engage With Individuals, Families, Groups, Organizations, and Communities

Specialized Practice Competency Description: Social workers understand that engagement is an ongoing component of the dynamic and interactive process of social work practice with, and on behalf of, diverse individuals, families, groups, organizations, and communities. Social workers value the importance of human relationships. Social workers understand theories of human behavior and the social environment, and critically evaluate and apply this knowledge to facilitate engagement with clients and constituencies, including individuals, families, groups, organizations, and communities. Social workers understand strategies to engage diverse clients and constituencies to advance practice effectiveness. Social workers understand how their personal experiences and affective reactions may impact their ability to effectively engage with diverse clients and constituencies. Social workers value principles of relationship-building and inter-professional collaboration to facilitate engagement with clients, constituencies, and other professionals as appropriate.

Competency Behaviors: (1) Appropriately engage and activate older adults, their families, and other care providers in the development and coordination of care plans that reflect relevant theoretical models and balance older adults' needs for care with respect for autonomy and independence. (2) Effectively utilize interpersonal skills to engage older adults, their families, and other care providers in culturally responsive, consumer-driven, and trauma-informed integrated care that addresses mutually agreed upon service goals and balances needs for care, protection, autonomy, and independence. (3) Establish effective and appropriate communication, coordination, and advocacy planning with other care providers and interdisciplinary care teams as needed to address mutually agreed upon service goals. Recognizing the complex nature of service engagement, ensure that communications with consumers and their families regarding service goals are both sensitive and transparent. (4) Manage affective responses and exercise good judgment around engaging with resistance, trauma responses, and other potentially triggering situations with older adults, their families, and other care providers. (CalSWEC, 2017, pp. 9–10)

Competency 7: Assess Individuals, Families, Groups, Organizations, and Communities

Specialized Practice Competency Description: Practitioners in aging utilize ecological-systems theory, a strengths-based and person/family-centered framework to conduct assessments that value the resilience of diverse older adults, families, and caregivers. They select appropriate assessment tools, methods and technology, and evaluate, adapt, and modify them, as needed, to enhance their validity in working with diverse, vulnerable and at-risk groups. The comprehensive biopsychosocial assessment takes into account the multiple factors of physical, mental and social well-being needed for treatment planning for older adults and their families. They develop skills in interprofessional assessment and communication with key constituencies to choose the most effective practice strategies. Gero social workers understand how their own experiences and affective reactions about aging, quality of life, loss and grief may affect their assessment and resultant decision-making.

Competency Behaviors: (1) Conduct assessments that incorporate a strengths-based perspective, person/family-centered focus, and resilience while recognizing aging related risk, (2) Develop, select, and adapt assessment methods and tools that optimize practice with older adults, their families, caregivers, and communities, and (3) Use and integrate multiple domains and sources of assessment information and communicate with other professionals to inform a comprehensive plan for intervention. (Council for Social Work Education, 2017, pp. 89–90)

Competency 8: Intervene With Individuals, Families, Groups, Organizations, and Communities

Specialized Practice Competency Description: Social workers understand that intervention is an ongoing component of the dynamic and interactive process of social work practice with, and on behalf of, diverse individuals, families, groups, organizations, and communities. Social workers are knowledgeable about evidence-informed interventions to achieve the goals of clients and constituencies, including individuals, families, groups, organizations, and communities. Social workers understand theories of human behavior and the social environment, and critically evaluate and apply this knowledge to effectively intervene with clients and constituencies. Social workers understand methods of identifying, analyzing, and implementing evidence-informed interventions to achieve client and constituency goals. Social workers value the importance of inter-professional teamwork and communication in interventions, recognizing that beneficial outcomes may require interdisciplinary, inter-professional, and inter-organizational collaboration.

Competency Behaviors: (1) In partnership with older adults and their families, develop appropriate intervention plans that reflect respect for autonomy and independence, as well as contemporary theories and models for interventions with older adults. Plans should:

+ Reflect cultural humility and acknowledgement of individualized needs;
+ Incorporate consumer and family strengths;
+ Utilize community resources and natural supports;
+ Incorporate multidisciplinary team supports and interventions;
+ Include non-pharmacological interventions; and
+ Demonstrate knowledge of poly-pharmacy needs and issues specific to older adults.

(2) Apply the principles of teaming, engagement, inquiry, advocacy, and facilitation within interdisciplinary teams and care coordination to the work of supporting older adults, family members, and other care providers to accomplish intervention goals and satisfy advanced care planning needs. (3) Effectively implement evidence-based interventions in the context of providing emergency response, triage, brief treatment, and longer-term care, and in the course of

addressing a range of issues presented in primary care, specialty care, community agency, inpatient, and palliative care settings. Interventions should be guided by respect for older adults' autonomy and independence and should include components such as psychoeducation, problem-solving treatment skills, symptom tracking, medication therapies, follow-up, and planning for evolving care needs. (4) Effectively plan for interventions in ways that incorporate thoughtfully executed transitions during time-limited internships, recognizing that consumer needs for support may continue beyond these time periods. (CalSWEC, 2017, pp. 12–14)

Competency 9: Evaluate Practice With Individuals, Families, Groups, Organizations, and Communities

Specialized Practice Competency Description: Social workers understand that evaluation is an ongoing component of the dynamic and interactive process of social work practice with, and on behalf of, diverse individuals, families, groups, organizations and communities. Social workers recognize the importance of evaluating processes and outcomes to advance practice, policy, and service delivery effectiveness. Social workers understand theories of human behavior and the social environment, and critically evaluate and apply this knowledge in evaluating outcomes. Social workers understand qualitative and quantitative methods for evaluating outcomes and practice effectiveness.

Competency Behaviors: (1) Record, track, and monitor consumer engagement, assessment, and intervention data in practice with older adults, their families, and other care providers accurately and according to field education agency policies and guidelines. (2) Conduct accurate process and outcome analysis of engagement, assessment, and intervention data in practice with older adults, their families, and other care providers that incorporates consumer perspectives and reflects respect for older adults' autonomy and independence. (3) Use findings to evaluate intervention effectiveness, develop recommendations for adapting service plans and approaches as needed, improve interdisciplinary team coordination and care integration, and help agency and community policies better support older adults, their families, and their formal and informal care systems. (4) Share both the purposes of such data collection and the overall results of data analysis with older adults, their families, and communities whenever possible, with the goal of engaging them more meaningfully in the evaluation process. (CalSWEC, 2017, pp. 14–15)

Learning Objectives

1. Learners will become aware of contextual and diversity factors to consider when engaging, assessing, intervening, and evaluating outcomes with older adults with mental health and substance use disorders.
2. Learners will identify screening tools for assessing mental health and substance use disorders among older adults.
3. Learners will identify appropriate evidence-based interventions.
4. Learners will understand the importance of referring older adult clients to appropriate technological and community resources and when to assist with coordination.
5. Learners will identify sources of transference and countertransference when working with older adults with mental health and substance use disorders.

Case Study

Ms. Tran is a 69-year-old divorced female living alone in a tri-level condominium she owns. She is a retired school teacher, has no children and no friends, and does not socialize with neighbors. She was born in Vietnam and came to the United States at the age of 6. Her parents are deceased, and she is estranged from her two siblings, who live on the East Coast. She was diagnosed with major depressive disorder at the age of 66, one year after retirement, and is enrolled in a local county mental health case management program. Ms. Tran was diagnosed with stage 4 breast cancer, had a double mastectomy, and was discharged with home health and a 24-hour live-in caregiver. Ms. Tran fired the caregiver upon arrival home. She stopped taking her antidepressant medications and, within one week, developed psychotic symptoms, including homicidal ideations toward her psychiatrist and suicidal ideations. The home health nurse ordered a social worker to evaluate for a psychiatric nurse, appropriateness of level of care, and community resources as the client was unable to secure food on a daily basis and meet basic needs. The home was cluttered, with cat urine and feces throughout the three levels of the condominium. The client stayed in her third-level bedroom, was disheveled with strong/foul odors, and presented with psychotic symptoms upon arrival by the social worker. Upon arrival, the client permitted the social worker to call her case manager at the local county case management for emergency psychiatric evaluation due to grave disability from a mental health condition exacerbated by a medical condition, with nonadherence of psychotropic medications. The county mental health case management team was nonresponsive to the emergent needs for a period of three working days, during which time the home health nurse brought food daily to the client. The physician ordered a follow-up order for the social worker, at which time the client's condition persisted. An emergency call was placed to her county mental health case management team, with no response. The county psychiatric evaluation team (PET) was contacted, and they were unable to send an evaluator for two days. The social worker called the physician and nurse, and the home health team determined an emergency call to the police for initiation of a 5150 was necessary for safety.

Assessing Context

Substance Use

Although research suggests that after young adulthood illicit drug use declines, according to a report from the Center for Behavioral Health Statistics and Quality, in 2014, more than 1 million older adults ages 65 and older were living with a substance use disorder and substance use disorders are projected to increase to 5.7 million older adults by 2020 (Mattson, Lipari, Hays, & Van Horn, 2017). Data from the report came from three data sources in the United States: the Substance Abuse and Mental Health Services Administration (SAMHSA), the Drug Abuse Warning Network (DAWN), and the National Survey on Drug Use and Health (NSDUH) (Mattson, Lipari, Hays, & Van Horn, 2017). One explanation for the anticipated increases in substance use disorders among older adults is the higher drug use of baby boomers (i.e. those born between 1946 and 1964) compared to prior cohorts and generations (Mattson, Lipari, Hays, & Van Horn, 2017). Between 2007 and 2014, approximately 16.2 million older adults ages 65 and older reported drinking alcohol in the past month, binge drinking was reported for 772,000, and heavy alcohol use was reported by 772,000 older adults; and in 2014, 6 million older adults used alcohol on a daily basis with an average of 1.8 drinks per day (Mattson, Lipari, Hays, & Van Horn, 2017).

Illicit drug use among older adults during 2014 at the same period was reported at 469,000 over the past month with drug use falling in nine categories of illicit drugs: marijuana, heroin, inhalants, cocaine, hallucinogens, tranquilizers, sedatives, pain relievers, and stimulants (Mattson, Lipari, Hays, & Van Horn, 2017). Marijuana use was the highest reported with 132,000 older adults reporting marijuana use over the past 30 days. In 2011, the number of emergency department visits related to drug use by older adults ages 65 and older was 750,529 (Mattson, Lipari, Hays, & Van Horn, 2017). On a daily basis, the highest number of emergency visits were related to illicit drug use (i.e., primarily pain relievers such as hydrocodone and oxycodone) (118 cases), followed by benzodiazepines (48 cases), alcohol combined with other drugs (25 cases), antipsychotics and antidepressants (23 cases), cocaine (13 cases), heroine (7 cases), marijuana (5 cases), and amphetamines and methamphetamines (2 cases) (Mattson, Lipari, Hays, & Van Horn, 2017).

Mental Health

According to the World Health Organization (2017), nearly 15% of adults ages 60 and older internationally live with a mental health disorder and 20% have either a neurological or mental health disorder (or one in five older adults globally). Total disability among older adults is approximately 6.6% due to mental health disorders, and the number of years living with a disability due to both neurological and mental health disorders is 17.4% (World Health Organization, 2017). Between 2015 and 2050, the population of older adults is anticipated to increase nearly 100% from 12% (i.e., 900 million) to 22% (i.e., 2 billion) (World Health Organization, 2017), making the need to understand contextual factors to inform best practices for addressing mental health disorders among older adults increasingly an issue of global importance. Approximately 5% to 7% of older adults internationally are living with dementia or depression, respectively, followed by 3.8% living with an anxiety disorder. In 2017, there were 50 million adults living with a diagnosis of dementia; those numbers are projected to increase to 82 million and 152 million by 2030 and 2050, respectively (World Health Organization, 2017), making the need for trained clinicians to work with older adults with dementia and neurological disorders an issue of global importance. Internationally, rates of depression among older adults is approximately 7% and accounts for 5.7 years of living with a disability (World Health Organization, 2017). In 2014, in the United States, the percentage of adults ages 50 and older with a serious mental illness increased nearly 20% between 2008 (2.5%) and 2014 (3.1%) (Substance Abuse and Mental Health Services Administration, 2015). In that same period, the percentage of adults ages 50 and older with any mental illness increased from 11.6% in 2008 to 12.3% in 2014 (Substance Abuse and Mental Health Services Administration, 2015). The percentage of adults ages 50 and older who have experienced a major depressive episode in the past year among adults ages 55 and older increased from 4.5% in 2005 to 5.2% in 2014 (Substance Abuse and Mental Health Services Administration, 2015). The percentage of adults ages 50 and older who experienced severe impairment due to a major depressive episode increased 26% from 2.6% in 2009 to 3.5% in 2014 (Substance Abuse and Mental Health Services Administration, 2015).

Co-Occurring Disorders

Comorbidity refers to having two or more physical health, mental health, or substance use conditions simultaneously. Comorbid substance use and mental health disorders, referred to as co-occurring disorders, or dual diagnosis in clinical settings, are estimated to affect approximately 7.9 million adults in the United States based on the 2014 NSDUH (Substance Abuse and Mental Health Services Administration, 2016). The NSDUH revealed that though the percentage of co-occurring disorders among the general population of adults 18 and older decreased slightly from 18.4% in 2008 to 18.2% in 2014, the percentage among adults ages 50 and older increased roughly 61% from 6.3% in 2008 to 10.3% in 2014 (Substance Abuse and Mental Health Services Administration, 2015). Older adults have an increased sensitivity to alcohol, putting them at higher risk for unintended injuries or accidents, and heavy drinking among older adults exacerbates chronic and mental health conditions such as high blood pressure, diabetes, mood disorders, osteoporosis, memory problems, and congestive heart failure (National Institute on Alcohol Abuse and Alcoholism, 2017).

Protective Factors

Clinicians working with older adults living with a substance use, mental health, and/or co-occurring disorder recognize that an assessment of protective factors—an important contextual factor—informs treatment planning and interventions with older adults and their families. Protective factors such as spirituality and resilience are linked to the well-being of older adults as well as maintaining a positive outlook on life despite changes, challenges, and transitions. For example, in a study of older adults residing in a skilled nursing facility, spirituality was associated with higher reported quality of life as indicated by statistically significant associations between quality of life and two measures of spirituality—"intrapersonal self-transcendence" and "meaning-in-life" (Haugan, Moksnes, & Løhre, 2016, p. 790).

Resilience is defined as "an individual's capacity to maintain stability, endure, and recover in light of negative life events" (Martin, Distelberg, Palmer, & Jeste, 2015, p. 2). Research on resilience with older adults has demonstrated that: (1) resilience is linked to "positive states of mental health that contribute to successful cognitive, emotional, and subjective aging;" (2) "resilience has been significantly associated with various characteristics of successful aging such as improved health, social involvement, and a positive outlook, regardless of income;" and (3) it is associated with a "higher life satisfaction in spite of physical disability" (Martin, Distelberg, Palmer, & Jeste, 2015, p. 3). Clinicians can assess and plan treatments to increase protective factors of older adults living with a substance use, mental health, or co-occurring disorder as research on three protective factors of resilience suggests that "individuals who possess these three protective factors: self-efficacy, optimism and/or a strong belief system, and emotional regulation are considered more likely to be resilient when faced with life's difficulties" (Martin, Distelberg, Palmer, & Jeste, 2015, p. 3). Nine additional resilience factors that clinicians identified in a qualitative meta-synthesis study examining resilience specific to older adults include: (1) having connections with external support (i.e., with friends, family, community, cultural/spiritual groups); (2) meaningfulness (i.e., the sense of a purpose in life arrived through spiritual or existential processes; (3) grit (i.e., having a sense of a strong will to live and adapt); (4) having a positive outlook on life; (5) prior experience with difficulties (i.e., the ability to adapt and adjust to changes, transitions, or losses in the past); (6) engaging in self-care; (7) autonomy or independence (i.e., the sense of control of one's life and having confidence loss); (8) acceptance of self and current transitions or changes; and (9) having altruistic qualities (Bolton, Praetorius, & Smith-Osborne, 2016). Using a strengths-based perspective, clinicians assess the protective factors of older adults when conducting biopsychosocial/spiritual assessments, engaging in treatment planning, and targeting interventions to build protective factors of older adults living with substance use, mental health, and/or co-occurring disorders.

Biopsychosocial/Spiritual Assessment

Following is an application of the Geriatric Biopsychosocial/Spiritual Assessment conducted by Ms. Tran's social worker.

Case Study Application

Box 7.1

Geriatric Biopsychosocial/Spiritual Assessment

Basic Demographic: 69-year-old female; Asian American; Vietnamese and English language; divorced; bachelor-level education

Referral Information: Referral generated from home health social worker

Cultural/Spiritual: Client's religious preference is Buddhism; no use of complementary or alternative medicine per client report

Social: [Relationships within family, social/diversity groups, and community]

- Divorced at age 45; no contact with two siblings who live on the East Coast; no children or friends; client fired 24-hour caregiver; client is isolated and does not participate in social activities

Financial: [Ability to provide basic needs and access health services]

- Ability to provide basic needs: Client is unable to secure food; her shelter and clothing are secure; however, she needs assistance with housekeeping and laundry
- Health insurance: Adequate—Medicare and AARP supplemental insurance
- Income sources: State retirement from the school pension program; savings less than $2,000; she has an IRA with more than $100,000

Environmental: [Personal safety, maintenance of residence, and safety of community]

- Current social context/environmental: At home alone
- Neighborhood safety: Adequate lighting, low crime in neighborhood
- Home safety: Slip rugs; clutter and cat feces and urine; handrails on stairs leading up to each of the upper two levels
- Access to guns: No guns or access to guns in the home
- Screen for abuse or neglect by self or perpetrated by others (APS SOC341 report if suspected): Report filed upon first assessment due to self-neglect (refusing care from caregiver for safety, grave disability, unable to secure food, and nonadherence with psychotropic medications)

Physical: [Individual function and disease morbidity]

- Health literacy and self-rated health: Client has low insight into health and mental health due to acute psychotic symptoms; client reports she does not have an advance directive, general power of attorney, or conservatorship; diagnosis is stage 4 breast cancer, post-double mastectomy, and major depressive disorder with psychotic features; medications: patient started on tamoxifen after surgery and had order in place for Prozac (nonadherent with both); functional health (ADLs, IADLs): independent with ADLs, needs assist with IADLs; no other chronic health, substance use, or mental health conditions; sexual health—inactive

Mental: [Mental status, depression, anxiety, and substance abuse]

- Standardized screening instruments: Client refused screening for depression
- Suicide risk assessment: Endorsed suicidal ideations
- Homicidal ideations: Endorsed homicidal ideations toward psychiatrist
- Substance use: None

Formulation/Evaluation: Adult Protective Services report; initiate 5150 with local law enforcement due to nonresponse to urgent psychiatric needs by both the county mental health PET and local county mental health case management offices

Treatment Planning: Collaborated with physician and nurse; reached out to county psychiatric services; social work initiated 5150 for emergency acute psychiatric needs of client with grave disability due to comorbid mental health and health conditions and medication nonadherence

Community Resource Needs: Collaboration with law enforcement, Adult Protective Services, and local county mental health case management team for disposition

Diversity–Cultural Competence/Spirituality/LGBT/Sexuality

For older adults with co-occurring disorders in prison institutional settings, integrated care (i.e., treatment that addresses substance use, mental health, and physical health) that provides treatment for co-occurring mental health and substance use disorders has been found to lead to decreased recidivism (i.e., arrests) and substance use (Substance Abuse and Mental Health Services Administration, 2016). Among the 23.4 million veterans in the Unites States, a common co-occurring disorder is a substance use disorder and mental health disorder, specifically post-traumatic stress disorder (PTSD), which has been reported among 33% of veterans (Substance Abuse and Mental Health Services Administration, 2016). Over a five-year period between 2005 and 2009, every 36 hours, one veteran committed suicide, for a total of roughly 1,100 veterans committing suicide (Substance Abuse and Mental Health Services Administration, 2017c). Veterans also benefit from integrated care services for treatment of co-occurring disorders, yet many do not seek treatment at health facilities operated by the Veterans Affairs (VA) Department (Substance Abuse and Mental Health Services Administration, 2017c). Therefore, collaboration between providers, veterans, their families, the VA, and agencies outside of the VA are critical for effective integrated care practices with veterans living with co-occurring, mental health, and/or substance use disorders.

In 2016, approximately 202,297 homeless adults were living with a mental health or substance use disorder, which is roughly one in five (Substance Abuse and Mental Health Services Administration, 2017a). The mortality rate for homeless individuals is four to nine times higher than in the general adult population, and they are at higher risk for multiple comorbidities of chronic health, mental health, and substance use disorders as well as violence (Substance Abuse and Mental Health Services Administration, 2017c). There are roughly 9 million lesbian, gay, bisexual, and transgender (LGBT) adults living in the United States—they are at a high risk for substance abuse and alcohol and tobacco use, with tobacco use among LGBT adults being twice that of the national average (Substance Abuse and Mental Health Services Administration, 2017c).

Clinicians recognize that culture impacts perceptions of self, outlook on life, and perceived well-being. Research suggests that there are variations related to cultural contexts clinicians should consider when understanding subjective reports of well-being and/or life satisfaction. For example, "in *independent* cultural contexts such as the United States, the person is regarded as separated from others and personal goals often are accorded priority over in-group goals, whereas in more *interdependent* cultural contexts such as Japan, the person is understood as connected to others and part of an encompassing social unit, wherein in-group norms have priority over personal needs" (Karasawa et al., 2011, p. 2). Additionally, the context of well-being differs across culture with an independent versus interdependent context. For example, subjective well-being in cultures that are independent rate well-being subjectively based on "high levels of autonomy;" "personal achievement;" "self-esteem;" and "high ratings of uniqueness, self-confidence, and self-motivation" (Karasawa et al., 2011, p. 2). The context of subjective reports by those from interdependent cultures consider more "social relational factors such as social harmony;" the "attainment of relational goals;" "socially engaging emotions;" and "perceived emotional support from close others" (Karasawa et al., 2011, p. 2). The context of culture is considered along with other diversity and biopsychosocial/spiritual factors obtained in the assessment phase when engaging in activities related to differential diagnosis.

Differential Diagnosis

In detecting mental health and substance use disorders among older adults, differential diagnosis informs treatment planning, interdisciplinary team planning, integrated care approaches, and selection of the best evidence-based interventions to present to the client for treatment decision making. With all *Diagnostic and Statistical Manual of Mental Disorders* (5th ed.; *DSM-V*) mental health disorders, there are specific criteria that must be ruled out and present to arrive at a specific diagnosis. For example, the condition must occur during a specific time period; certain behavioral and mood indicators must be present; the behavioral/mood indicators must result in occupational, social, educational, or vocational impairment; and the indicators must not be attributable to another mental health diagnosis/condition or a medical condition. A discussion of diagnostic criteria for anxiety, depression, dementia, delirium, and substance use disorders follows.

Anxiety

Anxiety disorders, as described by the American Psychiatric Association (2013) in the *DSM-V*, share excessive fear and anxiety features in behavioral impairments, with fear associated with threats that are perceived to be imminent and anxiety pertaining to threats that are anticipated in the future (American Psychiatric Association, 2013). The *DSM-V* outlines anxiety disorders developmentally based on the age of presentations; anxiety disorders relevant to older adults include specific phobia (i.e., fear or anxiety about specific situations or objects and/or avoidance behavior), social anxiety disorder (i.e., fear and avoidant behaviors about being rejected, offended, embarrassed, or humiliated by other people), panic disorder (i.e., fear of panic attacks that result in avoidance behaviors), agoraphobia (i.e., fear of two or more of the following situations: open spaces, public transportation use, places that are enclosed/confined, crowds or standing in lines, or venturing outside of the home), generalized anxiety disorder (to be reviewed later in this section), substance-/medication-induced anxiety disorder (i.e., anxiety and fear related to withdrawal of substance or medication), anxiety due to another medical condition (i.e., fear and anxiety responses that result from a chronic or life-threatening illness), other specified anxiety disorder, and unspecified anxiety disorder (American Psychiatric Association, 2013).

One of the most common forms of anxiety clinicians may see in clinical practice is that of generalized anxiety disorder (GAD). The criteria for a diagnosis of GAD is at least six months of worry or fear about activities or any event the older adult may engage in (category A); the client has a difficult time being able to take control of the state of worry (category B); at least three of six symptoms occur with the anxiety and fear: restlessness, fatigue, irritable mood, tension in the muscles, difficulty concentrating, and difficulty with sleep) (category C); there is significant social, occupational, or other impairment (category D); it is not attributable to a substance (category E); or a mental health disorder (category F) (American Psychiatric Association, 2013).

Depression

Depressive disorders, according to the American Psychiatric Association (2013), include a feature of mood among individuals reflecting sadness, emptiness, irritability, or changes to function due to cognitive and/or somatic symptoms. Similar to anxiety disorders, the *DSM-V* outlines depressive disorders developmentally. Depressive disorders relevant to older adults include major depressive disorder (to be reviewed later in this section), persistent depressive disorder (dysthymia) (i.e., two years of disturbances in mood), substance-/medication-induced depressive disorder (i.e., side effects from substances or prescribed medications), depressive disorder due to another medical condition (i.e., mood and behavior due to physiological responses of a medical condition), other specified depressive disorder (i.e., recurrent brief depression, short-duration depressive episode, or depressive episode with insufficient symptoms), and unspecified depressive disorder (i.e., when the clinician chooses not to specific why the diagnostic criteria are met) (American Psychiatric Association, 2013).

Dementia

Under the *DSM-V*, dementia falls under neurocognitive disorders as a major neurocognitive disorder (American Psychiatric Association, 2013). The diagnostic criteria include: changes in social cognition, executive function, language, motor perception, or complex attention from prior level contingent upon one of two additional criteria that (1) the clinician, client, or others notice changes or (2) there is a standardized clinical assessment or instrument documenting and substantiating the change in function (category A) (American Psychiatric Association, 2013). The second criterion (category B) requires impairment in instrumental activities of daily living (IADLs) (i.e., medication management, bill payment, phone calls to doctors, etc.) or activities of daily living (ADLs) (i.e., bathing, toileting, grooming, ambulating, etc.) (American Psychiatric Association, 2013). Additionally, the deficits in cognition are not attributable to delirium (category C) or another mental health disorder (category D) (American Psychiatric Association, 2013). Lastly, specifiers are added for clinicians to specify if the major and/or mild neurocognitive disorder is related to Alzheimer's disease, frontotemporal lobar degeneration, Lewy body disease, vascular disease, traumatic brain injury, substance/medication use, HIV infection, prion disease, Parkinson's disease, Huntington's disease, other medical conditions, etiologies of multiple origins, and unspecified origins (American Psychiatric Association, 2013).

Delirium

Delirium, like dementia, also falls under the new classification in *DSM-V* under neurocognitive disorders. The diagnostic criteria for delirium include both awareness and attention disturbances (category A); a change in baseline functioning for both awareness and functioning over a brief period of time with fluctuation noted throughout the day (category B); one additional disturbance observed in cognition (i.e., perception, language, disorientation, deficit in memory, or visual) (category C); criterion from category A and C are not best explained by a condition such as a coma or other pre-existing, evolving, or current disorder of a neurocognitive nature (category D); the disturbance is attributable to substance use/withdrawal, toxin, multiple etiologies, physical exam, or established history (category E) (American Psychiatric Association, 2013).

Substance Use Disorders

Substance use disorders are categorized under substance-related and addictive disorders in the *DSM-V*, which include 66 disorders ranging from alcohol; caffeine; cannabis; hallucinogen; phencyclidine; inhalant; opioid; sedative; hypnotic or anxiolytic; stimulant; tobacco; other and unspecified; and gambling disorders (American Psychiatric Association, 2013). Common characteristics of the 10 key classes of drugs include activation of the reward systems of the brain that lead to an individual neglecting of normal daily activities (American Psychiatric Association, 2013). Substance use disorders involve, under category A: difficulty controlling and cutting down substance use (criterion one); unsuccessful attempts to reduce consumption (criterion two); a significant amount of time spent obtaining, using, and recovering from the substance (criterion three); and daily activities performed by the individual revolve around the next use and craving the substance (criterion four) (American Psychiatric Association, 2013). The second grouping of substance use disorders considers social impairment under criteria five through seven (American Psychiatric Association, 2013). Specifically, for older adults, disturbances in social and occupational functioning (criterion five), continuance of use of the substance despite social and occupational disturbances (criterion six), and withdrawal and abandonment of social and occupational or recreational activities due to substance use (criterion seven) (American Psychiatric Association, 2013). Risky use is considered continued use in situations considered hazardous (criterion eight) and continued use despite known physical or psychological harm/risks (criterion nine) (American Psychiatric Association, 2013). And lastly, pharmacological criteria are considered tolerance (criterion 10) and withdrawal (criterion 11) (American Psychiatric Association, 2013). Clinicians present findings from differential diagnosis activities to the older adult client and interdisciplinary team to inform treatment planning and the presentation of the best interventions to inform treatment decision making with the older adult client.

Interdisciplinary Team Roles and Planning

To date, research suggests that integrated care approaches that involve interdisciplinary team member assessment, collaboration, coordination, treatment planning, and interventions between behavioral health (i.e., mental health and substance use disorders) and physical health (i.e., primary care) providers provide the best outcomes and is the most effective treatment model for adults living with comorbid behavioral and health conditions (Health Resources and Services Administration, 2017). Integrated care also involves collaboration and coordination of care across systems of care, such as with the instance of Ms. Tran, who required emergency psychiatric treatment services after her discharge home following a double mastectomy for breast cancer.

Integrated care occurs across settings, with demonstration projects after the Affordable Care Act of 2013 serving as exemplar models for integrating primary care into behavioral health settings, behavioral health into primary care settings, medical health homes, and within safety net provider (Health Resources and Services Administration, 2017). The Substance Abuse and Mental Health Administration and Health Resources and Services Administration (SAMHSA-HRSA) Center for Integrated Health Solutions outlines core competencies for providers of integrated behavioral health and primary care. The first competency, interpersonal communication, pertains to providing "anticipatory guidance for patients and caregivers," avoiding "confusing medical terminology," clearly explaining "medications and treatment options," and tapping "the patient's strengths to promote self-management and communicate positive views of aging" (Substance Abuse and Mental Health Administration and Health Resources and Services Administration, 2016, p. 8).

The second competency outlined by SAMHSA-HRSA for integrated behavioral health and primary care with older adults is collaboration and teamwork, which specifically involves having an "informed team approach to provide comprehensive services, with all team members aware of their responsibilities," "working relationships with other internal or external members of the team," listening to the older adult client and caregiver, and recognizing "that the desired outcome for older adults may be a change in function, not a change in symptoms" (Substance Abuse and Mental Health Administration and Health Resources and Services Administration, 2016, p. 8). The third competency, screening and assessment, recommends screening for "depression, anxiety, substance use, chronic pain, risk of falls" and any stressors that can increase fall risk; it includes recognizing gender and behavioral health symptoms that may be related to a physical health condition and differential diagnosis of dementia, delirium, and depression, as well as screening for and detecting elder abuse (Substance Abuse and Mental Health Administration and Health Resources and Services Administration, 2016, p. 9). The fourth competency for integrated care with older adults is care planning and care coordination, which includes the identification and use of peer support and aging networks and services, providing a warm handoff between different providers or agencies to ensure care continuity, collaboration with the pharmacist on medications, and offering follow-up care as appropriate (Substance Abuse and Mental Health Administration and Health Resources and Services Administration, 2016).

The fifth competency, intervention, recommends that the effective practices used with older adults be evidence based (Substance Abuse and Mental Health Administration and Health Resources and Services Administration, 2016). The sixth competency is cultural competence and adaption, involving accessibility for older adults with functional health limitations, respect and incorporation of cultural perspectives, and use of community resources to overcome any barriers to accessing care (Substance Abuse and Mental Health Administration and Health Resources and Services Administration, 2016). The seventh competency, systems-oriented practice, includes providers being knowledgeable about health and behavioral health services, insurances, and benefits (Substance Abuse and Mental Health Administration and Health Resources and Services Administration, 2016). Competencies eight and nine involve continuous quality improvement based on outcome data and informatics using electronic health records across providers, respectively (Substance Abuse and Mental Health Administration and Health Resources and Services Administration, 2016).

Pharmacotherapy

Drug therapies are often used as part of treatment for older adults living with a chronic health, mental health, substance use diagnosis, and/or comorbid conditions. Polypharmacy, or multiple medication use, becomes an issue for older adults when multiple providers prescribe medications without knowing what other physicians, psychiatrists, or providers have prescribed. Communication and collaborations with pharmacists and providers is important to prevent harmful effects of multiple medication use. Clinicians should be aware of the classes of medications used to treat various mental health, substance use, and comorbid conditions. Treatment of chronic and behavior conditions with older adults differs from how treatments are provided to younger adults (Goeres, Williams,

Eckstrom, & Lee, 2014). Two important ways the disposition of drugs is altered with older adults are: (1) "intestinal absorption may be delayed and drug metabolism and renal elimination may be decreased, leading to higher blood concentrations" and (2) "increased body fat and decreased total body water may change drug distribution" (Goeres, Williams, Eckstrom, & Lee, 2014, p. 2). Dose personalization is, therefore, recommended for pharmacotherapy treatment with older adults to maximize beneficial outcomes and minimize side effects (Schlender et al., 2017). Medication-assisted treatment (MAT) (i.e., behavioral therapy, psychotherapy, and medication therapy combined) is effective for treatment and recovery for adults with substance use disorders (Substance Abuse and Mental Health Services Administration, 2017b). Clinicians collaborate with nurses, physicians, and other providers to assist with developing medication lists, assessing adherence, monitoring mood and behavior indicators and the effectiveness or ineffectiveness of the medication in reducing/managing symptoms, and encouraging the use of one pharmacy for all medications.

Clinicians adhere to CSWE Gero Competency 1: Demonstrate Ethical and Professional Behavior, specialized practice behavior 5 to maintain relationships and understand the roles of other disciplines when working with older adults with mental health, substance use, and/or comorbid conditions and CSWE Gero Competency 6: Engage With Individuals, Families, Groups, Organizations, and Communities, specialized practice behaviors 1–4 (CalSWEC, 2017). Clinicians work with the interdisciplinary team to develop treatment plans and coordinate interventions with other disciplines (CSWE Gero Competency 7: Assess Individuals, Families, Groups, Organizations, and Communities, specialized practice behavior 3 and Competency: 8 Intervene With Individuals, Families, Groups, Organizations, and Communities, specialized practice behavior 2) (CalSWEC, 2017).

Ms. Edwards, a 71-year-old non-Hispanic White female who lived alone in a second-story apartment, had a home health nurse assisting her with medication management. Her primary care physician ordered home health due to his concern that Ms. Edwards was not appropriately managing her anxiety medication, Ativan; in the physician's referral, he reported that Ms. Edwards had been requesting refills before they were due for refill and would call the office demanding a refill. During a medication reconciliation of Ms. Edwards's medication, Ms. Edwards asked the nurse to call her physicians for more Ativan. The social worker was contacted for an assessment and discovered Ms. Edwards had a stockpile of several bottles of Ativan. Ms. Edwards reported she went to other doctors, got prescriptions of Ativan, and took them to different pharmacies to get filled and paid by cash. With the assessments completed by the nurse and social worker, a team conference was set up with the primary physician. The social worker, nurse, and physician in treatment planning determined the client should be further screened for a substance use disorder; the social worker would provide another visit to conduct further brief screening for substance use disorder and options for treatment; and the nurse was requested to continue with medication management and provide further follow-up on Ms. Edwards's report to the social worker that she had multiple anxiety medications.

Clinicians require knowledge and training in evidence-based interventions and best practices to respond to and treat older adults with substance use, mental health, and/or co-occurring or comorbid disorders.

Evidence-based Interventions

Motivational Interviewing

Motivational interviewing, developed by Rollnick and Miller (1995), is an evidence-based intervention for use with older adults living with mental health, substance use, and comorbid disorders. Motivational interviewing emphasizes client-centered techniques clinicians use to promote motivation to change from within the client, assess readiness to engage in change behavior, and work with both resistance and ambivalence of the client to change (Rollnick & Allison, 2004). For the intervention to be the most effective, the stance of the therapist should be geared toward the stage of change the client presents in from the transtheoretical and stages of change model (i.e., precontemplation, contemplation, preparation, action, and maintenance). In precontemplation, "the client is not yet considering change or is unwilling or unable to change" (Substance Abuse and Mental Health Services Administration, 1999, p. 31). Recommended strategies by the clinician for motivational interviewing for clients in precontemplation include: (1) "establish rapport, ask permission, and build trust;" (2) "raise doubts or concerns in the client about substance-using patterns" by "eliciting the client's perceptions of the problems" or "exploring pros and cons;" and (3) "express concern and keep the door open" (Substance Abuse and Mental Health Services Administration, 1999, p. 31). In contemplation, the client is open to change and acknowledges concerns but still has some ambivalence to change (Substance Abuse and Mental Health Services Administration, 1999). Motivational strategies clinicians can use with clients in contemplation include: (1) normalizing ambivalence on the part of the client, (2) helping the client "tip the decisional balance scales toward change" by "emphasizing the client's free choice, responsibility and self-efficacy for change," (3) eliciting statements from the client that convey intent and commitment to change, (4) eliciting treatment and self-efficacy expectations from the client, and (5) providing summaries to the client of their conveyed statements for change reflecting self-motivation (Substance Abuse and Mental Health Services Administration, 1999, p. 31).

Preparation involves a client considering plans to change with uncertainty on the necessary actions to engage in (Substance Abuse and Mental Health Services Administration, 1999). Motivational strategies clinicians can use with clients in the preparation stage of change include: (1) clarifying the "client's own goals and strategies for change," (2) "offer a menu of options for change or treatment," (3) "with permission, offer expertise and advice," (4) "consider and lower barriers to change," (5) "help the client enlist social support," (6) "explore treatment expectancies and the client's role," and (7) "elicit from the client what has worked in the past either for him or others whom he knows" (Substance Abuse and Mental Health Services Administration, 1999, p. 32). Clients in the action stage of change are actively taking steps to engage in change (Substance Abuse and Mental

Health Services Administration, 1999). Motivational strategies clinicians can use for clients in the action stage include: (1) "engage the client in treatment and reinforce the importance of remaining in recovery," (2) "support a realistic view of change through small steps," (3) "acknowledge difficulties for the client in early stages of change," (4) "help the client identify high-risk situations through a functional analysis and develop appropriate coping strategies to overcome these," (5) "assist the client in finding new reinforcers of positive change," and (6) "help the client assess whether she has strong family and social support" (Substance Abuse and Mental Health Services Administration, 1999, p. 32).

The maintenance stage of change involves clients who achieved and are maintaining the gains made to date for recovery, wellness, and abstinence (Substance Abuse and Mental Health Services Administration, 1999). Motivational strategies clinicians can use with clients in the maintenance stage of change include: (1) helping the client identify new positive reinforcers for pleasure and satisfaction, (2) supporting the lifestyle changes the client has made to maintain new behaviors and change, (3) assisting the client with exploring and identifying new coping strategies to manage potential high- and low-risk triggers for relapse of mental health or substance use disorders, (4) providing affirmations to reinforce client self-efficacy efforts, (5) continuing contact for counseling as needed with the client in recovery, and (6) exploring and reviewing goals the client has made for long-term recovery, wellness, and relapse prevention (Substance Abuse and Mental Health Services Administration, 1999).

The four key principles for practice include the following: express empathy, roll with resistance, support self-efficacy, and develop discrepancy (Rollnick & Allison, 2004). Express empathy involves empathic listening by the clinician, demonstrated through reflective listening, which involves "both simple summary statements" of what the client is conveying to the clinician, "designed to ensure parity with the client," and "more complex statements that enable the skilled counsellor to gently but directively highlight elements of the client's dilemma that might encourage resolution of ambivalence" (Rollnick & Allison, 2004, p. 109). Roll with resistance "highlights the need to avoid non-constructive conversations, which resemble a battle of wills" between the clinician and client (Rollnick & Allison, 2004, p. 109). Support self-efficacy involves the clinician supporting the client's internal conviction for change rather than the clinician's outer directive, as implemented in therapy—"suggestions are made and specific problems are discussed in the context of a brainstorming session in which the client is encouraged to take charge of decision-making" (Rollnick & Allison, 2004, p. 110). The fourth principle, develop discrepancy, involves the state of discomfort the client feels as a result of talking about and processing future goals and personal values; it arises when the client discovers the "contrasts between what the person wants from life and the self-destructive nature of the addiction problem" (Rollnick & Allison, 2004, p. 110). The discrepancy is viewed as an opportunity for change, allowing the client to see "how the problem might be at odds with what is dear to them and their hopes for the future" (Rollnick & Allison, 2004, p. 110).

The methods for motivational interviewing include empathic listening skills, eliciting self-motivating statements (change talk), and responding to resistance (Rollnick &

Allison, 2004). Empathic listening skills include: reflective listening, open questions, summarizing, and affirmations (Rollnick & Allison, 2004). Reflective listening is "the principal for conveying empathy with the client" (Rollnick & Allison, 2004) and involves a skill where the clinician demonstrates an accurate understanding of what a client has conveyed by "restating its meaning" (Substance Abuse and Mental Health Services Administration, 1999, p. 50). Open-ended questions "encourage the client to do most of the talking, help you avoid making premature judgements, and keep communication moving forward" (Substance Abuse and Mental Health Services Administration, 1999, p. 50). Summarizing consists of "distilling the essence of what the client has expressed and communicating it back; it serves as an opportunity for the clinician to be corrected if information they summarize is inaccurate" and helps the client "consider their own responses and contemplate their own experience" (Substance Abuse and Mental Health Services Administration, 1999, p. 52). Affirmations are used to build the self-efficacy of the client by acknowledging obstacles clients have overcome and experienced; they help clients "feel confident about marshaling their inner resources to take action and change behavior" through the clinician specifically "emphasizing their past experiences that demonstrate strength, success, or power" (Substance Abuse and Mental Health Services Administration, 1999, p. 52).

The second method, eliciting self-motivating statements (change talk) involves the task of "instead of presenting arguments for change to the client, the counsellor elicits these from the client" using more complex reflective listening statements, such as a "double-sided reflection, where the counsellor looks for contrasting feelings and captures them in a single brief statement" (Rollnick & Allison, 2004, p. 111). The third method, responding to resistance, involves a clinician's stance and approach that acknowledges and provides space for the client to be heard while maintaining respect and dignity for the client (Rollnick & Allison, 2004). The approach the clinician takes here is to come "alongside the client, thereby undermining the oppositional nature of the interaction" by using reflective listening (Rollnick & Allison, 2004, p. 111). A second effective evidence-based intervention is cognitive behavioral therapy.

Cognitive Behavioral Therapy

Cognitive behavioral therapy (CBT) is a "present-centered" and "problem-oriented" form of therapy that uses "verbal procedures and behavioral experiments to examine and test the validity and utility of the client's perceptions and interpretations of events" (Roberts & Yeager, 2006, p.368). In a review of 269 meta-analyses conducted on CBT with adult populations living with substance use, mental health, and comorbid disorders, very strong evidence exists for its effectiveness for disorders such as anxiety, substance use, depression, psychotic disorders and schizophrenia, bipolar and personality and eating, as well as other conditions such as general stress, chronic pain and fatigue, insomnia, and general medical condition-related distress (Hofmann, Asnaani, Vonk, Sawyer, & Fang, 2012). The key premise of CBT, according to Aaron Beck and Albert Ellis (the classical theorists of CBT), is that emotional and behavioral problems are attributable to maladaptive cognitions that include "general beliefs, or schemas, about the world, the self, and the future, giving rise to specific automatic thoughts in particular situations" (Hofmann, Asnaani, Vonk, Sawyer, & Fang, 2012, p. 427).

Clients are taught the cognitive model that facilitates insight among clients who are ready to engage in change behaviors. In therapy, clinicians work with clients to allow them to see the association between their interpretation of events around them due to automatic thoughts or schemas/beliefs about the world, their feelings/emotions associated with the event, and subsequent actions that result in maladaptive rather than adaptive behaviors. Clinicians work with clients to identify and understand their core beliefs/schemas and recognize how these core beliefs/schemas influence automatic thoughts and/or cognitive distortions leading to inaccurate interpretations about events. Clinicians further work with clients on strategies, such as cognitive restructuring, to replace these automatic and inaccurate thoughts and beliefs with those that are more realistic and accurate, resulting in more positive emotions and adaptive behaviors. For example, a client with a core belief that he or she is unworthy and unlovable may have an automatic thought that others will never love or accept him or her, leading to feelings of inadequacy and subsequent behaviors of avoidance in social situations. The clinician works with the client on a new core belief that he or she is lovable (core belief) and worthy of love (automatic thought), resulting in positive feelings (confident and adequate) and adaptive behavior (to approach others in social situations). Screening brief interventions and referral for treatment is a third evidence-based intervention clinicians working with older adults can be trained in.

Screening Brief Intervention and Referral for Treatment

Screening brief intervention and referral for treatment (SBIRT) is an evidence-based intervention used to screen, detect, prevent, and provide referrals for treatment for adults with risky substance use behaviors and/or substance use disorders. Screening and brief intervention (SBI) (1) "uses motivational approaches based on how ready the person is to change in behavior," (2) provides referral for treatment (RT) with "feedback and suggestions respectfully in the form of useful information, without judgement or accusations," and (3) "has been shown by research to be effective in reducing alcohol use and alcohol-related adverse consequences, including injury" (American Public Health Association, 2008, p. 2). SBIRT is an effective brief intervention for both males and females of all ages that has been shown to be effective in emergency and primary care settings (American Public Health Association, 2008). The first phase of treatment, screening, is not done to establish a diagnosis but rather to identify at-risk drinkers—based on the National Institute on Alcohol Abuse and Alcoholism (2017), for older adults who do not take medications, this means no more than three drinks per day and no more than seven drinks per week. Screening can be conducted with brief client self-administered or clinician-administered standardized instruments such as the 10-item alcohol use disorders identification test (AUDIT); the eight-item, multiple-question alcohol, smoking, substance involvement screening test (ASSIST); or the four-item cut down, annoyed, guilty, eye-opener (CAGE) screening (American Public Health Association, 2008).

The next phase of SBIRT involves conversations that last anywhere from five to 30 minutes where the clinician begins with providing feedback and information to the client based on the results from the drug and alcohol screening (American Public Health Association, 2008). The clinician provides brief psychoeducation on the risks and problems of use and heavy/high-risk drinking and reviews both the recommended guidelines for low-risk drinking and treatment options to stop use (American Public Health Association, 2008). The use of motivational interviewing and understanding of the stages of change informs SBIRT best practices. Clinicians, for example, "understand the client's view of drinking and increase his or her motivation to change" through techniques such as encouraging the client to explore the pros and cons of drinking, contributions of drinking to their problems currently, and how they may want to change both risks and behaviors related to drinking (American Public Health Association, 2008, p. 9). Motivational interviewing is also used by clinicians to "engage clients in a discussion that helps them come to their own decisions about drinking" (American Public Health Association, 2008, p. 9). When providing referrals for treatment, the following guidelines are recommended: (1) "provide clear and respectful advice, without judgement or blame, about the need to decrease risk by cutting down or quitting drinking and avoiding high-risk situations;" (2) "explore different options by listening to the person's concerns and clarifying his or her strengths, resources, and past successes;" (3) keeping in mind that the "best result is for clients to develop their own goals and a realistic plan of action to achieve them based on how ready they are to change; and (4) "the plan may involve reducing drinking somewhat or quitting altogether" (American Public Health Association, 2008, p. 9).

In the second visit with Ms. Edwards, the social worker obtained her consent to receive screening for substance use. In assessing where Ms. Edwards was in terms of the stage of change, Ms. Edwards presented initially as being in the precontemplation stage as she was initially resistant and denied "having a drug problem" when the social worker sought her consent for further screening. The clinician administered the ASSIST screening—her score of 34 placed her at high risk (scores of 27 and higher) for developing problems related to her current pattern of use of Ativan. Using motivational interviewing techniques, the social worker engaged Ms. Edwards in a 25-minute discussion surrounding her pattern of use. As the clinician worked through Ms. Edwards's resistance and explored her ambivalence, as well as the pros and cons to change, Ms. Edwards's motivation level toward change and insight about potential problems related to her use improved. Ms. Edwards decided she would like to know about treatment options. The continuity of care for substance treatment options were presented to Ms. Edwards, and she decided to start participating in an intensive outpatient program (IOP). She surrendered the bottles of Ativan she had stockpiled to her physician, who safely disposed of them. She was referred to a chemical dependence physician, who worked collaboratively with Ms. Edwards and her primary care physician to develop a treatment plan that would address her co-occurring anxiety and substance use. The fourth evidence-based intervention clinicians can be trained in to work effectively with older adults living with a substance use, mental health, or co-occurring/comorbid condition is mindfulness.

Mindfulness

In a systematic review of randomized controlled trials, mindfulness-based stress reduction (MBSR) was found to be effective in mental health improvement, and mindfulness-based cognitive therapy (MBCT) has been found to be effective in prevention of relapse for depression (Fjorback, Arendt, Ørnbøl, Fink, & Walach, 2011). Mindfulness interventions have been found to be effective in reducing symptoms in older adults with comorbid conditions as well. In a randomized control trial, 40 older adults were provided with an eight-week MBSR intervention and older adults had reductions in both loneliness and proinflammatory genes (Creswell et al., 2012). MBSR originated in the 1970s and incorporates Buddhist meditation techniques in an attempt to cultivate an individual's state of being mindful or presence in the here and now (Chiesa & Serretti, 2011). Mindfulness refers to "the development of a particular kind of attention characterized by a non-judgmental awareness, openness, curiosity, and acceptance of internal and external present experiences" (Chiesa & Serretti, 2011, p. 83). It incorporates three techniques: The first technique, the body scan, "involves a gradual sweeping of attention through the entire body from feet to head, focusing non-critically on any sensation or feeling in body regions and using periodic suggestions of breath awareness and relaxation" (Chiesa & Serretti, 2011, p. 84). The second technique, sitting meditation, "involves both mindful attention on the breath or on the rising and falling abdomen as well as on other perceptions" and awareness without judgment of one's "cognitions and of the stream of thoughts and distractions that continuously flow through the mind" (Chiesa & Serretti, 2011, p. 84). The third technique, hatha yoga, includes "breathing exercises, simple stretches, and posture designed to strengthen and relax the musculoskeletal system" (Chiesa & Serretti, 2011, p. 84). Clinicians assess and monitor all evidence-based interventions they use with older adults to determine the impact and effectiveness of the interventions and changing the desirable outcomes in line with the identified goals for treatment and plan of care.

Assessing/Monitoring Evidence-based Treatment Outcomes

Clinicians can use standardized assessment tools as baseline measures for mental health disorders, such as depression (i.e., PHQ-9 or Geriatric Depression Scale), anxiety (i.e., GAD-7), and substance use disorders (i.e., CAGE, ASSIST, or AUDIT screening tools), and monitor the effects of the intervention on improving the desired outcome.

Clinicians have an ethical responsibility to monitor and evaluate the treatment effectiveness of their interventions with an older adult. The monitoring and evaluation of treatment outcomes should adhere to CSWE Gero Competency 9: Evaluate Practice With Individuals, Families, Groups, Organizations, and Communities, specialized practice behaviors 1–4 (CalSWEC, 2017, pp. 14–15). Clinicians follow agency policies and guidelines in recording and monitoring treatment outcome data (specialized practice behavior 1); they ensure accuracy in their analysis of treatment phases and include client perspectives (specialized practice behavior 2); they use the findings to improve clinical practice, interdisciplinary collaboration, program development, and services by the community and agencies (specialized practice behavior 3); and they share the data with clients and their families with the goal of improving the data collection process (CalSWEC, 2017).

Community Resources/Interagency Coordination

Community resource coordination and interagency coordination for prevention, assessment, treatment, recovery, and wellness programs are essential to effective interventions with older adults presenting with mental health, substance use, or comorbid conditions. Knowledge of and established relationships with providers can lead to a warm hand-off for vulnerable older adults who are fearful of mental health or substance use treatment in an inpatient or outpatient chemical dependency, residential treatment, or sober living environment. Clinicians maintain current local listings of Alcoholics Anonymous (Al-Anon) and National Alliance on Mental Illness (NAMI) for education and support for family and significant others. Clinicians maintain up-to-date lists of community resources for clients to choose their preferred options, including resources such as, Narcotics Anonymous, or other self-help or 12-step programs for sponsors, recovery, and relapse prevention. Clinicians seek to become knowledgeable about insurance coverage for appropriate referrals to different mental health inpatient and outpatient partial hospitalization programs, intensive outpatient programs, clinics, county mental health, and private practice providers. Clinicians have awareness of county, state, and national resources, as well as application processes. Clinicians adhere to CSWE Gero Competency 8: Intervene With Individuals, Families, Groups, Organizations, and Communities, specialized practice behaviors 1–4 (CalSWEC, 2017, pp. 12–14). Clinicians are aware of potential transference and countertransference issues; technological resources for education, support, and advocacy; and potential legal or ethical issues that may present when working with older adults living with a substance use, mental health, or co-occurring/comorbid condition.

Transference/Countertransference

Clinicians working with older adults with mental health, substance use, and comorbid conditions adhere to CSWE Gero Competency 1: Demonstrate Ethical and Professional Behavior, specialized practice behaviors 1–6 to practice both ethically and professionally in all potential transference/countertransference issues between the clinician, client, and other providers (CalSWEC, 2017, pp. 1–2). Clinicians working with older adults with mental health and substance use disorders should be aware of the potential triggering of transference on the part of the client toward the clinician if the clinician reminds the client of another clinician he or she has worked with, favorably or unfavorably, in the past or if the clinician reminds the client of someone in the position of being a high-risk relationship trigger for relapse. For countertransference, the clinician may have experiences with a substance use or mental health condition or know someone who has, or the clinician may overidentify with the client and overinvest in the treatment, recovery, and aftercare plan for the client. The same may follow with personal attitudes and experiences about mental health and substance use disorders, the etiology of them, and/or any stereotypes about individuals living with a mental health, substance use, or co-occurring disorder. Awareness of the potential for transference/countertransference and mindfulness of strategies to address issues that present are essential to ethical and professional practice.

Technological Resources

Alcoholics Anonymous: https://www.aa.org/

Al-Anon family groups: https://findtreatment.samhsa.gov/locator/link-SPA

Mental Health America: http://www.mentalhealthamerica.net/

Narcotics Anonymous: https://www.na.org/

National Alliance for Medication Assisted Recovery: http://www.methadone.org/

National Alliance on Mental Illness: https://www.nami.org/

National Council on Alcoholism and Drug Dependence: https://www.ncadd.org/

Substance Abuse and Mental Health Services Administration: https://www.samhsa.gov/

SAMHSA: Behavioral health treatment locator: https://findtreatment.samhsa.gov/

SAMHSA: Mental health consumer assistance: https://findtreatment.samhsa.gov/locator/link-focMHCA

SAMHSA: Peer support (mental health): https://findtreatment.samhsa.gov/locator/link-focPeer

SAMHSA: Self-help groups addiction: https://findtreatment.samhsa.gov/locator/link-focSelfGP

SAMHSA: Service provider associations: https://findtreatment.samhsa.gov/locator/link-SPA

SAMHSA-HRSA Center for Integrated Health Solutions: Administration: https://www.integration.samhsa.gov/about-us/about-cihs

SAMHSA-HRSA Center for Integrated Health Solutions: Clinical practice: https://www.integration.samhsa.gov/clinical-practice

SAMHSA-HRSA Center for Integrated Health Solutions: Integrated care models: https://www.integration.samhsa.gov/integrated-care-models

SAMHSA-HRSA Center for Integrated Health Solutions: Screening tools: https://www.integration.samhsa.gov/clinical-practice/screening-tools

Legal/Ethical Considerations

When engaging older adult clients in motivational interviewing techniques, clinicians are reminded that when developing discrepancy, "its practice requires a sensitivity and ability to empathize that is critical for avoiding the ethical challenge that therapy should not be making clients feel uncomfortable," and the recommended guideline to manage this is "the more discrepancy is deployed, the deeper should be the quality of empathic listening" (Rollnick & Allison, 2004, p. 110). Clinicians should be aware of legal issues that older adult clients may be working through as a result of substance use, mental health, co-occurring, or comorbid conditions and work ethically with the client and other agencies to provide resources and support for addressing such issues (i.e., DUIs, court-mandated drug or alcohol counseling, medical bills from comorbid conditions or inpatient mental health or substance use, housing foreclosure or evictions, etc.). Clinicians adhere to CSWE Gero Competency 1: Demonstrate Ethical and Professional Behavior, specialized practice behaviors 1–7 to work ethically and professionally with older adults living with comorbidity, mental health, substance use, and co-occurring disorders.

Critical Thinking Activity/Discussion Questions

1. How are older adults with mental health disorders screened in your agency or community?
   a. What treatments and interventions are typically provided to organizations at your agency, in the local community, or in the state where you work with older adults?
   b. What resources are available?
   c. What legal/ethical issues have occurred that you are aware of, and how were they addressed?

2. How are older adults with substance use disorders screened in your agency or community?
   a. What treatments and interventions are typically provided to organizations at your agency, in the local community, or in the state where you work with older adults?
   b. What resources are available?
   c. What legal/ethical issues have occurred that you are aware of, and how were they addressed?

3. How are older adults with comorbid or co-occurring disorders screened in your agency or community?
   a. What treatments and interventions are typically provided to organizations at your agency, in the local community, or in the state where you work with older adults?
   b. What resources are available?
   c. What legal/ethical issues have occurred that you are aware of, and how were they addressed?

Self-Reflection Exercises

1. Critically examine your own attitudes and beliefs about mental health.
   a. What did you learn about mental health growing up?
   b. From whom did you learn it?
   c. How do those beliefs influence your perceptions of mental health today?
   d. How might those beliefs affect your ability to engage, assess, and intervene with older adults living with a mental health disorder(s)?

2. Critically examine your own attitudes and beliefs about substance use.
   a. What did you learn about substance use growing up?
   b. From whom did you learn it?
   c. How do those beliefs influence your attitudes about substance use today?
   d. How might those beliefs affect your ability to engage, assess, and intervene with older adults living with a substance use disorder(s)?

3. Critically examine your own attitudes and beliefs about comorbid or co-occurring disorders.
   a. What did you learn about comorbid or co-occurring disorders growing up?
   b. From whom did you learn it?
   c. How do those beliefs influence your attitudes about comorbid or co-occurring disorders today?
   d. How might those beliefs affect your ability to engage, assess, and intervene with older adults with high risks factors for sexual health?

References

American Psychiatric Association. (2013). *Diagnostic and statistical manual of mental disorders* (5th ed.). Arlington, VA: American Psychiatric Publishing.

American Public Health Association. (2008). *Alcohol screening and brief intervention: A guide for public health practitioners*. Washington DC: National Highway Traffic Safety Administration, U.S. Department of Transportation.

Bolton, K. W., Praetorius, R. T., & Smith-Osborne, A. (2016). Resilience protective factors in an older adult population: A qualitative interpretive meta-synthesis. *Social Work Research, 40*(3), 171–182.

CalSWEC. (2017). CalSWEC curriculum competencies for public child welfare, behavioral health, and aging in California. Retrieved from https://calswec.berkeley.edu/sites/default/files/2017_calswec_curriculum_competencies_0.pdf

Chiesa, A., & Serretti, A. (2011). Mindfulness-based interventions for chronic pain: A systematic review of the evidence. *The Journal of Alternative and Complementary Medicine, 17*(1), 83–93.

Council for Social Work Education. (2017). Specialized practice curricular guide for gero social work practice. Alexandria, VA: Council on Social Work Education.

Creswell, J. D., Irwin, M. R., Burklund, L. J., Lieberman, M. D., Arevalo, J. M., Ma, J., ... & Cole, S. W. (2012). Mindfulness-based stress reduction training reduces loneliness and pro-inflammatory gene expression in older adults: A small randomized controlled trial. *Brain, Behavior, and Immunity, 26*(7), 1095–1101.

Fjorback, L. O., Arendt, M., Ørnbøl, E., Fink, P., & Walach, H. (2011). Mindfulness-based stress reduction and mindfulness-based cognitive therapy: A systematic review of randomized controlled trials. *Acta Psychiatrica Scandinavica, 124*(2), 102–119.

Goeres, L. M., Williams, C. D., Eckstrom, E., & Lee, D. S. (2014). Pharmacotherapy for hypertension in older adults: A systematic review. *Drugs & Aging, 31*(12), 897–910.

Haugan, G., Moksnes, U. K., & Løhre, A. (2016). Intrapersonal self-transcendence, meaning-in-life and nurse–patient interaction: Powerful assets for quality of life in cognitively intact nursing-home patients. *Scandinavian Journal of Caring Sciences, 30*(4), 790–801.

Health Resources and Services Administration. (2017). What is integrated care? Retrieved from https://www.integration.samhsa.gov/resource/what-is-integrated-care

Hofmann, S. G., Asnaani, A., Vonk, I. J., Sawyer, A. T., & Fang, A. (2012). The efficacy of cognitive behavioral therapy: A review of meta-analyses. *Cognitive Therapy and Research, 36*(5), 427–440.

Karasawa, M., Curhan, K. B., Markus, H. R., Kitayama, S. S., Love, G. D., Radler, B. T., & Ryff, C. D. (2011). Cultural perspectives on aging and well-being: A comparison of Japan and the United States. *The International Journal of Aging and Human Development, 73*(1), 73–98.

Martin, A. V. S., Distelberg, B., Palmer, B. W., & Jeste, D. V. (2015). Development of a new multidimensional individual and interpersonal resilience measure for older adults. *Aging & Mental Health, 19*(1), 32–45.

Mattson, M., Lipari, R. N., Hays, C., & Van Horn, S. L. (2017). *A day in the life of older adults: Substance use facts* (Short Report). Rockville, MD: Center for Behavioral Health Statistics and Quality, Substance Abuse and Mental Health Services Administration. Retrieved from https://www.samhsa.gov/data/sites/default/files/report_2792/ShortReport-2792.html

National Institute on Alcohol Abuse and Alcoholism. (2017). Older adults. Retrieved from https://www.niaaa.nih.gov/alcohol-health/special-populations-co-occurring-disorders/older-adults

Roberts, A. R., & Yeager, K. (Eds.). (2006). *Foundations of evidence-based social work practice.* New York, USA: Oxford University Press.

Rollnick, S., & Allsion, J. (2004). What is motivational interviewing? In N. Heather & T. Stockwell (Eds.) *The Essential Handbook for Treatment of Alcohol Problems* (pp. 105-115). The Atrium, Southern Gate, Chichester, England: John Wiley & Sons Ltd

Schlender, J. F., Vozmediano, V., Golden, A. G., Rodriguez, M., Samant, T. S., Lagishetty, C. V., ... & Schmidt, S. (2017). Current strategies to streamline pharmacotherapy for older adults. *European Journal of Pharmaceutical Sciences. 111*, 432–442.

Substance Abuse and Mental Health Services Administration. (1999). *Enhancing motivation for change in substance abuse treatment* (Treatment Improvement Protocol (TIP) Series, No. 35.). Rockville, MD: Center for Substance Abuse Treatment. Retrieved from www.ncbi.nlm.nih.gov/books/NBK64967/

Substance Abuse and Mental Health Services Administration. (2015). Behavioral health trends in the United States: Results from the 2014 national survey on drug use and health. Retrieved from https://www.samhsa.gov/data/sites/default/files/NSDUH-FRR1-2014/NSDUH-FRR1-2014.pdf

Substance Abuse and Mental Health Administration and Health Resources and Services Administration. (2016). *Growing older: Providing integrated care for the aging population* (HHS Publication No. (SMA) 16-4982). Rockville, MD: Substance Abuse and Mental Health Services Administration.

Substance Abuse and Mental Health Services Administration. (2016). Co-occurring disorders. Retrieved from https://www.samhsa.gov/disorders/co-occurring

Substance Abuse and Mental Health Services Administration. (2017a). Homelessness and housing. Retrieved from https://www.samhsa.gov/homelessness-housing

Substance Abuse and Mental Health Services Administration. (2017b). Medication Assisted Treatment (MAT). Retrieved from https://www.integration.samhsa.gov/clinical-practice/mat/mat-overview

Substance Abuse and Mental Health Services Administration. (2017c). Other specific populations. Retrieved from https://www.samhsa.gov/specific-populations

World Health Organization. (2017). Mental health of older adults. Retrieved from http://www.who.int/mediacentre/factsheets/fs381/en/

CHAPTER 8

Chronic Illness and Disability

Chapter Overview

This chapter explores clinical practice with older adults living with a chronic illness and/or disability, presents evidence-based interventions for addressing living with a chronic illness and/or disability, and explores key domains to promote both effective clinical practice with older adults and optimal client outcomes.

CSWE Gero Competencies Highlighted

Competency 1: Demonstrate Ethical and Professional Behavior

> **Specialized Practice Competency Description:** Social workers understand the value base of the profession and its ethical standards, as well as relevant laws and regulations that may impact practice at the micro, mezzo, and macro levels. Social workers understand frameworks of ethical decision-making and how to apply principles of critical thinking to those frameworks in practice, research, and policy arenas. Social workers recognize personal values and the distinction between personal and professional values. They also understand how their personal experiences and affective reactions influence their professional judgment and behavior. Social workers understand the profession's history, its mission, and the roles and responsibilities of the profession. Social workers also understand the role of other professions when engaged in inter-professional teams. Social workers recognize the importance of lifelong learning and are committed to continually updating their skills to ensure they are relevant and effective.

> Social workers also understand emerging forms of technology and the ethical use of technology in social work practice.

Competency Behaviors: (1) Guided by ethical reasoning and self-reflection, demonstrate adherence to ethical frameworks and key laws, policies, and procedures related to aging, and the rights of older adults. (2) Engage in active dialogue with field faculty/instructors regarding aging field placement agency policies and culture around behavior, appearance, communication, and the use of supervision. (3) Develop and sustain effective collaborative relationships that respect older adults' needs for protection, self-determination, and the provision of services in the least restrictive environment possible with colleagues and community stakeholders, including older adults, their family members, other care providers, and Tribes. (4) Effectively manage professional boundary issues and other challenges arising in the course of aging-related work, particularly ambiguities presented by home visits, personal loss, trauma, and other highly involved and potentially emotionally triggering aspects of the work. (5) Develop and sustain relationships with members of interdisciplinary and integrated health care teams, including social workers, primary care providers, hospital staff, home health care providers, psychiatrists, psychologists, substance use disorder treatment staff, Tribal service providers, and others, that reflect clear understanding of their roles in providing care to older adults. (6) Demonstrate both knowledge of the history and evolution of social work practice related to aging and older adults in the United States and California, and a commitment to lifelong learning around this practice. (7) Follow all ethical guidelines and legal mandates in the use of technology in order to maintain the confidentiality of all personal, behavioral health, and health-related information. (CalSWEC, 2017, pp. 1–2)

Competency 2: Engage Diversity and Difference in Practice

Specialized Practice Competency Description: Social workers understand how diversity and difference characterize and shape the human experience and are critical to the formation of identity. The dimensions of diversity are understood as the intersectionality of multiple factors, including, but not limited to, age, class, color, culture, disability and ability, ethnicity, gender, gender identity and expression, immigration status, marital status, political ideology, race, religion/spirituality, sex, sexual orientation, and Tribal sovereign status. Social workers understand that, as a consequence of difference, a person's life experiences may include oppression, poverty, marginalization, and alienation as well as privilege, power, and acclaim. Social workers also understand the forms and mechanisms of oppression and discrimination and recognize the extent to which a culture's structures and values, including social, economic, political, and cultural exclusions, may oppress, marginalize, alienate, or create privilege and power.

Competency Behaviors: (1) Engage in critical analysis of the interpersonal, community, and social structural causes and effects of disproportionality, disparities, and inequities in the incidence and trajectory of aging-related care needs, housing, transportation, and resource access among older adults, their families, and their communities. (2) Evidence respectful awareness and understanding of the impact of being a member of a marginalized group on aging experiences, and accurately identify differences in access to and quality of available services for members of different communities and populations. (3) Demonstrate knowledge of diverse cultural norms and traditional methods of providing care to older adults, as well as an applied understanding of how these realities affect work with older adults from diverse backgrounds, their families, and their communities. (4) Develop and use practice methods that acknowledge, respect, and address how individual and cultural values, norms, and differences impact the various systems with which older adults interact, including, but not limited to, families, communities, primary care systems, mental and behavioral health care systems, and integrated care systems. (CalSWEC, 2017, pp. 3–4)

Competency 3: Advance Human Rights and Social, Economic, and Environmental Justice

Specialized Practice Competency Description: Social workers understand that every person regardless of position in society has fundamental human rights such as freedom, safety, privacy, an adequate standard of living, health care, and education. Social workers understand the global interconnections of oppression and human rights violations, and are knowledgeable about theories of human need and social justice and strategies to promote social and economic justice and human rights. Social workers understand strategies designed to eliminate oppressive structural barriers to ensure that social goods, rights, and responsibilities are distributed equitably and that civil, political, environmental, economic, social, and cultural human rights are protected.

Competency Behaviors: (1) Clearly articulate the systematic effects of discrimination, oppression, and stigma on the needs and experiences of older adults and on the quality and delivery of services available to them, and identify and advocate for policy changes needed to address these issues. (2) Advocate for changes in policies and programs that reflect a social justice practice framework for facilitating access and providing services to older adults, their families, and care providers, especially among underserved groups and communities. (3) Demonstrate the ability to work effectively in cross-disciplinary collaboration to develop and provide interventions that explicitly address the specific needs of diverse older adults, their families, and care providers. (4) Integrate into all aspects of policy and practice sensitivity to the reality that fundamental rights, including freedom and privacy, may be compromised for older adults engaged in care, and the goal that services should be provided in the least restrictive environment possible. (CalSWEC, 2017, pp. 4–5)

Competency 4: Engage in Practice-informed Research and Research-informed Practice

Specialized Practice Competency Description: Social workers understand quantitative and qualitative research methods and their respective roles in advancing a science of social work and in evaluating their practice. Social workers know the principles of logic, scientific inquiry, and culturally informed and ethical approaches to building knowledge. Social workers understand that evidence that informs practice derives from multidisciplinary sources and multiple ways of knowing. They also understand the processes for translating research findings into effective practice.

Competency Behaviors: (1) Demonstrate the ability to understand, interpret, and evaluate the benefits and limitations of various evidence-based and evidence-informed treatment models as they influence practice with older adults. (2) Engage in critical analysis of research findings, practice models, and practice wisdom as they inform aging related practice, including how research practices have historically failed to address the needs and realities of exploited and/or disadvantaged communities, and how cross-cultural research practices can be used to enhance equity. (3) Clearly communicate research findings, conclusions, and implications, as well as their applications to aging practice, across a variety of professional interactions with consumers, families, and multidisciplinary service providers. (4) Apply research findings to aging-related practice with individuals, families, and communities and to the development of professional knowledge about the needs, experiences, and well-being of older adults. (CalSWEC, 2017, pp. 5–6)

Competency 6: Engage With Individuals, Families, Groups, Organizations, and Communities

Specialized Practice Competency Description: Social workers understand that engagement is an ongoing component of the dynamic and interactive process of social work practice with, and on behalf of, diverse individuals, families, groups, organizations, and communities. Social workers value the importance of human relationships. Social workers understand theories of human behavior and the social environment, and critically evaluate and apply this knowledge to facilitate engagement with clients and constituencies, including individuals, families, groups, organizations, and communities. Social workers understand strategies to engage diverse clients and constituencies to advance practice effectiveness. Social workers understand how their personal experiences and affective reactions may impact their ability to effectively engage with diverse clients and constituencies. Social workers value principles of relationship-building and inter-professional collaboration to facilitate engagement with clients, constituencies, and other professionals as appropriate.

Competency Behaviors: (1) Appropriately engage and activate older adults, their families, and other care providers in the development and coordination of care plans that reflect relevant theoretical models and balance older adults' needs for care with respect for autonomy and independence. (2) Effectively utilize interpersonal skills to engage older adults, their families, and other care providers in culturally responsive, consumer-driven, and trauma-informed integrated care that addresses mutually agreed upon service goals and balances needs for care, protection, autonomy, and independence. (3) Establish effective and appropriate communication, coordination, and advocacy planning with other care providers and interdisciplinary care teams as needed to address mutually agreed upon service goals. Recognizing the complex nature of service engagement, ensure that communications with consumers and their families regarding service goals are both sensitive and transparent. (4) Manage affective responses and exercise good judgment around engaging with resistance, trauma responses, and other potentially triggering situations with older adults, their families, and other care providers. (CalSWEC, 2017, pp. 9–10)

Competency 7: Assess Individuals, Families, Groups, Organizations, and Communities

Specialized Practice Competency Description: Practitioners in aging utilize ecological-systems theory, a strengths-based and person/family-centered framework to conduct assessments that value the resilience of diverse older adults, families, and caregivers. They select appropriate assessment tools, methods and technology, and evaluate, adapt, and modify them, as needed, to enhance their validity in working with diverse, vulnerable and at-risk groups. The comprehensive biopsychosocial assessment takes into account the multiple factors of physical, mental and social well-being needed for treatment planning for older adults and their families. They develop skills in interprofessional assessment and communication with key constituencies to choose the most effective practice strategies. Gero social workers understand how their own experiences and affective reactions about aging, quality of life, loss and grief may affect their assessment and resultant decision-making.

Competency Behaviors: (1) Conduct assessments that incorporate a strengths-based perspective, person/family-centered focus, and resilience while recognizing aging related risk, (2) Develop, select, and adapt assessment methods and tools that optimize practice with older adults, their families, caregivers, and communities, and (3) Use and integrate multiple domains and sources of assessment information and communicate with other professionals to inform a comprehensive plan for intervention. (Council for Social Work Education, 2017, pp. 89–90)

Competency 8: Intervene With Individuals, Families, Groups, Organizations, and Communities

Specialized Practice Competency Description: Social workers understand that intervention is an ongoing component of the dynamic and interactive process of social work practice with, and on behalf of, diverse individuals, families, groups, organizations, and communities. Social workers are knowledgeable about evidence-informed interventions to achieve the goals of clients and constituencies, including individuals, families, groups, organizations, and communities. Social workers understand theories of human behavior and the social environment, and critically evaluate and apply this knowledge to effectively intervene with clients and constituencies. Social workers understand methods of identifying, analyzing, and implementing evidence-informed interventions to achieve client and constituency goals. Social workers value the importance of inter-professional teamwork and communication in interventions, recognizing that beneficial outcomes may require interdisciplinary, inter-professional, and inter-organizational collaboration.

Competency Behaviors: (1) In partnership with older adults and their families, develop appropriate intervention plans that reflect respect for autonomy and independence, as well as contemporary theories and models for interventions with older adults. Plans should:

- Reflect cultural humility and acknowledgement of individualized needs;
- Incorporate consumer and family strengths;
- Utilize community resources and natural supports;
- Incorporate multidisciplinary team supports and interventions;
- Include non-pharmacological interventions; and

Demonstrate knowledge of poly-pharmacy needs and issues specific to older adults. (2) Apply the principles of teaming, engagement, inquiry, advocacy, and facilitation within interdisciplinary teams and care coordination to the work of supporting older adults, family members, and other care providers to accomplish intervention goals and satisfy advanced care planning needs.

(3) Effectively implement evidence-based interventions in the context of providing emergency response, triage, brief treatment, and longer-term care, and in the course of addressing a range of issues presented in primary care, specialty care, community agency, inpatient, and palliative care settings. Interventions should be guided by respect for older adults' autonomy and independence and should include components such as psychoeducation, problem-solving treatment skills, symptom tracking, medication therapies, follow-up, and planning for evolving care needs. (4) Effectively plan for interventions in ways that incorporate thoughtfully executed transitions during time-limited internships, recognizing that consumer needs for support may continue beyond these time periods. (CalSWEC, 2017, pp. 12–14)

Specialized Practice Competency Description: Social workers understand that evaluation is an ongoing component of the dynamic and interactive process of social work practice with, and on behalf of, diverse individuals, families, groups, organizations and communities. Social workers recognize the importance of evaluating processes and outcomes to advance practice, policy, and service delivery effectiveness. Social workers understand theories of human behavior and the social environment, and critically evaluate and apply this knowledge in evaluating outcomes. Social workers understand qualitative and quantitative methods for evaluating outcomes and practice effectiveness.

Competency Behaviors: (1) Record, track, and monitor consumer engagement, assessment, and intervention data in practice with older adults, their families, and other care providers accurately and according to field education agency policies and guidelines. (2) Conduct accurate process and outcome analysis of engagement, assessment, and intervention data in practice with older adults, their families, and other care providers that incorporates consumer perspectives and reflects respect for older adults' autonomy and independence. (3) Use findings to evaluate intervention effectiveness, develop recommendations for adapting service plans and approaches as needed, improve interdisciplinary team coordination and care integration, and help agency and community policies better support older adults, their families, and their formal and informal care systems. (4) Share both the purposes of such data collection and the overall results of data analysis with older adults, their families, and communities whenever possible, with the goal of engaging them more meaningfully in the evaluation process. (CalSWEC, 2017, pp. 14–15)

Learning Objectives

1. Learners will become aware of contextual and diversity factors to consider when engaging, assessing, intervening, and evaluating outcomes with older adults with chronic illnesses and disabilities.
2. Learners will identify screening tools for assessing chronic illnesses and disabilities among older adults.
3. Learners will identify appropriate evidence-based interventions.
4. Learners will understand the importance of referring older adult clients to appropriate technological and community resources and when to assist with coordination.
5. Learners will identify sources of transference and countertransference when working with older adults with chronic illnesses and disabilities.

Case Study

Mrs. Fitzpatrick is a 79-year-old female, Caucasian, English-speaking widow residing in a first-floor condominium in a senior retirement community. Her spouse was an aerospace executive; he died five years ago from a stroke. Mrs. Fitzpatrick has a primary diagnosis of chronic obstructive pulmonary disease (COPD); her additional comorbid diagnoses include anxiety disorder and hypertension. Mrs. Fitzpatrick ambulates with a walker, is oxygen dependent after discharge from the hospital, and has been advised by her physician to stop smoking cigarettes. Mrs. Fitzpatrick has two children, a son aged 50 and daughter aged 45—both live in Northern California. Mrs. Fitzpatrick was an elementary school teacher for 40 years at a private school in her community prior to retirement; she has a bachelor degree in education. Mrs. Fitzpatrick has decided, after discharge from her recent hospitalization for pneumonia, to stop driving due to her concerns of slowed reaction time and difficulty seeing at night. She has been independent with shopping, cooking, transportation, and self-care up until her recent hospitalization for pneumonia. Mrs. Fitzpatrick's income is $1,275 in Social Security and $1,500 from her spouse's pension; she has more than $200,000 in savings; her condominium is paid for. Mrs. Fitzpatrick is experiencing increased anxiety and stress and, as a result, changes in activities of daily living (ADL) and instrumental activities of daily living (IADL) functioning after discharge from her hospitalization for pneumonia. The nurse and primary care physician requested a social work consultation to assess anxiety and readiness for smoking cessation, changes in ADL/IADL functioning, coping, and the need for community resources to assist with ADLs and IADLs.

Assessing Context

The definitions for the terms chronic condition and/or chronic disease vary. Both terms are frequently used interchangeably in literature, among governmental health organizations, and among medical professionals. The World Health Organization defines chronic disease as a type of noncommunicable disease that is "of long duration" with "generally a slow progression," such as cardiovascular diseases, diabetes, respiratory diseases, and cancers (2018b, para. 1). The National Center for Health Statistics defines chronic disease as "one lasting 3 months or more" (Bernell & Howard, 2016, p. 1). The Centers for Disease Control's National Center for Chronic Disease Prevention and Health Promotion uses the terms chronic disease and chronic conditions interchangeably, whereas the Centers for Medicare and Medicaid Services uses the term chronic condition consistently. The National Center for Chronic Disease Prevention and Health Promotion defines a chronic condition as one that lasts "a year or more and require[s] ongoing medical attention or that limit[s] activities of daily living" (2016, para. 1). The Centers for Medicare and Medicaid Services lists 18 chronic conditions:

> Alzheimer's disease and related dementia, arthritis (osteoarthritis and rheumatoid), asthma, atrial fibrillation, autism spectrum disorders, cancer (breast,

colorectal, lung, and prostate), chronic kidney disease, chronic obstructive pulmonary disease, depression, diabetes, heart failure, hepatitis (chronic viral B & C), HIV/AIDS, hyperlipidemia (high cholesterol), ischemic heart disease, osteoporosis, schizophrenia and other psychotic disorders, and stroke. (2017, para. 2)

Prevalence rates in 2015 for the top 10 chronic conditions among adults ages 65 and older in the United States are as follows: hypertension (58%), hyperlipidemia (47%), arthritis (31%), ischemic heart disease (29%), diabetes (27%), chronic kidney disease (18%), heart failure (14%), depression (14%), Alzheimer's disease and dementia (11%), and COPD (11%) (National Council on Aging, 2016).

Chronic diseases remain the leading cause(s) of death for older adults in the United States (National Council on Aging, 2016). In 2015, the top five causes of death for adults ages 65 and older (in order) were: heart disease, cancer, chronic respiratory disease, cerebrovascular disease, and Alzheimer's disease (National Center for Health Statistics, 2017). Chronic diseases account for a significant proportion of total health-care spending in the United States as well. According to an analysis conducted by RAND (2017) on the total health-care expenditures by number of chronic conditions adults in the United States are living with (i.e., inpatient and outpatient and across all payer types), 90% of all health-care expenditures in 2014 were accounted for by adults living with one or more chronic conditions. Roughly two-thirds of all health-care costs in the United States are attributed to costs for comorbid or multiple chronic diseases as well as roughly 93% of all expenditures by Medicare (National Council on Aging, 2016). As the number of chronic conditions an adult age 65 or older is living with increases, so do the risks for premature institutionalization, mortality, hospitalization, injury, and impact on functional health in daily activities (National Center for Chronic Disease Prevention and Health Promotion, 2016). Older adults with limitations in functional health, or disability, frequently require assistance from caregivers or other long-term care supports to remain safely in their home and prevent injury. Each year, one out of three older adults fall, which, in turn, increases their risk for hip fractures, institutionalization, social isolation, and depression (National Council on Aging, 2016).

According to the National Council on Aging (2016), 80% of older adults in the United States live with and manage at least one chronic health condition, and nearly 70% live with and manage two or more health conditions. According to the National Center for Chronic Disease Prevention and Health Promotion, three out of four adults ages 65 and older live with multiple chronic conditions (2016). Older adults living with chronic conditions and multiple chronic conditions face risks for limitations in ADLs and IADLs, both of which are measures of disability that can impact the quality of life of an older adult. In 2014, adults ages 65 and older living with and managing one or more chronic conditions and reporting limitations with ADLs or IADLs were 22% and 37%, respectively (RAND, 2017). Cognitive limitations can impact an older adult's ability to perform ADLs and IADLs. In 2014, 39% of adults ages 65 and older with one or more chronic condition reported cognitive limitations (RAND, 2017).

According to the Americans with Disabilities Act (ADA) of 1990, an individual living with a disability is defined as:

> A person with a physical or mental impairment that substantially limits one or more major life activities, or a person with a record of such a physical or mental impairment, or a person who is regarded as having such an impairment. (Northwest ADA Center, 2018, para. 1)

According to the American Community Survey (ACS), in 2016, approximately 35% of adults ages 65 and older were living with a disability (Kraus, Lauer, Coleman, & Houtenville, 2018). The prevalence rates for specific disabilities among adults ages 65 and older in 2016 are as follows: ambulatory (22.5%), hearing (14.6%), independent living (14.6%), cognitive (8.9%), and self-care (8.1%) (Kraus, Lauer, Coleman, & Houtenville, 2018). When engaging, assessing, and intervening with older adults, clinicians should pay close attention to the intersection of chronic illness and disability on the well-being and quality of life of the older adult.

Clinicians can assess frailty levels, comorbid chronic illnesses, functional health, as well as a history of falls to inform treatment planning and interventions with older adults to ensure a goodness of fit. Analysis of data from the National Health and Aging Trends Study, a national study of 7,439 older adults, reveals that older adults who are frail have higher prevalence rates of chronic illnesses in comparison to robust, or non-frail, older adults, and higher rates of falls and hospitalizations in the past 12 months (Bandeen-Roche et al., 2015). The study defines frailty using the physical frailty pheno-type (PFP), which includes five measures: (1) shrinking (i.e., body mass index of 18.5 or lower, loss of 10 or more pounds in the past 12 months); (2) exhaustion (i.e., decreased energy that impacts day-to-day functioning/participation in daily activities); (3) weakness, measured by hand grip strength; (4) low physical activity (i.e., not walking or participating in strenuous activities); and (5) slowness, measured by a low walking speed (Bandeen-Roche et al., 2015). Frail older adults are those who meet three to five criteria from the PFP; robust older adults are those who meet none of the PFP criteria (Bandeen-Roche et al., 2015). Fall prevalence rates (in the past year) are 54.9% for frail older adults in comparison to 18.1% of robust older adults (Bandeen-Roche et al., 2015). Hospitalizations are also higher for frail older adults in the past year in comparison to robust older adults—42.4% versus 11.1%, respectively (Bandeen-Roche et al., 2015). Prevalence rate comparisons for chronic illnesses between frail older adults and robust older adults are as follows: arthritis: 75.4% versus 40.9%; high blood pressure: 72.5% versus 56.2%; heart disease: 42.4% versus 16.2%; diabetes: 35.4% versus 17.2%; osteo-porosis: 31.8% versus 15.6%; lung disease: 26.2% versus 9.2%; probable dementia: 29.3% versus 2.7%; and stroke: 21.9% versus 4.7%, respectively (Bandeen-Roche et al., 2015). Frail older adults experience greater limitations in functional health (i.e., indicator of disability) and subsequently have higher prevalence rates of need for assistance with self-care, mobility, and household activities in comparison to robust and prefrail older adults (i.e., those who meet one to two PFP criteria) (Figure 8.1) (Bandeen-Roche et al., 2015).

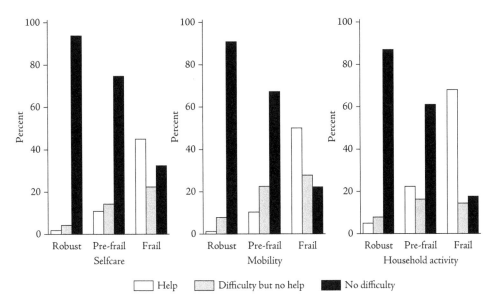

Help   Difficulty but no help   No difficulty

FIGURE 8.1. Disability Prevalence by Frail Status (n = 7,439)

Biopsychosocial/Spiritual Assessment Case Study Application

Following is an application of the Geriatric Biopsychosocial/Spiritual Assessment conducted by Mrs. Fitzpatrick's social worker.

Box 8.1

Geriatric Biopsychosocial/Spiritual Assessment

Basic Demographic: 79-year-old female, Caucasian, English-speaking widow; bachelor-level education

Referral Information: Nurse and primary care physician requested a social work consultation to assess anxiety, readiness for smoking cessation, changes in ADL/IADL functioning, coping, and the need for community resources to assist with ADLs and IADLs

Cultural/Spiritual: Client's religious preference is Christianity; no use of complementary or alternative medicine per client report

Social: [Relationships within family, social/diversity groups, and community]

- Widowed at age 74; has one sister in Northern California and one brother in Florida — she speaks to both weekly; two adult children live in Northern California; she has several friends from church and a bridge club at the clubhouse in her retirement community

Financial: [Ability to provide basic needs and access health services]

- Ability to provide basic needs: Client is able to secure food; her shelter and clothing are secure; however, she needs assistance with housekeeping, laundry, shopping, and transportation
- Health insurance: Adequate—Medicare and AARP supplemental insurance
- Income sources: $1,275 in Social Security and $1,500 from spouse's pension; she has more than $200,000 in savings

Environmental: [Personal safety, maintenance of residence, and safety of community]

- Current social context/environmental: At home alone
- Neighborhood safety: Adequate lighting, low crime in neighborhood
- Home safety: Slip rugs removed; no clutter; oxygen precautions followed; client has an electric stove and oven; concerns for safety with oxygen and smoking cigarettes
- Access to guns: No guns or access to guns in the home
- Screen for abuse or neglect by self or perpetrated by others (APS SOC341 report if suspected): No indicators of abuse or neglect

Physical: [Individual function and disease morbidity]

- Health literacy and self-rated health: Client has high health literacy, and self-rated health is good; client reports she does have an advance directive and general power of attorney, listing her son and daughter as agents; diagnosis is COPD, anxiety, and hypertension; medications: Advair COPD inhaler and Ativan for anxiety PRN (adherent with both); functional health (ADLs, IADLs): independent with ADLs, needs assistance with IADLs; no other chronic health, substance use, or mental health conditions; sexual health—inactive

Mental: [Mental status, depression, anxiety, and substance abuse]

- Standardized screening instruments: Moderate anxiety from GAD-7, score of 13; no indicators of depression
- Suicide risk assessment: Did not endorse suicidal ideations
- Homicidal ideations: Did not endorse homicidal ideations
- Substance use: None

Formulation/Evaluation: Assist with application for local transportation and part-time caregiver from local agency; one-on-one counseling for three weeks with cognitive behavioral therapy and mindfulness-based stress reduction to reduce anxiety symptoms

> **Treatment Planning:** Collaborated with physician, nurse, and physical and occupational therapists; social worker to assist with ensuring transportation and caregiver are implemented before discharge; one-on-one counseling for three weeks for anxiety and smoking cessation readiness
>
> **Community Resource Needs:** Assist with local transportation application; assist with setting up caregiver agency interviews with three agencies; referral for waterproof emergency response pendant through Lifeline for safety; chronic disease management program

Diversity–Cultural Competence/Spirituality/LGBT/Sexuality

When engaging, assessing, and intervening with older adults, clinicians must be aware of how diversity impacts the lived experience of an older adult client living with a chronic illness and/or disability. Health disparities and inequalities in the United States among minority populations are well documented in literature. The Centers for Disease Control (CDC) Office of Minority Health and Health Equity defines health disparities as "differences in health outcomes and their causes among groups of people" (2018, para. 1). Examples of disparities include differences in prevalence rates of diseases, access to preventive care, and mortality rates. Health inequalities are "avoidable, unfair differences in health status seen within and between populations" (Centers for Disease Control, 2013, p. 1). Health inequalities are further described by the World Health Organization as "systematic differences in health outcomes or in the distribution of health resources, arising from the social conditions in which people are born, grow, work, live, and age" (2018a, para 1). Those social conditions and other factors that influence health are referred to as social determinants of health—for example, access and quality of education and jobs, food and housing resources available, social support, culture, language, transportation, community-based services to support independent living, health-care service access, crime, socioeconomic status, technology access, social norms, and segregation of residences (Office of Disease Prevention and Health Promotion, 2018). Social determinants of health also include the "wider set of forces and systems shaping the conditions of daily life," such as "economic policies and systems, development agendas, social norms, social policies and political systems" (World Health Organization, 2018c, para. 1). The Healthy People 2020 initiative highlights five key areas of social determinants of health in an organizing framework to create objectives: economic stability; education; social and community context; health and health care; and neighborhood and built environment (Office of Disease Prevention and Health Promotion, 2018).

When engaging, assessing, and intervening with older adult clients, clinicians can be aware of and seek to understand from the client's narrative the particular social determinants influential to the client's health status and target micro, mezzo, and macro interventions to improve health outcomes and address inequities. Social determinants of health are attributable to a large proportion of health inequalities (Centers for Disease

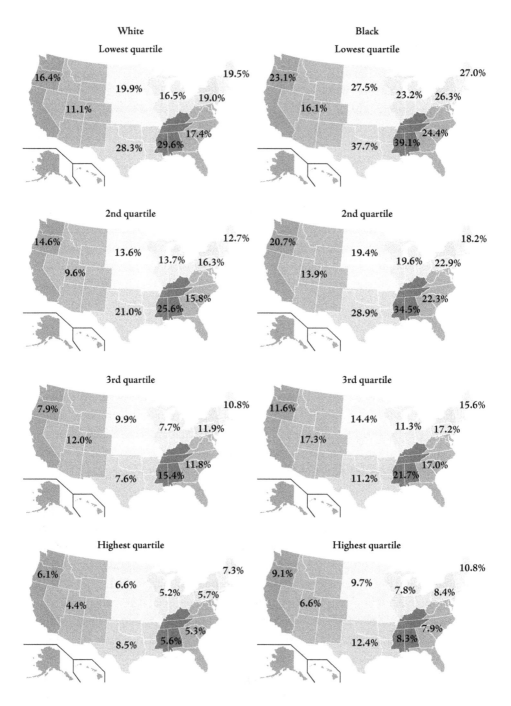

Control, 2013). A cross-sectional examination of the National Health and Aging Trends Study, a longitudinal study of 7,439 adults ages 65 and older across all regions of the United States, was supplemented by a two-hour interview with participants to examine frailty along with the existence of disparities by income, geographical region, ethnicity, and gender prevalence for adults 65 and older in the United States (Bandeen-Roche et al., 2015). Researchers found that among adults 65 and older in the United States, frailty was reported by 15.3% of older adults, pre-frailty 45.5%, and robust 39.2% (Bandeen-Roche et al., 2015). Frailty is an indicator of disability and subsequent need for ADL and IADL assistance (Bandeen-Roche et al., 2015). The former national study of older adults identified key disparities for vulnerable older adults:

> Higher frailty prevalence was observed among older persons, women and racial/ ethnic minorities, persons in residential care, and persons with lower incomes. The extent of variation was striking, with frailty prevalence 65%–85% higher for blacks and Hispanics than whites, more than twofold higher among those in residential care versus the community dwelling, and more than fourfold higher among the oldest age group relative to the youngest, and the lowest income quartile relative to the highest. (Bandeen-Roche et al., 2015, p. 1429)

Specifically, frailty increases with advancing age from 8.9% of adults ages 65 to 69 to 33.3% of oldest old adults ages 85 to 89 and 3.9% of oldest old adults ages 90 and older (Bandeen-Roche et al., 2015). Rates of frailty are higher for both non-Hispanic Black (22.9%) and Hispanic (24.6%) in comparison to non-Hispanic White and other races (13.8% and 13.7%, respectively) (Bandeen-Roche et al., 2015). The disparity reflecting regional, race/ethnicity, and income are represented in Figure 8.2; for all geographic and regional levels, frailty is lower among non-Hispanic White older adults in comparison to non-Hispanic Blacks (Bandeen-Roche et al., 2015). Frailty rates were higher in residential care settings (29.5%) in comparison to community settings (14.5%) (Bandeen-Roche et al., 2015). Lower income was also indicative of higher frailty rates, with frailty decreasing as income increased: lowest income quartile was 25.8%, second income quartile was 19.7%, third income quartile was 11%, and highest income quartile was 5.9% (Bandeen-Roche et al., 2015). An assessment of diversity factors informs interdisciplinary treatment planning.

Interdisciplinary Team Roles and Planning

Mr. Martinez was seen in the hospital by the social worker while recovering from his triple bypass surgery. In rounds, the attending physician and nurse presented his physical status and projected physical/medication needs postdischarge. The social worker was assigned to assist with assessing and identifying other postdischarge psychosocial needs and financial/ insurance/medication options. An immediate need for Mr. Martinez was to apply for state disability to establish an immediate link to Medi-Cal (i.e., Medicaid in California) insurance to cover his financial expenses at the hospital and postdischarge aftercare treatment once he returned home. Although Mr. Martinez lived in California, his hospitalization and surgery occurred before the implementation of the Affordable Care Act; therefore, he was without insurance and was established as a cash patient. He did have an immediate link, however, to state disability as he had been working for more than 45 years with state, local, and federal taxes taken out. The social worker assisted with completing the Employment Development Department (EDD) state disability application and had the attending physician complete sections to submit the application prior to discharge. Mr. Martinez's options were to apply for state disability under state disability insurance (SDI), which provides higher compensation than unemployment; Social Security Disability (SSD) and Supplemental Security Income; or early Social Security with a penalty. Mr. Martinez needed immediate financial resources to meet his household expenses and decided to apply for state disability first, followed by Social Security and Medicare A and B when he turned 65 in six months. The financial department at the hospital was contacted to assist with completing a Medi-Cal application that could be submitted with retrospective payment for the past 90 days once his state disability was approved. Medication assistance program applications were completed to assist with reduced medication costs for his postdischarge medications until his Medi-Cal took effect. A primary care physician was identified, and an appointment was scheduled three days after discharge within 20 minutes from Mr. Martinez's residence. His spouse was able to drive and assist with IADLs; Mr. Martinez needed supervision with bathing and grooming as his two weeks in the hospital left him frail and weak and using a walker for ambulation. Physical and occupational therapy worked with him in the hospital and home health nurse, physical, occupational therapist, and social worker evaluations were ordered for his discharge follow-up.

Interdisciplinary team communication, collaboration, and planning are key to successful care transitions and coordination of care from one system of care to another during an episode treatment. Fortunately, Mr. Martinez was highly motivated for treatment and was compliant with recommended care from each discipline. His spouse received caregiver training to assist him with postdischarge aftercare as well, and there were no barriers in accessing necessary financial and community resources to ensure positive health outcomes. In working in health and community-based settings with older adults, there are four key evidence-based interventions that can assist the client with managing chronic conditions and ensuring safety in the setting of the client's preference: motivational interviewing, solution-focused therapy, problem-solving therapy, and chronic disease management models.

Evidence-based Interventions

The use of evidence-based interventions to increase older adult clients' motivation to engage in change behaviors for managing chronic illnesses, implementing modifications for safety in the home (i.e., removal of slip rugs, proper lighting, handrails and grab bars, etc.), and accepting community resource/service assistance (i.e., personal care, transportation, case management, etc.) when unmet functional health needs are identified is essential to the safety, well-being, and quality of life of older adults. Clinicians can add an assessment of frailty levels, comorbid chronic illnesses, functional health, as well as a history of falls to inform treatment planning and interventions with older adults that provide a goodness of fit. Communication with other disciplines for corroboration of client self-reports and clinician assessment/observations further inform treatment planning.

Motivational Interviewing

The use of motivational interviewing by social workers with older adults has demonstrated effectiveness in improving the health status for adults with improved control of high blood pressure and blood sugar, lower cholesterol, and protective change behaviors such as increased physical activity, a healthy diet, and smoking cessation (Cummings, Cooper, & Cassie, 2009). Motivational interviewing, an evidence-based intervention developed by Rollnick and Miller, is defined as "a directive, client-centered counseling style for eliciting behavior change by helping clients explore and resolve ambivalence" (Rollnick & Allison, 2004, p. 107). Motivational interviewing emphasizes three key concepts: (1) readiness (i.e., the client's readiness to engage in change behavior assessed by the clinician using the stages of change or transtheoretical model), (2) ambivalence (i.e., the client's ambivalence about change behaviors), and (3) resistance (i.e., the client's "general reluctance to make progress, or as opposition to the counsellor or what the counsellor thinks is best, or as the client's expectations as to the posture of the agency the counsellor represents, or even, more traditionally, as denial") (Rollnick & Allison, 2004, p. 109). Mrs. Fitzpatrick was advised to stop smoking due to her primary diagnosis of COPD and postdischarge dependence on oxygen 24 hours per day. She was reluctant at the hospital to pursue options for smoking cessation; her safety at home due to oxygen dependence was a concern, as were preventing recidivism and complications to her health. Upon the initial assessment of Mrs. Fitzpatrick's readiness for smoking cessation in the hospital, she was in precontemplation as she denied that there would be safety concerns and stated she planned to go out onto the patio and leave her oxygen inside when she smoked as much as half a pack of cigarettes per day. Upon the initial home visit, she expressed ambivalence about changing as she stated she had been smoking for more than 50 years and was concerned that her anxiety would increase if she stopped smoking; she maintained a posture of resistance to change during the first home visit.

The key principles of motivational interviewing are express empathy, roll with resistance, support self-efficacy, and develop discrepancy (Rollnick & Allison, 2004). The method involves empathic listening skills, eliciting self-motivating statements—referred to as change talk, where the client presents reasons for change rather than the clinician—and responding to resistance (Rollnick & Allison, 2004). The use of simple and complex reflections as well as summaries by the clinician provide opportunities for the client to correct both reflections and summaries made (Rollnick & Allison, 2004). Express empathy is defined as a clinical technique "enhanced considerably by the use of reflective listening," which "involves both simple and summary statements, designed to ensure parity with the client, and more complex statements that enable the skilled counsellor to gently but directively highlight elements of the client's dilemma that might encourage resolution of ambivalence" (Rollnick & Allison, 2004, p. 109). The principles and skills of motivational interviewing used by the clinician during the three sessions with Mrs. Fitzpatrick proved effective in resolving her ambivalence about smoking cessation. During the first session, Mrs. Fitzpatrick expressed ambivalence and resistance to change related to a fear that smoking cessation would increase her anxiety and/or cause weight gain; she minimized safety concerns with smoking and oxygen use. During the second session, Mrs. Fitzpatrick transitioned from precontemplation to contemplation as she began expressing her own reasons for change, such as preventing hospitalization, preventing a heart attack or stroke, and an interest in improving her lung function by enrolling in a Better Breathing program offered at the hospital. By the third session, Mrs. Fitzpatrick transitioned to the action stage; her self-efficacy and confidence in moving forward with smoking cessation increased, and she requested the social worker contact her nurse and physician to begin smoking cessation treatment. Two follow-up visits were authorized to monitor Mrs. Fitzpatrick's anxiety, reinforce the use of coping skills and relaxation techniques, and assess smoking cessation compliance. Mrs. Fitzpatrick successfully transitioned to the maintenance stage of change with new confidence in her ability to maintain gains she made in treatment and better manage her symptoms. The combined use of motivational interviewing with solution-focused therapy can further facilitate an older adult's self-efficacy and motivation to identify solutions to address issues or problems they are experiencing related to living with a chronic illness, functional health declines, and/or other psychosocial issues.

Solution-focused therapy

Solution-focused therapy, developed by de Shazer and Berg in the 1980s, is a clinical approach that places emphasis on the clinician's facilitation and exploration with the client in discovering "what works (so that we could do more of it) rather than its opposite" to address issues the client presents to treatment; as such, the approach emphasizes solutions that make biopsychosocial/spiritual issues the client presents for treatment with better (de Shazer & Berg, 1997, p. 122). Solution-focused therapy is a client-centered model that emphasizes what clinicians and clients do together in treatment that is beneficial versus what the clinician does that is beneficial for the client (de Shazer & Berg, 1997). According to Bannink (2007), there is a clear difference in the therapeutic stance of the clinician between problem-focused and solution-focused approaches to treatment:

> Many differences exist between SFBT [Solution Focused Brief Therapy] and problem-focused types of psychotherapy which focus on in-depth exploration of the life history of the client and his family, problem description and data collection in a problem analysis, diagnosis made by the therapist, formulation of goals, treatment plan and interventions by the therapist, execution of interventions by the client and evaluation of the treatment. [With problem focused-approaches] the attitude of the therapist is "leading": he is the expert who advises the client. (p. 90)

Solution-focused therapy can be beneficial in inpatient and outpatient settings where an older adult newly diagnosed with a chronic illness, managing exacerbations of symptoms and/or subsequent changes in functional health chronic illnesses medical settings, receives brief therapy (sessions of one to six visits) with the clinician. Engagement and rapport building with a client in an initial outpatient clinical setting using solution-focused therapy often begins with one of two questions: "What brings you here?" or "What needs to come out of this session/these sessions?" (Bannink, 2007, p. 91). A suggested modification to direct these questions to specific chronic illnesses and functional health changes of older adults are: "What do you know about changes in your health status?" and "What do you need out of treatment?" These questions invite the client to describe in his or her own words presenting issues and to formulate solutions through goals to address them. The development of a goal for treatment should be SMART (i.e., one that is specific, measurable, attainable, realistic, and with a time frame). This process involves the client, rather than the clinician, "envisaging and describing what will be different in his life once the problem is solved" (Bannink, 2007, p. 91). The formulation of goals may involve the miracle question:

> Imagine a miracle occurring tonight that would (sufficiently) solve the problem which brought you here, but you were unaware of this as you were asleep: how in the morning would you notice that this miracle had taken place? What would be different? What would you be doing differently? What else? Who would be the next person to notice that the miracle has happened? How would this person notice? How would he react? (Bannink, 2007, p. 91)

The miracle question helps the client envision the change they desire; by engaging in this question, they are often able to more easily articulate specific actions and solutions to achieve the desired state/situation. Other techniques include: (1) assessing the client's motivation for change during the initial session, (2) inviting the client to share exceptions or "moments in the client's life when the problem does not occur or is less serious and who did or does what to make these exceptions happen," and (3) using scaling questions "to discover improvements between the application and the first meeting, which can be built upon; to measure progress in the therapy, and to measure and stimulate motivation and confidence that the problem can be solved" (involving a ranking on a scale of 1 to 10, with a lower score indicative of lower confidence and motivation of a problem being solved and a higher number indicative of greater confidence) (Bannink, 2007, p. 91). In traditional outpatient clinical settings, the clinician provides feedback to focus the client on further development or changes that can be made to reach the client's targeted goals, which involves the clinician leaving the room for a brief period and then coming back with compliments to the client and suggestions—compliments "emphasize what the client is already doing in order to solve his problems" and suggestions "indicate areas requiring attention by the client or possible further actions to solve the problems" (Bannink, 2007, p. 91). Feedback can be modified to the inpatient or outpatient setting with an older adult without the clinician leaving the room. Mr. Martinez presented with a specific issue that he sought information for and guidance from the clinician: adjusting to a nonwork role after bypass surgery and providing financially for his spouse due to his inability to return back to work. Mr. Martinez was motivated and clear about his goal for treatment: being informed about his options to provide financially after discharge. He formulated a specific goal for treatment to become educated about his income options and make a decision as to the best option to apply for within 48 hours prior to discharge. The clinician met with Mr. Martinez two days later, provided compliments for his actions and motivation to consider his best option, provided feedback on the pros and cons of each option, and assisted with ensuring his application for state disability was submitted prior to his discharge.

In a meta-analysis of the efficacy of SFBT in 21 international studies, SFBT was found to produce "equivalent results and, in some cases, positive changes occur in less time and, therefore, at a lower cost for users" than problem-focused treatments (Bannink, 2007, p. 90; Stams, Dekovic, Buist, & de Vries, 2006). In the meta-analysis, it was concluded that "SFBT does not have a larger effect than problem-focused therapy, (however) it does have a positive effect in less time and satisfies the client's need for autonomy more than do traditional forms of psychotherapy" (Bannink, 2007, p. 90).

Problem-Solving Therapy

Problem-solving therapy (PST) was developed in the 1970s by D'Zurilla and Goldfried to provide a "positive approach to clinical intervention that focuses on training in constructive problem-solving attitudes and skills" with the aim to "reduce psychopathology and to enhance psychological and behavioral functioning to prevent relapses and the development of new clinical problems" and to "maximize quality of life" (D'Zurilla & Nezu, 2010, p. 197). This approach grew out of the cognitive behavioral movement and emphasizes self-control of the client change behavior maintenance (D'Zurilla & Nezu, 2010). A myriad number of efficacy studies have been conducted to date; the research suggests PST is effective with older adults as an individual treatment or combined with other treatments; in primary care, outpatient, clinical, and other settings; with individuals, families, and groups; and for psychosocial and health conditions such as depression, anxiety and stress disorders, suicidal ideations, relationship issues, cancer, diabetes and other chronic health conditions, substance use, and obesity, as well as weight management (D'Zurilla & Nezu, 2010).

The five goals for PST are: "(1) Enhance one's positive problem orientation; (2) decrease one's negative orientation; (3) foster one's ability to apply rational problem-solving skills; (4) reduce one's tendency to avoid problem solving; and (5) minimize one's tendency to be impulsive and careless" (D'Zurilla & Nezu, 2010, pp. 209-210). The approach to problem solving emphasizes five key problem-solving skills clients must have to successfully implement the model; clinicians should review the following five skills with the client before engaging the client in PST using the seven steps of PST. These skills are intended to enhance client adaptation to their environments when seeking to address problems or issues they are experiencing:

A = Attitude. Before attempting to solve the problem, individuals should adopt a positive, optimistic attitude (i.e., problem orientation) toward the problem and their problem-solving ability.

D = Define. This step recommends that individuals, after adopting a positive attitude, define the problem by obtaining relevant facts, identifying obstacles that inhibit goal achievement, and specifying a realistic goal.

A = Alternatives. Based on a well-defined problem, persons are directed to generate a variety of different alternatives to overcome any identified obstacles and achieve the problem-solving goal.

P = Predict. After generating a list of alternatives, people are directed to predict both the positive and negative consequences of each alternative, and to choose the one(s) that has the highest probability to achieve the problem-solving goal, while minimizing costs and maximizing benefits.

T = Try out. When individuals have chosen a solution, they are then asked to try out the solution in real-life and monitor its effects. If they are satisfied with the results, the problem is solved and they should engage in self-reinforcement. If they are not satisfied, they are then directed to go back to the "A" step and search for a more effective solution. (D'Zurilla & Nezu, 2010, p. 212)

PST sessions generally range from 30 to 40 minutes in length and as a brief intervention, between four and 12 sessions (UCSF, 2011). When engaging in PST, the seven stages the clinician guides the client through are: "(1) selecting and defining the problem, (2) establishing realistic and achievable goals, (3) generating alternative solutions, (4) implementing decision making guidelines, (5) evaluating and choosing solutions (6), implementing the preferred solution, and (7) evaluating the outcome" (Substance Abuse and Mental Health Services Administration, 2016, para 1). Mrs. Robinson was a 66-year-old African American female who relocated from Alaska to live with her daughter, son-in-law, and two grandchildren due to multiple comorbid chronic health conditions (obesity, emphysema, insulin-dependent diabetes, hypertension, and oxygen dependence) and depression, which left her homebound and in need of assistance with ADLs and IADLs; she ambulates with standby assistance with a walker and uses a wheelchair when leaving the home. Mrs. Robinson was struggling with the sale of her home in Alaska and adapting to her new environment; she agreed to PST for four sessions in her home to address a specific problem she identified as the source of her depression. Mrs. Robinson had been living with her family for three months prior to the home visit by the clinician. Mrs. Robinson defined her greatest problem as her daughter wanting her to sell her home in Alaska and live permanently with her and her family (stage one). Mrs. Robinson made the goal of making a decision on whether to sell her home within 2 weeks (stage two). The solutions she developed were to sell her home and stay with her family or return back home to Alaska with a 24-hour caregiver (stage three). During treatment, Mrs. Robinson engaged in evaluating the solutions using decision-making guidelines to determine the feasibility of each solution, its impact on her and her family, and whether it met her goal (stage four) (UCSF, 2011). In the following session, Mrs. Robinson engaged in comparisons of the pros and cons of each solution, using a PST worksheet to list all of the pros and cons of each solution (stage five); she was encouraged to consider a solution with the most positive impacts and the least negative ones according to clinician guidelines (UCSF, 2011). In the next session, Mrs. Robinson made the decision to sell her home; from here, a list of all the actions she needed to engage in were documented; she asked that her daughter be present at the end of the session so she could share her decisions, necessary actions, and what her preferences were (stage six). In the last session, Mrs. Robinson was encouraged to evaluate the outcome of her decision (stage seven). Although the sale of her home and legal assistance with items she wanted to distribute to others would extend beyond treatment, Mrs. Robinson was satisfied with her decision and reported feeling better prepared to now adjust and adapt to her new environment and any available opportunities to improve her quality of life and well-being.

Chronic Disease Management Models

Chronic disease management models are an important component of tertiary interventions for maintenance of desired behavior changes and self-management of comorbid chronic illnesses and/or disability among older adults. Chronic disease self-management programs improve client self-efficacy, knowledge, and skills to manage and live with single or comorbid chronic illnesses, such as diabetes, arthritis, heart disease, stroke, or lung disease, which may impact their functional health and ability to perform ADLs and IADLs (Centers for Disease Control and Prevention, n.d.). The chronic disease self-management program was developed in 1996 after clinical trials conducted by Stanford University and consists of six sessions, two and a half hours in length, with trained leaders who are usually a social worker or nurse and peer educator (i.e., one living with a chronic illness) (Self-Management Resource Center, 2018). The educational topics include: "techniques to deal with problems such as frustration, fatigue, pain and isolation;" group member "appropriate exercise for maintaining and improving strength, flexibility, and endurance;" guidance on the "appropriate use of medications;" strategies and practice for interpersonal effectiveness for "communicating effectively with family, friends, and health professionals;" "nutrition, decision-making;" and "how to evaluate new treatments" (Self-Management Resource Center, 2018, para. 7). A meta-analysis of 23 clinical trials for the chronic disease self-management program was conducted to evaluate the program's efficacy on the following key outcomes: self-efficacy, psychological health status, physical health status, health behaviors, and health-care utilization (Centers for Disease Control, 2011). Key outcomes results are as follows: self-efficacy for managing a chronic illnesses improved moderately and significantly at four- to six- and nine- to 12-month follow-ups; psychological health status for depression and distress were significantly improved at four- to six- and nine- to 12-month follow-ups; physical health improvements for energy and fatigue were maintained through four- to six-month follow-ups; small to moderate improvements were noted for health behaviors (i.e., cognitive symptom management, exercises for strength/stretching, physician communication skills) at four- to six- and nine- to 12-month follow-ups; and changes in health-care utilization were minimal (Centers for Disease Control, 2011). Assessment of outcomes and monitoring of interventions is a key to best practice with older adults.

Assessing/Monitoring Evidence-based Treatment Outcomes

Clinicians follow CSWE Competency 9: Evaluate Practice With Individuals, Families, Groups, Organizations, and Communities to engage, assess, track, and monitor data for health promotion, wellness, and interventions for aging in place with older adults and their families that promotes chronic disease self-management behaviors to improve client self-efficacy, improvements in psychological and physical health, health behaviors, and communication with health-care professionals (specialized practice behaviors 1–2). Evidence-based chronic disease self-management programs, such as those developed by Stanford University, include evaluation tools clinicians can use to monitor and track initial outcomes and maintenance of key outcomes at four to six and nine to 12 months. Clinicians use the outcomes from evaluations and self-management programs to improve interdisciplinary care planning, treatment, and evaluation of interventions with older adults and their families and to engage them in processes related to chronic disease management and adapting to functional health changes/disability (specialized practice behaviors 3–4). In addition to monitoring outcomes, as part of best practice, clinicians identify, refer, and coordinate services among agencies/systems when appropriate.

Community Resources/Interagency Coordination

Clinicians working with older adults living with chronic illnesses and/or functional health changes/disabilities should be aware of local and national resources that an older adult can utilize to achieve their desired goals as well as interagency collaborations and web-based and other forms of chronic disease self-management using technology (CSWE Gero Competency 1: Demonstrates Ethical and Professional Behavior, specialized practice behaviors 3, 5, and 7).

Clinicians also ensure that older adults are in the least restrictive environment and that their human rights are not violated, that information for accessing necessary resources is not withheld by providers, and that access for necessary resources is advocated for (CSWE Competency 3: Advance Human Rights and Social, Economic, and Environmental Justice, specialized practice behaviors 2–4). Research-informed practice is engaged in when assessing, intervening, monitoring, and communicating/collaborating with other providers and systems to ensure desirable outcomes for chronic disease management, adaptation/resources for functional health changes/disability are met, and older adults participate autonomously in decision making (CSWE Gero Competency 4: Engage in Practice-informed Research and Research-informed Practice, specialized practice behaviors 3–4; CSWE Competency 6: Engage With Individuals, Families, Groups, Organizations, and Communities, specialized practice behaviors 1–4; Gero Competency 7: Assess Individuals, Families, Groups, Organizations, and Communities, specialized practice behaviors 1–3; CSWE Gero Competency 8: Intervene With Individuals, Families, Groups, Organizations, and Communities, specialized practice behaviors 1–4; and CSWE Gero Competency 9: Evaluate Practice With Individuals, Families, Groups, Organizations, and Communities, specialized practice behaviors 1–4).

Home health is a benefit provided under Medicare and other insurances for older adults with a skilled nursing or physical therapy need who require assistance in leaving the home. Home health emphasizes rehabilitation and is an intermittent service that has nurses, physical and occupational therapists, social workers, speech therapists, psychiatric nurses, and wound care ostomy nurses in some agencies, as well as home health aides for bathing assistance. The interdisciplinary home health team provides important home safety evaluations and recommendations for physical health and environmental safety. The team makes recommendations for environmental/home modifications to improve home safety, such as wheelchair ramps, lift chairs, stair lift chairs, removal of slip rugs, smoke alarms, and improvements in lighting. The interdisciplinary team provides evaluation and assistance with ordering specific durable medical equipment as well, such as shower and bath benches, grab bars, hospital beds, three-in-one commodes, walkers, and canes. Case management services may be received by the home health agency during the episode of treatment, and Area Agencies on Aging provide case management services for older adults in their respective service provider areas, referred to as SPAs. Other options for case management include private pay contractors and county, municipal, and community senior center programs serving older adults with chronic illnesses and/or functional health declines/disability. In all stages of treatment with older adults, clinicians also manage potential transference and countertransference issues that may present.

Transference/Countertransference

When working with older adults living with a chronic illness, comorbid chronic illness, and functional health changes/disability, transference and countertransference reactions must be managed by the clinician (CSWE Gero Competency 1: Demonstrate Ethical and Professional Behavior, specialized practice behaviors 1–6). Clinicians can engage in strategies such as supervision and appropriate peer consultation to process and manage transference and countertransference reactions. Clinicians working with older adults should be aware of the potential triggering of transference on the part of the client toward the clinician and countertransference toward the client by the clinician when assessing, intervening, treating, and evaluating chronic disease self-management behaviors and adaptations to functional health changes/disability. Clinicians identify and refer older adults and their caregivers to a range of technological resources that provide education, support, and assistance with various biopsychosocial/spiritual needs of older adults as they relate to chronic illnesses and/or disability.

Technological Resources

ADT Health: http://adtmedicalalert.com/?source=cad&DNIS=WEB0000678

Bay Alarm Medical: https://www.bayalarmmedical.com/free-quote/?affiliate_id=133989&utm_source=ConsumersAdvocate&utm_medium=desktop&utm_term

Consumer Advocates.org top 10 Home and Mobile Medical Alert Systems for Older Adults https://www.consumersadvocate.org/medical-alerts/a/best-medical-alerts?pd=true&keyword=%2Btop%20%2Bmedical%20%2Balert&gca_campaignid=176363822&gca_adgroupid=8306358062&gca_matchtype=b&gca_network=g&gca_device=c&gca_adposition=1t1&gca_loc_interest_ms=&gca_loc_physical_ms=9031548&&pd=true&keyword=%2Btop%20%2Bmedical%20%2Balert&gca_campaignid=176363822&gca_adgroupid=8306358062&gca_matchtype=b&gca_network=g&gca_device=c&gca_adposition=1t1&gca_loc_interest_ms=&gca_loc_physical_ms=9031548&gclid=EAIaIQobChMI0tLww7ev3wIV07fACh-1hcgauEAAYASAAEgJ_7PD_BwE

Chronic disease self-management: e-pill reminders: https://www.epill.com/timecap.html

GreatCall Lively Mobile: https://www.greatcall.com/landing/lively/medical-alert-v4

LifeFone: http://www.lifefone.com/landing/?st-t=ConsumersAdvocate&utm_source=-Consumers+Advocate&utm_medium=partner&utm_campaign=Home+DT

Life Station: https://brochure.lifestation.com/medical-alert-gl/?conid=15&device=c&matchtype=e&network=g&adposition=1t1&keyword=life%20station&gclid=EAIaIQobChMIhpCF-rev3wIVWLbACh3PFA3FEAAYASA-AEgICXfD_BwE

Medical Alert: https://medicalalert.com/consumersadvocatelp.html

Medical Care Alert: https://www.medicalcarealert.com/Articles.asp?ID=324

Medical Guardian: https://www.medicalguardian.com/help-me-choose/?aid=2022&subid=call%20button%20for%20elderly&subid2=desktop

Medisafe: Medication assistance/reminders: https://medisafe.com/

MedMinder: https://www.medminder.com/

MobileHelp: http://www.buymobilehelp.com/?utm_source=ConsumersAdvocate&utm_medium=desktop&utm_term=call%20button%20for%20elderly

Phillips Lifeline: https://www.lifeline.philips.com/?origin=2_us_en_s6jL_consumeradvocate&utm_campaign=5939

PillDrill: https://www.pilldrill.com/?gclid=EAIaIQobChMIvNbR1o-s2wIVhR9pCh-0v5gEIEAMYASAAEgKCCvD_BwE

PillPack: https://www.pillpack.com/?utm_source=healthline&utm_medium=display&utm_campaign=pillpackarticlecpa&c3ch=Display&c3nid=Healthline

Self-Management Resource Center (Stanford University): https://www.selfmanagementresource.com/

SMRC: Better Choice, Better Health—Arthritis or Healthier Living With Arthritis (Internet Arthritis Self-Management Program): https://www.selfmanagementresource.com/programs/online.programs/online-program-arthritis/

SMRC: Better Choices, Better Health or Healthier Living With Ongoing Health Problems (Internet Chronic Disease Self-Management): https://www.selfmanagementresource.com/programs/online.programs/chronic-disease

SMRC: Better Choices, Better Health or Healthier Living With Ongoing Health Problems (Internet Diabetes Self-Management Program): https://www.selfmanagementresource.com/programs/online.programs/diabetes/ Cancer: Thriving and Surviving Program Internet Program https://www.selfmanagementresource.com/programs/online.programs/cancer-survivors/

SMRC: Cancer: Thriving and surviving (CTS) program: https://www.selfmanagementresource.com/programs/small-group/cancer-thriving-and-surviving/

SMRC: Chronic disease self-management: https://www.selfmanagementresource.com/programs/small-group/chronic-disease-self-management/

SMRC: Chronic pain self-management: https://www.selfmanagementresource.com/programs/small-group/chronic-pain-self-management

SMRC: Diabetes self-management: https://www.selfmanagementresource.com/programs/small-group/diabetes-self-management/

SMRC: Online programs: https://www.selfmanagementresource.com/programs/online.programs/

SMRC Small Group Programs: https://www.selfmanagementresource.com/programs/small-group/

TabTime Vibrating Pill Reminder: https://tabtime.com/products/tabtime-vibrating-pill-reminder

Top 10 health and medical apps for Android: https://www.androidauthority.com/best-medical-apps-for-android-609131/

Weight Watchers Mobile (Weight Watchers International): https://www.weightwatchers.com/templates/marketing/marketing_utool_1col.aspx?pageid=1191351

Legal/Ethical Considerations

When engaging, assessing, intervening, and evaluating interventions with older adults for options to meet their chronic illnesses and functional health changes, clinicians ensure that services are tailored to meet cultural preferences of the older adult and promote self-determination in the least restrictive environment (CSWE Gero Competency 1, Demonstrate Ethical and Professional Behavior, specialized practice behavior 3 and CSWE Gero Competency 2: Engage Difference in Practice, specialized practice behaviors 3–4).

Clinicians ensure that, with all communications and referrals to other providers and agencies, they have client consent and follow organizational procedures and protocols and state and federal policies (Health Insurance Portability and Accountability Act, HIPPA) when transmitting clients' protected health information (PHI) and electronic health records. Clinicians assess for and provide advocacy when a client's rights secured under the ADA are violated (i.e., accessibility to buildings, sidewalks, bathrooms, transportation, etc.).

Critical Thinking Activity/Discussion Questions

1. How are older adults with chronic illnesses screened in your agency or community?
   a. What treatments and interventions are typically provided to organizations at your agency, in the local community, or in the state where you work with older adults?
   b. What resources are available?
   c. What legal/ethical issues have occurred that you are aware of, and how were they addressed?

2. How are older adults with functional health change/disabilities screened in your agency or community?
   a. What treatments and interventions are typically provided to organizations at your agency, in the local community, or in the state where you work with older adults?
   b. What resources are available?
   c. What legal/ethical issues have occurred that you are aware of, and how were they addressed?

3. How are older adults with chronic illnesses and functional health change/disabilities screened in your agency or community?
   a. What treatments and interventions are typically provided to organizations at your agency, in the local community, or in the state where you work with older adults?
   b. What resources are available?
   c. What legal/ethical issues have occurred that you are aware of, and how were they addressed?

Self-Reflection Exercises

1. Critically examine your own attitudes and beliefs about chronic illnesses.
   a. What did you learn about chronic illnesses growing up?
   b. From whom did you learn it?
   c. How do those beliefs influence your perceptions of chronic illnesses today?
   d. How might those beliefs affect your ability to engage, assess, and intervene with older adults living with a chronic illness(es)?

2. Critically examine your own attitudes and beliefs about disabilities.
   a. What did you learn about functional health changes/disabilities growing up?
   b. From whom did you learn it?
   c. How do those beliefs influence your attitudes about functional health changes/disabilities today?
   d. How might those beliefs affect your ability to engage, assess, and intervene with older adults living with a functional health change/disability?

3. Critically examine your own attitudes and beliefs about chronic illnesses and disability.
   a. What did you learn about chronic illnesses and functional health change/disability growing up?
   b. From whom did you learn it?
   c. How do those beliefs influence your attitudes about chronic illnesses and functional health change/disability today?
   d. How might those beliefs affect your ability to engage, assess, and intervene with older adults with high-risk factors for chronic illnesses and functional health change/disability?

References

Bandeen-Roche, K., Seplaki, C. L., Huang, J., Buta, B., Kalyani, R. R., Varadhan, R., ... & Kasper, J. D. (2015). Frailty in older adults: A nationally representative profile in the United States. *The Journals of Gerontology: Series A, 70*(11), 1427–1434.

Bannink, F. P. (2007). Solution-focused brief therapy. *Journal of Contemporary Psychotherapy, 37*(2), 87–94.

Bernell, S., & Howard, S. W. (2016). Use your words carefully: What is a chronic disease? *Frontiers in Public Health, 4,* 159. http://doi.org/10.3389/fpubh.2016.00159

CalSWEC. (2017). CalSWEC curriculum competencies for public child welfare, behavioral health, and aging in California. Retrieved from https://calswec.berkeley.edu/sites/default/files/2017_calswec_curriculum_competencies_0.pdf

Centers for Disease Control. (n.d.). Chronic disease self-management program (CDSMP). Retrieved from https://www.cdc.gov/arthritis/marketing-support/1-2-3-approach/docs/pdf/provider_fact_sheet_cdsmp.pdf

Centers for Disease Control. (2011). Sorting through the evidence for arthritis self-management program and chronic disease self-management program (CDSMP): Executive summary ASMP/CDSMP of meta-analyses. Retrieved from https://www.cdc.gov/arthritis/docs/ASMP-executive-summary.pdf

Centers for Disease Control. (2013). Fact sheet: CDC Health disparities and inequalities report—U.S. 2013. Some key factors that affect health and lead to disparities in health in the United States. Retrieved from file:///C:/Users/joosten_admin/Downloads/cdc_20865_DS1.pdf

Centers for Medicare and Medicaid Services. (2017). Chronic conditions. Retrieved from https://www.cms.gov/Research-Statistics-Data-and-Systems/Statistics-Trends-and-Reports/Chronic-Conditions/CC_Main.html

Council for Social Work Education. (2017). Specialized practice curricular guide for gero social work practice. Alexandria, VA: Council on Social Work Education.

Cummings, S. M., Cooper, R. L., & Cassie, K. M. (2009). Motivational interviewing to affect behavioral change in older adults. *Research on Social Work Practice, 19*(2), 195–204.

D'Zurilla, T. J., & Nezu, A. M. (2010). Problem-solving therapy. *Handbook of Cognitive-Behavioral Therapies, 3,* 197–225.

de Shazer, S., & Berg, I. K. (1997). "What works?" Remarks on research aspects of solution-focused brief therapy. *Journal of Family Therapy, 19*(2), 121–124.

Kraus, L., Lauer, E., Coleman, R., & Houtenville, A. (2018). *2017 disability statistics annual report.* Durham, NH: University of New Hampshire. Retrieved from https://disabilitycompendium.org/sites/default/files/user-uploads/AnnualReport_2017_FINAL.pdf

National Center for Chronic Disease Prevention and Health Promotion. (2016). Multiple chronic conditions. Retrieved from https://www.cdc.gov/chronicdisease/about/multiple-chronic.htm

National Center for Health Statistics. (2017). *Health, United States, 2016: With chart book on long-term trends in health.* Hyattsville, MD.

National Council on Aging. (2016). Healthy aging fact sheet. Retrieved from https://www.ncoa.org/wp-content/uploads/Healthy-Aging-Fact-Sheet-final-2018.pdf

Northwest ADA Center. (2018). Definition of disability. Retrieved from http://nwadacenter. org/toolkit/definition-disability

Office of Disease Prevention and Health Promotion (2018). Social determinants of health. Retrieved from https://www.healthypeople.gov/2020/topics-objectives/topic/ social-determinants-of-health

Office of Minority Health and Health Equity. (2018). Healthy equity. Retrieved from https:// www.cdc.gov/healthequity/index.html

RAND. (2017). Chronic conditions in America: Price and Prevalence. Retrieved from https:// www.rand.org/blog/rand-review/2017/07/chronic-conditions-in-america-price-and-preva-lence.html

Rollnick, S., & Miller, W. R. (1995). What is motivational interviewing? *Behavioural and Cognitive Psychotherapy, 23*(4), 325–334.

Rollnick, S., & Allison, J. (2004). Motivational interviewing. In N. Heather & T. Stockwell (Eds.), *The essential handbook of treatment and prevention of alcohol problems* (pp. 105–115). The Atrium, Southern Gate, Chichester, England: John Wiley & Sons Ltd John Wiley & Sons.

Substance Abuse and Mental Health Services Administration. (2016). National Registry of Evidence-based Programs and Practices: Problem-solving therapy. Retrieved from https:// nrepp.samhsa.gov/ProgramProfile.aspx?id=108#hide4

Self-Management Resource Center. (2018). Chronic disease self-management (CDSMP). Retrieved from https://www.selfmanagementresource.com/programs/small-group/ chronic-disease-self-management/

Stams, G. J., Dekovic, M., Buist, K., & de Vries, L. (2006). Effectiviteit van oplossingsgerichte korte therapie; een meta-analyse [Efficacy of solution-focused brief therapy: A meta-analysis]. *Gedragstherapie {Behavior Therapy]*, 39(2), 81–94.

UCSF. (2011). *Problem solving therapy for late life depression.* Retrieved from http://pstnetwork.ucsf. edu/sites/pstnetwork.ucsf.edu/files/documents/PST%20manual%20NEW%202012.pdf

World Health Organization. (2018a). 10 facts on health inequities and their causes. Retrieved from http://www.who.int/features/factfiles/health_inequities/en/

World Health Organization. (2018b). Noncommunicable diseases and their risk factors. Retrieved from http://www.who.int/topics/noncommunicable_diseases/en/

World Health Organization. (2018c). Social determinants of health. Retrieved from http:// www.who.int/social_determinants/en/

Credits

Figure 8.1: Karen Bandeen-Roche, et al., *The Journals of Gerontology*: Series A, vol. 70, no. 11, pp. 1431. Copyright © 2015 by Oxford University Press.

Figure 8.2: Karen Bandeen-Roche, et al., *The Journals of Gerontology*: Series A, vol. 70, no. 11, pp. 1430. Copyright © 2015 by Oxford University Press.

CHAPTER 9

Long-Term Care Planning

Chapter Overview

This chapter identifies strategies and best practices for engaging in long-term care planning with older adults, families, and loved ones and explores key domains to promote both effective clinical practice with older adults and optimal client outcomes.

CSWE Gero Competencies Highlighted

Competency 1: Demonstrate Ethical and Professional Behavior

Specialized Practice Competency Description: Social workers understand the value base of the profession and its ethical standards, as well as relevant laws and regulations that may impact practice at the micro, mezzo, and macro levels. Social workers understand frameworks of ethical decision-making and how to apply principles of critical thinking to those frameworks in practice, research, and policy arenas. Social workers recognize personal values and the distinction between personal and professional values. They also understand how their personal experiences and affective reactions influence their professional judgment and behavior. Social workers understand the profession's history, its mission, and the roles and responsibilities of the profession. Social workers also understand the role of other professions when engaged in inter-professional teams. Social workers recognize the importance of lifelong learning and are committed to continually updating their skills to ensure they are relevant and effective. Social workers also understand emerging forms of technology and the ethical use of technology in social work practice.

Competency Behaviors: (1) Guided by ethical reasoning and self-reflection, demonstrate adherence to ethical frameworks and key laws, policies, and procedures related to aging, and the rights

of older adults. (2) Engage in active dialogue with field faculty/instructors regarding aging field placement agency policies and culture around behavior, appearance, communication, and the use of supervision. (3) Develop and sustain effective collaborative relationships that respect older adults' needs for protection, self-determination, and the provision of services in the least restrictive environment possible with colleagues and community stakeholders, including older adults, their family members, other care providers, and Tribes. (4) Effectively manage professional boundary issues and other challenges arising in the course of aging-related work, particularly ambiguities presented by home visits, personal loss, trauma, and other highly involved and potentially emotionally triggering aspects of the work. (5) Develop and sustain relationships with members of interdisciplinary and integrated health care teams, including social workers, primary care providers, hospital staff, home health care providers, psychiatrists, psychologists, substance use disorder treatment staff, Tribal service providers, and others, that reflect clear understanding of their roles in providing care to older adults. (6) Demonstrate both knowledge of the history and evolution of social work practice related to aging and older adults in the United States and California, and a commitment to lifelong learning around this practice. (7) Follow all ethical guidelines and legal mandates in the use of technology in order to maintain the confidentiality of all personal, behavioral health, and health-related information. (CalSWEC, 2017, pp. 1–2)

Competency 2: Engage Diversity and Difference in Practice

Specialized Practice Competency Description: Social workers understand how diversity and difference characterize and shape the human experience and are critical to the formation of identity. The dimensions of diversity are understood as the intersectionality of multiple factors, including, but not limited to, age, class, color, culture, disability and ability, ethnicity, gender, gender identity and expression, immigration status, marital status, political ideology, race, religion/spirituality, sex, sexual orientation, and Tribal sovereign status. Social workers understand that, as a consequence of difference, a person's life experiences may include oppression, poverty, marginalization, and alienation as well as privilege, power, and acclaim. Social workers also understand the forms and mechanisms of oppression and discrimination and recognize the extent to which a culture's structures and values, including social, economic, political, and cultural exclusions, may oppress, marginalize, alienate, or create privilege and power.

Competency Behaviors: (1) Engage in critical analysis of the interpersonal, community, and social structural causes and effects of disproportionality, disparities, and inequities in the incidence and trajectory of aging-related care

needs, housing, transportation, and resource access among older adults, their families, and their communities. (2) Evidence respectful awareness and understanding of the impact of being a member of a marginalized group on aging experiences, and accurately identify differences in access to and quality of available services for members of different communities and populations. (3) Demonstrate knowledge of diverse cultural norms and traditional methods of providing care to older adults, as well as an applied understanding of how these realities affect work with older adults from diverse backgrounds, their families, and their communities. (4) Develop and use practice methods that acknowledge, respect, and address how individual and cultural values, norms, and differences impact the various systems with which older adults interact, including, but not limited to, families, communities, primary care systems, mental and behavioral health care systems, and integrated care systems. (CalSWEC, 2017, pp. 3–4)

Competency 3: Advance Human Rights and Social, Economic, and Environmental Justice

Specialized Practice Competency Description: Social workers understand that every person regardless of position in society has fundamental human rights such as freedom, safety, privacy, an adequate standard of living, health care, and education. Social workers understand the global interconnections of oppression and human rights violations, and are knowledgeable about theories of human need and social justice and strategies to promote social and economic justice and human rights. Social workers understand strategies designed to eliminate oppressive structural barriers to ensure that social goods, rights, and responsibilities are distributed equitably and that civil, political, environmental, economic, social, and cultural human rights are protected.

Competency Behaviors: (1) Clearly articulate the systematic effects of discrimination, oppression, and stigma on the needs and experiences of older adults and on the quality and delivery of services available to them, and identify and advocate for policy changes needed to address these issues. (2) Advocate for changes in policies and programs that reflect a social justice practice framework for facilitating access and providing services to older adults, their families, and care providers, especially among underserved groups and communities. (3) Demonstrate the ability to work effectively in cross-disciplinary collaboration to develop and provide interventions that explicitly address the specific needs of diverse older adults, their families, and care providers. (4) Integrate into all aspects of policy and practice sensitivity to the reality that fundamental rights, including freedom and privacy, may be compromised for older adults engaged in care, and the goal that services should be provided in the least restrictive environment possible. (CalSWEC, 2017, pp. 4–5)

Competency 4: Engage in Practice-informed Research and Research-informed Practice

Specialized Practice Competency Description: Social workers understand quantitative and qualitative research methods and their respective roles in advancing a science of social work and in evaluating their practice. Social workers know the principles of logic, scientific inquiry, and culturally informed and ethical approaches to building knowledge. Social workers understand that evidence that informs practice derives from multidisciplinary sources and multiple ways of knowing. They also understand the processes for translating research findings into effective practice.

Competency Behaviors: (1) Demonstrate the ability to understand, interpret, and evaluate the benefits and limitations of various evidence-based and evidence-informed treatment models as they influence practice with older adults. (2) Engage in critical analysis of research findings, practice models, and practice wisdom as they inform aging related practice, including how research practices have historically failed to address the needs and realities of exploited and/or disadvantaged communities, and how cross-cultural research practices can be used to enhance equity. (3) Clearly communicate research findings, conclusions, and implications, as well as their applications to aging practice, across a variety of professional interactions with consumers, families, and multidisciplinary service providers. (4) Apply research findings to aging-related practice with individuals, families, and communities and to the development of professional knowledge about the needs, experiences, and well-being of older adults. (CalSWEC, 2017, pp. 5–6)

Competency 6: Engage With Individuals, Families, Groups, Organizations, and Communities

Specialized Practice Competency Description: Social workers understand that engagement is an ongoing component of the dynamic and interactive process of social work practice with, and on behalf of, diverse individuals, families, groups, organizations, and communities. Social workers value the importance of human relationships. Social workers understand theories of human behavior and the social environment, and critically evaluate and apply this knowledge to facilitate engagement with clients and constituencies, including individuals, families, groups, organizations, and communities. Social workers understand strategies to engage diverse clients and constituencies to advance practice effectiveness. Social workers understand how their personal experiences and affective reactions may impact their ability to effectively engage with diverse clients and constituencies. Social workers value principles of relationship-building and inter-professional collaboration to facilitate engagement with clients, constituencies, and other professionals as appropriate.

Competency Behaviors: (1) Appropriately engage and activate older adults, their families, and other care providers in the development and coordination of care plans that reflect relevant theoretical models and balance older adults' needs for care with respect for autonomy and independence. (2) Effectively utilize interpersonal skills to engage older adults, their families, and other care providers in culturally responsive, consumer-driven, and trauma-informed integrated care that addresses mutually agreed upon service goals and balances needs for care, protection, autonomy, and independence. (3) Establish effective and appropriate communication, coordination, and advocacy planning with other care providers and interdisciplinary care teams as needed to address mutually agreed upon service goals. Recognizing the complex nature of service engagement, ensure that communications with consumers and their families regarding service goals are both sensitive and transparent. (4) Manage affective responses and exercise good judgment around engaging with resistance, trauma responses, and other potentially triggering situations with older adults, their families, and other care providers. (CalSWEC, 2017, pp. 9–10)

Competency 7: Assess Individuals, Families, Groups, Organizations, and Communities

Specialized Practice Competency Description: Practitioners in aging utilize ecological-systems theory, a strengths-based and person/family-centered framework to conduct assessments that value the resilience of diverse older adults, families, and caregivers. They select appropriate assessment tools, methods and technology, and evaluate, adapt, and modify them, as needed, to enhance their validity in working with diverse, vulnerable and at-risk groups. The comprehensive biopsychosocial assessment takes into account the multiple factors of physical, mental and social well-being needed for treatment planning for older adults and their families. They develop skills in interprofessional assessment and communication with key constituencies to choose the most effective practice strategies. Gero social workers understand how their own experiences and affective reactions about aging, quality of life, loss and grief may affect their assessment and resultant decision-making.

Competency Behaviors: (1) Conduct assessments that incorporate a strengths-based perspective, person/family-centered focus, and resilience while recognizing aging related risk, (2) Develop, select, and adapt assessment methods and tools that optimize practice with older adults, their families, caregivers, and communities, and (3) Use and integrate multiple domains and sources of assessment information and communicate with other professionals to inform a comprehensive plan for intervention. (Council for Social Work Education, 2017, pp. 89–90)

Competency 8: Intervene With Individuals, Families, Groups, Organizations, and Communities

Specialized Practice Competency Description: Social workers understand that intervention is an ongoing component of the dynamic and interactive process of social work practice with, and on behalf of, diverse individuals, families, groups, organizations, and communities. Social workers are knowledgeable about evidence-informed interventions to achieve the goals of clients and constituencies, including individuals, families, groups, organizations, and communities. Social workers understand theories of human behavior and the social environment, and critically evaluate and apply this knowledge to effectively intervene with clients and constituencies. Social workers understand methods of identifying, analyzing, and implementing evidence-informed interventions to achieve client and constituency goals. Social workers value the importance of interprofessional teamwork and communication in interventions, recognizing that beneficial outcomes may require interdisciplinary, inter-professional, and inter-organizational collaboration.

Competency Behaviors: (1) In partnership with older adults and their families, develop appropriate intervention plans that reflect respect for autonomy and independence, as well as contemporary theories and models for interventions with older adults. Plans should:

- Reflect cultural humility and acknowledgement of individualized needs;
- Incorporate consumer and family strengths;
- Utilize community resources and natural supports;
- Incorporate multidisciplinary team supports and interventions;
- Include non-pharmacological interventions; and
- Demonstrate knowledge of poly-pharmacy needs and issues specific to older adults.

(2) Apply the principles of teaming, engagement, inquiry, advocacy, and facilitation within interdisciplinary teams and care coordination to the work of supporting older adults, family members, and other care providers to accomplish intervention goals and satisfy advanced care planning needs. (3) Effectively implement evidence-based interventions in the context of providing emergency response, triage, brief treatment, and longer-term care, and in the course of addressing a range of issues presented in primary care, specialty care, community agency, inpatient, and palliative care settings. Interventions should be guided by respect for older adults' autonomy and independence and should include components such as psychoeducation, problem-solving treatment skills, symptom tracking, medication therapies, follow-up, and planning for evolving care needs. (4) Effectively plan for interventions in ways that incorporate thoughtfully executed transitions during time-limited internships, recognizing

that consumer needs for support may continue beyond these time periods. (CalSWEC, 2017, pp. 12–14)

Competency 9: Evaluate Practice With Individuals, Families, Groups, Organizations, and Communities

Specialized Practice Competency Description: Social workers understand that evaluation is an ongoing component of the dynamic and interactive process of social work practice with, and on behalf of, diverse individuals, families, groups, organizations and communities. Social workers recognize the importance of evaluating processes and outcomes to advance practice, policy, and service delivery effectiveness. Social workers understand theories of human behavior and the social environment, and critically evaluate and apply this knowledge in evaluating outcomes. Social workers understand qualitative and quantitative methods for evaluating outcomes and practice effectiveness.

Competency Behaviors: (1) Record, track, and monitor consumer engagement, assessment, and intervention data in practice with older adults, their families, and other care providers accurately and according to field education agency policies and guidelines. (2) Conduct accurate process and outcome analysis of engagement, assessment, and intervention data in practice with older adults, their families, and other care providers that incorporates consumer perspectives and reflects respect for older adults' autonomy and independence. (3) Use findings to evaluate intervention effectiveness, develop recommendations for adapting service plans and approaches as needed, improve interdisciplinary team coordination and care integration, and help agency and community policies better support older adults, their families, and their formal and informal care systems. (4) Share both the purposes of such data collection and the overall results of data analysis with older adults, their families, and communities whenever possible, with the goal of engaging them more meaningfully in the evaluation process. (CalSWEC, 2017, pp. 14–15)

Learning Objectives

1. Learners will understand the context of long-term care planning in the United States.
2. Learners will understand options for long-term care to inform treatment planning with older adults, including levels of care and financial options.
3. Learners will identify appropriate best practices for use with adults aging in areas of long-term care planning.

4. Learners will understand the importance of referring older adult clients and their family members to appropriate technological and community resources and when to assist with coordination to ensure long-term care needs are met.
5. Learners will identify sources of transference and countertransference when working with older adults to aging in areas of long-term care planning.

Case Study

Mr. and Mrs. Romano live in a three-level, 3,200-square-foot home, where they have resided for the past 50 years. They have three adult children, who live within a 20-minute radius, and six grandchildren. Mr. Romano was diagnosed with Parkinson's disease one year ago; he has comorbid heart disease. Mrs. Romano has comorbid diabetes, hypertension, and osteoarthritis. Mr. Romano is 75 years old and ambulates with a cane; he stopped driving after he was diagnosed with Parkinson's disease. Mrs. Romano is 74 years old and independent with activities of daily living (ADLs) and instrumental activities of daily living (IADLs); she still drives. Mr. and Mrs. Romano are first-generation Italian immigrants from Northern Italy; they emigrated to the United States when they were both children. They grew up in an Italian American community in San Pedro, California, and Mr. Romano worked with his father and took over the fishing business. Mrs. Romano was a homemaker; she is very active at the Italian American Club and her local perish. Their identified religious preference is Roman Catholic. Mr. and Mrs. Romano have strong ties to the community; they have recently decided that they would like to sell their home in preparation for changes in their health and functional health; they note the upkeep on the home has become increasingly difficult for them as well, as have the two flights of stairs in the home.

Assessing Context

In clinical practice with older adults in inpatient, outpatient, and community-based settings, long-term care planning can be defined as the process of identifying long-term care options to meet current or anticipated changes that result in a need for assistance due to functional health and/or changes in mental/cognitive functioning, biopsychosocial/spiritual, and environmental/safety needs of an older adult and subsequent referral, information and/or linkage to services, programs, and financial options available to meet professionally recommended and client-preferred options for long-term care. Long-term care planning always begins with a comprehensive biopsychosocial/spiritual assessment and is informed by a comprehensive geriatric assessment with findings and recommendations from the interdisciplinary team, as well as clinical expertise in providing a goodness of fit for services and options to meet the client's preferences for presenting needs and accessibility of long-term care services. Ideally, long-term care planning occurs before an older adult requires the need for services so that the older adult client is informed and empowered to participate in decision making regarding long-term care options as the needs present. Unfortunately, most often, it is after a discharge from a hospital for an episode of care that treatment for a chronic or new life-threatening illness, fall, or accident or during the hospitalization that long-term care is presented to an older adult. Long-term care planning in advance helps prepare older adults to know what their options are and empowers them to make informed decisions that support autonomy and independence while balancing safety and assistance needs for functional health and/or cognitive changes. For example, an older adult may be in need of long-term care services following a stroke after discharge from inpatient rehabilitation. The older adult may need assistance to meet functional health changes for ADLS, such as bathing, toileting, and grooming, and IADLs, such as transportation, shopping, meal preparation, laundry, and scheduling doctors' appointments. Or an older adult whose dementia progresses from mild to moderate or advanced may require minimal to full assistance with ADLs and IADLs.

In the development of an instrument for measuring behaviors of long-term care planning, it has also been defined as "actions of preparation for a future time when help with activities of daily living may be needed because of decrements in functional capacity" (Friedemann, Newman, Seff, & Dunlop, 2004, p. 521). Although to date a universal definition for long-term care planning does not exist, the concept of long-term care is well established. The National Institute on Aging defines long-term care as involving "a variety of services designed to meet a person's health or personal care needs during a short or long period of time. These services help people live as independently and safely as possible when they can no longer perform everyday activities on their own" (2017, para. 1). The World Health Organization further defines the context of long-term care systems as those that:

> enable older people, who experience significant declines in capacity, to receive the care and support of others consistent with their basic rights, fundamental freedoms and human dignity. These services can also help reduce the inappropriate use of acute health-care services, help families avoid catastrophic care expenditures and free women – usually the main caregivers – to have broader social roles. (2018, para. 1–2)

The World Health Organization acknowledges the context of uncertainty in predicting international long-term care needs as well as the intersection of poverty and socioeconomic status factors influencing the availability of long-term care services at national levels: "While global data on the need and unmet need for long-term care do not exist, national-level data reveal large gaps in the provision of and access to such services in many low- and middle-income countries" (2018, para. 2).

In the United States, most long-term care is provided in community-based settings by formal and informal caregivers. Informal and formal caregivers are defined as follows:

> informal caregiver—is an unpaid individual (for example, a spouse, partner, family member, friend, or neighbor) involved in assisting others with activities of daily living and/or medical tasks. Formal caregivers are paid care providers providing care in one's home or in a care setting (day care, residential facility, long-term care facility). (Family Caregiver Alliance, 2018, para. 1)

In 2015, over a period of 12 months, informal care to adults ages 50 and older was provided by 34.2 million informal caregivers; slightly less than half of all informal care was provided for adults with dementia and/or Alzheimer's disease (i.e., 15.7 million) (Family Caregiver Alliance, 2018). Long-term care services beyond formal and informal care in the United States are composed of five generally recognized categories of long-term care services: adult day service centers, nursing homes, residential care communities, home health agencies, and hospices (Harris-Kojetin et al., 2016). Data from the 2014 National Study of Long-Term Care Providers (NSLTCP) indicate the following utilization of the former five general categories of long-term care services from 2013 to 2014:

> there were an estimated 282,200 current participants enrolled in adult day services centers, 1,369,700 current residents in nursing homes, and 835,200 current residents living in residential care communities. In 2013, about 4,934,600 patients received services from home health agencies, and 1,340,700 patients received services from hospices. Together these five long-term care services sectors served about nine million (8,762,400) people annually. (Harris-Kojetin et al., 2016, p. 34)

It is projected that one out of two older adults in the United States will be in need of long-term care services in their lifetime (Business Wire, 2017). The estimated annual expenditure for long-term care services in the United States for 2013 to 2014 ranges between $210 billion and $317 billion (Harris-Kojetin et al., 2016); as the aging population increases through 2050, the demand for long-term care, as well as annual expenditures, will grow.

When engaging in long-term care planning, clinicians must first be aware of the levels of care for housing that an older adult may choose from to receive long-term care services. The lowest level of care is at the community level, where an older adult resides in either their own home or that of a friend or family member (i.e., house, townhome, condominium, apartment, or mobile home). At this level, a variety of home and community-based services are available to meet the myriad needs of older adults, allowing them to remain safely in the community-based setting of their preference through local community centers, Area Agencies on Aging-contracted case management services, private and public sector programs, and caregiver/respite programs. One complexity, however, is that the array of services, often fragmented, varies by urban, suburban, and rural areas, and they require multiple applications and coordination of efforts for implementation of services. According to an annual study of 30,000 long-term care providers across the United States, the average cost of private care in the United States is $23 per hour, a nurse home visit is $139, and the average cost of receiving 40 hours of in-home assistance each year ranged from $36,000 to $64,000, depending on the state and region (Business Wire, 2017). Section 8 low-income subsidized housing for adults ages 55 and older through local and state subsidized housing provides an affordable option for older adults to age in a setting that has rent control, subsidized housing for low-income residents (i.e., usually 30% of their income for rent), recreational activities, brief case management for community resources (i.e., meals, transportation), socialization activities and clubs/outings, options, a community club house, and other social activities. There are often long waiting lists for section 8 housing for adults ages 55 and older.

Assisted living is the next level up from the community-based level. Assisted living is designed generally as a setting for older adults who require assistance with some ADLs and IADLs. In general, the setting is apartment style, with residents having shared or private rooms; a shared community dining area is found in most facilities, where residents ambulate down for all three meals and snacks; assistance with medications is offered at many for an additional fee, as well as housekeeping, laundry, and personal care. The facilities may be a single level or multiple levels with elevators. When determining if assisted living is appropriate for a client, keep in mind that residents, in general, should be independent with ambulation or ambulate with a cane or a walker; clients who are wheelchair- or bedbound are not appropriate for most assisted living unless they have ample financial resources for supervision/assistance beyond what the assisted living facility provides. Most assisted living facilities provide recreational activities, religious services, and transportation for scheduled outings and/or day trips. Some have beauty shops for haircuts and fitness gyms for exercise. Memory units are available in some assisted living facilities, offering locked units to prevent wandering of ambulatory residents with dementia or other cognitive/neurological disorders. The monthly rate for and availability of assisted living facilities varies by state and region (urban, suburban, and rural). Some assisted living facilities provide Supplemental Security Income (SSI) rates for a shared or private room; given the for-profit nature of long-term care for older adults, most facilities have waiting lists for subsidized assisted living. In the Los Angeles, California, area, rates for a semiprivate room range for SSI subsidy at roughly $1,300 per month to upward of $4,000 to more than $10,000 for a private room, depending upon the facility, the amount of personal and functional health assistance needed, and amenities provided, as well as location. In the United States, the national average rate for a studio apartment at an assisted living facility in 2017 was $4,000 per month (Business Wire, 2017).

Board and cares, also referred to as six packs, are homes located in communities with as many as six residents and two to three 24-hour caregivers. Board and cares provide private and shared rooms, all meals, assistance with medications, and assistance with personal care (i.e., bathing, grooming, transferring, and toileting). Transportation to doctors' appointments is offered by some, usually for an extra fee. Supplemental social activities are recommended as group activities, socialization, and mental/cognitive stimulation activities beyond home health or hospice professionals are often not provided in board and cares. Board and cares do, however, provide residents with an opportunity for a home environment as opposed to an institutional/skilled nursing environment for older adults with dementia and/or functional health or mental health limitations that result in a need for moderate to maximum assistance with ADLs and IADLs. Board and cares are located in residential communities; they are most often single-level homes with wheelchair accessibility, and accommodations within the home are made to meet ADA requirements for wheelchair accessibility (i.e., raised commodes, grab bars, wheel-in showers, handheld shower heads, and accessibility in shared common rooms (i.e., living room and dining area, as well as patios). Board and cares are often privately owned, and the rates vary for private and shared rooms. Board and cares are most often financed through private pay unless an older adult has a link to veterans benefits or other long-term care insurances that assist with payment. The prices range in general from $2,000 to $10,000 per month.

The highest level of care, skilled nursing care, provides 24-hour care and supervision in an institutional setting with availability of skilled registered nurses (RNs), licensed vocational nurses (LVNs), and certified nursing assistants (CNAs); physical and occupational therapists and speech and respiratory therapists; and social workers or social service designees. Recreational therapists are offered in some, and physicians provide visits in many. An older adult can be ambulatory or bedbound; ambulatory older adults with dementia require a memory unit with locked doors to prevent wandering. Skilled nursing facilities have a community dining area for meals, or residents can have meals bedside. Full assistance with ADLs (i.e., toileting, grooming, ambulation, transferring, and bathing) is provided, and assistance with IADLs usually consists of medication assistance, arranging transportation for doctors' appointments, some assistance with shopping for personal care items as needed, laundry, and meals. Skilled nursing is financed through Medicare and other insurances for those with a three-day qualifying stay at an acute care hospital for transitional care; for those with a skilled need (i.e., nursing or physical therapy), Medicare pays for as many as 100 days per year. The remaining 265 days of the year can be financed privately out of pocket, with long-term care insurance, or through Veterans Administration long-term care pensions/programs; for older adults who meet the income test, Long-Term Medicaid subsidizes long-term care financing at a skilled nursing facility. Medicaid pays for 57% of long-term care at skilled nursing facilities, followed by private insurance companies and private payers at 29% and Medicare at 14% (American Health Care Association, 2018). Due to the for-profit nature of long-term care in the United States, the availability of long-term care beds for Medicaid subsidies is usually few with waiting lists. In fact, nationally, 70% of skilled nursing facilities are for profit, 24% are not for profit, and 6% are operated by a government agency (American Health Care Association, 2018). The national average rate in 2017 for a semiprivate room at a skilled nursing facility in the United States was $89,305, whereas private rooms averaged $102,900 per year (Business Wire, 2017).

Continuing care retirement communities (CCRCs) provide a setting for all levels of long-term care an older adult may need to transition to as his or her functional health and/or cognitive/neurological functioning changes. CCRCs offer independent living in apartments, assisted living, and custodial/skilled nursing care for the duration of the resident's lifetime. They are generally paid for with a sizable deposit as a down payment and monthly payments, similar to a mortgage or long-term lease contract. For example, in California, the down payment for a CCRC ranges from $100,000 to more than $1 million (California Advocates for Nursing Home Reform, 2008). There are more than 2,000 CCRCs in the United States, the average deposit being $250,000 (Wasik, 2016). As a part of best practice, clinicians identify cultural and diversity factors that impact long-term care planning processes.

Biopsychosocial/Spiritual Assessment

Following is an application of the Geriatric Biopsychosocial/Spiritual Assessment conducted by Mr. and Mrs. Romano's social worker.

Geriatric Biopsychosocial/Spiritual Assessment

Basic Demographic: Mr. and Mrs. Romano are 75- and 74-year-old Italian Americans; Mr. Romano was self-employed in the fishing industry prior to retirement and has an associate degree in business; Mrs. Romano has been a homemaker and has a high school education

Referral Information: Physician for long-term care planning after Mr. Romano's recent hospitalization for exacerbation of Parkinson's disease symptoms

Cultural/Spiritual: Roman Catholic—regular church attendance at local perish; both Mr. and Mrs. Romano accept their health diagnoses as "God's will;" they report no use of complementary and alternative medicine

Social: [Relationships within family, social/diversity groups, and community]

- Personal and family history: Client worked as a self-employed owner of a business in the fishing industry, and he retired at the age of 70; his spouse has been a homemaker since their marriage; they have three children and six grandchildren, who live locally; they have several friends in the community and through their local perish

- Both Mr. and Mrs. Romano maintain current relationships and contact with family, friends, social/diversity groups, and community groups; no caregiver stress noted

Financial: [Ability to provide basic needs and access health services]

- Clients have the ability to provide basic needs for housing, food, shelter, and clothing

- Health insurance: Current primary and secondary insurance provide essential benefits; there is adequate coverage with no gaps in coverage; and clients report co-pays and any out-of-network fees are manageable and medications are covered with no high co-pays

- Income sources: Social Security, pension, savings, and investments

Environmental: [Personal safety, maintenance of residence, and safety of community]

- Current social context/environmental: Clients live in a suburban neighborhood close to stores and recreational, faith, health, and community services

- Neighborhood safety: Low crime, street lighting, and paved roads and sidewalks with curb cuts

- Home safety: Clients have working smoke and carbon monoxide detectors and a fire extinguisher; lighting is adequate; no slip rugs; shower and toilet are accessible; there are no elevators or ramps to access the home, six small steps to front porch with handrail, and two flights of stairs in a three-level home
- Access to guns: No guns or access to guns
- No indicators of abuse or neglect by self or perpetrated by others

Physical: [Individual function and disease morbidity]

- Health literacy is adequate for both, self-rated health is good, clients have an advance directive and living will, clients have knowledge on their comorbid diagnoses as well as medications (and both are medication adherent); functional health: she ambulates independently and performs all ADLs and IADLs, he ambulated with a cane and needs assistance with transportation;

Mental: [Mental status, depression, anxiety, and substance abuse]

- Standardized screening instruments: Both clients are alert and oriented, no indicators of depression, anxiety, or cognitive deficits
- Suicide risk assessment: Low—clients do not endorse suicidal ideations and have no attempt history or history of suicidal ideations
- Homicidal ideations: Ruled out—clients do not endorse homicidal ideations
- One glass of wine per night with dinner reported by both clients

Formulation/Evaluation: Psychosocial support to process diagnosis and psychoeducation on Parkinson's disease; review options for long-term care and assist with the development of a client-centered long-term care plan; both clients are coping well overall and have an abundance of support from their family, faith, and community groups; they have an advance directive and living will in place

Treatment Planning: In consultation with physician, social work evaluation plus two additional visits for follow-up; family conference final visit

Community Resource Needs: Listings for assisted living, board and care, skilled nursing, and continuing care retirement centers; home- and community-based services; and Parkinson's Foundation and local Parkinson's disease support group

Diversity–Cultural Competence/Spirituality/LGBT/Sexuality

In clinical practice, the context of culture is an important determinant of long-term care decision making. The literature, as well as practice experience, suggests that Asian Americans, Hispanic Americans, and African Americans are less likely to consider placement in a residential setting due to the strong cultural preference of caring for aging parents. However, there are instances where the best efforts of family members to provide 24-hour care for their aging parent or family member are still not enough. In these situations, allowing space and time for the older adult client and his or her family members to vent and process the conflict between customs, practices, and cultural/family preferences and the older adult client's needs are crucial. There is oftentimes guilt and regret on the part of the family member(s) for agreeing to placement for the aging parent/family member and guilt by the aging parent/family member about the younger family member(s) needing to assist with care. These responses should be allowed time, space, and sensitivity for discussion and processing to ensure validation of the collective experiences. On the other hand, some families are unified in decision making and engage in collective decision making without experiencing guilt about placement of an aging loved one or receipt of care from family and loved ones. Using a strengths-based perspective, clinicians can tap into and bring the resiliency of the family to light, allowing them space to process and reconnect with their ability to respond to, adjust, and adapt to changes that they have worked through as a result of prior losses.

Mr. and Mrs. Romano, first-generation immigrants from Italy, had strong cultural preferences and customs of care for aging parents that conflicted with their decision not to "burden" their adult children and grandchildren with their day-to-day personal needs as their functional health needs changed over time due to their comorbid health conditions. They both wanted to stay close to their family, cultural and spiritual supports, and multiple friends. Their eldest daughter was adamant about having them move in with her, her spouse, and their two elementary school-aged children; she expressed a strong commitment to care for her parents as she observed her parents do for theirs. The pros and cons of each option were explored privately with Mr. and Mrs. Romano during the initial two visits at their home. For the final visit, they called all family members together for a family conference to inform them of their decision to sell their home and relocate to a local CCRC 20 minutes from their home. The clinician's role was to support the long-term care decision making of Mr. and Mrs. Romano and answer any questions that they could not for their family, per their request. Their two sons were very supportive of this decision; their eldest daughter still expressed a preference to care for them and an open-door invitation if they changed their mind, but she respected their final decision to have all-inclusive care at the local CCRC following the sale of their home. When engaging diversity in practice (CSWE Competency 2), clinicians follow specialized practice behaviors 1–4 to ensure that all long-term care planning and treatments respect the autonomy and cultural preferences of older adults (CalSWEC, 2017). Clinicians present to the interdisciplinary team relevant diversity factors that inform interdisciplinary team treatments and long-term care planning.

Interdisciplinary Team Roles and Planning

The interdisciplinary team plays a critical role in assessment, treatment planning, and subsequent recommendations for care and treatment for long-term care needs of older adults across the continuum of long-term care (i.e., community-based, assisted living, board and care, skilled nursing center, or continuing care retirement center). Physicians provide diagnoses and treatment of chronic and life-threatening diseases, as well as mental health, and/or other comorbid conditions that may contribute to an older adult's current or future long-term care needs. Physicians orders are required for home health, palliative care, and hospice care long-term care services. For older adults accessing adult day care centers, collaborative treatment planning with the primary care physician can enhance outcomes for biopsychosocial/spiritual well-being. Physical and occupational therapists play an important role in modifications for daily tasks of living and strengthening, balancing, and safety during ambulation and transfers. Both nutrition consultations and interventions, such as the use of food diaries and psychoeducation, can be beneficial for older adults with comorbid chronic conditions, such as diabetes, heart disease, and/or renal failure. Clinicians provide assessment, intervention, treatment, and coordination of services, recognizing the roles of other disciplines in meeting the long-term care needs of older adults at the desired level of care they prefer in the least restrictive environment (Gero Competency 1: Develop Professional and Ethical Behavior, practice behavior 5). They also develop and sustain collaborative relationships with older adults, their families, members of the interdisciplinary team, and other service providers to ensure self-determination of the older adults (Gero Competency 1: Develop Professional and Ethical Behavior, practice behavior 3). Clinicians identify and present to the interdisciplinary team and older adult client the best practices and interventions for long-term care planning.

Evidence-based Interventions and Monitoring of Best Practice Outcomes

Best Practices for Long-Term Care Planning

In a Cochrane systematic review of 19 studies composed of a combined total of more than 10,800 participants with chronic or long-term health conditions who received personalized care planning in either acute care, outpatient medical, or a community-based setting, personalized care planning was found to improve client key psychological outcomes (i.e., lower depression) and physical outcomes (i.e., improved control of asthma, improvements in blood glucose levels and diabetes, and lower blood pressure) (Coulter et al., 2013). Personalized care planning involves clinicians working collaboratively with older adult clients with chronic and long-term conditions to establish goals for treatment and consider treatment needs and current as well as future supportive services (Coulter et al., 2013). Personalized care planning involves seven key steps: (1) preparation (i.e., an initial visit to examine progress of management efforts for chronic or long-term conditions); (2) goal setting (i.e., establishing treatment goals that reflect the values and preferences of the client); (3) action planning (i.e., connection to and implementation of professional, peer, and/or other community-based services to facilitate goal attainment); (4) documentation (i.e., provider and client documentation to record progress toward treatment goals); (5) coordinating (i.e., the clinician ensuring that all professional, peer, and community-based services are accessible for the client and well coordinated); (6) supporting, which involves scheduled contacts between the client and clinician (in person, by phone, or by email or other electronic format) to engage in problem solving to ensure the client can attain desired treatment goals—it may involve "health coaching, motivational support, problem solving, or simply checking and reinforcing progress in implementing the agreed plan;" and (7) reviewing, which involves a meeting with the client and clinician to review the client's progress toward meeting goals and developing plans for the client's next actions or steps (Coulter et al., 2013, p. 8).

To date, evidence-based long-term care planning interventions and systematic reviews or controlled trials of such interventions are not well represented in literature. Similar to personalized care planning, long-term care planning should be tailored to the specific anticipated or current long-term care needs of the older adult client and involve collaboration between the client and the clinician in developing a plan that reflects the client's values and preferences. Two practice standards and guidelines developed from the National Association of Social Workers (NASW) can be used to inform best clinical practices for long-term care planning assessment, engagement, treatment, and evaluation: the NASW Standards for Social Work Services in Long-Term Care Facilities and the NASW Standards for Social Work Case Management.

NASW Standards for Social Work Services in Long-Term Care Facilities

According to the NASW, the primary role of social workers in long-term care settings are to "provide assessment, treatment, rehabilitation, and supportive care, and to preserve and enhance social functioning" through comprehensive interventions that include a "unique combination of physical, psychological, and social interventions and family support, the goal of which is to promote an optimal level of psychological, physical, and social functioning" (2003, p. 5). Although the standards were developed specifically for social work services in long-term care settings, they recognize the standards may be adapted to the context in which any of the five types of long-term care services are provided (i.e., adult day service centers, nursing homes, residential care communities, home health agencies, and hospices) to older adults in community-based, assisted living, board and care, or skilled nursing settings. An emphasis is placed on the clinician's role in addressing the following guiding principles for clinical practice in long-term care established by the NASW: (1) "the social and emotional impact of physical or mental illness or disability," (2) "the preservation and enhancement of physical and social functioning," (3) "the promotion of the conditions essential to ensure maximum benefits from long-term health care services," (4) "the prevention of physical and mental illness and increased disability," and (5) "the promotion and maintenance of physical and mental health and an optimal quality of life" (2003, p. 9). There are 11 standards established by the NASW for best practices in long-term care settings.

Standard 1: Ethics and Values: Focuses on ensuring self-determination and autonomy of the older adult client in following the Code of Ethics from the NASW as well as human rights, empowerment, and playing a role in improving organizational, community, and government policies (National Association of Social Workers, 2003).

Standard 2: Service Plan: Also referred to as the treatment plan, this includes the goals of treatment and objectives in the long-term care setting (National Association of Social Workers, 2003). For all long-term care housing settings, it includes the specific actions of the clinician, client, other members of the interdisciplinary team, family members, as well as services and timelines for initiating the treatment plan and implementing collaborative long-term care through local, state, and/or national service providers and funders.

Standard 3: Responsibility of Social Work Department: Includes quality assurance efforts put in place by the clinician to ensure the desired outcome(s) for the client outlined in the service or treatment plan are achieved (National Association of Social Workers, 2003).

Standard 4: Program Function: Includes the long-term care planning services and "direct services to residents, families, and other individuals involved with residents' care; advocacy; care planning, discharge planning and documentation" as well as mezzo and macro interventions that include "participation in policy and program planning; quality improvement; staff education pertaining to social services; liaison to the community; and consultation to other staff members" (National Association of Social Workers, 2003, p. 13).

Standard 5: Staffing: A standard that addresses education and training standards. Clinicians should have a bachelor or master's degree in social work and have competency/ training in long-term care for older adults (National Association of Social Workers, 2003) with an understanding of the five settings of long-term care, housing options, financing options, diversity/culture, Gero Competencies, etc.

Standard 6: Professional Development: Has to do with the clinician's required continuing education to stay informed on the latest treatments, intervention, policies, and programs for long-term care for older adults (National Association of Social Workers, 2003).

Standard 7: Personnel Policies and Procedures: Position descriptions should exist within organizations, clearly stating the qualifications of and responsibilities for those engaging in treatment of long-term care; these descriptions should be accessible by all disciplines (National Association of Social Workers, 2003) to improve efficiency in referrals for other disciplines.

Standard 8: Documentation: This should include all of the following:

> information related to the social and emotional functioning of the resident; relevant historical information regarding the resident and family and others involved with the resident's care; psychosocial assessments; the social work plan and specific goals; services provided and outcomes; and a summary of problems

and goals attained, as well as reasons for nonattainment of goals. Referrals to other agencies or resources should be documented in the resident's medical record and should include any ongoing follow-up or recommendations by an outside agency or individual. Notes shall be clear and concise. Progress notes, reports, and summaries of services shall be regularly recorded in the medical record and be consistent with all federal, state, and local legal and statutory, regulatory, and policy requirements and with the organization's or facility's policies on reporting, maintenance of and access to records, and confidentiality. (National Association of Social Workers, 2003, p. 18)

Standard 9: Work Environment: Includes work and space accessibility to the clinician by older adults and their families for in person conference, technology, and documentation (National Association of Social Workers, 2003).

Standard 10: Cultural Competence: Has to do with the clinician ensuring that services are delivered in accordance with the cultural preferences and needs of the client.

Standard 11: Interdisciplinary Collaboration: Has to do with a clear understanding of the roles and responsibilities of each discipline, communication, and collaboration in treatment planning with older adults for long-term care needs and services.

NASW Standards for Social Work Case Management

Applied to long-term care planning with older adults, the goals of social work case management include the clinician's ability to asses, engage, and intervene with older adult clients and their families to: "optimize client functioning and well-being by providing and coordinating high-quality services, in the most effective and efficient manner possible, to individuals with multiple complex needs" (National Association of Social Workers, 2013, p. 17). Strategies used to achieve long-term care goals with older adults include: (1) "strengthening the developmental, problem-solving, and coping capacities of clients," (2) "enhancing clients' ability to interact with and participate in their communities, with respect for each client's values and goals," (3) "linking people with systems that provide them with resources, services, and opportunities," (4) "increasing the scope and capacity of service delivery systems," (5) "creating and promoting the effective and humane operation of service systems," and (6) "contributing to the development and improvement of social policy" (National Association of Social Workers, 2013, p. 17). Social work case management emphasizes the following characteristics of social work practice with clients and families: person-centered services (that incorporate and are sensitive to the preferences of the client), the primacy of the social worker–client relationship (as without a relationship of trust and rapport, treatment cannot occur), the person-in-environment framework (in recognizing the intersectional factors that influence the context for long-term care services), the strengths perspective (in recognizing the resiliency of clients to resolve and respond adaptively to changes and transitions throughout the client's life course to date), and a collaborative teamwork with an interdisciplinary team (National Association of Social Workers, 2013).

The following standards for social work case management are similar to those previously described for social work in long-term care facilities.

Standard 1: Ethics and Values: Ensuring the NASW ethical principles for service, social justice, human dignity and worth, importance of human relationships, integrity, and competence (National Association of Social Workers, 2013).

Standard 2: Qualifications: The assurance that clinicians are qualified for and have the credentials and training to adhere to scope of practice and competence for engaging in long-term care planning for the long-term care services and context of the housing level of the client and client preferences (National Association of Social Workers, 2013).

Standard 3: Knowledge: Clinicians should have postgraduate training and experience in the application of it for human behavior; growth and development; behavioral health; physical health; family relationships; resources and systems; and the professional social work role (National Association of Social Workers, 2013).

Standard 4: Cultural and Linguistic Competence: The social work case manager's role is to ensure culturally and linguistic appropriate services that include establishing therapeutic and professional, collaborative relationships with clients, and interdisciplinary professionals for intervening within the intersectional contexts of diversity (National Association of Social Workers, 2013). Areas of diversity include:

> race, ethnicity, socioeconomic class, gender, gender identity, gender expression, sexual orientation, religion, age, health and family status; cognitive, physical, or psychiatric ability; and sensory differences, preferred language, migration background (within-country migration, immigration, refugeeism, and documentation status), degree of acculturation, level of formal education, and literacy (including health, behavioral health, and financial literacy). It can also include vocational affiliations, such as participation in the military or involvement in veterans' services. (National Association of Social Workers, 2013, p. 28)

Standard 5: Assessment: The social work case manager engages older adult clients and their families in "an ongoing information gathering and decision-making process to help clients identify their goals, strengths, and challenges" when engaging in long-term care planning (National Association of Social Workers, 2013, p. 30).

Standard 6: Service Planning, Implementation, and Monitoring: Includes person-centered treatment plans that consider any of the following activities: (1) "education and coaching in life skills," (2) "permanency, life span, and advance care planning," (3) "individual counseling and psychotherapy drawing on a variety of modalities, such as cognitive–behavioral or solution-focused approaches," (4) "couples and family counseling," (5) "family-team conferences," (6) "group interventions (such as psychotherapeutic groups, professionally facilitated psychoeducational groups, or peer-led support groups)," (7) "family caregiving support interventions," (8) "mediation and conflict resolution," (9) "crisis intervention," (10) "disaster planning and preparedness," (11) "advocacy on behalf of, and in collaboration with, clients," (12) "team, organizational, and inter-organizational service planning and collaboration," (13) "resource information and referral," (14) "systems navigation and coordination of services, especially during transitions of care or other significant life transitions," (15) "ongoing monitoring and evaluation of the service plan," and (16) "planning for service transfer or termination" (National Association of Social Workers, 2013, pp. 36–37).

Standard 7: Advocacy and Leadership: Requires clinicians to "advocate for the rights, decisions, strengths, and needs of clients and shall promote clients' access to resources, supports, and services" (National Association of Social Workers, 2013, p. 38).

Standard 8: Interdisciplinary and Interagency Collaboration: Requires clinicians to engage in collaborative practice with members of the interdisciplinary team and service providers across systems to ensure attainment of older adult clients' long-term care goals (NASW, 2013).

Standard 9: Practice Evaluation and Improvement: Involves the clinician's ongoing efforts to evaluate and monitor the effectiveness of their interventions with older adults for long-term care planning through activities such as: (1) "solicitation and incorporation of feedback from case management clients regarding the extent to which social work services have helped them identify and achieve their goals;" (2) "strategic planning to reach measurable objectives in program, organizational, or community development for case management clientele;" (3) "development of program budgets that take into account diverse sources of financial support for, and equitable allocation of resources among, case management clients," (4) "application of appropriate tools such as clinical indicators, practice guidelines, satisfaction surveys, and standardized performance assessments to evaluate client progress and satisfaction;" (5) "measurement of both process and outcome objectives;" (6) "practitioner, program, and organizational self-evaluation;" (7) "use of internal and external practice, program, or organizational evaluators;" (8) "use of peer review, supervision, and consultation with other social workers and across disciplines;" (9) "incorporation of evaluation practices in the service transfer or termination process;" (10) "analysis and use of professional literature to inform and improve case management practice;" (11) "participation in qualitative and quantitative social work research to strengthen the 44 evidence base for social work case management;" (12) "application of evaluation and research findings, including evidence-based practice, to facilitate client goal setting and to enhance practice and program quality and outcomes;" and (13) "dissemination of evaluative data to clients, payers, and other service providers on request, and with consideration for clients' rights to privacy and confidentiality" (National Association of Social Workers, 2013, pp. 43–44).

Standard 10: Record Keeping: Requires clinicians to document engagement, assessment, treatment, and evaluation, as well as termination activities (National Association of Social Workers, 2013).

Standard 11: Workload Sustainability: Requires, at a mezzo level, that clinician managers monitor caseloads of clinicians as well as appropriate measures for planning, monitoring, and evaluating case management efforts of clinicians (National Association of Social Workers, 2013).

Standard 12: Professional Development and Competence: Activities that clinicians engage in include but are not limited to: (1) "developments in social work theory and practice;" (2) "research developments related to case management practice and clientele;" (3) "policies and legislation affecting case management clientele and practice;" (4) "community resources, supports, and services available to case management clients;" (5) "issues and experiences specific to the social work case manager's specialty area services ... medical conditions, behavioral health, trauma, veterans' concerns;" (6) "cultural and linguistic competence, including concerns specific to case management population served;" (7) "ethics;" (8) "strengths-based models;" (9) "assessment of professional and personal strengths, learning needs, and goals as related to social work practice;" (10) "professional and personal self-care;" and (11) "technological advances related to the provision of case management" (National Association of Social Workers, 2013, p. 50).

As part of best practice, clinicians identify appropriate community-based services and programs to meet the long-term care needs of older adults and assist with coordination when appropriate.

Community Resources/Interagency Coordination

The identification of, referral to, and assistance with accessing necessary home- and community-based, as well as professional, services across agencies is a key component of long-term care planning. Referrals are tailored to the client's values and preferences, appropriate type of long-term care service(s) needed, and the housing level of the client. Respite care for caregivers, caregiver support and education groups, and options for private versus subsidized caregiving options to provide caregiver relief are important components of long-term care planning as well. When engaging in long-term care planning with older adults and their families, clinicians ensure that the autonomy and self-determination of the client are preserved; they also provide advocacy to ensure older adult clients have access to all necessary and available long-term care services and supports (CSWE Competency 3: Advance Human Rights and Social, Economic, and Environmental Justice, specialized practice behaviors 2–4). Clinicians are aware of potential transference and countertransference issues that may present when engaging, assessing, intervening, and evaluating long-term care planning interventions with older adults.

Transference/Countertransference

In providing long-term care planning with older adults in a variety of settings, clinicians are aware of potential transference and countertransference issues that may present in the therapeutic relationship and how to manage them. A client may experience transference toward the clinician if the clinician reminds him or her of encounters with other providers in the past around issues of long-term care, autonomy, and decision-making. Establishing rapport and trust during engagement can create an environment where an older adult is empowered to engage collaboratively in establishing long-term care goals and desirable services to meet long-term care goals. The clinician is also aware of potential countertransference reactions that may occur, such as the clinician overidentifying with a client who reminds him or her of a family member, friend, or previous client and/or his or her own values and preferences for long-term care services and supports (CSWE Gero Competency 1: Demonstrate Ethical and Professional Behavior, specialized practice behaviors 1–7). As part of best practice, clinicians identify appropriate technological resources and identify legal/ethical issues that may present when engaging in long-term care planning with older adults and their families.

Technological Resources

Administration on Aging: How much care will you need? https://longtermcare.acl.gov/the-basics/how-much-care-will-you-need.html

Administration on Aging: Long-Term Care: https://longtermcare.acl.gov/

Administration on Aging: Long-term care considerations for LGBT adults: https://longtermcare.acl.gov/the-basics/lgbt/index.html

Administration on Aging: The Basics: https://longtermcare.acl.gov/the-basics/

Administration on Aging: What is long-term care? https://longtermcare.acl.gov/the-basics/what-is-long-term-care.html

Administration on Aging: Where you can receive care? https://longtermcare.acl.gov/the-basics/where-can-you-receive-care.html

Administration on Aging: Who needs care? https://longtermcare.acl.gov/the-basics/who-needs-care.html

Administration on Aging: Who pays for long-term care? https://longtermcare.acl.gov/the-basics/who-pays-for-long-term-care.html

Administration on Aging: Who will provide your care? https://longtermcare.acl.gov/the-basics/who-will-provide-your-care.html

American Health Care Association: LTC Trend Tracker: https://www.ahcancal.org/research_data/trendtracker/Pages/default.aspx

Eldercare Locator: https://eldercare.acl.gov/Public/Index.aspx

Family Caregiver Alliance: Selected long-term care statistics: https://www.caregiver.org/selected-long-term-care-statistics

National Association of Area Agencies on Aging: https://www.n4a.org/

National Institute on Aging: What is long-term care? https://www.nia.nih.gov/health/what-long-term-care

Legal/Ethical Considerations

Clinicians engaging in long-term care planning with older adults and their families ensure that treatment plans reflect the client's right to self-determination, preferences, and values. They adhere to the Health Insurance Portability and Accountability Act (HIPPA) and obtain consents and releases from the client for the sharing of all patient health information and medical records needed in referring clients to long-term care services, providers, and support services. They provide advocacy for the client with family members and providers when the client's preferences for long-term care are not supported. Clinicians provide psychoeducation on the potential benefits of the array of options for long-term care services and support in meeting both professionally recommended safety needs of the client and meaningful services to the client consistent with desirable quality of life and well-being. They also ensure that their ethical rights are not violated and that all local, state, and federal ethical and legal standards are followed across settings and types of long-term care (CSWE Gero Competency 1:Demonstrate Ethical and Professional Behavior, specialized practice behaviors 1–7, CalSWEC, 2017).

Critical Thinking Activity/Discussion Questions

1. What treatments and interventions are needed for older adults in need of long-term care services?
2. What treatments and interventions are typically provided to organizations at your agency, in the local community, or in the state where you work with older adults?
3. What resources are available?
4. What legal/ethical issues have occurred that you are aware of, and how were they addressed?
5. How might you engage in advocacy to address any unmet needs or issues of older adults presenting with long-term care issues and needs?
6. How are older adults with long-term care service needs and issues engaged in decision making in your agency or community? What role can clinicians play in ensuring their participation in decision making?

Self-Reflection Exercises

1. Critically examine your own attitudes and beliefs about long-term care service needs for older adults.

a. What attitudes and beliefs do you have about long-term care services for older adults?
b. From what sources did these attitudes and beliefs develop?
c. How do those beliefs influence your perception on the appropriate housing levels and services and support to meet/address long-term care needs and issues among older adults?
d. How might those beliefs affect your ability to engage, assess, and intervene with older adults presenting with long-term care issues or needs?

2. What assumptions do you have about the long-term care practices of diverse clients? How can you work with cultural humility and competence to test those assumptions and provide culturally tailored and preferred long-term care planning interventions?
3. Imagine one of your parents or older adults in your family had a change in their functional health and or cognition. What preferences does your family have for long-term care? What are the roles of various family member? How can you manage potential countertransference when it comes to long-term care planning with clients/families similar to yours?

References

American Health Care Association. (2018). Fast facts: Nursing homes. Retrieved from https://www.ahcancal.org/research_data/trends_statistics/Pages/Fast-Facts.aspx

Business Wire. (2017). Lincoln Financial Group annual "What Care Costs" study indicates continued rise in long-term care costs in state-by-state comparison. Retrieved from https://www.businesswire.com/news/home/20170215005783/en/

California Advocates for Nursing Home Reform (2008). Continuing care retirement communities (CCRCs). Retrieved from http://www.canhr.org/CCRC/

CalSWEC. (2017). CalSWEC curriculum competencies for public child welfare, behavioral health, and aging in California. Retrieved from https://calswec.berkeley.edu/sites/default/files/2017_calswec_curriculum_competencies_0.pdf

Council for Social Work Education. (2017). Specialized practice curricular guide for gero social work practice. Alexandria, VA: Council on Social Work Education.

Coulter, A., Entwistle, V. A., Eccles, A., Ryan, S., Shepperd, S., & Perera, R. (2013). Personalised care planning for adults with chronic or long-term health conditions. *Cochrane Database of Systematic Reviews* (5)3, pp. 1-131.

Family Caregiver Alliance. (2018). Select long-term care statistics. Retrieved from https://www.caregiver.org/selected-long-term-care-statistics

Friedemann, M. L., Newman, F. L., Seff, L. R., & Dunlop, B. D. (2004). Planning for long-term care: Concept, definition, and measurement. *The Gerontologist, 44*(4), 520–530.

Harris-Kojetin, L., Sengupta, M., Park-Lee, E., Valverde, R., Caffrey, C., Rome, V., & Lendon, J. (2016). Long-term care providers and services users in the United States: Data from the National Study of Long-Term Care Providers, 2013–2014. *Vital Health Stat, 3*(38), x-xii.

National Association of Social Workers. (2003). NASW Standards for Social Work Services in long-term care facilities. Retrieved from https://www.socialworkers.org/LinkClick.aspx?fileticket=cwW7lzBfYxg%3d&portalid=0

National Association of Social Workers. (2013). NASW Standards for Social Work Case Management. Retrieved from https://www.socialworkers.org/LinkClick.aspx?fileticket=acrzqmEfhlo%3d&portalid=0

National Institute on Aging. (2017). What is long-term care? Retrieved from https://www.nia.nih.gov/health/what-long-term-care

Wasik, J. F. (2016). The everything-in-one promise of a continuing care community. Retrieved from https://www.nytimes.com/2016/02/27/your-money/the-everything-in-one-promise-of-a-continuing-care-community.html

World Health Organization. (2018). Ageing and life-course: Long-term-care systems. Retrieved from http://www.who.int/ageing/long-term-care/en/

CHAPTER 10

Advance Care Planning and End-of-Life Issues

This chapter identifies best practices for engaging in advance care planning with older adults, families, and loved ones; addresses interventions and culturally competent strategies for addressing end-of-life issues; and explores key domains to promote both effective clinical practice with older adults and optimal client outcomes, including quality of life and self-determination.

CSWE Gero Competencies Highlighted

Competency 1: Demonstrate Ethical and Professional Behavior

Specialized Practice Competency Description: Social workers understand the value base of the profession and its ethical standards, as well as relevant laws and regulations that may impact practice at the micro, mezzo, and macro levels. Social workers understand frameworks of ethical decision-making and how to apply principles of critical thinking to those frameworks in practice, research, and policy arenas. Social workers recognize personal values and the distinction between personal and professional values. They also understand how their personal experiences and affective reactions influence their professional judgment and behavior. Social workers understand the profession's history, its mission, and the roles and responsibilities of the profession. Social workers also understand the role of other professions when engaged in inter-professional teams. Social workers recognize the importance of lifelong learning and are committed to continually updating their skills to ensure they are relevant and effective. Social workers also understand emerging forms of technology and the ethical use of technology in social work practice.

Competency Behaviors: (1) Guided by ethical reasoning and self-reflection, demonstrate adherence to ethical frameworks and key laws, policies, and procedures related to aging, and the rights of older adults. (2) Engage in active dialogue with field faculty/instructors regarding aging field placement agency policies and culture around behavior, appearance, communication, and the use of supervision. (3) Develop and sustain effective collaborative relationships that respect older adults' needs for protection, self-determination, and the provision of services in the least restrictive environment possible with colleagues and community stakeholders, including older adults, their family members, other care providers, and Tribes. (4) Effectively manage professional boundary issues and other challenges arising in the course of aging-related work, particularly ambiguities presented by home visits, personal loss, trauma, and other highly involved and potentially emotionally triggering aspects of the work. (5) Develop and sustain relationships with members of interdisciplinary and integrated health care teams, including social workers, primary care providers, hospital staff, home health care providers, psychiatrists, psychologists, substance use disorder treatment staff, Tribal service providers, and others, that reflect clear understanding of their roles in providing care to older adults. (6) Demonstrate both knowledge of the history and evolution of social work practice related to aging and older adults in the United States and California, and a commitment to lifelong learning around this practice. (7) Follow all ethical guidelines and legal mandates in the use of technology in order to maintain the confidentiality of all personal, behavioral health, and health-related information. (CalSWEC, 2017, pp. 1–2)

Competency 2: Engage Diversity and Difference in Practice

Specialized Practice Competency Description: Social workers understand how diversity and difference characterize and shape the human experience and are critical to the formation of identity. The dimensions of diversity are understood as the intersectionality of multiple factors, including, but not limited to, age, class, color, culture, disability and ability, ethnicity, gender, gender identity and expression, immigration status, marital status, political ideology, race, religion/spirituality, sex, sexual orientation, and Tribal sovereign status. Social workers understand that, as a consequence of difference, a person's life experiences may include oppression, poverty, marginalization, and alienation as well as privilege, power, and acclaim. Social workers also understand the forms and mechanisms of oppression and discrimination and recognize the extent to which a culture's structures and values, including social, economic, political, and cultural exclusions, may oppress, marginalize, alienate, or create privilege and power.

Competency Behaviors: (1) Engage in critical analysis of the interpersonal, community, and social structural causes and effects of disproportionality, disparities, and inequities in the incidence and trajectory of aging-related care

needs, housing, transportation, and resource access among older adults, their families, and their communities. (2) Evidence respectful awareness and understanding of the impact of being a member of a marginalized group on aging experiences, and accurately identify differences in access to and quality of available services for members of different communities and populations. (3) Demonstrate knowledge of diverse cultural norms and traditional methods of providing care to older adults, as well as an applied understanding of how these realities affect work with older adults from diverse backgrounds, their families, and their communities. (4) Develop and use practice methods that acknowledge, respect, and address how individual and cultural values, norms, and differences impact the various systems with which older adults interact, including, but not limited to, families, communities, primary care systems, mental and behavioral health care systems, and integrated care systems. (CalSWEC, 2017, pp. 3–4)

Competency 3: Advance Human Rights and Social, Economic, and Environmental Justice

Specialized Practice Competency Description: Social workers understand that every person regardless of position in society has fundamental human rights such as freedom, safety, privacy, an adequate standard of living, health care, and education. Social workers understand the global interconnections of oppression and human rights violations, and are knowledgeable about theories of human need and social justice and strategies to promote social and economic justice and human rights. Social workers understand strategies designed to eliminate oppressive structural barriers to ensure that social goods, rights, and responsibilities are distributed equitably and that civil, political, environmental, economic, social, and cultural human rights are protected.

Competency Behaviors: (1) Clearly articulate the systematic effects of discrimination, oppression, and stigma on the needs and experiences of older adults and on the quality and delivery of services available to them, and identify and advocate for policy changes needed to address these issues. (2) Advocate for changes in policies and programs that reflect a social justice practice framework for facilitating access and providing services to older adults, their families, and care providers, especially among underserved groups and communities. (3) Demonstrate the ability to work effectively in cross-disciplinary collaboration to develop and provide interventions that explicitly address the specific needs of diverse older adults, their families, and care providers. (4) Integrate into all aspects of policy and practice sensitivity to the reality that fundamental rights, including freedom and privacy, may be compromised for older adults engaged in care, and the goal that services should be provided in the least restrictive environment possible. (CalSWEC, 2017, pp. 4–5)

Competency 4: Engage in Practice-informed Research and Research-informed Practice

Specialized Practice Competency Description: Social workers understand quantitative and qualitative research methods and their respective roles in advancing a science of social work and in evaluating their practice. Social workers know the principles of logic, scientific inquiry, and culturally informed and ethical approaches to building knowledge. Social workers understand that evidence that informs practice derives from multidisciplinary sources and multiple ways of knowing. They also understand the processes for translating research findings into effective practice.

Competency Behaviors: (1) Demonstrate the ability to understand, interpret, and evaluate the benefits and limitations of various evidence-based and evidence-informed treatment models as they influence practice with older adults. (2) Engage in critical analysis of research findings, practice models, and practice wisdom as they inform aging related practice, including how research practices have historically failed to address the needs and realities of exploited and/or disadvantaged communities, and how cross-cultural research practices can be used to enhance equity. (3) Clearly communicate research findings, conclusions, and implications, as well as their applications to aging practice, across a variety of professional interactions with consumers, families, and multidisciplinary service providers. (4) Apply research findings to aging-related practice with individuals, families, and communities and to the development of professional knowledge about the needs, experiences, and well-being of older adults. (CalSWEC, 2017, pp. 5–6)

Competency 6: Engage With Individuals, Families, Groups, Organizations, and Communities

Specialized Practice Competency Description: Social workers understand that engagement is an ongoing component of the dynamic and interactive process of social work practice with, and on behalf of, diverse individuals, families, groups, organizations, and communities. Social workers value the importance of human relationships. Social workers understand theories of human behavior and the social environment, and critically evaluate and apply this knowledge to facilitate engagement with clients and constituencies, including individuals, families, groups, organizations, and communities. Social workers understand strategies to engage diverse clients and constituencies to advance practice effectiveness. Social workers understand how their personal experiences and affective reactions may impact their ability to effectively engage with diverse clients and constituencies. Social workers value principles of relationship-building and inter-professional collaboration to facilitate engagement with clients, constituencies, and other professionals as appropriate.

Competency Behaviors: (1) Appropriately engage and activate older adults, their families, and other care providers in the development and coordination of care plans that reflect relevant theoretical models and balance older adults' needs for care with respect for autonomy and independence. (2) Effectively utilize interpersonal skills to engage older adults, their families, and other care providers in culturally responsive, consumer-driven, and trauma-informed integrated care that addresses mutually agreed upon service goals and balances needs for care, protection, autonomy, and independence. (3) Establish effective and appropriate communication, coordination, and advocacy planning with other care providers and interdisciplinary care teams as needed to address mutually agreed upon service goals. Recognizing the complex nature of service engagement, ensure that communications with consumers and their families regarding service goals are both sensitive and transparent. (4) Manage affective responses and exercise good judgment around engaging with resistance, trauma responses, and other potentially triggering situations with older adults, their families, and other care providers. (CalSWEC, 2017, pp. 9–10)

Competency 7: Assess Individuals, Families, Groups, Organizations, and Communities

Specialized Practice Competency Description: Practitioners in aging utilize ecological-systems theory, a strengths-based and person/family-centered framework to conduct assessments that value the resilience of diverse older adults, families, and caregivers. They select appropriate assessment tools, methods and technology, and evaluate, adapt, and modify them, as needed, to enhance their validity in working with diverse, vulnerable and at-risk groups. The comprehensive biopsychosocial assessment takes into account the multiple factors of physical, mental and social well-being needed for treatment planning for older adults and their families. They develop skills in interprofessional assessment and communication with key constituencies to choose the most effective practice strategies. Gero social workers understand how their own experiences and affective reactions about aging, quality of life, loss and grief may affect their assessment and resultant decision-making.

Competency Behaviors: (1) Conduct assessments that incorporate a strengths-based perspective, person/family-centered focus, and resilience while recognizing aging related risk, (2) Develop, select, and adapt assessment methods and tools that optimize practice with older adults, their families, caregivers, and communities, and (3) Use and integrate multiple domains and sources of assessment information and communicate with other professionals to inform a comprehensive plan for intervention. (Council for Social Work Education, 2017, pp. 89–90)

Competency 8: Intervene With Individuals, Families, Groups, Organizations, and Communities

Specialized Practice Competency Description: Social workers understand that intervention is an ongoing component of the dynamic and interactive process of social work practice with, and on behalf of, diverse individuals, families, groups, organizations, and communities. Social workers are knowledgeable about evidence-informed interventions to achieve the goals of clients and constituencies, including individuals, families, groups, organizations, and communities. Social workers understand theories of human behavior and the social environment, and critically evaluate and apply this knowledge to effectively intervene with clients and constituencies. Social workers understand methods of identifying, analyzing, and implementing evidence-informed interventions to achieve client and constituency goals. Social workers value the importance of interprofessional teamwork and communication in interventions, recognizing that beneficial outcomes may require interdisciplinary, inter-professional, and inter-organizational collaboration.

Competency Behaviors: (1) In partnership with older adults and their families, develop appropriate intervention plans that reflect respect for autonomy and independence, as well as contemporary theories and models for interventions with older adults. Plans should:

- Reflect cultural humility and acknowledgement of individualized needs;
- Incorporate consumer and family strengths;
- Utilize community resources and natural supports;
- Incorporate multidisciplinary team supports and interventions;
- Include non-pharmacological interventions; and
- Demonstrate knowledge of poly-pharmacy needs and issues specific to older adults.

(2) Apply the principles of teaming, engagement, inquiry, advocacy, and facilitation within interdisciplinary teams and care coordination to the work of supporting older adults, family members, and other care providers to accomplish intervention goals and satisfy advanced care planning needs. (3) Effectively implement evidence-based interventions in the context of providing emergency response, triage, brief treatment, and longer-term care, and in the course of addressing a range of issues presented in primary care, specialty care, community agency, inpatient, and palliative care settings. Interventions should be guided by respect for older adults' autonomy and independence and should include components such as psychoeducation, problem-solving treatment skills, symptom tracking, medication therapies, follow-up, and planning for evolving care needs. (4) Effectively plan for interventions in ways that incorporate thoughtfully executed

transitions during time-limited internships, recognizing that consumer needs for support may continue beyond these time periods. (CalSWEC, 2017, pp. 12–14)

Competency 9: Evaluate Practice With Individuals, Families, Groups, Organizations, and Communities

Competency 9 Specialized Practice Competency Description: Social workers understand that evaluation is an ongoing component of the dynamic and interactive process of social work practice with, and on behalf of, diverse individuals, families, groups, organizations and communities. Social workers recognize the importance of evaluating processes and outcomes to advance practice, policy, and service delivery effectiveness. Social workers understand theories of human behavior and the social environment, and critically evaluate and apply this knowledge in evaluating outcomes. Social workers understand qualitative and quantitative methods for evaluating outcomes and practice effectiveness.

Competency Behaviors: (1) Record, track, and monitor consumer engagement, assessment, and intervention data in practice with older adults, their families, and other care providers accurately and according to field education agency policies and guidelines. (2) Conduct accurate process and outcome analysis of engagement, assessment, and intervention data in practice with older adults, their families, and other care providers that incorporates consumer perspectives and reflects respect for older adults' autonomy and independence. (3) Use findings to evaluate intervention effectiveness, develop recommendations for adapting service plans and approaches as needed, improve interdisciplinary team coordination and care integration, and help agency and community policies better support older adults, their families, and their formal and informal care systems. (4) Share both the purposes of such data collection and the overall results of data analysis with older adults, their families, and communities whenever possible, with the goal of engaging them more meaningfully in the evaluation process. (CalSWEC, 2017, pp. 14–15)

Learning Objectives

1. Learners will understand the context for advance care planning with older adults across the continuum of health-care settings in the United States.
2. Learners will identify best practices for engaging in advance care planning with older adults across the continuum of health-care settings.
3. Learners will identify best practices for engaging, intervening, treating, and evaluating best practices for older adults and their families experiencing end-of-life issues.

4. Learners will understand the importance of referring older adult clients and their family members to appropriate technological and community resources and when to assist with coordination.
5. Learners will identify sources of transference and countertransference when working with older adults when engaging in advance care planning and/or addressing end-of-life issues.

Case Study

Mrs. Gonzalez, a 73-year-old Hispanic female, presented with edema and pulmonary edema; her primary symptoms were swelling of the arms and legs, nausea, chest pain, fatigue, decreased urine output, and high blood pressure. She was in the hospital for two weeks and diagnosed with end-stage renal disease. At discharge from the hospital, the attending physician ordered hemodialysis three times per week and home health services. She also had comorbid heart disease, hypertension, high cholesterol, and type 2 diabetes. She has not been compliant with diet or blood sugar testing. She had a heart attack at the age of 65. She is married with six children and 13 grandchildren, all of whom live within a 5-mile radius from her and her spouse. Mrs. Gonzalez was a homemaker and volunteered at her children's schools and her local perish. Mrs. Gonzalez has a large social support network of family and friends. Mrs. Gonzalez identifies as a devout Catholic and attributes her diagnoses to "God's will" in her life. She and her spouse own their own home; her spouse worked as a longshoreman. Mr. and Mrs. Gonzalez do not have a living will or advance health-care directive. The social worker was referred to the client for advance care planning as part of the home health interdisciplinary team.

Assessing Context

In the United States, since the 1970s, advance care directives have served within states as the primary means for allowing a client to convey their preferences for end-of-life and life-sustaining measures (Sabatino, 2007). Other forms of documentation include a living will or health-care power of attorney, both of which are usually drawn up by attorneys. Although the laws in each state vary when it comes to advance directives, generally the documents can be drawn up and become a legal document without an attorney, provided there are two nonfamily/health-care provider witnesses or a public notary and/ or the document is witnessed by a long-term care ombudsman if the client resides in a long-term care setting (i.e., board and care or skilled nursing facility). The client must be alert and oriented to sign, validate, and execute preferences outlined in the document as the document is a legal document and would be considered invalid for a client who has diminished cognitive capacity to legally sign the document. The prevalence rates of advance health-care directives completed by adults in the United States ranges from one in four Americans to one in three Americans. The prevalence rates of advance health-care directives in the United States, according to a meta-analysis of 148 studies comprising approximately 1.7 million adults, is slightly more than one in four adults (26.7%) (Yadav et al., 2017b). In another meta-analysis of 150 studies conducted between 2011 and 2016 with approximately 796,000 adults, the prevalence rate of adults with an advance directive was discovered to be one in three adults (36.7%) (Yadav et al., 2017a).

It is often within the context of being diagnosed with a long-term chronic or life-threatening illness that a client is engaged by a health-care professional in the process of advance care planning. Advance care planning most frequently occurs between a client and health-care provider to ensure that a client is aware of his/her options for end-of-life care treatments following an episode of care at an acute care hospital, outpatient primary or specialty care, or skilled nursing facility/transitional care unit. It can also take place at a board and care, assisted living and/or home, or other community-based settings. Advance care planning empowers older adults to consider their preferences for full life-sustaining treatment and technologies, or the lack thereof, consistent with his or her values and preferences that reflect personalized definitions of quality of life and achieving death with dignity. Completion of an advance health-care directive is one goal of advance care planning.

The advance health-care directive document, according to state statutes, outlines the authority of health-care agents or proxies when appointed by the client; the client's preferences for end-of-life treatment; any exceptions for the health-care agent's authority; and burial, autopsy, and organ donation preferences. The advance health-care directive ensures a client's right to self-determination in the event that they become incapacitated and unable to provide legal consent for treatment, or the lack thereof. The advance health-care directive ensures that the wishes of the client for end-of-life treatment or emergency life-sustaining treatment is documented and a clear agent(s) to carry out these wishes are identified. Clients with diminished capacity cannot legally agree to, consent, and sign an advance directive or other legal document. Substituted judgment may be considered to investigate the end-of-life care preferences of the client without an advance health-care directive in acute care settings or determined in client-centered conferences with the physician, nurses, social workers, family members, and, in some instances, a bioethicist. An advance health-care directive is not a physician's order for end-of-life care treatment options; rather, it is a statement of client preferences and the decision for whom the client appoints as the health-care decision maker or proxy in the event they are unable to sign consents. Some states use a physician's order for life-sustaining treatment (POLST). This document, unlike the advance health-care directive, is a physician's order that provides physician's orders for life-sustaining methods for the client, and the order follows the client across the continuum of health-care settings (i.e., emergency department, acute care, transitional care at a skilled nursing facility, or other rehabilitation) and across housing levels when emergency first responders arrive in a medical emergency (i.e., from the community-based settings, assisted living, board and care, continuing care retirement centers, and skilled nursing settings).

The National Institute on Aging defines advance care planning as the process in which a provider facilitates client knowledge about: (1) "the types of decisions that might need to be made, considering those decisions ahead of time, and then letting others know—both you family and your healthcare providers—about preferences;" (2) putting these preferences into "an advance directive, a legal document that goes into effect only if you are incapacitated and unable to speak for yourself" or it can take effect immediately (depending on state legal requirements for advance directives); (3) serving as a legal document to help "others know what type of medical care you want;" and (4) how an advance directive and advance care planning empower the older adult client to express his or her "values and desires related to end-of-life care" (2018, para. 3). Advance care planning is defined by the National Hospice and Palliative Care Organization as including the following goals: (1) "getting information on the types of life-sustaining treatments that are available," (2) "deciding what types of treatment you would or would not want should you be diagnosed with a life-limiting illness," (3) "sharing your personal values with your loved ones," and (4) "completing advance directives to put into writing what types of treatment you would or would not want should you be unable to speak for yourself" (2017, para. 2). An assessment of cultural and other diversity factors is a key best practice when engaging older adult clients and their families in advance care planning and end-of-life discussions.

Biopsychosocial/Spiritual Assessment

Following is an application of the Geriatric Biopsychosocial/Spiritual Assessment conducted by Mrs. Gonzalez's social worker.

Box 10.1

Geriatric Biopsychosocial/Spiritual Assessment

Basic Demographic: Mrs. Gonzalez, a 73-year-old Hispanic married female; speaks Spanish and English is a second language; has an eighth grade education

Referral Information: The social worker was referred to the client for advance care planning as part of the home health interdisciplinary team

Cultural/Spiritual: Mrs. Gonzalez identifies as a devout Catholic and attributes her diagnoses to "God's will" in her life

Social: [Relationships within family, social/diversity groups, and community]

- Mrs. Gonzalez has six children and 13 grandchildren, all of whom live within a 5-mile radius from her and her spouse; Mrs. Gonzalez was a homemaker
- She volunteered at her children's schools and her local perish; Mrs. Gonzalez has a large social support network of family and friends

---

Financial: [Ability to provide basic needs and access health services]

- Basic needs met for housing, clothing, food, and shelter
- Health insurance: International Longshoremen and Warehouse Union-Pacific Maritime Association (ILWU-PMA) welfare plan
- Income sources: Spouse's pension

Environmental: [Personal safety, maintenance of residence, and safety of community]

- Neighborhood safety: Crime level is low to moderate in the neighborhood
- Home safety: No slip rugs; grab bars are in place; controlled in nursing home environment
- No access to guns or gun ownership
- No indicators of abuse or neglect by self or perpetrated by others

Physical: [Individual function and disease morbidity]

- Moderate health literacy; poor self-rated health; no advance directive in place; she also has comorbid heart disease, hypertension, high cholesterol, and type 2 diabetes; she has not been compliant and has a history of non-adherence with diet or blood sugar testing; she had a heart attack at the age of 65; she is independent with ADLs and requires assistance with IADLs; she reports no sexual activity for years with spouse; no concerns verbalized

Mental: [Mental status, depression, anxiety, and substance abuse]

- No indicators of depression or anxiety; she is alert and oriented and competent to engage in decision making
- Suicide risk assessment: She does not endorse suicidal ideations and no history reported
- Homicidal ideations: Ruled out—no history of homicidal ideations
- No history of smoking; no alcoholic beverages for the past five years

Formulation/Evaluation: Advance care planning over two visits after initial evaluation as client requests family be present for two visits involving advance care planning; dietary consultation request

Treatment Planning: Social worker to provide advance care planning and will assist with documenting client's preferences to be notarized or signed by two nonfamily member witnesses; consultation with physician and nurse; a dietary consultation requested

Community Resource Needs: Legal referral for options for living will/trust; local community resources for transportation and support groups as needed; American Heart Association and American Diabetes Association for education, dietary, and other support

Diversity–Cultural Competence/Spirituality/LGBT/Sexuality

Clinicians must consider the context of culture, spiritual, and generational beliefs about advance care planning when engaging older adult clients in discussions on end-of-life-care decision making. In a qualitative study of 60 Chinese Americans, advance care planning was perceived as important to both younger and older generations, and both generations reported an interest in engaging in these discussions (Byon, Hinderer, & Alexander, 2017). However, hesitancy to engage in such discussion was reported and attributed to "expectations and obligations of Xiao (filial piety) in Chinese culture" (Byon, Hinderer, & Alexander, 2017, p. 83). It is the clinician's role to assess whether a client may have cultural customs and preferences for decision making that may range from decisions made individualistically or within the confines of the nuclear family, seen commonly in Western cultures such as the United States, or whether the client prefers to engage in collectivist decision making, engaging members of the immediate family, extended family, and/or faith/cultural/spiritual community.

In a meta-analysis of 33 studies that examined culturally diverse intersections for decision making at the end of life, the studies suggested that in comparison to non-Hispanic Whites, members of other racial or ethnic groups (i.e., African American, Asian, and Hispanic) had less knowledge about advance directives (Kwak & Haley, 2005). The formerly described meta-analysis revealed the following preferences across studies reviewed: (1) "African Americans were consistently found to prefer the use of life support;" (2) "Asians and Hispanics were more likely to prefer family-centered decision making than other racial or ethnic groups;" and (3) "variations within groups existed and were related to cultural values, demographic characteristics, level of acculturation, and knowledge of end-of-life treatment options" (Kwak & Haley, 2005). In some Asian cultures, decision making is deferred to the eldest son. From a survey of 250 adults in Taiwan, researchers concluded that "in a Confucian society, the family element often determines the course of decision and the patient's autonomy is overlooked"—the key decision maker is the "head of the family, not the patient himself or herself" and is the one who "usually makes the decision, especially when the medical decision has something to do with a life or death situation" (Tai & Tsai, 2003, p. 558).

Referring back the case study formerly presented, Mrs. Gonzalez expressed a preference to have her spouse and six children present for the initial discussion surrounding advance care planning and the follow-up session. Her preference was to be full code with all life-sustaining measures; she and her family members expressed that these options are consistent with their family traditions and cultural and spiritual beliefs and practices. The clinician plays a key role in assessing and examining the role of cultural diversity and other intersectional factors that influence the of end-of-life decision making of older adults and their families when engaging in advance care planning and end-of-life discussions (CSWE Competency 2). Clinicians adhere to specialized practice behaviors 1–4 to ensure that all care planning and treatments are culturally preferred and valued by the older adult and involve decision makers according to the older adult's preferences (CSWE Competency 2, CalSWEC, 2017).

Acculturation has been identified as a predictor of older Korean Americans' knowledge of and completion of an advance directive (Dobbs, Park, Jang, & Meng, 2015). In a nationally representative survey of adults ages 50 and older, non-Hispanic Whites were discovered to have higher prevalence rates of completed advance directives (44%) in comparison to African American and Hispanics (24% and 29%, respectively) (Huang, Neuhaus, & Chiong, 2016). When controlling for age, gender, religion, education, employment, access to the internet, "preferences for physician-centered decision making, and desiring longevity regardless of functional status," multivariate analyses reveal that in this sample of 2,154 adults ages 50 and older, "black older Americans remained significantly less likely than white older Americans to have an advance directive (odds ratio [OR] = 0.42, 95% confidence interval [CI] = 0.24–0.75), whereas the effect of Hispanic ethnicity was no longer statistically significant (OR = 0.65, 95% CI = 0.39–1.1)" (Huang, Neuhaus, & Chiong, 2016, p. 149). In a separate qualitative study using focus groups and semistructured interviews with African Americans seeking to understand their perceptions about advance directives, palliative and hospice care, the following themes emerged:

> Participants felt that advance care planning, palliative care, and hospice can be beneficial to African American patients and their families but identified specific barriers to completion of advance directives and hospice enrollment, including lack of knowledge, fear that these measures may hasten death or cause providers to deliver inadequate care, and perceived conflict with patients' faith and religious beliefs. (Rhodes et al., 2016, p. 510)

It cannot be emphasized enough that clinicians have an instrumental role in presenting to and advocating within the interdisciplinary treatment team the cultural and spiritual preferences of older adults when it comes to advance care planning and treatment options for end-of-life issues.

Interdisciplinary Team Roles and Planning

Interdisciplinary teams play an important role in providing advance care planning with older adults and their families. As formerly mentioned, it is quite common in the United States for advance care planning to be initiated when an older adult is diagnosed with a long-term chronic or life-threatening illness. It is most often the physician, nurse, and social worker who are involved in advance care planning. In acute care settings, advance care planning may be initiated by the physician for a social work consultation for an advance health-care directive. For clients referred to palliative care services, these discussions are frequently held in a scheduled family conference with the client and identified key decision makers identified by the client, as well as the palliative care team composed of a physician, nurse, social worker, and chaplain. In a study examining communication practices of physicians, social workers, and nurses around advance directives, it was concluded "social workers offer distinct skills in their advance directive communication practices and discuss advance directives more frequently than either physicians or nurses" (Black, 2005, p. 39). Communication processes in the former study included the following phases: "initiation of the topic, disclosure of information, identification of a surrogate decision-maker, discussion of treatment options, elicitation of patient values, interaction with family members, and collaboration with other health care professionals" (Black, 2005, p. 39).

Mr. Kim was referred to palliative care due to the attending physician's referral order that life support was futile treatment and the client would likely expire overnight. Mr. Kim suffered a major stroke and was placed on life support in the intensive care unit; the palliative care team was referred to meet with Mrs. Kim and her son to engage in end-of-life-care discussions, options, and advance care planning. During the family conference, the social worker observed that Mrs. Kim was visibly uncomfortable with the discussion and tearful; the social worker asked if she would like to end the meeting and meet privately with the social worker and her son, and she agreed. Mrs. Kim shared that as part of her Korean culture, she prefers to engage in collective decision making, including the family and members of her faith community; she and her son identified their religious preference of Christianity and stated they preferred to meet with their faith community before making a decision. The social worker informed the palliative care team of their decision, as well as the referring physician. The next morning, Mr. Kim's vitals and prognosis were improved; Mrs. Kim and her son decided to keep Mr. Kim as full code with all life-sustaining measures on the advance health-care directive. A week later, Mr. Kim was transferred to the medical surgery floor; he continued to make progress each day, eventually ambulating with a walker with standby assistance. After four weeks from admission, he was discharged to a transitional care unit for continued rehabilitative services. As part of best practice, clinicians are aware of and present to the older adult client and treatment team a range of options to inform decision making for both advance care planning and end-of-life issues.

Evidence-based Interventions

Respecting Choices, an evidence-based, internationally recognized advance care planning program, emphasizes person-centered care and shared decision making when engaging clients and families in discussion on end-of-life-care and preferences and values for advance health-care directives (Respecting Choices, 2017). It was recognized in 2011 as the national framework for advance care directives by the Australian government (Respecting Choices, 2017). It was also described in a report to Congress as an effective multicomponent intervention that (1) "included patient and provider education," (2) incorporates "changes in documentation policies and practices in order to alter community expectations and provider standards of care," and (3) it "demonstrated a nearly six-fold increase in advance directive completion and a match between treatments received and dying patients' wishes" in La Crosse, Wisconsin (U.S. Department of Health & Human Services, 2008, p. xv). In a systematic review of 16 studies using Respecting Choices and respective derivative models, researchers concluded, however, that "there is a low level of evidence that [Respecting Choices] and derivative models increase the incidence and prevalence of Advance Directive and Physician Orders for Life-Sustaining Treatment completion" (MacKenzie, Smith-Howell, Bomba, & Meghani, 2018, p. 897). The researchers concluded that using the Respecting Choices program within non-Hispanic White populations increases "patient–surrogate congruence" and that, overall, the "evidence is mixed, inconclusive, and too poor in quality to determine whether [Respecting Choices] and derivative models change the consistency of treatment with wishes and overall health-care utilization in the end of life" (MacKenzie, Smith-Howell, Bomba, & Meghani, 2018, p. 897).

A recent study designed to increase participation in advance care planning focused on increasing motivation through offering decision sets with more options for completing an advance directive (Courtright et al., 2017). In the randomized trial of 316 adults at 15 outpatient hemodialysis centers over a one-year period, clients were randomly assigned to receive an intervention using either a brief advance directive form or an intervention using comprehensive, expanded, or brief forms in advance care planning (Courtright et al., 2017). The key outcome was completion of an advance directive, and other outcomes included: "whether patients wanted to complete an advance directive, decision satisfaction, quality of life at 3 months, and patient factors associated with advance directive completion" (Courtright et al., 2017, p. 544). Although there was not a statistically significant difference between the groups receiving interventions with brief advance care directive forms or comprehensive, expanded, or brief advance directive forms, the intervention "did significantly increase the proportion of patients who wanted to complete an advance directive and took one home (71.9% in standard v. 85.3% in expanded, $P = 0.004$)" (Courtright et al., 2017, p. 544). For secondary outcomes, no statistically significant differences were found for "satisfaction ($P = 0.65$) or change in quality of life between groups ($P = 0.63$);" however, "a higher baseline quality of life was independently associated with advance directive completion ($P = 0.006$)" (Courtright, et al., 2017, p. 544). Offering options for older adults may not only increase completion rates for advance directive, but completion of advance directives may also lead to improvements in quality of life.

Other randomized trials have utilized video aids to inform advance care planning with older adults to select preferences if they were to later in life develop and be diagnosed with advanced dementia (Volandes et al., 2009). In the trial, participants—200 older adults ages 65 and older receiving outpatient primary care at one of four clinics in Boston—were randomly assigned to a verbal narrative group or a video support tool group (Volandes et al., 2009). Participants in both groups were asked to make end-of-life decisions in anticipation of developing advanced dementia. The three preferences for goals of care were: "life prolonging care (cardiopulmonary resuscitation, mechanical ventilation), limited care (admission to hospital, antibiotics, but not cardiopulmonary resuscitation), or comfort care (treatment only to relieve symptoms)" (Volandes et al., 2009, p. 1). In comparison to older adults who engaged in advance care planning with a verbal narrative format, more older adults who received the video support preferred comfort care (86% versus 64%, respectively) (Volandes et al., 2009). Older adults who received the narrative format were more likely than those with the video format to prefer limited care (19% versus 9%) or life-prolonging care (14% versus 4%) (Volandes et al., 2009). The findings suggest that the use of video tools to depict future scenarios may be useful in assisting older adults with making decisions on end-of-life preferences. However, it is important to keep in mind that all advance care planning should be individualized to the client's preferences, values, and definition of what constitutes quality of life for him or her.

A study conducted by the Veterans Administration sought to determine whether a "patient-facing, interactive advance care planning website called PREPARE plus an easy-to-read advance directive increase advance care planning documentation compared with an advance directive alone" with both interventions providing no clinician education (Sudore et al., 2017, p. 1102). The sample—414 older adult veterans with two or more chronic health conditions, two or more visits to the primary care physicians, and two or more visits to the emergency room or a clinic—was 20% female and 43% race other than non-Hispanic White (Sudore et al., 2017). Older adults who received the PREPARE intervention had completion rates of 35% in comparison to 25% for those who received only the advance care directive (Sudore et al., 2017).

According to Sorrell, though efforts to increase advance care planning have increased recently in the United States, "90% of individuals believe that talking to loved ones about end-of-life wishes is important, but only 27% have done so" (2018, p. 32). Advance care planning is an important intervention for documenting the end-of-life wishes of older adult clients. Clinicians can create opportunities for the older adult client to engage in such meaningful discussions with family members and other decision makers. It can be one of a number of meaningful means for achieving death with dignity, with the client being the author and holding the pen to determine and document those terms and share them with others. Too often, there is fear and apprehension surrounding talking about death in American culture. Advance care planning for some may not be enough to open the door to review, reminisce, and consider one's legacy in life. Reminiscence therapy is one way to engage an older adult in discussions about their life; it can provide an opportunity for addressing Erikson's developmental stage, integrity versus despair.

Reminiscence therapy originates from the work of Butler in the early 1960s when he proposed therapists shift their perception about reminiscence among older adults away from the prevailing view of reminiscence as a "psychological dysfunction" or "symptom" whereby the older adult was perceived as "living in the past" (Butler, 1962, p. 65). According to Butler, this predominant therapeutic stance or perception of reminiscence resulted in "the content and significance" of reminiscence of an older adult to be "lost or devalued" (1962, p. 65). To Butler, "life review" is "a naturally occurring process where the person looks back on his/her life and reflects on past experiences, including unresolved difficulties and conflicts" (Woods, Spector, Jones, Orrell, & Davies, 2005, p. 2). In a systematic review of four randomized clinical trials ($n = 144$), older adults diagnosed with dementia who received reminiscence therapy, with sessions ranging from four to six weeks, had improvements in both cognition and mood at the time of follow-up after the interventions and improvements in behavior function at the end of the intervention (Woods, Spector, Jones, Orrell, & Davies, 2005). Improvements were also noted for caregivers, with lower stress levels of strain and improvements of resident backgrounds for staff (Woods, Spector, Jones, Orrell, & Davies, 2005). Group reminiscence therapy has been found to be effective for the treatment of depression among older adults in long-term care-settings (Elias, Neville, &

Scott, 2015). In a meta-analysis of 128 studies with control group designs, older adults who received reminiscence interventions (n = 4,067) had statistically significant improvements in "ego-integrity, depression, purpose in life, death preparation, mastery, mental health, positive well-being, social integration, and cognitive performance" (Pinquart & Forstmeier, 2012, p. 10). To date, reminiscence therapy is also effective with older adults who are frail, as well as ethnically diverse older adults (Substance Abuse and Mental Health Services Administration, 2011). Reminiscence therapy involves "discussion of past activities, events and experiences, with another person or group of people," which often involves use of "aids such as videos, pictures, archives and life story books" (Woods, Spector, Jones, Orrell, & Davies, 2005, p. 2). Sessions may range from four to 10 weeks; group formats are often eight to 10 sessions. Clinicians require formal training to conduct reminiscence therapy.

Clinicians can also be trained in and use end-of-life evidence-based interventions, such as dignity therapy, that provide opportunities for older adults to engage in life review, reminisce, achieve dignity, and consider their life legacy. Dignity therapy, developed in 2002 by Harvey Chochinov, a psychiatrist and professor at the University of Manitoba, was designed to be used for clients in the last six months of life as an option for achieving dignity for clients. Dignity therapy (n = 108), when compared to both palliative care (n = 111) and client-centered care (n = 107) in a randomized clinical trial of terminally ill patients, was found to be statistically significant by patients as being "helpful (χ^2 = 35.501; p<0.001);" it improved their "quality of life (χ^2 = 14.520; p<0.001);" it helped them to achieve a "sense of dignity (χ^2 = 12.655; p = 0.002);" patients noticed a change in "how their family sees and appreciates them (χ^2 = 33.811; p<0.001);" and patients perceived that dignity therapy was "helpful to their family (χ^2 = 33.864; p<0.001)" (Chochinov et al., 2011, p. 2)

Chochinov describes dignity therapy as a way for clients to "speak on tape about various aspects of life they would most want permanently recorded and ultimately remembered" (2002, p. 2258). The intervention involves the clinician asking the client a series of questions (Figure 10.1) that are "based on the

FIGURE 10.1. Dignity Psychotherapy Question Protocol (Chochinov, 2002, p. 2258)

Dignity Psychotherapy Question Protocol

Can you tell me a little about your life history, particularly those parts that you either remember most or think are the most important?

When did you feel most alive?

Are there specific things that you would want your family to know about you, and are there particular things you would want them to remember?

What are the most important roles (eg, family, vocational, community service) you have played in life?

Why are they so important to you, and what do you think you accomplished in those roles?

What are your most important accomplishment, and what do you feel most proud of?

Are there particular things that you feel still need to be said to your loved ones, or things that you would want to take the time to say once again?

What are your hopes and dreams for your loved ones?

What have you learned about life that you would want to pass along to others?

What advice or words of guidance would you wish to pass along to your___(son, daughter, husband, wife, parents, other[s])?

Are there words or perhaps even instructions you would like to offer your family, in order to provide them with comfort or solace?

In creating this permanent record, are there other things that you would like included?

dignity model, which focus on things that they feel are most important and that they would most want their love one(s) to remember" (Chochinov, 2002, p. 2258).

According to Chochinov, though some clients may find meaning, dignity, and satisfaction with a life well lived through spiritual and cultural connections and relationships, dignity therapy can be another means for a client to process "whether or not they feel they have made an important contribution in life;" it can "engender a sense that they will leave something of value, whether to thank loved ones, ask for forgiveness, leave important information or instructions, or provide words of comfort" (2002, p. 2258). According to Chochinov, after completing the recorded interviews from the psychotherapy session with the client asking the series of questions, the audio recordings are transcribed and "then edited so that they read like well-honed narratives;" this document then becomes a "life manuscript" that "is returned to the patient, in most instances to be left for surviving loved ones" (2002, p. 2259). Dignity therapy, as an intervention, is a "therapeutic process" that "is intended to enhance a sense of meaning and purpose for dying patients" and provides "a lasting legacy for their loved ones;" thus, "patients may sense that their dignity has been duly honored and therefore enhanced" as a result of participating in dignity therapy (Chochinov, 2002, p. 2259). As part of best practice, clinicians monitor and assess outcomes of advance care planning and end-of-life interventions.

Assessing/Monitoring Evidence-based Treatment Outcomes

When engaging, assessing, and intervening with older adults with life-threatening or comorbid chronic illnesses, clinicians adhere to CSWE Gero Competency 1: Demonstrate Ethical and Professional Behavior to ensure that at the micro, mezzo, and macro levels, professional, ethical, and legal standards are followed when engaging diversity and difference in practice (CSWE Gero Competency 2) and that they engage in research and evidence-informed practice (Gero Competency 4) (CalSWEC, 2017). Clinicians engage in ongoing interactive evaluation, understand relevant theories pertaining to assessment and use of evidence-based interventions, and use this knowledge as well as knowledge about qualitative and quantitative methods to evaluate primary and secondary outcomes (CSWE Competency 9) (CalSWEC, 2017). Clinicians keep accurate records and monitor and track data on interventions (CSWE Competency 9, behavior 1) (CalSWEC, 2017) to ensure autonomy of older adult clients, and they include their perspectives as well as those of family members and members of the interdisciplinary treatment team in all analyses (CSWE Competency 9, behavior 2) (CalSWEC, 2017). Clinicians adapt the treatment plan as appropriate when monitoring its effectiveness and engage and share the results of such analyses with older adult clients, their family members, and members of the interdisciplinary treatment team (CSWE Competency 9, behaviors 3–4) (CalSWEC, 2017). Clinicians identify appropriate community resources to support advance care planning and end-of-life preferences and biopsychosocial/spiritual needs of older adults and their families.

Community Resources/Interagency Coordination

Clinicians should be aware of the range of community resources, programs, and services available to serve the diverse biopsychosocial/spiritual needs of older adults and their families surrounding interventions for advance care planning and end-of-life issues. Clinicians are aware of a range of options, from no-cost to private pay, to ensure older adults and their families have access to information and legal services when a client is in need of or prefers professional attorney services to draw up a living will, trust, general power of attorney, and/or conservatorship. Clinicians advance the human rights of older adults with end-of-life issues, chronic comorbid, and life-threatening illnesses and provide advocacy to ensure clients have access to necessary information and services to meet their full range of biopsychosocial/spiritual needs, promoting their safety, dignity, and quality of life (CSWE Competency 3: Advance Human Rights and Social, Economic, and Environmental Justice, specialized practice behaviors 2–4). Ms. Taylor, a 65-year-old non-Hispanic White single female with no children and no social support, was working as a secretary at an aerospace company. She was diagnosed with an aggressive form of breast cancer stage 3; her insurance company denied authorization of the necessary chemotherapy she needed, which targets the specific type of cancer she was diagnosed with. She had been off work for four weeks, and her employer was threatening to terminate her if she did not return back to work. The social worker assisted Ms. Taylor with gaining immediate access to a legal firm that specializes in cancer care; the attorney sent a letter to both her employer and the insurance company—within 48 hours, her insurance authorized the life-sustaining chemotherapy she needed, and her employer provided confirmation that her job would not be terminated and all accommodations she required according to the ADA would be followed upon her return.

Clinicians should be aware of eligibility criteria, insurances accepted, policies, and procedures, as well as local, state, and federal policies when providing referrals for community and other agencies to assist older adults with access to the range of services and programs to ensure end-of-life care that promotes well-being and quality of life. Clinicians are aware, for example, that older adults with chronic and/or life-threatening illnesses who choose to continue life-sustaining treatments may have home health services with a nurse, social worker, physical and occupational therapist, and home health aide when there is a clinical need. They may receive palliative care simultaneously for pain and symptom management, and if they choose to forgo life-sustaining treatments, they may choose to utilize hospice services and have medications and services provided at the home with biopsychosocial/spiritual treatment from a nurse, aide, social worker, chaplain or other spiritual care, and respite care. They should also be aware of the criteria—within states where it is legal—for physician aid in dying. Long-term care planning can be beneficial as well to provide a comprehensive range of options for clients and their families to choose from based on their preferences. Clinicians are also aware of potential transference and countertransference issues that may present when working with older adult clients, their families, and other providers surrounding advance care planning and end-of-life care.

Transference/Countertransference

Clinicians working with older adults and their families may experience both transference and countertransference when engaging, assessing, intervening, and evaluating outcomes for advance care planning and end-of-life issues. Clinicians utilize appropriate strategies for managing both transference and countertransference, such as supervision, case consultation, and/or counseling. Transference may present in the therapeutic relationship when the clinician reminds the client of a family member or provider they have worked with. The client may ask the clinician what they would do and become dependent upon the clinician to help with making decisions around advance care planning and end-of-life issues. Countertransference may be positive or negative; for example, a clinician may have a positive countertransference reaction toward an older adult client who resembles a family member or other client they have worked successfully with in advance care planning or end-of-life issues. The clinician may make assumptions, however, that the client may want similar support or interventions and lead the client toward similar decision making; therefore, the clinician must seek ways to manage the countertransference reactions so that the client receives client-centered care tailored to his or her unique preferences and values, respecting autonomy and independence when engaging the client in decision making. Negative countertransference may occur when the clinician directs a client toward decision making because the clinician has strong perceptions, values, or beliefs against what the client prefers. For example, if a client prefers no life-sustaining measures at all if they had a stroke and the clinician felt strongly against that personally, directing a client toward the clinician's preferences and values would be unethical. Active management of countertransference reactions is required for ethical and professional practice with the client (CSWE Gero Competency 1, specialized practice behaviors 1–7). Clinicians are aware of technological resources to provide education and support to older adults and their families, and they identify and provide advocacy to address potential legal/ethical issues that may present during an episode of care.

Technological Resources

American Academy of Hospice and Palliative Medicine: http://aahpm.org/

American College of Healthcare Executives: Decisions near the end of life: https://www.ache.org/policy/endoflif.cfm

American Medical Association: Ethics consultations: https://www.ama-assn.org/delivering-care/ethics-consultations

American Medical Association: Medical ethics: https://www.ama-assn.org/delivering-care/medical-ethics

Center to Advance Palliative Care: https://www.capc.org/

Compassion and Choices: https://www.compassionandchoices.org/

Dignity in Care: http://www.dignityincare.ca/en/

LifeBio: Engage and use reminiscence therapy to capture life stories: http://www.lifebio.org/health-care/senior-care-health/?gclid=EAIaIQobChMI_cCpscjK2wIVE57ACh-1IxgesEAAYAiAAEgLYWPD_BwE

National Association for Home Care and Hospice: https://www.nahc.org/

National Hospice and Palliative Care Organization: Advance care planning: https://www.nhpco.org/advance-care-planning

National Institute on Aging: Advance care planning: Healthcare directives: https://www.nia.nih.gov/health/advance-care-planning-healthcare-directives#what

Social Work Policy Institute: End-of-life care: http://www.socialworkpolicy.org/research/end-of-life-care.html

Legal/Ethical Considerations

Bioethical principles guide professional relationships in health settings between clinicians, providers, clients and their families, community-based providers, insurance companies, and other stakeholders. The four bioethical principles are autonomy, nonmaleficence, beneficence, and justice (McCormick, 2013). The first, autonomy, is a requirement for informed consent; it implies that "the patient has the capacity to act intentionally, with understanding, and without controlling influences that would mitigate against a free and voluntary act" (McCormick, 2013, para. 5). A clinician who directs a client toward their own values and preferences on end-of-life-care would be violating this bioethical principle in addition to the professional ethic of autonomy in the NASW. The second principle, nonmaleficence, requires clinicians and medical professionals to "not intentionally create a harm or injury to the patient, either through acts of commission or omission" and requires a provider to provide "a proper standard of care that avoids or minimizes the risk of harm" (McCormick, 2013, para. 8). A provider is considered "negligent if one imposes a careless or unreasonable risk of harm upon another," and this principle further "affirms the need for medical competence" (McCormick, 2013, para. 8). When engaging in advance care planning, to avoid harm, clinicians must: (1) be competent and trained in the interventions they provide, (2) work within their scope of practice and competence, and (3) not withhold information or mislead a client about an intervention, options, or other end-of-life services.

The third principle, beneficence, refers to the duty of clinicians and health-care providers to "be of a benefit to the patient, as well as to take positive steps to prevent and to remove harm from the patient;" additionally, "these duties are viewed as rational and self-evident and are widely accepted as the proper goals of medicine" (McCormick, 2013, p. 11).

In other words, clinicians and health-care providers have a duty to help a client in need of services from them. If the clinician is not trained in the intervention the client prefers and needs, to avoid harm, the clinician should assist the client with identifying a clinician or other provider who can. The fourth bioethics principle, justice, has to do with "a form of fairness," or as Aristotle once said, "giving to each that which is his due;" it further "implies the fair distribution of goods in society and requires that we look at the role of entitlement" (McCormick, 2013, para. p. 15). For clinicians, this principle is consistent with the NASW Code of Ethics justice principle: that clinicians provide advocacy and assistance with ensuring older adult clients have access to the end-of-life services and care they prefer and value.

When engaging, assessing, and intervening with older adult clients, their families, and myriad stakeholders, an ethical dilemma may arise. An ethical dilemma occurs when there is a decision that needs to be made or is recommended that conflicts with the client's values and preferences, the family members, providers, and/or any key stakeholders, laws, and policies. According to Allen, three conditions must be met for an ethical dilemma to occur: (1) "when an individual, called the 'agent,' must make a decision about which course of action is best," (2) "there must be different courses of action to choose from," and (3) "no matter what course of action is taken, some ethical principle is compromised" (2018, p. 2). A bioethicist may be consulted on cases where ethical dilemmas occur; they commonly are consulted on cases involving withdrawal or withholding of care, advance directives, physician-assisted death, quality of life, competency, informed consent, and pain management to help render ethical decision making. Mrs. Jones suffered a massive heart attack and stroke shortly after her 69th birthday. While in the intensive care unit, her organs began to shut down and the physician recommended removal of life support and requested a family meeting. Mrs. Jones, unconscious and unable to provide consent, had an advance directive with a preference for all life-sustaining measures. One of the client's health-care agents, the eldest son, agreed with the physician and wanted to remove life support, but the other, the eldest daughter, wanted to honor the client's wishes and continue with full life-sustaining measures. In this case, any solution or decision will result in conflicts in bioethical principles. If Mrs. Jones were removed from life support, it compromises the ethical principles of autonomy and justice. If she remained on life support, it compromises the ethical principles of maleficence and beneficence.

Clinicians should be aware of policy and laws such as the Patient Self-Determination Act of 1991, which requires all Medicare-certified providers (i.e., outpatient and inpatient) to provide information to patients about their rights to receive and complete an advance directive (Silveira, Wiitala, & Piette, 2014). If an older adult is not asked if he or she has an advance directive by Medicare-certified institutions, the provider/institution is in violation of the Patient Self-Determination Act. Clinicians should be aware of policies, procedures, and protocols at their agency and provide mezzo- and macro-level advocacy to improve such policies, procedures, and protocols to ensure they are compliant with the Patient Self-Determination Act. In states where it is legal, clinicians should be aware of state laws surrounding physician aid in dying policies, procedures, and protocols and work with their organizations and institutions to ensure compliance with state laws.

Physician aid in dying is "a process that has also been referred to as "assisted suicide" and "death with dignity" that "when adopted at the state level ... allows physicians to write a prescription for a terminally ill person to self-administer medication to end his or her life" (Dorn, 2018, p. 1). Following are a list of states and years that physician aid in dying polices were enacted: "PAD is legal in Oregon (since 1997), Washington state (2009), Vermont (2013), California (2016), Colorado (2016), the District of Columbia (2017), and Hawaii (effective in 2019);" legislation is pending in 20 states (Dorn, 2018, p. 1).

When assessing, engaging, and intervening with older adult clients and their families in advance care planning and on end-of-life issues, clinicians ensure that the intersections of culture and diversity are included in discussions, and clinicians often assist communication to the interdisciplinary team about cultural preferences, practices, and/or rituals the client and family prefer to plan for the future or engage in when decisions are being made about life and death.

Clinicians working with older adults and their families with advance care planning and end-of-life issues adhere to CSWE Gero Competency 1: Demonstrate Ethical and Professional Behavior, specialized practice behaviors 1–7 to ensure professional, ethical, and legal standards are practiced at micro, mezzo, and macro levels (CalSWEC, 2017).

Critical Thinking Activity/Discussion Questions

1. What interventions for advance care planning with older adults do you think are needed?
   a. What advance care planning interventions are typically provided to organizations at your agency, in the local community, or in the state where you work with older adults?
   b. What resources are available?
   c. What legal/ethical issues have occurred that you are aware of, and how were they addressed?
   d. How might you engage in advocacy to address any unmet needs of older adults in need of advance care planning?

2. What interventions for end-of-life issues with older adults do you think are needed?
   a. What end-of-life interventions are typically provided to organizations at your agency, in the local community, or in the state where you work with older adults?
   b. What resources are available?
   c. What legal/ethical issues have occurred that you are aware of, and how were they addressed? How should they have been addressed?
   d. How are older adults engaged in decision making for end-of-life issues in your agency or community?
   e. What role can clinicians play in ensuring their participation in decision making?

Self-Reflection Exercises

1. Critically examine your own attitudes and beliefs about advance care planning.
    a. What attitudes and beliefs do you have about advance care planning?
    b. From what sources did these attitudes and beliefs develop?
    c. How do those beliefs influence your perception on what interventions are needed for advance care planning today?
    d. How might those beliefs affect your ability to engage, assess, and intervene with older adults in need of advance care planning?

2. Critically examine your own attitudes and beliefs about end-of-life issues.
    a. What did you learn about end-of-life issues growing up?
    b. From what sources did you learn it?
    c. How do those beliefs influence your attitudes about care interventions for older adults surrounding end-of-life issues?
    d. How might those beliefs affect your ability to engage, assess, and intervene with older adults in need of interventions to address end-of-life issues?

3. Identify the advance directive form in your state. Or go to the five wishes website https://fivewishes.org/ and view a sample form.
    a. Print it, read through it entirely once, and then imagine that you yourself have made a decision to complete an advance health-care directive.
        i. Who would you select? A family member? A friend?
        ii. Do you want one or more people to make decisions? Will they agree to follow your wishes if you became cognitively incapacitated and could no longer consent to treatment?
        iii. What preferences do you have for life-sustaining treatments?
        iv. How do you define quality of life?
        v. Under what conditions would you want full life-sustaining treatments?
        vi. Under what circumstances would you want no life-sustaining treatments?
        vii. What are your preferences for your body after death? Cremation, burial, or spreading of ashes?
        viii. What cultural and spiritual practices would influence the rituals before your death? After your death?

References

Allen, K. (2018). What is an ethical dilemma? Retrieved from http://www.socialworker.com/feature-articles/ethics-articles/What_Is_an_Ethical_Dilemma%3F/

Black, K. (2005). Advance directive communication practices: Social workers' contributions to the interdisciplinary health care team. *Social Work in Health Care*, 40(3), 39–55.

Butler, R. N. (1963). The life review: An interpretation of reminiscence in the aged. *Psychiatry*, 26(1), 65–76.

Byon, H. D., Hinderer, K., & Alexander, C. (2017). Beliefs in advance care planning among Chinese Americans: Similarities and differences between the younger and older generations. *Asian/Pacific Island Nursing Journal, 2*(3), 83–90.

CalSWEC. (2017). CalSWEC curriculum competencies for public child welfare, behavioral health, and aging in California. Retrieved from https://calswec.berkeley.edu/sites/default/files/2017_calswec_curriculum_competencies_0.pdf

Chochinov, H. M. (2002). Dignity-conserving care—A new model for palliative care: Helping the patient feel valued. *JAMA, 287*(17), 2253–2260.

Chochinov, H. M., Kristjanson, L. J., Breitbart, W., McClement, S., Hack, T. F., Hassard, T., & Harlos, M. (2011). Effect of dignity therapy on distress and end-of-life experience in terminally ill patients: A randomised controlled trial. *The Lancet Oncology, 12*(8), 753–762.

Council for Social Work Education. (2017). Specialized practice curricular guide for gero social work practice. Alexandria, VA: Council on Social Work Education.

Courtright, K. R., Madden, V., Gabler, N. B., Cooney, E., Kim, J., Herbst, N., ... & Halpern, S. D. (2017). A randomized trial of expanding choice sets to motivate advance directive completion. *Medical Decision Making, 37*(5), 544–554.

Dobbs, D., Park, N. S., Jang, Y., & Meng, H. (2015). Awareness and completion of advance directives in older Korean-American adults. *Journal of the American Geriatrics Society, 63*(3), 565–570.

Dorn, C. (2018). An overview of physician aid in dying and the role of social workers. Retrieved from https://www.socialworkers.org/LinkClick.aspx?fileticket=1WNwr-xYTlY%3d&portalid=0

Elias, S. M. S., Neville, C., & Scott, T. (2015). The effectiveness of group reminiscence therapy for loneliness, anxiety and depression in older adults in long-term care: A systematic review. *Geriatric Nursing, 36*(5), 372–380.

Huang, I. A., Neuhaus, J. M., & Chiong, W. (2016). Racial and ethnic differences in advance directive possession: Role of demographic factors, religious affiliation, and personal health values in a national survey of older adults. *Journal of Palliative Medicine, 19*(2), 149–156.

Kwak, J., & Haley, W. E. (2005). Current research findings on end-of-life decision making among racially or ethnically diverse groups. *The Gerontologist, 45*(5), 634–641.

MacKenzie, M. A., Smith-Howell, E., Bomba, P. A., & Meghani, S. H. (2018). Respecting choices and related models of advance care planning: A systematic review of published evidence. *American Journal of Hospice and Palliative Medicine, 35*(6), 897–907.

McCormick, T. R. (2013). Principles of bioethics. Retrieved from https://depts.washington.edu/bioethx/tools/princpl.html

Pinquart, M., & Forstmeier, S. (2012). Effects of reminiscence interventions on psychosocial outcomes: A meta-analysis. *Aging & Mental Health, 16*(5), 541–558.

National Hospice and Palliative Care Organization. (2017). Advance care planning. Retrieved from https://www.nhpco.org/advance-care-planning

National Institute on Aging. (2018). Advance care planning: Healthcare directives. Retrieved from https://www.nia.nih.gov/health/advance-care-planning-healthcare-directives#what

Respecting Choices. (2017). About us. Retrieved from https://respectingchoices.org/about-us/

Rhodes, R. L., Elwood, B., Lee, S. C., Tiro, J. A., Halm, E. A., & Skinner, C. S. (2017). The desires of their hearts: The multidisciplinary perspectives of African Americans on end-of-life care in the African American community. *American Journal of Hospice and Palliative Medicine*, 34(6), 510–517.

Sabatino, C. P. (2007). *Advance directives and advance care planning: Legal and policy issues*. U.S. Department of Health and Human Services, Office of Disability, Aging, and Long-Term Care Policy. Washington, D.C.

Silveira, M. J., Wiitala, W., & Piette, J. (2014). Advance directive completion by elderly Americans: A decade of change. *Journal of the American Geriatrics Society*, 62(4), 706–710.

Sorrell, J. M. (2018). End-of-life conversations as a legacy. *Journal of Psychosocial Nursing and Mental Health Services*, 56(1), 32–35.

Substance Abuse and Mental Health Services Administration. (2011). *The treatment of depression in older adults: Selecting evidence-based practices for treatment of depression in older adults* (HHS Pub. No. SMA-11-4631). Rockville, MD: Center for Mental Health Services, Substance Abuse and Mental Health Services Administration, U.S. Department of Health and Human Services.

Sudore, R. L., Boscardin, J., Feuz, M. A., McMahan, R. D., Katen, M. T., & Barnes, D. E. (2017). Effect of the PREPARE website vs. an easy-to-read advance directive on advance care planning documentation and engagement among veterans: A randomized clinical trial. *JAMA Internal Medicine*, 177(8), 1102–1109.

Tai, M. C. T., & Tsai, T. P. (2003). Who makes the decision? Patient's autonomy vs. paternalism in a Confucian society. *Croatian Medical Journal*, 44(5), 558–561.

U.S. Department of Health & Human Services. (2008). Advance directives and advance care planning: Report to Congress. Retrieved from https://aspe.hhs.gov/basic-report/advance-directives-and-advance-care-planning-report-congress#preface

Yadav, K. N., Gabler, N. B., Cooney, E., Kent, S., Kim, J., Herbst, N., ... & Courtright, K. R. (2017a). Approximately one in three U.S. adults completes any type of advance directive for end-of-life care. *Health Affairs*, 36(7), 1244–1251.

Yadav, K. N., Gabler, N. B., Cooney, E., Kent, S., Kim, J., Herbst, N., ... & Courtright, K. R. (2017b). Prevalence of advance directives in the United States: A systematic review. *American Journal of Respiratory and Critical Care Medicine*, 195, pp. A4633–A4633.

Volandes, A. E., Paasche-Orlow, M. K., Barry, M. J., Gillick, M. R., Minaker, K. L., Chang, Y., ... & Mitchell, S. L. (2009). Video decision support tool for advance care planning in dementia: randomised controlled trial. *The BMJ*, 338, b2159. http://doi.org/10.1136/bmj.b2159

Woods, B., Spector, A. E., Jones, C. A., Orrell, M., & Davies, S. P. (2005). Reminiscence therapy for dementia. *The Cochrane Library*, Issue 2, pp. 1–34.

Credit

Figure 10.1: H.M. Chochinov, *Jama*, vol. 287, no. 17, pp. 2258. Copyright © 2002 by American Medical Association.

CHAPTER 11

Loss, Grief, and Bereavement

Chapter Overview

This chapter identifies normative and non-normative losses older adults often experience; types of grief and normal grief responses; interventions for addressing grief, loss, and bereavement among older adults; and explores key domains to promote both effective clinical practice with older adults and optimal client outcomes.

CSWE Gero Competencies Highlighted

Competency 1: Demonstrate Ethical and Professional Behavior

Specialized Practice Competency Description: Social workers understand the value base of the profession and its ethical standards, as well as relevant laws and regulations that may impact practice at the micro, mezzo, and macro levels. Social workers understand frameworks of ethical decision-making and how to apply principles of critical thinking to those frameworks in practice, research, and policy arenas. Social workers recognize personal values and the distinction between personal and professional values. They also understand how their personal experiences and affective reactions influence their professional judgment and behavior. Social workers understand the profession's history, its mission, and the roles and responsibilities of the profession. Social workers also understand the role of other professions when engaged in inter-professional teams. Social workers recognize the importance of lifelong learning and are committed to continually updating their skills to ensure they are relevant and effective. Social workers also understand emerging forms of technology and the ethical use of technology in social work practice.

Competency Behaviors: (1) Guided by ethical reasoning and self-reflection, demonstrate adherence to ethical frameworks and key laws, policies, and procedures related to aging, and the rights of older adults. (2) Engage in active dialogue with field faculty/instructors regarding aging field placement agency policies and culture around behavior, appearance, communication, and the use of supervision. (3) Develop and sustain effective collaborative relationships that respect older adults' needs for protection, self-determination, and the provision of services in the least restrictive environment possible with colleagues and community stakeholders, including older adults, their family members, other care providers, and Tribes. (4) Effectively manage professional boundary issues and other challenges arising in the course of aging-related work, particularly ambiguities presented by home visits, personal loss, trauma, and other highly involved and potentially emotionally triggering aspects of the work. (5) Develop and sustain relationships with members of interdisciplinary and integrated health care teams, including social workers, primary care providers, hospital staff, home health care providers, psychiatrists, psychologists, substance use disorder treatment staff, Tribal service providers, and others, that reflect clear understanding of their roles in providing care to older adults. (6) Demonstrate both knowledge of the history and evolution of social work practice related to aging and older adults in the United States and California, and a commitment to lifelong learning around this practice. (7) Follow all ethical guidelines and legal mandates in the use of technology in order to maintain the confidentiality of all personal, behavioral health, and health-related information. (CalSWEC, 2017, pp. 1–2)

Competency 2: Engage Diversity and Difference in Practice

Specialized Practice Competency Description: Social workers understand how diversity and difference characterize and shape the human experience and are critical to the formation of identity. The dimensions of diversity are understood as the intersectionality of multiple factors, including, but not limited to, age, class, color, culture, disability and ability, ethnicity, gender, gender identity and expression, immigration status, marital status, political ideology, race, religion/ spirituality, sex, sexual orientation, and Tribal sovereign status. Social workers understand that, as a consequence of difference, a person's life experiences may include oppression, poverty, marginalization, and alienation as well as privilege, power, and acclaim. Social workers also understand the forms and mechanisms of oppression and discrimination and recognize the extent to which a culture's structures and values, including social, economic, political, and cultural exclusions, may oppress, marginalize, alienate, or create privilege and power.

Competency Behaviors: (1) Engage in critical analysis of the interpersonal, community, and social structural causes and effects of disproportionality, disparities, and inequities in the incidence and trajectory of aging-related care needs, housing, transportation, and resource access among older adults,

their families, and their communities. (2) Evidence respectful awareness and understanding of the impact of being a member of a marginalized group on aging experiences, and accurately identify differences in access to and quality of available services for members of different communities and populations. (3) Demonstrate knowledge of diverse cultural norms and traditional methods of providing care to older adults, as well as an applied understanding of how these realities affect work with older adults from diverse backgrounds, their families, and their communities. (4) Develop and use practice methods that acknowledge, respect, and address how individual and cultural values, norms, and differences impact the various systems with which older adults interact, including, but not limited to, families, communities, primary care systems, mental and behavioral health care systems, and integrated care systems. (CalSWEC, 2017, pp. 3–4)

Competency 3: Advance Human Rights and Social, Economic, and Environmental Justice

Specialized Practice Competency Description: Social workers understand that every person regardless of position in society has fundamental human rights such as freedom, safety, privacy, an adequate standard of living, health care, and education. Social workers understand the global interconnections of oppression and human rights violations, and are knowledgeable about theories of human need and social justice and strategies to promote social and economic justice and human rights. Social workers understand strategies designed to eliminate oppressive structural barriers to ensure that social goods, rights, and responsibilities are distributed equitably and that civil, political, environmental, economic, social, and cultural human rights are protected.

Competency Behaviors: (1) Clearly articulate the systematic effects of discrimination, oppression, and stigma on the needs and experiences of older adults and on the quality and delivery of services available to them, and identify and advocate for policy changes needed to address these issues. (2) Advocate for changes in policies and programs that reflect a social justice practice framework for facilitating access and providing services to older adults, their families, and care providers, especially among underserved groups and communities. (3) Demonstrate the ability to work effectively in cross-disciplinary collaboration to develop and provide interventions that explicitly address the specific needs of diverse older adults, their families, and care providers. (4) Integrate into all aspects of policy and practice sensitivity to the reality that fundamental rights, including freedom and privacy, may be compromised for older adults engaged in care, and the goal that services should be provided in the least restrictive environment possible. (CalSWEC, 2017, pp. 4–5)

Competency 4: Engage in Practice-informed Research and Research-informed Practice

Specialized Practice Competency Description: Social workers understand quantitative and qualitative research methods and their respective roles in advancing a science of social work and in evaluating their practice. Social workers know the principles of logic, scientific inquiry, and culturally informed and ethical approaches to building knowledge. Social workers understand that evidence that informs practice derives from multidisciplinary sources and multiple ways of knowing. They also understand the processes for translating research findings into effective practice.

Competency Behaviors: (1) Demonstrate the ability to understand, interpret, and evaluate the benefits and limitations of various evidence-based and evidence-informed treatment models as they influence practice with older adults. (2) Engage in critical analysis of research findings, practice models, and practice wisdom as they inform aging related practice, including how research practices have historically failed to address the needs and realities of exploited and/or disadvantaged communities, and how cross-cultural research practices can be used to enhance equity. (3) Clearly communicate research findings, conclusions, and implications, as well as their applications to aging practice, across a variety of professional interactions with consumers, families, and multidisciplinary service providers. (4) Apply research findings to aging-related practice with individuals, families, and communities and to the development of professional knowledge about the needs, experiences, and well-being of older adults. (CalSWEC, 2017, pp. 5–6)

Competency 6: Engage With Individuals, Families, Groups, Organizations, and Communities

Specialized Practice Competency Description: Social workers understand that engagement is an ongoing component of the dynamic and interactive process of social work practice with, and on behalf of, diverse individuals, families, groups, organizations, and communities. Social workers value the importance of human relationships. Social workers understand theories of human behavior and the social environment, and critically evaluate and apply this knowledge to facilitate engagement with clients and constituencies, including individuals, families, groups, organizations, and communities. Social workers understand strategies to engage diverse clients and constituencies to advance practice effectiveness. Social workers understand how their personal experiences and affective reactions may impact their ability to effectively engage with diverse clients and constituencies. Social workers value principles of relationship-building and inter-professional collaboration to facilitate engagement with clients, constituencies, and other professionals as appropriate.

Competency Behaviors: (1) Appropriately engage and activate older adults, their families, and other care providers in the development and coordination of care plans that reflect relevant theoretical models and balance older adults' needs for care with respect for autonomy and independence. (2) Effectively utilize interpersonal skills to engage older adults, their families, and other care providers in culturally responsive, consumer-driven, and trauma-informed integrated care that addresses mutually agreed upon service goals and balances needs for care, protection, autonomy, and independence. (3) Establish effective and appropriate communication, coordination, and advocacy planning with other care providers and interdisciplinary care teams as needed to address mutually agreed upon service goals. Recognizing the complex nature of service engagement, ensure that communications with consumers and their families regarding service goals are both sensitive and transparent. (4) Manage affective responses and exercise good judgment around engaging with resistance, trauma responses, and other potentially triggering situations with older adults, their families, and other care providers. (CalSWEC, 2017, pp. 9–10)

Competency 7: Assess Individuals, Families, Groups, Organizations, and Communities

Specialized Practice Competency Description: Practitioners in aging utilize ecological-systems theory, a strengths-based and person/family-centered framework to conduct assessments that value the resilience of diverse older adults, families, and caregivers. They select appropriate assessment tools, methods and technology, and evaluate, adapt, and modify them, as needed, to enhance their validity in working with diverse, vulnerable and at-risk groups. The comprehensive biopsychosocial assessment takes into account the multiple factors of physical, mental and social well-being needed for treatment planning for older adults and their families. They develop skills in interprofessional assessment and communication with key constituencies to choose the most effective practice strategies. Gero social workers understand how their own experiences and affective reactions about aging, quality of life, loss and grief may affect their assessment and resultant decision-making.

Competency Behaviors: (1) Conduct assessments that incorporate a strengths-based perspective, person/family-centered focus, and resilience while recognizing aging related risk, (2) Develop, select, and adapt assessment methods and tools that optimize practice with older adults, their families, caregivers, and communities, and (3) Use and integrate multiple domains and sources of assessment information and communicate with other professionals to inform a comprehensive plan for intervention. (Council for Social Work Education, 2017, pp. 89–90)

Competency 8: Intervene With Individuals, Families, Groups, Organizations, and Communities

Specialized Practice Competency Description: Social workers understand that intervention is an ongoing component of the dynamic and interactive process of social work practice with, and on behalf of, diverse individuals, families, groups, organizations, and communities. Social workers are knowledgeable about evidence-informed interventions to achieve the goals of clients and constituencies, including individuals, families, groups, organizations, and communities. Social workers understand theories of human behavior and the social environment, and critically evaluate and apply this knowledge to effectively intervene with clients and constituencies. Social workers understand methods of identifying, analyzing, and implementing evidence-informed interventions to achieve client and constituency goals. Social workers value the importance of interprofessional teamwork and communication in interventions, recognizing that beneficial outcomes may require interdisciplinary, inter-professional, and inter-organizational collaboration.

Competency Behaviors: (1) In partnership with older adults and their families, develop appropriate intervention plans that reflect respect for autonomy and independence, as well as contemporary theories and models for interventions with older adults. Plans should:

+ Reflect cultural humility and acknowledgement of individualized needs;
+ Incorporate consumer and family strengths;
+ Utilize community resources and natural supports;
+ Incorporate multidisciplinary team supports and interventions;
+ Include non-pharmacological interventions; and
+ Demonstrate knowledge of poly-pharmacy needs and issues specific to older adults.

(2) Apply the principles of teaming, engagement, inquiry, advocacy, and facilitation within interdisciplinary teams and care coordination to the work of supporting older adults, family members, and other care providers to accomplish intervention goals and satisfy advanced care planning needs. (3) Effectively implement evidence-based interventions in the context of providing emergency response, triage, brief treatment, and longer-term care, and in the course of addressing a range of issues presented in primary care, specialty care, community agency, inpatient, and palliative care settings. Interventions should be guided by respect for older adults' autonomy and independence and should include components such as psychoeducation, problem-solving treatment skills, symptom tracking, medication therapies, follow-up, and planning for evolving care needs. (4) Effectively plan for interventions in ways that incorporate

thoughtfully executed transitions during time-limited internships, recognizing that consumer needs for support may continue beyond these time periods. (CalSWEC, 2017, pp. 12–14)

Competency 9: Evaluate Practice With Individuals, Families, Groups, Organizations, and Communities

Competency 9 Specialized Practice Competency Description: Social workers understand that evaluation is an ongoing component of the dynamic and interactive process of social work practice with, and on behalf of, diverse individuals, families, groups, organizations and communities. Social workers recognize the importance of evaluating processes and outcomes to advance practice, policy, and service delivery effectiveness. Social workers understand theories of human behavior and the social environment, and critically evaluate and apply this knowledge in evaluating outcomes. Social workers understand qualitative and quantitative methods for evaluating outcomes and practice effectiveness.

Competency Behaviors: (1) Record, track, and monitor consumer engagement, assessment, and intervention data in practice with older adults, their families, and other care providers accurately and according to field education agency policies and guidelines. (2) Conduct accurate process and outcome analysis of engagement, assessment, and intervention data in practice with older adults, their families, and other care providers that incorporates consumer perspectives and reflects respect for older adults' autonomy and independence. (3) Use findings to evaluate intervention effectiveness, develop recommendations for adapting service plans and approaches as needed, improve interdisciplinary team coordination and care integration, and help agency and community policies better support older adults, their families, and their formal and informal care systems. (4) Share both the purposes of such data collection and the overall results of data analysis with older adults, their families, and communities whenever possible, with the goal of engaging them more meaningfully in the evaluation process. (CalSWEC, 2017, pp. 14–15)

Learning Objectives

1. Learners will understand the context for grief, loss, and bereavement as it relates to older adults.
2. Learners will identify best practices for engaging, intervening, treating, and evaluating grief and bereavement interventions with older adults.
3. Learners will identify best practices for engaging in grief counseling and grief therapy with older adults.

4. Learners will understand the importance of referring older adult clients and their family members to appropriate technological and community resources and when to assist with coordination.
5. Learners will identify sources of transference and countertransference when working with older adults and engaging in grief counseling and grief therapy with older adults.

Case Study

Mrs. Welch, an 89-year-old non-Hispanic White female had a fall at home, which resulted in hospitalization and a diagnosis and treatment for a hip fracture prior to her discharge home. Mrs. Welch, a widow for one year, lives in a single-level home with a steep driveway and a flight of stairs leading to the front door. Mrs. Welch has two children and eight grandchildren. Her power of attorney and agent for health care are her son and daughter—they both live within one hour from Mrs. Welch. Mrs. Welch is a retired teacher; her spouse was an engineer. She retired at the age of 65; her spouse retired at the age of 70. Mrs. Welch was involved at the local senior center and her local Lutheran church; she volunteered in children's ministries every Sunday. After her spouse died a year ago, her children reported to the primary care physician and home health nurse that she started to withdraw from the family and slowly stopped volunteering at church and participating in activities at the senior center. They noted she also stopped having her hair done monthly at the local beauty shop, a ritual they report she engaged in since they could remember. Mrs. Welch has a housekeeper and hired a part-time caregiver to assist with meal preparation and errands during her rehabilitation from the hip fracture; she ambulates with a walker and is no longer driving. The physician requested a social work evaluation to assess the psychological and social functioning of Mrs. Welch.

Assessing Context

Loss, a universal experience, involves adjustment and adaptation to changes and transitions that arise throughout each person's life course. Such adaptations and adjustments occur most often when individuals experience either normative developmental losses or non-normative losses that may be unexpected, anticipated, ambiguous, complicated, and/or traumatic. Loss, as described by Silverman, "is not simply something that happens to us;" rather, it is "something we must make sense out of, give meaning to, and respond to" (2004, p. 226). Loss is commonly associated with various types of grief such as normal uncomplicated grief, anticipatory grief, complicated grief, or traumatic grief. Grief commonly refers to "the ways in which people express the feelings that arise after a death," such as "sadness, crying, despair" (Silverman, 2004, p. 226). Worden defines normal, uncomplicated grief as "a broad range of feelings and behaviors that are common after a loss," which may manifest under four categories: feelings, physical sensations, cognitions, and behaviors (2018, pp. 17–30). It is important to note that an older adult client may not experience all of the normal grief reactions. Emotional grief reactions include feelings such as "sadness, anger, guilt and reproach, anxiety, loneliness, fatigue, helplessness, shock, yearning, emancipation, relief, numbness" (Worden, 2018, pp. 18–23). Normal physical grief reactions include physical sensations such as "hollowness in the stomach, tightness in the chest, tightness in the throat, oversensitivity to noise, a sense of depersonalization, breathlessness, weakness in the muscles, lack of energy, dry mouth" (Worden, 2018, pp. 23–24). Normal cognitive grief reactions include cognitions such as "disbelief, confusion, preoccupation, sense of presence, hallucinations" (Worden, 2018, pp. 24–26). Normal behavioral grief reactions include behaviors such as "sleep disturbances, appetite disturbances, absentminded behavior, social withdrawal, dreams of the deceased, avoiding reminders of the deceased, search and calling out, sighing, restless hyperactivity, crying, visiting places or carrying objects that remind the survivor of the deceased, treasuring objects that belonged to the deceased" (Worden, 2018, pp. 26–31). Normal grief reactions are similar to diagnostic criteria for major depressive disorder in the *Diagnostic and Statistical Manual of Mental Disorders* (5th ed.; *DSM-V*). Clinician expertise with distinguishing between normal, uncomplicated grief versus major depressive disorder is essential to ensure that an older adult's normal grief reactions are not considered as pathologies. Normal, uncomplicated grief often occurs following a loss and does not cause impairment in social, occupational, or educational functioning.

Anticipatory grief occurs when the griever anticipates a future loss, such as anticipating the death of a loved one living with a life-threatening illness, the diagnosis of self with a life-threatening illness, a planned retirement, and/or other future losses such as an upcoming relocation of an older adult from their home to an assisted living setting or other long-term care setting. Worden distinguishes anticipatory grief from normal, uncomplicated grief as "many deaths occur with some forewarning, and it is during this period of anticipation that the individual begins the task of mourning and begins to experience various responses of grief" (2018, p. 202). Anticipatory grief can allow time for the older adult griever to have meaningful conversations, finish unfinished business, reconcile, and prepare in advance for the loss.

Complicated grief is defined as "a persistent form of intense grief in which maladaptive thoughts and dysfunctional behaviors are present along with continued yearning, longing and sadness and/or preoccupation with thoughts and memories of the person who died" (The Center for Complicated Grief, 2017, para. 6). For the survivor living with complicated grief, normal acute grief reactions do not subside and "grief continues to dominate life and the future seems bleak and empty" (The Center for Complicated Grief, 2017, para. 6). The survivor may have "irrational thoughts that the deceased person might reappear," and he or she often "feels lost and alone" (The Center for Complicated Grief, 2017, para. 6). The symptoms associated with complicated grief may manifest in a chronic nature, lasting for months or years. It may be delayed when the survivor does not allow time to accept the loss, experience, and adjust to the loss of a loved one, and he or she may not engage in cultural and spiritual norms and/or return back to work quickly, avoiding accommodation to the loss.

According to Jacobs, traumatic grief is defined as "a disorder that occurs after the death of a significant other" (2016, p. 24). The symptoms of traumatic grief include a core symptom, separation distress, and "bereavement specific symptoms of being devastated and traumatized by death" (Jacobs, 2016, p. 24). According to Jacobs, for diagnosis, "the symptoms must be marked and persistent and last at least 2 months" (2016, p. 24). Traumatic grief causes severe impairment, consistent with *DSM-V* criteria, in occupational, educational, and/or social functioning (Jacobs, 2016). Jacobs clarifies that traumatic grief does not necessarily result from violent deaths or homicides; for those vulnerable, such as older adults, traumatic grief may present "after deaths that are not conspicuously traumatic" (2016, p. 24). Worden underscores three key distinctions from Rando, Horowitz, and Figley's perspective to assist clinicians with recognizing the differences and similarities between trauma and grief (2018). First, "trauma without bereavement" occurs for the individual who "experiences a traumatic event that gives rise to trauma symptoms leading to diagnosis of posttraumatic stress disorder or acute stress disorder"—a client may present, for example, with comorbid symptoms of anxiety and depression, informing diagnosis (Worden, 2018, p. 7). For the first distinction, according to Worden, "the traumatic event has not led to any deaths and the person is dealing with one or more of the classic trauma symptoms (intrusion, avoidance, hyperarousal) without bereavement" (2016, p. 7). The second distinction, "bereavement without trauma," may present for a client who has "experienced the death of a loved one without experiencing trauma symptoms associated with the event," and in this situation, complicated grief or mourning would be more relevant to "complications after the loss" (Worde, 2018, p. 7). The third distinction, "traumatic bereavement," occurs when the client "experiences a death and there is something about the death itself (often violent deaths)" or there may be "something about the person's experience of the death (often related to an insecure attachment or conflicted relationship with the deceased" or "that gives rise to symptoms associated with trauma" (Worden, 2018, p. 7).

The terms bereavement, grief, and mourning are oftentimes used interchangeably; however, among grief theorists and clinicians engaged in grief and bereavement services, the terms are recognized as having distinct meanings and factors to consider with each client in the context of loss. Worden defines bereavement as the process that "defines the loss to which the person is trying to adapt" (2018, p. 17). The bereaved are those, therefore, who have experienced a loss; bereavement may also be considered as a state or period of adjustment and accommodation of a loss. Worden defines grief as "the experience of one who has lost a loved one to death" (2018, p. 17). Grief can also occur for losses other than death, however, such as loss of health, a home, or driving for an older adult. The proper ways to grieve emotionally, physically, cognitively, and spiritually are dictated by the cultural, spiritual, and social norms of the older adult griever. Grief is also recognized, according to Silverman, as a "normal, expected transition in the life cycle that is associated not only with strong feelings but also with change;" it is something we all "live through and learn to deal with" (2004, p. 226). Grief can be considered a "period of transition," or time of "loss and change," that may consist of "many crises and periods of stress" (Silverman,

2004, p. 232). In Western culture, grief, as well as death and dying, are experiences many are uncomfortable with or not prepared to acknowledge, validate, and normalize the grief responses and experiences of the griever. This holds true for all individuals across the life course in Western culture. Family members, friends, and society, for example, may minimize a loss or not provide support to the individual grieving—this is referred to as disenfranchised grief. Disenfranchised grief, according to Doka, is grief "that is not recognized, validated or supported in the mourner's social world;" it oftentimes involves instances where others do not see the loss as worthy of sympathy or condolence (Walter & McCoyd, 2015, p. 21). For older adults, normative losses—those that are developmentally expected in Western culture—may result in disenfranchised grief when an older adult's grief reactions are not validated or supported or when they are discounted. Normative losses include normal biological, cognitive, and physical changes associated with aging, retirement, downsizing of a home, relocation after retirement, being diagnosed with a chronic health condition, or loss of spouse or friends. Non-normative losses—losses that are not expected at this developmental stage to occur—may result in disenfranchised grief as well. Non-normative losses include being diagnosed with a life-threatening illness, a diagnosis of Alzheimer's disease or dementia, the loss of an adult child or grandchild, raising grandchildren, and/or being the victim of a crime, neglect, or violence. However, it is important to note that both normative or non-normative losses may produce other formerly described forms of grief for an older adult as well.

Doka describes five general categories of disenfranchised grief: (1) "grief where the relationship is not recognized" by society such as lesbian, gay, bisexual, transgender (LGBT) relationships and extramarital affairs; (2) "grief where the loss is not acknowledged by societal norms as a 'legitimate' loss," such as adoption, loss of a pet, or abortion; (3) "grief where the griever is excluded," such as older adults because they are "inaccurately not believed to experience grief;" (4) "grief where the circumstances of death cause stigma," such as alcoholism, suicide, or homicide; and (5) "grief expressed in nonsocially sanctioned ways," where the griever's grief responses are not in line with cultural or social norms of grief behaviors and responses (Walter & McCoyd, 2015, p. 21).

Mourning is defined as "the mental work following the loss of a loved one" (Silverman, 2004, p. 226). This involves adjusting to a world without the deceased, grief reactions and feelings, and changes in relational and developmental contexts (Silverman, 2004). According to Silverman, "mourning does not end, we do not 'recover,'" rather, we adapt, accommodate, change"—this accommodation to a loss is seen as a positive opportunity to change and grow in light of a loss; it "can be seen as a new beginning" (2004, p. 227). Grief and loss theorists and clinicians, rather than seeing an older adult who has lost a loved one as an event likely to lead to depression and despair, see the event, using a strengths-based approach, as one that has potential to lead the survivor into a transformation where rediscovery and reinvestments in self, others, and society can occur through the adaptation to such change as a result of loss. The loss of a loved one, especially a spouse, can trigger a spiritual process where the older adult searches for meaning, reconsiders, and/or redefines his or her identity and place in the family, community, and society.

Clinicians can assist older adult clients with this adaptation and change process by bearing witness to the loss; normalizing and validating it and providing psychoeducation on types of grief and normal grief reactions; and processing the loss to promote restoration through the accommodation process where the client can begin to reinvest in self, other, community, and society.

In considering the relational context of mourning, Silverman (2004) posits that in line with "symbolic interactionalism" theory, the social construction of self—an interactive process involving relationships with others, known to influence one's definition of self—also influences grief responses and mourning that occur in the context of "multiple mourners" (p. 227). The voices, or narratives, of multiple mourners comes from five sources: (1) "the family with its various members, whose roles are changed with the death;" (2) "the cultural or societal values, attitudes and mores of the larger society in which the family/mourners live frame and give direction to their grief;" (3) "a mourner's faith system directs how he or she gives meaning to death;" (4) "community resources may provide support and care;" and (5) "the deceased's role in the family needs to be considered, as does his or her legacy and the relationship that is lost and its impact on the mourners" (Silverman, 2004, pp. 226–227). This is consistent with social learning theory—in the context of grief, an individual learns from those models in the social network on the proper grief reactions, rituals, and customs and imitates these responses and norms when presented with loss. In light of loss, the griever seeks to find meaning and understand the world around him or her. Neimeyer describes this process as one in which the griever strives to "punctuate, organize, and anticipate their engagement with the world by arranging it in themes that express their particular cultures, families and personalities," which is also influenced by where the client is developmentally (Silverman, 2004, p. 227).

In considering the developmental context of mourning, where an older adult is developmentally "influences what he or she experiences as lost, how the lost relationship frames his or her sense of self, and how this self in relationship may change" (Silverman, 2004, p. 229). The processes that are associated with the developmental stage of the client affect the journey of grief, resolution of grief, and subsequent meaning and purpose through it (Silverman, 2004)—or, in some instances, the lack of meaning, especially in instances where an older adult client is experiencing traumatic or complicated grief. Erikson's developmental psychosocial crisis for older adults is integrity versus despair. An adaptive resolution of grief may lead to enhanced integrity of an older adult who, in time, finds a sense of meaning, purpose, and/or reinvestment in self, others, community, and society as a result of the adaptations and adjustment of loss. In contrast, an older adult with unresolved grief, complicated or traumatic grief, and/or ambiguous loss may experience difficulty in reaching the stage of accommodation, as coined by Silverman, where he or she reinvests in self, others, community, and society; in this instance, the older adult may be at risk for depression and/or despair, characteristic of Erikson's developmental stage.

Biopsychosocial/spiritual factors also play a role in understanding the context of grief and loss among older adults; as such, clinicians must assess these factors comprehensively before formulating a treatment plan and identifying treatment options. Screening tools, the

DSM-V, and key grief and loss supplemental questions are recommended tools to inform assessment of grief reactions and the types of grief an older adult client presents with.

Biopsychosocial/Spiritual Assessment

Walter and McCoyd (2016) present a biopsychosocial/spiritual and life course perspective that underscores the biological, psychological, and social effects of grief with the intersection of the developmental stage of the client. Biological effects of grief that clinicians should be aware of include: an understanding that higher mortality rates are associated with bereavement and that "interactions of emotions, stress, trauma, and physical health are mediated through the immune, genetic, hormonal/biochemical, and neurological functions" (Walter & McCoyd, 2016, p. 4). In terms of neurological effects of grief, MRI scans have shown that with grief, regions of the brain play a role in memory and storytelling about lives, specifically "the posterior cingulate cortex, the cerebellum, and the inferior temporal gyrus" (Walter & McCoyd, 2016, p. 5). Grief also affects brain changes in the way that the "amygdala interacts with the dorsolateral prefrontal cortex" (Walter & McCoyd, 2016, p. 5). Despite the association most people make between positive emotions and health, research suggests that it is a "mix of positive and negative emotions" that promotes good health (Walter & McCoyd, 2016, p. 4). However, negative emotions related to grief have been found to affect physical health through a reduction of the "immune system's efficiency" that provokes "inflammation, which has negative cardiovascular and neurological effects" (Walter & McCoyd, 2016, p. 4). With knowledge about genetics and the role of epigenetics (i.e., gene–environment interactions), physical health, and neurological impacts, as well as predisposing genetic risk factors understood through a family history assessment, clinicians can assist clients with understanding how stressors related to grief responses, symptoms, and reactions may be associated with what the client comes in for treatment of. Clinicians can provide psychoeducation on the interactions and presentation of physical and psychological symptoms in the context of predisposing genetic risk and protective factors.

Psychological/biological factors related to grief responses affect the cardiovascular system through hormonal and neurotransmitter changes with cortisol, "norepinephrine and ephedrine," triggered by stress related to grief (Walter & McCoyd, 2016, p. 5), and subsequent activation of fight-or-flight responses activated in the sympathetic and parasympathetic nervous systems. The psychological effects of grief are also influenced by the developmental stage and cognitive functioning of the griever and "nearly always entails psychic pain, challenges in coping, and irritation, sadness, and rumination" (Walter & McCoyd, 2016, p. 6). Grief is also understood to interact with time, such as with anniversary dates of the loss of a loved one or other loss (Walter & McCoyd, 2016). Rando, for example, "recognized that grief continues to be felt long after the acute phase resolves" (Walter & McCoyd, 2016, p. 6). Prescriptive timelines (i.e., a certain number of days, weeks, months, or years) on grief resolution can, therefore, result in misperceptions on the part of a clinician that a client's grief responses are maladaptive when the grief responses may fall within normal cultural/spiritual customs and rituals where the deceased is remembered and celebrated. Cumulative and prior losses impact the resolution of a current loss. Cumulative losses may exacerbate the intensity of grief reactions and symptoms and/or "impede coping with new losses" (Walter & McCoyd, 2016, p. 7).

Social factors and "rituals are fundamental to most important transitions, including those provoked by loss and death," illustrated in memorials, funerals, wakes, or other ceremonies that may be "grounded in religious" or cultural practice and "a community of believers" that "provide a deeply social way of mourning losses" (Walter & McCoyd, 2016, p. 7). Cultural, spiritual, religious, and familial rituals are useful "in both allowing a griever to have a sense of control and to lower levels of grief and mourning" (Walter & McCoyd, 2016, p. 7). The assumptions and beliefs a client has about society and the world (i.e., whether it is safe, predictable, just) may become threatened when a client experiences traumatic grief. Depending on the client, loss may cause a client to both adjust to the loss of a loved one and often to revise his or her view of the world in light of the loss (Walter & McCoyd, 2016). This may intersect with spiritual views, and a client may draw closer to spiritual and religious beliefs in an attempt to find meaning through the loss or he or she might turn away from or abandon those beliefs and practices. These changes, adjustments, and revisions in light of loss are normal social and psychological processes. When engaging and assessing an older adult client, clinicians recognize that the degree to which responses and symptoms are adaptive or maladaptive and pathological or nonpathological must be understood in the context of the intersections of culture, diversity, and spirituality; prior losses and responses to those losses; and the developmental stage of the client.

Following is an application of the Geriatric Biopsychosocial/Spiritual Assessment conducted by Mrs. Welch's social worker.

Box 11.1

Geriatric Biopsychosocial/Spiritual Assessment

Basic Demographic: Mrs. Welch is an 89-year-old non-Hispanic White female; she is a widow, speaks English, and has a bachelor degree

Referral Information: The physician requested a social work evaluation to assess the psychological and social functioning of Mrs. Welch

Cultural/Spiritual: Mrs. Welch identifies with the Lutheran faith; she has not attended church for the past three months

Social: [Relationships within family, social/diversity groups, and community]

- Mrs. Welch has two children and eight grandchildren, all who live within one hour from her; Mrs. Welch taught third grade in a local public school

---

- She volunteered in children's ministries at her Lutheran church and participated in social activities at the local senior center until shortly after her spouse died a year ago; Mrs. Welch has a support network composed of family, friends from church, and the local senior center; she has not been socializing with friends at church or the senior center since her spouse died

Financial: [Ability to provide basic needs and access health services]

- Basic needs met for housing, clothing, food, and shelter
- Health insurance: Medicare and California State Teachers' Retirement System (CalSTRS)
- Income sources: Social Security from spouse, savings, and pension from CalSTRS

Environmental: [Personal safety, maintenance of residence, and safety of community]

- Neighborhood safety: The crime level is low in the neighborhood; community watch signs are around neighborhood; there is lighting on streets
- Home safety: No slip rugs; grab bars are in place, as well as shower bench and handheld shower head
- No access to guns or gun ownership
- No indicators of abuse or neglect by self or perpetrated by others

Physical: [Individual function and disease morbidity]

- High health literacy; good self-rated health; advance directive and living will in place; Mrs. Welch has osteoarthritis and was hospitalized after a fall at home and diagnosed with a hip fracture; she requires minimal assistance/supervision with ADLs presently and assistance with some IADLs; she reports no sexual activity for years prior to death of spouse and no current sexual partners

Mental: [Mental status, depression, anxiety, and substance abuse]

- She scored a 4 on the PHQ-9 screen for depression, indicative of mild depression; she does not want to take antidepressant medications; no indicators of anxiety; she is alert and oriented and competent to engage in decision making
- Suicide risk assessment: She does not endorse suicidal ideations, and no history is reported
- Homicidal ideations: Ruled out—no history of homicidal ideations
- No history of smoking and no alcoholic beverages

Formulation/Evaluation: Mrs. Welch presents with prolonged unresolved or chronic grief symptoms characteristic of complicated grief; her score on the PHQ-9 is indicative of minimal depression; upon evaluation, Mrs. Welsh revealed she has not been able to talk about the death of her spouse, and her adult children were present for the first visit and requested assistance with encouraging her to get back to her normal activities; social worker met privately with Mrs. Welsh who stated the source of her minimal depression has been unresolved grief over the loss of her spouse; Mrs. Welsh consented to grief and bereavement counseling for five sessions

Treatment Planning: Collaboration with physician, nurse, and physical therapist on treatment plan; five additional sessions with social worker for grief and bereavement counseling and psychoeducation; monitor symptoms of depression and complicated grief

Community Resource Needs: Referral for support group and drop-in counseling as needed, local transportation services, emergency response pendant, and home-delivered meals

Screening Tools

With the recognized overlap in symptoms between normal, uncomplicated grief, complicated grief, major depression, post-traumatic stress disorder (PTSD), and traumatic grief, screening tools have been developed to further assist clinicians with differential diagnosis. The Texas Revised Inventory of Grief is a 13-item inventory tested with older adults using a five-point Likert scale that assesses a client's "present feelings" of normal grief (American Psychological Association, 2018b). The Inventory of Complicated Grief (ICG), a 19-item inventory with strong internal consistency and test-retest reliability, assesses complicated grief symptoms (i.e., anger, hallucinations, and disbelief) using a five-point Likert scale—it has strong reliability and assesses indicators of pathological grief, such as anger, disbelief, and hallucinations (American Psychological Association, 2018b). The ICG format includes "first-person statements concerning the immediate bereavement-related thoughts and behaviors of the client" (American Psychological Association, 2018a, para. 1). The Traumatic Grief Inventory Self-Report Version (TGI-SR), an 18-item measure, was designed to assess the new category in *DSM-V* for persistent complex bereavement disorder (PCBD) and prolonged grief disorder (PGD), a new category for the *International Classification of Diseases 11 (ICD-11)* (Boelen & Smid, 2017). The PCBD has strong concurrent validity and internal consistency (Boelen & Smid, 2017).

A grief and loss assessment, along with screening tools and the *DSM-V* for differential diagnosis, can aide the clinician in diagnosis and treatment panning with an older adult. The grief and loss assessment should include: a history of losses throughout the life course; past attempts to resolve grief symptoms from prior losses and the results; cultural and spiritual customs and rituals surrounding grief; recent or ongoing losses; key grief symptoms and duration of symptoms; and the impact of grief symptoms on physical, psychological, social, and spiritual functioning. The grief and loss assessment can aide the clinician in identifying client strengths and developing a culturally preferred and meaningful treatment plan, and it informs differential diagnosis of *DSM-V* disorders and/or diagnostic categories.

When making a diagnosis of grief an older adult client presents with, there are two diagnoses in the *DSM-V*: uncomplicated bereavement (V62.82, Z63.4), characteristic of normal grief reactions, which should be further differentiated from major depressive disorder single episode, and PCBD for traumatic, complicated grief listed under other specified trauma- and stressor-related disorder (309.89, F43.8, category 5, condition for further study) (American Psychiatric Association, 2013). Uncomplicated bereavement includes normal grief reactions of an individual experiences the death of someone they know (American Psychiatric Association, 2013). Many of the normal grief reactions are similar to diagnostic criteria in a major depressive episode, such as "feelings of sadness and associated symptoms such as insomnia, poor appetite, and weight loss" as well as "depressed mood" (American Psychiatric Association, 2013). Unlike uncomplicated bereavement, Prolonged Complicated Bereavement Disorder (PCBD) causes impairment in social, educational, or occupational functioning. Under other specified trauma and stressor-related disorder in the *DSM-V*, Prolonged Complicated Bereavement Disorder is listed as a specifier and condition under further study (American Psychiatric Association, 2013). One criterion that must be satisfied is that the individuals symptoms are related to the death of a close friend or family member (American Psychiatric Association, 2013). A second criterion is that the individual must experience at least one of the following grief related symptoms most of the time daily for 12 months or longer: (1) "persistent yearning/longing for the deceased," (2) "intense sorrow and emotional pain in response to the death," (3) "preoccupation with the deceased," or (4) preoccupation with the circumstances of the death" (American Psychiatric Association, 2013). A third criterion is that an individual must experience 6 or more complicated grief symptoms for 12 month or more" (American Psychiatric Association, 2013). Additional criterion include impairment or distress in social functioning, at work or at school; and the bereavement is not consistent with norms of the family, society, or culture of the individual (American Psychiatric Association, 2013). This condition under further study also has a trauma specifier if trauma symptoms are present for the individual in addition to the complicated grief symptoms related to the death of a family member or close friend (American Psychiatric Association, 2013).

Although not included in the *DSM-V*, Prolonged Grief Disorder (PGD) is a grief disorder under review for addition to the *ICD-11*, the proposed criteria for *ICD-11*, and *DSM-V* follow (Prigerson et al., 2009, p. 9):

TABLE 11.1   Criteria for PGD proposed for *DSM-V* and *ICD-11*.

Category	Definition
A.	Event: Bereavement (loss of a significant other)
B.	Separation distress: The bereaved person experiences yearning (e.g., craving, pining, or longing for the deceased; physical or emotional suffering as a result of the desired, but unfulfilled, reunion with the deceased) daily or to a disabling degree.
C.	Cognitive, emotional, and behavioral symptoms: The bereaved person must have five (or more) of the following symptoms experienced daily or to a disabling degree:

1. Confusion about one's role in life or diminished sense of self (i.e., feeling that a part of oneself has died)

2. Difficulty accepting the loss

3. Avoidance of reminders of the reality of the loss

4. Inability to trust others since the loss

5. Bitterness or anger related to the loss

6. Difficulty moving on with life (e.g., making new friends, pursuing interests)

7. Numbness (absence of emotion) since the loss

8. Feeling that life is unfulfilling, empty, or meaningless since the loss

9. Feeling stunned, dazed or shocked by the loss

D. Timing: Diagnosis should not be made until at least six months have elapsed since the death.

E. Impairment: The disturbance causes clinically significant impairment in social, occupational, or other important areas of functioning (e.g., domestic responsibilities).

F. Relation to other mental disorders: The disturbance is not better accounted for by major depressive disorder, generalized anxiety disorder, or posttraumatic stress disorder.

Diversity–Cultural Competence/Spirituality/LGBT/Sexuality

The context of grief, bereavement, and mourning experiences as well as normal grief reactions vary across cultures. Clinicians should participate in ongoing continuing education on cultural competency, diversity, and inclusion and strive to develop cultural humility. A clinician meets a client where the client is in his or her journey of grief and allows the older adult client to educate the clinician about his or her narrative on proper grief reactions, roles, behaviors, customs, and rituals. The context of culture and spirituality serves as a guide for the griever, enabling him or her to have a sense of what to expect, how to respond (i.e., behaviorally, emotionally, cognitively, spiritually), who responds, how long, and how frequent after a loss. In assessing the intersection of culture and spirituality factors of the client and gaining a sense of their narrative and experiences, clinicians can serve as facilitators in the resolution of grief, helping the older adult client discover a sense of how to navigate through, accept, process the pain of the loss, adapt, and reorganize after a loss. In the absence of ritual, clinicians can help guide a client to create ritual that is meaningful to him or her. For example, some common Western rituals are visiting a gravesite and reading a poem or letter to the deceased, lighting candles at the location where a loved one may have died suddenly, memorials, and funerals. Cultural rituals surrounding grief "whether in the form of a Catholic funeral mass, Jewish Shivah, or secular memorial service, serve both integrative and regulatory goals by providing a structure for the emotional chaos of grief, conferring a symbolic order on events, and facilitating the construction of shared meanings among members of the family, community, or even nation" (Neimeyer, Prigerson, & Davies, 2002, p. 237). Clinicians should also be aware that the expression of grief, in mind and body, may vary across cultures. Walter and McCoyd (2016) note that in Western cultures, physical health is often equated to relating to the body and psychological health to the mind. Many Eastern cultures understand well-being as the interaction of mind and body, and normal grief reactions may present somatically with physical symptoms such as a stomachache, physical pain, or a headache.

An older adult may experience ambiguous loss or disenfranchised grief when he or she experiences inconsistencies between current grief reactions and what is expected for normal grief reactions established by his or her culture, religious/faith community, country of origin, family, and/or those in the developmental stage/generation (Walter & McCoyd, 2016). The rules and norms for normal grief reactions, mourning rituals, and customs vary across cultures and are socially constructed, as noted by Walter and McCoyd: The "norms and rules about losses to be mourned and the people entitled to mourn them (and for how long) are social creations not artifacts of biology or individual psychology" (2016, p. 7). Traditional expressions of grief among Native Hawaiians include "wailing (uwe), chanting rituals (oli), and physical degradation of the mourner;" and "burial practices;" and the "O'hana (family, including extended family) process and storytelling" are "two of the major ways people in Hawaii express their grief" (Pentaris, 2011, p. 53).

In the United States, Hispanic clients may have immigrated from or be descendants of immigrants from "Mexico, Cuba, the Dominican Republic, Nicaragua, Colombia, El Salvador, Guatemala, Chile, Perú, and the U.S. Commonwealth of Puerto Rico, among others" (Houben, 2011, p. 4). Clinicians cannot assume that each Hispanic client will have similar grief responses, symptoms, or rituals. One commonality in Hispanic cultures is "personalismo, which means relationships that are warm and personal," in relationship to how "Hispanics experience grief, they expect health care providers to be caring, show empathy, and be respectful of their beliefs, many of which have to do with their religious and cultural traditions" (Houben, 2011, p. 4). In addition, the family is important, and they expect clinicians "to take into account the needs of the family members" when working through grief (Houben, 2011, p. 4). Another commonality among Hispanic clients "is the familial hierarchal rule of respeto, or 'respect,' which can play a vital role in the grieving process" (Houben, 2011, p. 7). According to Houben, Hispanic clients may seek therapy from a clinician for grief for two reasons: (1) "they do not want to be a burden to their family, so they want to feel better" and (2) "in the presence of their family members they pretend to be strong, when in reality they feel a tremendous pain in their hearts" (2011, p. 7). Houden further recommends when working with grieving Hispanic clients that clinicians recognize that "each Hispanic/Latino person displays unique responses and engages in unique practices regarding his or her loss" (Houben, 2011, p. 7).

Similarly, clinicians should not make assumptions about normal grief responses, customs, rituals, and practices of Asian Americans and, as suggested by Houden (2011), recognize that each client has his or her unique set of grief responses, practices, and beliefs. Grief rituals, customs, and practices are diverse as many Asian Americans are first-generation immigrants or a descendant of an immigrant from Eastern Asia (i.e., China, Taiwan, Japan, Korea), South Central Asia (i.e., Bangladesh, India, Iran, Nepal, Pakistan), South Eastern Asia (i.e., Myanmar, Cambodia, Laos, Philippines, Thailand, Vietnam), or Western Asia (i.e., Iraq, Israel, Lebanon) (Migration Policy Institute, 2018a). The grief and mourning practices of Chinese "are characterized by a relatively strong emphasis on extensive, ritualized, and culturally reinforced expressions of grief" with "the most intensive mourning rituals usually occur[ring] during the first seven weeks of bereavement," "further mourning practices continuing for 100 days and sometimes longer," and "ceremonial practices to honor deceased relatives [continuing] regularly for years beyond the death" (Bonanno, Papa, Lalande, Zhang, & Noll, 2005, p. 88). Chinese have unique mourning practices as well, which are "aimed more at honoring and comforting the deceased and promoting his or her transition to the spirit realm" and emphasize "cultural connectedness" as well "the continuation of the relationship with the deceased" (Bonanno, Papa, Lalande, Zhang, & Noll, 2005, p. 88).

Grief rituals, customs, and normal grief responses also vary among African Americans in the United States; as such, clinicians must recognize that each client has a unique way of responding to and recovering from loss. Like other ethnic groups in the United States, an African American client's customs, practices, expression of grief, and rituals may be influenced by the region he or she was born in in the United States (North, South, East, West), as well as religious or spiritual practices and beliefs. African Americans' grief practices and rituals may also be influenced by cultural practices from the country he or she immigrated from or is a descendant of—for example, North Africa (i.e., Egypt, Morocco, Sudan, other) (Migration Policy Institute, 2018b), South Africa, the Caribbean or Latin America, Haiti, Jamaica, or other countries such as Europe or Canada (Population Reference Bureau, 2018). Rosenblatt and Wallace, in describing the grief experiences of African Americans in a qualitative study of 27 African Americans in the United States, underscore the importance for the clinician to create respectful space for the narrative to come forth following a death; the narrative "gives meaning to the person who died, the dying, the death, the grieving, the family aftermath of the death" and is "often about the larger societal context for the loss and grieving," where grieving often reflects a "collective loss from the ongoing oppression" that influences the grieving process (2013, p. xx). Specific grief practices and rituals that emerged from these interviews include: (1) communal grieving "from the significance of food made available following a service to the psychological and historical underpinnings of elaborate funeral ceremonies" and (2) features of mourning practices that include "adaptation of African customs in the context of predominantly Christian rituals, resulting in distinctive practices of 'praying a loved into heaven' and 'homegoing' celebrations" (Rosenblatt & Wallace, 2013, p. viii).

A grief and loss assessment can assist the clinician with gaining an understanding of the older adult client's grief and loss history, strengths and resiliency, and rituals and customs that can provide direction, comfort, and meaning to the bereaved during or after an ongoing ambiguous, future anticipated, or past loss or death. The clinician assesses and examines the role of cultural diversity and other intersectional factors that influence the older adult client's acceptance, adjustment, adaptation, accommodation, and resolution of grief of older adults and their families when engaging in treatment planning and interventions (CSWE Competency 2). Clinicians ensure that all care planning and treatments are culturally preferred and valued by the older adult and that they involve family members and others based on the older adult's preferences (CSWE Competency 2, practice behaviors 1-4, CalSWEC, 2017).

Interdisciplinary Team Roles and Planning

Clinicians, as global assessors, play a large role in recognizing loss, grief, and bereavement among older adults. Clinicians inform the interdisciplinary team about the client's grief, loss, and bereavement practices, beliefs, and rituals to inform treatment planning, ensuring client self-determination in treatment options based on the unique grief preferences, values, and practices of the client (CSWE Gero Competency 1: Demonstrate Ethical and Professional Behavior, specialized practice behavior 5; CSWE Gero Competency 2: Engage Diversity and Difference in Practice, specialized practice behavior 4; CSWE Gero Competency 8: Intervene With Individuals, Families, Groups, Organizations, and Communities, specialized practice behaviors 1–3; and CSWE Gero Competency 9: Evaluate Practice With Individuals, Families, Groups, Organizations, and Communities, specialized practice behaviors 1-3). Clinicians also work collaboratively with physicians and psychiatrists to ensure the appropriate diagnosis of an older adult presenting with grief symptoms. Clinicians provide advocacy and work collaboratively across disciplines to ensure the grief, loss, and bereavement resources preferred by the client are accessible (CSWE Gero Competency 3: Advance Human Rights and Social, Economic, and Environmental Justice, specialized practice behaviors 2–4). For older adults adjusting and adapting to a loss, clinicians can work with the interdisciplinary team to encourage older adults to engage in health-protective factors that can be beneficial, such as a lean diet with fruits, vegetables, grains, and lean meats; exercise; screenings and checkups from physicians; engaging in self-care activities; getting outdoors during daylight; and intaking sources of food with B vitamins, omegas, and antioxidants or supplements (McCoyd & Walter, 2016). Clinicians also identify best practices for the treatment of grief, loss, and bereavement with older adults.

Evidence-based Interventions and Best Practices

According to Worden (2018), treatment of normal, uncomplicated grief and normal grief reactions can be facilitated with grief counseling; however, "most people are able to cope with these reactions and address the four tasks of mourning on their own, thereby making some kind of adaptation to the loss" (p. 83). The four tasks of mourning that serve as goals for grief counseling are: (1) "increasing the reality of the loss;" (2) helping the older adult "deal with both the emotional and behavioral pain;" (3) helping the older adult "overcome various impediments to readjustment after the loss;" and (4) helping the older adult client "find a way to maintain a bond with the deceased while feeling comfortable reinvesting in life" (Worden, 2018, p. 84). According to Neimeyer in a systematic review of grief counseling for uncomplicated grief, clinical trials including grief counseling "are typically ineffective, and perhaps even deleterious, at least for persons experiencing a normal bereavement" (2000, p. 541). Most older adults, when connected to family, friends, faith, cultural, as well as community support systems, are able to resolve their uncomplicated grief symptoms associated with loss without the assistance of a grief counselor. Psychoeducation of normal, uncomplicated grief; support groups; and connecting an older adult to friends, family, faith, cultural, and community-based support can be beneficial in the resolution of grief.

In the treatment of complicated grief with older adults, as suggested by Worden, grief therapy interventions that focus on complicated mourning of four types may be more appropriate: (1) "the complicated grief reaction is manifested as prolonged grief" or chronic grief; (2) "it manifests as delayed grief;" (3) "it manifests as an exaggerated grief response; or (4) "it manifests through some masked somatic or behavioral symptom" (2018, p. 153). Chronic grief occurs in individuals who are aware that they have not resolved their grief according to cultural norms (Worden, 2018). Delayed grief occurs when there is "insufficient grieving" to a loss that may be due to "a lack of social support, a lack of social sanction… the need to be strong for someone else, or feeling overwhelmed by the number of losses" (Worden, 2018, p. 154). Exaggerated grief occurs when the griever experiences "excessive depression, excessive anxiety, or some other feature usually associated with normal grief behavior manifested in an exaggerated way so that the person is dysfunctional and a psychiatric disorder" may apply (Worden, 2018, p. 154). Masked grief occurs when an older adult experiences behavioral or somatic symptoms and is "not aware that unresolved grief is the reason behind their symptoms" (Worden, 2018, p. 154). In a systematic review of randomized trials of grief counseling and grief therapy, grief therapy was found to be "more beneficial and safer for those who have been traumatically bereaved" (Neimeyer, 2000, p. 541). Worden outlines 10 procedures for grief therapy: (1) "rule out physical disease," especially among clients presenting with normal grief symptoms of a physical nature; (2) "set up the contract and establish an alliance" as grief therapy often occurs in the context of private practice; (3) "revive memories of the deceased" through storytelling and reminiscing about positive and mixed memories of the deceased; (4) "assess which of the four mourning tasks the patient is struggling with;" (5) "deal with affect or lack of affect stimulated by memories;" (6) "explore and defuse linking objects," which include transitional objects or mementos that aide the survivor in maintaining a relationship with the deceased; (7) "help the patient acknowledge the finality of the loss;" (8) help the patient design a new life without the deceased;" (9) "assess and help the patient improve social relationships;" and (10) "help the patient deal with the fantasy of ending grieving" (Worden, 2018, pp. 157–167).

There are four key Western theoretical task-based frameworks that can inform treatment planning and interventions with older adults experiencing loss, grief, and bereavement, and the themes across the theories overlap. Clinicians must keep in mind that some of these tasks may not conform to the spiritual or cultural norms, beliefs, and practices of diverse older adult clients. Worden defines four key tasks of mourning: (1) "to accept the reality of the loss," which involves reduction of denial and acceptance of the death of a loved one; (2) "to process the pain of grief," involving reduction of normal grief reactions of a cognitive, physical, behavioral, or psychological nature; (3) "to adjust to a world without the deceased," involving external, internal, and spiritual adjustments; and (4) "to find an enduring connection with the deceased in the midst of embracing on a new life" (Worden, 2018, pp. 39–50). Mrs. Welch experienced difficulty accepting the death of her spouse; although she did eventually accept his loss, she did not have an outlet for processing the pain until she began grief counseling with the social worker. Although she experienced chronic complicated grief, she longed to regain a sense of herself again, and she set goals to start resuming some activities one week at a time—this facilitated her adjustment to the world without her spouse. In finding a connection with her spouse, she drew from her spirituality—her Lutheran faith; she believed that he was in heaven and that she could maintain a connection with him through prayer and going into the den where he often spent several hours a day reading.

In her work with terminally ill patients, Elisabeth Kübler-Ross introduced a stage-based theory, the five stages of death and dying, which have been applied to a variety of losses since. The five stages do not occur sequentially; in fact, the stages can occur simultaneously, and not all clients experience all five stages. The first stage, denial, "is usually only a temporary defense for the individual;" here, the griever may have a disbelief about the loss happening to him or her, and they may see it as a mistake (Hebert, Moore, & Rooney, 2011, p. 326). The second stage, anger, occurs when a client recognizes "that they can no longer continue in denial" (Hebert, Moore, & Rooney, 2011, pp. 326–327). This may emerge, but not always, once the reality of the loss has set in. In this stage, it is not uncommon for the client to have "misplaced feelings of resentment" (Hebert, Moore, & Rooney, 2011, pp. 326–327). The griever may be angry at the loved one who died, they may be angry about their own loss, and they may be angry at helping professionals or those they perceive played a role in the death or loss. The third stage, bargaining, is thought to occur as one recognizes that death is inevitable; here, a client may engage in the "usual form of the dialogue…to bargain for extended life in exchange for a reformed lifestyle" (Hebert, Moore, & Rooney, 2011, p. 327). For example, a client may bargain with God or a deity for extra time for good behavior. The fourth stage, depression (for a dying client), was thought by Kübler-Ross to occur when the client "begins to understand the certainty of death and may refuse treatments/medications and visitors" (Hebert, Moore, & Rooney, 2011, p. 327). The client may become silent and withdrawn, or he or she may have other symptoms of depression. The final stage, acceptance (for the dying client), occurs when the client "begins to come to terms with his or her mortality or that of loved ones" (Hebert, Moore, & Rooney, 2011, p. 327). Mrs. Welch reported that when her spouse first died, she experienced a state of disbelief (denial). In her sessions with the social worker, she recalled asking God why he did not take her first (bargaining). She indicated, however, that because of her Lutheran faith, she was able to accept her spouse's death and that, painful as it was, she believed he was in heaven and that she would see him again there one day (acceptance). She did not report experiencing any anger toward her spouse, self, others, or God.

According to Silverman, "responding to any loss takes place over time," and it "can be divided into phases during which people do the 'work' of the transition" (Silverman, 2004, p. 236). She notes that change phases reflect "the negotiation and renegotiation that we do all of our lives as we deal with what is happening to us and what has happened to us" (Silverman, 2004, p. 237). The first phase, impact, occurs when a client, presented with the notification of a death or loss, faces the reality of it within hours, days, or months (Silverman, 2000). The processes involved in impact may include numbness, which is common upon initial notification where shock may set in, anxiety, or depression (Silverman, 2000). Silverman notes that when a "mourner is initially numb and in shock, it may be totally impossible, at one level, to accept the reality of the death" (2004, p. 236). In this phase, the clinician can provide interventions to reduce denial, connecting the client with family, friends, and faith, cultural, and social communities and support. The second phase, recoil, involves feelings processes where the mourner begins to grapple with survivorship; here, the client is invited to identify, express, and share his or her feelings (Silverman, 2000). It is thought that once the reality of a death has set in, the mourner then starts to process how they will survive without his or her loved one. The third phase, accommodation, involves processes involved for the mourner to find meaning in adjustment to the loss (Silverman, 2000). This phase involves the processes of finding meaning and purpose in the life of the mourner in light of the loss, meaning making or continuing a bond with the deceased, and in the contexts of self, others, community, and society (Silverman, 2000).

Rando outlines six R processes categorized under three phases—avoidance, confrontation, and accommodation:

Avoidance Phase

1. Recognize the loss- The bereaved must acknowledge and understand the reality of the death.

Confrontation Phase

1. React to the separation- The bereaved must experience the pain of the loss, give it expression and mourn secondary losses.
2. Recollect and re-experience the deceased and the relationship. The bereaved is to review and remember the relationship realistically and also review and re-experience the emotions that arise as they remember the relationship.
3. Relinquish the old attachments to the deceased and the old assumptive world. The bereaved is to let go of previous bonds and beliefs and develop a "new normal" with new relationships and attachments.

Carolyn Ambler Walter and Judith L. M. McCoyd, *Grief and Loss Across the Lifespan: A Biopsychsocial Perspective*, pp. 15. Copyright © 2016 by Springer Publishing Company.

Accommodation Phase

1. Readjust to move adaptively into the new world without forgetting the old. The bereaved is to revise his or her assumptive world; develop a new relationship with the deceased; adopt new ways of being in the world and form an identity not predicated on the presence of the deceased.
2. Reinvest. This is a time to invest in new relationships and roles and indicates a resolution to active grieving. (Walter & McCoyd, 2016, p. 15)

According to Rando (1986), the six R processes lead toward healing and grief resolution. Clinicians can use this model to guide grief counseling interventions as to which phase the client's journey of grief may be characteristic of. Psychoeducation on the grief models can also be used with grief counseling and therapy, informed by cultural and spiritual beliefs and practices of the client. Clinicians continually monitor the effects of all interventions that target specific grief, loss, and bereavement symptoms of older adult clients.

Assessing/Monitoring Evidence-based Treatment Outcomes

When engaging, assessing, and intervening with older adults with loss, grief, and bereavement, clinicians follow competencies for ethical and professional behavior as well as ethical and legal standards (CSWE Gero Competencies 1–2) at micro, mezzo, and macro levels when engaging diversity and difference in practice (CSWE Gero Competency 2) and research as well as evidence-informed practice (Gero Competency 4) (CalSWEC, 2017). Clinicians engage in ongoing interactive evaluation, recognize limitations with grief theories with diverse populations, use best practices and evidence-based interventions, and evaluate outcomes qualitatively and quantitatively (CSWE Competency 9, CalSWEC, 2017). Clinicians not only keep accurate records, monitor, and track data on interventions (CSWE Competency 9, behavior 1, CalSWEC, 2017), but they also ensure that the grief, loss, and bereavement narratives emerge for the older adult client and preserve older adult client autonomies with inclusion of the perspectives of family and the interdisciplinary treatment team in all analyses (CSWE Competency 9, behavior 2, CalSWEC, 2017). In monitoring treatment effectiveness, clinicians adapt the treatment plan as needed and appropriate; they share their analysis with older adult clients, their family members, and members of the interdisciplinary treatment team (CSWE Competency 9, behaviors 3–4, CalSWEC, 2017). Clinicians identify appropriate community-based programs and services and assist with coordinating such services when appropriate to meet the grief, loss, and bereavement needs of older adult clients.

Community Resources/Interagency Coordination

Clinicians working with older adults in need of grief, loss, and bereavement support and interventions are aware of local community, county, state, and national resources and services available to assist them, collaboratively work with other service providers and agencies, and provide advocacy to ensure that clients have access to the necessary resources, support, and services to assist them with grief, loss, and bereavement collaborations (CSWE Gero Competency 1: Demonstrate Ethical and Professional Behavior, specialized practice behaviors 3, 5, and 7; CSWE Competency 3: Advance Human Rights and Social, Economic, and Environmental Justice, specialized practice behaviors 2–4; and CSWE Gero Competency 4: Engage in Practice-informed Research and Research-informed Practice, specialized practice behaviors 3–4). Mrs. Welch received referrals from the social worker after the home grief counseling sessions were terminated; she was referred to a local grief support group and center for drop-in counseling as needed, local transportation services, an emergency response pendant for home safety, and home-delivered meals to assist with an option for lunch. Clinicians should be aware of local, state, and federal resources to assist older adult clients with loss, grief, and bereavement needs. Clinicians are also aware of potential transference and countertransference issues that present when working with older adult clients with grief, loss, and bereavement needs.

Transference/Countertransference

Clinicians recognize and engage in active management of countertransference reactions as required for ethical and professional practice with the client (CSWE Gero Competency 1: Demonstrate Ethical and Professional Behavior, specialized practice behaviors 1–7). A client who has experienced a similar loss, grief, or bereavement issue as the clinician may experience transference, and the clinician working with an older adult client may experience countertransference when working on loss, grief, and bereavement issues. Mr. Schwartz's wife, age 69, in the intensive care unit on life support after a massive stroke, did not want to be on life support if she were diagnosed with a condition resulting in cognitive impairments. Mr. Schwartz was the legal decision maker and power of attorney for health care and was faced with the decision to honor the wishes of his spouse and remove her from life support. The social worker had a similar experience as Mr. Schwartz with a close family member and also had to make a decision to remove life support from a loved one to follow the loved one's wishes. The social worker was aware of potential countertransference and processed it with a social work colleague to ensure that it did not interfere with the clinician's interventions with Mr. and Mrs. Schwartz. Clinicians are aware of technological resources for support and education as well as potential legal/ethical issues they may present when working with older adults with grief, loss, and bereavement needs.

Technological Resources

Better Help: Online grief counseling: https://www.betterhelp.com

Grief.com: Bereavement groups and online resources: https://grief.com/group-resources/

Grief.com: Best and worst things to say to someone in grief: https://grief.com/10-best-worst-things-to-say-to-someone-in-grief/

Grief.com: Grief counselor directory: https://grief.com/grief-counselor-directory/

Grief.com: Resources: https://grief.com/resources/

Grief.com: Support group directory: https://grief.com/grief-support-group-directory/

Grief in Common: http://www.griefincommon.com/

Healthful Chat: Bereavement and grief chat room: http://www.healthfulchat.org/bereavement-chat-room.html

Legal/Ethical Considerations

Clinicians working with older adults with loss, grief, and bereavement issues follow CSWE Gero Competency 1: Demonstrate Ethical and Professional Behavior, specialized practice behaviors 1–7 to ensure professional, ethical, and legal standards are practiced at micro, mezzo, and macro levels (CalSWEC, 2017) in private practice, group settings, within interdisciplinary team treatment planning meetings, with referrals to other service providers, and with family members of the older adult, respecting any limits to confidentiality preferred by the older adult client. Mrs. Welch did not want her family members to be aware of her feelings and work with the social worker during grief counseling sessions; as such, privacy of such details was maintained by the social worker, and family members were advised that such information was confidential per the client's request.

Critical Thinking Activity/Discussion Questions

1. What interventions for loss and grief with older adults do you think are needed?
   a. What interventions are typically provided by organizations at your agency, in the local community, or in the state where you work with older adults?
   b. What resources are available?
   c. What legal/ethical issues have occurred that you are aware of, and how were they addressed?
   d. How might you engage in advocacy to address any unmet needs of older adults in need of interventions to address loss and grief?

2. What interventions for bereavement with older adults do you think are needed?
   a. What bereavement interventions are typically provided at your agency, in the local community, or in the state where you work with older adults?
   b. What resources are available?
   c. What legal/ethical issues have occurred that you are aware of, and how were they addressed? How should they have been addressed?

    d.   How are older adults engaged in bereavement support at your agency or in your community?

    e.   What role can clinicians play in ensuring access to bereavement support for older adults?

3.   Conduct a Google search for local grief, loss, and bereavement services and programs in your community, county, and state.

    a.   What types of programs and services are available?

    b.   Are they sufficient?

    c.   What gaps are there in services and programs to meet older adults grief, loss, and bereavement needs?

Self-Reflection Exercises

1.   Critically examine your own attitudes and beliefs about loss and grief.

    a.   What attitudes and beliefs do you have about loss and grief?

    b.   From what sources did these attitudes and beliefs develop?

    c.   How do those beliefs influence your perception on what interventions are needed for loss and grief interventions and support today?

    d.   How might those beliefs affect your ability to engage, assess, and intervene with older adults in need of loss and grief services and support?

2.   Critically examine your own attitudes and beliefs about bereavement support.

    a.   What did you learn about bereavement support growing up?

    b.   From what sources did you learn it?

    c.   How do those beliefs influence your attitudes about care interventions for older adults surrounding bereavement support?

    d.   How might those beliefs affect your ability to engage, assess, and intervene with older adults in need of interventions to address bereavement?

References

American Psychiatric Association. (2013). *Diagnostic and statistical manual of mental disorders* (5th ed.). Arlington, VA: American Psychiatric Publishing.

American Psychological Association (2018a). Inventory of complicated grief. Retrieved from http://www.apa.org/pi/about/publications/caregivers/practice-settings/assessment/tools/complicated-grief.aspx

American Psychological Association (2018b). Texas revised inventory of grief. Retrieved from http://www.apa.org/pi/about/publications/caregivers/practice-settings/assessment/tools/texas-grief.aspx

Boelen, P. A., & Smid, G. E. (2017). The traumatic grief inventory self-report version (TGI-SR): Introduction and preliminary psychometric evaluation. *Journal of Loss and Trauma, 22*(3), 196–212.

Bonanno, G. A., Papa, A., Lalande, K., Zhang, N., & Noll, J. G. (2005). Grief processing and deliberate grief avoidance: A prospective comparison of bereaved spouses and parents in the United States and the People's Republic of China. *Journal of Consulting and Clinical Psychology, 73*(1), 86.

CalSWEC. (2017). CalSWEC curriculum competencies for public child welfare, behavioral health, and aging in California. Retrieved from https://calswec.berkeley.edu/sites/default/files/2017_calswec_curriculum_competencies_0.pdf

Council for Social Work Education. (2017). Specialized practice curricular guide for gero social work practice. Alexandria, VA: Council on Social Work Education.

Hebert, K., Moore, H., & Rooney, J. (2011). The nurse advocate in end-of-life care. *The Ochsner Journal, 11*(4), 325–329.

Houben, L. M. (2011). *Counseling Hispanics through loss, grief, and bereavement: A guide for mental health professionals.* New York, NT: Springer Publishing Company.

Jacobs, S. (2016). *Traumatic grief: Diagnosis, treatment, and prevention.* Philadelphia, PA: Taylor & Francis.

Migration Policy Institute. (2018a). Asian immigrants in the United States. Retrieved from https://www.migrationpolicy.org/article/asian-immigrants-united-states

Migration Policy Institute. (2018b). Middle Eastern and North African immigrants in the United States. Retrieved from https://www.migrationpolicy.org/article/middle-eastern-and-north-african-immigrants-united-states

Neimeyer, R. A. (2000). Searching for the meaning of meaning: Grief therapy and the process of reconstruction. *Death Studies, 24*(6), 541–558.

Neimeyer, R. A., Prigerson, H. G., & Davies, B. (2002). Mourning and meaning. *American Behavioral Scientist, 46*(2), 235–251.

Pentaris, P. (2011). Culture and death: A multicultural perspective. *Hawaii Pacific Journal of Social Work Practice, 4*(1), 45–84.

Population Reference Bureau. (2018). Immigration and America's black population. Retrieved from https://www.prb.org/blackimmigration/

Prigerson, H. G., Horowitz, M. J., Jacobs, S. C., Parkes, C. M., Aslan, M., Goodkin, K., ... & Bonanno, G. (2009). Prolonged grief disorder: Psychometric validation of criteria proposed for DSM-V and ICD-11. *PLoS Medicine, 6*(8), e1000121.

Rando, T. (1986). *Loss and anticipatory grief.* Lexington, MA: Lexington Books.

Rosenblatt, P. C., & Wallace, B. R. (2013). *African American grief.* New York, NY: Routledge.

Silverman, P. R. (2000). *Never too young to know: Death in children's lives.* New York, NY: Oxford University Press.

Silverman, P. R. (2004). Bereavement: A time of transition and changing in relationships. In J. Berzoff & P. R. Silverman (Eds.), *Living with dying: A handbook for end-of-life healthcare practitioners.* Columbia University Press.

The Center for Complicated Grief. (2017). Key definitions. Retrieved from https://complicatedgrief.columbia.edu/professionals/complicated-grief-professionals/overview/

Walter, C. A., & McCoyd, J. L. (2016). *Grief and loss across the lifespan: A biopsychosocial perspective*. New York, NY: Springer Publishing Company.

Worden, J. W. (2018). *Grief counseling and grief therapy: A handbook for the mental health practitioner*. New York, NY: Springer Publishing Company.

CHAPTER 12

Caregiving

Chapter Overview

This chapter identifies issues related to caregiving for older adults, presents evidence-based interventions for addressing caregiving, and explores key domains to promote both effective clinical practice with older adults and their caregivers.

CSWE Gero Competencies Highlighted

Competency 1: Demonstrate Ethical and Professional Behavior

Specialized Practice Competency Description: Social workers understand the value base of the profession and its ethical standards, as well as relevant laws and regulations that may impact practice at the micro, mezzo, and macro levels. Social workers understand frameworks of ethical decision-making and how to apply principles of critical thinking to those frameworks in practice, research, and policy arenas. Social workers recognize personal values and the distinction between personal and professional values. They also understand how their personal experiences and affective reactions influence their professional judgment and behavior. Social workers understand the profession's history, its mission, and the roles and responsibilities of the profession. Social workers also understand the role of other professions when engaged in inter-professional teams. Social workers recognize the importance of lifelong learning and are committed to continually updating their skills to ensure they are relevant and effective. Social workers also understand emerging forms of technology and the ethical use of technology in social work practice.

Competency Behaviors: (1) Guided by ethical reasoning and self-reflection, demonstrate adherence to ethical frameworks and key laws, policies, and procedures related to aging, and the rights

of older adults. (2) Engage in active dialogue with field faculty/instructors regarding aging field placement agency policies and culture around behavior, appearance, communication, and the use of supervision. (3) Develop and sustain effective collaborative relationships that respect older adults' needs for protection, self-determination, and the provision of services in the least restrictive environment possible with colleagues and community stakeholders, including older adults, their family members, other care providers, and Tribes. (4) Effectively manage professional boundary issues and other challenges arising in the course of aging-related work, particularly ambiguities presented by home visits, personal loss, trauma, and other highly involved and potentially emotionally triggering aspects of the work. (5) Develop and sustain relationships with members of interdisciplinary and integrated health care teams, including social workers, primary care providers, hospital staff, home health care providers, psychiatrists, psychologists, substance use disorder treatment staff, Tribal service providers, and others, that reflect clear understanding of their roles in providing care to older adults. (6) Demonstrate both knowledge of the history and evolution of social work practice related to aging and older adults in the United States and California, and a commitment to lifelong learning around this practice. (7) Follow all ethical guidelines and legal mandates in the use of technology in order to maintain the confidentiality of all personal, behavioral health, and health-related information. (CalSWEC, 2017, pp. 1–2)

Competency 2: Engage Diversity and Difference in Practice

Specialized Practice Competency Description: Social workers understand how diversity and difference characterize and shape the human experience and are critical to the formation of identity. The dimensions of diversity are understood as the intersectionality of multiple factors, including, but not limited to, age, class, color, culture, disability and ability, ethnicity, gender, gender identity and expression, immigration status, marital status, political ideology, race, religion/spirituality, sex, sexual orientation, and Tribal sovereign status. Social workers understand that, as a consequence of difference, a person's life experiences may include oppression, poverty, marginalization, and alienation as well as privilege, power, and acclaim. Social workers also understand the forms and mechanisms of oppression and discrimination and recognize the extent to which a culture's structures and values, including social, economic, political, and cultural exclusions, may oppress, marginalize, alienate, or create privilege and power.

Competency Behaviors: (1) Engage in critical analysis of the interpersonal, community, and social structural causes and effects of disproportionality, disparities, and inequities in the incidence and trajectory of aging-related care

needs, housing, transportation, and resource access among older adults, their families, and their communities. (2) Evidence respectful awareness and understanding of the impact of being a member of a marginalized group on aging experiences, and accurately identify differences in access to and quality of available services for members of different communities and populations. (3) Demonstrate knowledge of diverse cultural norms and traditional methods of providing care to older adults, as well as an applied understanding of how these realities affect work with older adults from diverse backgrounds, their families, and their communities. (4) Develop and use practice methods that acknowledge, respect, and address how individual and cultural values, norms, and differences impact the various systems with which older adults interact, including, but not limited to, families, communities, primary care systems, mental and behavioral health care systems, and integrated care systems. (CalSWEC, 2017, pp. 3–4)

Competency 3: Advance Human Rights and Social, Economic, and Environmental Justice

Specialized Practice Competency Description: Social workers understand that every person regardless of position in society has fundamental human rights such as freedom, safety, privacy, an adequate standard of living, health care, and education. Social workers understand the global interconnections of oppression and human rights violations, and are knowledgeable about theories of human need and social justice and strategies to promote social and economic justice and human rights. Social workers understand strategies designed to eliminate oppressive structural barriers to ensure that social goods, rights, and responsibilities are distributed equitably and that civil, political, environmental, economic, social, and cultural human rights are protected.

Competency Behaviors: (1) Clearly articulate the systematic effects of discrimination, oppression, and stigma on the needs and experiences of older adults and on the quality and delivery of services available to them, and identify and advocate for policy changes needed to address these issues. (2) Advocate for changes in policies and programs that reflect a social justice practice framework for facilitating access and providing services to older adults, their families, and care providers, especially among underserved groups and communities. (3) Demonstrate the ability to work effectively in cross-disciplinary collaboration to develop and provide interventions that explicitly address the specific needs of diverse older adults, their families, and care providers. (4) Integrate into all aspects of policy and practice sensitivity to the reality that fundamental rights, including freedom and privacy, may be compromised for older adults engaged in care, and the goal that services should be provided in the least restrictive environment possible. (CalSWEC, 2017, pp. 4–5)

Competency 4: Engage in Practice-informed Research and Research-informed Practice

Specialized Practice Competency Description: Social workers understand quantitative and qualitative research methods and their respective roles in advancing a science of social work and in evaluating their practice. Social workers know the principles of logic, scientific inquiry, and culturally informed and ethical approaches to building knowledge. Social workers understand that evidence that informs practice derives from multidisciplinary sources and multiple ways of knowing. They also understand the processes for translating research findings into effective practice.

Competency Behaviors: (1) Demonstrate the ability to understand, interpret, and evaluate the benefits and limitations of various evidence-based and evidence-informed treatment models as they influence practice with older adults. (2) Engage in critical analysis of research findings, practice models, and practice wisdom as they inform aging related practice, including how research practices have historically failed to address the needs and realities of exploited and/or disadvantaged communities, and how cross-cultural research practices can be used to enhance equity. (3) Clearly communicate research findings, conclusions, and implications, as well as their applications to aging practice, across a variety of professional interactions with consumers, families, and multidisciplinary service providers. (4) Apply research findings to aging-related practice with individuals, families, and communities and to the development of professional knowledge about the needs, experiences, and well-being of older adults. (CalSWEC, 2017, pp. 5–6)

Competency 6: Engage With Individuals, Families, Groups, Organizations, and Communities

Specialized Practice Competency Description: Social workers understand that engagement is an ongoing component of the dynamic and interactive process of social work practice with, and on behalf of, diverse individuals, families, groups, organizations, and communities. Social workers value the importance of human relationships. Social workers understand theories of human behavior and the social environment, and critically evaluate and apply this knowledge to facilitate engagement with clients and constituencies, including individuals, families, groups, organizations, and communities. Social workers understand strategies to engage diverse clients and constituencies to advance practice effectiveness. Social workers understand how their personal experiences and affective reactions may impact their ability to effectively engage with diverse clients and constituencies. Social workers value principles of relationship-building and inter-professional collaboration to facilitate engagement with clients, constituencies, and other professionals as appropriate.

Competency Behaviors: (1) Appropriately engage and activate older adults, their families, and other care providers in the development and coordination of care plans that reflect relevant theoretical models and balance older adults' needs for care with respect for autonomy and independence. (2) Effectively utilize interpersonal skills to engage older adults, their families, and other care providers in culturally responsive, consumer-driven, and trauma-informed integrated care that addresses mutually agreed upon service goals and balances needs for care, protection, autonomy, and independence. (3) Establish effective and appropriate communication, coordination, and advocacy planning with other care providers and interdisciplinary care teams as needed to address mutually agreed upon service goals. Recognizing the complex nature of service engagement, ensure that communications with consumers and their families regarding service goals are both sensitive and transparent. (4) Manage affective responses and exercise good judgment around engaging with resistance, trauma responses, and other potentially triggering situations with older adults, their families, and other care providers. (CalSWEC, 2017, pp. 9–10)

Competency 7: Assess Individuals, Families, Groups, Organizations, and Communities

Specialized Practice Competency Description: Practitioners in aging utilize ecological-systems theory, a strengths-based and person/family-centered framework to conduct assessments that value the resilience of diverse older adults, families, and caregivers. They select appropriate assessment tools, methods and technology, and evaluate, adapt, and modify them, as needed, to enhance their validity in working with diverse, vulnerable and at-risk groups. The comprehensive biopsychosocial assessment takes into account the multiple factors of physical, mental and social well-being needed for treatment planning for older adults and their families. They develop skills in interprofessional assessment and communication with key constituencies to choose the most effective practice strategies. Gero social workers understand how their own experiences and affective reactions about aging, quality of life, loss and grief may affect their assessment and resultant decision-making.

Competency Behaviors: (1) Conduct assessments that incorporate a strengths-based perspective, person/family-centered focus, and resilience while recognizing aging related risk, (2) Develop, select, and adapt assessment methods and tools that optimize practice with older adults, their families, caregivers, and communities, and (3) Use and integrate multiple domains and sources of assessment information and communicate with other professionals to inform a comprehensive plan for intervention. (Council for Social Work Education, 2017, pp. 89–90)

Competency 8: Intervene With Individuals, Families, Groups, Organizations, and Communities

Specialized Practice Competency Description: Social workers understand that intervention is an ongoing component of the dynamic and interactive process of social work practice with, and on behalf of, diverse individuals, families, groups, organizations, and communities. Social workers are knowledgeable about evidence-informed interventions to achieve the goals of clients and constituencies, including individuals, families, groups, organizations, and communities. Social workers understand theories of human behavior and the social environment, and critically evaluate and apply this knowledge to effectively intervene with clients and constituencies. Social workers understand methods of identifying, analyzing, and implementing evidence-informed interventions to achieve client and constituency goals. Social workers value the importance of interprofessional teamwork and communication in interventions, recognizing that beneficial outcomes may require interdisciplinary, inter-professional, and inter-organizational collaboration.

Competency Behaviors: (1) In partnership with older adults and their families, develop appropriate intervention plans that reflect respect for autonomy and independence, as well as contemporary theories and models for interventions with older adults. Plans should:

- Reflect cultural humility and acknowledgement of individualized needs;
- Incorporate consumer and family strengths;
- Utilize community resources and natural supports;
- Incorporate multidisciplinary team supports and interventions;
- Include non-pharmacological interventions; and
- Demonstrate knowledge of poly-pharmacy needs and issues specific to older adults.

(2) Apply the principles of teaming, engagement, inquiry, advocacy, and facilitation within interdisciplinary teams and care coordination to the work of supporting older adults, family members, and other care providers to accomplish intervention goals and satisfy advanced care planning needs. (3) Effectively implement evidence-based interventions in the context of providing emergency response, triage, brief treatment, and longer-term care, and in the course of addressing a range of issues presented in primary care, specialty care, community agency, inpatient, and palliative care settings. Interventions should be guided by respect for older adults' autonomy and independence and should include components such as psychoeducation, problem-solving treatment skills,

symptom tracking, medication therapies, follow-up, and planning for evolving care needs. (4) Effectively plan for interventions in ways that incorporate thoughtfully executed transitions during time-limited internships, recognizing that consumer needs for support may continue beyond these time periods. (CalSWEC, 2017, pp. 12–14)

Competency 9: Evaluate Practice With Individuals, Families, Groups, Organizations, and Communities

Specialized Practice Competency Description: Social workers understand that evaluation is an ongoing component of the dynamic and interactive process of social work practice with, and on behalf of, diverse individuals, families, groups, organizations and communities. Social workers recognize the importance of evaluating processes and outcomes to advance practice, policy, and service delivery effectiveness. Social workers understand theories of human behavior and the social environment, and critically evaluate and apply this knowledge in evaluating outcomes. Social workers understand qualitative and quantitative methods for evaluating outcomes and practice effectiveness.

Competency Behaviors: (1) Record, track, and monitor consumer engagement, assessment, and intervention data in practice with older adults, their families, and other care providers accurately and according to field education agency policies and guidelines. (2) Conduct accurate process and outcome analysis of engagement, assessment, and intervention data in practice with older adults, their families, and other care providers that incorporates consumer perspectives and reflects respect for older adults' autonomy and independence. (3) Use findings to evaluate intervention effectiveness, develop recommendations for adapting service plans and approaches as needed, improve interdisciplinary team coordination and care integration, and help agency and community policies better support older adults, their families, and their formal and informal care systems. (4) Share both the purposes of such data collection and the overall results of data analysis with older adults, their families, and communities whenever possible, with the goal of engaging them more meaningfully in the evaluation process. (CalSWEC, 2017, pp. 14–15)

Learning Objectives

1. Learners will understand the context for caregiving of older adults in the United States.
2. Learners will identify screening tools to assess caregiver stress to prevent burnout when caring for older adults.

3. Learners will identify appropriate evidence-based interventions for caregivers of older adults.
4. Learners will understand the importance of referring caregivers of older adult clients to appropriate technological and community resources and when to assist with coordination.
5. Learners will identify sources of transference and countertransference when working with caregivers of older adults.

Case Study

Ms. Swanson, a 73-year-old non-Hispanic White female, was the caregiver for her partner, Ms. Jones, a 72-year-old non-Hispanic White female. Ms. Swanson and Ms. Jones were both attorneys, they have no children, they both identify as being lesbian, they have been in a relationship for 40 years, and they both have a living will and trust with each as the full power of attorney for the other. While on vacation in South America, Ms. Jones became ill. They flew back to the United States, and Ms. Jones' symptoms continued to worsen over a few days—she became disoriented, refused to eat, and complained of chest and back pain; she was also experiencing anxiety. Ms. Jones had been diagnosed with high blood pressure at age 50. Ms. Swanson took her to see the primary care physician, who requested Ms. Jones be taken to the emergency room—she was in a hypertensive crisis with blood pressure of 180/120, putting her at risk for a stroke. While hospitalized, she suffered a stroke. She remained hospitalized for four weeks; she was in the intensive care unit after going into cardiac arrest and was placed on a ventilator and respirator. She remained in the inpatient stroke rehabilitation unit for two weeks and was discharged home with an order for a home health nurse, physical therapist, occupational therapist, speech therapist, social worker, and home health. The stroke resulted in right-sided weakness and aphasia; she was wheelchair bound and required full assistance with all activities of daily living (ADLs) and instrumental activities of daily living (IADLs) at the time of discharge. A part-time caregiver was hired to assist Ms. Swanson with Ms. Jones's care. Ms. Jones and Ms. Swanson lived in a large four-bedroom home with one flight of stairs to the upstairs; the bedrooms and full bathrooms were all upstairs. There were five steps to the front porch and a paved sidewalk to the driveway.

Assessing Context

A caregiver is defined as "an unpaid individual (for example, a spouse, partner, family member, friend, or neighbor) involved in assisting others with activities of daily living and/or medical tasks" (Family Caregiver Alliance, 2016, p. 1). The former definition of caregiver is also commonly referred to an informal caregiver, whereas formal caregivers are "paid care providers providing care in one's home or in a care setting (day care, residential facility, long-term care facility)" (Family Caregiver Alliance, 2016, p. 1). In the United States, over a 12-month period, there are roughly 34.2 million informal caregivers providing functional health assistance to an adult age 50 or older (Family Caregiver Alliance, 2016). Most caregivers provide care to one adult (82%), whereas others provide care to two to three (15%) or more than three (3%) (Family Caregiver Alliance, 2016). The estimates of informal caregiving for adults with dementia or Alzheimer's disease is roughly 15.7 million (Family Caregiver Alliance, 2016). The economic value of informal care was estimated to be $470 billion in 2013, and the estimated value of informal caregiving in 2014 for adults with dementia or Alzheimer's disease was $217.7 billion in the United States (Family Caregiver Alliance, 2016).

Females represent 75% of all informal caregivers and are estimated to spend "50 percent more time providing care than males" (Family Caregiver Alliance, 2016, p. 2). The types of functional health tasks males and females assist with tend to follow not follow traditional gender norms with female caregivers as they assist more than males with caregiving tasks that can be physically strenuous, such as ADLs (i.e., toileting, transferring, bathing, dressing, eating), whereas males are "more likely to help with finances, arrangement of care, and other less burdensome tasks" (Family Caregiver Alliance, 2016, p. 2). One study found that females spend approximately 22 hours on caregiving each week in comparison to males who spend slightly more than 17 hours per week on caregiving (Family Caregiver Alliance, 2016). Other research suggests that males and females have similar rates in time spent caregiving (Family Caregiver Alliance, 2016). Among informal caregivers ages 75 and older, the research suggests that both males and females provide "equal amounts of care" (Family Caregiver Alliance, 2016, p. 2). These gender differences in informal caregiving are important for clinicians to recognize when working with older adults to ensure not only that the functional health needs of the older adult are being met but also that options for respite care and formal caregiving to supplement care and prevent burnout for the caregiver are explored, as well as appropriate interventions and services to assist with the tasks of caregiving.

For caregivers of adults with complex chronic care, research suggests that "46% perform medical and nursing tasks" and more than 96% assist with functional health needs for "activities of daily living (ADLs) such as personal hygiene, dressing and undressing, getting in and out of bed" and "instrumental activities of daily living (IADLs) such as taking prescribed medications, shopping for groceries, transportation, or using technology, or both" (Family Caregiver Alliance, 2016, p. 3). Most caregivers (43%) provide ADL assistance with transferring from the bed to a chair and back to bed, 78% of caregivers assist with the IADL task transportation, 76% assist with the task of shopping, and 72% assist with the task of housekeeping (Family Caregiver Alliance, 2016). In working with caregivers of older adults, clinicians should understand the context that assumption of a caregiver role may come from a belief that no one else can provide the care or they may feel a sense of pressure to assume the role of caregiver—more than 57% of caregivers report that the assumption of the role of caregiving is imposed by themselves (Family Caregiver Alliance, 2016). The disbelief that others can perform the roles and finances influence the assumption of a caregiving role as 43% of caregivers report that caregiving tasks "are their personal responsibility because no one else can do it or because insurance will not pay" for a formal caregiver (Family Caregiver Alliance, 2016, p. 4). Pressure by the care recipient or a family member to assume the caregiving role is reported by 12% and 8% of caregivers, respectively (Family Caregiver Alliance, 2016). These pressures may create or add to strains in family communication and functioning, feelings of guilt by the older adult care recipient or caregiver, and reluctance to accept care due to role reversal, especially when the care providers are adult children.

Overall, the majority (48%) of caregivers fall between the ages of 18 to 49 years of age, and 34% are ages 65 and older; the average caregiver age is 49.2 (Family Caregiver Alliance, 2016). However, the number of hours spent providing care increases with age, with adults ages 75 and older providing the most hours of care each week (34.5 hours), followed by adults ages 65 to 74 (30.7 hours), adults ages 55 to 64 (25.3 hours), and adults ages 45 to 54 (25.8 hours) (Family Caregiver Alliance, 2016). Older caregivers are at risk of not tending to their own health and biopsychosocial/spiritual needs when they devote nearly a full week's worth of care to their spouse or partner; middle-aged adults may experience added health and mental health risks with the pressure of caring for an aging parent or in-law in addition to working and caring for dependent children.

Caregiver burden has been defined by Zarit, Todd, and Zarit (1986) as: "The extent to which caregivers perceive that caregiving has had an adverse effect on their emotional, social, financial, physical, and spiritual functioning" (as cited in Adelman, Tmanova, Delgado, Dion, & Lachs, 2014, p. 1053). Using a strengths-based perspective, clinicians recognize that not all caregiving experiences lead to caregiver burden by caregiving spouses or partners or their children or grandchildren, but they may be perceived by the caregiver as rewarding, an honor, part of a cultural or family tradition, and a way to model care for family members to younger generations. Caregiver burden is, however, associated with provision of care to a care recipient with complex chronic care needs. Several clinical trials have been conducted to date examining caregiver burden associated with a care recipient with Alzheimer's disease, stroke, or cancer (Adelman, Tmanova, Delgado, Dion, & Lachs, 2014). Clinicians should be aware of the risk factors associated with caregiver burden to ensure they are assessed and appropriate interventions and supportive resources are provided to reduce caregiver burden and stress.

Risk factors for caregiver burden can be categorized under four key domains: demographic, clinical outcomes, psychosocial, and caregiving context (Adelman, Tmanova, Delgado, Dion, & Lachs, 2014). The demographic domain includes: "female sex, low education, and cohabitation with care recipient" (Adelman, Tmanova, Delgado, Dion, & Lachs, 2014, p. 1054). The impact of caregiver burden on the clinical outcomes of caregivers includes: (1) "a 63% increased risk of death," (2) "caregiver weight loss," (3) higher incidence of "low self-care behaviors and ignoring self-health," and (4) sleep deprivation, which is common in "caregivers of dementia patients who have disruption to the sleep-wake cycle" (Adelman, Tmanova, Delgado, Dion, & Lachs, 2014, p. 1054). The risk factors for the psychosocial domain include: (1) "depression and depressive symptoms identified as a risk factor and outcome of caregiver burden;" (2) "using a smaller number of coping strategies (e.g., seeking advice, exercising) associated with caregiver burden in caregivers of dementia patients;" (3) a "greater likelihood of experiencing caregiver burden in caregivers who perceive distress in the care recipient;" (4) "social isolation and decreased social activity;" (5) anxiety, which is "an outcome of caregiving in caregivers to advanced cancer care patients;" and (6) suicide, which is "an outcome of caregiver burden" (Adelman, Tmanova, Delgado, Dion, & Lachs, 2014, p. 1054). The fourth domain of caregiver burden, the caregiving context, consists of risk factors for caregiving burden in the following contexts: (1) "duration in the caregiving role and hours spent caregiving associated with caregiving burden;" (2) financial stress, which is "a risk factor for caregiver burden and an outcome of caregiver burden;" (3) "lack of choice in becoming a caregiver;" and (4) "inability to continue regular employment" and in contexts when "more than 1 caregiver exists, the family member who is not regularly employed is more likely to assume the caregiving role" (Adelman, Tmanova, Delgado, Dion, & Lachs, 2014, p. 1054). Clinicians can use screening tools to assist with caregiver burden assessment. Clinicians also assess the diversity and cultural factors of the caregiver to inform treatment planning.

Biopsychosocial/Spiritual Assessment

Following is an application of the Geriatric Biopsychosocial/Spiritual Assessment conducted by Ms. Swanson's social worker.

Box 12.1

Geriatric Biopsychosocial/Spiritual Assessment

Basic Demographic: Ms. Swanson is a 73-year-old female who identifies as a lesbian and lives with Ms. Jones, her partner of 40 years; Ms. Swanson speaks English as her primary language; she is non-Hispanic White; and she practiced law for 45 years with a law degree from Yale

Referral Information: Primary care physician and home health nurse requested social work referral for caregiver resources due to strained communication between Ms. Swanson and Ms. Jones, supportive and educational resources, and community-based resources for accessibility to home

Cultural/Spiritual: High literacy and knowledge about stroke and rehabilitation; practices no complementary and alternative medicine; no identified faith

Social: [Relationships within family, social/diversity groups, and community]

- Worked in law for 45 years; partially retired, working 24 hours per week; no children
- Has several friends, including co-workers, neighbors, and community members at the local homeless shelter she volunteers for; her domestic partner, Ms. Jones, recently suffered a stroke and is at home recovering from the stroke and is receiving home health before transitioning to outpatient rehabilitations

---

Financial: [Ability to provide basic needs and access health services]

- Basic needs for housing, food, and clothing are met; Ms. Swanson and Ms. Jones own their own home; Ms. Swanson has hired a part-time caregiver after Ms. Jones's discharge from acute care to assist with ADLs and during transportation to doctor's appointments
- Both Ms. Swanson and Ms. Jones have Medicare primary and Blue Cross secondary for insurances; co-pays and fees are manageable
- Income sources: Social Security, pension, savings, and investments

Environmental: [Personal safety, maintenance of residence, and safety of community]

- Lives with domestic partner in a two-level home
- Lighting on the streets, neighborhood watch, low crime
- Home safety: Smoke and carbon monoxide detectors and fire extinguisher are operable; adequate lighting throughout the home; physical therapist recommended removal of slip rugs in the kitchen, which patient complied with and removed; shower and toilet accessibility: a shower bench was ordered and a detachable shower head; no elevators—one flight of stairs to upstairs, five steps to front door with handrail, no ramps to access home
- No guns in the home
- Screen for abuse or neglect by self or perpetrated by others: No evidence or suspicion of abuse or neglect by self or others

Physical: [Individual function and disease morbidity]

- Ms. Swanson has a high level of health literacy; her self-rated health is "excellent;" she and Ms. Jones, her domestic partner, have a living will and trust; she is knowledgeable about her partner's stroke diagnosis, prognosis, and recovery; she and her partner were sexually active until Ms. Jones became ill while on vacation

Mental: [Mental status, depression, anxiety, and substance abuse]

- Standardized screening instruments: No indicators of mild cognitive impairment, no indicators of depression or anxiety, and scores in normal range for both screenings; mild caregiver burden detected with Zarit Burden Inventory, score = 22 out of 88
- Suicide risk assessment: Ruled out—does not endorse suicidal ideations and no history of suicide attempts or plans
- Homicidal ideations: Ruled out—does not endorse homicidal ideations and no history of homicidal ideations
- Substance use: One alcoholic beverage per day with dinner; no use of drugs

Formulation/Evaluation: Respite care; support group for caregivers; stroke support group for client and partner; options to improve accessibility of home

Treatment Planning: Consultation with physical therapist, nurse, and primary care physician; social worker to assist with information and access to support groups for caregivers and stroke; transportation with wheelchair accessibility; three sessions of counseling with Ms. Swanson and Ms. Jones to engage, assess, treat, and evaluate supportive counseling and care coordination with vendors for accessibility to and from home; monitor perceived caregiver burden

Community Resource Needs: Caregiver support group; stroke support group; formal care agencies to increase assistance for partner; wheelchair-accessible transportation and vendors for chair lift from downstairs to upstairs and wheelchair ramp for front porch

Screening Tools

The Zarit Burden Interview is a commonly used 22-item inventory used:

> by providers and agencies working with older adults to assess caregiver burden using scaled responses from 0 to 4 (Never to Nearly Always). (American Psychological Association, 2018)

The Zarit Burden Interview has good to excellent reliability, with alphas ranging from .88 to .91; adequate validity (r=.71); and good reliability for personal strain (alpha=.80) and role strain (alpha=.81) (Kuhlenschmidt & Wants, 2001).

Diversity–Cultural Competence/Spirituality/LGBT/Sexuality

In the United States, self-identification as lesbian, gay, bisexual, and transgender (LGBT) is reported by approximately 9% of informal caregivers (Family Caregiver Alliance, 2016). It is estimated that roughly 3 million adults ages 55 or older reside in the United States and the number is projected to double in size over the next 20 years (Family Caregiver Alliance, 2016). In a study comparing the number of hours spent on caregiving among LGBT, it was found that gay, bisexual and/or transgender and heterosexual males, gay, bisexual and/or transgender males provided more hours of care in comparison to heterosexual males (41 hours versus 29 hours, respectively) (Family Caregiver Alliance, 2016). Additionally, more gay males are caregivers in comparison to lesbian or bisexual caregivers, with gay males "spending over 150 hours per week in this capacity, compared to 3% of lesbian and 2% of bisexual respondents" (Family Caregiver Alliance, 2016, p. 3). Cultural competence and humility, diversity, and inclusion training, as well as engagement, assessment, intervention, and evaluation skills and techniques, are essential for clinicians to build rapport and intervene effectively with LGBT older adult caregivers as research suggests that "20% of older LGBT individuals and 44% of older transgender individuals feel their relationship with their healthcare provider would be adversely affected if their health provider knew their sexual orientation/gender" (Family Caregiver Alliance, 2016, p. 3). LGBT older adults are also at risk for having unmet caregiving needs as they are "twice as likely to age as a single person, twice as likely to reside alone, and three to four times less likely to have children" (Family Caregiver Alliance, 2016, p. 3).

Returning to the case study, neither Ms. Swanson, the informal caregiver, nor Ms. Jones, the care recipient, had children to assist with the presenting, unexpected caregiving needs of Ms. Jones. The social worker assisted both Ms. Swanson and Ms. Jones with developing a preferred treatment plan that included additional formal care, respite care, and support groups for Ms. Swanson and sessions with the social worker to problem solve and process presenting biopsychosocial/spiritual needs and legal and relationship strains resulting from Ms. Jones' sudden stroke. With a limited amount of informal caregiving support available beyond that of Ms. Swanson, the couple opted to bring in more formal care for respite for Ms. Swanson and ADL as well as IADL assistance for Ms. Jones. Within four weeks of implementing increased formal care and attendance to support groups for caregivers by Ms. Swanson and attendance to a stroke support group by both Ms. Swanson and Ms. Jones, both reported improvements in the communication and quality of their relationship, well-being overall, quality of life, and feeling prepared and knowledgeable on the trajectory of recovery for stroke survivors and their caregivers.

Higher prevalence rates for caregiving are reported among Hispanic adults (21%), African American adults (20.3%), and Asian American adults (19.7%) in comparison to non-Hispanic Whites (16.9%) (Family Caregiver Alliance, 2016). Non-Hispanic White caregivers tend to be older (average age 52.5 years) in comparison to Asian Americans (average age 46.6 years), Hispanics (average age 42.7 years), and African Americans (average age of 44.2 years) (Family Caregiver Alliance, 2016). The race/ethnicity reported in the United States among caregivers is non-Hispanic White at 62%, Hispanic at 17%, African American at 13%, and Asian American at 6% (Family Caregiver Alliance, 2016). Hours spent on high-burden caregiving is highest among African American (77% or 30 hours per week) and Hispanic caregivers (45% or 30 hours per week) in comparison to non-Hispanic White (33% or 20 hours per week) and Asian American caregivers (30% or 16 hours per week) (Family Caregiver Alliance, 2016). Demand for African American caregivers are high with more than half reporting that they fall into the sandwich genera-tion, providing care for one or more older adult family members and dependent children simultaneously; living with and providing 20.6 hours of care; and/or maintaining full or part-time employment while balancing caregiving (66%) (Family Caregiver Alliance, 2016). African American caregivers also provide more assistance (41%) with the physically strenuous tasks of caregiving (i.e., three ADLs) than both non-Hispanic Whites (28%) and Asian Americans (23%) (Family Caregiver Alliance, 2016).

When engaging, assessing, intervening, and evaluating best practice with older adults and their caregivers, clinicians seek to understand the life histories, experiences, prefer-ences, opportunities, and barriers to caregiving for older adult clients and their caregivers to provide interventions valued and preferred by the client and beneficial to the caregiver

(CSWE Competency 2: Engage Diversity and Difference in Practice, specialized practice competency 2, behavior 3). Clinicians seek to gain knowledge and understanding from the client about his or her experiences and intersections with disparities and inequities that may impede successful opportunities to provide care for an older adult in areas such as health care, housing, and home- and community-based services (specialized practice competency 2, behavior 1). When engaging, assessing, intervening, and evaluating practice with diverse older adults and their caregivers, clinicians demonstrate respect of the cultural norms, beliefs, and practices of diverse older adults and the influence on interactions of the older adult with various micro, mezzo, and macro systems (specialized practice competency 2, behavior 4). Clinicians inform the treatment plan of the cultural and diversity preferences and needs of informal caregivers of older adults.

Interdisciplinary Team Roles and Planning

Interdisciplinary teams play an essential role in the well-being and quality of life of informal caregivers of older adults. Clinicians engage, assess, intervene, and evaluate interventions with informal caregivers of older adults to ensure that key objectives and goals for treatment are accomplished. When planning and implementing interventions, clinicians are aware of best practices and evidence-based interventions to meet the biopsychosocial/spiritual needs and to ensure a goodness of fit between recommended caregiver support services with the caregivers' preferences, values, and culture to ensure self-determination of caregivers in endorsing and accessing home- and community-based supportive services and programs (CSWE Gero Competency 1: Demonstrate Ethical and Professional Behavior, specialized practice behavior 5; CSWE Gero Competency 2: Engage Diversity and Difference in Practice, specialized practice behavior 4; CSWE Gero Competency 4: Engage in Practice-informed Research and Research-informed Practice, specialized practice behavior 3; CSWE Gero Competency 6: Engage With Individuals, Families, Groups, Organizations, and Communities, specialized practice behaviors 1–4; CSWE Gero Competency 7: Assess Individuals, Families, Groups, Organizations, and Communities, specialized practice behavior 3; CSWE Gero Competency 8: Intervene With Individuals, Families, Groups, Organizations, and Communities, specialized practice behaviors 1–3; and CSWE Gero Competency 9: Evaluate Practice With Individuals, Families, Groups, Organizations, and Communities, specialized practice behaviors 1–3). Both Ms. Swanson and Ms. Jones were comfortable in communicating their preferences and needs to the interdisciplinary team. New formal caregivers received training from nursing, physical and occupational therapists, and the home health aide for bathing. The social worker assisted with vendors to help make the home accessible with a chair lift from the first floor to the second floor, as sleeping in the same room was a goal for both Ms. Jones and Ms. Swanson, rather than having a hospital bed on the first floor of their home. The occupational and physical therapists further assisted with durable medical equipment, safety, and interventions to improve Ms. Jones's ability to participate in ADLs. A local community-based senior service agency was contracted to build a wheelchair ramp on the front porch, ensuring Ms. Jone's accessibility to and from the home. Clinicians are aware of evidence-based options for caregivers to receive best practices and essential support.

Evidence-based Interventions

Individual and Group Psychoeducation

Psychoeducation is defined as an evidence-based, "professionally delivered treatment modality that integrates and synergizes psychotherapeutic and educational interventions" and incorporates "both illness-specific information and tools for managing related circumstances" with an emphasis on a "holistic and competence-based approach, stressing health, collaboration, coping, and empowerment" with "the patient/client and/or family" considered as partners in treatment with clinicians (Lukens & McFarlane, 2004, pp. 205–206). Psychoeducation, consistent with the social work profession, is strengths based; it is an effective brief intervention that is present focused and based on the "premise that the more knowledgeable the care recipients and informal caregivers are, the more positive health-related outcomes" there will be for both (Lukens & McFarlane, 2004, p. 206). Psychoeducation has been used effectively across contexts and systems levels of both health and behavioral health (Lukens & McFarlane, 2004). Psychoeducation incorporates problem-solving skills and role playing using techniques from cognitive behavioral therapy, allowing caregivers and care recipients to review and practice new skills in a safe, therapeutic environment (Lukens & McFarlane, 2004).

Psychoeducation can be done individually with clients or in group settings. Group settings provide additional support through opportunities for caregivers and/or care recipients to engage in "within-group dialogue, social learning, expansion and support and cooperation, the potential for group reinforcement of positive change, and network building" (Lukens & McFarlane, 2004, p. 206). Psychoeducation promotes the use and practice of coping skills, and narrative psychoeducation models further assist the caregiver and/or care recipient to "recognize personal strengths and resources and generate possibilities for action and growth" (Lukens & McFarlane, 2004, p. 206). Randomized trials using psychoeducation have been proven effective for caregivers of care recipients with schizophrenia (i.e., decreases in health-related illness and increased well-being) and care recipients (i.e., improvements in symptoms and social functioning) (Lukens & McFarlane, 2004). Randomized trials have been conducted on care recipients living with cancer; improvements have been found in quality of life, lower levels of anxiety, distress, and longevity in professionally led groups (Lukens & McFarlane, 2004). A study examining informal caregivers of care recipients with cancer who have participated in psychoeducation groups has shown improvements in caregiver mood disturbances and increased perceived emotional support (Lukens & McFarlane, 2004).

Savvy Caregiver is an evidence-based psychoeducation program composed of a "12-hour course with the aims of introducing family caregivers to the caregiving role, providing them with the knowledge, skills, and attitudes needed to carry out that role, and alerting them to self-care issues" (Hepburn, Lewis, Sherman, & Tornatore, 2003, p. 908). The learning objectives of the Savvy Caregiver program include: (1) "acknowledge the disease," (2) "make the cognitive shift," (3) "develop emotional tolerance," (4) "take control," (5) establish a realistic care goal," (6) "gauge the care recipient's capabilities," (7) "design opportunities for satisfying occupation," and (8) "become a sleuth" (Table 12.1) (Hepburn, Lewis, Sherman, & Tornatore, 2003, p. 910).

TABLE 12.1   Caregiving Learning Objectives in the Savvy Caregiver Curriculum

Objective	Description
Acknowledge the disease	Understand and come to grips with the disease that is affecting the person. Recognize it is not personal—it is the disease and not the person that is causing difficulties.
Make the cognitive shift	Develop a strategic sense of what cognitive losses are occurring and how caregiver behavior has to adapt to these as they take place and progress.
Develop emotional tolerance	Recognize the central role of confusion in dementia and how it contributes to troubling behaviors (e.g., shadowing or repetitive questioning). Appreciate the care recipient's need for emotional stability in the face of confusion. Accept the caregiver's role of providing calm and stability.
Take control	Understand that dementia gradually erodes autonomy. Appreciate the social and emotional difficulties involved in taking control of another adult (thinking of the other as somehow not equal). Recognize the need to take control and be willing and able to do so.
Establish a realistic care goal	Accept that striving to ensure as good a quality of life as possible is the most realistic goal for caregiving. Recognize that rehabilitation, restoration, or retardation of disease progress are not feasible goals and let go of them, when applicable.
Gauge the care recipient's capabilities	Be able, using an occupational-therapy-based staging system, to estimate the care recipient's capacity for involvement in tasks and activities (kind, complexity, duration, etc.).
Design opportunities for satisfying occupation	Be able, based on the estimate of capability, to design tasks or activities in which the person can become engaged and which she or he will enjoy. Be able to communicate effectively with the person to promote and maintain involvement.
Become a sleuth	Adopt a problem-solving approach to caregiving, one that involves being able to stand back from the situation (emotionally), create hypotheses about causes of behavior, formulate and try out responses, observe and learn from results, and repeat the sequence as needed.

Source: Kenneth W. Hepburn, et al., "Caregiving Learning Objectives in the Savvy Caregiver Curriculum," *The Gerontologist*, vol. 43, no. 6, pp. 910. Copyright © 2003 by Oxford University Press.

The Savvy Caregiver program has been successfully adapted to brief formats in urban settings. In a collaborative pilot study, investigators of the University of Southern California Edward R. Roybal Institute and Alzheimer's Greater Los Angeles provided an adapted brief version of the Savvy Caregiver program with three sessions rather than 12, referred to as the Savvy Express (Aranda & Cherry, 2018). With roughly 30,000 caregivers of older adults in the Greater Los Angeles area, this program sought to improve the psychological and physical well-being of informal caregivers of older adults, referred to as care partners. The care partners' racial/ethnic identification (n=116) was 41% non-Hispanic White; 21% Latino/a and Hispanic; 20% African American; and 16% Asian American (Aranda & Cherry, 2018). The care partners' average age was 64 years old (range of 26 to 93), nearly 15 years higher than the national average age of 49.2 years old (Family Caregiver Alliance, 2016). There were more female care partners (81%) than males (Aranda & Cherry, 2018), which reflects a rate slightly higher than the national average of females comprising 75% of all informal caregivers (Family Caregiver Alliance, 2016). Immigrants comprised 19% of all care partners (Aranda & Cherry, 2018). The care partners reported providing care to a parent (44%), spouse (39%), or other family member (17%) (Aranda & Cherry, 2018). The average number of hours spent each week on care was 25 hours, with 32% of all care partners providing 24-hour care (Aranda & Cherry, 2018). The primary diagnosis of care recipients was Alzheimer's disease at 47% and other dementias at 34% (Aranda & Cherry, 2018).

Care partners completed "3 interviews: at baseline, immediately after the classes ended, and 3 months after baseline" (Aranda & Cherry, 2018, p. 1). The key outcomes from the Savvy Express program include statistically significant improvements in the following key outcomes for care partners: (1) competence "about oneself as a care partner;" (2) management in terms of "learning as much as one can about the illness;" (3) meaning, composed of two components—"reduction of expectations" and "making positive comparisons;" (4) depressive symptoms measured with the PHQ-9; and (5) anxiety symptoms measured with the GAD-7 (Aranda & Cherry, 2018, p. 2). Care providers were also assessed for changes in their reactions to the care recipients' behavioral and memory problems. The researchers found statistically significant "lower reactions" for: (1) "overall reaction: feeling bothered or distressed by memory and behavioral problems" and (2) "specific symptoms: feeling distressed by the family members' memory, depression," or "disruptive behavior" (Aranda & Cherry, 2018, p. 2).

Medical Family Therapy

According to Linville, Hertlein, and Lyness, medical family therapy (MedFT) "bridges psychosocial and physical health, examining the correlations between family, context, and an individual's physical functioning, offering family therapy interventions for medical illnesses" (2007, p. 85). MedFT provides an advantageous interdisciplinary team approach, combining expertise between mental health and medical professionals. Interventions occur between clients, their families, and mental health/social work clinicians trained in client and family biopsychosocial/spiritual engagement, assessment, diagnosis, treatment, and evaluation, along with medical providers trained in physical health, diagnosis, treatment, and evaluation. It is defined as "an approach to health care from a biopsychosocial/spiritual perspective, informed by systems theory, spanning across a variety of clinical settings, where" (1) "the patient's interpersonal relationships are believed to play a key role" and (2) "collaboration exists between the family therapist and other health care practitioners," which emphasizes interdisciplinary psychotherapy and medical interventions (Linville, Hertlein, & Lyness, 2007, p. 86). In a meta-analysis of MedFT studies conducted between 1965 and 2004, family interventions combined with medical interventions are effective at improving outcomes for caregivers with cardiovascular and neurological disorders as well as clients with obesity and anorexia nervosa and among those who are caregivers of a family member with dementia (Linville, Hertlein, & Lyness, 2007).

In a study conducted among experts in MedFT composed of faculty and doctoral students from marriage and family therapy, nursing and other medical fields, clinical and developmental psychology, education, and family studies, the key skills of clinicians conducting MedFT were identified (Tyndall, Hodgson, Lamson, White, & Knight, 2014). The key competency areas for clinicians to develop skills to engage in MedFT include: medical culture and collaboration, clinical care or therapy skills, family systems and therapy knowledge, relationship and health training, theoretical competence in the biopsychosocial/spiritual perspective, intervention for physical health and mental health, and self-care (Tyndall, Hodgson, Lamson, White, & Knight, 2014).

Specific skills for medical culture and collaboration include: (1) "the ability to communicate with providers," (2) "act as a facilitator between providers and patients and their families," and (3) "maintain an awareness of the cultural differences within a medical environment as compared to a traditional therapy setting" (Tyndall, Hodgson, Lamson, White, & Knight, 2014, p. 181). Clinical care or therapy skills identified included: "being skilled at systemic therapy, integrated care, empowering patients, general family therapy skills, and being culturally competent," as well as having treatment planning skills. Closely related to clinical skills was treatment planning (Tyndall, Hodgson, Lamson, White, & Knight, 2014, p. 181). Additional skills include family systems and therapy knowledge—specifically, clinicians should have knowledge and experience with "collaboration, coordinated/integrated delivery systems/services, and the overlap of medical and mental health problems," and clinicians engaging in MedFT "should have competency in advanced application of family systems concepts developmentally to acute, chronic, and terminal illness" (Tyndall, Hodgson, Lamson, White, & Knight, 2014, p. 181). Clinicians should also be competent in relationship and health training—specifically, "training in health and relationships" and "knowledge of common diseases" (Tyndall, Hodgson, Lamson, White, & Knight, 2014, p. 181). Knowledge of systems theory, the biopsychosocial/spiritual perspective, and agency as well as communion objectives are essential skills for clinicians to engage in MedFT (Tyndall, Hodgson, Lamson, White, & Knight, 2014). Lastly, clinicians should be competent and able to educate others on the biopsychosocial/spiritual perspective and self-care activities and strategies (Tyndall, Hodgson, Lamson, White, & Knight, 2014).

The goals of MedFT include: (1) "better coping with a chronic illness or disability," (2) "less conflict about handling a medical regimen," (3) "better communication with physicians," and (4) "more acceptance of a medical problem that cannot be cured, or help with making lifestyle changes" (Doherty, McDaniel, & Hepworth, 1994, p. 39). The two objectives that underlie the former goals are: promoting agency and communion (Doherty, McDaniel, & Hepworth, 1994). Promoting agency can be understood as: (1) "active involvement in, and commitment to, one's own care;" (2) "a sense of making personal choices in dealing with illness and the health care system, both of which often contribute to feelings of passivity and lack of control;" (3) "helping the patient and family set limits on the amount of control the illness or disability has over their lives, as in a decision to proceed in some fashion with holiday celebrations despite the partial incapacitation of a family member;" (4) "helping the family to negotiate for more information or better care arrangements with health professionals;" and (5) interventions where the clinician promotes "the agency of the patient vis-à-vis other family members," often involving "boundary setting on family members' helpfulness, or assertively asking for help, as when the caretaker of a patient with Alzheimer's disease is coached on insisting on family assistance" (Doherty, McDaniel, & Hepworth, 1994, pp. 39–40). The second objective of MedFT, communion, "refers to the emotional bonds that are often frayed by illness, disability, and contact with the health care system; it involves a "sense of being cared for, loved, and supported by family members, friends, and professionals" (Doherty, McDaniel, & Hepworth, 1994, p. 40).

Four strategies are suggested for clinicians engaging in MedFT: (1) "accepting that there is a patient (i.e., the family and larger system are worked with in terms of this fundamental starting point)," (2) "working with the illness as part of the system (i.e., they encourage the discussion of beliefs about the illness and the treatment, and help families accept the reality of the illness in their lives)" (3) "routinely collaborating with medical professionals (i.e., the therapist needs the medical professionals as much as vice versa, for information, consultation, and support," and (4) "working with developmental issues in individuals, families, illnesses, and caregiving systems," which involve a focus on "(a) the developmental progression of the illness and its psychosocial corollaries, (b) the interaction between the illness phase and individual and family developmental issues, and (c) the interaction of all of these and the developmental dynamics of the caregiving system" (Doherty, McDaniel, & Hepworth, 1994, p. 41–43).

Other Evidence-based Interventions

A meta-analysis of 55 studies (43.6% were randomized trials, 23.6% multiple observations, 12.7% quasi-experimental, and 11% cross-sectional or other) conducted between 2008 and 2012 on interventions for caregivers ages 50 and older found that most interventions (60%) were psychosocial in nature with support and counseling (20%) or education and training (40%) interventions (Heller, Gibbons, & Fisher, 2015). The remaining studies emphasized government programs (23.6%) with care coordination or supportive services (14.5%) or home and financial support (9.1%) (Heller, Gibbons, & Fisher, 2015). Other interventions included writing programs, an exercise intervention by phone, videophones, and home-based literature (Heller, Gibbons, & Fisher, 2015). The key caregiver outcomes focused on both caregiver mental health (58.2%)—specifically stress, depression, and anxiety—and caregiver appraisal (58.2%) with stress, burden, and satisfaction outcomes (Heller, Gibbons, & Fisher, 2015). Other key outcomes of caregivers included health (14.5%), care recipient outcomes (14.5%), and access to support (12.7%) (Heller, Gibbons, & Fisher, 2015).

In the studies, the government care coordination interventions included transition support from acute care for caregivers of a family member with dementia, telephone interventions for dementia care, and home medical care (Heller, Gibbons, & Fisher, 2015). The government care coordination programs increased caregiver access to support; use of community-based resources; satisfaction, skills, and knowledge; and decreased caregiver burden and mental health symptoms (Heller, Gibbons, & Fisher, 2015). The government home and financial support interventions emphasized respite care; the key outcomes for caregivers included "maintaining and improving quality of life, relief of psychological stress, decreased caregiver burden, and increased access to supports" (Heller, Gibbons, & Fisher, 2015, p. 336). The psychosocial interventions for education and training included education on topics such as "communication, wellness, medication management, community resources, care recipient behavior," self-care, and information about the care recipient's chronic illness or disease and/or functional health/disability, use of a specific program, Resources for Enhancing Alzheimer's Caregiver Health (REACH), or psychoeducation (Heller, Gibbons, & Fisher, 2015). The key outcomes for the former psychosocial interventions for caregivers included improvement in the health of the caregiver; decreased mental health symptoms (depression) and caregiver burden (strain, burden, and stress); and increased confidence in the use of effective coping strategies and ability to care for the care recipient, social support, and communication (Heller, Gibbons, & Fisher, 2015). The psychosocial support and counseling interventions emphasized support groups and one-on-one counseling focused on improving the well-being and quality of life of caregivers (Heller, Gibbons, & Fisher, 2015). The interventions included cognitive behavioral therapy by phone, spirituality and religion, family counseling, in-person counseling and support groups, and web-based support (Heller, Gibbons, & Fisher, 2015). The key outcomes from the interventions with caregivers included "decreased depression, strain and burden, and increased life satisfaction, well-being, and self-efficacy" (Heller, Gibbons, & Fisher, 2015, p. 337). Clinicians monitor and track caregiver outcomes throughout treatment.

Assessing/Monitoring Evidence-based Treatment Outcomes

Clinicians engage, assess, track, and monitor data for caregiver interventions that seek to improve the well-being and quality of life of caregivers and address caregiver burden, mental health, coping skills, and other biopsychosocial/spiritual needs (CSWE Competency 9: Evaluate Practice With Individuals, Families, Groups, Organizations, and Communities, specialized practice behaviors 1–2). Clinicians use the outcomes from evaluations of caregiver interventions to improve interdisciplinary care planning, treatment, and evaluation of outcomes with caregivers of older adults and engage them in processes related to achieving and maintaining well-being and quality of life (CSWE Competency 9: Evaluate Practice With Individuals, Families, Groups, Organizations, and Communities, specialized practice behaviors 3–4). Clinicians are aware of appropriate community-based services and programs to meet the needs of informal caregivers and assist with coordination and access to such services as appropriate.

Community Resources/Interagency Coordination

Clinicians working with caregivers of older adults are aware of the range of caregiver options for respite care, support as well as individual and group counseling, and financial and legal resources available to achieve well-being and quality of life consistent with their values, preferences, and desired goals, and they collaborate with other agencies (CSWE Gero Competency 1: Demonstrates Ethical and Professional Behavior, specialized practice behaviors 3, 5, and 7). Clinicians assist and provide advocacy for caregivers of older adults with accessing desired programs, information, and legal and supportive services; advance the human rights of caregivers; and ensure that caregivers of older adults receive information to enable them to support an older adult in the least restrictive environment (CSWE Competency 3: Advance Human Rights and Social, Economic, and Environmental Justice, specialized practice behaviors 2–4). Clinicians also engage in research-informed practice (CSWE Gero Competency 4) in communication and collaborative efforts between the caregiver, interdisciplinary team, and interagency provider systems (specialized practice behaviors 3–4).

When working with informal caregivers of older adults to promote biopsychosocial/spiritual well-being and quality of life, clinicians adhere to CSWE Gero Competencies in all phases of treatment, including engagement (CSWE Gero Competency 6: Engage With Individuals, Families, Groups, Organizations, and Communities, specialized practice behaviors 1–4) by ensuring self-determination and participation in decision making of older adults and their caregivers and assessment (CSWE Gero Competency 7: Assess Individuals, Families, Groups, Organizations, and Communities, specialized practice behaviors 1–3) by using a strengths-based perspective that emphasizes resilience of informal caregivers and older adults when using assessment tools and informing the client, caregiver, and interdisciplinary team of all findings to inform selection of best practices and evidence-based interventions for treatment (CSWE Gero Competency 8: Intervene With Individuals, Families, Groups, Organizations, and Communities, specialized practice behaviors 1–4). Clinicians engage in developing treatment plans and implementing evidence-based treatments that are preferred by the informal caregiver and that provide a goodness of fit for the informal caregivers presenting biopsychosocial/spiritual needs; communicate and coordinate treatment with the interdisciplinary team and other service providers; and engage in evaluation of desirable outcomes and dissemination and communication of such findings with the caregiver and the interdisciplinary team

(CSWE Gero Competency 9: Evaluate Practice With Individuals, Families, Groups, Organizations, and Communities, specialized practice behaviors 1–4). Clinicians are aware of potential transference and countertransference issues that may present in the therapeutic relationship when working with informal caregivers of older adults.

Transference/Countertransference

When working with informal caregivers of older adults to promote well-being and quality of life, clinicians identify and manage potential sources of transference and countertransference that may present in the therapeutic relationship by engaging in supervision, peer consultations, journaling, counseling, and/or other strategies (CSWE Gero Competency 1: Demonstrate Ethical and Professional Behavior, specialized practice behaviors 1–6) (CalSWEC, 2017). Clinicians manage triggers for transference and countertransference to promote their quality of life and well-being (CSWE Gero Competency 6: Engage With Individuals, Families, Groups, Organizations and Communities, specialized practice behavior 4). Clinicians are aware of technological resources and potential legal/ethical issues that may occur when working with informal caregivers of older adults.

Technological Resources

AARP: Family caregiving: https://www.aarp.org/caregiving/?intcmp=AE-CAR-LRS-IL

AARP: Resources caregivers should know about: https://www.aarp.org/caregiving/local/info-2017/important-resources-for-caregivers.html

American Caregiver Association: https://www.americancaregiverassociation.org/

Caregiver Action Network: http://caregiveraction.org/resources/agencies-and-organizations

Family Caregiver Alliance: https://www.caregiver.org/

National Alliance for Caregiving: https://www.caregiving.org/

National Council on Aging: Resources: https://www.ncoa.org/audience/older-adults-caregivers-resources/?post_type=ncoaresource

Well Spouse Association: https://wellspouse.org/

Legal/Ethical Considerations

When communicating with caregivers of older adults, older adult care recipients, other family members, other care providers, interdisciplinary team members, and/or home- and community-based and interagency providers, clinicians adhere to federal and state laws to protect the privacy and confidentiality of the caregivers of older adults' electronic health and medical records and communications (CSWE Gero Competency 1: Demonstrate Ethical and Professional Behavior, specialized practice behaviors 1, 3, and 7). Clinicians follow organizational, community, county, state, and federal procedures, protocols, policies, and laws to ensure the protection of older adult caregivers' protected health information. Clinicians provide advocacy to improve such procedures and protocols when flaws are identified that violate the ethical and legal rights to privacy and confidentiality of caregivers' protected health information; they further advocate for plans that ensure self-determination and promote tailoring to meet cultural and diversity preferences (CSWE Gero Competency 1: Demonstrate Ethical and Professional Behavior, specialized practice behavior 3 and CSWE Gero Competency 2: Engage Difference in Practice, specialized practice behaviors 3–4).

Critical Thinking Activity/Discussion Questions

1. How are older adult caregivers screened in your agency?
   a. What treatments and interventions are typically provided to caregivers at your agency/organization?
   b. What other resources are available?
   c. What legal/ethical issues have occurred that you are aware of, and how were they addressed?

2. How are older adult caregivers screened in your community or state?
   a. What treatments and interventions are typically provided at community and state levels for caregivers of older adults?
   b. What other resources are available?
   c. What legal/ethical issues have occurred that you are aware of, and how were they addressed?

3. Conduct a Google search to identify the caregiver resources in your community, county, and state.
   a. What types of programs and services are available?
   b. Are there eligibility criteria and/or fees associated?
   c. Are the services and programs sufficient?
   d. What hours are the services provided during the day, evening, and weekend?
   e. What types of services or programs are needed?
   f. Who could you work with to plan caregiver services to address the gaps you identified?

Self-Reflection Exercises

1. Critically examine your own attitudes and beliefs about caregiving for an older adult's wellness.
    a. What did you learn about caregiver responsibilities, tasks, and roles growing up?
    b. From whom did you learn it?
    c. How do those beliefs influence your perceptions on caregiving today?
    d. How might those beliefs affect your ability to engage, assess, and intervene and evaluate best practices with older adults and their caregivers?

2. Critically examine your own attitudes and beliefs about gender norms associated with caregiving for an older adult.
    a. What did you learn about the gender norms of caregiving growing up?
    b. From whom did you learn it?
    c. How do those beliefs influence your attitudes about gender norms in the care of older adults today?
    d. How might those beliefs affect your ability to engage, assess, and intervene with older adults and their caregivers?

References

Adelman, R. D., Tmanova, L. L., Delgado, D., Dion, S., & Lachs, M. S. (2014). Caregiver burden: A clinical review. *JAMA*, *311*(10), 1052–1060.

Aranda, M. & Cherry, D. (2018). A class for families caring for loved ones with memory loss: Findings from Savvy Express. Retrieved from https://roybal.usc.edu/wp-content/uploads/2018/06/Savvy-Express-Info-Sheet-Updated-Final.pdf

American Psychological Association. (2018). Zarit Burden Inventory. Retrieved from http://www.apa.org/pi/about/publications/caregivers/practice-settings/assessment/tools/zarit.aspx

CalSWEC. (2017). CalSWEC curriculum competencies for public child welfare, behavioral health, and aging in California. Retrieved from https://calswec.berkeley.edu/sites/default/files/2017_calswec_curriculum_competencies_0.pdf

Doherty, W. J., McDaniel, S. H., & Hepworth, J. (1994). Medical family therapy: An emerging arena for family therapy. *Journal of Family Therapy*, *16*(1), 31–46.

Family Caregiver Alliance. (2016). Caregiver statistics: Demographics. Retrieved from https://www.caregiver.org/caregiver-statistics-demographics

Heller, T., Gibbons, H. M., & Fisher, D. (2015). Caregiving and family support interventions: Crossing networks of aging and developmental disabilities. *Intellectual and Developmental Disabilities*, *53*(5), 329–345.

Hepburn, K. W., Lewis, M., Sherman, C. W., & Tornatore, J. (2003). The Savvy Caregiver program: Developing and testing a transportable dementia family caregiver training program. *The Gerontologist*, *43*(6), 908–915.

Kuhlenschmidt, S., & Wants, R. A. (2001). Review of memory and behavioral problems and the burden interview. In B. S. Plake & J. C. Impara (Eds.) *The fourteenth mental measurements yearbook*. Buros Institute of Mental Measurements. Lincoln Nebraska: University of Nebraska-Lincoln.

Linville, D., Hertlein, K. M., & Lyness, A. M. P. (2007). Medical family therapy: Reflecting on the necessity of collaborative healthcare research. *Families, Systems, & Health, 25*(1), 85.

Lukens, E. P., & McFarlane, W. R. (2004). Psychoeducation as evidence-based practice: Considerations for practice, research, and policy. *Brief Treatment and Crisis Intervention, 4*(3), 205.

Tyndall, L., Hodgson, J., Lamson, A., White, M., & Knight, S. (2014). Medical family therapy: Charting a course in competencies. In *Medical Family Therapy* (pp. 33–53). Cham, Switzerland: Springer International Publishing.

Zarit, S. H., Todd, P. A., & Zarit, J. M. (1986). Subjective burden of husbands and wives as caregivers: a longitudinal study. *The Gerontologist, 26*(3), 260–266.

CHAPTER 13

Mezzo Practice

Program Planning and Management in Organizations and Communities

Chapter Overview

This chapter identifies mezzo-level strategies and skills for social workers engaged in program planning and management in organizations and communities serving older adults.

CSWE Gero Competencies Highlighted

Competency 1: Demonstrate Ethical and Professional Behavior

Specialized Practice Competency Description: Social workers understand the value base of the profession and its ethical standards, as well as relevant laws and regulations that may impact practice at the micro, mezzo, and macro levels. Social workers understand frameworks of ethical decision-making and how to apply principles of critical thinking to those frameworks in practice, research, and policy arenas. Social workers recognize personal values and the distinction between personal and professional values. They also understand how their personal experiences and affective reactions influence their professional judgment and behavior. Social workers understand the profession's history, its mission, and the roles and responsibilities of the profession. Social workers also understand the role of other professions when engaged in inter-professional teams. Social workers recognize the importance of lifelong learning and are committed to continually updating their skills to ensure they are relevant and effective. Social workers also understand emerging forms of technology and the ethical use of technology in social work practice.

Competency Behaviors: (1) Guided by ethical reasoning and self-reflection, demonstrate adherence to ethical frameworks and key laws, policies, and procedures related to aging, and the rights

of older adults. (2) Engage in active dialogue with field faculty/instructors regarding aging field placement agency policies and culture around behavior, appearance, communication, and the use of supervision. (3) Develop and sustain effective collaborative relationships that respect older adults' needs for protection, self-determination, and the provision of services in the least restrictive environment possible with colleagues and community stakeholders, including older adults, their family members, other care providers, and Tribes. (4) Effectively manage professional boundary issues and other challenges arising in the course of aging-related work, particularly ambiguities presented by home visits, personal loss, trauma, and other highly involved and potentially emotionally triggering aspects of the work. (5) Develop and sustain relationships with members of interdisciplinary and integrated health care teams, including social workers, primary care providers, hospital staff, home health care providers, psychiatrists, psychologists, substance use disorder treatment staff, Tribal service providers, and others, that reflect clear understanding of their roles in providing care to older adults. (6) Demonstrate both knowledge of the history and evolution of social work practice related to aging and older adults in the United States and California, and a commitment to lifelong learning around this practice. (7) Follow all ethical guidelines and legal mandates in the use of technology in order to maintain the confidentiality of all personal, behavioral health, and health-related information. (CalSWEC, 2017, pp. 1–2)

Competency 2: Engage Diversity and Difference in Practice

Specialized Practice Competency Description: Social workers understand how diversity and difference characterize and shape the human experience and are critical to the formation of identity. The dimensions of diversity are understood as the intersectionality of multiple factors, including, but not limited to, age, class, color, culture, disability and ability, ethnicity, gender, gender identity and expression, immigration status, marital status, political ideology, race, religion/spirituality, sex, sexual orientation, and Tribal sovereign status. Social workers understand that, as a consequence of difference, a person's life experiences may include oppression, poverty, marginalization, and alienation as well as privilege, power, and acclaim. Social workers also understand the forms and mechanisms of oppression and discrimination and recognize the extent to which a culture's structures and values, including social, economic, political, and cultural exclusions, may oppress, marginalize, alienate, or create privilege and power.

Competency Behaviors: (1) Engage in critical analysis of the interpersonal, community, and social structural causes and effects of disproportionality, disparities, and inequities in the incidence and trajectory of aging-related care

needs, housing, transportation, and resource access among older adults, their families, and their communities. (2) Evidence respectful awareness and understanding of the impact of being a member of a marginalized group on aging experiences, and accurately identify differences in access to and quality of available services for members of different communities and populations. (3) Demonstrate knowledge of diverse cultural norms and traditional methods of providing care to older adults, as well as an applied understanding of how these realities affect work with older adults from diverse backgrounds, their families, and their communities. (4) Develop and use practice methods that acknowledge, respect, and address how individual and cultural values, norms, and differences impact the various systems with which older adults interact, including, but not limited to, families, communities, primary care systems, mental and behavioral health care systems, and integrated care systems. (CalSWEC, 2017, pp. 3–4)

Competency 3: Advance Human Rights and Social, Economic, and Environmental Justice

Specialized Practice Competency Description: Social workers understand that every person regardless of position in society has fundamental human rights such as freedom, safety, privacy, an adequate standard of living, health care, and education. Social workers understand the global interconnections of oppression and human rights violations, and are knowledgeable about theories of human need and social justice and strategies to promote social and economic justice and human rights. Social workers understand strategies designed to eliminate oppressive structural barriers to ensure that social goods, rights, and responsibilities are distributed equitably and that civil, political, environmental, economic, social, and cultural human rights are protected.

Competency Behaviors: (1) Clearly articulate the systematic effects of discrimination, oppression, and stigma on the needs and experiences of older adults and on the quality and delivery of services available to them, and identify and advocate for policy changes needed to address these issues. (2) Advocate for changes in policies and programs that reflect a social justice practice framework for facilitating access and providing services to older adults, their families, and care providers, especially among underserved groups and communities. (3) Demonstrate the ability to work effectively in cross-disciplinary collaboration to develop and provide interventions that explicitly address the specific needs of diverse older adults, their families, and care providers. (4) Integrate into all aspects of policy and practice sensitivity to the reality that fundamental rights, including freedom and privacy, may be compromised for older adults engaged in care, and the goal that services should be provided in the least restrictive environment possible. (CalSWEC, 2017, pp. 4–5)

Competency 4: Engage in Practice-informed Research and Research-informed Practice

Specialized Practice Competency Description: Social workers understand quantitative and qualitative research methods and their respective roles in advancing a science of social work and in evaluating their practice. Social workers know the principles of logic, scientific inquiry, and culturally informed and ethical approaches to building knowledge. Social workers understand that evidence that informs practice derives from multidisciplinary sources and multiple ways of knowing. They also understand the processes for translating research findings into effective practice.

Competency Behaviors: (1) Demonstrate the ability to understand, interpret, and evaluate the benefits and limitations of various evidence-based and evidence-informed treatment models as they influence practice with older adults. (2) Engage in critical analysis of research findings, practice models, and practice wisdom as they inform aging related practice, including how research practices have historically failed to address the needs and realities of exploited and/or disadvantaged communities, and how cross-cultural research practices can be used to enhance equity. (3) Clearly communicate research findings, conclusions, and implications, as well as their applications to aging practice, across a variety of professional interactions with consumers, families, and multidisciplinary service providers. (4) Apply research findings to aging-related practice with individuals, families, and communities and to the development of professional knowledge about the needs, experiences, and well-being of older adults. (CalSWEC, 2017, pp. 5–6)

Competency 5: Engage in Policy Practice

Specialized Practice Competency Description: Social workers understand that human rights and social justice, as well as social welfare and services, are mediated by policy and its implementation at the federal, state, and local levels. Social workers understand the history and current structures of social policies and services, the role of policy in service delivery, and the role of practice in policy development. Social workers understand their role in policy development and implementation within their practice settings at the micro, mezzo, and macro levels and they actively engage in policy practice to effect change within those settings. Social workers recognize and understand the historical, social, cultural, economic, organizational, environmental, and global influences that affect social policy. They are also knowledgeable about policy formulation, analysis, implementation, and evaluation.

Competency Behaviors: (1) Demonstrate familiarity with relevant statutes, civil codes, and roles of relevant policy entities, including, but not limited to:

- The Older Americans Act
- The Elder Justice Act
- The Patient Protection and Affordable Care Act
- Other local, state, and federal legislation and policies related to older adults
- SAMHSA, HRSA, DHHS, CMS, AoA, and other federal entities
- CDHCS, CDMHC, CHHS, and other state entities
- The National Council on Aging and other advocacy organizations.

(2) Understand and adhere to local policies and procedures that influence community practice with older adults, their families, and other care providers. (3) Engage with the political and legislative arena of aging through involvement with relevant activities, including, but not limited to:

- Maintaining ongoing familiarity with changes to legislation that impacts older adults and the rationale for such changes;
- Reading, analyzing, and communicating in speech and writing about proposed legislation relevant to the aging field; and
- Attending Legislative Lobby Day events in Sacramento.

4) Utilize policy knowledge to effectively develop, implement, and evaluate agency, local, state, and federal policies in the course of aging-related practice. (CalSWEC, 2017, pp. 7–8)

Competency 7: Assess Individuals, Families, Groups, Organizations, and Communities

Specialized Practice Competency Description: Practitioners in aging utilize ecological-systems theory, a strengths-based and person/family-centered framework to conduct assessments that value the resilience of diverse older adults, families, and caregivers. They select appropriate assessment tools, methods and technology, and evaluate, adapt, and modify them, as needed, to enhance their validity in working with diverse, vulnerable and at-risk groups. The comprehensive biopsychosocial assessment takes into account the multiple factors of physical, mental and social well-being needed for treatment planning for older adults and their families. They develop skills in interprofessional assessment and communication with key constituencies to choose the most effective practice strategies. Gero social workers understand how their own experiences and affective reactions about aging, quality of life, loss and grief may affect their assessment and resultant decision-making.

Competency Behaviors: (2) Develop, select, and adapt assessment methods and tools that optimize practice with older adults, their families, caregivers, and communities. (Council for Social Work Education, 2017, pp. 89–90)

Competency 9: Evaluate Practice With Individuals, Families, Groups, Organizations, and Communities

Specialized Practice Competency Description: Social workers understand that evaluation is an ongoing component of the dynamic and interactive process of social work practice with, and on behalf of, diverse individuals, families, groups, organizations and communities. Social workers recognize the importance of evaluating processes and outcomes to advance practice, policy, and service delivery effectiveness. Social workers understand theories of human behavior and the social environment, and critically evaluate and apply this knowledge in evaluating outcomes. Social workers understand qualitative and quantitative methods for evaluating outcomes and practice effectiveness.

Competency Behaviors: (1) Record, track, and monitor consumer engagement, assessment, and intervention data in practice with older adults, their families, and other care providers accurately and according to field education agency policies and guidelines. (2) Conduct accurate process and outcome analysis of engagement, assessment, and intervention data in practice with older adults, their families, and other care providers that incorporates consumer perspectives and reflects respect for older adults' autonomy and independence. (3) Use findings to evaluate intervention effectiveness, develop recommendations for adapting service plans and approaches as needed, improve interdisciplinary team coordination and care integration, and help agency and community policies better support older adults, their families, and their formal and informal care systems. (4) Share both the purposes of such data collection and the overall results of data analysis with older adults, their families, and communities whenever possible, with the goal of engaging them more meaningfully in the evaluation process. (CalSWEC, 2017, pp. 14–15)

Learning Objectives

1. Learners will become aware of mezzo-level management and supervision styles, competencies, and strategies for professional development in organizations serving older adults.
2. Learners will become aware of mezzo-level skills to engage in program planning and evaluation in organizations serving older adults.

3. Learners will identify appropriate organizational-level advocacy skills to ensure the needs of older adults and their families are ethically addressed.
4. Learners will understand the importance of conducting a needs assessment of a community to inform program planning of programs and services for older adults.
5. Learners will identify appropriate community advocacy skills to engage and collaborate with stakeholders when planning community-based programs to serve older adults and/or advocate for policy changes.

Organization Management and Supervision

According to the U.S. Bureau of Labor Statistics (2018), in 2016, there were 682,100 social work jobs in the United States and the projected job growth rate exceeds all other occupations for 2016 to 2026, with a projected 16% job growth increase. There were 650,000 social workers at the BSW and MSW level in 2015 and 350,000 licensed social workers (Council on Social Work Education, 2017). There is a clear need for trained social workers in the workforce in the United States. According to the NASW Workforce Study of 2017 of social work graduates, a nationwide survey in the United States, 92% of all MSW graduates are engaged in direct practice with individuals, families, and/or groups after graduation in comparison to mezzo-level practice with communities comprising 2.6% of positions entered by MSW graduates. Although the percentage of social workers entering management positions after graduation is commonly lower than those entering clinical positions, clinicians interested in securing management and leadership positions can benefit from research and training on successful leadership styles as well as management competencies established for the social work profession.

Clinicians entering into mezzo-level settings serving older adults require a combination of both clinical as well as management/supervisory skills to remain competitive in and secure management and supervisory positions in the workforce. In mezzo-level practice, clinicians may be promoted into the role of a clinical manager or supervisor of an organization serving older adults and their families especially after gaining clinical experience and obtaining licensure. Others may have received management training in their graduate education and sought such training in their field experiences. Regardless of the entry pathway into management and supervisory positions and roles, there are key leadership styles that are indicative of executive-level social work professionals (Goldkind & Pardasani, 2013). In a survey of the more than 1,600 executive directors of health and human service agencies, 393 social work administrators in a national sample completed the Multifactor Leadership Questionnaire (MLQ), a 45-item questionnaire, to determine the effective leadership styles of executive-level social workers (Goldkind & Pardasani, 2013). The sample consisted of PhD, JD, MSW, and BA degree social work executives (Goldkind & Pardasani, 2013). The MLQ measures nine factors of leadership: "idealized influence (attributed)," idealized behavior, inspirational motivation, intellectual stimulation, " individual consideration, contingent reward, management by exception (active), management by exception (passive) and laissez-fairre leadership" (Goldkind &

Pardasani, 2013, p. 580). The nine factors of leadership are grouped into six domains of leadership, which include:

Charisma/Inspirational – Provides followers with a clear sense of purpose that is energizing; a role model for ethical conduct which builds identification with the leader and his/her articulated vision. This factor (style) comprises idealized influence (both attributed and behavior) and inspirational motivation.

Intellectual Stimulation – Gets followers to question the tried and true ways of solving problems; encourages them to question the methods they use to improve upon them.

Individualized Consideration – Focuses on understanding the needs of each follower and works continuously to get them to develop to their full potential.

Contingent Reward – Clarifies what is expected from followers and what they will receive if they meet expected levels of performance.

Active Management-by-Exception – Focuses on monitoring task execution for any problems that might arise and correcting those problems to maintain current performance levels.

Passive Avoidant – Tends to react only after problems have become serious to take corrective action and may avoid making any decisions at all. This factor comprises management by exception (passive) and laissez-faire leadership styles. (Goldkind & Pardasani, 2013, p. 580)

Social work executives with an MSW were more likely to rate themselves as having transformational or charismatic leadership styles, and those with a JD were the least likely to rate themselves as a charismatic/transformational leader (Goldkind & Pardasani, 2013). Executives with a PhD rated themselves as being an effective leader more than those with a JD, MSW, or BSW (Goldkind & Pardasani, 2013). Passive avoidant executives tended to have a BSW, whereas those with an MSW were the least likely among all educational levels of social work executives to rate themselves as passive/avoidant leaders (Goldkind & Pardasani, 2013). Executives with an MSW were satisfied more with their leadership style than those with a PhD (Goldkind & Pardasani, 2013). The study provides clear implications for the importance for social work programs in undergraduate, graduate, dual-degree, and post-graduate levels to prepare social workers with both educational/curricular and direct training in developing effective leadership skills and styles.

The Network for Social Work Management developed competencies for social workers pursuing management and supervisory positions. The competencies, which present a framework for both essential skills for leadership in nonprofit and for-profit agencies, as well as a self-assessment for manager development by supervisors, cover four key domains with respective competencies and performance indicators for "Executive Leadership, Resource Management, Strategic Management and Community Collaboration" (The Network for Social Work Management, 2015, p. 1). Competencies for executive leadership and example performance indicators applied to organizations serving older adults follow. Competency one "establishes, promotes, and anchors the vision, philosophy, goals, objectives, and values of the organization" and involves performance indicators such as the establishment of the organizational mission, values, and relevance to older adults and needs for community-based services for older adults (The Network for Social Work Management, 2015, p. 4). Competency two "possesses interpersonal skills that support the viability and positive functioning of the organization" and involves performance indicators such as a commitment to advancing the organization's values, philosophy, and mission to serve older adults while serving as a model, team player, and inspiration to supervisees and other stakeholders (The Network for Social Work Management, 2015, p. 4). Competency three "possesses analytical and critical thinking skills that promote organizational growth" and involves performance indicators such as the manager/supervisor's knowledge of finances, budget, and allocation of organizational resources to meet diverse needs of older adults (The Network for Social Work Management, 2015, p. 5). Competency four "models appropriate professional behavior and encourages other staff members to act in a professional manner" and involves performance indicators such as modeling and promoting ethical conduct by the social work manger/supervisor, integrity promotion for the agency, professional development, continuing education, and triaging skills for ambiguous situations involving work with older adults and their families (The Network for Social Work Management, 2015, p. 5). Competency five "manages diversity and cross-cultural understanding" and involves performance indicators such as culturally appropriate services, competence by staff, and creating an environment to embrace and learn about diversity and adapt services appropriately when working with older adults and their families (The Network for Social Work Management, 2015, p. 6). Competency six "develops and manages both internal and external stakeholder relationships" and involves performance indicators such as assessing, communicating, and collaborating with external and internal stakeholders at local, state, and national levels, as appropriate, to ensure service needs are adequate for older adults and their families (The Network for Social Work Management, 2015, p. 6). Competency seven "initiates and facilitates innovative change processes" and involves the social work manager/supervisor staying abreast of current evidence-based interventions for treatment with older adults and their families; it also involves stakeholder perspectives with planning and implementation as performance indicator examples (The Network for Social Work Management, 2015, p. 7). In relation to older adults, Competency eight involves social work executives recognizing unmet needs of older adults as well as service gaps and providing advocacy for "public policy change and social justice at national, state, and local levels" (The Network for Social Work Management, 2015, p. 7). Competency nine "demonstrates effective interpersonal and communication skills" and involves performance indicators including the social work executive's ability to articulate to stakeholders the vision and mission of the organization serving older adults sensitively and competently (The Network for Social Work Management, 2015, p. 8). Competency 10 "encourages active involvement of all staff and stakeholders in decision-making processes" and includes performance indicators such as having older adults included in stakeholder collaborations, involving all stakeholders in program changes, and seeking their buy in (The Network for Social Work Management, 2015, p. 8). Competency 11 "plans, promotes, and models life-long learning practices" and involves the social work executive engaging in continued leadership education, providing continued education and encouragement to staff to receive higher education degrees to ensure current best practices based on evidence are provided to older adults in programs, and providing supervision to staff (The Network for Social Work Management, 2015, p. 9). In addition to executive leadership, social work executives should also have competency in resource management within the organization.

The second key domain, resource management, is composed of four competencies: Competency 12 "effectively manages human resources;" competency 13 "effectively manages and oversees the budget and other financial resources to support the organization's/ program's mission and goals to foster continuing program improvement and accountability;" competency 14 "establishes and maintains a system of internal controls to ensure transparency, protection, and accountability for the use of organizational resources;" and competency 15 "manages all aspects of information technology" (The Network for Social Work Management, 2015, pp. 10–11). Competency 12 performance indicators include ensuring the work environment is positive for older adults and staff; exercising fairness in recruiting, training, evaluating, and promoting staff; ensuring a diverse staff to meet the needs of diverse older adult clients; and ensuring the environment does not discriminate against older adult clients or staff (The Network for Social Work Management, 2015). Performance indicators for Competency 13 include managing and monitoring revenue, expenditures, allocation of resources, and outcomes to ensure that the program services are meeting the needs of older adult clients and are consistent with the organization's goals and mission (The Network for Social Work Management, 2015). Competency 14 involves performance indicators for social work managers to develop budgets for the programs and services for older adults, manage risks ethically to protect against liability, maintain accurate financial records, maintain equipment and facilities where services are provided, and establish a revenue accountability system (The Network for Social Work Management, 2015). Competency 15 performance indicators involve a social work manager's ability to incorporate appropriate technological resources to assist the organization in improving processes, tracking program delivery, and monitoring older adult outcomes to ensure that quality services are provided in an efficient manner (The Network for Social Work Management, 2015). In addition to resource management, a third key domain of social work executive competencies is strategic management.

The third key domain, strategic management, involves five competencies and respective performance indicators. Competency 16, fundraising, involves behaviors and actions where the social work manager "identifies and applies for new and recurring funding while ensuring accountability with existing funding systems" (The Network for Social Work

Management, 2015, p. 12). The respective performance indicators include developing a philanthropy culture, working with funders in private and public sectors, applying for grants, and collaborating with appropriate government organizations to fund or partner in provision of programs for older adults (The Network for Social Work Management, 2015). Competency 17, marketing and public relations, occurs when the social work executive "engages in proactive communication about the agency's products and services" (The Network for Social Work Management, 2015, p. 12). The performance indicators include establishing positive relationship with all external constituents, using electronic media, establishing guidelines for communication with constituents, maintaining those relationships, and instilling confidence in the constituents that the organization is competent and trustworthy in providing superior services to older adults (The Network for Social Work Management, 2015). Competency 18 "designs and develops effective programs" and includes performance indicators such as the planning, design, and implementation of programs to meet the needs of diverse older adults; ensuring programs reflect the mission and goals of the organization and are evidence-based with best practices for older adults; and establishing methods and procedures for data entry, collection, tracking, monitoring, and evaluation to ensure the desired effects of the program are being achieved and to ensure the quality of services provided (The Network for Social Work Management, 2015, p. 13). Competency 19 "manages risk and legal affairs" and involves performance indicators involving the social work manager establishing policy procedures and protocols to protect and prevent against potential risk; monitoring all areas within the organization where the potential for risk exists; and ensuring "adherence to all laws, regulations, contracts, and legal agreements" (The Network for Social Work Management, 2015, p. 13). Competency 20 "ensures strategic planning" and involves performance indicators of the social work manager's ability to plan for the success and future of the organization serving older adults; involves staff in the identification of potential areas for growth of the organization as well as planning for short-term, intermediate, and long-term goals to achieve the mission of the organization; and establishes a clear business plan to accomplish goals, objectives, and activities outlined in the strategic plan (The Network for Social Work Management, 2015, p. 13).

Community collaboration, the fourth key domain, is essential to both the future of the organization and potential success by the social work manager to implement the strategic plan formerly described in the third domain, strategic management. The visibility, buy-in, trust, and confidence in the organization by the community, stakeholders, and other constituents is necessary for the long-term sustainability of an organization serving older adults. The fourth key domain involves one competency and respective performance indicators. Competency 21 "builds relationships with complementary agencies, institutions, and community groups to enhance the delivery of services" and involves the performance indicators of a social work manager to work effectively, creating alliances with multiple constituents, such as "businesses, institutions of higher learning, local educational agencies, child care centers, health and human services, employment and job training centers, boards, and other agencies," to assess the needs of older adults, as well as to "enhance program resources, and improve services" to older adults and their families (The Network for Social Work Management, 2015, p. 14).

The Network for Social Work Management recommends the following practices for social work executives, managers, and supervisors to enhance their continued career development: (1) networking with colleagues; (2) provide feedback on performance by supervisors, peers, subordinates, and others; (3) mentoring; and (4) action learning ("progressive job responsibilities/challenging job assignments, hardships, personal reflection/journaling") (2015, p. 18). Additionally, program planning and evaluation skills are essential for all social work executives and managers working in organizations serving older adults as described in competency 18—they are responsible for planning and developing effective programs for older adults.

Program Planning, Logic Models, and Evaluation

According to Timmreck (2003), "planning, program development, and evaluation emerged in the 1980s as a key component of health education and health promotion" and both "planning and evaluation skills are necessary to successful" promotion, education, and prevention services (2003, p. xv). Many programs and services for older adults emphasize health education, prevention, wellness, and other health/behavioral health promotion activities. Timmreck (2003) presents a simple-to-follow 10-step model for program planning that social work administrators, executives, and/or managers can follow in planning a program at their organization. According to Timmreck (2003), step one is to establish a mission statement for the program, which is the main purpose of the program or idea that is "usually based on a general observation, an obvious seen need or interest, or a need assessment or result" (p. 30); "sets forth the basic purpose of the project or program and distinguishes it from other programs;" and "identifies the scope of the program and provides overall direction to the project, program, or service" (p. 33). This differs from the general mission statement of an organization but is often related to the types of services set forth in the organization mission statement philosophy, which tends to be more global and broad. Step two involves completing an "assessment and evaluation of organization, inventory of resources, and review of regulation and policies"—this step includes an internal assessment, external assessment, consideration of organization resources, and a review/consideration of regulations and policies (Timmreck, 2003, pp. 38–39). The social work manager should answer the following two questions for the internal assessment: (1) "does the organization have the ability and resources to do the project?" and (2) "does anyone care if the project is done, i.e., administrators or elderly recipients?" (Timmreck, 2003, p. 38). The resources to consider include: "money and finances; building space; personnel; equipment and materials; transportation; expertise; motivation and commitment; management audit; support for: organization, community/consumer, employees, board" and "plan for evaluation process" (Timmreck, 2003, p. 39). The external assessment requires the social work manager to answer the following four questions: (1) "will the community accept and support the project?" (2) "what are the government regulations affecting the project?" (3) "what are the legal issues?" and (4) "are there any zoning considerations?" (Timmreck, 2003, p. 38). Considerations for the social worker in planning the program for regulations and policies include two key areas, according to Timmreck: (1) "what are the governmental limitations, restrictions, barriers and requirements?" and (2) "what are the policy limitations, restrictions, barriers and requirements?" (2003, p. 39).

Step three involves writing the specific goals and objectives for "need assessments and feasibility studies" and subsequent planning questions for a needs assessment, which include: (1) "what are the overall goals of the needs assessment?" (2) "what needs to be planned using the needs assessment, and what can objectives be written for?" (3) "what specific needs are addressed or ascertained that objectives can be written for?" (4) "what are five to ten general areas the need assessment is to cover?" (5) "what type of need assessment is appropriate for the project at hand?" (6) what specific activities need to be considered and included?" (7) "what activities and objectives need to be accomplished in developing the need assessment form?" and (8)"what specific items or issues need to be included in the need assessment form or process?" (Timmreck, 2003, pp. 67–68).

Step four involves developing and conducting a needs assessment, which is covered in the subsequent community section.

Step five involves determining and setting priorities (Timmreck, 2003, p. 120). What this entails for the social work manager is a consideration of the following: (1) "what are the major gaps in existing services and programs?" (2) "in addition to the gaps in services, what are the all-important identified needs for services and programs that your organization can provide?" and (3) the social worker then makes "decisions, ascertains needs," and sets priorities (Timmreck, 2003, p. 120).

Step six involves writing the goals and objectives for the program once approved by upper administration (Timmreck, 2003). A program goal "reflects the intention of social workers within the program" (Grinnell, Gabor, & Unrau, 2010, p. 57). According to Grinnell, Gabor, and Unrau (2010), all program objectives directed at behavior, knowledge, and effects developed by social workers should be SMART (i.e., specific, measurable, attainable, realistic, with a time frame). A SMART objective that is specific considers "Who? (target population) and What? (action/activity)" and is measurable, addressing whether "the objective is measurable? And if appropriate, how much change is expected?" (Grinnell, Gabor, & Unrau, 2010, p. 61). Social workers writing a SMART objective also consider whether the objective is achievable with the following question: "can the objective be realistically accomplished given the program's current resources and constraints?" (Grinnell, Gabor, & Unrau, 2010, p. 61). Social workers also factor in the realistic nature of the program by writing an objective that both "addresses the scope of the program and proposes reasonable programmatic steps" and has a time frame or a "timeline indicating when the objective will be met" (Grinnell, Gabor, & Unrau, 2010, p. 61).

Step seven involves the activities and procedures for implementing the program (Timmreck, 2003). In step seven, social work administrators answer two key questions: (1) "what needs to be one first? What needs to be done before other activities can take place?"

and (2) "what items or processes need to take place before others can start?" (Timmreck, 2003, p. 138). This step involves a clear depiction of the specific interventions, actions, and activities the program will deliver to older adults; it also outlines clear plans for appropriate outcome measures and indicators, as well as clear methods for data collection at intake and throughout the program to monitor implementation of the program with older adults that will later be used for program evaluation.

Step eight, "develop timeline charts," has to do with the social worker creating and developing charts that detail the specific activities, responsibilities, and actions of various staff to ensure that the program is implemented as planned (Timmreck, 2003).

Step nine, "implementation of the project" entails three key activities: (1) "make final preparation, and plan marketing, community education, an open house, and so on;" (2) "be sure all equipment, services, utilities, licenses, and permits are in place;" and (3) "open the project or service" to older adult clients (Timmreck, 2003, p. 170). Implementation is "the process of putting a project, service, or program into effect to fulfill the planning process and accomplish the setting up and management of the execution of the project" (Timmreck, 2003, p. 170).

The last step, step 10, "evaluation and feedback," requires the social work administrator to consider the following: (1) "are the objectives being met?" (2) "are the activities effective and efficient?" (3) "are timelines being met" (4) "is there a regular formal evaluation system in place, and is it used seriously?" and (5) "conduct impact evaluation and outcome evaluation?" (Timmreck, 2003, p. 186).

According to Grinnell, Gabor, and Unrau, all "evidence-based programs have logic models" that are "tools that help people physically see the interrelations among the various components of programs" at an organization (2010, p. 68). Logic models in social services are "concept maps with narrative depictions of programs in that they visually describe the logic of how social service programs are conceptualized and operationalized" (Grinnell, Gabor, & Unrau, 2010, p. 68). Logic models are presented in columns, which are read from left to right under five areas: resources/inputs, activities, outputs, outcomes (the short-term changes in an older adult client), and impact (which often includes intermediate- and long-term outcomes on expected desirable outcomes for older adult clients, the organization, and/or the community). Logic models visually illustrate the planning phase of program development and implementation under the first two columns. The first column on the left, resources referred to as inputs, include all resources necessary to develop and operate a program (Grinnell, Gabor, & Unrau, 2010). Inputs include a program budget, space, or facilities to run the program in, all staff and/or human resources to implement the program, financial resources, organizational resources, and research required to plan and develop the program (Royse, Thyer, & Padgett, 2010). The second column (to the right of inputs), activities, includes all of the interventions (i.e., counseling, support groups, health, and/or nutrition screening, etc.), services provided in the program, as well as the actions, events, and tasks involved in implementing the program (Royse, Thyer, & Padgett, 2010). The intended outcomes or results of the program are captured in the remaining three columns. The third column, outputs, refers to the "countable products that result from activities (e.g., the number of pamphlets distributed, the number of individual therapy sessions held, the number of clients transported to the day treatment program)," the number of participants attending a group psychoeducation session, etc. (Royse, Thyer, & Padgett, 2010). The fourth column, outcomes, includes all changes in older adult participants that are expected to occur as a result of participating in the program, such as decreased depression, lower anxiety, lower blood pressure, or management of diabetes. The fifth column, impact, includes changes the program are expected to lead to as a result of older adults participating in the program, including intermediate outcomes such as improved life satisfaction, improved quality of life, prevention of hospitalization, maintenance of desired behaviors, attitudes and changes in knowledge, and long-term impacts such as lower health-care costs or the ability of older adult participants to age in place. An example logic model adapted from the Kellogg Foundation (2004) is illustrated in Figure 13.1 from the National Council on Aging's fall prevention coalition logic model for states.

Evaluation involves an examination of whether the goals, objectives, and desirable outcomes of the program for older adults have been achieved. Most commonly, social work administrators consider either or both process and outcome evaluations. A process evaluation includes "procedures, policies, work flow, materials, personnel management, performance appraisals, programmatic performance, quality, administrative effectiveness and efficiency, and other administrative inputs of the implementation process" (Timmreck, 2003, p. 188). Process evaluations allow social work administrators to track the implementation of a program and make modifications to program inputs, activities to improve outputs, and/or short-term outcomes. An outcome evaluation, on the other hand, involves an assessment and analysis of the final outcome of the program activities in creating the desired changes in older adult participants outlined in the goals and objectives of the program. Outcome evaluation is concerned with determining whether the desired changes in behavior, attitudes, and knowledge of older adult participants has been attained. Outcome evaluations, therefore, look at the short-term, intermediate, and long-term outcomes and/or the impact of a program. In addition to program planning and evaluation skills, social workers should be trained in and familiar with organizational advocacy skills to ensure that older adult clients have access to and receive necessary services and programs that can improve their well-being and quality of life.

Organizational Advocacy Skills

According to Jansson, social workers use four key advocacy skills whether they are engaging in micro, mezzo, or macro advocacy: (1) "value-clarifying skills to determine whether to initiate an advocacy intervention in the first place and to conduct their advocacy ethically," (2) "political or influential skills to surmount the disinclination of specific individuals to agree with specific policy advocacy initiatives," (3) "analytic skills to analyze situations and issues to decide what remedies will improve the well-being of specific individuals," and (4) "interactional skills to communicate effectively to persuade others to take specific

FIGURE 13.1. Fall Free Logic Model (National Council on Aging, 2018)

	Inputs	Outputs			Outcomes		
	Using These RESOURCES	We Will Engage in These ACTIVITIES (examples)	And Produce These PRODUCTS	To REACH	Which Yield These Short-Term OUTCOMES	And These Medium-Term OUTCOMES	With These Ultimate Long-Term OUTCOMES
	Data • Injury • Death • Hospitalization • ED • EMS • Program costs • Health care costs Partnerships • Public health • Aging • Health care Programs and Services • Exercise programs • Medication reviews • Vision screening • Home assessments • PT and OT Funding • Core injury • Title IIID • Foundations • Grants • Health care reimbursement	Gather and analyze falls surveillance and cost data Develop statewide awareness campaign • Incorporate unified falls prevention (FP) messaging • Discuss evidence-based (EB) programs Train stakeholders on advocacy, policy changes, and community planning Train stakeholders on FP, EB programs and services Review/adopt EB interventions	Summary of data PSAs, videos, brochures, presentations, flyers, toolkits, training, webinars Compendium of products, EB programs, and services available in the community Policy briefs, fact sheets, etc., for appropriate audiences	Adults 65+ Consumers Health care providers Children of parents in the 65+ Community Caregivers Community service providers Policymakers State Coalition Members Evaluation	Improved surveillance, analysis, and reporting of data Increased public and stakeholder (e.g., policymakers) awareness and appreciation of FP and EB programs and services Increased organizational capacity to provide EB programs and services Increased health care provider knowledge of falls risks and appropriate EB programs and services	Improved integration of program and cost data in decision-making Increased/new fall prevention policy within different sectors Increased participation in EB FP programs Increased numbers of older adults and caregivers making appropriate behavior changes Increased engagement of policymakers Increased numbers of older adults screened for falls risks and referred to appropriate EB programs and services	Demonstration of positive return on investments Recognition that falls are preventable and are not a normal part of aging Incorporation of FP into organizational, health care, and community plans/policies/practices Provision and use of a wide range of FP programs and services in most counties Decrease in falls, fall-related injuries, and fall-related deaths Increase in life expectancy, independence, and quality of life

actions" (2016, p. 57). Jansson further describes eight tasks that advocates at micro, mezzo, and macro levels engage in, referred to as challenges: "challenge 1: deciding whether to proceed;" "challenge 2: deciding where to focus;" "challenge 3: securing attention (i.e., obtaining recognition that a client has an unresolved problem from other staff in an agency [micro] or securing decision makers' attention for a policy issue or problem [mezzo/macro];" "challenge 4: analyzing or diagnosing why a client has an unresolved problem [micro] or why a dysfunctional policy has developed [mezzo/macro];" "challenge 5: developing a strategy to address a client's unresolved problem [micro] or a proposal to address a policy-related problem [mezzo/macro];" "challenge 6: developing support for their strategy to resolve a client's unresolved problem [micro] or to enact a policy proposal [mezzo/macro];" "challenge 7: implementing their strategy [micro] or their enacted proposal [mezzo/macro];" and "challenge 8: assessing whether their implemented strategy [micro] or enacted policy has been effective [mezzo/macro]" (2016, p. 57).

At the case level within an organization, social workers engage in "micro policy advocacy when they advocate for specific individuals or families to help them obtain services, rights, opportunities, and benefits that they would (likely) not otherwise receive and that would advance their well-being" (Jansson, 2016, p. 58). Take, for example, an older adult client whose insurance company is not authorizing a life-saving cancer treatment. A social worker, acting as a micro-level policy advocate, could work with the client to file an appeal and contact a cancer legal advocate if necessary to ensure the older adult client has access to necessary treatments. Social workers also work as mezzo-level policy advocates and may present due to flaws in policies, protocols, and/or procedures within an organization that impact the care and/or continuity of care for older adult clients and their caregivers. According to Jansson, social workers "engage in mezzo policy advocacy at the organizational level when they seek to change dysfunctional policies in agencies" that "impede the provision of service, benefits, and opportunities, as well as the protection of client's rights" (2016, p. 58). The dysfunctional policies may include any of the following policies within an organization: "standard operating procedures, budgets, mission statements and organizational culture, eligibility requirements, selection of staff, allocation and training of staff, evaluation procedures, planning mechanisms, official organizational policies" (Jansson, 2016, p. 58). For example, a social worker on the medical surgery floor discovers that older adult clients are not being asked upon admission through the emergency room of an acute care hospital whether they have an advance health care directive and, if they do not, whether they would like assistance with completing one. The social worker could work with his or her supervisor, managers, and administrators to improve and modify the emergency department intake procedures and protocols to become compliant with the Health Insurance Portability and Accountability Act (HIPAA) of 1996. The changes would be updated in the official organizational policy and procedures manual as well as the unit procedures and protocol manuals, and in-service education could be provided to train all staff on the updated policy, procedures, and protocols for advance health care directives.

Jansson (2016) identified seven red flag or core problem areas that represent potential issues social workers can be on alert for that may signal a need for their involvement in advocacy at micro, mezzo, and/or macro levels, which can be applied to any service delivery context. Applied to health care, the first core problem, ethical rights, may be a red flag alert signaling social work advocacy around areas such as: obtaining informed consent for treatment, necessary medical information to inform decision making (i.e., "risks, diagnosis, prognosis, discussion of treatment planning and timeline"); confidentiality of protected health information, client competency to provide informed consent, and advance health care directives (Jansson, 2016, p. 68). The second core problem, quality of care, involves advocacy needed due to observations of a "lack of evidence-based healthcare, medical errors, whether to have specific diagnostic tests, fragmented care," and "nonbeneficial" or futile treatment (Jansson, 2016, p. 68). The third core problem, cultural content of care, considers a lack in providing information (printed and oral) in the older adult client's language; "communication with patients with limited literacy or health knowledge;" "religious, spiritual, and cultural practices;" and "use of complementary and alternative medicine" (Jansson, 2016, pp. 68–69). The fourth core problem, preventive treatment, may involve red flag signals for advocacy surrounding the lack of preventive screening for wellness; overlooking modifiable risk factors such as "smoking, obesity, lifestyle, substance use;" "chronic disease care;" and "immunizations" (Jansson, 2016, p. 69). The fifth core problem, affordability or access to care, involves identifying and providing advocacy with problems such as "financing necessary healthcare and medications;" the "use of publicly funded programs" and affordability of co-payments as well as eligibility criteria that may exclude those older adults with the greatest risk and need for services; and "coverage from private insurance companies," which often entails an advocacy need due to an insurance company not authorizing a necessary treatment or medication that is nonformulary to the insurance plan (Jansson, 2016, p. 69). The sixth problem, mental health conditions, involves several potential problematic areas a social worker may need to provide advocacy for in health-care settings with older adults: "screening for specific mental health conditions," "treatment of mental health conditions while hospitalized," "follow-up treatment for mental health conditions after discharge," "mental distress stemming from health conditions," "availability of individual counseling and/or group therapy," and "availability of support groups" (Jansson, 2016, p. 69). The seventh core problem, community-based health care, involves identifying and advocating when problems occur surrounding "discharge planning;" "transitions between community-based levels of care;" "referrals to services in communities;" "reaching out to referral sources on behalf of the patient, such as coordinating services, providing a warm handoff, and monitoring or assessing services;" and "assessment of home, community and work environments" (Jansson, 2016, p. 69).

Community

At community levels, there are three key domains social work clinicians should have skills in to work effectively in macro practice: conducting a needs assessment, engaging and collaborating with community members and other constituents, and community advocacy.

Needs Assessment

A needs assessment is conducted to determine the needs of members of a community for programs and services. A thorough needs assessment is a key component of program planning in that the data and results help social work managers and administrators identify service gaps for older adults. All community-based organizations should conduct needs assessments on a regular basis to ensure that their services and programs are tailored to the diverse needs of the older adults residing in the catchment area and services are provided to older adult participants. Needs assessments help program planners and developers understand the demographics of the target population (i.e., gender, age range, race/ethnicity, marital status, language, education, and socioeconomic status); presenting health and nutritional needs; psychological/emotional, social, and spiritual needs and strengths; and more practical information to ensure that the target population has access to the programs and services (i.e., transportation, caregiver assistance, sliding scale, or free services). Needs assessments are defined as "attempts at estimating deficiencies" such as "unmet needs, gaps in services, or problems that have not been previously recognized" (Royse, Thyer, & Padgett, 2010, p. 55). There are eight key steps social work administrators and managers can use to conduct a needs assessment. The task for step one involves considering the parameters of the needs assessment; in this step, the first goal is to understand "the purpose of the needs assessment" (Royse, Thyer, & Padgett, 2010, p. 60). Is the purpose, for example, to plan new services, improve existing services, or understand existing services in the community and/or gaps in services for programs that serve older adults? In step one, the second goal of a needs assessment is to specify "the level of assessment (statewide, community, neighborhood)" (Royse, Thyer, & Padgett, 2010, p. 60). This will influence the stakeholders involved in the needs assessment as well as target interviewees. The third goal is to identify the relevant stakeholders "to include clients or potential clients, program staff, key community leaders, state officials," funders, business owners, other programs, and/or administrators (Royse, Thyer, & Padgett, 2010, p. 60). The fourth goal is to consider the resources that are available to conduct the needs assessment as well as prepare a budget for it (Royse, Thyer, & Padgett, 2010). The fifth goal of step one is to develop a timeline for the planning, implementing, and disseminating of the results of the needs assessment to various stakeholders (Royse, Thyer, & Padgett, 2010).

Step two involves gathering information to inform decision making; in this step, social workers simply consider the question "what do you need to know?" (Royse, Thyer, & Padgett, 2010). What do you need to know, for example, about potential new older adult participants, former participants of other programs, gaps in services, existing services and costs associated with them, preferences for services of older adults, preferences by administrators to meet goals and objectives of the agency, and/or requirements of funders for specific types of services? Step three follows from step two—it involves determining "whether the information needed already exists" to inform decision making or whether it "can be obtained with your resources" (Royse, Thyer, & Padgett, 2010). For example, if the social worker's agency has existing reports or if data from a national repository or local governmental or community organization exists that can be obtained for a fee.

In step four, the needs assessment instrument, measurement methods, and procedures are designed (Royse, Thyer, & Padgett, 2010). In developing the instrument, social workers can determine whether an existing needs assessment with strong reliability and validity exists, whether to use former needs assessments from the agency, or whether to modify an instrument to include supplemental questions to obtain specific information relevant to decision making. Social workers also need to consider whether quantitative, qualitative, and/or mixed methods will be used and whether the needs assessment will be conducted in person (face-to-face interviews or focus groups), by mail, and/or online. Step five involves collection of data outlined by the methods and procedures in step four, entry of data, and analyzation of data for the needs assessment (Royse, Thyer, & Padgett, 2010). Next, the research report from the needs assessment is prepared (step six), followed by dissemination of the report to "key stakeholders to obtain their feedback" (step seven), and lastly, a final formal dissemination of the findings to all other interested stakeholders in a presentation, executive summary, or both (step eight) (Royse, Thyer, & Padgett, 2010).

Engagement/Collaboration

In the social work profession, community engagement and collaboration efforts are often aimed at efforts to improve conditions for vulnerable, marginalized, oppressed, and stigmatized populations. Efforts at the community level consider the residents' or specific target population's well-being and quality of life; safety; health; environmental/ living conditions; access to resources and services to meet basic, health, and behavioral health needs; ensuring financial security, employment, and vocational skills for residents necessary for upward mobility; promoting equality; and addressing civil and ethical rights violations and social injustices through mezzo-level advocacy strategies, interventions, tactics, and skills—for example, civic engagement; grassroots initiatives; community collaborations; coalitions; and national, state, county, and local collaborative initiatives. Social work advocates recognize that engagement and collaborative efforts at the mezzo level of the community require the involvement of multiple stakeholders of residents in the community or neighborhood, service providers, local and/or county officials, law enforcement, task forces, health and human services, and business owners. According to Jansson, advocates at the community level must "be familiar with the fabric of those communities where they engage in community-based work...they have to be versed in developing and maintaining coalitions...they also need skills in working with the mass media, often coaching community members in organizing press conferences, writing press releases, and talking with reporters;" and, in some instances, they have to escalate "conflict to draw attention to specific issues," "to pressure local officials and organizations," and "to get coverage from the mass media" (2011, p. 425).

Collaborations between organizations and stakeholders in communities are often planned and perform specific tasks to ensure the provision of specific services (Jansson, 2016 to residents of a community or specified target population(s) within a community. In some instances, services may be mandated due to national or state policies. One such example is integrative collaborative care, a best practice model for treating comorbid and co-occurring health, substance use, and mental health conditions involving six different levels of collaboration from minimal collaboration (i.e., with providers in separate locations, making referrals to each other and having infrequent contact) within a community (level one) to fully integrated and co-located care where all providers are in the same space and meet face to face to assess, plan with, and treat older adults (level six) (Heath, Wise, Romero, & Reynolds, 2013).

In their discussion of a multidisciplinary model for community collaborative problem solving, Lasker and Weiss describe three proximal outcomes that can inform both practice and research on multidisciplinary collaborative processes to address health issues at community levels: (1) "empower individuals by getting them directly and actively involved in addressing problems that affect their lives;" (2) "create bridging social ties that bring people together across society's dividing lines, build trust and a sense of community, and enable people to provide each other with various kinds of support;" and (3) "create synergy—the breakthroughs in thinking and action that are produced when a collaborative process successfully combines the knowledge, skills, and resources of a group of diverse participants" (2003, p. 21). The model (Figure 13.2), referred to as the *Model of Community Health Governance,* presents a flowchart social work leaders and managers can use to inform their community-level mezzo practice interventions using collaborative problem solving to address a specific issue in the community, such as community health (Lasker & Weiss, 2003). The following mezzo-level policy advocacy skills described by Jansson and Heidemann (2016) can be used by social workers in community engagement and collaboration efforts.

FIGURE 13.2. Model of Community Health Governance (Lasker & Weiss, 2003, p. 18)

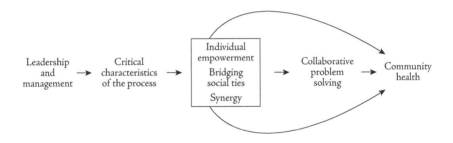

Community Advocacy Skills

Jansson and Heidemann describe five key skills social workers should have to engage in mezzo-level (community) policy advocacy: "initiating, influencing, negotiating and bargaining, mediating conflicts," and "communicating" (2016, pp. 108–109). The initiating skill involves advocates' initiation of interventions designed to change policies—"this is a critical skill, because failure to take initiative often means the wishes of other individuals and officials prevail *even when they lead to dysfunctional policies*" (Jansson & Heidemann, 2016, p. 108). This skill requires advocates to be assertive while professionally bringing issues to the table without starting a conflict (Jansson & Heidemann, 2016). The influencing skill has to do with the ability of the advocate to "influence other people to work with them to change specific policies" (Jansson & Heidemann, 2016, p. 108). Influence can come from having established professional working relationships with a variety of community constituents and consumers, a positive image, a good reputation and credibility, and internal and external resources of the advocate and the organization he or she represents. The negotiating and bargaining skill enables advocates to "negotiate and bargain with agency and community leaders to achieve their policy goals" (Jansson & Heidemann, 2016, p. 108). This skill involves knowing the perspectives and positions of stakeholders, potential responses to your position/proposal for change by various stakeholders, collaboration, and the art of recognizing when negotiation is most appropriate or feasible for achieving incremental, minor, or major policy changes. When stakeholder conflicts occur, the mediating conflicts skill enables advocates to (1) "mediate by identifying points or issues that competing groups have in common," (2) "help participants identify compromises," and (3) "use process skills in task groups and committees to facilitate positive outcomes" (Jansson & Heidemann, 2016, p. 109). Advocates use communicating skills with "concerned citizens, agency heads, community leaders, public officials and other people who can help resolve specific issues" (Jansson & Heidemann, 2016, p. 109). Jansson and Heidemann underscore that the communication skills used by mezzo-level advocates differ from those used by clinicians at micro/case levels as mezzo-level advocates: (1) "often want to analyze broader issues that impact the quality and nature of services and programs," (2) "want data that shed light on the nature of specific issues," (3) "want to examine policy and program options," and (4) "want to know the cost of proposed reforms" (2016, p. 109).

Technological Resources

Association for Community Health Improvement: Community Health Assessment Toolkit: http://www.healthycommunities.org/Resources/toolkit.shtml

Center for Community Health and Development: Cultural competence (Sections 1–11): https://ctb.ku.edu/en/table-of-contents/culture/cultural-competence

Centers for Disease Control and Prevention: Communities of Practice: Develop SMART objectives: https://www.cdc.gov/phcommunities/resourcekit/evaluate/smart_objectives.html

Centers for Disease Control and Prevention: Communities of Practice: Resource kit: https://www.cdc.gov/phcommunities/resourcekit/index.html

Centers for Disease Control and Prevention: Framework for program evaluation: https://www.cdc.gov/eval/framework/index.htm

National Association of County and City Health Officials: Mobilizing for action through planning and partnerships (MAPP): https://www.naccho.org/programs/public-health-infrastructure/performance-improvement/community-health-assessment/mapp

National Association of Social Workers: Advocacy: https://www.socialworkers.org/Advocacy

National Association of Social Workers: Policy issues: https://www.socialworkers.org/advocacy/policy-issues

National Association of Social Workers: Social justice: https://www.socialworkers.org/Advocacy/Social-Justice

The Network for Social Work Management: https://socialworkmanager.org/

The Network for Social Work Management: Competencies: https://socialworkmanager.org/competencies/

The Network for Social Work Management: Programs: https://socialworkmanager.org/programs/

The Network for Social Work Management: Resources: https://socialworkmanager.org/resources/

Critical Thinking Activity/Discussion Questions

1. Consider your role as a potential or current social work executive, manager, or supervisor at an organization serving older adults.
   a. Which of the six leadership styles described by Goldkind and Pardasani (2013) characterizes your leadership style? Are you satisfied with your current leadership style: yes or no? Describe why.
   b. Review the competencies of social work managers and supervisors described by the Network for Social Work Management. In which competencies do you need further professional development? How will you seek education/training to further develop these competencies?

2. Identify an organization where treatment of older adults occurs in a service-delivery context you are familiar with or want to learn more about/work in (i.e., long-term care, health care, mental health, substance use, inpatient/outpatient, private practice, a specific community-based organization, integrated health-care clinic, adult day health-care center, home health, or hospice agency, etc.).
   a. What type of program could be beneficial to older adults served by the organization that are not currently provided by the organization?
   b. Apply each of Timmreck's (2003) 10 steps to plan the program for your organization.
   c. Create a logic model for the program you are planning.
   d. Discuss whether a process evaluation, outcome evaluation, or both would be beneficial.
   e. Which mezzo-level skills described by Jansson (2016) could assist your efforts?

3. Identify a community or neighborhood with which you would like to engage in collaboration and community-/neighborhood-wide service planning.
    a. Discuss how you could conduct a needs assessment of the community or neighborhood using the seven steps described by Royse, Thyer, and Padgett (2010).
    b. Discuss engagement and collaboration strategies you could employ to plan services to meet a need in the community or neighborhood for older adults.
    c. Which mezzo-level policy advocacy skills described by Jansson (2016) could assist your efforts?

Self-Reflection Exercises

1. Consider an organization where treatment of older adults occurs in a service delivery context you are familiar with or want to learn more about/work in (i.e., long-term care, health care, mental health, substance use, inpatient/outpatient, private practice, a specific community-based program, integrated health care, etc.).
    a. Refer back to Jansson's (2016) seven core problems presented in this chapter. Identify potential and/or observed problems for each of the seven core problems in the service context that may signal a red flag for a social worker to provide advocacy.
    b. What advocacy skills do you need to engage in advocacy at the organizational level?
    c. What resources are available/do you need to support your advocacy efforts?
    d. Reflect on the NASW Code of Ethics, and consider the pros and cons of providing advocacy for the issue you identify.

        i.   What risks are there in not providing advocacy? To older adults? To the organization as whole?
        ii. What benefits are there for older adults? The organization?
        iii. Consider the pros and cons as a professional for providing advocacy or not providing advocacy to address the issue (i.e., concerns of retaliation, being fired, safety, loss of license, adherence to the NASW Code of Ethics, job satisfaction, etc.).
        iv. How would you proceed after weighing the pros and cons?
        v.   Who could you consult to inform your decision making on best practices for your advocacy plan that adheres to the NASW Code of Ethics?

2. Identify an issue or problem that occurs for older adults in communities (in urban, rural, suburban, or residential settings). Review the NASW Code of Ethics. Consider each of the following:
    i.   What risks are there in not providing advocacy? To older adults? To the community as whole?

ii. What benefits are there for older adults, the community, and for you yourself in providing advocacy?

iii. Consider the pros and cons as a professional for providing advocacy or not providing advocacy to address the issue.

iv. How would you proceed after weighing the pros and cons?

v. Who could you consult to inform your decision making on best practices for your advocacy plan that adheres to the NASW Code of Ethics?

References

CalSWEC. (2017). CalSWEC curriculum competencies for public child welfare, behavioral health, and aging in California. Retrieved from https://calswec.berkeley.edu/sites/default/files/2017_calswec_curriculum_competencies_0.pdf

Council on Social Work Education. (2017). Profile of the social work workforce. Retrieved from https://www.cswe.org/Centers-Initiatives/Initiatives/National-Workforce-Initiative/SW-Workforce-Book-FINAL-11-08-2017.aspx

Goldkind, L., & Pardasani, M. (2013). Social workers as senior executives: Does academic training dictate leadership style? *Advances in Social Work*, (14)2, 573–593.

Grinnell Jr, R. M., & Unrau, Y. A. (2010). *Social work research and evaluation: Foundations of evidence-based practice*. New York, NY: Oxford University Press.

Heath, B., Wise Romero, P., & Reynolds, K. (2013). *A standard framework for levels of integrated care*. Washington, DC: SAMSHA-HRSA Center for Integrated Health Solutions.

Jansson, B. S. (2011). *Improving healthcare through advocacy: A guide for the health and helping professions*. Hoboken, NJ: John Wiley & Sons.

Jansson, B. S. (2016). *Social welfare policy and advocacy: Advancing social justice through 8 policy sectors*. Los Angeles: Sage Publications.

Jansson, B. S., & Heidemann, G. (2016). Engaging in mezzo policy advocacy. In B. S. Jansson (Ed.) *Social welfare policy and advocacy: Advancing social justice through 8 policy sectors* (pp. 107–135). Los Angeles: Sage Publications.

Lasker, R. D., & Weiss, E. S. (2003). Broadening participation in community problem solving: A multidisciplinary model to support collaborative practice.

National Council on Aging. (2018). Falls free logic model. Retrieved from https://www.ncoa.org/resources/falls-free-logic-model/

Royse, D., Thyer, B., & Padgett, D. (2010). *Program evaluation: An introduction*. Belmont, CA: Wadsworth.

The Network for Social Work Management. (2015). Human services management competencies. Retrieved from https://socialworkmanager.org/competencies/professionals/

Timmreck, T. C. (2003). *Planning, program development, and evaluation: A handbook for health promotion, aging, and health services*. Sudbury, MA: Jones & Bartlett Learning.

U.S. Bureau of Labor Statistics. (2018). *Occupation outlook handbook: Social workers*. Retrieved from https://www.bls.gov/ooh/community-and-social-service/social-workers.htm

Credits

Figure 13.1: National Council on Aging, www.ncoa.org/resources/falls-free-logic-model/. Copyright © 2018 by National Council on Aging.

Figure 13.2: Roz D. Lasker and Elisa S. Weiss, *Journal of Urban Health*, vol. 80, no. 1, pp. 18. Copyright © 2003 by Springer Nature.

CHAPTER 14

Macro Practice

Policy Advocacy at County, State, Federal, and Global Levels

Chapter Overview

This chapter identifies macro-level policy advocacy skills and strategies social workers engaged in service delivery and advocacy with older adults can develop and engage in for policy advocacy strategies at local, state, federal, and global levels.

CSWE Gero Competencies Highlighted

Competency 1: Demonstrate Ethical and Professional Behavior

Specialized Practice Competency Description: Social workers understand the value base of the profession and its ethical standards, as well as relevant laws and regulations that may impact practice at the micro, mezzo, and macro levels. Social workers understand frameworks of ethical decision-making and how to apply principles of critical thinking to those frameworks in practice, research, and policy arenas. Social workers recognize personal values and the distinction between personal and professional values. They also understand how their personal experiences and affective reactions influence their professional judgment and behavior. Social workers understand the profession's history, its mission, and the roles and responsibilities of the profession. Social workers also understand the role of other professions when engaged in inter-professional teams. Social workers recognize the importance of lifelong learning and are committed to continually updating their skills to ensure they are relevant and effective. Social workers also understand emerging forms of technology and the ethical use of technology in social work practice.

Competency Behaviors: (1) Guided by ethical reasoning and self-reflection, demonstrate adherence to ethical frameworks and key laws, policies, and procedures related to aging, and the rights of older adults. (2) Engage in active dialogue with field faculty/instructors regarding aging field placement agency policies and culture around behavior, appearance, communication, and the use of supervision. (3) Develop and sustain effective collaborative relationships that respect older adults' needs for protection, self-determination, and the provision of services in the least restrictive environment possible with colleagues and community stakeholders, including older adults, their family members, other care providers, and Tribes. (4) Effectively manage professional boundary issues and other challenges arising in the course of aging-related work, particularly ambiguities presented by home visits, personal loss, trauma, and other highly involved and potentially emotionally triggering aspects of the work. (5) Develop and sustain relationships with members of interdisciplinary and integrated health care teams, including social workers, primary care providers, hospital staff, home health care providers, psychiatrists, psychologists, substance use disorder treatment staff, Tribal service providers, and others, that reflect clear understanding of their roles in providing care to older adults. (6) Demonstrate both knowledge of the history and evolution of social work practice related to aging and older adults in the United States and California, and a commitment to lifelong learning around this practice. (7) Follow all ethical guidelines and legal mandates in the use of technology in order to maintain the confidentiality of all personal, behavioral health, and health-related information. (CalSWEC, 2017, pp. 1–2)

Competency 2: Engage Diversity and Difference in Practice

Specialized Practice Competency Description: Social workers understand how diversity and difference characterize and shape the human experience and are critical to the formation of identity. The dimensions of diversity are understood as the intersectionality of multiple factors, including, but not limited to, age, class, color, culture, disability and ability, ethnicity, gender, gender identity and expression, immigration status, marital status, political ideology, race, religion/spirituality, sex, sexual orientation, and Tribal sovereign status. Social workers understand that, as a consequence of difference, a person's life experiences may include oppression, poverty, marginalization, and alienation as well as privilege, power, and acclaim. Social workers also understand the forms and mechanisms of oppression and discrimination and recognize the extent to which a culture's structures and values, including social, economic, political, and cultural exclusions, may oppress, marginalize, alienate, or create privilege and power.

Competency Behaviors: (1) Engage in critical analysis of the interpersonal, community, and social structural causes and effects of disproportionality, disparities, and inequities in the incidence and trajectory of aging-related care needs, housing, transportation, and resource access among older adults, their families, and their communities. (2) Evidence respectful awareness and understanding of the impact of being a member of a marginalized group on aging experiences, and accurately identify differences in access to and quality of available services for members of different communities and populations. (3) Demonstrate knowledge of diverse cultural norms and traditional methods of providing care to older adults, as well as an applied understanding of how these realities affect work with older adults from diverse backgrounds, their families, and their communities. (CalSWEC, 2017, pp. 3–4)

Competency 3: Advance Human Rights and Social, Economic, and Environmental Justice

Specialized Practice Competency Description: Social workers understand that every person regardless of position in society has fundamental human rights such as freedom, safety, privacy, an adequate standard of living, health care, and education. Social workers understand the global interconnections of oppression and human rights violations, and are knowledgeable about theories of human need and social justice and strategies to promote social and economic justice and human rights. Social workers understand strategies designed to eliminate oppressive structural barriers to ensure that social goods, rights, and responsibilities are distributed equitably and that civil, political, environmental, economic, social, and cultural human rights are protected.

Competency Behaviors: (1) Clearly articulate the systematic effects of discrimination, oppression, and stigma on the needs and experiences of older adults and on the quality and delivery of services available to them, and identify and advocate for policy changes needed to address these issues. (2) Advocate for changes in policies and programs that reflect a social justice practice framework for facilitating access and providing services to older adults, their families, and care providers, especially among underserved groups and communities. (3) Demonstrate the ability to work effectively in cross-disciplinary collaboration to develop and provide interventions that explicitly address the specific needs of diverse older adults, their families, and care providers. (4) Integrate into all aspects of policy and practice sensitivity to the reality that fundamental rights, including freedom and privacy, may be compromised for older adults engaged in care, and the goal that services should be provided in the least restrictive environment possible. (CalSWEC, 2017, pp. 4–5)

Competency 5: Engage in Policy Practice

Specialized Practice Competency Description: Social workers understand that human rights and social justice, as well as social welfare and services, are mediated by policy and its implementation at the federal, state, and local levels.

Social workers understand the history and current structures of social policies and services, the role of policy in service delivery, and the role of practice in policy development. Social workers understand their role in policy development and implementation within their practice settings at the micro, mezzo, and macro levels and they actively engage in policy practice to effect change within those settings. Social workers recognize and understand the historical, social, cultural, economic, organizational, environmental, and global influences that affect social policy. They are also knowledgeable about policy formulation, analysis, implementation, and evaluation.

Competency Behaviors: (1) Demonstrate familiarity with relevant statutes, civil codes, and roles of relevant policy entities, including, but not limited to:

- The Older Americans Act
- The Elder Justice Act
- The Patient Protection and Affordable Care Act
- Other local, state, and federal legislation and policies related to older adults
- SAMHSA, HRSA, DHHS, CMS, AoA, and other federal entities
- CDHCS, CDMHC, CHHS, and other state entities
- The National Council on Aging and other advocacy organizations.

(2) Understand and adhere to local policies and procedures that influence community practice with older adults, their families, and other care providers. (3) Engage with the political and legislative arena of aging through involvement with relevant activities, including, but not limited to:

- Maintaining ongoing familiarity with changes to legislation that impacts older adults and the rationale for such changes;
- Reading, analyzing, and communicating in speech and writing about proposed legislation relevant to the aging field; and
- Attending Legislative Lobby Day events in Sacramento.

(4) Utilize policy knowledge to effectively develop, implement, and evaluate agency, local, state, and federal policies in the course of aging-related practice. (CalSWEC, 2017, pp. 7–8)

Learning Objectives

1. Learners will become aware of macro-level policy advocacy skills for legislative levels (county, state, federal, and global).

2. Learners will become aware of macro-level framework for international-level policy advocacy.
3. Learners will become aware of macro-level issues affecting older adults.
4. Learners will understand frameworks for developing and writing a policy issue brief addressing macro-level issues affecting older adults.

Policy Advocacy Skills and Strategies

Advocates seeking to propose new policy proposals or modify existing policies affecting older adults at legislative and international levels must both understand specific skills required of macro-level policy advocates as well as competencies and the context for macro-level policy advocacy at legislative levels within the United States and internationally.

Macro-Level Policy Advocacy Skills

Jansson (2016) describes specific skills macro-level policy advocates should have to engage in advocacy at legislative and international levels. The first skill, *developing an overarching strategy*, involves seven steps: (1) "organizing a team or coalition that will spearhead the project, with leadership provided by an existing advocacy group or by a new group;" (2) "establishing policy goals, such as whether to advocate incremental change or basic change;" (3) "specifying a proposal's content," which often includes a policy issue brief; (4) "establishing a style," such as conflictual or nonconflictual;" (5) "deciding who does what, including who meets with specific people, who makes certain presentations, who does the research, and who develops a list of supporters; (6) implementing "the strategy using the various influence and power resources;" and (7) "revising the strategy in light of changing events as the process unfolds" (Jansson, 2016, p. 155). The second skill, "*diagnosing who stands where—and recruiting people to a cause*," involves assessing stakeholders and identifying who supports, does not support, or is moderate/undecided on the issue; it also involves recruiting legislators who have the power and influence to persuade other legislators to support the policy advocacy proposal (Jansson, 2016, p. 156).

The third skill, "*framing issues to gain support*," involves using key words in describing policy advocacy proposals salient to legislators and their constituents, such as "prevention, improving health, increasing opportunity, increasing upward mobility," or "increasing fairness" (Jansson, 2016, p. 156). The fourth skill, "*networking and coalition building*," involves the cultivation of relationships within networks that can be drawn upon as a strategy to lower opposition to the policy advocacy proposal (Jansson, 2016, p. 156). The fifth skill, "*managing conflict*," involves the advocates' use of strategies to manage opposition to the policy proposal, such as persuading "specific legislators that their views of a policy proposal are based on incorrect assumptions about it or knowledge of it," stressing "specific facets of the proposal that spur opposition to it," seeking "support from influential legislators who are widely admired by other legislators," modifying proposals to decrease the controversial nature of it, touching bases "with likely opponents or swing voters so that they can decrease the level of their opposition to them," and/or anticipating "opposition by examining prior voting patterns of legislators on similar policy proposals" (Jansson, 2016, p. 157).

The sixth skill, *"using procedural power,"* involves strategies to promote passage of a measure they support, such as convincing "prominent and influential legislators to sponsor their legislation," attempting to "route their measures to those legislative committees and subcommittees that will be favorable to them," and making efforts to "get hearings for their policy proposals before legislative committees" (Jansson, 2016, p. 157). The seventh skill, *"developing and using personal power resources,"* involves the building of credibility by the advocate in the eyes of legislators through a history of transactions using "personal power resources" to gain credibility of stakeholders and decision makers that policy advocates seek to influence (Jansson, 2016, p. 157). Personal power resources include: (1) "expertise based on our professional and other knowledge;" (2) "reward power to the extent that other people believe we have and will use inducements," such as recognition, friendship, favors, or increased support from their constituents; (3) "coercive power to the extent that other people believe we can withhold inducements or impose penalties, such as excluding them from deliberations, harming their reputations," or decreasing support from their constituents; (4) "authority to the extent that others believe we hold powerful or influential positions that might ultimately help or harm them;" (5) "charisma to the extent that other people respond positively to our requests because of our personal qualities;" and (6) substantive power "as other people come to see us as able to improve policy proposals or to make changes in them that are viewed as correctable or advisable" (Jansson, 2016, pp. 157–158).

The eighth skill, *"developing credible proposals,"* involves the policy advocates' ability to "demonstrate that they will be effective in addressing specific problems or issues" through demonstrated support of experts, research, and funders (Jansson, 2016, p. 158). The ninth skill, *"negotiating skills,"* involves the advocates' ability to be an effective negotiator, allowing for appropriate give and take and making concessions artfully to ensure the proposal moves forward with support (Jansson, 2016, p. 158). The 10th skill, *"developing power by changing legislator's environment,"* involves strategies to influence legislators' decisions on a policy proposal, such as placing "pressure on them by using social media to lead many people to send them messages on Facebook, Twitter, and other social media sites—messages that urge them to take or refrain from specific actions...working with advocacy groups" to place pressure on legislators; "participating in electoral politics;" organizing "specific parts of legislators' constituencies, such as homeless people, low-income people," or "residents of public housing;" and/or raising "funds for specific constituencies" (Jansson, 2016, p. 158). The 11th skill, *"developing personal connections,"* involves developing personal "relationships with public officials;" "learning their hobbies, discovering mutual friendships, and seeing them at a number of occasions;" or empathizing "with them about the significant challenges public life brings to them, such as the loss of autonomy, hectic work schedules, and exposure to criticism in the mass media" (Jansson, 2016, pp. 158–159).

Jansson (2011) also describes four basic skills and accompanying competencies for each that macro-level policy advocates should have to address issues at legislative and international levels affecting older adults. The first, *"analytic skills,"* involves skills at evaluating social issues, developing proposals to address them, analyzing the extent of the issue, identifying potential barriers to "policy implementation," and developing "strategies for assessing programs" (p. 86). The accompanying competencies for analytic skills for policy advocates follow:

> developing a proposal, calculating tradeoffs, using social science research, conducting a marketing study, using the internet, working with budgets, finding funding sources for specific projects, diagnosis audiences, designing a presentation, diagnosing barriers to implementation, designing strategy to improve implementation, developing political strategy, analyzing the content of policies and issues, designing policy assessments, and selecting a policy practice style (Jansson, 2011, pp. 89–90).

The second basic skill, *"political skills,"* involves both the development and use of power as well as implementing an appropriate "political strategy" (Jansson, 2011, p. 86). The competencies that accompany political skills, according to Jansson, include: "using the mass media," "taking a personal position," "advocating a position with a decision maker," "seeking positions of others," "empowering others," "orchestrating pressure on decision makers," finding resources to fund advocacy projects," "developing and using personal power resources," "donating time/resources to an advocacy group," advocating for the needs of a client," "participating in a demonstration," initiating litigation to change policies," "participating in a political campaign," and "voter registration" (2011, pp. 88–89).

The third basic skill, *"interactional skills,"* involves persuasion skills to gain support for a policy proposal and participating in "task groups, such as committees and coalitions" (Jansson, 2011, p. 86). Specific competencies for interaction skills that policy advocates should possess include: "coalition building," "making a presentation," building personal power," "task group formation and maintenance," and "managing conflict" (Jansson, 2011, p. 90). The fourth and final basic skill, *"value-clarifying skills,"* enables policy advocates to "identify and rank relevant principles when engaging in policy practice," which involves one competency, "engaging in ethical reasoning," in both community and public settings (Jansson, 2011, pp. 86–90).

With a basic understanding and development of the key skills required of macro-level policy advocates as basic skills and relevant competencies to the strategy for addressing an issue affecting older adults, social work advocates can assess the context and prepare to develop their policy advocacy strategy and/or proposal.

Legislative-Level Context (Municipal, County, State, Federal)

Clinicians may choose to engage in macro-level advocacy at legislative levels when they determine that the micro-level and mezzo-level advocacy efforts are insufficient to address an issue affecting older adults at municipal, county, state, or federal levels and or macro-level policy advocacy is part of an overall advocacy plan involving a combination of micro- and/or mezzo-level advocacy along with macro-level policy advocacy. Clinicians must first have a basic understanding of the policy context. Jansson describes necessary information all clinicians should know about the macro-level context before formulating a policy advocacy proposal or plan: "the executive branch of government; legislatures; advocacy groups; elected officials; connections among interest groups, legislators, and bureaucrats…public opinion, regulations, and legal action" (2016, pp. 138–146). Clinicians must have a basic understanding of the executive branch of government, which includes: "elected officials (heads of government, including mayors, governors, and presidents; legislators (at the local, state, and federal levels); and people appointed to special bodies" (Jansson, 2016, p. 138). When identifying appropriate stakeholders to target policy proposal to, clinicians should also be aware of key unelected officials as well as lobbyists and/or special interest groups. Unelected officials include those appointed by local government officials, such as civil servants (Jansson, 2016). Lobbyists and interest groups include those who "represent a wide range of corporations, unions, professions, and nongovernmental organizations," such as the National Association of Social Workers (NASW) (Jansson, 2016, p. 138). They should understand the legislative process and be aware of how legislative proposals are introduced and become laws at local, state, and national levels (Jansson, 2016). The legislature "are usually divided into two houses, such as the House of Representatives and the Senate at the federal level, or the Senate and the Assembly at the state level" (Jansson, 2016, p. 139). Advocates may work with specific advocacy groups to formulate policy advocacy proposals and demonstrations to bring an issue affecting older adults into the eye of the public by developing policy issue briefs presented through the media, social media, news conferences, at Senate or House hearings, or at local-level town halls, city councils or chamber of commerce meetings. Advocacy groups "may be community groups, coalitions, think tanks, public interest groups, or professional groups," such as the American Association of Retired Persons (AARP), National Council on Aging, Justice in Aging, and NASW (Jansson, 2016, p. 142). In understanding the perspectives of elected officials, Jansson recommends the following strategies to help advocates: "study the following: public opinion polls; recent outcomes of other elections in comparable districts; the mail you receive; the views of subgroups within your constituency;" and "the preferences of state or national organizations" (2016, p. 143). For example, the NASW has position statements and letters to officials for a variety of issues affecting vulnerable, marginalized, stigmatized, and oppressed populations. Clinicians should be aware of and identify potential collaborative connections among special interest groups, bureaucrats, and legislators as "they can be tapped" into "for technical advice or for the support of a specific measure" (Jansson, 2016, p. 145). Clinicians should be aware of the vulnerability of bureaucrats "to public opinion because scandals or unpopular decisions can ruin political appointees' and even civil servants' careers" (Jansson, 2016, p. 145). Additionally, legislators who seek re-election often align their decisions with their constituents, voters, and/or other supporters. Regulations "shape the content of specific publicly funded programs because they define the program details not contained in the statutes that established them" and legal action may be a means for achieving policy advocacy goals of advocates (Jansson, 2016, p. 145).

Global-Level Advocacy Framework

The ability of a policy advocate to get a global policy initiative considered is often dependent on the skill of the advocate in developing a strategy that makes the proposal a priority for international legislators to adopt. Shiffman and Smith (2007) developed a framework policy advocates can draw from in developing policy advocacy strategies that address the political context of international advocacy. They describe four key categories that advocates should consider when developing strategies and proposals to secure international decision makers' attention and ultimately increase the likelihood that their strategy or proposal will be adopted: (1) *"actor power,"* described as "the strength of the actors involved in the initiative;" (2) *"ideas,"* described as "the power of the ideas they use to portray the issue;" (3) *"political contexts,"* described as "the nature of the political contexts in which they operate;" and (4) *"issue characteristics,"* described as "characteristics of the issue itself" and summarized in Figure 14.1 (Shiffman & Smith, 2007, p. 1370). For each of the four categories, Shiffman and Smith (2007) identify specific factors that advocates can consider that shape the political priority of an issue they seek to change at an international level. Although the framework was created for global health initiatives, it can be adapted to other international issues affecting older adults such as poverty, abuse and/or neglect, homelessness, long-term care needs, mental health, substance use, and/or co-occurring disorders.

The first category, *actor power,* has four specific factors for advocates to consider in developing international strategies and proposals to address issues affecting older adults: "policy community cohesion, leadership, guiding institutions," and "civil society mobilization" (Shiffman & Smith, 2007, p. 1371). Factor one, *policy community cohesion*, involves the extent of agreement on the salience of an issue and actions to address it among stakeholders involved at an international level, such as the World Health Organization, United Nations, nongovernmental organizations, government organizations and officials, academic institutions and scholars, and funders. According to Shiffman and Smith, "policy communities that agree on basic issues such as how the problem should be solved are more likely to acquire political support than are those that are divided by such issues;" this is often due to the nature of politicians to be "more likely to listen to those in agreement as authoritative sources of knowledge" (2007, p. 1371). Factor two, *leadership*, involves leaders who are credible and accepted members of the political community that provide a strong vision and plan for the policy proposal (Shiffman and Smith, 2007). Factor three, *guiding institutions*, says that those who coordinate and implement the policy proposal or strategy to address an issue (Shiffman and Smith, 2007) are essential to the maintenance and monitoring of any programs or solutions to ensure desired goals and outcomes (short-term, intermediate, and long-term impact) are reached. Factor four, *civil society mobilization*, involves allying with grassroots organizations to increase the likelihood that political stakeholders will adopt the proposal or strategy (Shiffman and Smith, 2007).

FIGURE 14.1. The Four Categories for the Framework on Determinants of Political Priority for Global Initiatives (Shiffman & Smith, 2007, p. 1371)

	Description	Factors shaping political priority
Actor power	The strength of the individuals and organisations concerned with the issue	1. Policy community cohesion: the degree of coalescence among the network of individuals and organisations that are centrally involved with the issue at the global level 2. Leadership: the presence of individuals capable of uniting the policy community and acknowledged as particularly strong champions for the cause 3. Guiding institutions: the effectiveness of organisations or coordinating mechanisms with a mandate to lead the initiative 4. Civil society mobilisation: the extent to which grassroots organisations have mobilised to press international and national political authorities to address the issue at the global level
Ideas	The ways in which those involved with the issue understand and portray it	5. Internal frame: the degree to which the policy community agrees on the definition of, causes of, and solutions to the problem 6. External frame: public portrayals of the issue in ways that resonate with external audiences, especially the political leaders who control resources
Political contexts	The environments in which actors operate	7. Policy windows: political moments when global conditions align favourably for an issue, presenting opportunities for advocates to influence decision makers 8. Global governance structure: the degree to which norms and institutions operating in a sector provide a platform for effective collective action
Issue characteristics	Features of the problem	9. Credible indicators: clear measures that show the severity of the problem and that can be used to monitor progress 10. Severity: the size of the burden relative to other problems, as indicated by objective measures such as mortality levels 11. Effective interventions: the extent to which proposed means of addressing the problem are clearly explained, cost effective, backed by scientific evidence, simple to implement, and inexpensive

The second category, *ideas*, has two factors for policy advocates to consider: the *"internal frame"* (factor five) and *"external frame"* (factor six) (Shiffman & Smith, 2007, p. 1371). Shiffman and Smith note that "frames that resonate internally … unify policy communities by providing a common understanding of the definition of, causes of, and solutions to the problem," whereas "frames that resonate externally … move essential individuals and organizations to action, especially the political leaders who control the resources that initiatives need" (2007, p. 1372). The third category, *political contexts*, also has factors for policy advocates to consider in developing policy proposals and strategies to address an issue affecting older adults: *"policy windows"* (factor seven) and the *"global governance structure"* (factor eight) (Shiffman & Smith, 2007, p. 1372). Policy windows is the context in which an issue has salience worldwide and creates a window for movement on a strategy of policy by advocates with decision makers and leaders at national and international levels, such as the AIDs epidemic (Shiffman & Smith, 2007). Policy windows frequently open after natural disasters, after "discoveries" such as a new medication to cure a disease or vaccination, or during forums such as conferences or summits held by the United Nations or World Health Organization (Shiffman & Smith, 2007, p. 1372). The global governance structure is the "set of norms, shared beliefs on appropriate behavior" and "the institutions that negotiate and enforce these norms," such as those enforced and monitored in "international treaties, laws, and declarations" for sectors such as "trade, the environment and health" (Shiffman & Smith, 2007, p. 1372).

The fourth category, *issue characteristics*, has three factors for policy advocates to inform the framing of their strategy or policy advocacy proposal to address an issue affecting older adults: *"credible indicators"* (factor nine), *"severity"* (factor 10), and *"effective interventions"* (factor 11) (Shiffman & Smith, 2007, p. 1372). *Credible indicators* have to do with the fact that when there are credible indicators of an issue established through research that are measurable, policymakers may be more inclined to adopt the proposal due to the severity of the issue being confirmed and developed measures being readily available for monitoring the short-term, intermediate, and long-term outcomes of an initiative proposed to address the issue (Shiffman & Smith, 2007, p. 1372). Severity has to do with the magnitude of the problem, prevalence, and incidence in comparison to other issues international and national decision makers are faced with making decisions about—those that may "cause substantial harm, as indicated by subjective measures such as numbers of deaths, are more likely to attract resources than are those that do not, since policymakers will perceive harmful problems as more serious" (Shiffman & Smith, 2007, p. 1372). Effective interventions—which have been scientifically proven through research, are efficient and cost effective, have identifiable outcome measures, and are easy to implement and monitor—are more likely to be adopted by policymakers than those that lack an evidence base (Shiffman & Smith, 2007, p. 1372).

At international, national, state, and local levels, policy advocates for older adults should be aware of key macro issues that affect older adults that influence their overall well-being and quality of life.

Macro Issues Affecting Older Adults

In the United States, among macro issues that have been predominant over the past two decades, health-care reform has received much debate and attention, particularly with concerns about the growth and rising costs of Medicare and Medicaid programs, rising national health-care costs, and projected new beneficiaries receiving Social Security due to baby boomers entering into retirement and/or semiretirement. Solvency of both Medicare and Social Security programs has been the source of much debate over the past 20 years as well. Additionally, with recessions and the Great Recession, continued cuts to programs for older adults garnished attention. Specifically, ensuring the continued funding of the aging network programs offered under the Administration on Aging's (AoA) network of Area Agencies on Aging that fund vital community-based programs that enable older adults to age in place with their biopsychosocial/spiritual needs met, such as home-delivered meals, legal services, housing assistance, protective services, long-term care ombudsman services, and caregiver and respite care programs. By conducting a comprehensive search of the literature, advocates can identify issues they can provide macro-level policy advocacy to address at micro, mezzo, and macro levels locally, nationally, and internationally. Financial security and the issue of poverty has been a macro policy issue in the United States for decades; programs such as Social Security and Supplemental Security Income (SSI) have been projected to go bankrupt for the past two decades as baby boomers retire and the dependency ratio of beneficiaries to workers increases. Ensuring adequate cost of living adjustments and solvency of these key financial safety net programs are critical to the well-being and health of older adults.

Health-Care Reform

Enacted in 2010, the Patient Protection and Affordable Care Act, signed into law by President Barack Obama, represented landmark health-care reform in the United States, equivalent in size and significance to the passage of Medicare and Medicaid signed into law by President Lyndon B. Johnson in 1965 (Centers for Medicare and Medicaid Services, 2018a). The Patient Protection and Affordable Care Act opened up immediate cost savings for older adults with prescription medications through a rebate the first year of implementation, followed by closing of the donut hole or coverage gap for out-of-pocket expenses beneficiaries incurred for medications. Myriad preventive and wellness screening and services were added for Medicare beneficiaries to ensure the screening, detection, and treatment of chronic illnesses among older adults. Denial of coverage for pre-existing coverage was a key provision as well, ensuring that older adults with chronic and life-threatening illnesses could not be denied for having a pre-existing condition. Another key provision placed greater accountability on federal agencies to collect data that could be used to track, monitor, address, and prevent health disparities by collecting data on ethnic and racial minority status, disability, primary language, sex, and developing measures to collect data that could be used to understand and address health disparities for lesbian, gay, bisexual, and transgender (LGBT) older adults (Office of Minority Health, 2017).

According to President Obama, the law also began "the process of transforming health care payment systems, with an estimated 30% of traditional Medicare payments now flowing through alternative payment models like bundled payments or accountable care organizations," contributing to a "sustained period of slow growth in per-enrollee health care spending and improvements in health care quality" (2016, p. 525).

The proposed American Health Care Act, which the House of Representatives passed on May 4, 2017, but not the Senate, would not have changed reductions to Medicare spending established under the Affordable Care Act to Medicare benefit or Advantage plans (Kaiser Family Foundation, 2018a); however, with an age tax provision, it could have allowed insurance companies to charge older adults five times more for their premiums than premiums under the Affordable Care Act (National Council on Aging, 2017). On February 9, 2018, President Donald Trump signed the Bipartisan Budget Act of 2018 into law, which introduced changes to Medicare Part D enacted (Kaiser Family Foundation, 2018b) and ended the individual mandate from the Affordable Care Act. Advocates for older adults must continue to monitor health-care reform initiatives, identify the impact on older adults, and provide advocacy to prevent enactment of provisions that have negative impacts on the health and well-being of older adults. To inform micro-, mezzo-, and macro-level advocacy, advocates should have a basic understanding of both Medicare and Medicaid and stay up to date on current benefits provided by the respective programs.

Medicare

Until 2003, Medicare had three key health-care coverage parts referred to as Part A (acute care), Part B (outpatient care), and Part C (Medicare Advantage programs). In 2003, with the enactment of the Medicare Modernization and Prescription Drug Act, Part D (prescription drug coverage) was added as a key benefit for Medicare beneficiaries. Medicare Part A covers stays in acute care hospitals and other inpatient settings; skilled nursing facilities, when there is a qualifying stay from an acute care hospital; hospice; and some home health care (Kaiser Family Foundation, 2017a). Beneficiaries may have deductibles ($1,340 in 2018) for some benefits and co-insurances for inpatient and skilled nursing stays that exceed normal lengths of stay (Kaiser Family Foundation, 2017a). Medicare Part B covers outpatient services including primary care and specialty care, preventive and other outpatient services, as well as home health care (Kaiser Family Foundation, 2017a). Medicare B generally has a co-insurance of 20% (Kaiser Family Foundation, 2017a), which is why it is important for older adults who have Medicare as their primary insurance to have a secondary insurance that picks up the 20%; otherwise they are responsible for paying the 20% as a co-payment. Part B benefits are available to beneficiaries for a premium ($134 monthly in 2018) (Kaiser Family Foundation, 2017a). For low-income beneficiaries with SSI and Medicaid, the Part B premium is paid, and beneficiaries referred to as dual eligible enrollees (Medicare/Medicaid) typically have full coverage for outpatient services. Part C, Medicare Advantage, comprises 33% of Medicare beneficiaries (roughly 19 million in 2017) (Kaiser Family Foundation, 2017a). With Part C Medicare, beneficiaries can enroll in a health maintenance organization (HMO) that often offers benefits, such as health club membership, and manages the beneficiaries of Medicare Part A, Part B, and Part D, with many services providing preauthorization from insurance and an order from the primary care physician. Medicare beneficiaries who elect to enroll in Part C Advantage programs may also enroll in a preferred provider organization (PPO), which allows them to receive outpatient specialty services without a referral from the primary care physician and preauthorization from the insurance company. With PPOs, there may be co-insurances and deductibles that are higher for providers who are out of network compared to in network.

Medicare beneficiaries electing a Part C Advantage program may also enroll in a private health plan. All three options (HMO, PPO, and private) provide Part A and B benefits, with most Part C plans also providing Part D benefits (Kaiser Family Foundation, 2017a). Medicare Part D, a voluntary prescription drug benefit, had 42 million beneficiaries enrolled in 2017 benefits (Kaiser Family Foundation, 2017). Part D plans, through "stand-alone prescription drug plans (PDPS) and Medicare Advantage drug plans (MA-PD plans)," unless a beneficiary meets low-income criteria, require "monthly premiums and cost sharing for prescriptions, with costs varying by plan," and "those who do not receive low-income subsidies pay 5 percent of total drug costs after reaching the catastrophic coverage threshold" (Kaiser Family Foundation, 2017a, p. 4). Premiums for Part D in 2018 ranged from $13 monthly to $74.80 monthly for beneficiaries with high incomes (Kaiser Family Foundation, 2017a). Provisions within the Bipartisan Budget Act of 2018 are projected to change Medicare Part D in the following ways: The coverage gap will be closed in 2019 rather than 2020 by "accelerating a reduction in beneficiary coinsurance from 30 percent to 25 percent;" beginning in 2018, manu-facturers of brand-name medications will increase discounts from 50% to 70%; in 2019, biosimilars will begin to be "treated the same as other brand-name drugs in the Part D coverage gap, with manufacturer discounts of 70 percent;" and both Part B and Part D will see income-related premium increases from the initial 80% to 85% for individual beneficiaries with incomes of $500,000 or more or couples with incomes of $750,000 or more (Kaiser Family Foundation, 2018b).

Eligibility criteria for Medicare includes: older adults and their spouses if either had 10 years or 40 quarters of tax contributions for Medicare; disabled adults ages 65 or younger who contributed 10 years of Medicare tax contributions; and individuals with end-stage renal disease (U.S. Department of Health and Human Services, 2018b). In 2017, older adults comprised 49.8 million of the total 58.5 million Medicare beneficiaries (Centers for Medicare and Medicaid Services, 2018c).

Medicaid

Medicaid is a key safety net health insurance program for low-income beneficiaries. In September 2018, more than 66 million individuals were enrolled in Medicaid based on data collected from 49 states by the Centers for Medicare and Medicaid Services (2018b). In 2018, older adults represented 6 million of the total 75.1 million Medic-aid beneficiaries (Centers for Medicare and Medicaid Services, 2018c). According to the Centers for Medicare and Medicaid Services, "federal law requires states to cover certain groups of individuals," such as with the following mandatory eligibility groups: blind, disabled, older adults who meet SSI requirements, "low income families, qualified pregnant women and children, and individuals receiving Supplemental Security Income (SSI)" (2018d, para. 2–6).

Each state determines the types of optional benefits and services they will offer Medicaid beneficiaries, such as physical and occupational therapy, medications, and case management; however, all states are required to provide mandatory benefits, such as "inpatient and outpatient hospital services, physician services, laboratory and x-ray services, and home health services" (Centers for Medicare and Medicaid Services, 2018b). Although the federal government sets the minimum standards for Medicaid programs overseen by states, states have flexibility over eligibility, benefits, premiums and cost sharing, delivery system and provider payment, and waivers (Figure 14.2) (Kaiser Family Foundation, 2017b). States often further devolve Medicaid programs and Section 1115 waiver programs down to the county level, where local decision makers can tailor services to the needs of beneficiaries within a county/municipality.

FIGURE 14.2. State Responses to Program Options in Medicaid

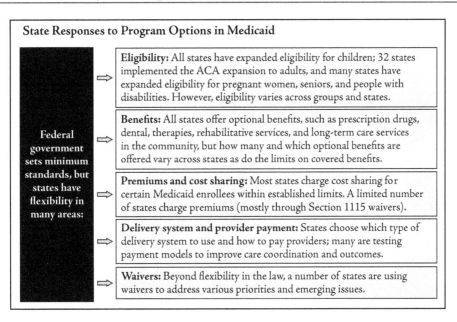

Eligibility for Medicaid for older adults is based on qualified citizenship (i.e., born in the United States or in a qualified immigrant category for citizenship) though states generally offer emergency Medicaid for immigrants without citizenship. The eligibility for older adults is also based on income; some older adults may meet low-income eligibility requirements and have co-insurances or deductibles they have to pay out of pocket each month before Medicaid picks up remaining costs for benefits incurred that month. The federal poverty level (FPL) is used to calculate eligibility for Medicaid; in 2018, the FPL for an individual was $12,140 annually and $16,460 for a couple and in both Alaska and Hawaii, the FPL amounts are higher (U.S. Department of Health and Human Services, 2018a). Advocates can screen older adults' income to determine eligibility for Medicaid by considering the following income and asset tests follow: (1) Qualified Medicare Beneficiaries (QMB) "100% of FPL + $20:" monthly income of $1,032 and asset limits of $7,560 for individuals or monthly income of $1,392 and asset limits of $11,340 for couples; (2) "Specified Low-Income Beneficiaries (SLMB) 120% of FPL + $20:" monthly income of $1,234 and asset limits of $7,560 for individuals or monthly income of $1,666 and asset limits of $11,340 for couples; and (3) "Qualified Individuals (QI) 135% of FPL + $20:" monthly income of $1,386 and asset limits of $7,560 for individuals or monthly income of $1,872 and asset limits of $11,340 for couples (Centers for Medicare and Medicaid Services, 2018b).

The monthly share of costs and co-insurances can create financial burdens and dilemmas for vulnerable low-income older adults who are below, at, or just above the FPL. For some older adults, with each addition of a new medication or required treatment for a chronic or life-threatening illness, they become faced with making decisions between treatment and health care or paying rent or a utility bill or purchasing food. Mr. Jones, a 73-year-old non-Hispanic White male, was one such client. He lived alone, was single, received Social Security/SSI, was a dual-eligible enrollee (Medicare/Medicaid), and his income was $875 per month at the time the social worker saw him. He was living in a studio apartment with a shared bathroom for three other tenants and paid $575 per month for rent. He had no children, and his two siblings lived out of state. He had been on a waiting list for subsidized low-income housing for seven years. His budget for food, transportation, medications, and utilities was $300 per month. He had heart disease and diabetes and had just been diagnosed during a recent hospitalization with chronic obstructive pulmonary disease (COPD) and began using a walker at that time. The social worker was referred to Mr. Jones because he had not filled his medications; the social worker found out two of the new medications were nonformulary and his insurance did not cover them. The social worker called the pharmacist and requested the pharmacist contact Mr. Jones's physician to identify a medication covered under his insurance. Mr. Jones informed the social worker that his income barely met his expenses each month and he could not afford the cost of one of the medications—an inhaler for his COPD. With Mr. Jones's consent, the social worker enrolled him in a local Medi-Cal (the name of Medicaid in California) Section 1115 case management waiver program that assisted him with affordable low-cost transportation, low-cost congregate and home-delivered meals, an emergency response pendant, and discounted utility rates for low-income older adults. They also assisted him with obtaining a section 8 voucher close to the local senior center. He also qualified for an in-home supportive services caregiver to assist him with IADLs such as shopping, laundry, and getting him to his doctors' appointments. At the time of his discharge by the social worker, Mr. Jones was attending the senior center twice a week and began attending the Better Breathers Club and Pulmonary Education Program at the local hospital. It is the availability of programs provided by the AoA and

Aging Network providers, such as those accessed by Mr. Jones, that ensures older adults can remain in the community with their needs met and out of institutions. The need for advocacy of continued funding is critical to continuance of such programs for vulnerable older adults such as Mr. Jones.

Funding Administration on Aging Programs

Another key area advocates can target macro-level advocacy efforts toward is that of maintaining requested funding to the Administration on Community Living (ACL) to ensure that programs for older adults and their caregivers administered by the AoA under the Older Americans Act are not cut. The budget request to Congress from the ACL for fiscal year 2017 was $2.076 billion, representing an increase of $28.4 million from the budget in 2016 that was enacted (Administration for Community Living, 2017). In 2018, the ACL requested a budget of $1.851 billion, a decrease of "$109,666,242 below the annualized FY 2017 Continuing Resolution level" (Administration for Community Living, 2018a, p. 3). The budget request by the ACL to Congress for 2019, $1.781 billion, represents a "decrease of $171,582,000 below the FY 2018" (Administration for Community Living, 2018b, p. 3). With the recent trend of decreased budgets to the ACL, there is a clear need for advocacy to ensure that services provided to older adults and their families, critical to the well-being of older adults, continue to receive full funding.

The AoA is "one of the Nation's largest providers of home and community-based care for older persons and their caregivers" (Administration for Community Living, 2018c, p. 1). Cuts to programs and services provided by AoA networks put older adults at risk for having unmet needs, hospitalizations, and/or premature institutionalization. The Older Americans Act of 1965 established the AoA; it is an agency located within the U.S. Department of Health and Human Services (HHS) (Administration for Community Living, 2018c). The AoA partners with the National Aging Network, "which consists of 56 State Units on Aging, 629 Area Agencies on Aging, 256 Tribal and Native organizations, 20,000 service providers, and thousands of volunteers" (Administration for Community Living, 2018c, p. 1). The mission of the AoA is to "develop a comprehensive, coordinated and cost-effective system of home and community-based services that helps elderly individuals maintain their health and independence in their homes and communities" (Administration for Community Living, 2018c, p. 1).

The partnership of the National Aging Network and AoA, often referred to as the Aging Network, provides services to older adults and their families through grants to states authorized under the Older Americans Act, categorized under six core services: support; nutrition; preventive health; national family caregiver support; elder rights; and service to Native Americans, Native Hawaiians, and Native Alaskans (Administration for Community Living, 2018c). The first core service, *support services*, includes home- and community-based services such as transportation; adult day care; referral and information through programs such as 211 for health and human services; and in-home care (Administration for Community Living, 2018c). The second core service, *nutrition services*, provides congregate (i.e., at a senior center, adult day care, or other community setting) and home-delivered meals (Meals on Wheels) (Administration for Community Living, 2018). The third core service, *preventive health services,* includes programs and services that "promote healthy lifestyles through physical activity, appropriate diet and nutrition," health screenings, and education on the importance of engaging in health prevention activities daily (Administration for Community Living, 2018c, p. 2). The fourth core service, *National Family Caregiver Support program,* offers caregivers and family members "individual and group counseling...training for caregivers, and respite care" (Administration for Community Living, 2018b, p. 2). The fifth core service, *elder rights services,* includes services such as "pensions counseling, legal assistance," "elder abuse investigations" in community settings, and the "Long-Term Care Ombudsman program" to investigate complaints in long-term care settings (Administration for Community Living, 2018c, p. 2). The sixth core service, *service to Native Americans, Native Hawaiians, and Native Alaskans,* provides outreach and support to address the "high prevalence of chronic diseases, the challenges of accessing care and support for persons living in rural settings, and the environmental impact on health" (Administration for Community Living, 2018c, p. 2). Policy advocates can also focus their efforts on issues pertaining to Social Security and SSI.

Social Security and Supplemental Security Income

Social Security and SSI are essential income sources for older adults. In June 2018, 47.3 million older adults ages 65 and older received Social Security, with 45.1 million receiving Social Security alone, 987,000 receiving SSI alone, and 1.3 million receiving both Social Security and SSI (Social Security Administration, 2018a). Social Security has commonly been referred to as one of the three key legs of retirement, along with pensions, savings and investments. The fourth leg of retirement, work, may be a personal choice for some or a necessity for many low-income older adults to meet their basic needs. Following the Great Depression in the United States, President Roosevelt signed into law the Social Security Act on August 14, 1935 (Social Security Administration, 2018b). Prior to the passage, in 1934, President Roosevelt formed a committee on economic security to "develop a comprehensive social insurance system covering all major economic hazards with a special emphasis on unemployment and old age insurance" (Social Security Administration, 2018b, para. 4). Adults who are at least 61 years and 9 months of age can apply for Social Security; benefits can start at the age of 62 or up to the age of 70 (Social Security Administration, 2018c). Those who apply earlier than full retirement age (ages 66 to 67, depending on the year they are born) have reduced benefits (Social Security Administration, 2018d). SSI provides a supplement to Social Security for those older adults at or below the FPL with limited resources, or it provides an income to older adults ages 65 and older with both limited income and resources who are U.S. citizens or in an eligible immigrant category (Social Security Administration, 2018e). The resources counted for SSI eligibility in 2018 was $2,000 for individuals and $3,000 for couples (Social Security Administration, 2018e). If an older adult who is not eligible for Social Security is receiving general relief and food stamps, those benefits discontinue once the

SSI benefits begin. Both Social Security and SSI beneficiaries are eligible for Medicare; however, older adults who are only eligible for SSI (i.e., spouse and applicant did not work long enough to be eligible) typically receive only Medicaid unless they have a health condition or disability qualifying them for Medicare, such as end-stage renal disease or blindness. To receive Social Security, older adults or their spouse need to have worked in a job at least 10 years or 40 quarters with Social Security taxes deducted. Older adults who are widows or widowers whose spouse earned Social Security may receive survivor benefits. Advocates interested in efforts to ensure these two vital financial security programs remain solvent and are not cut for older adults can monitor proposals affecting the Social Security trust fund and get engaged in local, state, and national efforts.

As part of macro practice, advocates can develop policy issue briefs for: legislative advocacy to inform and/or garnish the attention of stakeholders and the public about an issue affecting older adults requiring action; to raise the awareness of and interest in joining in an advocacy effort to address the issue with other professional and advocacy groups; to share policy briefs through social media and the press to gain mass attention to the issue; and writing issue briefs for professional journals and advocacy organizations.

Developing a Policy Issue Brief

Policy advocates require basic skills to successfully prepare a policy issue brief that will get the attention of the intended target audience. Policy briefs should have clear language, avoid the use of jargon; present a clear and logical argument for change; use evidence to support the arguments; and provide charts or graphs as visual aids when appropriate to summarize data or key points. Policy issue briefs generally start off with a description of the issue that includes the context, affected population, scope of the problem, argument for why action change must occur, and the recommended policy action. The brief should provide a summary of the magnitude or significance of the issue, using prevalence and incidence data. Policy briefs present options available to address the issue and provide a clear argument supporting the option recommended by the advocate(s). The length of the policy issue brief depends upon the purpose and intended audience. For example, a policy issue brief may be short—one to two pages if the target audience is legislators and the purpose is for lobbying. For policy issue briefs with a target audience such as administrators or executives of health-care organizations with a purpose of summarizing a new policy such as the Affordable Care Act and how it impacts current procedures, policies and protocols, the policy brief may be extensive in length and begin with an executive summary of one to two pages. Two frameworks follow that advocates can use for developing policy issue briefs. Both frameworks can be modified to the target audience and purpose of the policy issue brief.

Jansson defines a policy brief used for legislative lobbying as one that "comprises an analysis of an existing law, their proposal, why they want to change the existing policy, and the likely objections to their policy" (2011, p. 408). Before preparing a policy issue brief for legislative lobbying, Jansson (2011) recommends, because many legislators are lawyers, that advocates seek opinion from legal experts on the issue early on to best frame the issue brief with awareness of how implementation of the policy advocacy proposal would affect existing laws. Once advocates know the issue affecting older adults they seek to provide policy advocacy for, they can state to targeted stakeholders in the policy issue brief: (1) "what they are concerned about;" (2) "how their issue affects other areas, such as likely costs and effects on other programs or laws;" (3) "an array of possible remedies with their likely costs and implementation problems; (4) "an initial proposal (not yet in the form of a legislative bill) that addresses the problem;" and (5) "the likely arguments of opponents" (Jansson, 2011, p. 408). The policy issue brief for legislative lobbying should be no more than one to two pages in length to increase the likelihood a busy legislator will read the issue brief in its entirety (Jansson, 2011). The policy issue brief is a tool used by advocates to orient legislators to the position of the advocate(s) (Jansson, 2011). The legislative lobbying policy issue brief should further be written in the context of considering other likely policy solutions brought forward by opponents to the advocates' recommended policy option (Jansson, 2011). The following framework is a tool for writing a policy issue brief—it should contain the following succinct information: (1) a statement of the *"policy issue"* and "recommendations" for policy action to address the issue (i.e., the proposed action); (2) a *"summary and analysis of issues"* describing the "current situation," the optimal situation, and what is needed to address the issue; (3) a summary of *"available options"* to address the issue, listing the pros and cons of each option to address the issue (here the advocate can select existing policy options to address the issue, modify a current policy option or law, or present a new policy option to address the issue); (4) the *"recommendation"* from the formerly summarized available policy options and a rationale for why it is the best option; and (5) *"implementation factors"* outlining succinctly the impact of the policy on other laws once implemented (Jansson, 2011, pp. 409–411).

The second framework, a four-step model for writing a health policy brief, may also be useful for advocates interested in writing policy issue briefs one to four pages in length to address health-related issues affecting older adults. Wong, Green, Bazemore, and Miller note five different types of health policy briefs advocates may select from: (1) a "policy one-pager" that has a target audience of professionals/peers, such as "family medicine providers, others in primary care;" (2) a "policy brief" up to four pages in length that targets "policy makers, health professionals, and journalists;" (3) a "policy white paper" that may be 10 or more pages in length targeting "policy makers and health professionals;" (4) a "research brief" approximately six pages in length targeting "local policy and community decision makers, health and environment professionals;" and (5) an "issue brief" nine pages or more in length targeting "policymakers, journalists, and the general public" (2017, p. 23).

The four steps to writing a health policy brief, summarized in Table 14.1, include: step 1: "define the problem," step 2: "state the policy," step 3: "make your case," and step 4: "discuss the impact" (Wong, Green, Bazemore, & Miller, 2017, pp. 22–23). Advocates can use a variety of technological resources to inform their policy advocacy efforts. Example policy briefs may be found at the Urban Institute's website and Kaiser Family Foundation, as well as social justice briefs on the NASW's website.

TABLE 14.1   Four Steps to Writing a Health Policy Brief (Wong, Green, Bazemore, & Miller, 2017, pp. 22–23)

Step	Instructions for Writing the Step
Step 1: Define the problem	a. What is the issue or the problem? Why is it important? b. Why now? Who is impacted and who cares? c. When defining your problem, be specific to your audience and clearly frame the issue. Who has the influence to make a change that will address this problem? [Note:] If the audience is expected to be policymakers (and their staff), community leaders (grassroots), industry or nongovernmental organization executives, the problem should be defined in terms relevant to their policy intervention, respectively.]
Step 2: State the policy	a. Identify 1–3 specific policy actions that will address the problem. [Note:] In a focused policy brief, the goal is to limit the menu of potential actions to target a policy approach of interest.]
Step 3: Make your case	a. Display and describe relevant data using 1–2 figures or tables. b. Declare potential bias based on the data sources. c. Refer to other related policies that are not discussed. Redirect to other policy references when possible or appropriate.
Step 4: Discuss the impact	a. Briefly discuss the implications of both action and inaction. b. Analyze estimated pros and cons of the policy action. c. Consider intended and unintended consequences. d. Address opposing arguments. e. Conclude with a restatement of how this policy specifically addresses this problem.

Source: Shale L. Wong, et al., "Four Steps to Writing a Health Policy Brief," *Families, Systems, & Health*, vol. 35, no. 1, pp. 22-23. Copyright © 2017 by American Psychological Association.

Technological Resources

Administration for Community Living: https://www.acl.gov/about-acl/administration-aging

American Association of Retired Persons: https://www.aarp.org/about-aarp/policies/

American Planning Association: https://www.planning.org/policy/

American Society on Aging: http://www.asaging.org/key-initiatives

Centers for Medicare and Medicaid Services: https://www.cms.gov/

Kaiser Family Foundation: https://www.kff.org/

Mental Health America: Advocacy Network: http://www.mentalhealthamerica.net/issues/advocacy-network

National Association of Social Workers: Advocacy: https://www.socialworkers.org/Advocacy

National Association of Social Workers: Policy issues: https://www.socialworkers.org/advocacy/policy-issues

National Association of Social Workers: Social justice: https://www.socialworkers.org/Advocacy/Social-Justice

National Council on Aging: For advocates: https://www.ncoa.org/for-advocates/

Older Persons Advocacy Network: http://www.opan.com.au/

The Urban Institute: https://www.urban.org/

Critical Thinking Activity/Discussion Questions

1. Identify an issue affecting older adults that you could engage in policy advocacy in at a legislative level.
   a. Why is it important?
   b. How many older adults are impacted by the issue?
   c. Is it a local, county, state, national, and/or international issue?
      i. What evidence is needed to demonstrate that it is an issue?
   d. What do you think should be done to address the issue?
   e. Who should be involved in addressing the issue?

2. Describe how you would apply each of the seven skills described by Jansson (2016) that macro-level policy advocates should have to engage in legislative advocacy.
   a. Developing an overarching strategy—consider how each of the seven steps applies to your advocacy strategy:
      i. How might the steps look different if your advocacy plan targeted a specific community, city, county, state, or nation?
   b. Diagnosing who stands where and recruiting people to a cause:
      i. Who are the key stakeholders? Supporters? Opponents?
      ii. Which legislators or decision makers would you like to persuade?
   c. Framing issues to gain support:
      i. Which key words are important to include to make the proposal salient to legislators, decision makers, and/or their constituents?
   d. Networking and coalition building:
      i. Which networks or coalitions could be beneficial to your advocacy plan?
   e. Managing conflict:
      i. Which strategies could be useful to manage opposition to your strategy?

f. Using procedural power:
 i. Which strategies could you use to promote passage of the measure/strategy you support to address the issue?
g. Developing and using personal power resources:
 i. Which personal power resources can be helpful in your strategy?

3. Identify an issue affecting older adults internationally that you would like to provide policy advocacy for.
 a. Apply the policy advocacy framework developed by Shiffman and Smith (2007) to develop a policy strategy to address the political context of the issue.
  i. For each of the four categories—*actor power* (factors 1–4), *ideas* (factors 5–6), *political contexts* (factors 7–8), *and issue characteristics* (factors 9–11)—apply the issue affecting older adults internationally to the respective factors shaping the political priority.

Writing a Policy Issue Brief

1. Consider an issue affecting older adults you would like to provide legislative advocacy for.
 a. Develop a policy issue brief using Jansson's (2011) policy brief framework.
  i. Write a statement of the *policy issue* and recommendations for policy action to address the issue (i.e., the proposed action).
  ii. Write a *summary and analysis of issues* describing the current situation, the optimal situation, and what is needed to address the issue.
  iii. Write a summary of *available options* to address the issue, listing the pros and cons of each option to address the issue.
  iv. Write about your *recommendation* from the formerly summarized available policy options and a rationale for why it is the best option.
  v. Write the section for *implementation factors* outlining succinctly the impact of the policy on other laws once implemented.

2. Consider a health-related issue affecting older adults you would like to provide advocacy for.
 a. Develop a health policy brief using Wong, Green, Bazemore, and Miller's (2017) four-step framework.
  i. Step 1: Define the problem.
   1. What is the issue or the problem? Why is it important?
   2. Why now? Who is impacted and who cares?
   3. When defining your problem, be specific to your audience and clearly frame the issue. Who has the influence to make a change that will address this problem?
  ii. Step 2: State the policy.

        1. Identify one to three specific policy actions that will address the problem.
- iii. Step 3: Make your case.
  1. Display and describe relevant data using one or two figures or tables.
  2. Declare potential bias based on the data sources.
  3. Refer to other related policies that are not discussed. Redirect to other policy references when possible or appropriate.
- iv. Step 4: Discuss the impact.
  1. Briefly discuss the implications of both action and inaction.
  2. Analyze estimated pros and cons of the policy action.
  3. Consider intended and unintended consequences.
  4. Address opposing arguments.
  5. Conclude with a restatement of how this policy specifically addresses this problem.

References

Administration for Community Living. (2017). Fiscal year 2017 ACL budget statement. Retrieved from https://www.acl.gov/node/82

Administration for Community Living. (2018a). Fiscal year 2018 Administration for Community Living justification of estimates for appropriations committees. Retrieved from https://www.acl.gov/sites/default/files/about-acl/2017-11/FY2018-ACLBudgetJustification.pdf

Administration for Community Living. (2018b). Fiscal year 2019 Administration for Community Living justification of estimates for appropriations committees. Retrieved from https://www.acl.gov/sites/default/files/about-acl/2018-05/FY2019ACL-CJ3.pdf

Administration for Community Living. (2018c). Administration on Aging fact sheet. Retrieved from https://www.acl.gov/news-and-events/fact-sheets/publications-and-fact-sheets#AoAfs

CalSWEC. (2017). CalSWEC curriculum competencies for public child welfare, behavioral health, and aging in California. Retrieved from https://calswec.berkeley.edu/sites/default/files/2017_calswec_curriculum_competencies_0.pdf

Centers for Medicare and Medicaid Services. (2018a). CMS' program history. Retrieved from https://www.cms.gov/About-CMS/Agency-Information/History/index.html

Centers for Medicare and Medicaid Services. (2018b). September 2018 Medicaid and CHIP enrollment data highlights. Retrieved from https://www.medicaid.gov/medicaid/program-information/medicaid-and-chip-enrollment-data/report-highlights/index.html

Centers for Medicare and Medicaid Services. (2018c). CMS fast facts. Retrieved from https://www.cms.gov/Research-Statistics-Data-and-Systems/Statistics-Trends-and-Reports/CMS-Fast-Facts/index.html

Centers for Medicare and Medicaid Services. (2018d). Eligibility. Retrieved from https://www.medicaid.gov/medicaid/eligibility/index.html

Jansson, B. S. (2011). *Becoming an effective policy advocate: From policy practice to social justice.* Belmont, CA: Brooks Cole Cengage Learning.

Jansson, B. S. (2016). Engaging in macro policy advocacy. In B. S. Jansson (Ed.), *Social welfare policy and advocacy: Advancing social justice through 8 policy sectors* (pp. 137–162). Los Angeles: Sage Publications.

Kaiser Family Foundation. (2017a). An overview of Medicare. Retrieved from https://www.kff.org/medicare/issue-brief/an-overview-of-medicare/

Kaiser Family Foundation. (2017b). Current flexibility in Medicaid: An overview of federal standards and state options. Retrieved from https://www.kff.org/report-section/current-flexibility-in-medicaid-issue-brief/

Kaiser Family Foundation. (2018a). Compare key elements of ACA repeal and replace proposals with new interactive tool. Retrieved from https://www.kff.org/health-reform/press-release/compare-key-elements-of-aca-repeal-and-replace-proposals-with-new-interactive-tool/

Kaiser Family Foundation. (2018b). Summary of recent and proposed changes to Medicare prescription drug coverage and reimbursement. Retrieved from https://www.kff.org/medicare/issue-brief/summary-of-recent-and-proposed-changes-to-medicare-prescription-drug-coverage-and-reimbursement/

National Council on Aging. (2017). Straight talk for seniors: The American Health Care Act. Retrieved from https://www.ncoa.org/blog/straight-talk-seniors-american-health-care-act/

Obama, B. (2016). United States health care reform: Progress to date and next steps. *JAMA, 316*(5), 525–532.

Office of Minority Health. (2017). Data collection standards for race, ethnicity, primary language, sex and disability status. Retrieved from https://minorityhealth.hhs.gov/omh/browse.aspx?lvl=2&lvlid=23

Shiffman, J., & Smith, S. (2007). Generation of political priority for global health initiatives: A framework and case study of maternal mortality. *The Lancet, 370*(9595), 1370–1379.

Social Security Administration. (2018a). Monthly statistical snapshot, June 2018. Retrieved from https://www.ssa.gov/policy/docs/quickfacts/stat_snapshot/index.html

Social Security Administration. (2018b). Social Security history. Retrieved from https://www.ssa.gov/history/orghist.html

Social Security Administration. (2018c). CMS Fast Facts. Retrieved from https://www.cms.gov/Research-Statistics-Data-and-Systems/Statistics-Trends-and-Reports/CMS-Fast-Facts/index.html

Social Security Administration. (2018d). When to start receiving retirement benefits. Retrieved from https://www.ssa.gov/pubs/EN-05-10147.pdf

Social Security Administration. (2018e). You may be able to get Supplemental Security Income (SSI). Retrieved from https://www.ssa.gov/pubs/EN-05-11069.pdf

U.S. Department of Health and Human Services. (2018a). Poverty guidelines. Retrieved from https://aspe.hhs.gov/poverty-guidelines

U.S. Department of Health and Human Services. (2018b). Who is eligible for Medicare? Retrieved from https://www.hhs.gov/answers/medicare-and-medicaid/who-is-elibible-for-medicare/index.html

Wong, S. L., Green, L. A., Bazemore, A. W., & Miller, B. F. (2017). How to write a health policy brief. *Families, Systems, & Health, 35*(1), 21.

Index

CPSIA information can be obtained
at www.ICGtesting.com
Printed in the USA
LVHW061937010223
738434LV00011B/21